INTRODUCTION
TO
CHRISTIAN
DOCTRINE

INTRODUCTION
TO
CHRISTIAN DOCTRINE

JOHN LAWSON

FRANCIS ASBURY PRESS
of Zondervan Publishing House
Grand Rapids, Michigan

FRANCIS ASBURY PRESS is an imprint of
Zondervan Publishing House
1415 Lake Drive, S.E.
Grand Rapids, Michigan 49506

Library of Congress Cataloging in Publication Data
Lawson, John.
    Introduction to Christian doctrine.
    Reprint of the 1967 ed. published by Prentice-Hall, Englewood Cliffs,
N.J., under title: Comprehensive handbook of Christian doctrine.
    Includes index.
    Theology, Doctrinal–Introductions. 2. Theology, Methodist. I. Title.
BT65.L38   230   80–24909
ISBN 0-310-23204-X

Printed in the United States of America

86 87 88 89 90 91 92 / 9 8 7 6 5 4 3 2 1

*to my friends
Claude and Sue Thompson,
faithful witnesses to the Gospel*

Preface

The purpose of this book is to provide initial reading in the systematic study of Christian theology, framed as far as possible in non-technical language, yet of sufficient scope to provide the foundation for more detailed study of particular theological subjects.

The need for such a book presented itself to the mind of the present writer because of his impression that much conventional teaching of systematic theology, particularly in the more academic type of institution, invites students to run before they can walk. Theological specialists are commonly possessed by the natural desire to talk to their students principally about those specialties which are the subjects of their own research. Discussion therefore tends to centre upon 'the modern movement,' and the writings of those celebrated academic theologians who for decades past have occupied the stage of theological controversy. This interest is legitimate in its due place, but labours under the grave disadvantage of a failure to communicate to the normal inexperienced student. The beginner is confronted with a strange technical jargon, often including words used in a sense misleadingly different from that which they carry in ordinary speech. Theological language appears to have little connection with the way in which we express ourselves in customary worship. This can easily lead to mental confusion, and to the acquiring of that 'little knowledge' which is proverbially 'a dangerous thing.' Students can make havoc of their faith through picking up ill-digested scraps of radical theories.

Concealed beneath this failing there is another, more far-reaching, which we are all aware has deeply affected much conventional religious teaching in colleges, universities, and seminaries. This is that theological discussion has tended to centre around the opinion of men, albeit in many cases men of brilliant intellect. This has led to the frequent neglect of that well-established system of Christian doctrine based upon the divine revelation recorded in Holy Scripture. Theology of this man-centred type plainly provides no sufficient basis for the devotional life, or for the constructive preaching of the Gospel in the congregation. In the present day it needs constantly to be affirmed that the reason for theological study is not some sort of intellectual ball-game, to be carried on for its own sake, and for mental stimulation. We theologians are concerned with the training of men and women to be effective Christian witnesses. Our ultimate business is always the salvation of souls, and the deepening of the spiritual life.

However, it is one's conviction that the true defence against confused, reduced, and un-evangelical theology is not a retreat into Christian obscurantism. We are not to retire from 'the modern discussion' as from a thing impious and defiling, in order to confine ourselves to the constricted ground of the advocacy of some denominational, or even narrow sectarian, school of thought. This would be to create the false and very damaging impression that evangelical Christians are what they are because they are timid and defensive souls, lacking in intellectual or social enterprise. Advocates of the true Gospel need to take their bold stand in the wide world, and hold conversation with all comers!

With these needs in mind, the present author has taken it as his aim to give within the compass of a single volume at least the essential minimum of treatment of all the important elements of the Christian system of theology. A serious attempt has been made to state these points in non-technical language. However, it is hoped that the more knowledgeable reader will recognize that the theological issues themselves have not been over-simplified. Thus the treatment, though designed for those relatively new to the study of theology, is not purely elementary. It is intended to lead on to, and to make intelligible, later and more detailed study.

A second feature is that the whole of the traditional and Scriptural system of theology, like the orthodox and catholic formulae of that ancient and undivided Church which is the Mother of us all, and the later insights of classic evangelical theology, are treated quite seriously as beliefs which can be fully accepted by intelligent modern Christians. Indeed, they can be more than merely accepted. They form the fitting intellectual substratum for spiritual experience and vital Christian devotion. Some will therefore judge this book to be broadly 'conservative.' The author trusts that it will be adjudged to be an enlightened, moderate, and constructive conservatism. Furthermore, at various points an attempt is made to give at least a brief, and a dispassionate, statement of the objections which have been raised to the traditional system by modern critics. It is hoped that this will help the reader to understand what the modern discussion is about, and to evaluate the critics aright.

A third feature is that in important cases where leading historic Christian denominations have professed differing convictions, a statement is made of varying standpoints. The ecumenical movement has indeed been hailed by some as 'the great new fact of our times,' but the movement has not always found favour in evangelical circles because unwise advocates of good-will and reconciliation between the various branches of the Church have not infrequently based their case on indifference to theological truth. Some ecumenists have professed a reduced and emasculated theology, lapsing at times into a vague Christianized humanism. Clearly this is not the way forward into that form of Christian unity which is according to God's will! The present volume has therefore attempted to provide for evangelical readers a brief, but it is hoped also a dispassionate and accurate, statement of the doctrine of other parts of the Church, making plain both the many and important matters in which we are all happily at one, and also the significance of those issues where we are not at one. It is hoped that this will help to dispel uninformed prejudice, and facilitate constructive discussion. There are also some matters in which not all evangelical Christians are agreed, for example, the doctrine of predestination, and the precise manner of the Lord's Second Advent. Again, statements of various views have been placed side by side, so as to help the reader to form a judgment as to what is the most reasoned exposition of Scripture.

Throughout the book, of course, care has been taken to give full Scripture references. It is hoped that the reader will dutifully examine all these, because the aim of this book is not to press the claims of a party view-point, or of a passing theological tendency, but to give an outline of the historic, continuing, balanced, reliable, and Scriptural tradition of Christian belief, stated in a form which may make it intelligible in the present day. This is indeed an ambitious aim! The writer does not flatter himself that he has everywhere succeeded, but he commends his work to the Christian public as a part of his due service to his Lord, and to the Church.

Contents

Chapter Three

The Word of the Cross

65

Chapter Four

The Power and the Wisdom

96

Chapter Five

The Spirit of the Lord

III

Chapter Six

The People of God

126

Chapter One

Belief in God

I believe in God the Father Almighty,
maker of heaven and earth

I. I Believe

A. Definition of Faith

The word "faith" is commonly used in two different senses, which must
be carefully distinguished.

1. There is the body of teaching about God, Christ, man, and salvation,
which is the intellectual substratum to religious devotion and obedience.
This is "The Faith," as in Galatians 1:23; Ephesians 4:5; Jude 3.

2. There is the human experience of being confronted immediately by
God in the secret place of the heart, of being held by Him, and of holding
on to Him in trust, depending upon Him in all things. At its deepest this is
the experience of union in loving personal trust with the God who has made
Himself known in His crucified and risen incarnate Son. This is "faith":
Christian saving faith (see pp. 221–22).

To bring out something of the importance of this distinction of usage
it will suffice to say that the teacher who claims, quite rightly, that true
religion is founded upon objective facts and sound reason, is arguing in terms
of (1). The teacher who maintains, equally rightly, that mere orthodoxy
does not make a man into a Christian, but that he must come to a living
personal faith, is discussing the matter in terms of (2). Neither side
logically needs to deny what the other says about Christian belief, but they

1

may seem to be contrary, on account of differences in usage of the word "believe."

B. The Ground of Faith

The vast majority of Christian believers do not come to their religious faith by being argued into it, either by texts from the Bible or by venerable ecclesiastical authority or by the latest learned book. Commonly they start with the experience of worship, though some would emphasize the place of ethical experience. In some moment of worship, either prayer or the devotional reading of the Bible or the sacrament or song, or in the challenge of awakening preaching, the soul becomes aware of the sense of the presence of God, with a solemn and mysterious awe. Normally the first stages of this divine encounter happen when children are taken to church by their parents, or pray at home, before they have any self-conscious and reasoned thought on the subject. Sometimes there is also in adult life a conscious crisis of divine encounter. This walk of the soul with God is immediate, personal, and mysterious. Like an ear for music or an eye for beauty, this form of "faith" is a gift which some few persons appear to enjoy to an exceptional extent, and which makes them the rightful spiritual leaders of their fellows. Many more possess it to a more moderate extent, though the gift may be developed by training and discipline, while a few sadly and mysteriously appear to enjoy it hardly at all.

Religion, therefore, normally starts with what may be termed "the devotional experience." The thoughtful person, who wishes to bring his whole life to a rational system, then naturally proceeds to reflect about this experience. He will examine it critically to determine whether it is indeed a reasonable and trustworthy form of human experience, or a subjective delusion. He will draw out its logical conclusions, and frame them in terms of the apparatus of thought proper to his time. Thus a *theology* is formed.

C. Religious Authority

We cannot escape the question whether or not it is possible to be certain about religion, and if so, what the organ of this certainty is. In times when the Christian witness has been faced by a searching challenge, those parts of the Church have endured best which have made the most satisfactory appearance of speaking to the people with a reasonable yet confident authority. At the same time, the circumstance that there are competing systems of authority shows that it is not easy to define the proper nature of Christian certainty. The confusion arises because, corresponding naturally to the two uses of the word "faith" which we have noticed, there are two chief aspects of religious authority.

1. There is the authority which can bring to the inquirer a rational degree of certainty that he has a sound grasp of "The Faith," considered as a body

of doctrine. Within this sphere authority is a matter of fact, not of feeling, and the organ of it is largely corporate, rather than purely individual.

For the Christian, The Faith is based in the first place upon the record of the facts about Christ: namely, the account of the preparation of the world for His coming, His spiritual background, His wonderful birth and life, His character, teaching, death, and resurrection. The only record of these facts is in the Bible, and therefore The Faith is founded on the Bible. Hence is deduced the traditional Christian position that every true Christian doctrine must be in accord with Scripture. However, the Bible was written by men who in the main were more interested in spiritual devotion and moral obedience than in systematic theology. Their doctrine is implicit more often than explicit. Therefore the Bible needs to be interpreted, that one may verify the historical facts about Christ, and understand aright the spiritual and theological implications of what He was and what He did. The doctrine implicit in Scripture requires to be made explicit, and to be focused into carefully framed and unambiguous terms. Simple Christian believers do not necessarily need to understand this technical theology in order to come to God in Christ, and to partake of salvation. The preaching of the gospel is based on the plain facts of The Faith, as recorded in Scripture, not on the theological theories constructed to explain the facts. Nevertheless, a teacher of The Faith must seek to understand this theology, for only so can he give reliable guidance on the way his hearers are to understand the facts recorded in the Bible.

This interpretative and safeguarding activity of the theologian is an activity of divinely guided reason, and is in the last resort a scholarly activity. It is therefore a corporate activity. Christian truth is rich and various. Some parts of it make a natural appeal to some individuals, and some to others. Therefore there may be an apparent tension between the Christian Faith as it is understood by one historical period or school of thought, and by another. The apprehension of Christian truth proper to men of many different temperaments, casts of mind, walks of life, and social and racial backgrounds, needs to be brought together into a developing world-wide consensus of Christian thought, under the guidance of the Holy Spirit. Theologians supplement one another, correct one another, and discipline one another, by heeding the long experience of the past, and by maintaining intellectual and spiritual fellowship with one another in the present. Purely individualist thought is ever in danger of being found partial, unbalanced, subjective, and erroneous. Corporate thought is well considered, balanced, comprehensive, and reliable. Thus if correct doctrine and morals are to be established from the Bible it requires to be interpreted by the Church. The guide into a rational degree of certainty on points of doctrine is the witness of Scripture, interpreted and understood by the reasoning activity of the living tradition of the whole Church, guided as she is by the

Holy Spirit. That which is accepted as The Faith by the whole of the universal, or Catholic, Church is the reliable and orthodox Faith, that is to say, the Catholic Faith.[1]

Christian teachers who speak of religious authority in terms of the Church and her historic creed, and who uphold religious certainty with the threefold cord of Scripture, tradition, and reason, have in mind chiefly the kind of authority which can assure the inquiring mind regarding "The Faith."

2. We then ask what sort of authority can hope to bring to the human soul certainty in "faith," that is, in the experience of the divine encounter, in reverence, trust, love, and obedience. This is a very different matter! A teacher may be thoroughly versed in knowledge of the Bible and of theology, and so have a most authoritative grasp of "The Faith," and yet have in his own life no vivid sense of God, no compelling urge for obedience to God, and no power to communicate the sense of God to others. His religion is a dry academic orthodoxy. What is it, then, which can quicken "The Faith," so that it makes personal appeal in the human heart, and gives birth to "faith"?

The quickening of faith is nothing less than the immediate activity of God Himself upon the human heart. Faith is a gift, and the gift of faith is the work of the Holy Spirit (1 Corinthians 12:3; Ephesians 2:8). The "seeing eye," to which God is the most pressing reality of life, is akin to the artist's view, the musician's ear, or the poet's tongue. It is a wonderful faculty, which can indeed be developed and trained by disciplined human response, but which is itself an implanted "gift." The means which God uses to quicken the gift of faith are very commonly corporate—the Christian family and school, the evangelistic service, or the sacraments of the Church. Nevertheless, though the means to the gift are corporate, the gift itself is essentially individual. Each man meets God in the loneliness of his own heart. No man can go proxy for another in this solemn transaction. The time and the manner in which the gift is bestowed remains a divine mystery (John 3:8).

Those who insist that true spiritual religion is individual and personal,

---

[1] The word "Catholic" suffers seriously from confusion, through being used in varying senses. The Roman Catholic calls his own communion "the Catholic Church" to register the claim that his is the only properly ordered and authenticated Church. Though he will acknowledge that his "separated brethren" are in a real sense Christians, and are in some sense a part of the Church, yet he has to maintain that their parts of the Church are not properly ordered and disciplined. Many Protestants, who do not acknowledge this claim, call the Roman Catholic Church "the Catholic Church" as a matter of common but theologically careless parlance. In this book, where the Roman Catholic Church is referred to, it is always spoken of as such. By "the Catholic Church" is meant the whole body of historic and orthodox Christianity, of which the Roman Catholic Church is an important part. "The Catholic Faith" is the faith of the Catholic Church, that is, the fundamental body of orthodox and essential belief which unites all the parts of the Catholic Church, as distinct from particular theological opinions emphasized by particular denominations or schools of thought (see p. 143).

and not just a matter of the Church, with her sacraments, institutions, and creeds; and that certainty in the religious life is founded upon "personal experience," are trying to say just this.

Summary of Divergence: Doctrines of Authority

a. Traditional

The general attitude of the ancient Church was that true doctrine is founded on Scripture, and that the Church, as the guardian of Scripture, is the authoritative interpreter of Scripture. The organ of this authority is particularly the episcopate, and the writings of the authoritative Church fathers of bygone ages. The bishops who are in succession to the apostles, particularly as they meet together in council, reliably interpret Scripture, so as to guard the Church from heresy. In particular, an Ecumenical (universal) or General Council of bishops, speaking for the whole Church, is empowered under the guidance of the Holy Spirit to make a fully authoritative determination of orthodox faith or practice for the universal Church. This is still the attitude of the Eastern, or Orthodox, Churches. They account the first seven General Councils of the Church, which took place before the division of the Eastern and Western (or Latin) Churches, to be true Ecumenical Councils. Since then it has not been possible to hold any councils fully authoritative for the universal Church. Thus continuing ecclesiastical authority is in abeyance. Authority rests on antiquity.

b. Roman Catholic

In western Europe during the Middle Ages the Pope was gradually accorded a greater share of the determining power within the Council of Bishops, until the Papacy became the predominating voice of ecclesiastical authority. A Roman Catholic would affirm that this development was the rightful and necessary outworking of the promise which Christ made to St. Peter (see p. 141). The aftermath of the disputes attendant upon the Protestant Reformation made it necessary for the Roman Catholic Church at the Council of Trent (1546–1563) further to define her doctrine of religious authority. It was there decided, in antithesis to Protestantism, that there is a twofold organ of dogmatic authority in the Church. Written Scripture and the unwritten tradition of the Church are in partnership. The ancient fathers of the Church may also be cited as a true authority. It is not the position of the Roman Catholic Church that ecclesiatical authority can determine doctrine in opposition to Scripture. It is affirmed that all true Christian doctrine is in accord with Scripture. Nevertheless, the tradition of the Church is a true authority in its own right, so that ecclesiastical authority is not limited simply to the power to interpret Scripture.

It is noteworthy that some modern Roman Catholic and Protestant discussion of the relation of Scripture to tradition appears to be moving to a position of greater mutual understanding, and perhaps ultimately to common ground. Thus Protestant New Testament scholarship is familiar with the circumstance that Christian faith was first transmitted in unwritten tradition, and that this was later recorded as the apostolic writings. On the other hand, some Roman Catholic scholars may now be found to restate the position of the Council of Trent in the following way. God's Christian revelation was in the first place the impact of the person and acts of Christ. The single witness to this revelation was in the first place the oral tradition of the Church, and was then recorded in the writings of the New Testament. The tradition of the Church guaranteed these writings and determined the authoritative canon of the New Testament. Furthermore, the New Testament can only be understood in light of the faith and life of the community which gave it birth. It is not the case that some Christian doctrines are supported by Scripture and others by the tradition of the Church. Written tradition, interpreted aright in the necessary context of the unwritten but living tradition of the Church, is the witness to the unified Christian Faith. A salient example of this process in action is the argument stated in relation to our Lord's institution of the Eucharist (see p. 143). The foundation for the Church's belief is our Lord's recorded words of institution, but these precious yet enigmatic words require to be interpreted in light of the evident conviction and usage of the ancient Church.

The growing predominance of the Papacy within the Council of Bishops culminated in the promulgation of the dogma of the Infallibility of the Pope, at the Vatican Council of 1870. This dogma does not involve the claim that all papal pronouncements of every sort are free from error. The doctrine thus defined is that when, after all the authorities within the Church have duly conferred, the Pope as earthly head of the Church determines the considered mind of the Church upon some matter of faith or morals by an authoritative public statement on behalf of the Church, then that pronouncement is final and without error, and is to be accepted by all the faithful as fully authoritative. It is noteworthy that the recent Vatican Council has to some extent balanced and complemented this doctrine by a new affirmation of the ancient position that all bishops are teaching and governing bishops in their own right, by succession from the apostles. Thus their right authoritatively to confer in a General Council is a real one, though the Pope is still the acknowledged infallible head. Furthermore, in scholarly Roman Catholic circles an increasing effort is being made to vindicate the position that ecclesiastical authority is not to be used to silence the new findings of reverent and sober Biblical scholarship. Thus the scriptural element in religious authority is also being reaffirmed within the Roman Catholic Church.

c. Protestant

The classic Protestant doctrine of religious authority is expressed in the phrase *"sola Scriptura"*—*Scripture alone*. It is not intended by this formula to assert that the meaning of every part of the Bible is self-evident, so that the corporate scholarly activity of interpretation is unnecessary. What is meant is that Christian scholars should not bring their human opinions or prepossessions to the Bible, but should reverently seek to be molded in their thinking by the Bible, which alone is the God-given authority within the Church. It is affirmed that if, under the guidance of the Holy Spirit, the careful student of the Bible seeks to interpret obscure passages of Scripture in the light of plain ones, and texts of secondary import in light of leading texts, that then the whole will fall into place. The Bible will thus constitute a self-sufficient authority on Christian faith and practice.

Note on the above.

It would appear to the present writer that the validity of the classic Protestant doctrine of religious authority is more clearly seen when it is applied to that aspect of authority which has been defined under point (*C2*), that is, the authority which brings "saving faith," rather than "The Faith."

Experience shows that one of the chief means which God uses to bring the experience of the divine encounter is the devotional reading and evangelical preaching of the Bible. The great prophetic and devotional chapters of both the Old Testament and the New are full of a sense that the most pressing reality of life is a God of sovereign majesty and love. As we look on the work of a great and sensitive artist we come to appreciate a beauty in a landscape or a face, which unaided we would never have fully observed. As we look in company with the artist, and through his eyes, we begin to see. In the same way, as we look out on life as it is seen from the viewpoint of the Bible writers we see it as it truly exists under the eye of God. Supremely, it is by seeing Christ in all His beauty and majesty that man meets God (Matthew 11:27; John 1:14, 18). Clearly, the Gospel record is the secure ground for this distinctively Christian form of religious experience. Thus the proverbial "open Bible" in the hand of the humble believer can and does speak with an immediate divine authority. Christ steps out of the page, and makes Himself real to the heart.

It has to be admitted that "the open Bible" in the hand of the simple believer does not of itself suffice to guarantee that he will come to a sound grasp of Christian doctrine. When the great Protestant Reformers speak of the right of the private believer to read the Bible, and of the sufficiency of Scripture for salvation, they tacitly assume that the reader already has an effective grasp of "The Faith." He accepts the Church, and her creed and sacraments, and reads the Bible from this believing point of view. Yet as he reads he is seeking to go on from "The Faith" to *faith,* to the saving "faith which works by love." He is not seeking to establish a purely private and individual authority for Scripture exposition or for doctrine (2 Peter 1:20).

d. Anglican

The doctrine of religious authority developed in the Church of England, following the Reformation period, represents a characteristic effort to find a mediating position between the Roman Catholic and classic Protestant views. In substance it followed the ancient traditional position, but sought to find a clearer vindication for the primary authority of Scripture than was apparent in much current Roman Catholic teaching. It has been held that authority rests upon the threefold foundation of Scripture, tradition, and reason. In matters of doctrine, morals, and Church practice which appear to be securely determined by Scripture, Scripture is affirmed to be the sufficient and final authority. However, there are other matters which are not clearly determined by Scripture, and here tradition, that is, the general usage and consensus of the Church, is of effective authority. It is characteristic of the Anglican position regarding tradition that chief weight is given to the usage and consensus of the first four or five Christian centuries, to the Church fathers of this early period, and to the first four Ecumenical Councils. It has been felt that the ancient Church was more manifestly united, and more free from corrupt accretions, than in later centuries. Ecclesiastical tradition originating only from the Middle Ages has been an object of reserve, or even suspicion, in contradistinction to the Roman Catholic position. The third element of reason finds place in that Scripture is to be expounded always according to competent and honest learning, and that traditional usages and ideas are to be placed under critical scrutiny. That which is ancient is to be followed where possible, but not simply because it is ancient.

Summary of Divergence : Existential Theology

a. Definition

Thinkers and philosophers have usually assumed that "behind" or "above" the world of matter and space and events passing around us, there is an invisible order of universal principles, which are intellectual or spiritual. By careful rational thought, or by the sudden enlightenment which comes in the moment of meditation, it is possible for man to grasp something of these principles, and so come to an understanding of the "meaning" of the world and of human life. The so-called existentialist philosophy is a mode of thought which repudiates this endeavor to rise above our existence in this world to a general intellectual order. It regards as a fruitless task the search for an overarching speculative "meaning." All that man can do is to receive the immediate impact of experience, and to find himself as a human being by resolutely reacting to it. Existentialist theology is a modern attempt to use this philosophy as a thought form for the expression of the essential Christian message.

b. Affirmative Statement

The exponents of this theology affirm that the existentialist philosophy is the mode of thought natural to the modern man in the age of science. Therefore if Christian faith is to be made intelligible to him, so as to win his respect as credible, it must be rendered into the thought forms of this system, in the same way that Christian theology has employed other current philosophies in past periods.

It is also affirmed that this position accords with biblical thought, and with the earliest Christian thought. The Hebrews, unlike the Greeks, were not interested in abstract speculative thought, or in the reflective search for a supposed "higher" order of general intellectual principles. In biblical thinking, God always acts immediately upon the world and upon man, while the concern of the man of God is always with immediate devotional experience and moral obedience, not with speculative doctrine. Thus biblical thought is "existential," as was the thought of the first Church. The first disciples did not first receive a doctrine that their Lord was divine by nature, and then on this account go on to worship Him and trust Him as divine. It was the other way about. They received an immediate experience that in the life of Christ God had met them in His person, His love, and His saving power. Out of this existential experience they confessed Him in trust and worship as their divine Lord, and from this point elaborated the doctrine of His divine nature.

Existential theology strongly emphasizes that it is not possible to "prove" the truth of the Christian religion either by arguments from the probability of historical fact (for example, efforts to demonstrate the fact of Christ's physical resurrection), or by arguments to demonstrate the reasonableness of the system of Christian doctrine (for example, by the traditional "proofs of the existence of God"). The sole and sufficient ground of the Christian Faith is the act of faith, that is, the response in decision, love, and trust, made when God encounters man.

c. Critical Statement

The exponent of the traditional Christian Faith can allow that this case is one aspect of the truth. Thus "Christian existentialism" may in some writers be no more than an exaggerated statement of the traditional Christian position that the essence of Christian faith is not just the acceptance of a body of speculative doctrine, but includes a life of personal trust in, and obedience to, the Saviour. So it is possible for an uneducated believer, who does not understand Christian theology, to be a genuine Christian. However, from the point of view of the established Christian system, the existential scheme, if taken to an extreme, comes dangerously near to an attempt to maintain "faith" (that is, loving and obedient trust in God) apart from its necessary intellectual and rational foundation in "The Faith" (that is, the Church's historic witness to the facts about Christ, and the doctrine formulated to expound and safeguard the meaning of these facts).

Some would question whether modern man is in fact so captivated by the existential philosophy that it is necessary to make a radical reconstruction of the Christian Faith in order to communicate it to him. However, it is to be accepted that Hebrew and biblical thought is concrete rather than abstract, practical and devotional rather than speculative. Furthermore, the faith of the first Church in her divine

Lord did apparently grow up in just this way. The experience of salvation was the cause, and the doctrine to expound this experience the consequence (see pp. 42–43, 47). Again, the Church from the very beginning has been aware that the most compelling demonstration of even so remarkable a fact as Christ's empty tomb will not drive unbelieving men to have faith (Luke 16:31; see pp. 101–2). Nor have the wiser theologians of the Church ever assumed that arguments in support of Christian belief, no matter how cogent, will ever of themselves suffice to constrain men from unbelief.

However, many writers who style themselves as Christian existentialists, finding natural allies in the "demythologizing" exegetes of the New Testament (see pp. 35–36), appear to go much further than this, and to advance upon what the traditional theologian regards as most dangerous ground. For example, arguing from the admitted fact that some heard the message of the empty tomb, yet did not receive faith, it has been affirmed that the supposed fact of the empty tomb is not important for faith, or even, to push the matter to the extreme, that the empty tomb is not a fact. So it has been taught that Christ died on the Cross and moldered in the tomb, while the disciples, reflecting upon His morally victorious life, received an "existential" experience that He had triumphed over death, and constructed the legend of the empty tomb in order vividly to symbolize this conviction of faith, and to communicate it to others. This is a salient example of a general treatment. So the Christ of historical fact more or less withers away, while a "Christ of faith," known chiefly or solely in the heart, remains.

To the traditional Christian this appears an incredible account of the origin of the Christian Faith and the Christian Church, and of the New Testament literature (see pp. 194–200). He feels that apart from the marvelous facts of God's action in history Christian faith would not have come into existence. Apart from continued belief in the historical facts faith will not continue. Furthermore, he will affirm that this is to make the Christian religion into a matter of subjective opinion. It ceases to be a gospel of God's saving power in Christ, actually exerted in the course of the history of this world, in which man can trust. It becomes at best a call to man to follow in his own strength a body of ethical teaching, at worst an invitation that he expose himself to autosuggestion, or even mass hysteria. To knock away the appeal to proved historical fact, and to the rational system of doctrine, in the supposed interests of "faith" is to make the Christian religion into something quite other than it has always been, and entirely to denature it as a religion of grace (see pp. 83–84).

II. God the Father Almighty

A. *Definition*

God may be defined in the broadest terms as the uncaused cause of all things which exist. He is the ultimate origin and sovereign governing principle of all.

B. *Transcendence and Immanence*

Christian theology holds that God is transcendent. This means that He is more than the governing principle of all things. He exists in His own right, apart from His creation. Thus there is a great division of existence between God, who from eternity alone is self-existent, and all other things which exist. The universe is His creation, and He is superior to it and in control of it. He existed in full perfection of being before the universe came into existence. This carries the implication that God is a spiritual being. That is to say, He does not have any kind of material body, and does not exist in any manner of place, any more than His being is confined to time.[2]

Christian theology also holds that God is immanent, which means that the transcendent God is not remote from the created universe, as though He cannot have direct contact with it, and act in it and through it. The Christian believes that God is in constant sovereign control of everything which exists, from the vastest galaxies to the most minute atomic particles. The natural laws which all these things obey are not a mere lifeless and careless mechanism. They are an expression of His control.

C. *A Personal God*

It is a fundamental article of the Christian Faith that God is a personal God. This means that the transcendent God is a thinking and feeling being, who knows Himself to be Himself, a being separate from and superior to His creation, of which He is the intelligent sovereign ruler. The contact and control of the immanent God is an intelligent and thoughtful control, not a bare law of action (Matthew 10:29). God is indeed the principle of existence and of "values," moral, intellectual, and aesthetic. He is (to use the phrase popularized by Tillich) "the ground of being." Yet Christian theology has insisted that language of this kind, though not untrue, should not be used in such a way as to obscure the vitally important truth that God is also a thinking, feeling, living, active being, who is personally interested in us. It is almost superfluous to cite texts to illustrate this doctrine, for it is the presupposition of every part of the Bible. The leading and most striking biblical phrase to express the idea of a personal God is "the living God" (Deuteronomy 5:26; Jeremiah 10:10; Acts 14:15). The most important consequence for religion of the personal nature of God is that it is possible for man to have personal fellowship with Him (Exodus 33:11). Thus worship is not just meditation about God. It is communion with God. It is to express the idea that God is personal that Christian theology speaks of God as "He," not "It."

---

2 The charge has sometimes been leveled by critics against traditional Christianity that it has taught that God exists in a place "above" or "beyond" the universe, which view must now be given up as unscientific. This would appear to be an injustice. Simple and uneducated Christians may indeed often have pictured God as in some sort of remote place, but such a view has never been part of the Christian system, as correctly understood. It is however difficult to do without a *symbolical* use of such terms as above.

D. The Father

The distinctive Christian title for God, as He is known as the creator and governor of the universe, is "the Father." This was the usage Christians learned from our Lord (Matthew 6:9). In the family a father is the source of his child. He is superior to his child, in a position of government over him, and of responsibility for him. He is also a loving and self-sacrificing superior. The word "Father" as applied to God therefore aptly indicates the two contrasting propositions that God is the one who gives to us our being, infinitely superior to us, the governor at whose absolute disposal we are, and also that He loves us and is interested in us with personal and sympathetic care.

E. Almighty

This word, as used in Christian thought, indicates that God is the sovereign ruler of all things. There is no power outside Himself which can frustrate His purpose (Isaiah 43:13). There is no sphere of existence where His law does not fully apply (Psalm 139:7–12). The word does not mean that God is a God of arbitrary might, who is unaccountable in His dealings with man, or that there is no conceivable thing which God cannot do. He is a morally and rationally accountable God, who is never inconsistent with Himself (2 Timothy 2:13). Thus even God cannot make man both morally free and also incapable of sinning. In creating man He has for an entirely good and wise end used His sovereign will to limit somewhat the exercise of His own sovereignty. In consequence, it is possible for events to happen in a world ruled by a sovereign God which are nevertheless not the direct will of God, though they are permitted by Him.

F. The Use of Symbolical Language

The use of the term "Father" introduces the reader to the employment in theology of symbolical language. Symbolism is a form of expression which, superficially at any rate, appears to be alien to the factual and "common-sense" language natural to the modern world. It is therefore often a subject of misunderstanding.

It is clear that to call God "the Father" is to take a word out of human experience, and to make of it a comparison or imaginative mental picture of that which is beyond direct human experience. This is what is meant by saying that the term "Father" as theologically applied to God is a *symbol*. The word "Father" is not a factual description of God, to be taken literally. The nature of God is beyond direct human experience of this world, and therefore He cannot be described in matter-of-fact language. His nature is to be set forth in the medium of imaginative word pictures. This principle of symbolic expression holds true of all those parts of Christian doctrine which concern matters which are outside the sphere of direct human experience, such as the beginning and the end of the creation, the origin of evil, and the destiny of the human soul.

Some critics[3] have argued that in attempting to discuss heavenly things Christian theology is guilty of using words in variable, unreal, and misleading senses, and is entangled in radical intellectual stultification. Thus if the word "Father" is taken seriously it would appear to indicate that the Christian thinks of God as a superior kind of man. God is the comforting "image" of a protective being which the subconscious mind has suggested after the image of man himself. In response the theologian attempts to clarify his case, and, as the critic will claim, conducts a partial forced retreat. He now allows that God is indeed a Father, but not as a human father is a father. God has no body, and has not procreated us. Yet, the theologian argues, he rightly uses the highest aspects of human nature as a symbol.

The critic's attack may then be renewed by speaking of the proverbial innocent child, dying painfully of some horrible disease. How is this consistent with a doctrine of God's fatherly love? So the theologian restates his case yet again, allowing that the word "love" is also a symbol when applied to God. There are indeed dark things in life which one finds hard to understand, yet the believer trusts that God's wisdom is higher than ours. He loves, but he does not love as a human father loves. He loves with a higher, though at times a mysterious, love. Thus the skeptic's charge is that in Christian theology the proper meaning of language has been eroded, inch by inch, in "the death of a thousand cuts." The theologian is seeking to know the unknowable, and to conceal his obscurity of thought by playing fast and loose with words.

In replying to this charge the Christian has first to admit that there is an element of truth in it. The theologian does indeed need at times to use symbolical language. Furthermore, a word drawn from the language of experience, and used as a symbol, does have a special meaning attached to it for this purpose. This meaning must be understood if the symbolism is to convey truth and not error. The symbol must not be taken in its matter-of-fact sense. So much is to be allowed. However, it is a common but serious confusion to speak of "mere" symbolism, as though literal and matter-of-fact language represents secure and rational knowledge, whereas symbolical language represents the fanciful, the unsubstantial, the unimportant. In every branch of knowledge the higher truths have to be expressed in symbolism appropriate to the subject. This is true in science. The initial stages of research are matter-of-fact: weighing, measuring, counting, directly or indirectly. The higher stage is a formula to demonstrate a general principle deduced from the experimental data. A scientific formula is a particular kind of *symbol*. This is the case with religious thought also. By the use of meaningful imaginative symbols the mind can advance from the world of immediate spiritual experience into the realm of spiritual principles. The comparison is never entirely adequate. Symbolism does not give a perfect knowledge of the world of God. Yet we need not feel that it leaves man

---

[3] Logical positivists.

with an illusion. The Christian believes that it gives man the most real knowledge of heavenly things which he can have in this world, and knowledge which will not be discredited when he comes to higher knowledge in heaven.

III. Arguments for the Existence of God

A. Fundamental Assumptions

Around us is the *universe*—the physical universe known to science. It comprises everything which exists physically from galaxies to atomic particles, including all living creatures, and man. It can be assumed by the thinker, as he takes up from the very start the process of thought, either that the universe corresponds to a rational plan, or that it does not. There seem to be no other possible basic assumptions. We may say that there is no prior train of argument which can be used either to prove or to disprove either of these fundamental assumptions. This is where the process of thought arises. The validity of the assumptions can only be tested by considering the final result which issues from proceeding upon them.

1. If it be assumed that the universe corresponds to a rational plan these consequences appear to follow: (a) Objects do not exist, nor events happen, without a sufficient prior cause.[4] (b) The process of rational thought corresponds to the very nature of existence, and if carried out correctly can lead to knowledge of ultimate principles of the truth regarding existence. Careful examination of the physical universe, and correct argument from the data observed, can rise above the universe, and lead to knowledge of the plan to which the universe corresponds. (c) This basic assumption of a rational plan to the universe makes possible the scientific outlook. (d) It also, so the Christian affirms, makes possible religious knowledge.

2. If, on the other hand, it is assumed that the physical universe does not correspond to a rational plan, an alternative set of consequences appears to follow: (a) There is no ground for assuming that objects or events correspond to a sufficient rational cause, so it is a waste of time to inquire why objects exist or events happen. (b) The reasoning human mind does not necessarily correspond to the nature of things. Therefore there is no ground for supposing that thought can lead to the knowledge of general and eternal principles of truth. (c) This reduces philosophy to the mere discussion of what one decides different words shall mean, and how logical argument ought to be arranged. (d) Science is reduced from a way of

---

[4] A critic may observe at this point that strictly speaking it is not possible to prove that event A (commonly called the "cause") *makes* event B (commonly called the "effect") happen. All we can say is that so far as we can observe, when event A happens event B always happens immediately afterwards. There is an observed fixed pattern of behavior. The affirmation that this pattern of behavior *is* fixed is one of the chief principles of physical science. However, we are not arguing this point here, regarding "causation." What we are stating is that the fixed pattern of behavior itself does not exist without a sufficient rational cause to make it happen.

fundamental understanding to a mere description of the universe, and to practical methods of making machines. (e) Religion is reduced to a set of unsubstantial subjective feelings.

Thus alternative (2) yields a radical skepticism regarding abstract thought or eternal spiritual principles. The Christian theologian has to admit that it is not possible by logical argument to drive the radical skeptic off his chosen ground. As we have stated above, it is a basic assumption made before the process of argument starts. Nevertheless, one is confident that this solution to the problems of thought will not permanently hold the allegiance of thinking humanity. It is a solution which chiefly commends itself in a period of strain and disillusionment, when men are inclined to despair of coming to an understanding of human life. However, the thinking mind has a deep implanted desire to see all things reduced to order and rational principles, and demonstrated as the outcome of an intelligible plan. This desire will not permanently be denied by an *a priori* assurance that this cannot be done. In particular, if science itself is not a system for the understanding of existence, the ground is cut away from beneath the feet of the radical skeptic himself, for he claims to base himself upon "the scientific attitude"!

The theologian, then, will take up alternative (1) as for him the truly constructive intellectual attitude. He will assume that the universe corresponds to a rational plan. One does not look for a logical proof of this, argued from prior principles. The "proof" of the rightness of this assumption must be provided by experience of where the process of thought leads in the end. It will stand or fall by the degree of justice which it does to the existence of the human mind, and by the satisfaction which it brings to the desire of the mind to see reason and order displayed in all things.

B. General Statement

If the universe corresponds to a rational plan the following train of consequences is to be observed.

1. That which exists in the universe known to experience and to science must have a sufficient cause. Objects do not exist meaninglessly, or by accident.

2. The universe is a unity. The most careful scientific examination appears to indicate that the same coherent reign of law runs through all things, from the heavenly galaxies to the atoms, and throughout all time. Therefore the sufficient source and plan of all must be *one*.

3. The universe appears not to suffer from any kind of limitation or constraint. The power behind it completely suffices for all its needs. The law of its action is constant, unerring, and exact. Therefore the source and plan of all must be unlimited in power, infinite and constant in wisdom.

4. The universe appears to have a purpose or destination. In its development one stage naturally and fittingly leads to another, which is the climax of all that has gone before. Thus the evolution of stars produced a planet

suited to the existence of organic life, and organic life then duly appeared to fulfill the development of the planet. The evolution of organic life under the influence of successive changes of environment on the earth at length came to its climax in an organism, man. He was adapted in body, nerve, and sense to be the potential medium of personal, rational, and moral life. Personal life then duly awoke, and man became man, fulfilling the previous organic development. The process has continued in the development of man. If the whole train of development, from beginning to end, corresponds to a sufficient cause and rational plan, it would appear that the earlier stages have been undergone in order that the later and higher may arise. Therefore the source and plan of all must have purpose.

5. The crown of the development of the physical universe is apparently man. He is a *personal* being. That is to say, he is self-conscious, thinking, feeling, and capable of moral choice. Man is also in part a spiritual being. These higher and nobler faculties of his, which make him human, are not merely part of the material body, though they work through it. The sufficient and rational cause of this effect must be at least as rich in being as man. Therefore the source of all is a Person, not merely a law of existence. He is a spiritual being, invisible, not having a material body, and not confined to time and space. Presumably this originating Person is altogether richer in personality than even the noblest of men, at a higher level of self-consciousness, more profound in thought, more pure and strong in feeling. He is not merely the impersonal "soul of the world," but a personal God who knows Himself as separate in existence from the world which He has created, and which He rules with sovereign power.

6. In the minds of men there are thoughts of goodness, truth, and beauty, which are the highest qualities of human life. If existence is a rational thing, these qualities cannot exist by accident, with no sufficient cause. They cannot be in the nature of an illusion. Therefore in the mirror of the mind of man they must form as the imperfect reflection of qualities of perfect goodness, truth, and beauty which exist in the mind of God.

Summary. We here have formulated in general terms the Christian argument for the existence of God, who is the all-wise and all-powerful spiritual and personal creator and ruler of the universe, and the ground and source of all goodness, truth, and beauty.

C. Traditional Statements

This argument has in the Church been traditionally formulated in a number of so-called "proofs of the existence of God."

1. ONTOLOGICAL ARGUMENT. The word "ontological" is derived from the Greek verb for "to be," "to exist." This is the argument from the very nature of existence, and is in fact the traditional statement of the basic assumption of the rationality of existence. Deeply implanted in the mind of man there is the idea that God exists, and that He is one and all-sufficient, and good. It is argued that this demonstrates that such a God actually does exist. We

have the idea of a perfect being, and a necessary part of this perfection is that He should actually exist. This mode of argument was first clearly stated by St. Anselm of Canterbury (1033–1109), in his book *Proslogion,* and this argument was the effective starting point of the great medieval venture of Christian philosophy known as Scholasticism. The ontological argument was later notably restated by the French philosopher and mathematician, Descartes (1596–1650), who argued that because the thoughts of goodness and truth in the mind of man are so distinct and clear they must correspond to reality.

It is easy for the skeptic to object that in thinking of God man may very possibly be the victim of subjective illusion. Thus critics have correctly argued that the idea in one's mind that a proverbial beautiful island exists beyond the farthest seas by no means demonstrates that it is there. However, the Christian will answer that he is not arguing about the existence of mundane objects such as this. He is concerned with the noblest and most profound thoughts which have moved in the minds of the greatest, the most sensitive, and the most rational of men. To affirm that these thoughts do not correspond substantially to the very nature of existence, but are of the nature of a profound illusion, overthrows the integrity of the thinking mind. It seems to presuppose that man himself, considered as a thinking person, is an unworthy illusion. The mind will not finally accept this conclusion, compelling though it may seem to some able and sincere men. Radical skepticism starts by acclaiming the worth of "reason," but ends in overthrowing much of the process of thought itself.

2. COSMOLOGICAL ARGUMENT. The word "cosmological" is derived from *cosmos,* the Greek word for the world, and particularly the world of nature considered as an orderly system. The existence of God is here argued from the evidence of order in the universe. The creation shows too much of majesty, wisdom, and wonder to be the result of an accident. Its existence declares the existence of an all-wise Creator, in the same way that if one discovered a delicately made watch on a desert island one would presume that an intelligent man had left his handiwork there, for a watch could not be the result of chance. This is a natural form of argument, and is repeatedly declared in the Bible (for example, Psalm 19:1–4, 94:9; Acts 14:17; Romans 1:19–20). It was notably restated by St. Thomas Aquinas (1225–1274), the classic figure of Scholasticism, that is, of the philosophical theology of the Schoolmen, or leading teachers of the medieval universities.

The chief thing to be said here is that the impressiveness of this argument largely depends upon what one assumes to be the proper end of existence. The argument from the majesty and order of the heavenly bodies, and of the rule of law in nature, is indeed impressive. Question arises chiefly when one considers sentient animal life, and in particular, self-conscious and sensitive human life. Animal existence is full of the strain and competition of "nature red in tooth and claw," while human experience is darkened by suffering, and by suffering which often cannot well be explained as due to the disordering of God's good order by the sin of man. There is also the fiendish ingenuity of some parasites, which to some would almost seem to speak of an intelligent designer of evil, as well as of good. One does not claim that every hard question can be completely answered, but the chief consideration here is that in his objection the "this-worldly" thinker almost instinctively makes the tacit assumption that the highest good in life is an untroubled existence in comfort, free from anxiety and pain. If this be so, it is then clear that the basic design of life is not completely good, for the order of nature is not as free from strain and pain as it could conceivably be. However, it can be argued that in the highest sense of the word it is good for man to have his bodily existence in a certain state of insecurity, so as to remind him of spiritual values beyond the bodily. Also there may be spiritual good to be gained by the discipline of uncomfortable effort, and by the patient endurance of pain. If this be so, the argument from wise design is much more obvious. It is the Christian, who has seen the wisdom of God revealed in the Cross of Christ, and in the Christian life of "cross-bearing," who is more likely to see things this way.

3. TELEOLOGICAL ARGUMENT. The term "teleological" is derived from the Greek *telos,* the end or aim of a process. The existence of God is argued from the appearance of developing purpose in the universe, because a sense of rational purpose in the development of the world of nature speaks of an origin in an intelligent mind.

In the modern period this argument has been assailed in the name of the scientific doctrine of organic evolution. Most of the traditional teleological arguments were based upon the admittedly wonderful adaptation of living creatures to their habitat, and of organs to their proper use. Thus Newton, to an eminent degree a man of science, could declare: "Was the eye contrived without skill in optics, or the ear without knowledge of sounds?" However, the doctrine of evolution through natural selection seems to show that living creatures adapt themselves automatically to their environment. Some have argued that this abolishes the idea of intelligent design in nature, and speaks of an eye which has designed itself, without recourse to a Designer having knowledge of optics. It is, however, not necessary to draw this conclusion. It can be argued that there is still room in the system for an intelligent original Designer of the whole evolutionary process (see pp. 26–27).

4. MORAL ARGUMENT. It is argued that there is within the heart of man a most majestic voice, which tells him that he must do that which he knows to be right.[5] This is a mark of the existence of a God whose will is the moral

---

[5] Though it need not be supposed that there is a divine voice which immediately informs man what in fact is right. Views of right appear to depend directly on background, the tradition of society, experience, and education, though this process is doubtless ultimately guided by God.

law for mankind. This form of argument is largely associated with the teaching of the German philosopher Kant (1724–1804), who demonstrated the difficulties in the traditional Scholastic arguments for the existence of God, and sought instead to base his system upon the moral argument.

C. Summary and Evaluation

We can see that the cosmological, teleological, and moral arguments rest upon the basic and *a priori* ontological argument. If it be granted that the mind of man is a real spiritual entity, and that the higher flights of the human intellect give some reliable grasp of reality, then the arguments have much force. However, if the mind of man itself is pronounced to be somewhat in the nature of an illusion, then the arguments lose their force. It is not surprising, therefore, that religious skeptics have in the modern situation largely followed those schools of psychological thought which maintain that the mind of man is not a directing spiritual entity, but a passing phenomenon set up by the physical and nervous activity of the body, which alone is "real." In the eyes of the Christian, belief in God is a fundamentally rational belief, and acceptable to the candid mind, because of the rational and humane view of life which it engenders. The religious basic assumption enshrines rationality and goodness as the very principle of existence, and as the purpose of human life.

Arguments for the existence of God will not suffice to constrain the mind of the man who lacks the sense that the spiritual is real. He may bring himself to agree with the logic of the argument, but he cannot take the initial evidence seriously as evidence. To the Christian, however, it is a mark of the goodness and wisdom of God that it is thus impossible to produce an absolutely coercive proof of the religious position, because it is this alone which guarantees that man's faith and love of God shall be free. A man confronted by a theorem in geometry is not free to reject the proof. If he will not agree he proves himself either deficient in understanding or deliberately dishonest. God never drives the unbeliever into a corner like this. However pressing be the arguments in favor of the reasonableness of religion (and they are cogent, and even majestic in their force), there always remains some genuine difficulty to which the skeptic can reasonably cling, and which preserves to him an admitted intellectual right to continue to be a skeptic. It is a Christian view that a good and wise God has allowed this, so that whenever man opens his heart to the Father in faith and love it shall always be freely, for the sake of faith and love. However, the arguments here summarized to appear to be an important part of the foundation of Christian theology. They enable the thoughtful man to assure himself that in practicing the discipline of worship, and in living by trust in God, he is acting in a thoroughly rational manner.

Summary of Divergence: Modern Unbelief and the Doctrine of God

Practical materialism is not new. In the past millions who have professed a belief in the existence of God have found their lives dominated practically by the pursuit of the good things of this world— its comforts, its security, its prestige. Nor in the history of thought is theoretical materialism any new thing. There have always been some to argue that the universe of matter and of physical force is the only thing which really exists. However, it is clear that today practical materialism is much more widespread than it has ever been before, particularly in advanced industrial societies. A majority of the population of many of the world's most advanced countries has ceased to pray or to attend worship with any regularity, without any apparent sense of loss. Most of these people would not positively say that they are unbelievers, but their religion is inhibited from practise. Some other advanced countries, in particular the United States, retain a great deal of popular churchgoing. Yet many critics would affirm that much of this is superficial escapism, and would hold that men who do not possess the intellectual courage to face the testing problems of the modern age seek a spurious emotional release by a spare-time resort to modes of worship which are appropriate only to a bygone and simpler age. Still more significant is the fact that theoretical materialist thought is more widespread than ever before, and enjoys much intellectual prestige. There is not only the influence of avowed materialist philosophies, and in particular the dialectical materialist doctrine of Marxism. Of perhaps even more force is the indirect persuasion of the unspoken materialist assumptions of many prominent literary figures and publicists.

The general materialist argument is that in the childhood of the race man found himself helpless and frightened in a mysterious and perilous world. It was comforting to suppose that some great "father figure" of superior power and wisdom invisibly supervised and protected the tribe. Therefore the subconscious mind, in search of that which would give emotional security, naturally suggested that this being actually exists. Since then new discoveries have brought into being new ways of earning a living, and these in turn new forms of society. Each of these successive forms of society have required certain rules of thought and action to make them work, and the subconscious mind has naturally suggested that these rules are "right," and "the will of God." Thus religion has gradually accumulated. Yet "the spiritual" does not actually exist, but is only an insubstantial shadow cast in the mind of the race by the physical business of living. In the modern scientific age, it is argued, man is no longer a child, but an adult. He has the power to understand the universe, so that it is no longer mysterious. He has the power to control it, so that he is no longer helpless before the forces of nature. Therefore he no longer needs religion, which may have been relatively beneficial or at least inevitable at one time, but is now outworn.

A practical rejoinder of the religious believer to this materialist argument is that the alleged "adulthood" of the race has not in fact produced emancipation into a more rational and humane form of living. Much popular religion of the past, including some which passed as Christian religion, was in fact degrading superstition which held mankind in bondage to unreason, fear, and cruelty. However, the abolition of these ancient superstitions has only left room for the world to be filled with other superstitions, such as fanatical revolutionary movements, hysterical nationalism, the adulation of popular figures in amusement and sport, and the frantic cult of material "status symbols." These have been found just as fertile as anything in the past to engender cruelty, fear, and unreason.

a. The Doctrine of God: The Call for a Restatement

It is affirmed by some critics that the decline of a vivid sense of the unseen world and of a vital belief in God which is characteristic of the modern age is due in the first place to a mental picture of God which is no longer credible. Traditional theology has spoken of God as though He were a kind of invisible man of great power and knowledge, who dwells in some sphere which is "above" our own, or "beyond" it. The scientist, on the other hand, knows that there is no sphere of existence "above" or "beyond" the universe. He does not take so exalted a view of puny human nature, existing in this tiny world, as to find it fitting to use human comparisons as symbols to set forth the nature of God. If the Christian religion is to be respected, theology must therefore be drastically reconstructed, so as completely to avoid any phrase which may be misunderstood as teaching that a "man-like" God exists in some form of "place." Rather is He to be spoken of as "the ground of being," as "that which gives value to existence."

Furthermore, in the coming adulthood of the race man will find less and less sense of reality in definite acts of prayer, and particularly in traditional communal religious ceremonial. His contact with God must rather be an attempt to express spiritual value in the course of ordinary daily life, and in useful humane social service. This concept of a life of devotion to the principle of value has been described as "religionless Christianity" ("religion" in this phrase being used in the sense of Christianity as expressed in formal speculative dogmatic statements, and in definite clerically organized acts of public worship). In this way alone can the essential spirit of Christ live on in the modern world.

These ideas are particularly associated with the writings of Tillich and Bonhoeffer, and have been widely discussed in relation to the popular book *Honest to God*.

b. Man's Sense of God: A Rejoinder from Christian Tradition

The exponent of the traditional system of Christian theology must first admit that among simple-minded Christians in the past, and to some extent even today, God has been thought of as "like a man," and as dwelling in some sort of glorious "place." However, this is no true or necessary part of Christian theology. The Bible does not, when correctly understood, speak of God as though He had a body, or experienced human emotions. On the contrary, instructed Christians in every age have been perfectly well aware that God is a spiritual being, and is not to be thought of as existing in space or time. Thus the critic is criticizing something which in fact is not part of the Christian system.

However, the idea of God can only be expressed in symbolical language, and the framing of this symbolism is a much more subtle undertaking than the critic is disposed to assume. It is to be allowed that God is "the ground of being," and "that which gives value to existence." What is said under this heading is a part of the Christian system, and is true so far as it goes. However, taken in isolation this language comes dangerously near to reducing the concept of God to that of a bare principle of existence. The idea of the sovereign transcendence of God, and above all, of the personal nature of God, is obscured. This shuts the door upon the most valuable feature of the Christian religion, the sense of personal communion in worship and prayer with the personal Living God of the Bible. God becomes an object of meditation, not of loving and obedient devotion.

Furthermore, it may be argued, whatever may be the case with a small minority of highly gifted intellectuals, who may perhaps be moved to a sense of deep personal release by abstract thought, God must be symbolized in vivid and realistic terms if the thought of Him is to be made real to the mind of man, though admittedly these realistic symbols are not to be misunderstood in a crude and material sense. Thus it is almost inevitable in worship to say "Lift *up* your hearts!" though the throne of God's majesty is not "up" in a place. We cannot avoid saying "Come Lord!," though He does not have to move from another sphere in order to answer the prayer. And it is right to use the noblest aspects of human nature as our highest symbols of God's nature, so as to speak of Him as "Father," and of His "love," though these are only comparisons, not to be taken humanly and literally. If this vivid language is forbidden ordinary people cannot think about God at all.

Furthermore, the exponent of Christian tradition will urge that it is not in fact true that men of the age of science cannot accept the symbolical language of the Christian Faith, as it is reflected in accepted doctrine and traditional modes of worship. Some indeed do not appear to possess the sense of God, and find no sense of reality in acts of prayer and worship. However, it is quite the reverse with many others who are fully attuned to the characteristic modern and scientific method and outlook. They understand, and can with intellectual honesty use, the traditional symbolism. In prayer and Christian worship they do find a sense of personal communion with God. In this way they enjoy the advantage that they are joined in fellowship with other and simpler believers, who perhaps in their own devotional lives take some of the traditional Christian language in a less reflective sense.

Thus, we may argue, the failure to hold some of the modern generation to the Christian Faith is not due to a radical fault in Christian theology or worship. It is perhaps an accompaniment of the dislocation of the times, something serious indeed, but passing. Some would argue that the drift of so many from customary Christian worship is not a revolt against Christian faith as such, but only against the Church, considered as a socio-political group. In many lands the formerly unprivileged classes have turned against the former "establishment." The Church appeared in their eyes to be part of this "establishment," and so they have simply turned from the Church. Furthermore, the industrialized masses have had their imagination bemused by the triumph of the material. The city man works at a machine or a desk. He amuses himself with a mechanical gadget. Everything in the city street is made by man, and has its price. Man is hemmed in by the material, so that by comparison the sense of the unseen has become vague and uncertain, and therefore worship seems like "talking into the air." Nevertheless, as man adjusts to his changed surroundings these disorders may pass, and religion will again win a hearing if the Church maintains her witness.

IV. Revelation and Inspiration

A. Revelation

The use of the word "revelation" indicates that man only has knowledge of God because God of His free grace chooses to make it known. The Christian answer to the question, "Canst thou by searching find out God?" (Job 11:7) is "No." God belongs to a sphere of existence outside man's this-worldly experience. He is great and holy, whereas man is frail and sinful, separated from God by a great gulf both of intellectual and moral blindness (Isaiah 6:5). Man could discover nothing about God had not God of His goodness first made Himself known.

The word can be used in two senses. "Revelation" is the process by which God makes Himself known. "The revelation" is the divine truth thus made known. Revelation is often classified in two parts.

1. GENERAL REVELATION. This is the divine truth made known through the general order of nature, including the social, moral, and aesthetic life of man. It is all that truth which has been considered in relation to the evidence for the existence of God. This evidence is a revelation. The heavens only declare the glory of God because God has created them to be an expression of His mind. The mind of man can only see God's glory in the heavens because God of His goodness has made the mind capable of doing so. Thus all is of God, a gift of free grace, a self-disclosure. Yet it is also a *general* revelation, made to all men. It is the knowledge of God which can be attained by every honest and candid mind, quite apart from Christ or the Bible (Romans 1:19-20).

That part of religion which is based on the general revelation is natural religion. This is not specifically Christian, but is "the religion of all reasonable men." Examples of natural theology are a belief in one just and good God, the claims of morality, and the expectation of a future life.

2. SPECIAL REVELATION. This is the self-disclosure of God to man through the Bible, and supremely, in Christ. To the Christian this special and specifically Christian revelation conveys to man a body of truths more sublime than the general revelation. Examples of such truths are the Trinity, the Incarnation, and the Atonement. Indeed, the special revelation is not only a body of truth about God. It is essentially a *personal* disclosure of God in Christ. At the center of divine revelation we meet a Person, though He brings the declaration of a doctrine.

That part of religion which is based on the special revelation is known as revealed religion.

Summary of Divergence: Catholic and Protestant Views of Natural Religion

There is a significant difference of emphasis at this point.

a. Catholic[6] tradition affirms that natural theology, which may be deduced by reason from the character of God's creation, and which may be known outside the specifically biblical revelation known to the Church, is of distinct value to the soul of man. It is, as it were, the due setting, in which the precious jewel of revealed theology is displayed. Intellectual arguments to explain and vindicate natural religion are an important contribution to the understanding of Christian theology, though the higher and distinctively Christian truths of revelation extend beyond the power of human reason.

b. Protestant tradition, seeking to vindicate the primacy of faith, lays less emphasis upon natural religion, and some schools of Protestant thought have looked upon it with suspicion. Thus Protestantism in general gives a smaller place to human reason in the construction of theology. It is allowed that reason can discern evidence for some important truths about God, but it is emphasized that these are not those distinctive Christian truths concerning the gospel of grace, whereby man comes to salvation. Man can only savingly know God by means of the divine gift of faith. An extreme form of this position may be seen in the so-called existential theology (see pp. 8–9).

B. Inspiration

This word indicates the doctrine that God, by His grace through the operation of the Holy Spirit, quickens the human faculties He has given to men, in order that they may more readily understand and accept what He has

---

6 Including Catholic tradition held outside the Roman Catholic Church.

revealed (1 Corinthians 2: 9–11). Sinful man is by nature in a state of partial blindness to spiritual things. Inspiration comes to his assistance. Divine inspiration should not be regarded as the suspension of natural human faculties. It is the stimulation of human faculty by God's action, so that man may come closer to his divinely intended power of understanding. Inspiration makes man more fully human, not less.

It is the usual Christian belief that divine inspiration extends to some extent to all good and wise men who desire to know the truth, including believers in other religions. However, to the Christian the most particular and important work of inspiration was the writing of the Bible, and since that time, the continued guidance of the Church in understanding it.

V. Maker of Heaven and Earth

A. Creation

By "creation" is meant the principle that the universe exists solely because the sovereign God wills that it should exist, and that His will is the sufficient ground for its existence (Genesis 1:1; Psalm 33:6; Revelation 4:11). The main interest of Christian thought has been to symbolize as adequately as possible the absolute sovereignty of God. Thus it is the generally accepted Christian teaching that the creation is not eternal. It had a beginning, and before time began God was alone in glory (Psalm 90:2). He also has the power to bring the creation to an end (Isaiah 51:6; Revelation 20:11). To affirm, with some thinkers, that God is eternally creative borders upon the supposition that He is the Creator by the inward necessity of His being, with the implied conclusion that the creation is in some way necessary to His self-fulfillment. Christian thought rejects the latter suggestion, as it appears to infringe upon God's divine sovereignty and self-sufficient perfection. Nor is divine creation an activity upon previously existing matter. It is creation in the proper sense of the word, that is, creation "from nothing."

Summary of Divergence: Doctrines of Creation

a. The Ancient Church

The interest of the ancient Church in framing the first clause of the Creed, quoted at the beginning of this chapter, was to repel Gnosticism. The Gnostics of the early centuries claimed to illuminate the Christian Faith with "knowledge" (gnosis). Basing their ideas upon presuppositions about the nature of God drawn from contemporary secular, and therefore nonbiblical, thought, they taught that the Supreme God was transcendent, but not immanent (see p. 11). He (or rather, "It") could not have contact with anything so ignoble as the material creation, which must therefore be the handiwork of an intermediary being who proceeded indirectly from the highest God. Thus the bungling god of creation, mentioned in the Old Testament, is not the Christian God the Father. Christianity was cut off from its Jewish roots, and the Jewish Scriptures discarded. The Church firmly denied all this, and her interest was to affirm in the strongest possible manner the biblical doctrine that the Christian Father was "the creator of heaven and earth." However, the ancient Church was quite familiar with the idea that the authoritative Scriptures, including the creation narratives, may rightly be interpreted in a symbolic or allegorical sense.

b. Classic Protestantism

The traditional Protestant position regarding creation has been to emphasize as strongly as possible the full authority and integrity of Scripture. Many have felt that this involves interpreting the Genesis creation narratives in a manner as near to the literal as possible, particularly as and when traditional theology was apparently assailed by evolutionary concepts. However, within the conservative evangelical school there is still a degree of liberty of interpretation as to how far some of the details of the narrative may be taken in a symbolic sense without detracting from the inspiration of Scripture. For example, the "days" of creation may not be periods of twenty-four hours (2 Peter 3:8).

c. Genesis and Evolution

The generally accepted findings of astronomy, geology, and biology affirm that the universe gradually developed into its present form over an immensely long period of time, and furthermore, that the human race, considered as a physical organism, evolved like other organisms from an animal ancestry. It is not possible to reconcile this view of nature with the Genesis creation narrative, interpreted literally. This would appear to involve that the Christian theologian should revive and greatly extend the ancient doctrine that the early chapters of Genesis can rightly be expounded symbolically or allegorically, as divinely inspired and authoritative parables of spiritual principles. They are not to be taken literally, in contradiction to secure scientific findings.

The doctrine of evolution does not of itself exclude the general idea of divine creation. Even if it be allowed to the scientific determinist that the whole process of the development of stars, the world, and organic life upon it, from beginning to end is an unbroken chain of mechanistic necessity, even so the whole process still, it may be argued, requires a sufficient First Cause (see pp. 14–16). Evolution is a method of describing the manner in which God created the universe, but does not abolish the Creator. Nor do the findings of physical science of themselves require a complete mechanistic necessity. This doctrine would appear to be a matter of philosophical assumption rather than of scientific fact, and the Christian may affirm that it is possible to defend the idea that God is in intelligent control of the processes of nature (see pp. 28–29). In particular, it may never be possible to produce scientific evidence which will completely illuminate the change by which man became man. The awakening in a purely animal subman of those distinctively human faculties of personal self-consciousness, morally responsible choice, and the potentiality of communion with God, was not a physical or material change. No fossil evidence of it can ever be discovered! It is perfectly reasonable for the Christian to see in the creation of man (that is, in the raising of the race to the "human" level), a special, significant, and mysterious divine intervention in the evolutionary process.

B. Natural Law

The traditional Christian doctrine of the divine government of the world and of God's immanence within it (see p. 11) has been strongly questioned by some because of the scientific conception of natural law[7] and of the general scientific doctrine of the continuity of nature. We must first define the scientific term "natural law." For example, if one pumps twice the quantity of air into a vessel the pressure on the walls is doubled. If the quantity be increased to three times, the pressure is tripled, and so on. This happens in an orderly way. It happens in reverse when the air is let out. It happens similarly with a container of a different shape, or with a gas other than air. In particular, it happens in the same way in a year's time, or in another country, and however many times the experiment is performed. Such an observation that events happen in a fixed and orderly manner is called a natural law. Each natural law is a particular example of the general scientific principle of the continuity of nature. Scientific investigation has demonstrated fixed laws governing even the most complicated events, and the further the investigation is taken the more fully is the reign of fixed natural law displayed and confirmed.[8]

This scientific conception of the reign of natural law is an idea of great importance to Christian belief. To the believer the continuity of nature is a token of the constancy and rationality of God's own being and purpose. He is shown by His handiwork to be trustworthy and constant. He never performs an unaccountable action. He is never taken by surprise in events, or under the necessity of changing His mind. To the religious skeptic, on the other hand, these same facts may be viewed as a token that the whole universe, throughout its entire course of existence, is a fixed train of cause and effect, for all the causes of events are but the effects of causes which were before them. The universe is, as it were, a great machine, with every action predetermined by an iron law of necessity. The life of man is likewise determined. He may fancy he is free to choose, but this is an illusion. He

---

7 The phrase "natural law" is here used in its ordinary modern scientific sense. This is to be distinguished from the classical sense of "natural law" as the principles of reason and morality implanted in man's nature.

8 Strictly speaking it is not the concern of physical science to discuss the ultimate reason *why* natural phenomena occur in this orderly manner. This is the business of philosophy. Science is concerned with revealing and applying patterns of orderly behavior.

acts in terms of his environment and his inherited character, which character
is molded by previous environment. Thus the mind, with its sensation of
freedom, is by some explained away as the illusory subjective effect of
psychological causes. Thus a law of necessity denies human moral freedom.
The doctrine of scientific determinism tends towards the notion that the
thinking mind and all ideas of "the spiritual" are unreal. Even if the idea
of God is not in principle abolished, the doctrine is denied of a God who
can care for man and answer prayer.

C. Providence

A Christian answer to this difficulty regarding God's government of the
universe and natural law is that if it is once allowed that there is a thinking
mind behind the universe, there is then no need to suppose that God is
a prisoner of the machine which He has made. It is true that "mind" does
not "break" natural law, but it can cooperate with it and work through it
to bring about events which would not have happened had not the thinking
mind been at work. For example, when a plane flies through the sky an event
takes place which would not have happened had nature been left to itself,
and which the science of a former day would quite possibly have stated to
be contrary to well-known natural laws. Yet the reign of natural law has not
been broken. Natural law has been understood and used by the mind of man
to produce a new and significant event, which has to a small extent changed
the apparently fixed course of nature. If our limited human minds can
"work through" the law of nature to a small extent, surely the infinite mind
of God can do the same to a much more commanding degree!

The thoughtful Christian will prefer not to say that God "suspends" the
law of nature, for that reign of natural law is fixed by Him and is an
expression of His being. Yet He can prevailingly work through it to bring
things to pass which would not happen were nature left to itself. What
physical science says about the exactitude of the machine of nature is to be
accepted as true so far as it goes, within the scope of scientific experiment.
However, it is the faith of the Christian that there is another sphere of
activity by no means contradictory to this, yet interpenetrating it and
superior to it. God can work through the natural order of the world in
which we live to care for His children, to answer prayer, and to uphold
the cause of right with resources of which the men of this world cannot take
account. This is the belief in divine *providence* (Psalm 124:1-3; Matthew
6:25-33).

There is indeed an element of mystery in the operation of providence.
God does not always guide and bless His own in the way which they
themselves desire (2 Corinthians 12:7-10). Yet experience shows that He
does guide and bless. It is surely an excess of dogmatism on the part of the
skeptic to affirm that a divine action cannot happen in the world because
we men cannot fully understand the manner of it! Particularly is this so in

light of the amazing and unforeseen advances of scientific knowledge, which bring home to us how little we really know about nature. It is significant that in recent years the more thoughtful scientist is often much less inclined than formerly to affirm that the universe is a closed system of mechanical necessity.

D. Miracles

If God can work through the natural order to care for His own and to accomplish His will, it is surely reasonable to suppose that He can on occasion work some outstanding act of providence—an act of deep spiritual significance, completely outside man's understanding and beyond man's ordinary expectation. Such an exceptional providence may be called a *miracle*. A miracle, therefore, is best not described as a "breach" or "suspension" of the natural order, though this phrase has often been used in theology. Yet it is a wonderful act worked by the God who is in sovereign control of nature.

It is to be expected that miracles should occur at times of high spiritual crisis in the life of humanity, when God is especially vindicating His purpose, and in the lives of especially devoted men and women, who are to an outstanding degree the instruments of His purpose. The experience of the Church affirms that this has actually been the case. To the Christian the chief historical occasion when it will be found fitting for miracles to have occurred is the life of Christ Himself, for His earthly career was to a unique degree the divine intervention into this world. This brief discussion of general principles is inadequate to cover the contentious issue of the attitude of the thoughtful Christian to the miracles recorded in the Bible. This will be referred to when we consider the character of the Gospel narrative and the doctrine of Christ's resurrection (see pp. 105–8).

E. The Natural and the Supernatural

1. THE SUPERNATURAL AND BIBLICAL THOUGHT. The idea of a God who is able by His power mysteriously to overrule the natural order with His providential government has traditionally been expressed in theology by the contrast between the lower order of the natural and the higher of the supernatural. This notion of a "two-story" universe is derived from Greek thought, rather than from the Bible. The ancient Hebrews were largely deficient in the means of expressing the idea of "indirect causation," that is, the conception that natural events happen according to a self-acting natural law, so that God is responsible for the event only in the modified and indirect sense that He has created the world in the way He has. Thus it was hard for them to say that something "happened" without saying that God caused it. Many phrases in the Bible which appear strange to us bear the mark of this difficulty, and it is important for this principle to be kept in mind as one reads the Bible. Thus the statement "the Lord hardened Pharaoh's heart"

(Exodus 7:13) is not far in intention from "Pharaoh's heart became hardened" (but in a world where every event is overruled by God).

Therefore the biblical writers are not at home with the inquiry "Is this event natural or supernatural?" Thus the standing still of the sun recounted in Joshua 10:12–13 would have been regarded as a wonderful sign from God, but hardly as "supernatural," for to them it was not "the natural order" for the sun to rise normally. The Hebrews thought of the sun as rising each day by a direct divine act, though on this day God acted differently. This consideration, which is admittedly not very easy to grasp by the average modern mind, has an application to the modern discussion. Some critics, who have wished to expel the miraculous as far as possible from the Christian system, have argued that the theologian will not speak of "the supernatural" because this is not a biblical concept. This appears to be a most misleading, or even disingenuous plea. The idea of "the supernatural" is indeed alien to the Bible, but not at all because the idea of "miracle" is not there. In a natural order where everything is thought of as caused by God, every event is on the verge of miracle. It is impossible honestly to cite the Bible on behalf of nonmiraculous Christianity. However, in our modern thinking the well-known contrast between "the natural" and "the supernatural" provides a convenient means for discussing the miraculous element in the Christian religion.

2. THE DIFFICULTY OF THE SUPERNATURAL. Without a doubt, many people find a real element of difficulty as they approach the supernatural or miraculous element in the Bible and in the Christian Faith. The believer may have no great difficulty in arguing to himself in principle that if there is indeed a sovereign and personal God in control of the world it is reasonable to suppose that He should be able to work a miracle. Furthermore, faith may command assent to some few salient miracles, such as the incarnation and Christ's resurrection, which appear to be required by the Christian Faith. Yet the Bible contains many other stories of marvelous occurrences, such as sudden deliverances in answer to prayer, miracles of healing, visions of angels and of the divine glory, and the like. These are so outside our own experience, and contrast so strongly with the mentality inculcated by the study of natural science, that candidly it taxes the imagination to accept them, and we almost wish that they were not part of the Scripture! This is a difficulty we must try to face.

In the first place, it is not necessary for the man who prizes a thoughtful and honest mind to feel that he must come to the Scripture and to the Christian creed with strong antisupernaturalistic bias. This is not required by the scientific mentality. The advance of scientific knowledge itself, which has opened our eyes to all manner of possibilities and laws which were undreamed of a few years ago, or which were even confidently denied by the science of the time, has enforced the mystery of the universe. We dare not say that the infinite mind of God, working through the laws of nature, cannot perform marvelous actions simply because the knowledge of today is not able to comprehend them. At the same time, we need not go to the other extreme and insist as a matter of faith that every detail of every wonder-story which has come down from the past must be taken literally. Allowance must be made for the prosupernaturalistic bias of ancient times. In antiquity men loved stories of wonders as a natural support to faith, so it is not surprising that the accounts of outstanding events and of holy men should have come down to us associated with accretions which may perhaps be legendary. Yet it is an excess of skepticism to dismiss the event, or the man, as unhistorical because every detail cannot be insisted upon. Each case is to be considered on its merits.

Allowance must also be made for different modes of describing the same event. It does not follow that an ancient account of a remarkable and significant event is unreliable simply because it is framed in thought forms entirely different from those of the present day. For example, it is related that travelers through Switzerland in the Middle Ages came back with reports that it was a land of gloom and horror. The imagination of those days peopled the wild mountains with dragons, and fear closed the eye of the beholder to the beauty which we see. Nevertheless, these accounts are reliable as evidence that such a place as Switzerland was visited by certain travelers. The difference is one of psychological approach, not of fact. So likewise we have to realize that were a modern man, with the typical modern mentality, able to be present at some of the great and mysterious events of the Biblical narrative, he might well describe them in a manner very different, and much less pointedly supernatural. Yet he would still bear witness to the fact, and its wonder, and its spiritual significance.

F. Angels

Christian thought has traditionally affirmed that God's creation includes all things, "visible and invisible." The physical universe of matter and force is not all that exists. There are also thinking, feeling, and morally responsible personal beings which do not have material bodies like ours. Presumably they may have nobler powers of mind and spirit than ourselves. These are the angels, who are frequently mentioned in the Bible as the messengers of God (for example, Luke 1: 26; Hebrews 12:22). Although the spectacular ninefold Heavenly Hierarchies of "Thrones, Dominations, Princedoms, Virtues, Powers," so prominent in the thought and art of the Middle Ages, can hardly be urged in these prosaic days as a serious part of Christian doctrine, yet there is no need to retreat to the other extreme, and to dismiss the whole matter as childish fantasy. The facts of the unseen world can only be set forth in symbolical language, and the question is then raised as to what is the most adequate symbolism. At the least, the concept of angels expresses the principle that man is not the highest and noblest of God's created servants, or the center of the universe. Cynics have often falsely charged

Christian theology with teaching just this presumptuous notion. Furthermore, there are many to whom this system of symbolism makes the unseen world a pressing reality, and this is all to the good. It can hardly be claimed that the existence of angels is a doctrine contrary to science, for if they have no material bodies their existence can neither be proved nor disproved by the methods of physical science. It is a question of inherent spiritual probabilities. These probabilities seem to make it quite reasonable to speak about angels, though we need not imagine them according to the conventional pictures.

Readings

a. Some other general handbooks.

Barth, K., *Dogmatics in Outline,* trans. G. T. Thompson. London: SCM Press, 1957.

Pike, J. A., and W. N. Pittinger, *The Faith of the Church.* New York: The National Council, Protestant Episcopal Church, 1951.

Quick, O. C., *Doctrines of the Creed.* London: Nisbet and Company, Ltd., 1938. (More detailed.)

Whale, J., *Christian Doctrine.* New York: The Macmillan Company; London: Cambridge University Press, 1941.

b. On the matter of Chapter I.

Temple, W., *Nature, Man, and God.* London: Macmillan & Co., Ltd.,1951.

Trueblood, D. E., *Philosophy of Religion.* New York: Harper & Row, Publishers, 1957.

Richardson, A., *Christian Apologetics.* New York: Harper & Row, Publishers, 1948. (Defense of Christian belief.)

Chapter Two

The Jesus of History

I believe in Jesus Christ, His only Son, our Lord;
who was conceived by the Holy Ghost,
born of the Virgin Mary

I. Historical Religion

In the second clause of the Apostles' Creed the Christian Faith comes down from heaven to earth. The doctrine of God, and of His relation to the world, concerns unseen realities. To set these forth, symbolism is to be used, mental pictures that it to say, framed out of man's experience in this world, to bring home fully to the mind and the imagination that which is beyond immediate experience. Furthermore, arguments to vindicate the intellectual honesty of the Christian symbolism of God are questions of abstract thought. Thus the first clause of the Creed is a matter of mental construction. However, it has traditionally been an essential characteristic of the Christian Faith to affirm that The Faith is not simply a construction of the human mind, resting for its authority upon the goodness and wisdom of those who have thought it out. In the last resort it is not a philosophy, or a set of doctrines, or a system of ethics, though all these are intimately associated with it. Rather is it an authoritative witness to events which actually happened, which are the saving acts of God performed in the course of the history of this world. And the greatest subject of debate between traditional and critical opinion within the Church concerns these two allied issues: "To what extent is the Christian Faith founded on historical fact?" and "What do we mean by 'historical' fact?"

As we turn from these questions of mental construction to the historical inquiry "Did it really happen?" we turn from that which is in general "religious," or "spiritual," to that which is specifically *Christian*. Certainly there are many sincere and good men who do not accept the recognizable Christian doctrinal tradition about Jesus. There is a long spectrum of religious conviction extending from unorthodox denominations which describe themselves as Christian, through Jews, Moslems, to the ethnic religions, great and small. It is certainly no part of the business of the Christian theologian to deny that there are elements of authentic truth in all these systems, and much genuine human goodness among the people who uphold them. There is the ground common between all those who in various ways uphold the religious or spiritual view of life. However, as we pass from the first to this second chapter, we pass definitely from this common ground to that which is specifically Christian. Many who are not Christians well know what it is to live by religious faith, but it is only specifically Christian faith if it is faith in God as He has made Himself known to man in Jesus Christ, the divine Son, incarnate, crucified, and risen. This illustrates what is meant by the statement that the center of the Christian revelation is not a doctrine, but a Person.

In what has been written in the first chapter regarding existential theology (see pp. 8–9) we have already hinted at a problem which comes fully into the open here, as we turn expressly to the Christian Faith as an historical religion. In the current discussion of this matter two issues are closely associated: "What is the relation of Christian saving faith to the Jesus of history?" and "What are we to think of the Gospel narratives as historical sources?"

Summary of Divergence : Christian Faith and the Historical Jesus

a. Traditional Position

i. Christianity is the religion of the Incarnation (see pp. 49–50). The act of the Incarnation is itself the supreme example of the sacramental principle (see pp. 163–65) that God, who has created the material world as an expression of Himself, uses the material for spiritual purposes. In the Incarnation of His Son, God united Himself actually and personally with His handiwork, so that He lived a genuine human life in real human conditions, in our world. Thus it is essential that the story of Christ's birth, life, teaching, wonderful works, death, and resurrection must be taken seriously as real history. However, these divine acts in history are not barely wonderful events. They are events possessing an inward spiritual meaning to be discerned by faith, which is a divine gift (see pp. 221–23). On the one hand, God acts spiritually upon the inward man of the mind, the moral will, and the heart, to make him altogether a better man. Yet the spiritual action is mediated to man through the material action. A bare knowledge of the material divine act by itself does not save man. The effect must come home to the inner man of the heart by moving the mind, will, and affections to loving trust and obedience. Yet the inward, and in a sense subjective, effect could not take place without a knowledge of the objective historic divine work. Salvation is not merely subjective, a state of feeling and willing into which man stirs himself by autosuggestion. It is a personal response to that which God has actually *done* for man, in His Son.

ii. Therefore the Scripture witness to the facts about Christ must be read as history. This history is the essential foundation of true Christian doctrine. The Scripture records the historical preparation of the world for the coming of Christ, and likewise the apostolic witness to Christ, when at length he came; His birth, life, death, and resurrection. This testimony to Christ is in fact the element in Scripture which makes it into the Church's authoritative book. The ancient Church gave large scope to allegorical exegesis, and at times seemed more concerned to discover what parables of spiritual truth could be drawn from the narrative, than to emphasise the historical character of the narrative. Traditional Protestantism, on the other hand, wishing to safeguard the primary authority of Scripture, has tended to give principal emphasis to the historical reliability of the narrative. Frequently this interest has been manifested in the form of the doctrine of the literal inerrancy of Scripture (see p. 186). Nevertheless, the difference has always been one of emphasis rather than of principle. The general Christian tradition on both sides has affirmed that the Scripture is a sufficient account of historical events, and that these historical events are of importance because they are God's expression of an inward and spiritual work.

b. A Critical Position: "Demythologizing"

i. Critical New Testament scholars and theologians have observed that in the New Testament the Christian message is framed in terms of a view of the world order very different from that which is acceptable to an educated man of today. God is spoken of as though the throne of His majesty were above the azure dome of the heavens, and that He can visit the world with the fullness of His salvation at a future point in time. There is also a vivid conception of "angels" as the messengers of God, and of mental and physical disorder as due to "demons." All this mental furniture is frankly incredible today, and must be changed and modernized. If the scientific man is to accept the Christian message, the essential of that message must be rendered into terms of the universe as we know it to be, and of human psychology as at present accepted.

ii. A word which has been prominently used in this connection, particularly by R. Bultmann and his disciples, is "demythologization." The word "myth" has been adopted from the study of anthropology and comparative religion, where the primary sense is "the narrative that belongs to a ritual which sets forth some part of man's life experience." More generally a myth may be spoken of as an imaginative story which symbolizes a set of ideas or values.[1] Jesus thought and spoke in terms of the myth of a descent from heaven, which is the abode of God, and of the overthrow of Satan and his minions in this world. This clothing, now outworn, is to be stripped off, and the essential message reclothed in a myth, or symbolic expression, suitable to our own mental climate. The attempt to do this is called demythologization, which is not to be misrepresented as a mode of dismissing the Gospel narrative as unworthy of consideration, but rather as the opposite. It is an attempt to bring the inward meaning of the narrative to the serious consideration of the modern man.

iii. Akin to this is the fact that the element of physical miracle, so prominent in the Gospel narrative, is a great stumbling-block to the modern reader (see pp. 27–28). It is not so much that the modern believer cannot accept the idea of a wonderful divine action which works man's salvation, but that he must view it as an action which takes place only in the inward man of the mind, the will, and the heart. He cannot allow it to be intimately associated with a "physical miracle," that is, a supposed event which would have been observable by the methods of physical science, had there been a scientific observer present, and yet which is alien to the scientific world view. It will make the Gospel more likely to win the intellectual respect of the thoughtful man if it be judiciously emptied of this element of physical miracle.

It is clear that there is a considerable degree of association between points (ii) and (iii), because those elements in the Gospel narrative answering to the myth which was proper to antiquity are also largely the elements presupposing physical miracle.

iv. Relief is to be found for these obstacles to faith by considerations arising out of what is known of the teaching processes and literary conventions of antiquity. These were quite different from our own, and allowance must be made for this in the interpretation of the New Testament. This may perhaps best be illustrated from a few examples. The ancients thought in pictures, and were not so aware as we are of a clear distinction between that which is historically correct and that which is symbolically expressive. Thus it was natural to them to construct an imaginative story, which to us reads like an "event," in order vividly to symbolize an idea, and so commend it to the faith of the hearer. So it may be argued that in writing Matthew 27:51, "the veil

---

[1] The present writer must say that he feels it to be unfortunate that so much confusion has been introduced into the theological world by the use of the word "myth," in connection with the Gospel, in a sense subtly and misleadingly different from that in which it is used in common intelligent parlance. To non-professionals a myth is an unhistorical fantasy, a story which is not to be taken seriously as a source of truth. Thus to speak of the Gospel narrative as framed in myth almost irresistibly conveys the idea that it is a naïve story from the childhood of the race, historically unreliable, and spiritually worthless. This is not in fact the intention. In critical writing, no necessary judgment is passed upon the historical reliability or spiritual value of a narrative by the use of the term "myth." Thus it is possible to affirm that the Gospel narrative contains an element of myth, and also to affirm that this particular myth is largely historically reliable, and spiritually most valuable. However, critical theologians have created a very serious problem of communication here.

of the temple was rent in twain from the top to the bottom," the
Evangelist was not interested in this as a visible and physical event, and
conceivably did not even intend it in this sense. It is intended as a
parable of the idea that in Christ's death the way of access to God,
formerly symbolized as closed by the curtain which shut off the Holy
of Holies in the Temple, is now laid open to all believers. Similarly,
a narrative can on occasion have a touch added to it, in order to bring
out more clearly the Christian claim that an Old Testament prophecy
was fulfilled by Christ. Thus the curious attempt in Matthew 21:7 to
represent that Jesus rode into Jerusalem on two asses is to be explained
as due to a misunderstanding of the prophecy referred to in Zechariah
9:9. At least some details of the apparent "event" were in fact constructed out of the prophecy. Furthermore, a story of parabolic meaning
can have its details filled out in retelling it, so as to bring out more
clearly the teaching which the teller feels is implied. Thus in the parable
of the great feast, as recounted by St. Luke, there is a second summons
to the vagrants of the city (14:23), which clearly is intended to
symbolize the great Gentile mission of the Church. On the other hand,
in the more Jewish St. Matthew's Gospel nothing is said about this
second invitation, but the guest who has come in without a wedding
garment is expelled (22:11-12). This touch is introduced in order to
indicate that some minimal degree of legally correct conduct is required
of the Christian (compare Acts 15:19-20).

Again, just as an ancient Greek historian can survey the military
situation before a battle by the convention of composing a speech and
putting it into the mouth of the general, so the New Testament writers
can symbolize the spiritual situation by constructing a scene or a
sermon. Thus it may be argued that many sayings of Jesus, otherwise
arranged by Luke, have been arranged by Matthew in the form of
"the Sermon on the Mount" to indicate that the teaching of the Lord
is the "Mountain of the Law" of the New Covenant, the Beatitudes
being the equivalent of the Ten Commandments. There was no thought
of pious fraud in the employment of all these methods, even though
this so naturally suggests itself to our minds, accustomed as we are to
entirely different literary conventions. It was just the natural and
accepted method of the time, which must be understood and allowed
for, not condemned.

Finally, there is an over-all consideration arising from the method of
literary investigation known as "form criticism." The Gospels were not
written from verbatim accounts of the life of Christ, recorded with the
biographical interest of giving later generations material for compiling
"Lives of Christ." Some only of the facts about Jesus and His teaching
were remembered by the Church and recorded, and then not in order.
These were those facts which served as the means for preaching the
Gospel and winning the hearers to Christian faith. Thus the whole
narrative has been filtered through the group mind of the believing
community, which has gradually arranged the general presentation
and order and adjusted the details of the separate narratives, the more
clearly to bring out these preaching and teaching interests. The con-

sequence is that what we meet in the Gospels is not a supposed reliably biographical "Jesus of history," but the Church's "Christ of faith."

Thus the critic can explain those mythic and miraculous elements in the Gospel narrative which are to us such a stumbling-block as going back only to the believing mind of the Church, as it expressed itself in the means natural to the time. There is no necessity to suppose that Jesus actually said all these things, or that His life was actually accompanied by all these miracles.

v. The result of all is the following general account of the historical origin of the Christian religion. Doubtless Jesus of Nazareth was a man of most commanding personality, and impressive spiritual insight as a teacher. After His death His disciples realized that personal contact with Him had brought to them a most moving and lasting sense of the presence and power of God. They had been assured of divine forgiveness, and that they were even now partakers of God's kingly rule over the world. They were possessed of a sense of loving fellowship with the God they had come to know through Christ, and they lived in a state of vivid expectancy of the completion of God's triumph. This, their "existential encounter" with God in Christ, *was* God's historic saving act, wrought out in this world. The first Church expressed this faith in its "kerygma" (Greek for "thing preached"; translated "preaching" in 1 Corinthians 1:21). The kerygma, or message, was finally recorded in writing, in the New Testament. How many of the Gospel events, pronouncements, ethical maxims, parables, and miracles (including the resurrection itself) are authentic historical reminiscences, and how far they represent the construction of the Church as it sought to symbolize and commend its faith, is a matter of uncertainty. Doubtless both elements are present in the Gospel narrative which we have received, but the character of each particular text is a matter of inherently varied scholarly judgment. Yet in the last resort this is a matter of interest only to academic scholarship, and not to religious faith, for the object of our faith is "the Christ of faith."

c. A Mediating Position

i. There are grave disadvantages both to the strictly traditional and to the extreme critical positions. In the case of the first, in order to safeguard the traditional judgment as to what is involved in the authority of the New Testament as the source of an historical faith, it is apparently necessary to reject as utterly mistaken a large number of scholarly judgments regarding the character of the Gospel narrative, even when these appear to be securely grounded, and widely accepted by cautious and moderate opinion. In the case of the second position, the Christian faith is revolutionized into something radically different from what it has always been understood to be, from the New Testament period up to the present century. If the critic still affirms that he upholds the Christian Faith as an historical religion, he is using the word "historical" in an entirely novel sense.

ii. The doctrine of the wholehearted "demythologizing" and "existential" critics is a radical departure from the historic tradition. The essential spiritual value of the traditional position that The Faith is based upon an objective act of God performed upon the plane of history, is that this is the factor which constitutes Christianity a religion of grace (see pp. 83–84) and of real divine redemption. Here is a witness to something which God in Christ actually *did* in our world, making our human situation different. To make oneself by faith one with this historic and victorious Christ is to partake of "a power *not ourselves* that makes for righteousness." However, if there is in fact no objective divine act, but only a powerful existential impression upon the minds of the first disciples, then there is no redeeming power from outside the human situation. To make onself by faith one with this "Christ of faith," a figure constructed out of the devout imagination of the Church, is in reality only an attempt to rally one's own moral will and love toward God by an exercise of psychological autosuggestion. In this case, the claim that by the agency of the Holy Spirit the Church's worship brings communion with a living and victorious Savior is a spurious claim! Christian worship is in the last resort an exercise in communal autosuggestion. The Church's autosuggestion may be unusually enlightened in moral and intellectual content, a venerable, beautiful, and disciplined system. Yet it is autosuggestion still. There is nothing *there*! This is indeed a radical departure.

iii. It would also appear that the attempt of "existential" Christianity to retreat from "physical miracle" to the inward life of the mind, the moral will, and the spirit, is an illusory relief. This position is inherently unstable. Even if a few astute academics, their minds sharpened to fine intellectual distinctions, can for a time sustain their religious faith upon it, it is only for a time. And experience shows that most people cannot so sustain their faith. The case in point is surely Christ's resurrection. It would at first sight seem attractive to some that the victory of the living Christ over the bondage of sin should be preached as an "existential" one only, wrought in the mind of the disciples, but unencumbered by the miracle of the empty tomb. However, if one presses the inquiry of why the physical miracle of the resurrection should thus be considered an encumbrance to faith, the answer surely is that "physical miracle" is forbidden by that mechanistic philosophy which cannot allow that there is a thinking mind (God) in control of nature (see pp. 27–28). And if one accepts the mechanistic philosophy, it will forbid thinking minds to the disciples, and to believers since, just as surely as it will forbid the empty tomb! The mechanistic way of looking at nature explains away the inward life of the heart and mind of man as a complicated chemical and electrical reaction, determined by physical forces. In fact, either one allows that the thinking mind of man is real, and also that there is a God who can, operating through the laws of nature, work a miracle— or else, logically, one denies both propositions.

iv. However, on the other side, it is to be admitted that these novel and critical methods of New Testament investigation possess some real measure of validity. Otherwise they would not have made their wide scholarly appeal. It can be agreed that the processes very briefly summarized in paragraph (b [iv]) above did take place in the formation of our Gospel narratives, and that real account must be taken of this in reliable interpretation. It is not necessary in the supposed interests of the authentic historic Faith to deny outright the findings of modern critical scholarship. All that is requisite is that these methods be not pressed to the extreme, in the manner of some of their most eminent exponents, such as the Bultmannians. Thus it should prove possible both to give a dispassionate reading to work of New Testament scholarship, and also to defend the dogmatic substance of the traditional and historic Christian Faith. This is a central and moderating position.

v. It is clear that there is an inherent tendency for certain critical methods of New Testament investigation to proceed to an extreme. First one minor feature of the accepted Gospel narrative is explained away as taking its origin in the interpretative and preaching interests of the mind of the early Church, and then another, and another, until the reliable historic Christ virtually vanishes. It may be asked, if the validity of these scholarly techniques be once allowed in principle, what is there to prevent this drift to extremism? An answer worthy of consideration is that the findings of a critical scholar are at least as much due to the philosophy of life which motivates him, and to the attitude of mind which he brings to his study, as to the character of the factual evidence.

Clearly, in the world of honest scholarship objective facts are sacred. Such facts include the existence, the contents, and the date of some manuscript or other piece of historical evidence. However, the mentality which is applied to this evidence is something *adopted* by the scholar, and which therefore can be called in question, or changed. It is never self-evident. And the orthodox Christian believer has just as much right to his philosophy and general attitude of mind as has the radical critic, or the skeptic. He has behind him the immense and impressive consensus and the long-tested endurance of the accepted Christian tradition. This is an important circumstance which must never be forgotten in reading the impressive works of learned men. One rightly respects erudition, and some learned writers of great repute are admittedly very radical in their criticisms. It must, however, always be remembered that they are not radical simply because they are deeper scholars than those somewhat more conservative. They are radical largely because of the initial subjective presuppositions which they have brought to the study of the objective facts.

The method of scholarly research is the comparison of biblical texts with each other, and of biblical with nonbiblical sources, to determine which may have influenced which in the evolution of the tradition. Each of these acts of comparison is a judgment which reflects the underlying philosophy or general approach of the scholar in question. Thus a learned volume of 200 pages, each with ten footnotes giving references, appears at first sight to present an irrefragable case of 2,000 separate pieces of evidence. Actually there is one piece of *determinative* evidence

—the particular mentality of the scholar who has made all the 2,000 judgments! This is why the evidence can be arranged in so many different ways.

The response of prudent Christian thought is not impatiently to reject the whole concern of critical scholarship as unreliable, irreverent, and dangerous to faith. Yet on the other hand, one certainly need not feel overawed into the abandonment of the historic Christian Faith simply because some extreme critic is a writer of great repute. More mature experience indicates that what is required is on the one hand respect for these illustrious figures, but also that they be viewed in the proper perspective from the vantage ground of the well-tried Christian tradition. In the past many stimulating schools of "modern theology" have gone all the way down one extreme track or another. After the experience of many years it has generally been shown that there was some aspect of truth in almost all, but never the whole of the truth. Those who on the one hand have candidly considered what the new school of thought has to offer in the understanding of the Christian system, but who on the other hand have treated the new school with cautious reserve, refusing to revolutionize traditional Christian theology because of it, are generally found, when the whole discussion is over, to have represented the most complete intellectual integrity and the fullest Christian wisdom.

vi. SUMMARY. If a mediating position is adopted it would appear that the New Testament account of Christ is not dispassionate biography, but an attempt so to present the facts about Christ as to win converts to Christian faith. Nevertheless, this does not imply that the account of the facts is radically unsatisfactory as historical evidence. The narrative has passed through the mind of the believing Church, which has introduced certain interpretative elements. However, these concern nonessential features. The main lines of the Gospel portrait of Christ are to be accepted as reliable, as an account of His character, teaching, death, and resurrection. They form a sufficient basis for the historic faith.

Particular leading examples of the issues discussed arise in connection with the doctrines of the Virgin Birth, Christ's resurrection, and the Second Advent.

A number of other important issues regarding the historical character of the Gospel narrative are more conveniently treated in the chapter on the Bible (see pp. 194–200).

II. Jesus Christ, His Only Son, Our Lord

The faith that in the person of Jesus God Himself had met mankind and performed His saving act in this world, came to birth in the fellowship of the disciples. The stages of the process may be traced out in the titles given to Jesus in the New Testament.

A. Jesus

This is the name given to our Lord in infancy (Luke 2:21), and speaks to us of our Lord as a man among men. The use of this human and personal name symbolizes to us the first stage of the meeting. Men first encountered Christ as one of themselves (Matthew 13:54–57). "Jesus" is the customary English rendering of the Greek name which in turn represents the Hebrew name which we read in our English Old Testament as "Joshua." Both names mean "Saviour," and our Lord was thus named after the hero who brought the tribes of Israel into the promised land (Joshua 1:1–9; compare Acts 7:45; Hebrews 4:8). There were other people with the same name (Colossians 4:11).

B. Jesus as a Prophet

1. The growing impression which Jesus made upon those who met Him was that He was a man of commanding personality, who possessed an unique grasp of spiritual things. He reminded men of the old prophets, upon whom the Spirit of the Lord descended to enable them to declare a word from God with authority. In particular, they were amazed at His power to heal, and to cast out demons. So He was hailed as a prophet (Matthew 16:13–14; Mark 6:15; Luke 7:16).

2. Answering to our Lord's human office as a prophet, is the circumstance that He received as preparation for His public ministry the typical prophetic equipment of a baptism of the Spirit of the Lord (Mark 1:9–11). Traditional Christian doctrine has decisively rejected the supposition that in this experience a certain ordinary man Jesus "became" the Christ, for this would be to make our Lord no more than an inspired man. The notion that the divine Spirit indwells all men to some extent, and Christ to the fullest extent, is not the accepted Christian doctrine of Incarnation, for such a doctrine does not represent the *union* of humanity with God. The Church teaches that the union of human and divine was complete from the first moment of Christ's conception in the Virgin's womb. We may say that He gradually became aware of His unique nature and office, and that He became aware of this through the operation of His natural human faculties. Doubtless the illumination which came at His baptismal inspiration was a decisive stage in this self-realization. Nevertheless, our Lord came to this realization on account of what He already was by nature.

C. The Christ

1. The New Testament word "Christ" is the Greek equivalent of the Hebrew word "Messiah," both words meaning "the anointed one." Anointing with oil was in Bible days the rite for consecrating a king (as in 1 Samuel 16:1–13), just as it still is in the British coronation service. Prophets and priests could also be anointed. It was a part of the Jewish faith that God had given to them the Davidic dynasty of kings as the center

of their nationhood, and had promised, in token that He would bless and protect His people through all time, that He would preserve to Israel a king of the house of David (1 Chronicles 17:9–14; 2 Chronicles 6:16). Politically speaking this hope had long and miserably failed, but their faith taught the Jews, in their subjection to pagan overlords, that God would vindicate His promise by doing with supernatural power what manifestly could not be done by political. God would set up His own "Anointed One," His king, His Messiah. Thus many of the Jewish people in the time of Christ were living in a state of expectancy for the coming of the Messiah. He could be thought of in terms of a coming prophetic, priestly, or angelic figure. However, the idea which more immediately lies behind the New Testament doctrine of our Lord is that the awaited Messiah was God's anointed king, the bringer of God's kingdom and the fulfiller of the ancient promises.

This hope took various forms. The Messiah could be thought of as a man descended from David, but equipped with the fullness of divine power (Isaiah 9:2–7, 11:1–3), or as a completely supernatural figure who had dwelt in glory with God, and who would descend to earth. His kingdom could be expected on this earth, when the creation was divinely restored (Isaiah 11:4–16), or it could bring the history of this world to an end, and exist in a new age. The hope could be given an inferior tone, largely nationalistic, and concentrated upon the victory, prosperity, and happiness of God's chosen people in that day. Yet there were men of spiritual insight whose hope for the unveiling of God's glory was by the restoration of His people to holiness and obedience to Himself, and that this restoration should be the means of divine blessing to all nations (Micah 4:1–4). This messianic hope was a most important part of the background of our Lord's ministry.

2. The first decisive stage in the growth of Christian faith among the community of our Lord's disciples occurred when first St. Peter, and then others, realized that the prophet who had so impressed them was in fact the long-expected Messiah, the Christ (Matthew 16:13–16). This involved a confession that Jesus was much more than a prophet, though it did not of itself necessarily involve the doctrine that He is divine. A Jew would quite possibly have described the expected Messiah as God's personal representative on earth, but not as divine in the later Christian sense. However, though Jesus was a very striking personality, He was very different from the military Messiah of much current expectation, and to come to this realization was a mark of very real spiritual insight, and the token that St. Peter and the others were inspired by God (Matthew 16:17). Thus the original feature of the distinctive Christian confession of faith is that Jesus is the Christ, and those who first made this confession under the leadership of St. Peter constitute in a real sense the foundation of the Church (Matthew 16:18–19).

3. THE SON OF MAN. This title was among those which could be used for the expected Jewish Messiah. It probably takes its rise from Daniel 7:13, where "a son of man," (that is, a noble *human* shape; compare Psalm 8:4)

stands for God's coming world kingdom, in the same way that the four bestial monsters of verses one to seven stand for the four pagan world empires of ancient times. This thought was developed in the period between the Old and New Testaments. In particular, in the so-called Book of Enoch (46:1–4; 62:2, 5, 9, 14), the "Son of Man" has been turned from the personification of God's kingdom into a supernatural person, God's king. He is destined to come from the presence of God upon the clouds of heaven and to set up God's kingdom.

The importance of this title is that it is the one which our Lord Himself chose regularly to refer to Himself (for example, Matthew 16:13; Mark 2:10). By this He clearly intended to claim that He was the Messiah (Mark 8:38, 14:61–62).[2] However, it seems to have been a somewhat vague title, and a somewhat guarded claim (John 12:34). It apparently lacked the ready-to-hand military and nationalist associations of the familiar title "Son of David," which was the natural one to find upon the lips of the enthusiastic crowd (Matthew 21:9). Perhaps Christ chose it as a part of His policy of avoiding a popular messianic rebellion (John 6:15), and also used it as a title into which He might more readily pour the notion of the nonmilitary and spiritual deliverer. Certainly when He used it He was often speaking of His humility and sufferings (for example, Mark 10:45, 14:41).

4. THE GOSPEL OF THE KINGDOM. This central doctrine is intimately associated with the confession that Jesus is the Messiah because it is the essential office of the Messiah to bring in the kingdom. Modern humanitarian reformers have often spoken of the kingdom of God as though it were the ideal social order of universal human brotherhood and right, set up by human effort in social reform. We cannot doubt that it is one of the aims of God to stir men up to strive for social right, and so to set up an improved social order. In a sense, then, activities for social reform may be a mark of the kingdom. Nevertheless, this reformist doctrine can easily obscure the fact that the New Testament kingdom of God is the action of God and the gift of God. In the Old Testament the kingdom of God is the sovereign power of God whereby He rules the world. It is exerted in the world of men to rescue the distressed cause of right, and in this way to vindicate the fact that He is king (Psalm 145:11–14; Daniel 2:44, 7:14). The central theme of the preaching of Jesus was the gospel (that is, good news) of the coming of this long-expected kingdom (for example, Luke 4:43). This answers exactly to the doctrine that Jesus is the Messiah, or Christ.

This doctrine has received much attention in the modern world of New

---

[2] Radical critics would largely deny this. The tendency would be to affirm that the quotation from Daniel was first viewed by the Church as a "prophecy of Christ," and then read on to the lips of our Lord to express their faith (see discussion on pp. 36–38). Indeed, some would say that our Lord did not describe Himself as "Son of Man," but that the title was attributed to Him by the early Church and placed upon His lips in the narrative.

Testament studies under the title of the *eschatological* view of the mission and teaching of Jesus. Eschatology is the doctrine of "the end"; that is to say, of the end of this present Age, and of the coming of the Day of God which will bring the unveiling of God's sovereignty, the overthrow of the power of wickedness, and the redemption of God's people. Clearly, our Lord's teaching was vitally concerned throughout with the arrival of the Day of God, and the first Christians lived in vivid expectation of it (Acts 17:30–31, 24:25; Romans 13:11–14). Thus Christ's gospel of the kingdom was largely eschatological, rather than social and reformist.

In many passages our Lord appears to teach that the long-expected Day of God had now arrived. God's sovereign redeeming power was at that moment immediately available (Mark 1:14–15). Because Jesus was with men the kingdom was with men (Luke 17:21, "for in fact the kingdom of God is among you," N.E.B.). Jesus taught that His wonderful acts of healing, casting out devils, and preaching were the very tokens that God's victorious power was now at work in the world (Luke 7:19–23, 11:15–22). God's amazing gift of the kingdom was now near at hand, only waiting for men believingly to grasp it (Matthew 13:44–46).

In some other passages Jesus appears to speak of the kingdom as future. He is to come, and to come very soon, in power and glory, to bring God's judgment and redemption (Matthew 10:23; Mark 9:1, 14:62; Luke 9:26–27). The circumstance that, until they were gradually taught otherwise by experience (compare 2 Peter 3:1–9), the early Christians did largely live in a state of expectancy to see their Lord come in judgment at an early date, would on the face of it seem to confirm the impression that He actually taught something of this sort. To the Christian believer, at least, this is a matter of some perplexity, in view of the fact that Christ did not so come. A variety of views have been put forward to account for this.

The most radical critics have stated that Jesus was an enthusiastic visionary who proclaimed, sincerely enough, that the Day of God was very soon to come, possibly with Himself as judge, but that He was mistaken. However, there was much of more permanent spiritual value in the message of Jesus, which lived on in the mind of the Church, even though experience compelled the Church to reconstruct much of the Lord's original teaching. One who accepts the divine lordship of Christ can hardly accept unreservedly this view, which is apparently destructive of the doctrine that our Lord is God's very revelation of Himself, and the authoritative spiritual leader of mankind. However, it is possible to resolve the difficulty by allowing that the apparent disparity between what our Lord originally meant and what the Church later understood Him to have said arose through difference in thought forms.

It may reasonably be argued that Christ, using the imaginative language of the prophets, symbolized that which is very certain and very urgent by speaking of the event as though it were very near. However, the disciples did not always very fully and very spiritually understand Him. Their minds were to some extent clouded with Jewish messianic dreams (Acts 1:6), and so in their recollection and interpretation of the teaching of their Master they made His prophetic urgency a whole degree more visible and material and "near in time," than He had intended. Although Jesus freely used the eschatological language of the tradition which lay behind Him, it is also reasonable to suppose that a person of His creative spiritual insight should have used this stirring imagery in the most spiritual sense of which it is capable, and not in a naïve and materialistic manner. Consistent with this supposition is the witness in the Gospels that Christ very positively forbade His disciples to give themselves over to curious speculations as to the exact time of this supposed sudden event (Mark 13:32–37; Luke 17:20–21). Attempts to calculate the "times and seasons" have always been an integral part of the less thoughtful and more naïve and materialistic type of eschatological expectation among both Jews and Christians. Our Lord showed Himself fully aware of this danger, so we need hardly suppose that He Himself was guilty of falling into it.

Possibly the best construction to be placed upon all the variety of sayings recorded in the Gospels, interpreted in light of both the spirit of our Lord and the experience of the Church, is that Christ taught that the kingdom is both present and future. It was truly present and active in His presence, but in an initial and relatively inconspicuous stage. And this authentic "seed" of the kingdom was destined to grow and to prevail in the earth, until the whole world order should be transformed and glorified by the full unveiling of God's sovereign power, and the open manifestation of the fact of Christ's presence (Matthew 13:31–32, 24:27) (see pp. 247–48). Thus the long expectation of God's people was both realized in Christ and yet remains to be realized. That future tremendous and mysterious realization of the Christian hope is to be awaited in solemn expectancy, yet not speculated about as though it were sudden or soon.

5. The church and the kingdom. Jesus also spoke many times of "entering" the kingdom (Matthew 7:21, 21:31; Mark 9:47, 10:14–15; Luke 16:16), or of "being in" it (Matthew 11:11; Luke 22:29–30). It has authoritative "keys" of admission and exclusion (Matthew 16:19, 23:13). This indicates that in addition to the primary eschatological meaning of the kingdom as "the sovereignty of God" there is a second and derived meaning in the mind of our Lord. The kingdom has a proper sphere of action in the world of men. Though God rules all men, He has a special instrument for exercising that sovereignty as it is unveiled in Christ. This is the disciplined company of those who acknowledge Jesus as the Christ, and trust in God's redeeming act performed in Him. Thus the Church, though not itself the kingdom of God as some traditional theology has claimed, is the instrument of the kingdom. It is the community of the kingdom, called into being by the King for the extension of His rule.

D. The Lord

The developing devotion and religious thought of the New Testament Church is reflected in the use of this title for Christ, for the name "Lord" seems to carry implications going beyond that of "Messiah." The deepest conviction of the Christians was that Jesus had done for them what only God can do. In response they regarded Him as man can rightfully think only of God. In union with Christ they had been united with God, for He had conquered the guilt and power of sin and evil. Therefore they trusted Christ for salvation. They made implicit obedience to Him their rule of life. Their attitude toward Him was one of unreserved loving trust and adoration. In fact, the language of worship came instinctively to their lips as the Church gathered together to hold communion with Him. It was this experience which was the foundation for the Church's claim that Christ was higher in dignity even than the Messiah of Jewish expectation. The conviction was symbolized in the title "Lord," which indicates the object of one's religious devotion, and trust for eternal salvation. Thus, while the first primitive confession which united the Church was "Thou art the Christ," the characteristic creedal confession of the New Testament Church is "Jesus is Lord" (Acts 2:36; Philippians 2:11). This word probably has its roots in both the Jewish and the Gentile backgrounds of the Church.

1. Among other uses of the word "Lord" in Gentile religion, the pagan mystery religions commonly referred to their divinities, in whom the devotee trusted for salvation, by the title "Lord." St. Paul shows himself aware of this, and stresses both the comparison and the contrast. The one and only true "Lord" and object of devotion is Jesus, the Christ (1 Corinthians 8:5-6).

2. Furthermore, the Greek translation of the Old Testament, in common use at that time both by the Jews and by the Church, rendered the sacred name of God by the word "Lord," just as does our English Old Testament. That the Christians were able to use the same divine name for Jesus shows how far their thought had moved. It took the later Church much time and care to think out a precise theological formula by which they could say that their Lord was divine in the full sense of the word, and also safeguard the basic truth that God is one. However, we see here in the New Testament a clear witness to the fundamental convictions which made the doctrine of the Holy Trinity necessary to the Church, as a way of drawing out clearly the implications of Scripture.

E. The Divine Son

The doctrinal conviction of the New Testament Church, springing out of her profound experience of saving union with God in Christ, is supremely expressed in this title. It speaks still more exactly of the doctrine of the divinity of Christ. In calling on Jesus as Lord, that is, as the object of religious devotion and trust, the Christian had accepted an attitude to Christ which man can only rightly adopt to God. The word "Son" crystallized their conviction that they were correctly guided in doing this. A son has the same equality of human nature as his father. They are of "one flesh and blood." This is applied symbolically to Christ. Thus the doctrine of the divine sonship of Christ symbolizes the idea of equality of divine status with God the Father (Matthew 11:25–27; Luke 20:9–13; John 1:18, 3:16; Acts 9:20; Hebrews 1:1–2; 1 John 4:10).

F. The Word of God

Here is an alternative way of defining the divine nature of Christ. The Greek word for "word" (in English letters written "logos") was capable of an interesting and subtle variety of meaning. "Logos" can mean "reason," the activity of the thinking mind, and also "a word." Reason is a purely spiritual thing, whereas a word is both spiritual and material, for it is reason expressing itself outwardly by means of a sound, and so entering another thinking mind. This usage provides an important method of symbolizing the relationship which exists between God the Creator and Jesus Christ. The Creator is the intelligent thinking mind which exists behind the universe. He is logos, reason. The creation in all its order and beauty, together with all the noble works of the mind of man, is the outward expression in material form of the divine reason. Thus the world is a word from God. However, the coming of Jesus Christ into the world is the supreme example of this general principle of the spiritual expressed through the medium of the material. The divine reason, who is the Creator, united Himself with human nature, so that a being lived on earth who was in a special sense both spiritual and material, because He was both God and man. Thus Christ is in a unique sense the Word of God. This way of thinking first comes to light in the prologue to St. John's Gospel, a passage which has always greatly appealed to philosophically minded theologians (John 1:1–5, 9–14).

This Greek idea of the Logos is also clearly linked with an Old Testament one. The prologue to the Fourth Gospel, opening as it does with the words "in the beginning," is designed to take the mind of the reader back to the first words of the creation story in Genesis. Here God "said, Let there be light" (Genesis 1:3; compare Psalm 33:6). The word of God, therefore, is much more than the expression of knowledge. It is the word of a sovereign king. It is an executive word, which causes something to happen. Thus to speak of Christ as the Word of God symbolizes the doctrine that He is the effective agent of creation (John 1:3) and also of restitution and judgment (Revelation 19:13).

This theology of Christ as the Logos of God is of importance chiefly in that it may be used to connect the special revelation of the work of Christ with the general revelation which comes through the intellectual and artistic activities of all mankind. The divine reason which has moved all true philosophers took on human form in a unique manner in Christ. Thus all the cultural activities of mankind lead up to Christ, and He is the focus of them all. Ancient Greece prepared the way for the gospel, just as did the Hebrew prophets. Learning, art, and science are part of the business of the Christian. However, this logos theology is not complete and self-sufficient, and needs to be balanced by the doctrine of Christ as the divine Son. Taken by itself it too easily represents Christ as simply the climax of the revelation of divine truth. Our Lord indeed is this, but still more, He is the agent of a divine redeeming historical work in the world.

III. The Incarnation

We now turn from the basic Christian convictions about our Lord, born of the experience of divine salvation, and recorded in the New Testament, to the precise theological formulae which the Church later developed in order clearly to bring out the implications of the New Testament witness. The doctrine of the divine Son as He exists in glory is more conveniently treated when we consider the doctrine of the Trinity. We now outline the Christian doctrine of the divine and human natures of the incarnate Lord.

A. The Incarnation

This word is devived from the Latin *carnis*, "flesh," and means "becoming flesh" (compare John 1:14). The Christian doctrine of the Incarnation is that the divine Son, who from all eternity is God in the same full sense that the Creator-Father and the Holy Spirit are divine, completely and permanently joined Himself to our genuine human nature, so as to form one real person who was at once both fully divine and fully human. In this way God joined Himself to the human race, His handiwork, and lived a real human life in this world (Philippians 2:5–11; Hebrews 1:1–8, 5:5–8). This doctrine is both the foundation of the whole classic Christian system and the chief cause of offense in the Christian system to naturalistic thinkers who conceive of the universe as a closed mechanistic system. The personal visit of God to His own creation is the cardinal example of a divine intervention into the affairs of men. It is the supreme miracle, which if accepted makes credible at least the possibility of other miracles. The Church originally sought to frame in systematic and unambiguous language the implications of her basic conviction that in Christ God had come to man and had done for man what only God can do. The doctrine of the Incarnation is required if Christianity is to retain its character as a religion of real historical divine redemption.

Any adequate doctrine of salvation appears to require two affirmations regarding our Lord. He must be divine, in the proper sense of the word, or His life, death, and resurrection is not the divine saving action in the world. And He must be human, in the proper sense of the word, or His saving action is not within the world of our human affairs, and has nothing to do with us. A teacher who is prepared to regard Christianity as no more than a philosophy of life or an ethical system can very well find himself content with a view of Christ which represents Him as the perfectly inspired man, and the bringer of the supreme revelation of God's will. In every age, however, teachers who have fully appreciated the Christian religion as a gospel of real redemption have affirmed the Incarnation. Here is "the great divide" between the broadly spiritual and humane view of life and the specifically *Christian* view.

By way of clarification we may outline some views of Christ which do *not* represent the Christian doctrine of the Incarnation, and which were held by some in the ancient world or which are current today. (The names given to some of these in footnotes are the technical terms used in historical theology, and are listed here for the sake of identification when they are found in theological literature.)

1. VIEWS WHICH DO NOT DO JUSTICE TO CHRIST'S FULL DIVINITY. (a) The Holy Spirit who inspires all true prophets descended in the fullest possible measure upon the righteous man Jesus, so that He became the Christ.[3] (b) There is a divine "spark" in the nature of all good men, and particularly in the great saints of mankind, who are in this sense "incarnations" of the divine. Christ was the supreme example of this general divine indwelling.[4] (c) At the beginning God the Father created an intermediate being who was higher in spiritual dignity than any other created soul, but less than the supreme and uncreated God. This being became incarnate.[5]

2. VIEWS WHICH DO NOT DO JUSTICE TO CHRIST'S TRUE HUMANITY. (a) The incarnate Son, being divine, did not have a real and material body. It was a "spiritual" phantom which only appeared to go through the motions of physical life (compare 1 John 4: 1–3).[6] (b) Christ's humanity consisted only of a physical body and animating nervous system, but lacked the higher directing faculties of reason and responsible moral will. These latter were supplied by the indwelling divine principle.[7] (c) The humanity was swallowed up in the divinity, so that it was in effect no longer itself, "like a drop of vinegar in the ocean."[8] (d) Christ's human mental and moral experience was radically different from our own, and was, in effect, only an appearance put on for the purpose of acting the part of a man. Thus, being God, He knew everything perfectly without learning, and did not share the natural knowledge of His time. He only seemed to learn by asking questions. So also, being God, He could not *really* be tempted by evil. It was only an appearance put on for the sake of the disciples. Such notions reflect a naïve and unin-

---

3 Adoptionism.
4 Found in pantheistic systems like Theosophy.
5 Arianism, and original Unitarianism.
6 Docetism.
7 Apollinarianism.
8 Monophysitism.

structed reverence for our Lord's divine nature. The witness of the New
Testament should be taken quite seriously (Luke 2:52, 4:1–13, 22:39–46;
Hebrews 4:15, 5:7–8).

3. A VIEW WHICH DOES NOT DO JUSTICE TO THE UNITY OF THE HUMAN
AND DIVINE. The fully human and fully divine natures went about together,
in somewhat the same way as a man's shadow goes about with him. The
two natures were united only in the sense that they always had the same
moral will, and so acted together, almost in the manner of identical twins,
who may find themselves always in perfect rapport with one another.[9]

B. The Homoousios Clause

The newcomer to theology may well form the judgment that doctrinal
formularies such as the above are extremely abstract and remote, and that
the ancient fathers of the Church who disputed about them were employed
in a task spiritually most unprofitable. A clearer appreciation of the process
which lies behind the orthodox doctrine of the Church may be gained by
a consideration of the origin of one salient clause of the Creed.

In A.D. 317 Arius, a scholarly presbyter of the church of Alexandria, in
Egypt, aroused controversy by teaching which he considered gave a reasonable explanation of the person of Christ. Actually it was a doctrine of Christ
adjusted to notions of the nature of God derived from a background in the
secular culture of the day, rather than from the Bible. Arius taught that
before the world was created, and before time began, the Father, who alone
is the absolute, unmoved, and unknown God, *created* His Son, who is far
higher in spiritual rank than any other created being, and who was the
agent of the creation of the rest of the world. The Son might truly be called
"divine," and worshipped, but He was not divine in the same full sense as
the Father is divine. This Son became incarnate by indwelling an animated
human body, taking the place in it of the higher spiritual faculties. This
subtle explanation was clearly an innovation, contrary to the original New
Testament faith in a divine Lord and Savior; yet it proved very difficult to
exclude by quoting texts, or by the established creedal formularies.

There was thus a long and obscure theological controversy, the turning
point of which was the first General Council of the Church, which met at
Nicea in Asia Minor in 325. Arius and those who sympathized with him
were here condemned. The confession adopted to state the Church's faith
was an eastern baptismal creed, into which was inserted the Greek word
homoousios, "of the same substance," despite the objection of some that this
was a novel and nonbiblical word. This operative keyword later appeared
in a fuller creed, which by long tradition is recited in the eucharistic liturgy
as the "Nicene" Creed, and which goes back to the second General Council
of the Church, of Constantinople, in 381. It is the word translated *"being of*

---

9 Nestorianism.

one substance" with the Father. The intention of this word is to affirm beyond question that God the Son, who became incarnate as our Lord Jesus Christ, is divine in the fullest and most exact sense of the word, even as the Father is divine.

Since that time this Creed has won increasing prestige as a canon of orthodox Christian faith. It is today accepted as such by the Roman Catholic and the Eastern, or Orthodox, Church; by Anglicans, and other denominations descended from them, such as Methodists; by Lutherans, by Reformed or Presbyterians; and it is assented to in more general terms by many other Christian denominations. In our own time the "Nicene" Creed, with this word as its focus, has been accepted by the Ecumenical movement as the doctrinal confession which more than any other expresses the underlying unity in faith of the divided parts of the Church. It is the Creed which symbolizes the faith which is based on the Incarnation.

Looking back now, from the vantage ground of the centuries, one may affirm that the Church of the fourth century was providentially guided by the Holy Spirit in this perplexed choice. Christian existentialists argue that it is not possible to express Christian faith in abstract speculative terms drawn from Greek thought, such as "substance." However, if it is allowed that Christian faith may be expressed in these classic terms, then this authoritative Creed will be seen to express the underlying spiritual intention of the New Testament. Had the subtle doctrine of Arius been allowed, nonbiblical views of the nature of God would have been admitted to dominate Christian theology. This reduced doctrine of Christ would have perhaps sufficed to proclaim our Lord as the supreme revelation of God, and the supreme teacher. It would not have sufficed as the basis for the preaching of Christianity as a religion of real redemption from sin, by faith in a divine saving action in Jesus Christ. Christianity would have evaporated gradually into an humane but ineffectual philosophy. This is a single salient example illustrating the general process of the establishment in the ancient and undivided Church of the orthodox body of Christian doctrine.

C. *Kenosis*

In summary, the person of our Lord consists in the divine Son, who has fully, truly, and permanently united with Himself genuine human nature, like ours save that it is sinless, yet without either the divine nature ceasing to be divine, or the human nature ceasing to be human. Thus as one person, alike human and divine, God united Himself with the human race, and conquered the guilt and power of sin, as man and for man. Nothing can wholly take away from the mystery of this central proposition of distinctive Christian theology. Nevertheless, men will continue to ask, "How can this be?" Intellectual caution and reverent reserve is necessary in seeking to answer this question. Just as it is impossible fully to understand the genius of Shakespeare, so it is still more impossible fully to comprehend the inner workings of the mind of Jesus of Nazareth. And it is still more impossible fully to comprehend the nature of the divine. Nevertheless, the Christian believes that God has revealed certain things, and that they are recorded in the New Testament.

God the Son, as divine, exists in eternal and changeless bliss, and in that bright glory upon which man cannot look. His being is not material, and is unlimited to space and time. He has all power, and knows all things, past, present, and future. It is clear that these qualities cannot exist in a human being. Jesus of Nazareth was confined to one time and place, a man spiritually majestic indeed to those who knew Him, but of humble station, inconspicuous in the wider world of human affairs, and not significantly recorded by the secular historians of His time. The glory was hidden, and the power. Furthermore, the New Testament witnesses that our Lord's mind and spirit worked in a truly human way. He apparently shared the natural knowledge of the times. For example, He spoke of what we call "psychological disorder," in the manner of His time, as demon-possession (Mark 5:1-13). This was the case even with natural knowledge on subjects connected with religion, though it was combined with matchless spiritual insight. Thus He was content to echo the general traditional judgment of His times that David was the author of the Psalms (Mark 12:35-37). The divine omniscience was hidden.

Our Lord also knew what it was to have a truly human religious experience. Thus in company with other worshipers He went to the synagogue (Luke 4:16). Like other devout men, He looked up to the heavenly Father with reverence and obedience (Mark 14:36), and modestly forbade men to give undue reverence to Himself, for worship is due only to God (Matthew 19:16-17). He lived a life of trustful prayer (Luke 6:12). Though those who knew Him bore witness of the marvel of His sinlessness, yet He could on occasion face temptation, and temptation that was grim and sore (Luke 22:39-44). This would appear to involve us in the surmise that He who by virtue of His divine nature was incapable of falling to temptation (James 1:13), in His human consciousness was unaware of this invulnerability, otherwise He could not have been truly tempted. Most mysterious of all, He who was by nature perfectly united with God could on one dreadful occasion share the darkest of human experiences. Upon the Cross, and fully one there with the human race in shame and guilt, He felt separated from God (Mark 15:34). Thus even the divine spiritual serenity could be shadowed. It was impossible for Him to be genuinely human without the hiding of these bright glories.

There is, however, a divine glory which we can imagine as consistent with the genuine human experience of a perfect man. We have never encountered it, because we have never seen sinless humanity. Nevertheless, we can imagine it as in principle capable of existence. This is the divine glory of perfect love to all men, of unerring moral insight within the scope of the natural circumstances of life, and of complete moral triumph in face of temptation. This divine-human glory did fully shine forth in Christ (John 1:14; 2 Corinthians 4:6; Hebrews 1:3). Therefore the divine-human person, though limited in glory, may truly be spoken of as divine (Colossians 2:9).

This doctrine that in becoming incarnate the divine Son "emptied Himself of all but love" is called *kenosis*, that is, "emptying."[10] Clearly some form of self-emptying is necessary in any intelligible doctrine of the Incarnation, but the doctrine needs carefully to be guarded against the supposition that in order to become man the divine Son temporarily "de-goded" Himself. The two chief safeguards are, first, that this limitation of glory was not one imposed upon the divine Son by any force of necessity. It was His own sovereign action of infinite condescension (John 10:17–18). In the second place, the divine Son did not undergo any kind of alteration in His divine nature when He became incarnate. Heaven, the throne of God's majesty, is not a place, but if the metaphor be allowed, the divine Son was still as fully "in heaven" during the time of the Christ's life on earth as He was before, and has been since.

D. Communicatio Idiomatum

A further consequence of the idea of Incarnation may be shown by explaining the technical term *communicatio idiomatum,* "communication of properties." The union of human and divine into one genuine human-divine person is so intimate that that which may be said of the human, or of the divine, may truly be said of the whole person. Therefore, what is properly said of the one nature of Christ may, by application, be said of the other nature. Thus, Christ suffered and died by virtue of His human nature. The divine, considered as the divine, exists forever in bliss, and cannot suffer or die. Nevertheless, the divine-human person suffered and died, and therefore the sufferings may be called the sufferings and death of God. This is not to say that God "as He is in Himself" is invaded by suffering, but that as He exists in His Son incarnate He condescends to suffer. Here is an expression of the paradox of the Incarnation. Thus the language of Christian devotion can sing of Christ on the Cross:

Impassive, He suffers; immortal, He dies.

The principle of the communication of properties also works the other way. We may truly say that in Christ our human nature triumphed over sin and

---

10 Compare the original Greek of the opening clause of Philippians 2:7, commonly rendered "He made himself of no reputation" (K.J.V.). This is literally "He emptied Himself."

death, in token that by divine grace we may triumph. However, the triumph of the one divine-human person was by virtue of the divinity.[11]

IV. Conceived by the Holy Ghost, Born of the Virgin Mary

A. Traditional Doctrine

The manner in which the divine and human natures in our Lord were joined at the Incarnation was that Christ was born of a human mother without the intercourse of any human father, by the special divine action of the Holy Spirit (Matthew 1:18: Luke 1:34). Thus Christ's human nature had a human mother, but no human father. From the Godhead Christ took the divine nature of the Son. From a human mother He took His real human nature.

B. Theological Significance of This Doctrine

1. The essential principle of the Incarnation is the personal union of God with His own handiwork. This is the occasion of the entry of God into His world for the purpose of breaking the fateful train of cause and effect which comes from the sinful past of the race, so as to give humanity a new redeemed beginning in a power not its own. This incarnational principle is symbolized by a birth into the human race which was both in one aspect like every other birth and in another different from every other birth. Christ wrought out the saving act of God by making Himself one with man in every sphere of human life, at the price of self-humiliation, patient endurance, and suffering; so that as man He might in every sphere of life give perfect and victorious obedience to God. His miraculous birth was a decisive act in that career of sacrificial self-identification with mankind. He who made Himself one with man in the useful toil of the workshop, the common worship of the synagogue, and the pain and disgrace of the Cross, made Himself fully one with man also in the humility of an infant birth and in the happiness of a godly home. This birth is a token of the principle of continuity with humanity, of identification. Yet the one who made Himself one with man was not just another man. He was also radically different from all men, the divine-human Man who brings from outside this world a new divine beginning for the race. Thus He was really born of a real

---

[11] Another example of the communication of properties, which is a prominent part of some traditions of Christian thought, is the application to our Lord's holy Mother of the title "Theotokos" (in Greek), or "Genetrix Dei" (in the Latin Mass), which is commonly but not very adequately translated "Mother of God." The correct sense is "the God-bearer." Clearly, only the human nature of our Lord was born of the Virgin Mary, for the divine nature is eternally begotten of the Father. Nevertheless, the one divine-human person was truly born. In this sense the Virgin Mother is the "Bearer of God." The use of this title "Theotokos" is the Church's way of saying that it is not the case that a purely human baby was born, who later *became* divine. The Babe of Bethlehem was the incarnate Son from the very beginning of His human existence.

mother, and did not descend from heaven suddenly as an angel. Yet He was also born by a mysterious divine action, answering to a new divine intervention into human affairs.

2. Another theological truth symbolized by the Virgin Birth is that God performs His saving intervention through the method of human cooperation. God's entry into the race was not sudden, inexplicable, blinding in glory. He entered the human race in the normal way, working through and not suspending the natural order. We are not indeed expressly told in the Gospel record that the Virgin was given the opportunity of refusing the wonderful providence which confronted her. Yet this is to be understood, for God does not need to ask questions of this sort. The Christian believes that God chose for this incomparable destiny a woman whose response He foreknew would be the immediate impulse of self-yielding to the divine calling, in the spirit of trustful, grateful, and willing obedience (Luke 1:38). The cooperative obedience of the Virgin Mary is the essential significance of the story of the Annunciation. Here we see the supreme example of the general principle of human cooperation with God. To yield oneself up to God in loving and trustful obedience, to be used by Him with a power not one's own for the accomplishment of a mighty divine purpose, is the essential of what it means to be a Christian believer. The obedience of the Virgin is the great example of this general Christian principle, for she by her cooperation was revealed as the chosen instrument of God's mightiest action, the Incarnation itself.

Summary of Divergence: Attitudes Toward the Doctrine of the Virgin Birth

Few major doctrines of the Christian Faith have been more subjected to attack, and have found more widespread rejection in liberal theological quarters, than the belief in our Lord's Virgin Birth. In natural reaction to this, theological conservatives, in their desire to uphold a doctrine affirmed to rest upon the authority of Holy Scripture, have made a particular point in requiring acceptance of the historicity of this event. There is therefore special need for a dispassionate approach to this subject. In the first place, it has candidly to be admitted that there are some difficulties in the biblical account. In consequence, those who call the accepted belief in question are not necessarily merely trifling with the authority of the Bible. On the other hand, if we are candid we also have to allow that much of the force behind the attack upon this doctrine often comes from the antisupernaturalistic bias of many critics. We believe that the thoughtful man will avoid this bias (see pp. 28, 30–31). The tacit assumption has been widespread that the more miracles are emptied out of the Christian message, the more likely it is to prove acceptable to the thinking man of today. Yet a case can certainly be made that this assumption is in fact contrary to experience.

It has been discussed whether the Virgin Birth is an "essential" doctrine. The answer surely is that the credibility of this doctrine rests upon the fact of the Incarnation itself, not vice versa. We can in principle imagine that the Incarnation could have taken place by the divine Son uniting to Himself human nature which had a human father as well as a human mother. Indeed, many critics of the traditional doctrine argue that our Lord's true humanity is more firmly established if He had a human father, though the orthodox doctrine also has always strongly affirmed Christ's full and true humanity. In this sense the doctrine of the Virgin Birth is less "essential" than the admittedly essential doctrine of the Incarnation. The Christian system does not collapse if this particular article be denied. Nevertheless, if the greater miracle of the Incarnation be once acknowledged, it becomes possible to imagine that the lesser miracle of the Virgin Birth took place also. And the orthodox can argue with some show of reason that it is appropriate to suppose that the Man who, though truly human, was different from every other man, should be both truly born of a woman and also born in this unique and mysterious way.

a. A Critical View of the Virgin Birth

A radical criticism of the traditional doctrine, proceeding on the lines of the demythologizing exegesis of the New Testament (see pp. 35–36), is commonly made on the following lines. The Church of the first days was possessed of a deep faith that in Christ, crucified and risen, a new principle of life had been brought into the world (Romans 6: 8–11). His coming into the world was the starting point of a new human race, composed of those who were united to Him by faith (1 Corinthians 15: 22). In order vividly to express to the mind of faith this idea of a new principle of life, and a fresh human start, and effectually to preach it to the hearers, the religious consciousness of the first Church suggested the symbol of the Virgin Birth. The details of this myth were drawn from the background of the times and the common heritage of ancient religion, the chief constituent elements being mythological legends of the miraculous births of various semidivine heroes, and also the desire to find fulfillment of Old Testament prophecies (in particular, the Septuagint text of Isaiah 7: 14). If one inquires whether the framers of this preaching regarded it as historical or not, the answer is that they were not interested in this issue. The characteristic modern interest in the difference between factual history and religious symbolism passed them by. Their concern was to present their faith as vividly as possible in a striking imaginative narrative. So we may today share in the faith of the ancient Church that Christ brought a new beginning for the human race, but we need not try to defend this story as history, for this is really foreign to the intention of those who first told it. And to acknowledge that the story is unhistorical makes the Gospel more acceptable to the typical modern mind.

b. Historical Discussion of the Virgin Birth

Those who uphold the long-accepted doctrine of the Church will affirm that the above is a construction not in fact developed out of the appropriate evidence, but read into the scriptural evidence with the aid of a modern speculative theory which is quite alien to the mind of the ancient Church. There is no evidence that any of the early Christians who mentioned the Virgin Birth had any idea other than that it was an actual historical event. We who are so far off can hardly know more of the historical probability than they who were near. It is therefore necessary to weigh up just what the evidence amounts to.

i. Two of the four Gospels contain clear references to the Virgin Birth (Matthew 1:18–25; Luke 1:31–35). The other two Gospels say nothing of the life of Jesus before the opening of His public ministry, so it is only natural to find that this event is unmentioned. Their silence is not definite evidence against this belief.

ii. It would seem that there were some Christians in the very early days of the Church who either did not know of this doctrine, or who knowing it, were nevertheless content to speak of Joseph as in some sense the "father" of Jesus. The evidence for this is that the First and Third Gospels, which themselves plainly intend to affirm this belief, have incorporated in them narratives from the earlier Christian community, which employ these looser modes of expression. The editing has not been careful to bring the earlier and later narrative to one consistent whole. In particular, the two genealogies of Christ (Matthew 1:1–17 and Luke 3:23–38) are traced through Joseph, which only makes sense in a Christian circle which regarded Joseph as the father of Jesus. So also Luke 2:27 and 41 speak of the "parents" of Jesus, and our Lord's Mother is represented as saying, "Thy father and I have sought thee sorrowing" (Luke 2:48).

This undoubted element of confusion plainly indicates to many critics that there was an original Christianity which did not teach this doctrine. This shows that it was a later development, which in turn is evidence that it is unhistorical. A possible answer is that this measure of apparent confusion and silence is much what one would have expected. In the first place, although such events as Christ's death and resurrection were from the beginning integral to the Christian preaching, so that it never spread anywhere without knowledge of them, Christ's wonderful birth was at the very first a piece of relatively private information, known only to a few. It therefore spread after a "time-lag," leaving some at the first who did not know of it. That some at first did not know does not of itself suffice to prove that the event did not take place, or serve to overthrow the positive testimony in other passages of Scripture.

iii. It is to be admitted that there is a large degree of silence in the New Testament regarding the Virgin Birth. Thus two of the four Gospels are content to pass over Christ's birth and infancy, and St. Paul says nothing unambiguous on this matter. This surely indicates to the impartial mind that the doctrine of the Virgin Birth was not as prominent in the first days of the Church as it later became. Yet this position does not of itself prove that the doctrine is unhistorical, particularly when one may observe an undoubted dogmatic interest in the early Church which tended to prevent this doctrine being voiced as readily and widely as it might otherwise have been. The essential point of the first preaching was that Jesus, though crucified, had been vindicated as the Messiah of Jewish expectation by the fact of the resurrection, supported by the argument from prophecy fulfilled (Acts 2:22–36). In light of this, there was the strongest possible incentive to represent Jesus as the descendant of David, born in Bethlehem (Matthew 2:1–6; Luke 2:1–7; Hebrews 7:14). The doctrine of the Virgin Birth was in a sense an unwelcome modification of this position, for it involved the implication that Jesus was a descendant of David only in a figurative sense. (We get a token of this adjustment in Luke 3:23.)

It is not impossible that St. Paul himself was the most illustrious theologian who found himself in this ambiguous position, which may help to explain his awkward silence. The apostle to the Gentiles to the end clung to the original Christian view that the Jewish people, children of Abraham by physical descent, retained a special place in God's plan of salvation (Romans 11:11–15, 25–32). He could emphasize that his Lord was the Messiah of Jewish expectation, "of the house of David" (Romans 1:3). He would perhaps therefore find it hard to give prominence to the doctrine of the Virgin Birth. It has very commonly been assumed that the weight of dogmatic prepossession was an influence which caused this doctrine to spread in the early Church, with the implication that its acceptance was due to "wishful thinking." Actually it can be well argued that in the very first days of the Church, at least, the weight of dogmatic prepossession was exerted in the other direction. The Christians came to accept the Virgin Birth not because they wished it to be true, but because the evidence supported the "awkward fact."

iv. It has often been argued that the doctrine of the Virgin Birth represents an infiltration of pagan thought into the Christian Church. There are two chief considerations here. First, pagan mythology contained stories of heroes or demigods coming into existence through miraculous births.[12] This idea suggested itself to Christians of Gentile background as a suitable way of expressing the divine honor due to their Lord. Second, much Gentile religious thought was strongly dualist in character, and conceived of the material as the opposite to the spiritual, and consequently of the physical body as the enemy of the higher life of the soul. With these presuppositions, sexual procreation, being passionate and bodily, was easily represented as essentially sinful. Virginity was the higher spiritual state. Therefore the doctrine of the Virgin Birth suggested itself to the Christian consciousness as a way of enhancing the doctrine of the sinlessness of Christ.

A rejoinder to this very common form of argument is that the doctrine of the Virgin Birth does not appear to have arisen principally in the background of Gentile Christianity. In the Church of later centuries

---

12 The legends referred to in Greek mythology were of gods taking human form so as to have intercourse with women, who then gave birth to "heroes" in a manner analogous to Genesis 6:1–4. This is the idea of a divine-human birth, but not exactly of a virgin birth.

the importance of this doctrine was sometimes emphasized for reasons connected with the notion that sex is "unspiritual," and that the Virgin Birth guarantees the sinlessness of Christ. Yet this was long after the New Testament was written and long after this doctrine had become a part of regular Christian teaching for other reasons. These ascetic influences may therefore at times have enhanced the place of the doctrine, but this is a very different thing from the claim that they *originated* it. If the Virgin Birth of Christ were found to be first spoken of many years later, and in Churches of predominantly Gentile background, this would indeed be a suspicious circumstance. However, the Christians of this early pre-New Testament period, even if not all of Hebrew physical descent, were predominantly of the Jewish religion. That is, the original Church was securely based upon a Jewish religious background and framed its institutions and doctrine upon Jewish and biblical ideas. In this background there was not the slightest inclination to look on pagan mythology with anything but contempt. It would hardly be adopted into Christian doctrine. In the Old Testament, furthermore, there is no notion whatever that celibacy is a purer spiritual state than marriage. The Bible is indeed a great book of families, and a chief sign of God's blessing upon the righteous is to have a long posterity. It is very significant that the clearest New Testament reference to the Virgin Birth is the one which occurs in the most Jewish-Christian of the Gospels (Matthew 1:18–25). The circle which first treasured this story had no bias whatever in favor of virginity as a holier state than matrimony.

v. Another form of argument to explain the development of the doctrine of the Virgin Birth is that it arose out of the attempt to find a "prophecy fulfilled" in the Septuagint (traditional Greek translation) of Isaiah 7:14. This reads "Behold, a virgin shall conceive, and bear a son." If this could be applied to the birth of Christ there was supplied a wonderful mark of divine prescience in this Old Testament passage, which was taken as a proof of the inspiration of Scripture, and a vindication of Scripture's witness to Christ. Thus the Christians read the Old Testament text into the life of Christ.

It is to be accepted that the early Christians did search through the Old Testament with great care to find examples of "prophecies fulfilled." Isaiah 7:14 was in fact to them one of the most impressive examples. However, the weakness of the case here is that so far as one can judge the events were the other way around! There appears to be no particular evidence before the time of Jesus that Isaiah 7:14 was interpreted as a prophecy of the birth of the expected Messiah. Thus the event of our Lord's Virgin Birth was believed in first, and this prophecy interpreted in this way in light of it, not vice versa.

vi. SUMMARY. There are admitted obscurities in the Scripture witness to the doctrine of the Virgin Birth. Therefore it is well not to be too dogmatic. The balance of historical evidence is such that the historic character of the doctrine can be defended out of the New Testament, but not placed beyond dispute. It is incautious for the modern critic to claim to know more about it than writers who may quite possibly have known the only person who could have given direct testimony! (Compare Acts 1:14.) The argument shows how much the result of the investigation depends upon the prepossessions in the mind of the reader. One who comes with a bias against the miraculous, and an acceptance of extreme critical theories, will have no difficulty in finding grounds for objection to the traditional doctrine. On the other hand, one who starts with a reverence for the authority of Scripture as it has been transmitted to us, and for the integrity of the Church's Creed, will find equally good ground for upholding the Virgin Birth as a historical event as well as a divine sign.

C. Further Doctrine Concerning the Virgin

1. HER TITLE. Much traditional Christian devotion has expressed the reverence which is due to our Lord's holy Mother, because of her unique relationship to the divine-human person, by referring to her as the Blessed Virgin Mary. This scriptural title is derived from Luke 1:48.

2. THE IMMACULATE CONCEPTION. Much traditional Christian theology has sought to safeguard the sinlessness of our Lord's humanity by the doctrine that the Virgin, from whose human nature our Lord's humanity was derived, was herself conceived without stain of original sin (traditional proof-text: Luke 1:28, 42).

3. THE PERPETUAL VIRGINITY. Another traditional opinion which has been widely held is that the Virgin never had any sexual relations with her spouse Joseph. This makes it necessary to affirm that the "brethren" and "sisters" of Christ mentioned in the New Testament (Matthew 12:46, 13:55; Galatians 1:19) were not, as one would perhaps naturally assume from the narrative, the children born to Mary and Joseph after the birth of our Lord, but were "cousins," or possibly Joseph's children by a previous wife. The background to this doctrine is clearly an attempt to vindicate the perfect spirituality of the Virgin in terms of a conviction that virginity is a higher spiritual state than matrimony. This idea was very natural in days when monasticism and clerical celibacy so largely prevailed in the Church.

4. THE ASSUMPTION. This traditional doctrine affirms the opinion that after her apparent death, or "sleep," the body of the Virgin did not suffer normal decay, but was spiritually glorified and carried up into heaven to be united directly with her soul. Thus she is taught to be in a condition analogous to the presence of the ascended Christ in heaven (traditional proof-text: Psalm 45:9-15).

5. ROMAN CATHOLIC DOGMA. These doctrines of the Immaculate Conception, the Perpetual Virginity, and the Assumption of the Blessed Virgin Mary have been generally held as matters of pious opinion in the Catholic Church since the Middle Ages. The doctrine of the Immaculate Conception was declared by the Roman Catholic Church to be a dogma of the Faith by a papal bull in 1854, and the Assumption in 1950. A non-Roman Catholic

should understand what this step involves. It does not mean that the papal authorities exerted authority to compel Roman Catholics to believe what they previously did not believe. Roman Catholics have accepted these doctrines as a part of their system of belief for many centuries. The promulgation of these doctrines as dogmas of the Faith means that they are now to be regarded as more than accepted opinion. They are to be taught as essential doctrines of the Faith, to deny which involves a formal charge of heresy.

6. A PROTESTANT STATEMENT. As doctrine and devotional practice connected with the Virgin is one of the chief grounds for the alienation which still often exists between the Roman Catholic and the Protestant Churches, and is also sometimes a cause of reserve and misunderstanding between Eastern Orthodox and Protestants within the Ecumenical movement, this discussion may be closed with a representative statement of the Protestant position.

Honor is due to our Lord's holy Mother in view of fact that she was chosen by God for this unique connection with the miracle of the Incarnation, that she typifies to us to an eminent degree the principle of Christian discipleship, and that she is a symbol of Christian womanhood and the Christian home. Nevertheless, the Protestant feels himself bound to maintain, in all charity, that many customary marks of reverence paid to the Virgin in Roman Catholic worship are regrettably easy to be misunderstood as divine worship by untheologically-minded believers. This is indeed a matter of proportion, rather than of clear spiritual principle, and need not of itself alienate Christian brothers. One may accept the statement of competent Roman theologians that these honors are distinct from, and less than, the worship which is due only to God. Furthermore, the circumstance that a piece of religious.symbolism is capable of being misunderstood does not of itself suffice to condemn it, for it is sadly true that the customs of every part of the Church are susceptible of perversion. Yet there is a matter of proportion. The thoughtful Protestant is bound to persist in his conviction that when every allowance is made for legitimate divergence of taste in religious symbolism, the Roman Catholic Church often errs in too easily tolerating, particularly among the simple-minded populations of backward countries, devotional language and practices which may obscure the fact that divine worship is to be offered only to God—the Father, Son, and Holy Spirit.

It is less often considered that there is a deeper cause of division in the Church. It will be found harder to remove because it is a matter of theological principle. One judges that the Roman theologian would defend these doctrines principally on the ground that they symbolize the high honor which is to be paid the Virgin on account of her unique connection with our Lord's humanity, and her position as the eminent type of the Christian saint. In doing this Roman theology has dangerously obscured the difference between doctrine which is symbolically true and that which is true as historical fact. Events which purport to have taken place upon the plane of history are affirmed for a symbolic reason, and affirmed without historical evidence appropriate to the case. The traditional Protestant way of stating this objection is to say that these three doctrines are unscriptural. What is at the bottom of the objection, when it is rightly understood, is legitimate fear lest the historical nature of the Christian religion be assailed. Christian speculation cannot thus take liberaties with history.

The situation has been rendered more acute, from the point of view of orthodox Protestantism at least, by the Roman Church taking action separate from the rest of Christendom to declare that the Immaculate Conception and the Assumption are essential dogmas of the faith. The circumstance that Roman Catholics hold some ideas which appear to the Protestant to be erroneous is not necessarily a barrier to spiritual recognition, if these are only matters of pious opinion which the Protestant is himself not called on to accept. However, if they are to be regarded as essential dogmas it would seem that fellowship can only be established if the Protestant will join in acknowledging them. This is what he cannot do. Here, in the Protestant view, is a regrettable and serious breach in the Church.

7. RADICAL LIBERAL VIEW. Those radical Protestants who have taken up the view of the Virgin Birth outlined in (a), page 57, and of the resurrection outlined in (a), page 103, do not to the same extent feel the force of this traditional Protestant objection to "unscriptural" Roman Catholic dogma. This is because they do not look upon the Christian Faith as a whole as "historical" in the traditional sense, and are therefore less concerned about this distinction between those articles of the Creed which affirm historical facts and those which affirm intellectual constructions. To the radical, the New Testament narratives of the Virgin Birth and the empty tomb are symbolic constructions, rather than accounts of facts, and therefore may be viewed as standing on much the same ground in this respect as the Roman Catholic dogmas of the Immaculate Conception and the Assumption. However, whether the radical liberal Protestant is really nearer to the Roman Catholic in ecumenical understanding is another matter, seeing that the Roman Church is so firmly committed to the traditional position that the Christian Faith is a historical revelation, founded upon the facts of the life of Jesus recorded in the Gospels.

Readings

Baillie, D. M., God *Was in Christ*. London: Faber & Faber, Ltd., 1948.
Boslooper, T., *The Virgin Birth*. Philadelphia: Westminster Press, 1962. (Critical.)
Bright, J., *The Kingdom of God*. Nashville: Abingdon Press, 1953.
Cullmann, O., *The Christology of the New Testament*. trans. S. C. Guthrie and C. A. M. Hall. Philadelphia: Westminster Press, 1959.

Edwards, D., *The Virgin Birth in History and Faith*. London: Faber & Faber, Ltd., 1943. (Defends the doctrine.)

Hodgson, L., *And Was Made Man*. London: Longmans, Green & Company, Ltd., 1928.

Hunter, A. M., *The Work and Words of Jesus*. London: SCM Press, 1951.

Perrin, N., *The Kingdom of God in the Teaching of Jesus*. Philadelphia: Westminster Press, 1963.

Temple, W., *Christus Veritas*. London: Macmillan & Co., Ltd., 1954.

Chapter Three

The Word of the Cross

He suffered under Pontius Pilate,
was crucified, dead, and buried;
He descended into Hell

I. The Suffering Christ

It is not for nothing that the characteristic symbol of the Christian Faith is the Cross. Many systems of religion, of philosophy, and of ethics have honored the figure of the martyr, and have shown themselves familiar with the sad truth that it often falls to good and wise men to suffer, and sometimes to suffer because they are wise and good. However, other faiths regard this suffering as the tragic accident which may overtake the prophet of righteousness. Christianity is distinguished by its insistence that the sufferings of the righteous Lord were of the very essence of what He came to do. The symbol of martyrdom is not merely the memorial of a cruel and unjust death, which took the leader away from His disciples and brought His work to an end. The history of the world is full of such sad stories. In the Christian Faith the token of martyrdom is the symbol that the Master has accomplished His work. Thus the Cross is central.

How characteristic this is of Christianity may be illustrated in a number of ways. In the first place, it was utterly unexpected. The Hebrew people were long prepared by historical experience for the coming of the Messiah. In countless ways their religious ideas and institutions and their Scriptures provide the source and background for Christianity, without which the Christian Faith and the Christian Church cannot be understood. Yet the idea that the expected Messiah should conquer, not by the unveiling of God's

65

power and glory, but by suffering, was hidden from the people. The inspired writer of Isaiah 53 may have had a passing and partial glimpse of this idea, but it was beyond his readers and passed largely uncomprehended. It was not until our Lord Himself realized that this passage was the Old Testament's clearest picture of the essential principle of His mission, and applied it to Himself (Luke 22:37; compare Isaiah 53:12; Luke 24:26–27), that the Christians were able to read in it the mysterious doctrine of a suffering Messiah (Acts 8:30–35). So it is today. The figure of Jesus of Nazareth is almost universally respected and admired among fair-minded and humane men and women of every school of thought. However, when He is respected it is commonly as a martyr, a suffering hero in the painful upward march of humanity. Yet to admire Him in this way alone is completely to miss the point of His mission in the world. It has to be admitted that the distinctive Christian doctrine of Christ as a divine sacrifice for sin is still a stumbling block to the average intellectual person (1 Corinthians 1:18–25). The "word of the Cross" is often viewed as an antiquated dogma having no contact with modern thought and conditions, and hardly worthy of notice; or else it is misrepresented in an impossibly naïve way, and then dismissed; or it is treated as utterly repulsive and degrading.

Several facts already observed set the stage for this central point of Christian doctrine. First we have seen that the argument for the goodness and wisdom of God as evidenced in the order of nature is marred by the presence of disorder within the order. In particular, there is the fact that human life is everywhere darkened by evil and woe. In the second place, the doctrine of the Incarnation is required by the circumstance that the Christian Gospel does not look upon our Lord only as the bringer of a perfect revelation and doctrine. He is the worker in this world of a divine saving act of redemption from sin. And in the third place, our Lord's making Himself one with man involved self-humiliation, endurance, pain, and disgrace. We must now draw out the implications of these facts.

II. The Mystery of Evil

A. Evil and Sin

The construction of the doctrine of a Savior requires first the consideration of what it is from which man needs to be saved. Evil is a comprehensive term, which includes everything in life which appears to be inconsistent with the good and wise plan of a God of holy love. It comprises the suffering which exists in the animal world, together with all human suffering in body and mind, due to natural calamity, disease and death, human stupidity, weakness and mismanagement, and to deliberate wrongdoing and cruelty. The concept of evil also includes the notion of sin, that is, of rebellion against the moral and spiritual order of God. Clearly, the presence of evil is the great and final mystery of life. It is to be noted, however, that this mystery, which darkens the minds and spirits of so many with frustration, bewilderment, rebellion, and unbelief, is a mystery which is created by the doctrine of the goodness and wisdom of the one sovereign God. Religious systems which teach the existence of two equal and eternal principles in conflict with one another, of good and evil, or the existence of many divinities, with wills in conflict with one another and perhaps of uncertain moral character, do not find the existence of evil so great an offense. It is simply something natural and inevitable, which has to be endured as best one can. It is a reflection of the Christian doctrine of God which causes so many to find in the manifest evil of life a temptation to religious unbelief.

Furthermore, conventional minds are chiefly perplexed at the spectacle of the suffering and woe which afflicts the bodies and minds of the race, and which makes life uncomfortable. To the Christian, however, the darkest mystery is the existence in the world of moral and spiritual evil, of sin. It is at first sight very hard to see how a God of holy love can allow continued rebellion against His own goodness, when its fruit is the degradation of the human spirit. One of the most significant aspects of Christian theology is its claim that it can in part illuminate this problem. Even if it cannot give a complete answer to every question which the mind can suggest, it can give an answer sufficient to arm man with courage for the battle of life.

Much human suffering is due to sin. This is very plain in the case of the grief and pain which arises from evil institutions such as war and oppression, from social neglect, from wrongdoing in the family circle, and from the disease which often springs from bad habits and dissipation. It is reasonable also to suppose that generations of living in defiance of God's health-giving laws has to some extent disordered or contaminated the human stock, so that many persons who are not personally "sinners" to any exceptional degree suffer from disease. Another factor is that it is sin which chiefly makes physical death into a sometimes fearsome experience. That the life of the body should come to an end, and leave room in the world for others, is in itself a good thing, and consistent with the Christian view of God. That this end should fill men with fear and grief is due to evil. The idea that the very order of nature itself, including animal as well as human life, has to some extent been disordered as a result of sin, so that the marks of God's goodness and wisdom in it are partially hidden, is an interesting speculation which often proves attractive to the religious mind (Genesis 3:16–19). St. Paul seems to have entertained some such doctrine (Romans 8:20–22).

It is an idea very natural to a simple-minded faith that a God of right who rules the world will certainly visit high-handed sin with the punishment of calamity, whereas the righteous will be rewarded with peace and prosperity in the end (Psalm 37). The Old Testament's more mature reflection upon this problem, particularly in the Book of Job, is that human life does not work out in this way. In large-scale human affairs there seems to be a power which sets a certain limit to the overflowing of human wickedness. Human systems which flourish by oppression and cruelty do seem to contain within themselves the seeds of their own decay, though perhaps only after many centuries. The Christian can rightly treat this as a mark of the divine government of the world. God will not allow His purpose for the world to be entirely frustrated by the disobedience of man. The prophetic view of history, that world powers of evil will in the end be destroyed and God's people blessed, is justified by events. Yet apparently God does not step in suddenly to take away from evil men their power to do evil. Therefore the Church, or the "righteous" nations, cannot trust that obedience to God will supernaturally protect the righteous from martyrdom, or from the calamities of defeat and adversity. The religion of the Cross, which has as its symbol the spectacle of the entirely Righteous One suffering the most unjust of all possible fates, stands as a plain rebuke to any such facile views of human destiny.

To the Christian, then, the deep problem of evil is not the problem of suffering, so much as that of sin.

B. Definitions of Sin

There is much unfortunate confusion about what is meant by "sin."

1. MORAL VIEW. This is the "common-sense" view which we have to use when we seek to frame rules of social obligation and legal justice for the community. In this view sin is an action for which a man is morally accountable, in the sense that he freely did it, knowing it to be wrong in light of the accepted standards of the community of which he is a part. This definition is legitimate for certain important purposes. If it be allowed, then "sin in ignorance" or "sin under compulsion" is a contradiction in terms, and so is sin in a child who has not come to years of moral responsibility. This standard of sin is also one which varies with every form of society.

2. RELIGIOUS VIEW. The man who discovers himself in the presence of God finds himself overcome by the sense of his own utter moral unworthiness (Isaiah 6:5). Even though he knows of no particular sinful action for which he is personally responsible, he is yet appalled at the gulf which yawns between a frail human being, dim of vision and compromised in standards, and the bright glory of the God of holy love. This gulf represents sin in the profounder sense of the word, in the religious or spiritual sense. Christian theology frequently employs the term in this way, and a common cause of misunderstanding is provided when the "common-sense" moral view of sin is taken from the general background of secular thought and read into the language of theology.

C. Sin as Pride

The average humane man, when asked what is the key to all virtue, will probably answer, "love." The Christian, will say "humility." By Christian principle the mainspring of sin is pride. At first sight this may seem to be an ignoble and unwelcome proposition, but experience illustrates what the Church has tried to say at this point. By way of example, commercial advertisers are not concerned with a theological view of human nature, but by trial and error they have discovered a practical technique of persuading people to buy goods. The standard appeal is that to possess this expensive article will make others envy one, and give status, or that to adopt some custom will make one socially acceptable, and that to decorate oneself in this way will make one the object of desire to the opposite sex. It is confidently assumed that men and women crave to live secure in their self-esteem, and to feel that those around them hold them in esteem. We instinctively yet quite irrationally live with ourselves in the center of the picture, and we trust that others will contribute to our welfare. This is what Christian theology means by pride.

Pride is to be condemned because it gives an utterly unrealistic view of life. In actual fact, the center of existence is the God of glory. Man is His microscopic creature. The least that is due to God is a life of obedient service, and any welfare which man can enjoy comes from God. Humility simply means recognizing that this is so. It is a step of spiritual realism, which is essential if life is to be restored to its proper order. Thus sex is not sinful. The desire of man for woman is in itself neither good nor bad, but natural. The self-regarding view of life, which allows a man or woman to look upon the sexual relation as a means whereby one may exploit another for one's own satisfaction is what makes the fatal difference between morally constructive marital happiness and foul lust. So also, property is not sinful. However, the attitude to life which sees oneself in the center corrodes socially constructive labor with that sordid spirit of competitive avarice which will corrupt and disintegrate any form of human society. This happens in human affairs even on the largest scale. Social wrongs continue even in the most advanced and humane societies because so many decent and well-meaning people tend unthinkingly to vote for candidates who tell them pleasing half-truths which minister to their self-esteem, in preference to those who dare to tell them the unflattering truth.

If this be so, then sin is essentially religious and spiritual. It consists in a wrong relationship to God, in a failure to acknowledge Him as the center of reverence, trust, obedience, and love. This is a conclusion against which normal human nature fights, and the reason is not far to seek. If sin is merely wrong action, or a wrong habit, then man may hope to improve himself by suitable moral effort, by superior education, and by providing a more helpful environment. This hope, which is the expectation for human improvement natural to humane and enlightened people who do not live by Christian faith, is a hope which itself ministers to man's self-esteem. But if sin is a wrong inward relationship with God, then man is crushed and helpless, unless God of His grace does something for him. Once a man realizes that God is in fact not the center of his reverence, trust, obedience, and love, he is in the condition of one who knows that he is color-blind, or has no ear for music. He is beset with a disability from which he cannot free himself.

D. The Fall

This stern and realistic doctrine about sin is set forth in the opening chapters of the Bible. The student of comparative religions will see that the stories in the early chapters of the Bible have parallels in the folklore of many primitive peoples. Originally these narratives were "tell-me-why stories," recited to set at rest the unsatisfied curiosity of men with questioning minds who found themselves in a mysterious world, and to give some sort of answer to such questions as "Why are men ashamed when caught naked?" "Why do we have to work?" "Why is the man the head of the tribe?" "Why is childbirth painful?" and so forth. Yet this undoubted similarity in form to the legends of the nations obscures to the mind of many investigators the deep spiritual significance of the biblical narrative. The Genesis story is marked as altogether superior to its parallels by the majestic sense of God which moves through the story, and by its understanding of the workings of the human heart. Built upon the foundations of ancient story there is an authentic word from God which can still help twentieth-century man toward an understanding of life. This is a good illustration of what is meant by the inspiration of the Bible.

Thus we read that man was created superior in talent to the rest of creation. In particular, he was endowed with the capacity for fellowship with God (Genesis 1:26-28). However, he wished to lift himself above his natural state of creaturely dependence (3:1-6). The spiritual result of this attempt at self-exaltation was humiliation, and shame when found in the presence of the holy God (3:7-10). A dreadful train of cause and effect was now revealed, for the first result of spiritual alienation from God is the alienation even of man from wife (3:12-13). The pair self-righteously blame one another, or the Tempter, rather than themselves. A further result is the labor, frustration, pain, and inequity of life (3:16-19). An apparently small sin leads in the next generation to a great one, and family bickering gives place to murder. The unrighteous man slays the righteous, and for the very reason that he is righteous (4:1-10). This crime deepens the curse on mankind (4:11-13). The children of the murderer increase in number, in wealth, in power, in culture, and above all in vainglory (4:16-24, 11:1-4). The final result is social wrong, which stinks to high heaven and is recompensed by overflowing calamity (6:1-13, 11:5-9). Here is the Bible's most revealing natural history of sin. We may recognize that this is the way in which sin operates in personal and social life today.

E. The Natural Man

By "the natural man" Christian theology means humanity as it is ordinarily found, but apart from God's redeeming act in Christ. Our Lord's judgment upon the human race was that it is evil, but that good is present as well (Matthew 7:11). At first sight this looks rather like the commonly accepted easy-going judgment that "Nobody is perfect," but "there is some good in everybody." However, Christian theology wishes to make it plain that the undoubted element of good which is found in all normal men, including men who are certainly not Christians, is not their own good, regarding which they can feel satisfaction in the presence of God. It is the gift of God's grace, even to those who do not recognize it for what it is. Even the decent and humane "natural man," when considered in isolation, is radically alienated from God (1 Corinthians 2:14). However, the usual Christian position has been that in fact men cannot thus be viewed in isolation, for the grace of God is operating in a preliminary way upon all who have not deliberately hardened themselves to good (John 1:9; Romans 1:20). This divine grace which *goes before,* and in a sense prepares the way for, the specific Christian operation of grace has often been called prevenient grace.[1]

F. The Bondage of the Will

Christian doctrine maintains that the will of the natural man is in a condition of bondage, so that of himself man is not able to turn to God and serve God (Romans 7:14–24; Galatians 5:17). This does not mean that Christian theology is determinist. The doctrine of the bondage of the will does not deny what is usually called "free will" and "moral responsibility." Ordinary men outside Christ have a true freedom to choose between one course and another, and between right and wrong, to such an extent that God can fittingly hold them morally responsible, looking with approval upon right, and punishing that which is wrong. All the moral exhortation of the Bible presupposes this (Deuteronomy 30:15–20; Ezekiel 33:1–19; Luke 12:47–48; Romans 3:5–8). Nor is this true freedom of choice confined only to mundane and trivial affairs of no deep moral significance. A man can, by and large, resolve to obey the law of the land in honesty and public spirit. God requires this and approves of it (Romans 13:1–7). What man cannot do of his own unaided will, apart from divine grace, is so to obey God, and so to please Him, as to accomplish his own eternal salvation (Luke 18:9–14, 25–27; Romans 7:24–25; Ephesians 2:8). He is not free to do this. However, even in this high matter man is not utterly helpless and hopeless, in the sense that there is nothing constructive which he can do. He may wait upon God in the obedience of prayer and good-doing, confident that

---

[1] In old-fashioned books, "preventing grace." To *prevent* is literally "to go before." See also pages 214–15.

God will approve of him. And in God's good time He will visit him with the opportunity of receiving grace (Acts 10:1-6) There is thus no place for indiscipline and apathy in the lives of those who would find the way of salvation.

G. Entire Depravity

Christian doctrine of the Augustinian school,[2] which has sought to emphasize man's need of grace in the strongest possible terms, has naturally also spoken in the gravest terms of the sinful weakness of the race. The phrase "entire depravity" has often been used in this connection. If by this term it is intended to teach that the man who is outside Christian grace has a moral will entirely and unreservedly turned to evil, so that he can do nothing to which the holy God can give any degree of approval, most Christian theologians would hardly seek to defend this doctrine. In defense Augustinians would, however, cite such a text as Genesis 6:5. However, if the phrase "entire depravity" be taken to mean that the natural man is alienated from God in every sphere of his life, so that there is no moral action which he can perform of his own strength, however desirable or praiseworthy, which is entirely untarnished and pleasing to God, then the doctrine surely is to be defended as realistic. Taken thus it emphasizes that there is no residual area in the life even of the good and upright man which is exempt from the general impossibility that man can do something to accomplish his own salvation. It is not the case that grace merely assists frail man to come more easily and surely to a salvation to which he can by a very great effort attain in his own strength.

H. The Flesh

This term in the New Testament can express the notion of "frail humanity," in contradistinction to the glory of God (Mark 13:20, 14:38; John 6:63; Romans 3:20; 1 Corinthians 15:50; Galatians 1:16). However, the word can also often be used, particularly by St. Paul, as the opposite to the "the spirit." This may easily convey to the reader the mistaken impression that the apostle, and Christian theology following him, teaches that it is the physical constitution, with its natural and animal feelings and desires, which is the essentially sinful element in man. This carries the idea that the body is in some way the enemy of the soul, and that salvation concerns only the immaterial part of man's nature. This way of thinking is contrary to the doctrine that man's body as well as his "soul" is the handiwork of God, and is called to sanctification and destined to salvation. Actually a careful reading of what St. Paul has to say indicates that among the "works of the flesh" he enumerates purely mental and spiritual sins as well as bodily ones, and that the "works of the spirit" include the activities of the body (Galatians 5:16-26). Thus "the flesh" is human nature, and

---

2 See pages 209-12.

the whole of human nature, body or mind or spirit, insofar as it exists in alienation from God, and in rebellion against God.

I. The Universality of Sin

This doctrine is a matter of empirical observation. If there is to be found anywhere a man who professes that he is morally perfect, so that he has no need of a guilty conscience about anything which he thinks or does, those who know this man well are probably quite sure that he is suffering from a sinful delusion! Contrariwise, there is the man whose character appeals to those who know him well as that of a saint, so that they would even venture the judgment that he is uncompromised with sin. This man will be the first to confess that he has a dreadful struggle with many secret temptations. Such are the facts which show that sin is universal, so that all men and women without exception desperately require salvation (Psalm 143:2; Romans 3:9-12).

J. Original Sin

This doctrine is required as the consequence of the universality of sin. The circumstance that every child born into this world, no matter how wisely nurtured and educated, sooner or later falls into some sin, or at least is beset by temptation which can only be resisted by divine grace, seems to show that there is born into every member of the race a bias of nature. This bias makes it inevitable that he will sin, apart from grace. By way of illustration, if a coin were tossed many thousands of times, and were observed to come down "heads" just occasionally, at irregular intervals, it might be argued that the overwhelming proportion of "tails" was no more than the result of a remarkable run of chance, and that in principle it was still equally possible at every successive toss for the coin to come down "heads." However, if the coin *always* came down "tails," one would judge that there was a bias about this particular coin, which compelled it to fall in this way. In the same way, if it were observed that a few of the noblest of men succeed in turning always to the good, it might then reasonably be argued that all the remainder of the race in principle was born capable of remaining sinless also. That the majority of those who were capable of choosing good had to some extent chosen evil would just be an unfortunate circumstance. However, the observed fact that the human coin invariably comes down "tails" seems to indicate that it does so because by nature it must. There is a bias toward sin in each man, because he is a part of a sinful human stock. Thus sin is "original" to him. That is to say, it is part of his constitution from the very beginning.

This theological term can easily prove misleading because of the two usages of the word "sin" (see p. 68). Original sin is not a sinful action for which the man in question is personally responsible. Rather is it the raw material for sinful actions, and the bias which makes them inevitable in human life. Indeed, if the narrowly moral view of sin is adopted, "original sin" is a contradiction in terms. If it is "original" or inborn in one, it is not anything which one has done of free will, knowing it to be wrong. Therefore, it is not a "sin." And if it is a "sin," then it must be something one has done, and so it cannot be "original." Here is probably a chief reason why so many find such difficulty in the Christian doctrine of original sin.

However, if the religious or spiritual view of sin be allowed, then this doctrine is a profound though dreadful truth. The shameful gulf between man's murky and compromised existence and the bright glory of the God of holy love is an inborn and universal factor of human nature. The unrealistic and morally vitiating instinct to view life with one's self as the center naturally appears in its rudimentary form as soon as the growing child awakes to his first moral choices. And as the growing man and the human race in its advance of knowledge come to the awareness of greater powers, the awakening of each one brings the temptation to give way to the self-regarding attitude. Thus as men become more clever, more powerful, and richer, they do not become wiser or better or more humane. The old battle is joined again and again on new ground.

The idea of original sin answers to the conception of the solidarity of the race, rather than that of heredity. There is no particular evidence from experience to show that moral character, or weakness of character, is inherited from one's parents. Original sin is therefore best not regarded as a "thing" attached to man's physical constitution, and inherited through procreation. It would seem to be found in each one of us anew, yet found there because we are part of a race which is collectively fallen. This at least would appear to be the most reliable exposition of such a text as 1 Corinthians 15:22, "For as in Adam all die, even so in Christ shall all be made alive." Adam (the name means "the man") has been chosen by St. Paul as a *type* of the fallen human race. In Genesis 3:1-19 Adam disobeyed God, and brought ruin upon himself. This is a true picture of what the whole human race has done collectively, and each man individually as a part of the race. Thus we are "in Adam." It is noteworthy that in the other passage where Paul employs this doctrine of the human race "in Adam," he does not say that "death" (moral and physical ruin) was inherited by all men by physical generation. It comes upon all because all are members of a race which has collectively sinned (Romans 5:12). We may reject the notion which has been held in some quarters that the sexual act is in itself of the nature of sin, so that those who are born as a result of it inherit the taint of original sin. This appears to be dishonorable to man's body, which is God's handiwork, and to the method which He has established for the continuance of the human race. Nor is this a legitimate exegesis of Psalm 51:5. This text is a poetical way of confessing that man's alienation in spirit from God, which fills him with shame, is part of his constitution from his earliest days.

K. Original Guilt

Traditionally it has been taught that the stain of original sin renders man guilty in the sight of God, and worthy of punishment, quite apart from any actual sins of thought or word which he may have committed. Several alternative views are to be distinguished here.

Summary of Divergence : The Guilt of Original Sin

a. Sacramental View

Long-established Catholic tradition has held that every human being coming into the world is contaminated by the guilt of original sin. Men may only be placed in the sphere of full Christian salvation by incorporation into Christ by Holy Baptism, in which God releases man from this guilt (see pp. 168–69). It does not follow, however, that all the unbaptized inevitably go to the eternal damnation of hell.

b. Augustinian View

The characteristic emphasis of the full Augustinian theology (see pp. 209–12), for example, as notably developed in Calvinism, is that on account of its descent from sinful Adam, and its collective sinfulness, the whole human race is in the eyes of a holy God necessarily the object of just condemnation and punishment (Romans 3:5–6). Only the elect are delivered from this just punishment of universal damnation by the sovereign grace of God (see p. 211).

c. A Moderating Restatement

Much modern thought has found itself uneasy about both these traditional positions. It would be argued by some that the main reason for the development of the sacramental view has been the desire of Catholic churchmen to find a strong theological reason for upholding the dignity and necessity of the custom of infant baptism. The custom of infant baptism was first based upon natural grounds of family solidarity (see p. 171). Afterward the idea of the washing away of the guilt of original sin suggested itself as a reason of principle for the accepted custom. The Augustinian doctrine has also been criticized as a precarious speculative construction developed upon the Christian doctrine of salvation by grace (see pp. 208–9). Therefore we find that some people, both from the Catholic and Evangelical sides, have come to the judgment that the guilt of original sin is ethically a dubious notion which is perhaps best abandoned, or at least modified. The notion of guilt, in its full and proper sense, would seem to be a moral idea, and to correspond to the moral view of sin. A just God could hardly hold man guilty, in the sense of holding him liable for punishment, on account of an inborn taint of nature for which he has no personal responsibility. As man finds himself in the presence of the holy God he may rightly feel himself utterly ashamed and humiliated because of his moral infirmity, and for his membership in the sinful race. Yet this is shame rather than guilt. He is called upon to feel guilt only for those actual sins for which he knows himself to be personally responsible. However, the abandonment of the notion of original guilt in no way detracts from the doctrine that all men need salvation, for all have in fact committed actual sin.

L. The Origin Of Sin: The Fall

Christian doctrine does not profess to explain the ultimate reason why man should have sinned, and why moral evil should have its foothold in a world created and ruled by a good God. Thus, however literally the Genesis account of the Fall be taken, this does not seek to explain why there should have been a Tempter present in the garden, and why Adam and Eve should have so unaccountably fallen to his wiles. The Bible contents itself with saying that this was so. The ultimate origin of sin remains a dark mystery.

There are a few Scripture passages which have been cited in support of the doctrine that some of the angels first sinned against God in the heavenly sphere, and were cast down from the presence of God by way of punishment (Isaiah 14:12; 2 Peter 2:4; Jude 6). Most people would today feel that taken by themselves such texts provide an insecure foundation, for they are poetical figures. In justice to this idea it should be said, however, that if there are such beings as angels (see pp. 31–32), that is, morally responsible intelligent beings, belonging to a sphere of existence other than our own, it is inherently possible that some of them, being morally free, should have sinned. And a "fallen angel," an intelligent being of superhuman powers but of sinful and depraved will, would be a "devil," that is, a superior directing intelligence of evil. The natural order, which seems to display so many marks of God's goodness and wisdom, also contains mysterious tokens of disorder, or natural evil (see pp. 66–67). These are sometimes of an extraordinarily ingenious type, and almost look like the work of a satanic intelligence, corrupting the handiwork of God. Furthermore, evil in human affairs sometimes seems so pervasive and persistent that it would appear to be more than the result of the actions of individual men. It seems reasonable to believe in a corporate human evil, and perhaps in a superhuman conspiracy of evil. Possibly, then, the New Testament doctrine of superhuman satanic intelligences is as reasonable as any abstract philosophical speculation in description of the cosmic operation of evil (Ephesians 6:12). However, it is clear that to press back the origin of evil and sin into the unseen world still does not provide an ultimate reason for evil. One has explained why there should be a Tempter, but not why he should have fallen in the first place, or have succeeded in his temptations of mankind.

By the nature of things, there can never be any secure scientific evidence regarding the first mental and spiritual awakenings of the race, a change which could leave no physical evidence (see p. 78). Thus, when an evolutionary doctrine of the origin of the human race is accepted, the ultimate origin of evil is equally a mystery. The first evidence we have concerning the ideas which moved in the minds of primitive men seems to show that sin was already a dark fact of human life. Science does not know what happened upon the stage before the curtain first went up on the intellectual history of the race. The ultimate origin of evil is therefore a matter of philosophical speculation, but not the direct concern of Christian theology. However, Christian theology cannot accept those philosophical speculations which would explain away sin as not real, or as not truly sinful.

Summary of Divergence : Doctrines of the Fall

a. New Testament and Primitive Christian

The clearest New Testament doctrine is that of Adam as a "type." It was doubtless accepted in the primitive Church that the early chapters of Genesis were literal history, and that Adam and Eve were the first real parents of the race. However, the effective theological interest in the biblical narrative was as a divinely inspired symbol of spiritual principle. The story of Adam and Eve is a picture of what the race has done, and every man in the race (see pp. 85–86).

b. Traditional

Beginning with the writer Tertullian (working around A.D.200), and coming to clear expression in St. Augustine of Hippo (354–430), we find the traditional doctrine that the disobedience of the first parents of the whole race produced a physical, mental, and spiritual deterioration and contamination of human nature as originally created by God, as well as punishment by the withdrawal of the fullness of divine grace from man. This disability has been inherited in the human stock ever since, and explains why the whole human race is weak before temptation, and subject to the just judgment of God. Coupled with this is an emphasis upon the extreme heinousness of the first sin, which was such as to merit this universal punishment. This exposition is clearly linked with an emphasis that Adam and Eve were literally and historically the physical ancestors of the whole race.

The Scholastic theologians of the Middle Ages elaborated this doctrine by maintaining a difference between the "image of God" and the "likeness of God" mentioned in Genesis 1:26. The "image of God" refers to those superior powers natural to man, which make him different from and superior to the animals. Such are reason, speech, moral choice, and the power to be religious. The "likeness of God" was a supernatural gift of divine grace granted to man to lift him up to perfect communion with God, and fill him with "original righteousness." At the Fall the "image of God" was deteriorated, and the "likeness of God" entirely lost. It may be doubted whether this is correct exegesis of the original sense of the Biblical text. However, this construction does correspond to the fact that sin spiritually alienates man from

God, and also damages to some extent his natural powers of body and mind. Yet it does not completely dehumanize him.

c. Evolutionary

A number of attempts have been made to restate the doctrine of the fall in terms of an evolutionary origin of man, so as to preserve the religious values of the doctrine as a part of the Christian system, but to allow acceptance of the findings of natural science regarding the physical origins of the human race. A word of caution is necessary in the approach to this subject, the discussion of which has often generated more heat than light. Granted that man's physical frame has evolved from an animal ancestry which he holds in common with the anthropoid apes, it would appear than man's animal ancestors have been evolving on a track separate from that of the apes for a period of time enormously long compared with that period (very short by standards of geological time) during which the human race has been recognizable as "man." This long period is not so far spanned by a complete and self-evident chain of fossil "missing links." The evidence of a physical relationship to the apes is far more the indirect evidence of present structure, including that of the foetus, and of vestigial remains. There is thus a large element of mystery remaining in the physical "descent of man," and that mystery is at its greatest in that part of most interest to the Christian, namely, the awakening of man to become an intelligent and morally responsible being. Clearly by the nature of things there can be no fossil remains of this nonmaterial change. Therefore, while mystery remains, there is always the possibility that science may drastically revise her findings in ways at present unforeseeable. Nothing is easier than for those who would impugn the findings of natural science in the supposed interests of traditional religious opinions, on the one hand, or for the less thoughtful writers of "popular science," on the other, to pontificate in these matters beyond the secure evidence. The wise reader will remember that from the scientific point of view we do not altogether know how man became man, and perhaps never will. There is certainly room both to respect the secure findings of natural science, and also to accept the rise of man as a marvelous divine act.

Scientific evidence would appear to indicate that the faculty of reason, and of responsible choice, first awoke in primitive men who physically were substantially similar to modern man. Before this awakening, which the Christian may reasonably claim was a distinct creative act, man was presumably animal, neither morally good nor bad, but nonmoral. When God evoked His "image and likeness" man became human and responsible. He became a potential moral agent. At this critical stage the infant moral sense was to some extent defying the inherited current of natural instinct. Some have claimed that this would make it inevitable that the first choice to be made would be sinful. For example, an early moral crisis would occur when conscience first ruled that each member of the hunting pack should no longer scramble for his own fill when the prey was killed, but should make room for the weak and the aged. The same action which had for uncounted generations been neither morally good nor bad, but nonmoral, was now sinful. Yet it was inevitable that this sin should be committed, because it was not to be expected that infant conscience should at the first attempt entirely succeed in rebuking inborn animal instinct. This early and apparently trival sin to some extent alienated man from God, and weakened his power to resist further temptation. This opened the door to sin.

Thus we have an evolutionary hypothesis of the origin of sin, which appears to make sin an inevitable stage in the evolution of good. This is very near to the notion that sin is not really sinful, which in turn is an idea that Christian theology cannot admit. There is, however, one forgotten factor in this symbolic construction. If this first moral choice was presided over by the foreseeing providence of a God of holy love, He would surely have so supported infant but innocent man with His grace that this all-decisive moral test was an equitable one, and not foreordained to failure. It must have been possible in principle for primitive but as yet undepraved man to have chosen good, and thus to have made further good choices possible. The dark mystery of the origin of sin remains, therefore. We can reasonably argue that God had to make man free, and therefore capable of moral evil, if he was to be capable of moral good. Why man should in fact have used this divine endowment of moral responsibility to defile himself remains the final irrationality of human experience.

III. Suffered Under Pontius Pilate

A. The Occasion of Christ's Death

It seems clear that the real reason why Christ was put to death was that He too pointedly challenged the pride, position, and interests of the accepted religious teachers and ecclesiastical authorities of His day. However, the legal responsibility for the execution rests upon the Roman administration of the province of Judea (Luke 23:13-25; John 18:28-32). Thus He "suffered under Pontius Pilate." The barbarous punishment of crucifixion was not part of the more humane Jewish law, and was introduced by the Romans for the more terrifying execution of rebels and disobedient slaves. The victim normally lingered for a long time and died by slow exhaustion, so that the Roman guards were surprised and moved to superstitious awe by the circumstance that Jesus died so suddenly, and in the fullness of His strength (Mark 15:37, 39, 44). To the pious Jew the chief horror of crucifixion, however, was that it appeared to involve the curse of Deuteronomy 21:23. Thus it was not only a death in agony and disgrace. It also entailed excommunication from Israel. The reader should remember what unfortunate misunderstanding can be caused by saying unguardedly that Christ was put to death "by the Jews." Historically this was largely so. Nevertheless, the sins which crucified Christ have been seen in the life of every nation alike, and still are, so that the spiritual guilt of His death is in principle a universal guilt, and not particularly Jewish. It is much more accurately Christian to say:

> O Jesus, my hope,
> For me offered up,
> Who with clamour pursued Thee to Calvary's top.

B. *The Meaning of Christ's Sufferings*

1. OBEDIENCE. The first New Testament thought to be considered is that Christ's suffering and death is a sacrifice of obedience. God has made man, and therefore everything which man is and has is by right entirely at God's disposal. If man is to please God and to live in a secure relation of friendship with Him, he must obey God. Thus God graciously admits His people into a Covenant with Himself, freely pledging His word to bless and protect them. The condition of this Covenant is obedience to God's revealed Law (Exodus 24:7; Micah 6:6–8). A sacrifice may be defined as the God-appointed way in which man is to offer himself to God and come to God in fellowship.[3] Therefore the essential sacrifice is the life of moral obedience, and the ceremonial sacrifices of religious ordinance are a means to this end (Micah 6:6–8). However, the one thing which man cannot do is to obey God as He ought to be obeyed. He cannot keep his part of the Covenant, and so man is alienated from God (Jeremiah 31:32).

The essential purpose of the Incarnation was that God's Son came to do as perfect man what frail and sinful man must do, but cannot. As man, genuinely one of us, He offered to the Father in heaven the sacrifice of a life of sinless obedience (Mark 8:31, 14:36; John 4:34, 5:30, 6:38; Philippians 2:8; Hebrews 5:7–8; 1 Peter 2:23).

One of the chief significances of the Gospel record is that it shows with tragic clarity how God's Son as man met all those influences of moral compromise, and all those entrenched powers of wickedness, which have so largely governed human affairs in every age, and which daunt men from rising to a noble and morally constructive life. Our Lord encountered first the disillusioning slowness of men to respond to the call of the good (Mark 6:6). He tasted the bitterness of spiritual loneliness and of shameful betrayal (Matthew 23:37, 26:40; Luke 22:61; John 6:67). He came also into collision with the authority of religious systems which had lost their vision, and with the power of rulers who heeded policy rather than principle (Luke 6:11; John 19:12). He experienced weariness and the grim force of temptation (Luke 22:39–44; Hebrews 5:7–9). This whole manner of life found its fitting climax in the awesome mystery of death, and death in torment, unmerited disgrace, and spiritual darkness (Mark 15:34; Philippians 2:8). In every successive crisis of this career Christ continued in sinless and loving

---

[3] For an explanation of the idea of "sacrifice," see pages 87–88.

obedience to the heavenly Father and in love toward man (John 4:34). Where men commonly stumble into disappointment, cynicism, and compromise, Jesus walked erect and victorious (Luke 9:51; 1 Peter 2:21–24). This is the sacrifice of sinless obedience which opens the door into the presence of the holy God (Hebrews 4:14–16, 9:14).

2. CHRIST THE VICTOR. A further basic New Testament theology of the suffering and death of Christ is that here was the victory of the power of God, the power of moral obedience and long-suffering love, against all the evil forces which tyrannize over mankind. The imaginative but concrete symbolism natural to the mind of those times depicted these forces as spiritual entities, and sometimes as demonic beings. This makes many significant texts in the New Testament somewhat obscure to the modern mind, which tends to think of man's spiritual foes in terms of abstract principles and social influences. However, if the effort is made to translate out of the idiom of one age into the idiom of another, the New Testament doctrine of *Christus Victor* becomes plain and impressive. It may be reconstructed from texts drawn from the writings of St. Paul, who gives us the fullest material. However, the same principle is found underlying the doctrine of other parts of the New Testament.

Paul teaches that sinful man is in bondage in the first place to satanic intelligences, great and small (2 Corinthians 4:4; Galatians 4:3; Ephesians 2:2, and 6:12). Christ as man put Himself into the sphere of influence of these forces, which crucified Him (1 Corinthians 2:6–8). His resurrection was the mark of victory over them. The demons were dragged off like prisoners in a Roman Triumph (Colossians 2:15).

Man was also in bondage to the curse of the Law of Moses, placed upon the disobedient (Galatians 3:10). A slavish fear of offending God could darken the spirit of the Jew. By no means all Jews felt like this about their ancestral religion, but rather rejoiced in it as their pride and strength. St. Paul, however, most significantly did so find the religion of law to be a bondage which filled him with an agony of spiritual frustration (Romans 7:7–24). Christ was born as one of those who owed a duty of obedience to the Law (Galatians 4:4–5). He suffered the punishment marked out by the Mosaic Law as an accursed and excommunicate death (Galatians 3:13). When He rose in triumph the crucified was vindicated as the Messiah (Acts 2:23–24, 36), and the curse of the Law was shown as of no effect (Romans 7:4, 10:4; Galatians 3:13).

Another human bondage was that of sin (Romans 5:21, 8:3). Christ crucified was one with man in his most tragic lot (Romans 8:3; 2 Corinthians 5:21). Christ was tempted to the uttermost, yet did not sin, and rose in triumph, so that He can be assailed by sin no more (Romans 6:10, 8:3; 1 Corinthians 15:56–57). This was the divine victory over yet another adversary.

The last dread enemy of mankind is death (Romans 5:14; 1 Corinthians 15:26). Christ laid Himself open to the attack of this foe also, and died as men die, in torment and darkness (Philippians 2:8). The power of death was conquered by the risen Christ (Romans 6:9–10; 1 Corinthians 15:55–57).

The modern man does not typically think of his own bondage in these New Testament terms, but it is possible to see that Christ's life of obedience was a life of victory over those same social forces which visit us with frustration (compare what has been said above in paragraph 1 on Christ's obedience). His resurrection was a pledge of this victory. Thus New Testament thought can effectively be translated into modern terms.

3. DIVINE IDENTIFICATION WITH MAN. The Incarnation was the divine act of identification with man, that is, of God "making Himself one" with the human race. Identification is the essential spiritual principle by which alone one man can hope to bear the moral burden and fight the moral battle of another. This is always done at the price of self-sacrifice. Thus for example, a patriot sees his native land about to be occupied by an invading tyrant. He may be able to escape, take his professional skill with him, and earn a comfortable living in another land. Or he may voluntarily choose to remain with his fellow countrymen less fortunate than himself, so that he may use his talents to organize their resistance. By remaining with his fellow countrymen, that is, by identifying himself with them, he is able to take upon himself a major share of their common struggle, and so strengthen each one of them in his own share. This he does at the price of his own suffering, of his voluntary self-sacrifice. In one way or another every effort to lift the human race morally and spiritually has worked through the medium of identification, and has involved this price.

The Incarnation, and the human career which followed from it, is the supreme example of this action. In order that by the power of His long-suffering and holy love God might conquer as man, and for man, God's Son made Himself one with man. He shared a lowly birth and home. He humbled Himself to commonplace work among men (Mark 6:3). He graciously received social outcasts, though their ways and standards must have revolted Him, and this also cost Him His reputation (Matthew 9:10–12; Luke 7:36–50). He was glad to go with the people to their accustomed worship, though the doctrine of their teachers must always have seemed spiritually dim to His clear eyes (Luke 4:16). Here was indentification at a cost, but still more costly was His death upon the Cross. The Son of God made Himself one with humanity in its last and lowest experiences; in agony, in humiliation, in disgrace, in spiritual darkness, and in death (2 Corinthians 5:21). Furthermore, human beings are joined one to another in confidence and love by the power of sympathy, and sympathy means "suffering with" one's fellow. So God in Christ conquered the power of evil in this world by a method which unveiled His divine sympathy. That He chose this costly way is the supreme pledge of God's goodwill toward man;

of His grace, His preparedness to forgive, His love (John 3:16; Romans 8:31–39; Galatians 2:20; 1 John 4:9).

4. THE REDEEMING SUFFERINGS OF CHRIST. We may now connect what has been said about man's sinful condition, and what has been established from the New Testament regarding the sufferings and death of Christ, in order to show how God's action meets man's need. Man's moral and spiritual need is twofold. Corresponding to this need there is in the life and death of Christ a twofold work of God.

If it is asked why ordinary men do not rise above their dead selves to better things, the first answer is that they have despaired of the power of good. Primitive men continue in cruel or degrading social customs through superstitious fear of evil spirits, yet the sophisticated men of the modern world are in substantially the same bondage. They too are aware of an outward force of evil constraining them from doing the good their better natures tell them they ought to do. They fear to stand for right because of what may happen to them socially, economically, or politically. The world of human affairs therefore seems to be in the grip of social and economic forces which are malign, frustrating, vast, and impersonal, and which are so nearly irresistible that it hardly seems worth while to risk all for the cause of right. This same sense of defeat reigns in the human heart. The common experience of those who have tried to reform their own lives is so disappointing that nothing would surprise them more than suddenly to find themselves keeping their own sincere good resolutions. In face of all these powers men have said: "It's no good." Here is bondage to the *power* of sin, to an objective power reigning in the world of men.

Those who have thought more deeply about life are aware that there is a problem more tragic even than the power of sin. This is the *guilt* of sin. Here is the enemy within. He who has once opened his heart and mind a little to the vision of how noble it is to follow the good, and who then candidly looks upon what he has made of his own life—the petty compromises he has knowingly allowed, his liability to mixed motives even in the most sacred of actions, the unworthy thoughts which creep unbidden into the secret imagination, and the haunting realization that even that which he sincerely accounts to be good may in God's sight be stained with evil—this man has surely said in his heart: "How God must despair of me and despise me: more even than I despise myself! Even if He could help me, I have no standing before Him to ask Him to do it. I am not clean enough within to aspire nobly after that which is noble. *Oh I'm no good!*" Here is bondage to the *guilt* of sin. This bondage answers to the spiritual or religious definition of sin, as the former bondage did to the moral.

The act of God in Christ fulfills both these needs. In the first place, Christ's life of sinless obedience is the mark that by the power of God, humanity when joined to God can conquer the power of sin. This decisive battle is a sure token that God can win the whole campaign. It is no longer necessary to say "It's no good"; for here is a proof that God can make a difference to human life, and in the human situation. In the second place, the sympathy of God, the pledge of His understanding and forgiving love, enables man, despite the past, to dare to come for God to do for him what He has offered to do. Even as the words "Oh, I'm no good" rise bitterly from the heart, man is emboldened by the spectacle of God in Christ making Himself one with man, even in man's compromise and shame. Though man is what he is, the door is open for him to come. Thus Christ crucified wipes away the barrier of guilt, as well as breaks the bondage of sin.

> Be of sin the double cure,
> Cleanse me from its guilt and power.

5. THE OBJECTIVE AND SUBJECTIVE WORK OF CHRIST. It would seem that any adequate view of the meaning of the saving act of God in Christ crucified must comprise these two sides, and keep them in balance. If man is to be redeemed he needs to be given a reasonable ground for assurance that God has actually conquered the objective power of evil, once and for all, as a matter of historical fact. It is not sufficient to see in the Cross the revelation of a doctrine, the appeal of a good example, or the psychological stimulus of warm and loving sentiment. There must be this divine *objective* "finished work," done "once and for all." Yet by itself knowledge of the objective work is orthodoxy, and not "the faith that works by love."[4] The victorious act of God in Christ needs to be brought home to the inner man of the heart, to his affections, to his moral will. It must make a *subjective* appeal. The breaking of the power of sin chiefly corresponds to the objective aspect, the wiping away of the guilt largely to the subjective, though the two are intimately connected.

6. IDENTIFICATION WITH CHRIST. It will be asked what difference a divine act performed in Galilee and Jerusalem more than nineteen hundred years ago can make to the moral and spiritual life of a man in Europe or America, living in the entirely different social circumstances of the modern age. Failure of understanding at this point is without a doubt one of the main reasons why genuine Christianity does not make a deeper and wider impact. Any explanation of the connection between the work of God in Christ then, and His work in the lives of men now, depends upon the principle of the solidarity of the race.[5] Christ made Himself one with us in order to do this thing, and by making Himself one with us He opened the door for us in turn to make ourselves one with Him. And if we make ourselves one with Him, or identify ourselves with Him, we can share in the fruit of His victory.

It is said that we live in an age of "mass humanity." In the sense that the typical modern man works in the vast ant heap of a factory or office

---

4 Galatians 5:6.
5 The work is also the operation of the Holy Spirit (see p. 116).

building, commutes to a spreading and formless suburb, watches with millions of others the same TV program, and has his habits of food and clothing dictated by mass publicity, the present is the age of "the mass man." This disguises the still more significant fact that the men and women who form these masses are frequently living in a state of extreme, and indeed often excessive and unhealthy, social isolation. A large part of the ills of modern industrial society appear to spring from this isolation. People are obsessed with the idea of "living their own lives in their own way." Their society is broken up into the smallest-sized family groups, which even then all too often do not possess the merit of enduring stability. The larger groups which in the past have normally given to men support, restraint, and guidance, such as the securely consolidated town or village community, or the traditional communal religion, have suffered a loosening of their bonds. It is important to remember that the ancient world, which is the background both of the Bible and of the development of Christian doctrine, was in contrast possessed by a very commanding sense of the natural solidarity of the race. If this principle of solidarity is forgotten, Christ's work cannot be made intelligible. Also, the chief promise of the Christian religion is that it can bring all men back to a new and rich solidarity, though at a higher spiritual and ethical level than the old.

In the broadest terms the principle of Christian salvation is this. In Christ the sovereign power and long-suffering love of God won the decisive battle over the power of sin. Because Christ did this as man, and for man, in a solidarity of suffering and triumph with the race, the door is now open for all men to make themselves one with Christ. All those who do so share in the fruit of the victory. In company with Christ each one can then conquer in the battle of life, by His power. As with the power, so it is with the guilt of sin. Christ as man offered to the Father the well-pleasing sacrifice of sinless obedience. Because He did it as man, all those who make themselves one with Him can go with Him and share in the sacrifice, and find that the deep gulf of alienation from God is banished. The barrier of guilt is thrown down, and the door is open for man to have fellowship with God. In Christ, God as man came to meet man. All those who identify themselves with Christ in a strong solidarity can therefore meet with God. Thus the effect of the initial, decisive, all-important, historical, "once-for-all" action of God in first-century Palestine is mediated to all mankind in every age and place. The way in which this happens is more fully described in the discussion of the doctrines of faith and of the Church (see pp. 155–56, 221–23).

The New Testament doctrine of "identification with Christ" may be explained by a discussion of the text, "For as in Adam all die, even so in Christ shall all be made alive," (1 Corinthians 15:22). Genesis 2:7, 19–23, describes Adam as the ancestor of the human race, the name "Adam" meaning "the man." Therefore in the thought of St. Paul, Adam is the "type" of the race. Adam is the figure whose action represents what the whole human race in its solidarity has done, and every individual man within that solidarity. Adam disobeyed, and in consequence "died," that is, brought upon himself alienation from God, moral degradation, and calamity. This is St. Paul's way of saying that the human race taken as an organic whole, and likewise every member of the race considered as an individual, has disobeyed, and dies. Each individual who disobeys makes himself one with Adam, and takes for himself his own share of the common death (Romans 5:12).

The whole race is "in Adam" not just by heredity, but by the much more profound spiritual principle of solidarity. St. Paul doubtless did believe that Adam was in fact the physical ancestor of the whole race, but his theological thought is not solely dependent upon this. This is not what he is saying here. All men are not "in Adam" in the sense that all the millions of acres of a new variety of wheat which is someday to cover the prairie are "in" the single first grain, as it lies in the hand of the plant breeder. They are "in Adam" in somewhat the sense that every citizen of the United States may be said to be "in" the President when his signature finally brings into action some new legislation. His action represents the action of the whole nation, and of every citizen within the nation, so that its effect is binding upon all in this great solidarity. In like manner, every man who by penitence, obedience, and faith, truly makes himself one with Christ in the great new Christian solidarity is "in Christ." Christ's saving action then truly and spiritually represents his own action, and each man shares in the blessing of Christ's action.

C. New Testament Words

It is necessary to explain some of the chief New Testament words used to set forth various aspects of the saving work of Christ.

1. ATONEMENT; RECONCILIATION. These two words have the same meaning in the New Testament. The word "atonement" occurs in the familiar English translation (K.J.V.) of the New Testament in Romans 5:11, but the same Greek word is translated "reconciliation" in 2 Corinthians 5:18, 19. The origin of the word "atonement" is "at-one-ment," that is, a "making at one." The verb "to atone" could in Elizabethan English be used of persons who had quarrelled, in the sense of "to reconcile" them. Thus the act of God in Christ produces the reconciliation of man to God, and is so called "the atonement." It is to be noted that the New Testament speaks of the reconciliation of man to God, not of God to man (2 Corinthians 5:19, 20).

2. PROPITIATION. This word has often been taken to imply the notion of the offering of a gift or bribe to an angry divinity, in order to appease him. This has produced a reaction in the minds of some, who have turned away from the idea of "propitiation" as unethical and unspiritual. The Greek word in question can indeed bear this sense of "appeasement" in

pagan writing, but it would appear to be established that the general sense in the Greek Old Testament, or Septuagint, which is much more determinative for the New Testament, is at an higher level. The basic biblical sense of the word rendered "to make propitiation" would seem to be "to perform an act whereby religious defilement is removed." In the earlier stages of religion this defilement was thought of chiefly in terms of ceremonial taboo, and "to make propitiation" was then to perform the customary ceremony of "spiritual disinfection." It was later realized by the Hebrews that it is *sin* in the moral and spiritual sense, and not merely breach of ceremonial taboo, which defiles man before God. The purification therefore had likewise to be a moral and spiritual one. It was seen that only God can do this, for only God can forgive sin against Himself. The verb "to make propitiation" then took on a higher usage, and came to be used of God in the sense of "to forgive," or "to provide a means by which guilt may be removed." Thus the familiar K.J.V. of Romans 3:25, "Whom God hath set forth to be a propitiation," may be rendered, "For God designed him to be the means for expiating sin" (N.E.B.). The work of Christ is the God-appointed means whereby the guilt and defilement of sin may be wiped away. Hence the Cross is a propitiation.

3. RANSOM. The original meaning of this word was that of the price paid to secure the release of a captive or the freedom of a slave. It would appear, however, that in the New Testament the word has become generalized to convey the idea of "the means of release," without necessarily being associated with the notion of "a price paid." Thus when our Lord describes His death as a ransom (Mark 10:45) we are not called upon to ask: "To whom was the price paid?" Rather does the phrase convey that Christ's death is the means whereby man is released from bondage to his spiritual adversaries.

4. SACRIFICE. This is perhaps the most profound and comprehensive word used in the New Testament to expound the saving act of God in Christ. There has been much discussion of what "sacrifice" meant in the religion of primitive men, and also in the Old Testament which is the background for the thought of the New Testament. This subject is to a certain extent a matter of surmise, because the ancient world was content to carry out its religious rites because they were customary and sacred, and has not left us critical accounts of why they did what they did. However, there would be a good deal of agreement about three general ideas regarding sacrifice.

(1) A man wishes to dedicate one of his possessions to God. He therefore offers some part of it to God as an "acted prayer" dedicating the whole. (2) A man realizes that all that he has and is belongs to God, and should be offered to Him. He therefore takes some highly significant object in his possession and sacrifices it as an "acted prayer" of his self-offering to God. (3) To share a meal together unites men in the sacred bond of host and guest, and is the means of fellowship. Man desires to have a secure bond

of goodwill with God, and to enjoy fellowship with Him. He therefore provides a sacrifice, part of which is offered to God, and part of which is eaten by the worshippers as a sacred meal of fellowship. Thus he "has a meal with God." In general, therefore, a sacrifice is the God-appointed means whereby man may offer himself to God in dedication and obedience, and hold fellowship with God. Christ in His life and death is clearly the supreme sacrifice. He is the one who actually and perfectly does what the ancient Jewish sacrifices only aspired to do.

This doctrine is particularly worked out in the Epistle to the Hebrews. The master theme here is that the Jewish sacrifices, with their approach to God in solemn ceremonial, were the preparatory earthly shadows, spiritually valid but only partial, of the entirely effective spiritual sacrifice of obedience to God which Christ on earth as man offered to God, and which He still offers in heaven. That Christ is both Himself the high priest, and His life of obedience the sacrifice which He offers, carries the implication that His saving work is essentially an act of self-sacrifice.

In the Jewish religion the high priest was a man among men, and like them frail and tempted. Therefore he was a suitable representative to appear before God of behalf of the people. In the person of the high priest the whole solidarity of the people appeared before God (Hebrews 5:1-3). On the great Day of Atonement this human high priest went with the blood of a divinely ordained ceremonial sacrifice into the Holy of Holies, which to the people symbolized the most immediate presence of God (9:1-7). This was the approach of the ancient people of God to their God in self-dedication, obedience, and communion, but enacted according to a preparatory and shadowy earthly copy which lacked the fullness of divine saving power (9:7-10, 10:1-4). Christ came and brought these old sacrifices to their proper climax by offering on earth a sacrifice which fully corresponds to the spiritual ideal of sacrifice as it exists in heaven, that is, in the mind of God. This true spiritual sacrifice brings the fullness of divine saving power.

The divine Son (1:2-3) took upon Himself human nature like ours, so that He might make Himself fully one with us (2:14, 17). Standing thus on our ground He fought our battle for us, and conquered in the wonder of a sinless life (4:15). In language which clearly points back to the scene in Gethsemane (Luke 22:39-46), the writer shows that Christ offered to the heavenly Father the sacrifice of a life of perfect obedience, even to suffering and death (5:7-8). This spiritual sacrifice, which was so much better than the ceremonial sacrifice, was in fact the sacrifice appropriate to the New Covenant of inward spiritual religion of which Jeremiah had spoken (8:6-12). Because this sacrifice was offered by one who was truly man, and who was therefore man's true representative, the effect of it can belong to all men (2:9, 18). By His endurance Christ has conquered the power of Satan for us (2:14), and has set man free from fear and death (2:15).

In the power of this victory the risen and glorified Christ ascended to heaven, to appear before the throne of the majesty of God. As the Jewish high priest went sacramentally into the earthly Holy of Holies, so Christ has gone into the true holy place. He has gone there as man, and therefore He is mankind's fitting representative before God, the true high priest of the New Covenant (4:14; 7:23-27; 8:1-2; 9:11-12, 15; 12:24). This true heavenly priesthood fittingly corresponds to the old earthly priesthood, but is of new and mysterious divine origin, and of an altogether higher spiritual dignity (5:10, 7:1-21). The heavenly high priest has offered Himself in sacrifice, and this self-sacrifice suffices to open the door for man to have true spiritual communion with the Most High God (9:24-26, 10:19-22). Thus Christ is the "captain" of our salvation (2:10, 5:9, 12:2), a word which can be rendered "leader" (N.E.B.), or perhaps "pioneer," and which can be used to describe the "founding father" of a tribe or city constitution. He is the one who at a great cost has first trodden the path which we men must tread if we are to come to God (6:20), "blazing the trail" for us. This makes it possible for us to tread the path also, if by faith we make ourselves truly one with Him in the body of His Church (10:19-25). Faith in God has ever been the guiding principle and bond of union of the true Israelites among God's ancient people. An enriched, confirmed, and more spiritual faith is the possession of the Church, which is the due spiritual heir of the ancient chosen people (11:39-12:2, 22-23). The Church is likewise the guardian of the Eucharist, which is the Christian act of sacrificial worship (13:9-10).

This noble and spacious structure of Christian thought is one of the great creative elements of New Testament writing. It demonstrates for us the potentialities of that sacrificial language regarding the death of Christ, which meets us in a scattered and less developed form in other parts of the New Testament. It has been most influential in the Church of later times, in the development of thought regarding the atonement and the Eucharist.

IV. Theologies of the Atonement

The Christian doctrine of the atonement has been expressed in various ways in different periods of the Church's life.

A. Ancient Thought

It is often said that during the first thousand years of the Church's life the ransom theory of the atonement ruled, the point of ancient controversy being whether the ransom of Christ's death was paid to God the Father or to the Devil. This gives the impression that Christian thought on this important doctrine was somewhat crude and immature. In fact, however, the Church of the Roman Empire contained many theologians who were men of deep culture and of great powers of thought. In general these follow the New Testament, and speak of the saving act of God in Christ as an actual conquest of the powers of evil which enslave men. As there was in those days a vivid sense of the existence of personal demonic powers, the conquest of Satan is naturally spoken of, and the despoiling Satan of his victims. Many vivid metaphors are used to enforce this idea, including that of ransom. A transaction is often depicted in which Christ offers His priceless soul to Satan in return for the freeing of his prisoners, after which Satan finds that he cannot hold the prize he has grasped! The theological worth of this admittedly quaint language can only be appreciated when it is realized that these metaphors are not more than the "sermon illustrations" used to expound a mature view of the work of Christ, which is dominant in the New Testament itself, and which goes back to our Lord's own view of His activity (Matthew 12:25–29). This is the doctrine of Christ as the Victor.

B. Satisfaction

In the centuries which followed the fall of the Roman Empire in the west there was a natural decay of all branches of learning, and very little constructive work in systematic theology was attempted. However, the Easter faith in Christ crucified and risen, the conqueror of Satan, sin, and death, the dread enemies of mankind, lived on in Church worship and popular piety, as it always has done. With the dawn of the Middle Ages we find the gradual rebirth of civilized social institutions, and with them a distinctive Christian culture. Naturally this was accompanied by the rise in educated circles of a more reflective form of Christian faith, and in course of time, of a vigorous theological life in the medieval universities. As a part of the medieval Scholastic theology we find the first of the great theologies of the atonement, namely, the satisfaction theory. This was pioneered by St. Anselm of Canterbury (1033–1109), and displaced the ancient ransom theory. Satisfaction ("making enough") is essentially the New Testament doctrine of Christ's death as a representative sacrifice,[6] but expressed in terms natural to those whose thought regarding the solidarity of the human race was molded by the institutions of medieval feudalism.

St. Anselm taught that sin is an affront to God's honor and to the divine order of the universe. Due satisfaction is to be made for this affront before it is seemly, or morally right, for God to forgive. Such submission of obedience must be made as will vindicate God's credit as the rightful and righteous ruler of the world. Sinful man is neither able nor worthy to offer himself to God in satisfaction for sin. He has no ground of standing before his king. A man, *and a sinless man,* must in obedience offer himself up to the glory of God before God can fittingly receive man. Therefore God Himself must become man, so that as man He may Himself do this. Moreover, the satis-

---

[6] Compare what has been written above (pp. 88–89) on the theology of the Epistle to the Hebrews.

faction for man's sin can only rightly be offered *by man:* by one who is the authentic representative of the fallen race. Therefore the divine Son fully identified Himself with mankind in its shame and woe, which is the fitting punishment for sin, and in submission freely offered Himself up to the glory of the Father. Thus by Christ's suffering and death the means was provided by God for man's forgiveness, and for his restoration to a secure status in the sight of God. The Cross was a satisfaction for sin.

This scheme, with God almost in the position of a feudal lord adjusting his differences with disobedient and disrespectful vassals, may appear to some people to be archaic. Nevertheless it has the spiritual value of giving a clear witness to the basic idea of our Lord's representative sacrifice, and to that principle of human solidarity in Him without which it is impossible to understand the atonement.[7] Satisfaction is an exposition of the Cross which to an eminent degree accords with the visible Church's sense of organic solidarity, as she joins in her sacramental worship. Thus the Eucharist, which is the earthly Church's sacrificial rite, is the means by which Christians make themselves one body with Christ, as He, the great high priest in glory, offers to the Father the one and only prevailing heavenly sacrifice.[8] Thus the medieval satisfaction theology harmonized naturally with the chief contemporary form of worship, namely, the sacrifice of the Mass.[9]

C. Substitution

This theology, which rose to prominence in Protestant circles at the Reformation period, in its original form states that the attitude of a holy God toward the sinner is necessarily that of wrath, which works punishment. A just God cannot forgive unless due punishment for sin is exacted; but the love of God provided the means for this by sending the incarnate Son, who as man bore upon the Cross the penalty, and suffered the curse, of the sins of the whole race. Because Christ was God as well as man, the merit of this divine suffering was so great as to suffice for the due punishment of the sins of all men. All those who by faith make themselves one with Christ, their meritorious Federal Head, share in His merit by virtue of their

---

[7] Thus it is to be observed that some of the best modern theology of the atonement is a restatement in more modern thought forms of the conception of representative sacrifice and of satisfaction.

[8] So the Consecration Prayer in the liturgy of the English Church runs: He "made there, by His one oblation of Himself once offered, a full, perfect, and sufficient sacrifice, oblation and *satisfaction,* for the sins of the whole world."

[9] The continuity in saving efficacy, yet difference in historical operation, between the "once-for-all" sacrifice of the incarnate Son on Calvary, and the constantly renewed sacrifice of the Mass has been traditionally expressed in Roman Catholic theology by calling the former the "bloody sacrifice" and the latter the "unbloody sacrifice." Some Roman Catholic theology has at times spoken of the Mass as a "repetition" of Calvary, but this dubious phrase can easily obscure the unique character of God's saving act in the incarnate Son, and would not appear to be acceptable to the most reliable Roman Catholic theologians.

solidarity with Him, and so receive forgiveness and reconciliation to God. Thus man is saved by the transfer of the penalty of sin to Christ, and the "imputation" of, or accounting of, the merits of Christ to man. This theology has been traditional in orthodox Protestantism.

In the modern period this theology has been criticized under various heads. (1) Some people feel that it appears to make the justice and the love of God quantities opposite to one another, and thus to introduce a division into the nature of God Himself. (2) The transfer of punishment, and of the merit of Christ's sufferings, appears to some to be an ethically dubious doctrine. (3) It has been observed that the New Testament "wrath of God" is not a personal attitude of divine anger toward the sinner, but a nemesis, or self-acting train of cause and effect, which brings retribution upon the sinner (Romans 1:18–32). So it is the action of God to deliver from the wrath, not to bring it upon man (1 Thessalonians 5:9). Thus the substitutionary theology has been restated in the form of the so-called *governmental* theories. These are based upon the undoubted truth that even the God of love cannot forgive in such a way as to allow man to suppose that sin is condoned. God's strict moral government of the world must be fully vindicated before sin can be freely pardoned. Christ indeed bore the penalty of sin upon the Cross, but to satisfy the claims of justice before God and man, rather than to turn away the anger of God from man.

It will be seen that this theology answers to the Christianity of individual conversion, as satisfaction does to the religion of corporate sacramental worship. It serves strongly to emphasize the facts of personal guilt, of personal moral responsibility before God, and of personal liability to punishment. It gives the believer a ground for assurance that his own guilt is set aside by God, and his own liability liquidated. Because Christian salvation is individual as well as communal there is here an important aspect of truth, and the preaching of substitution has been blessed by God in evangelistic preaching. However, it will surely be agreed that the presentation of the Cross should be such as to encourage men, united in the body of Christ, to say "He died for *us,* and for each one as a member of that body," as well as the individual "He died for me." The older theologies have much to contribute here.

D. Moral Influence

This presentation of the Cross is essentially a feature of modern theology, particularly in "liberal" circles, though it was notably advanced in the medieval period by Abelard (1079–1142). The basis of this exposition is the doctrine that Christ crucified is a compelling demonstration in human terms of how sin and the sinner appear in the sight of the God of holy love. The rejection of Christ is the supreme token of man's repulse of God's offered love, and of the spite which the sinner does to the divine grace. This will move the heart of man to shame and penitence. The self-sacrifice and forgiveness of Christ is likewise the supreme token of God's forgiving love, and of His preparedness to receive the penitent sinner. This enables the penitent to return to God despite the sorry past and accept forgiveness.

It is clear that there is truth here also. Here is the atonement expounded in psychological terms, as substitution is in judicial. In fact, the moral influence theology of the atonement answers almost entirely to the *subjective* side of the atonement (see p. 84). It concerns the mental process by which the saving act of God can make an appeal to the human personality, rather than the nature and importance of the saving act itself. Taken in isolation the moral influence theology is thus in danger of representing the Cross as an appeal to sentiment, or as the revelation of a truth. It does not convey the essential Christian conception of an historic divine act in Christ, whereby the power and guilt of sin are effectually destroyed. Nevertheless, the moral influence theology helps to illuminate the manner in which the historic divine act can make an appeal to the human personality, and influence it morally and spiritually. Thus this school of thought is really an adjunct to the other systems, and a valuable adjunct, but not a sufficient doctrine on its own.

E. Summary

It is to be observed that any preaching of the Cross can be blessed by God for the salvation of souls if it can convey to man a reasonable ground for supposing that in Christ God has actually done everything which needs to be done to dispel the guilt and destroy the power of sin, and to enable man to come to God and receive forgiveness. It is therefore most unfitting to dispute around the foot of the Cross, as though one theory alone were a legitimate part of the Gospel. There are elements of value in all these approaches, or they would never have made their historic appeal. The Christian teacher should reverently seek among these elements to make his presentation of the underlying scriptural witness as profound, intelligible, and winning as possible.

V. Dead and Buried, He Descended Into Hell.

This clause of the Creed was very important in old times, but in the modern world is often the occasion of unfortunate misunderstanding. However, the desire of the Church to find a theological meaning symbolized in Christ's sojourn in the grave during the period between His crucifixion and resurrection is more than fanciful curiosity. The underlying spiritual principle of the Incarnation is the self-identification of the divine Son with mankind. He made Himself one with man in infancy, in childhood, in the labor of manhood, in the worship of His people, in temptation, in agony, in spiritual darkness, and in death. The last act of this process is that He made Himself one with the dead as they await the general resurrection. As He conquered for man in all these other phases of human experience, so He conquered in the grave.

The spiritual condition of the departed is not open to direct human experience, and therefore is not capable of description in matter-of-fact language. Christian doctrine has to be deduced from spiritual principles, and symbolized in imaginative language. The Church has inherited two traditions of symbolism, both of which are legitimate and have their own spiritual value, and are indeed complementary to one another. The form of symbolism which comes more naturally to most modern minds is derived in part from the Bible, but in part also from the philosophical thought of the Greeks. It considers the souls of the departed in Christ as now existing in the spiritual sphere, which is not a "place." They are in a state of enhanced personal awareness, spiritual blessedness, and communion with God. There is, however, alongside this a purely Hebraic and biblical system of symbolism, which speaks of the dead as awaiting the general resurrection, and the coming Day of God. Those who wait in the world of the departed are indeed not in a state of suspended animation, but their full spiritual blessedness in the presence of God awaits the Day of the Lord. The traditional doctrine which we are now to consider is framed in terms of this second and biblical system of symbolism. It is a pity that its value is concealed from the minds of some who see no further than the symbolical language of this article of the Creed, and who dismiss the matter as a piece of archaic and naïve mythology left over from the childhood of the Church.

In the familiar English Bible two quite different Greek words are translated "hell." There is *Hades,* the world of the departed, or the grave, where the dead await the resurrection, as in Luke 16:23 and Acts 2:31; and there is *Gehenna,* the place of punishment of the finally impenitent, after the Judgment, as in Matthew 5:22, 29; Mark 9:43. It is important to remember that this clause of the Creed refers to our Lord's descent into Hades, the world of the departed, not into Gehenna. This translation will seem less remarkable when it is remembered that in Tudor English, into which the Apostles' Creed was translated from the Latin, the word "hell" had a much broader meaning than it does today in our common speech. It meant simply "a covered place."[10] The Christian doctrine is, then, that our Lord spent the time before His resurrection with all the rest of the departed, however we may conceive of their mode of existence. This was the last fitting act of identification with man, which enabled Him to conquer for man in this mysterious sphere also.

Christian thought on this subject has followed the course of 1 Peter 3:19–20, which teaches that Christ "went and preached unto the spirits in prison." The Church from the beginning had a very strong sense of

---

[10] Thus the old English occupational surname *Hellier* designated a man who thatched houses, and who *covered* them.

continuity with the ancient people of God. The saints and heroes of old Israel were seen as the spiritual ancestors of the Church, and therefore the Christian mind was much exercised as to the possibility of the salvation of righteous men of old time, who lived before the saving act of God in Christ was performed. The doctrinal solution was that those who because of their faithfulness were virtually "Christians before the time" would be found in the end to belong to Christ. In 1 Peter the "spirits in prison," to whom Christ went, would appear to be the unrighteous who were drowned in the Deluge, and who are here apparently given an opportunity for repentence. However, in Christian tradition they have been seen as those prisoners of Satan and the grave who were worthy to be called into Christ's kingdom. The effect is the same either way. The possibility of salvation in Christ is taken backwards in time to the beginning of God's people. Here is the theme of "The Harrowing of Hell," so prominent in medieval mystery plays and religious art. Christ the strong man, who has bound Satan (Luke 11:21–22), is depicted as descending with His angels into the world of the grave, there to spread the victory of the Cross and to release Satan's prisoners. He takes Adam and Eve by the hand, and lifts them out to salvation. Thus interpreted, this clause of the Creed speaks of the principle that Christian salvation potentially extends to every human soul who in the end will be found to have accepted Christ in penitence and faith, even though some were not apparently believers in this life. There is a real and lasting spiritual value in this belief, even though some people may not appreciate the way in which it has traditionally been expressed.

Readings

Aulén, G., *Christus Victor*. New York and Toronto: The Macmillan Company, 1945.

Brunner, H. E., *Man in Revolt,* trans. O. Wyon. New York: Charles Scribner's Sons, 1939.

Hodgson, L., *The Doctrine of the Atonement*. London: Nisbet and Co., Ltd., 1951; New York, Charles Scribner's Sons, 1951.

Newbigin, L., *Sin and Salvation*. Philadelphia: Westminster Press, 1957.

Robinson, H. W., *Redemption and Revelation in the Actuality of History*. New York and London: Harper & Row, Publishers, 1942.

Scott, C. A. A., *Christianity According to St. Paul*. London: Cambridge University Press, 1932.

Taylor, V., *Jesus and His Sacrifice*. London: Macmillan & Co., Ltd., 1937.

Chapter Four

The Power and the Wisdom

The third day He rose again from the dead,
and ascended into heaven,
and sitteth on the right hand of the Father

I. He Rose Again

The art of scratching rude words on buildings is a very ancient one. On a site belonging to the early Christian centuries there was found a rough drawing of a man kneeling before an ass's head stuck upon a pole, with the words: "Alexamenos worships his god." Alexamenos was doubtless a Christian, and those who were jesting at his expense have left a record of how the ancient world viewed the Cross. The mind of the time could worship "the genius of the emperor" and see something of true divinity in the impressive symbol of universal government. But crucifixion was not a hallowed thing to those who from time to time could actually see the grisly spectacle! It was a horrid death reserved by calculated sadism for the humiliation and torment of rebels and disobedient slaves. There was nothing of dignity there, and for the Christian to proclaim in Christ crucified and risen the act of God was so contrary to every presupposition of reasonable men that the idea was "too funny for words." In that miracle-believing age most men had no difficulty whatever in accepting the proposition that the gods could, if they wished, raise a man from the dead. Nevertheless, the gospel of the resurrection was the subject of ribald mirth (1 Corinthians 1:18, 21–24).

Long centuries of Christian culture have made the unbelieving world more polite. The figure of Jesus of Nazareth is almost universally respected, and even loved, even among those who do not believe in Him. However, the gospel of the resurrection is today just as completely "foolishness" in the eyes of the world of polite unbelief as it was when St. Paul preached in Athens, the university city of the ancient world (Acts 17:32). That Christ should have risen from the dead is contrary to every normal presupposition of the modern man. This is why the modern Christian, like the ancient martyr Church, finds himself "swimming against the tide." Secular writers will in their philosophical works or literary articles readily agree to classify Jesus with Socrates, a revered martyr in the painful upward march of truth and social right, or with St. Joan of Arc, a figure of purity perishing cruelly at the hand of ignorant and prejudiced men. Yet for them to accept the empty tomb is too great a burden. Special resistance is reserved for this doctrine.

The reason for this is not far to seek. The victory of God's power and love is a hidden victory. To the Apostle the Christian gospel is "the mystery" (Romans 16:25; 1 Corinthians 2:7; Ephesians 1:9, 3:9–10). It is a piece of divine knowledge so wonderful that the most acute human intelligence could never have discerned it, had not God willed

To make the joyful secret known

by a special act of revelation (1 Corinthians 2:9–10). And the victory of the Cross is the central point of this mystery. That the Cross is a victory is by no means obvious. On the surface it appears exactly the opposite. The Cross looks like the most signal defeat of God's power and love. Our Lord is the one who, in His unselfish purity of intention and sympathetic friendliness, *ought* to have won all hearts, and He has been more than decisively repulsed. If whatever is good in the human heart cannot be won by this matchless appeal, how can it ever be won? The Cross viewed as the most shameful of martyrdoms is a token of the utter unworthiness of human nature and of the black despair of mankind. To see it as a victory requires the divine gift of faith. It requires an opening of the eyes to discern that which is not in accord with the common sense of ordinary people, either in the ancient world or in the modern. Here is the place of the resurrection. It is the conquering sign wrought by God to show that the victory of the Cross *is* a victory, and that Christ's sacrifice of obedience sufficed in its high purpose. Thus traditional Christianity has always affirmed that the gospel of Christ crucified stands or falls with the resurrection (1 Corinthians 15:14, 17).

II. The Doctrine of the Resurrection

A. The Third Day

According to the usual tradition, our Lord's last supper was the Passover meal (Luke 22:1, 7, 13, 15).[1] He died before sunset on what we now call

---

[1] The Fourth Gospel places the last supper one day earlier (John 13:1).

Friday, that is, before the Jewish Sabbath commenced (Luke 23:44, 54; John 19:31, 42). It will be remembered that the Jews counted each new day as beginning at sunset (Genesis 1:5). He rose "upon the first day of the week, very early in the morning" (Luke 24:1), that is, after the Sabbath was ended. Thus Christ was in the tomb during part of two days and the full day between. According to the Jewish computation the resurrection was thus upon "the third day" (Acts 10:40; 1 Corinthians 15:4).

B. A Reversal to Death

The essential meaning of Christ's resurrection is that it was the reversal of His death. It was the abundantly triumphant "more-than-reversal" of the death of shame (Romans 6:8–9). We must speak with reserve concerning an unparalleled event of this sort. The resurrection narrative is the record of men who are seeking to describe that for which they have no adequate words. We have no right to expect common-sense coherence in every detail. Furthermore, the account was written for the purpose of proclaiming the Faith, and not in order to anticipate the detailed critical questions of a later age. Therefore we need not be surprised that there is variation as to whether one or two angels were seen (Mark 16:5; Luke 24:4), or even in the more important issue as to whether the resurrection appearances were all in Galilee, as appears to be implied by Mark 16:7; or all in Jerusalem, according to the Lukan narrative; or in both places, according to Matthew and John. We cannot know more about the resurrection than is written, and the element of mystery is bound to remain. Nevertheless, this does not necessarily hold in question the reality of the event itself.[2]

Taken at its face value the New Testament narrative appears to indicate quite decisively, on the one hand, that the resurrection was not simply an impressive vision of Christ in glory, which convinced the first disciples that their Lord was triumphant over death, even though the body lay corrupting in the grave. The tomb was empty (Mark 16:6), and the risen Christ possessed that which truly corresponded to the body which had died (Luke 24:36–43; John 20:27). We may also surmise that perhaps St. Paul was aware that there was a mysterious but important difference between the resurrection appearances to the first disciples, and his own decisive experience on the Damascus road. As he writes to the Corinthian Christians he knows that the original qualification for the office of apostle was ability to bear witness to the fact of Christ's resurrection (Acts 1:21–22). These apostles had later made their own the characteristic work of the traveling preacher and founder of churches. Paul had in fact excelled in this work, and in this sense was an "apostle" (1 Corinthians 15:10). Yet he knows full well that those who did not favor his policy of Gentile freedom from circumcision

---

[2] A discussion of the general trustworthiness of the Gospel narrative recording our Lord's life and teaching will be found in the chapter dealing with the Christian doctrine of the Scriptures (pp. 197–200).

could point to the fact that he did not possess that original qualification for the work of apostleship. He had not witnessed the resurrection.[3] Hence the care with which he repeatedly rehearses the story of the Damascus road, and of the vision which had commissioned him to his preaching ministry (Acts 26:16–18). It was to him the spiritual equivalent of having seen an appearance of Christ in resurrection glory. Yet it was not more than an *equivalent.* This perhaps is the force of his curious phrase in 1 Corinthians 15:8: "And last of all He was seen of me also, as of one born out of due time." By his vision he was born into the company of the apostolic witnesses, yet he was only just born alive. He dare not claim to his Corinthian Christians that he had seen the Lord in His resurrection body, in the same way as had the original witnesses listed in 15:1–7. There was a mysterious but important difference between Christ's resurrection in a glorified body and even the most impressive of visions.

However, the Gospel narrative on the other hand indicates that the resurrection body of our Lord was a glorified body. It was not barely the body of flesh and blood which had died, now come to life again in the same condition as before. The Lord could appear and disappear, and even those who knew Him well did not always immediately recognize Him (Luke 24:15–16, 31). The resurrection body indeed corresponded to the body which had died. Christ was no disembodied ghost. Yet it corresponded at an altogether higher state of glory. Christ's resurrection body was thus a body which answered appropriately to the principle of triumphant "more-than-reversal" of death. St. Paul again struggles with the problem of expression. Writing to the Corinthians he plainly reinterprets the Jewish hope of resurrection in terms of the one resurrection which had actually taken place, and speaks of the paradox of a "spiritual body" which shall belong to the believer in the Day of God (1 Corinthians 15:35–53). The implication is that this was the manner of body in which Christ rose from the dead: no mere body of resuscitated flesh and blood, but a body answering fittingly to the body of flesh and blood, yet answering equally to the glory of the Day of the Lord. Naturally the mind is left with all manner of unsatisfied inquiries, but this is inevitable as man confronts the mystery of God's immediate and unique saving act in history.

C. A Symbolic Act

If it is asked why God should have chosen to signify in this, and in no other way, that the Cross was a victory and not a defeat, the answer is to be sought in terms of the manner in which the Jewish people thought of human nature and personality. We today usually think of human nature as a nonmaterial "soul," which is the essential man, dwelling in and expressing

---

[3] However, those who affirm that the original resurrection appearances to the Twelve were a vision only, similar to St. Paul's experience on the Damascus road, would point to 1 Corinthians 9:1 as implying a claim that he was a witness of the resurrection, in the same manner as the original apostles.

itself through a material body, which is the necessary temporary companion of the soul in this life but not the real "personality." This is a thought form learned from the Greeks, and it is important to remember that it is not biblical.[4] The ancient Hebrews did not divide man into body and soul in this way, but looked upon human nature as unitary. All that we think of as together comprised in the terms of "body and soul," or "body, mind, and spirit," were by them conceived of simply as "the man," so that it would not have been natural for them to speak of the immaterial part of human nature as "the essential man."[5] Thus to the Hebrews, for the surviving immaterial "spirit" of a man to visit this world from the world of the dead, apart from the body, would not have been seen as the triumph of that man over death. It would be the survival of a ghost, of the mere partial shadow of the man.

In terms of this way of thinking the symbol of "triumph over death" is clearly not "survival of the soul in heaven," but rather *resurrection:* that is, the raising to life of the body which has died, and its reunion with the animating "breath of life." We thus find that the Hebrew expectation of the glorious life of the Day of the Lord is framed in terms of the resurrection of the body (Daniel 12:2).[6] This expectation could be interpreted by superficial minds in a crudely materialistic way, or by the more thoughtful as the resurrection of a human body mysteriously adapted for the glories of the messianic kingdom. It was to these Hebrew people, thinking in this way, that God gave His sign. He spoke as they were able to understand. Thus Christ was raised from the dead as the due token of victory over death. God placed His stamp of approval upon the expectation of resurrection, and also confirmed a "spiritual" interpretation of resurrection, in the sense that the body which rose was not barely the body of flesh and blood physically resuscitated, but a glorified body. We have to speak with reverent reserve concerning these mysterious things, but this would appear to accord with the witness of the New Testament, if the narrative be taken at its face value.

D. The Preaching of the Resurrection

The early sermons recorded in the Acts of the Apostles are not verbatim reports. Furthermore, it was a common and quite permissible literary device in antiquity for an author to compose a speech representing his view of a given historical situation, and place it in the mouth of the character concerned. Thus many critics would argue that these early sermons are not

---

[4] This does not necessarily involve that this way of thinking is wrong or that it is not a proper part of Christian theology.

[5] We are reminded that this view of human nature is not unreasonable by the investigations of modern psychology, which have illustrated how intimately the development of the mental life and the "personality" is connected with the action of the physical nervous system.

[6] This doctrine received much development in the period of time between the composition of the Old and the New Testaments.

the very words used by the apostles on these occasions. Even so, they are something of at least equal value, for they are a valid representation to us of the way in which the Christian gospel was preached by the Church in its first days. The apostolic argument is that by His glorious resurrection Jesus had been divinely vindicated as the Christ, even though He had suffered the fate, almost unbelievably paradoxical for the Messiah, of a cursed death (Acts 2:22-24, 32-36; 3:14-15; 4:10). To this is added a second line of argument, the "argument from prophecy." The Christians, reading the Scriptures in the light of their faith, could find many passages which spoke plainly to them of the doctrine of the crucified and risen Messiah. Therefore the mysterious paradox had been foreseen by the wisdom of God, and must be reverently accepted upon the authority of Scripture as the wonderful counsel of God (Acts 2:25-31, 34-35; 3:18, 21-25; 4:11, 24-28).

E. A Sign to Faith

It is most significant for the understanding of the whole spirit of the Christian faith that our Lord in His resurrection glory did not show Himself to confound Pilate or Caiaphas, but only to His broken-hearted yet loving disciples. To our Lord His "mighty works" were full of meaning. They were marks that in His person the kingdom of God was at work among men (Matthew 11:2-5, 12:28; Luke 11:20). Yet He seems to have sought to avoid creating the impression among the crowd that He was a worker of prodigies, or was the man to bring men bread on easy terms or victory over their enemies (John 6:14-15, 26-27). Instead, He bade men so far as possible keep His works of mercy secret (Matthew 8:4; Mark 8:26). In particular, He did not work miracles to produce faith in unbelievers, but invited men to have faith before He worked the wonder (Matthew 9:27-31; Mark 5:35-36). The man to whom is granted a wonderful work is he who cries out in his distress: "Lord, I believe; help Thou mine unbelief" (Mark 9:17-27). In Christ we see that God first invites man to respond to the initiative of His grace by opening his mind and heart in trust and love. He seeks that man should respond freely for the sake of love. The man who cooperates this far with God's act can then receive a mightier act of divine goodness and power which will increase and confirm his faith.

This progression of divine initiative and of free human response is illustrated in the story of our Lord's transfiguration.[7] This impressive sign was not given until the disciples had first, and without a sign, confessed that their Master was the Messiah (Mark 8:27-29). The wonderful work cannot be performed until men have first confessed the faith solely on account of the impression which our Lord's character and teaching had freely and

---

[7] Even if the order of this narrative is due to the Evangelists, the circumstance that they placed these elements of the story in this order is a token of the way in which they understood the mind of their Lord.

thoughtfully made upon their minds. Then, and only then, is it spiritually fitting that they should receive a miraculous confirmation of faith (Mark 9:1–8). This sign is not given so that the tale can be recounted to others as a wonder-story (9:9), but because their faith is presently to be sorely tested (9:30–32). On the other hand, for men to desire a sign as the condition for faith is the mark of unbelief (Matthew 12:38–39), while the desire to constrain unbelieving men by the working of a staggering miracle is the temptation of Satan himself (Matthew 4:5–7).

The climax of this process is the resurrection itself. The resurrection appearances were granted to men and women who freely had believed, whose faith was crushed by the devastating spectacle of their Lord's accursed death, yet whose hearts still cried out to believe because they were moved by love (Luke 24:18–25, 30–32). Doubting Thomas was allowed to see the Lord's glory, not simply because he was possessed of doubt which needed to be dispersed, but because despite his doubt he did not doubt utterly, and so remained with the disciples. The Lord came to him because He knew that he was, even in his "unbelief," prepared to come to faith if he saw (John 20:24–28). Thus the resurrection was a sign of Messiahship given to faith, and this faith is not a gift merely implanted in passive man. It is *evoked* by God.

F. The Pledge of Eternal Life

It can be argued that if God is good and reasonable in His dealings with men there must be, beyond this life, an eternal life with God (see pp. 257– 58). This degree of faith is confirmed by the resurrection, and raised from a reasonable supposition to a confident hope which is the comfort of man in darkness and bereavement. That God could raise Christ from the dead is the supreme "case in point" (1 Corinthians 15:20–23, 55–58).

III. The Resurrection as Fact and as Symbol

In the accepted Christian system our Lord's resurrection is an outstanding instance of the general principle that God mediates the spiritual through the material (see p. 164). On the one hand, God's pledge of Christian faith is an historical act. It is a mysterious physical miracle, in that Christ rose from the dead. On the other hand, to Christian faith the value of the resurrection is not in the outward and physical act as such, but in the inward and spiritual principle which is symbolized by the act. Perhaps many, filled with curiosity, looked into the empty tomb and simply did not know what to make of it. The factual evidence of the resurrection did not produce faith, but only bewilderment. As the early evangelists discovered by experience, demonstration of the outward fact of the resurrection does not by itself constrain men to have faith (Luke 16:31). Yet the Church has always affirmed that the inward faith could not have arisen in the first place apart from the outward and physical sign of God's saving act. And without it faith cannot be sustained today. This has been the subject of widespread modern controversy.

Summary of Divergence: the Character of the Resurrection Gospel

a. A Critical View

The following points are presupposed as the basis for discussion. One assumes what has been established regarding the literary methods of the ancient world and the manner in which the original Christian tradition could have been modified in expression by transmission through the believing group mind of the ancient Church (see pp. 36–37, 38). Furthermore, the early Christian preaching was expressed in terms of "myth" belonging to those times (see pp. 35–36). Again, if Christian faith is to be made acceptable in the modern world the element of "physical miracle" must so far as possible be eliminated, because the scientific mentality assumes the doctrine of the continuity of nature and cannot accept the notion of a miracle (see pp. 27–28). Thus in a modern presentation of the gospel the resurrection is to be expounded apart from the miracle of the empty tomb, because this would have been a physical event.

The critical case, then, is as follows. The New Testament Church became aware as a matter of immediate and incontestable experience that their Lord was present with them after His death, alive, victorious over all evil, and the mediator to them of the very presence of God.[8] This momentous experience of divine "life out of death" was in fact itself God's historic saving act, and the foundation of the gospel. The group mentality of the first circle of believers then naturally and spontaneously constructed the imaginative narrative or "myth" of the angelic messengers, the empty tomb, the visible appearances of Christ, the mark of the nails, Christ's meals with His disciples, and the like, in order to give vivid expression to their faith that the living and victorious Lord was with them. There was no element of deception in this. It was simply the natural and inevitable way in which people of that place, time, and culture clothed their thoughts so as to grasp their faith for themselves and communicate it to others. Yet today we are mistaken if we seek to take the narrative literally, so as to speak of the empty tomb as a physical fact. If it be inquired what actually happened after the burial of Christ to generate the experience of the present and living Lord, the answer has to be given that we simply do not know, and by the nature of the case cannot know, beyond the vaguest of surmise. The Gospel narrative gives the witness of the Church to its faith in Christ, but not to "facts" about the resurrection in the sense of historical or scientific facts. To press an inquiry after these is alien to the sense of the story, and obscures to our mind the nature of the Gospel witness.

---

8 To use the current phrase, they knew this "existentially."

b. A Rejoinder

The upholder of the traditional Christian system will first emphasize that the above exposition of Christianity, now widespread in many critical circles, is not simply a reinterpretation of the Christian Faith into the language of the modern day. It is a radical transformation of the whole Christian religion into something entirely different from what it has always been. It is a denial of the basic incarnational principle, that the God who made the material world, and who indwells and works through it, uses material means for the accomplishment of His spiritual ends (see pp. 23–24, 34). This attempt to withdraw God's saving act into the invisible world of the mind, and away from the material world, is an inherently unstable and illusory way of seeking to safeguard the spiritual (see p. 39). It is likewise a move whereby the Christian message ceases to be a gospel of divine grace, for there is now no longer reliance upon an objective divine saving work, but only an invitation to spiritual autosuggestion (see p. 39). Yet the true gravamen of all these objections is that the underlying demand for a Christian preaching free from the offensive "physical miracle" of the empty tomb in fact answers to a God-denying mechanistic view of the universe. We are back in the sphere of basic assumptions about life and thought (see pp. 14–15). The upholder of Christian tradition affirms that the radical critic's extreme reconstruction does not in fact spring out of the relevant evidence. It arises from the mind which he brings to the evidence. The tacit assumption throughout is that although there may be a God who gives existence to the world, there is no Living God who can perform a miracle of grace for the salvation of man.

The exponent of historic Christianity is well content that with the miracle of the empty tomb the Christian Faith should come into open and irreconcilable conflict with materialist and mechanistic views of the universe. Here in fact is a basic choice between faith or unbelief, which has to be made one way or the other. Practical experience of Christian advocacy shows that the obscuration of this issue by the construction of a "nonmiraculous" view of Christianity does not increase one's chance of winning to Christian faith men of a scientific background. If there is a sovereign personal God in control of the world, then He could have raised Christ from the dead, even though we cannot understand the manner. In this case, the plain Gospel evidence is at least credible, even though it is not to be read uncritically. And if we live in a world in which it is possible for God to become incarnate, and within this world perform His mighty act, then clearly He can perform other providential and saving acts. The doctrine of the empty tomb stands as the uncompromising rebuke to mechanistic philosophies. The whole spiritual attitude to life is in a sense pledged for the Christian by the gospel of Christ's miraculous resurrection.

In the first days of the Church the Christian Faith was distinguished from competing pagan Mysteries and Gnostic systems by its historical character. This principle has continued to work out in the long experience of the Church, and still continues in present developments. It has often happened that Christian teachers, moved by a perfectly sincere desire to make the Christian Faith more acceptable to the general body of reasonable men, have attempted to accommodate it to some extent to secular intellectual presuppositions. The effect has always been to tone down the rugged and challenging "supernatural" element. The Christian preaching has then inevitably, though perhaps insensibly and over a long period of time, drifted into a high-minded and idealistic call to men that they revere the spirit of Christ, seek to follow His example, and attempt to live by obeying His commandments. Thus the Christianity which slips away from the miracle of the Incarnation, which regards Christ as the supremely God-inspired man, and which to match this is content to say that the resurrection is true only symbolically, ceases to be a religion of grace. High-minded idealism then gradually ebbs out into discouragement, and thence to spiritual impotence. It is not possible permanently and convincingly to preserve the resurrection faith apart from acceptance of the actual and physical symbolic resurrection fact. Revivals of vital Christianity, on the other hand, of whatever brand of churchmanship, return to the challenging religion of the "supernatural" divine act in Christ, for this alone is the religion of grace.

IV. The Evidence for the Resurrection

A. Both those who uphold the long-established Christian Faith and the advocates of modern critical theories often find it hard to approach this subject dispassionately. After all, fundamental attitudes to life and to religious faith are laid bare here. Just as the critic tends to struggle against the evidence because he is aware that to accept Christ's miraculous physical resurrection would be a painful invasion of his intellectual pride, so the orthodox believer instinctively and passionately clings to every bit of evidence because he feels that the overthrow of this belief would be to him a crushing spiritual blow. Nevertheless, the effort to be candid must be made. Christianity is an historical religion, and therefore the theologian is committed at the very center of his faith to an honest evaluation of historical evidence. The truth must be told, even if it prove painful to conventional piety.

B. The charge often made against the historical narrative of the resurrection is that it was a gradually accumulating wonder-legend, born out of the attempt of unsophisticated minds to express their unbounded reverence for their Lord. A common form of argument is that the disciples could not bring themselves to believe that one so noble could be humbled in death. When they fled back to Galilee warm sentiment and nostalgia overwhelmed them, and they became hysterical. Thus they saw visions of Christ (as so many have seen all down the centuries), which convinced them that He was victorious over death. Their courage and faith consequently revived, and in the passionate strength of sincere and high-minded delusion they went out to conquer the world. This is the general line of argument for an "explanation" of the rise of Christianity in terms of "natural causes," and some such notion commonly lies hidden under the surface in "nonmiraculous" accounts of Christian faith.

The force of this attack lies in a number of facts which have to be admitted. The mentality of the time did welcome "wonder-stories" and did construct myths and legends. People have at times seen visions, and fanatical enthusiasm, high-minded or otherwise, can unite men into a close brotherhood and inspire them to heroic morale. Religious devotion has crystallized around many figures besides Christ, and legendary accretions do gather around the great figures of history. On the other side is the circumstance that the story of the resurrection was not a gradually accumulating legend. In the narratives of the lives of such prophetic figures as the Buddha and Francis of Assisi, there is usually first the original stratum giving an account of a man very striking indeed in personality but relatively nonmiraculous. In later strata of the traditional narrative, pious imagination has been active to increase the element of wonder-legend. Christian literature, from the so-called "apocryphal Gospels" onward, bears witness to the fact that ever-elaborating legends did grow up around the figure of Christ, just as one could have expected.[9] However, there is no evidence in the New Testament literature of an earlier nonmiraculous stratum lying hidden beneath the present narrative and bearing witness to an original Christian preaching of a "simple human Jesus."

From the very beginning the Christian gospel centered around the proclamation of the resurrection. The fact of the resurrection itself was not a gradually accumulating legend, though legends accumulated around it later. The resurrection, furthermore, was preached not first in another city some miles away, or some few years later, by which time the factual evidence might have become a little obscured. It was preached in Jerusalem within a very short time of the crucifixion, in the presence of many who had seen Jesus on the Cross, and with Joseph's tomb around the corner. If the bitter and resourceful enemies of Christianity had at that juncture produced the corpse, the high-minded delusion would have been dispelled, the mass hysteria would have been chilled, the fanatical morale of the Christians would have been shattered, and the infant "faith" would have been stillborn. That the first Christian preaching was of this character and survived this searching ordeal indicates to many candid minds that the Easter sepulchre was in fact empty. If this argument is allowed, the narrative is to be trusted as a sufficient historical testimony to the fact of the resurrection, even though a critical scholar would not take every accompanying detail literally.

The vulgar notion that the Christians first launched their faith in sincere

---

[9] Thus many cautious and relatively conservative critics would be prepared to view a narrative such as Matthew 27:51–53, or possibly John 19:34, as a beginning to this process.

delusion, and later contrived to hide the body of Jesus so as to preserve the credit of their movement and the morale of their admiring followers, is one of the miracles of unbelief. Scheming miracle-mongers have been known in the long and mixed history of the Church. There have also been well-intentioned and pious men of confused counsels, who have considered that a modicum of deception might be justified as good for the Christian cause. But men do not emerge from this shady background to become conquering heroes for Christ. It is psychologically impossible to suppose that the apostles, harboring the grisly secret of a concealed corpse, received strength to live lives of heroic devotion and to die the deaths of martyrs for a Christ whom they knew had not risen from the dead, and that no one ever betrayed the deception.

There is also the confirming argument of the Church's long experience of the new life in Christ. That the historic Church has adapted herself to ever-new environments, and has renewed herself from time to time, rising to new spiritual life from out of institutional corruption, and so has endured to the present day, is a remarkable phenomenon. This is no sufficient proof of the truth of the Christian religion. In a perverse world many errors have shown something of this strange power of self-renewal. Furthermore, the hostile critic would claim that ineluctable fate has in these better-educated days at length apparently caught up with the Church, and that it is dying out. He may be wrong, but he has sufficient superficial appearance of truth in his boast to deter the Christian from too lightly claiming that Christianity must be true because it works. Nevertheless, the Church is much more than an institution which has shown great power of self-perpetuation. Christian faith has shown itself to be the world's longest-sustained, and most wide-spread and various, spring of new life for the race. Despite the manifest sins of those who have called themselves Christians it has been history's major influence to bring spiritual renewal, intellectual emancipation, and moral and human advance.

One is aware that there are some materialists and secular humanists who will passionately deny this, and who will cite evidence to show that historic Christianity has been a source of superstition, repression, and cruelty. The failings and sins of some who have called themselves Christians are such that this case cannot lightly be dismissed. The Christian answer is that these are the failings of social groups of Christians, behaving in the manner common to social groups, but not of the faith and spirit of Christianity itself. Essential Christianity has shown itself, and does still show itself, to be this life-giving power, but the claim can be tested only by experience. To the Christian it is impossible to imagine that this beneficent wave of new life in Christ can spring from a radical and rather pathetic illusion. In a rational world an effect requires a sufficient cause, and the cause of mankind's oft-tested hope of renewal is God's victorious act. The individual believer who experiences the power of the resurrection in his own life can assure himself that he is not the victim of a beautiful but unsubstantial illusion, because he does not stand alone. His private devotional experience is declared to be valid because it echoes the experience of the great body of believers. That great historic Church Universal has been tested not by pious sentiment, but by the most searching ordeals of history.

V. He Ascended Into Heaven

A. A Symbolic Act

We read that for a period of forty days, which in the language of Scripture stands for a substantial and significant period of time, the risen Christ from time to time appeared to His disciples in the glory of His resurrection body. At the end of this period He disappeared for the last time in a special manner. He did not just vanish as before, but disappeared into the clouds of heaven (Acts 1:1–11; compare Luke 24:50–52). This was a symbolic action, and is not to be taken so literally as to involve the idea that heaven is a place above the blue sky.

The essential factor surely is that the mind of that time thought of heaven, the seat of God's majesty, as "up," though it was also taught that God did not have a body, and therefore discriminating minds even in those days would not think of God as existing in a *material* place. Indeed, we still instinctively symbolize spiritual *exaltation* as "up," saying "Lift *up* your hearts!" and the mind of that time did so even more vividly. God, as always, spoke to men as they were able to understand. Our Lord's glorious ascension was a parable acted in terms of this idea. He vanished in such a way as to impress upon the apostles that the reason they were to see Him no more on earth in His glorious resurrection body was that He had gone to be with the majesty on high, in glory. The historical redeeming act of God, which had to be performed once and for all within the limitations of time and place, was now triumphantly completed. All that remained for Christ was to reign in glory, and to distribute to His believers the fruits of His victory (1 Corinthians 15:25; Ephesians 1:20–22, 4:8–12; Philippians 2:9–11; Colossians 3:1; Revelation 5:1–10, 19:11–16).

B. "Sitteth on the Right Hand of the Father"

This phrase is symbolical and is certainly not to be taken literally, for God the Father, who does not exist in a "place," does not sit on a "throne," and has no "body" or "right hand." In an earthly court the place to the right hand of the monarch was the place of chief honor, where might sit the heir to the throne, the queen, or the chief minister. The right hand was likewise the strong hand, which held the sword. Thus "the right hand" is the due symbol of majesty, power, authority, and glory (Psalm 45:9, 98:1, 110:1). This clause of the Creed vividly expresses the universal sovereignty of Christ. By an inconceivable act of self-humiliation He made Himself man, that as man He might perform the saving act of God. Yet this historical act was temporary. We are not to think of our Lord now as humiliated, as suffering human limitation, as tempted, as the object of our compassion. He is the object of our reverence, for with the Father and the Holy Spirit He reigns over all things in eternal and coequal glory.

C. The Heavenly High-Priesthood of Christ

This doctrine has already been introduced in exposition of the Epistle to the Hebrews, regarding our Lord's death as a sacrifice (see pp. 88–89). Some implications should be noticed. It is the Christian faith that the Incarnation has not been brought to an end by Christ's ascension into glory. The union of humanity and divinity is permanent, for Christ reigns in glory in His glorified manhood (Hebrews 10:12–13). There are two points at which this doctrine needs to be guarded against misunderstanding. To say that Christ's glorified humanity is "in heaven" does not involve that heaven is a place, or that Christ's glorious body occupies space. Furthermore, the permanence of this union of human and divine does not involve any kind of change in the nature of the Godhead, for God is by definition perfect, and therefore eternally the same. The divine Son, the second person of the Trinity, who continued to be equally "in heaven" during the time of the Incarnation on earth, has united humanity to Himself, but this change does not affect His divine nature considered in its own right. Rather it is a change of the humanity. Christ's human nature is unchanged after the Incarnation. Considered in isolation it is still fully human. Nevertheless, in the Person of the incarnate Son, human nature is promoted in honor by being associated with the divine.

An important aspect of this doctrine is the doctrine of the heavenly high-priesthood of Christ. By the Incarnation, God by His infinite condescension came near to mankind in sympathy. The ascension of Christ to glory, and consequent withdrawal from the Church of the presence of Christ in His resurrection body, does not mean that this sympathy is likewise withdrawn and that God has again become distant in majesty. Rather does it mean that united to the nature of the God who reigns in glory, there is that to which frail man can with confidence make the appeal of sympathy. The humanity, which in the days of Christ's flesh was so sympathetic that social outcasts dared ask Him to be one of their company, is there still enshrined in the holy place, though now glorified. Thus the ascension has not made God distant, but has made Him for all time approachable. The high priest is there, a genuine representative of the human race, opening the door for man in Him to come to God (Hebrews 2:18; 4:14–16; 7:24–26; 8:1–2; 9:11–14, 24; 10:19–22). The ascension consequently speaks both of Christ's majesty and conquering power and of His tender and understanding sympathy, and in Christian thought unites these two qualities (Revelation 5:5–6).

Readings

Baillie, J., *And the Life Everlasting*. New York: Charles Scribner's Sons, 1933.
Filson, F. V., *Jesus Christ the Risen Lord*. New York: Abingdon Press, 1956.
Ramsey, M., *The Resurrection of Christ*. Philadelphia: The Westminster Press, 1946.

Chapter Five

The Spirit of the Lord

And I believe in the Holy Ghost

I. The Holy Ghost

A. The Name

In Tudor English the word "ghost" simply meant "spirit." Thus in the Communion exhortation of the Book of Common Prayer we have the phrase "He may receive the benefit of absolution, together with ghostly counsel and advice, to the quieting of his conscience." When the Bible and the liturgy were translated into English, the title "Holy Ghost" was naturally and freely employed, and has molded the customary language of worship ever since.

B. Definition

The Holy Spirit, the third person of the Trinity, is the personal Agent by whom God the Father and God the Son more expressly and effectually operate in the world, and in the world of men. The divine work most particularly in mind is that of man's Christian salvation, though it is not confined to this. The distinctive work of the Holy Spirit operates in the Church of every time and place, and in the personal religious experience of every believer in the Church. He mediates the sense of Christ risen and glorified, and continues in present experience the effect of the saving work accomplished once and for all in the incarnation, atonement, resurrection, and ascension of our Lord. Thus the Christian doctrine of the Holy Spirit sets forth the connection

111

between the historic work of God performed in Palestine in the first century and His practical saving operation in the world of men today. A clear doctrine of the Holy Spirit preserves the believer from confusing Christian faith with dogmatic orthodoxy or pious Christian antiquarianism, and safeguards Christian worship from degenerating into formal ceremonialism or even into magic. This doctrine is essential to vital, personal, converting, and morally active Christianity.

II. The Holy Spirit in the Old Testament

A. The phrase "the Holy Spirit" is by origin a striking Old Testament metaphor to convey the idea of "God in action in the world." Thus there is a clear and important doctrine of the Holy Spirit in the Old Testament, though distinctively Christian elements are added to it in the New. This symbolical language is a comparison from human experience. To the biblical writers "the breath" was "the life" of man. While a man breathes, he lives. When he exerts himself, his breathing is strengthened. When he breathes out for the last time, he dies. "The breath" makes the mysterious difference between a man and a corpse. This thought form is applied in the Old Testament to God. He is the Living God, and so He has "breath." When God specially exerts Himself to perform some wonder, this is "the strong breath of God," that is, "the Spirit of the Lord." It will be appreciated that "breath" and "spirit" are alternative renderings of the same word in the Hebrew Old Testament and in the Greek New Testament. We have the same usage in English, where "to inspire" medically means "to breathe in" but can also be used in a spiritual sense. "To expire" means both medically "to breathe out" and also generally "to die."

B. The act of divine creation was the work of the Spirit (Genesis 1:2; Psalm 33:6; Isaiah 40:13).

C. The Spirit called, inspired, and equipped the prophets and heroes of Israel (for example, Judges 6:34, 14:6; Isaiah 61:1; Ezekiel 11:5, among many passages).

D. It was expected that a special outpouring of the Spirit would be the equipment of the Messiah when He came (Isaiah 11:2).

E. It was expected that the day of the messianic kingdom would be accompanied by a great outpouring of the prophetic Spirit, not only upon the few, as in the past, but upon all the redeemed people of Israel (Joel 2:28–29).

F. Considered as a man, an Israelite among Israelites, our Lord Himself was the climax of the prophets. Therefore the Holy Spirit came upon Him at the opening of His public ministry to equip Him for this prophetic and teaching office (Mark 1:9–12; compare Hebrews 1:8–9).

III. The Pentecost Experience

A. The Pentecost experience (Acts 2:1–21) has often been spoken of as the birthday of the Christian Church. However, it is not to be looked upon as an isolated event. Indeed, some would argue that what we have in Acts 2 is a symbolic representation of the general state of spiritual experience and preaching activity of the Church in her very first days, in a scene which is largely constructed by St. Luke. Nevertheless, it is reasonable to suppose that the first emergence of the Church, in her triumphant experience of the risen Christ, from dubious and timid hiding to confident and courageous public witness, would be the occasion of special divine equipment. We may continue to speak of a "day of Pentecost," even though many other days witnessed a substantially similar experience, as is shown in the New Testament itself (for example, Acts 4:31). In the same way, St. Peter's famous sermon (Acts 2:14–36) is by some scholars understood, not so much as a verbatim report of what he said on this actual occasion, but as a construction to represent the mode of Christian preaching in those first decisive days. Theologically speaking this is even more valuable, for this and other early sermons in Acts do, we believe, correctly represent the experience and belief of the first Church.

It is open to discussion how far the "rushing mighty wind" and the "cloven tongues" are to be understood as phenomena which could be heard and seen physically (see pp. 29, 31). Visions undoubtedly do occur, but how they occur is a mysterious subject, and the way in which they are described depends to an unusual degree upon the customary thought forms of the beholders. Nor need the reader be unduly puzzled by the circumstance that St. Luke's account appears to read as though "the gift of tongues" consisted in utterance in a variety of foreign languages (vv. 6–8), whereas the actual description we have of this "gift" indicates quite plainly that it was ecstatic and unintelligible speech (1 Corinthians 14:1–23). Perhaps both propositions are true, the latter historically, the former symbolically. The "speaking in an unknown tongue" was perhaps not the gift of speech in a foreign language, yet the Church did speak to men of many lands, races, and languages. St. Luke sees this symbolized in the first and normative preaching of the gospel. The pilgrims of Israel from many lands, including many who were not of Jewish faith (Acts 2:10), were at the first preaching joined to the Church, which is the true Israel. This is an expressive picture of what had actually happened in the evangelistic experience of the Church.

B. We may see from the Pentecost sermon that the essential faith of the apostles was that their Lord Jesus, though crucified, was nevertheless the Messiah, the bringer of the promised kingdom. They were assured of the inconceivable paradox in the first place by the experience of the resurrection (vv. 22–24, 32–33, 36), with the compelling supporting evidence that this wonderful event could be found spoken of in sacred prophecy (vv. 25–31, 34–35). In this conviction the apostles found themselves with a certainty of the presence, the favor, and the redeeming power of God, which nothing could destroy. Men brought up upon the Old Testament recognized this experience. It was "like the old prophets again." This was a manifest out-pouring of "the Spirit of the Lord." The messianic promise in Joel was fulfilled, because the prophetic Spirit rested upon every member of the new Israel of God (vv. 16–21).

C. Those who had known so well what it was to have Jesus in the company recognized the Pentecost experience in another way, which was new and even more full of meaning to them. It was "like Jesus with them again," though there was no one to see. When Jesus was at their head they felt strong for anything (John 11:16). When He was taken from them, they were crushed and beaten men (Mark 14:50; John 20:19). When they knew He was with them again in resurrection victory, their faith and courage sprang to life again (John 20:26–28). The Pentecost experience was like this, only more so, even though there was now no visible presence of the risen Christ. Therefore they naturally spoke of the Spirit of Pentecost, not only in Old Testament terms as "the Spirit of the Lord," but also in New Testament terms as "the Spirit of Jesus" or "the Spirit of Christ" (Philippians 1:19; Galatians 4:6). Indeed, "the Spirit of God" and "the Spirit of Christ" are virtually indistinguishable in usage (Acts 16:6–7; Romans 8:9).

D. Thus in Christian thought the Old Testament phrase, "the Spirit of the Lord," conveying the idea of "the manifested presence and power of God," is extended. The Holy Spirit is the agent who mediates to the Church in present experience the sense of the presence and power of God *as He is known in Jesus Christ,* and as He comes to man and performs His saving act in His incarnate Son.

IV. Aspects of the Doctrine of the Holy Spirit

A. His Person

It is Christian teaching that the Holy Spirit is a divine person, together with the Father and the Son. It is for this reason that the divine Agent is always spoken of as "He" and not as "It." This again is symbolic language, being a comparison drawn from human experience and applied to God. It is not intended to say that the Holy Spirit is masculine, but that He is a divine person, not merely an impersonal divine influence. Thus the God of creation is not the bare "creative principle" necessary to explain the existence and order of the universe. In Christian and biblical thought He is "the Living God," a personal God who has created the universe by an act of knowledge and will. When the Spirit, who is the creative "hand" or "arm" of the Lord, acts (Isaiah 48:13), there is always a sovereign person acting. It is often loosely said that there is a divine spirit in all men, and in particular in all good men. The impression may be created thereby that the Holy Spirit is simply a name for the higher faculties of the human personality. This is a confusion which is condemned by Christian theology. There are indeed these nobler faculties of human nature, which are part of man's natural existence and which are bestowed by God. Yet when the Holy

Spirit inspires prophets, saints, philosophers, and artists, there is present a divine person, quite distinct from the human personality, yet holding communion with it, who by His "personal influence" quickens the natural human faculties to their endeavors.

In particular, when the Holy Spirit mediates Christian salvation to man through the preaching of the word, and the sacraments and worship of the Church, it is not to be supposed that there is a kind of "spiritual electricity" flowing down an ecclesiastical wire. This is an example of the impoverished thought which may allow Christian rites to degenerate into formality or even into magic. God does not save man by infusing into his personality a mysterious heavenly substance which acts as a sort of spiritual preservative. It is by a powerful and transforming process of "personal influence" that He changes man in personal character, moral will, and responsible ethical action. We may conceive of this as analogous to the way in which a man of noble character may assist his friend by being constantly near to him in personal presence and personal sympathy. Thus when God in Christ visits the company of His people in the Church's ministry of word and sacraments, and brings to them their share of Christian salvation, there is always an invisible *person* there, never a mere invisible "thing." The divine agent is a person. All these important ideas are summed up in the doctrine of the personal existence of the Holy Spirit.

B. The *Filioque Clause*

The original form of the Nicene Creed declares of the Holy Spirit that He "proceedeth from the Father." This is what is still said by the Eastern, or Orthodox, Church. Following St. Augustine's teaching the Western and Latin-speaking Church sought to emphasize the strict equality of the Father and the Son by teaching that the Spirit proceeds also from the Son. This doctrine eventually crept into the Nicene Creed as it is said in the Western Church, with the result that our Creed runs: "who proceedeth from the Father and the Son," the added words being a translation of the Latin word *filioque*. It may be claimed that the doctrine represented by this addition is sound and scriptural. It helps to emphasize that it is God *in Christ* who acts for man's salvation, and that God the Son is divine in the same full sense as is God the Father. The Orthodox Church of course fully accepts both these positions. However, it is a great pity that this divergence should have appeared in the Creed, which otherwise is one of the most significant marks of the unity of the Catholic Church. The Eastern Church has much justice in her objection that this addition, though not false, is unauthorized.

C. The *Paraclete*

This Greek word is more commonly applied to the Holy Spirit, though it can also be used of the divine Son (1 John 2:1). It means, by derivation, "a person called to one's aid." Thus it can commonly carry the legal meaning of "the knowledgeable and influential friend one takes to court," that is, an *advocate*. This is the traditional translation used when the word is applied to Christ, as in 1 John. When applied to the Holy Spirit (John 14:16, 26; 15:26; 16:7) the traditional translation has been "Comforter." This beautiful word is, however, somewhat misleading in modern ears. In Tudor English the verb "to comfort" (from the Latin *fortis*, "strong") retained much of its original meaning of "to strengthen." Thus for a disloyal person "to comfort the king's enemies" meant "to aid and abet" them. If this sense be taken, there is not so much difference between "Comforter" and "Advocate." Thus they can be alternative translations for the same Greek word.

In light of this we see that the operative word in John 14:16, "And I will pray the Father, and He shall give you another Comforter, that He may abide with you for ever," is *another*. In the days of His flesh our Lord was the one who by His presence with His disciples, and by His personal influence, made them strong for the battle of life with a moral power which was not their own. He was the Paraclete, the Strengthener, the Comforter. However, by the nature of things, this saving activity had to come to an end. God's saving act in His incarnate Son, performed once for all as man and for men, had to take place upon the plane of history. It was done at one certain time and place, and therefore at no other. Nevertheless, God's saving activity in Christ is to be available to all men who will accept it, equally and without distinction in every time and place and circumstance. Therefore the once-for-all decisive historic act of God had to come to its due end, and its place be taken by the continuing and universal act of God in Christ. The Paraclete, who is the incarnate Son, ascended to glory. And another gracious divine presence like His, that is to say, another *Paraclete,* was given "that He may abide with you for ever." Thus the Holy Spirit is the one who carries on universally and to the end of time the work of Christ in the heart.

D. *The Holy Spirit and the Risen Christ*

It is hardly surprising that people untutored in theology often find their minds in confusion as to the distinction between the Holy Spirit and the presence of the risen Christ invisibly with His Church. When the Church prays to her Lord:

> Present we know Thou art,
> But O Thyself reveal!

the Holy Spirit is the Agent who answers the prayer, and who works in the heart the conscious sense of communion with the Christ who is always present, whether or not man is conscious of Him. Thus devotionally speaking, there is no distinction which we can experience between the Holy Spirit and the risen Christ. Yet theologically speaking, there is a distinction *in thought*. The Son represents the saving presence of the Supreme God in the world of men, but as incarnate, and as performing the saving work once for all. The Spirit represents the same saving presence in the world, but as performing the saving work in the heart, and in the Church, invisibly, and in every time and place, on account of what was performed once for all by the incarnate Son.

V. The Work of the Holy Spirit

A. The work of the Holy Spirit is in no sense limited to the Christian salvation of men, or to the Church. Whenever and wherever the one triune God acts He acts wholly, and not in part. In a true sense the whole creation and providential government of the world is an act of God through the Spirit. So is the spiritual guidance of the hearts and minds of all men, and particularly of the spiritual leaders of mankind, whether or not they name the name of Christ. However, to the Christian the supreme example of "God in action in the world" is the work of salvation and the mediation of that salvation to men. Therefore Christian theology sees the operation of the Spirit most particularly in all the high points of the life of the Church, and at all the decisive moments in the spiritual experience of the believer.

B. The Holy Spirit, who rested upon the first apostles, called and equipped those who were later joined to the apostolic office (Acts 13:2), as well as other ministers in the Church (Acts 6:3; compare 1 Timothy 4:14). The whole New Testament Church was possessed of a vivid sense of being indwelt and guided by the Holy Spirit. He was, as it were, the atmosphere of the Church's life, so that the company of believers were "in the Spirit" (Romans 8:9-13). He bestowed upon the Church the fullness of spiritual "gifts," devotional, moral, and intellectual (1 Corinthians 12:4-14).

C. The Holy Spirit, who is the Spirit of prophecy which inspired the Old Testament (2 Peter 1:21), likewise inspired the authors of the apostolic writings and guided the Church in the selection of them to form the canon of New Testament Scripture (John 14:26). Thus the whole Bible is the gift of the Holy Spirit to the Church.

D. The Holy Spirit guides the Church, and in particular the fellowship of reverent and learned teachers within the Church, to fuller understanding of God's revelation declared in Christ and preserved in Holy Scripture (John 16:13-15). Thus as the truth of Christ is applied to the ever-changing issues of life there is accumulating in the experience of the Church through the centuries an ever-enriched body of Christian teaching. This is, however, always to be securely attached to the original historic revelation, and the tradition of the Church is therefore to be a continuous and consistent scriptural tradition. The leading points of focus of this process of the formulation of Christian doctrine are the General Councils of the ancient and undivided Church. In these councils the teaching voice of the whole Church is more expressly heard, exposing and rebutting error, and clarifying the intention of Scripture and of the existing tradition of doctrine, by the authoritative formulation of a new doctrinal statement, which is henceforth a part of the faith of the Church. It is the traditional faith of the Church that these General Councils were effectually guided by the Holy Spirit, so that their doctrinal formulations are to be accepted as fully authoritative for the Church. For a further summary of divergent views of ecclesiastical authority see pages 2–8.

E. The Holy Spirit works in the believer a renewed and righteous character of love, purity, and unselfishness (Galatians 5:16–17, 22–25). He is the guiding principle of all Christian conduct, teaching man what is right, and giving him power to do it. Thus all true Christian morality is a "work of the Spirit," and this it is which makes the Christian obligation of obedience to the divine moral law a nobler and more spiritual thing than mere legal obedience for the sake of duty, in hope of reward or fear of punishment. The Spirit enables man to obey for the sake of love.

F. The Holy Spirit guides the Church, and in particular the fellowship of authorized and responsible pastors in the Church, to an understanding of how this "spiritual law" is to be applied to the ever-changing issues of life. The moral and disciplinary standard declared by the Church is the effective standard which the conscientious man may be expected to understand and accept. Thus it is the moral standard by which God judges his actions (John 20:21–23).

G. The Holy Spirit calls men to the sacred ministry, and to other branches of Christian service. He also guides the Church in her responsible task of deciding whether those who profess this call, and who offer themselves to the Church, are indeed so qualified by divine call and by gifts and graces of character as to make it right to admit them and authorize them for their office. In principle it is essential to the rightful making of a Christian minister that he be first called by God (Hebrews 5:4), for no man is good or wise enough to be qualified as a volunteer, by his own wisdom or goodness. He can only act or speak for God if he goes as one sent by God.

H. In the consecration of bishops and the ordination of presbyters and deacons, the Holy Spirit, working through the due laying on of hands, inwardly stamps or seals the ministers of Christ to the end that their ministerial actions may be in due ecclesiastical order in the Church, and as such the objects of God's promise to give grace to believing men through the ministrations of the Church (1 Timothy 4:14).

I. The Holy Spirit gives grace to all Christ's servants, and in particular to those ordained to the sacred ministry, to enable them effectually to preach the gospel, and to give pastoral counsel in faith and morals, to the people for whom they bear responsibility. It is, we believe, a fact of experience that if Christ's servants fully open their hearts to Him in consecration the Holy Spirit can actually quicken their powers of understanding and utterance, and enable them on occasion to speak words of persuasion with a power not their own. There is, however, a deeper and more general principle expressed in the proposition that the Holy Spirit grants special grace to those ordained to the Christian ministry. The minister is deeply aware that he himself is a sinful man, in desperate need of that which he offers to others. So far as his own attainments in the Christian life are concerned he has no right to offer good advice to others, and the preacher's own words convict him of hypocrisy. Nevertheless, it is his duty to speak because God has sent him, and the Church has commissioned him with responsibility for those to whom he speaks. Thus the divine equipment alone qualifies him to say, fittingly, that which no man is fit to say. That he can exercise a useful ministry is an act of divine grace, through the operation of the Holy Spirit.

J. The Holy Spirit operates through the sacraments to make of them effectual and operative means of grace to the believing Church, and to every faithful soul (Acts 2:38, 19:5–6). (See also pp. 165, 169.)

K. The Holy Spirit prompts men to accept the gospel when it is preached to them, and moves them to faith in Christ (1 Corinthians 12:3). It is a fact of familiar experience that not all who hear of Christ believe, and that some who wish they could open their hearts to Christ in loving trust find they cannot do so, at least at that moment (see pp. 222–23). Man's will for good is in bondage, and his spiritual faculties weak, so it is idle for him to delude himself that he can turn to Christ in penitent faith as and when he will. He can only do so when God effectually calls, by the agency of the Spirit.

L. The Holy Spirit stimulates and guides man's power of prayer (Romans 8:26).

M. It is a truth particularly emphasized by some branches of evangelical Christianity that it is a work of the Holy Spirit in the heart of the believer to give to him a witness of his adoption, and of assurance of his salvation (Romans 8:14–17). (See also p. 228.)

N. The Holy Spirit operates in Confirmation, and in other rites of dedication leading to the status of communicant Church membership, to seal these vows and to enable those who have pledged their allegiance to Christ and His Church to do what they have promised (Acts 8:14–17, 19:6).

VI. Summary: The Christian Doctrine of God, the Holy Trinity

A. Now that the doctrine of the person and work of God the Father, God the Son, and God the Holy Spirit has been defined, the Christian

doctrine of God may be summarized by a treatment of the doctrine of
the Holy Trinity. The newcomer to theology often makes the objection
that this part of Christian teaching is abstract, speculative, and needlessly
hard to understand. It is first to be remembered that it is idle to expect
a *simple* doctrine of God. The world in which we live is a very wonderful
and intricate thing, and the mind of man is of limited capacity to understand
it. Therefore every branch of human study runs off into mystery at some
point. For example, only a select few have intellect sufficient to master
the most advanced branches of higher mathematics, and they only after
long and careful training. If it once be allowed that the mind of God is
the law which lies behind all the laws of nature, then the residual mystery
of mathematical law is only one single small part of the mystery of the
mind of God. God cannot be fully grasped by the human mind, and any
language framed to symbolize His nature must be such as to remind man
of this fact. That is to say, the symbol is "difficult."

Through the centuries, and today, many schools of thought have sought
to frame a "simple" doctrine of God, the general line of approach being
that He is the solitary and remote Sovereign Potentate, or perhaps even
only an impersonal first principle, who has partially revealed Himself from
time to time in the leading teachers of mankind. This is a conception of
God which makes an incarnation and a divine act of redemption inconceivable. In fact, the mystery of God has been "simplified," and the doctrine
of God made more easy to expound, by the expedient of ignoring some
of the facts about Him which the Christian is particularly anxious to affirm.
The attraction of such a "simple" doctrine of God will, we believe, be
found superficial. Many of the heresies which troubled the ancient Church
arose as the result of perfectly sincere efforts to frame Christian doctrine
in terms of a "reasonable" and "scientific" conception of God, such as
would be easy to expound as a basis for a doctrine of God and the world.
These systems of theology were found unsatisfactory because in the attempt
to make clear and simple the doctrine of God as the creator and governor
of the world they denatured the doctrine of salvation by a divine act in
Jesus Christ, God's incarnate Son. It was to safeguard the truths of salvation
that the Church, as it were, in part turned her back upon a "simple"
and "scientific" doctrine of God, and went to the world with the admittedly
mysterious doctrine of the Holy Trinity. Thus the wise student of theology
should be prepared to come to this doctrine with an open and sympathetic
mind. Its presence in the Christian system is not an intellectualist perversity,
but an attempt to safeguard the interests of the gospel.

B. The converse may be seen if the doctrine of the Trinity is approached
from the historical point of view, and the question raised concerning by
what process it came to be framed. The Church certainly did not start
with a speculative theory of the nature of God, framed for speculative
reasons. She started with the direct experience that in Christ God had

visited man and done for him what only God can do (see pp. 47–48). Thus from experience was framed the doctrine that Christ is the divine Son. The primitive Church went before the world preaching two imperative religious interests—from its Jewish background in the Scriptures, that there is but one sovereign God; and from its experience of salvation, that Jesus Christ is divine. As and when the Church developed the talent and leisure for intellectual speculation it was realized that there is a tension between these two interests. How could they both be fully safeguarded? Thus the fathers of the Church had to construct a doctrine of God which would enable them to say that their Lord was a divine Saviour, in the full and proper sense of the word, and at the same time make it plain that there is only one God. The fruit of this admittedly exacting intellectual quest is the doctrine of the Trinity.

C. The underlying issue may be stated in this way. It is the Christian conviction that God has made Himself known to man in a threefold way. There is God as He is seen in the creation and government of the universe. Our Lord taught us to call the Creator-God "our Father" (Matthew 6:9), so that the most distinctive Christian title for God is "the God and Father of our Lord Jesus Christ" (Romans 15:6; Ephesians 1:3). In the second place, there is God as He became incarnate, lived for a span of years in Galilee and Jerusalem, taught, died, and rose again. He is described as the divine Son (John 1:18; Hebrews 1:1–3). And in the third place, there is the Spirit of God, who is also the Spirit of Christ (Romans 8:9; Galatians 4:6; 1 Peter 1:11), who is the personal agent by whom the activity of the Father and the Son is applied to the lives of men and women.

The question which then faces the theologian is this: "Are we to believe that in this threefold experience the Supreme God has really visited man, and actually revealed His nature to him? Or is the threefold experience a mere concession to human ways of thought, and to human frailty; so that it is by way of an illusion, which leaves the Supreme God still out of touch with man, unknown and unknowable?" The doctrine of the Trinity is the Church's attempt to give a full and clear affirmative to the former proposition. It is a way of saying that God's showing of Himself to man as Father, Son, and Holy Spirit profoundly corresponds to the inmost nature of the Supreme God as He really exists "in Himself," from eternity to eternity. The alternative is clear, and is destructive of the whole Christian position that the Gospel is the message of a divine visit to this world, and of a divine act in this world. To deny the doctrine of the Trinity logically involves that the Supreme God is a remote God who has not come to encounter man and show Himself to man in a personal incarnation. All He has done is to give passing and partial glimpses of Himself.

It must be made plain that Christian theology does not claim that the Supreme God has made Himself *fully* known in the experience of God as the Father, the Son, and the Holy Ghost. This would not be possible, because God "as He is in Himself," being infinite, is not wholly within the grasp of limited human knowledge. There is no claim to know all there is to know about God, but only that God has made Himself known as fully and adequately as is possible in human terms, and that this knowledge is real and secure knowledge, having in it no element of illusion. It is the conviction of the Church that when in heaven believers are able to see God as He really is, they will find God's revelation of Himself to man in terms of Father, Son, and Holy Spirit to be fully vindicated and confirmed, though it will doubtless be transcended by a fuller knowledge which is inherently impossible to man in this finite life. There will be much to learn, but nothing to unlearn.

D. There is also the converse to this. The Supreme God has made Himself known in this threefold way for a reason which is fundamental to the nature of existence. It is the faith of the Church that He has come to man in the experience of this world, as Father, Son, and Holy Spirit, because His heavenly and eternal nature "as it is in itself" is like this. Thus from one point of view the doctrine of the Trinity is the last point of Christian doctrine. It is the sublimest effort of the mind of man, under divine inspiration, to climb up from the facts of immediate religious experience to speculation about the nature of God. Yet as the complement to this manward aspect there is the Godward aspect. From this point of view the doctrine of the Trinity is the first and fundamental point of Christian doctrine. The revelation in history has taken place in the way it has because this most fully corresponds to the nature of God from eternity.

E. The formula adopted by the Church as authoritative for the doctrine of the Holy Trinity is "One divine *substance,* three divine *persons.*" The sense of both these symbolical terms needs to be defined if the formula is to be expressive. In each case the word is used in a special way, somewhat different from the ordinary sense.

Substance. The modern man instinctively thinks of a "substance" as a solid body, having size and weight. Clearly this sense cannot apply to the invisible and omnipresent God. The word "substance" as used here derives from the traditional philosophy of the Church, and indicates the essential nature of a thing, the possession of which constitutes what it is. It has no material connotation. The possession of the *spiritual* "substance" of divinity constitutes a being divine. To say that there is but one divine substance is a convenient and exact way of saying that there is but one God. To say that Father, Son, and Holy Ghost each possess the divine substance means that each is in the fullest and most proper sense divine.

Person. This is admittedly one of the more difficult of theological terms for the modern mind to grasp, because one who is not grounded in systematic theology almost instinctively makes of it the equivalent of the modern term "personality." To do this is to obscure the doctrine of the Trinity and to make the idea of the "Three-One" logically impossible. The modern psychological notion of "personality" includes the ideas of self-consciousness, exclusiveness, and autonomy. A personality knows himself to be himself, and as such, distinct from all other things. By consequence, he has the sensation of a kind of mental "wall" around himself, which shuts other things out. He also has the sensation of choice. He is aware that he is not wholly passive before the force of circumstance. He has within himself certain resources of will, which can at least attempt to give direction to his activity. It is clearly an error to apply all these notions unmodified to the three persons of the Godhead. To say that God is three "personalities" would be to imagine Him as a "committee" of three separate Gods, who are only "one" in the very reduced sense that they have the same policy and action in making and governing the world. This is not the Christian doctrine of the Trinity. The three divine persons are not as separate from one another as would be three personalities, in the modern sense. Yet this is not a sign that the word "person" is here being used in a reduced, denatured, and misleading sense.

When in the ancient Church the word "person" was first adopted to designate the Three it was a legal term. It denoted a legal "party," in the sense of an individual, or group of individuals, who could possess a piece of property or be a party in a legal action. In usage it has become enriched since then, and one might say that as used in the trinitarian formula it includes the conception of self-consciousness, but not that of exclusiveness. We may symbolize the Three as "knowing" one another, but not as "shutting one another out." The divine persons are not exclusive, like human personalities, but inclusive. They "take one another in," and presuppose one another's existence, so that by the nature of existence they have but one will and action.

Here is symbolic language constructed from a comparison with human experience. A human personality comes to the experience of self-consciousness by "hitting up against" other personalities, discovering them to be there, learning that they are different and also autonomous, and by making room for them. From this experience we instinctively associate the idea of exclusiveness with personality. Yet this is a mark of the limitation of human personality, and of the fact that it has to develop. The most developed and perfect human personalities we know are not the most exclusive, those who have the toughest spiritual "wall" around themselves. They are those who have most completely transcended this limitation of growth, and who have become the most inclusive. The most completely "personal" persons we know are not the most fiercely autonomous, but those who are most completely united in mutual accord and sympathy with other persons round about them. Developed personality starts with self-consciousness, but it moves from bare self-consciousness to personal communion.

This surely is a parable of the nature of God, whose infinite, eternal, and unchanging existence is altogether superior to the necessity of *developing* a self-consciousness by contact with existence outside Himself. The three divine persons are not at all exclusive. By the law of their existence they are eternally, completely, and unchangeably inclusive. Thus the Three are more closely identified with one another than any human personalities we can imagine. Yet this does not imply that the Three are less "personal" than would be three perfectly loving human personalities. They are more fully "personal" because they are less separate than humans. Such is the highest attempt of the human mind to symbolize the nature of God. Here we may imagine the possibility of the Supreme God being both Three and One.

F. In summary, the doctrine of the Holy Trinity is the logical background in speculative thought for the devotional doctrine that God is love. It has been said that the only difficult Christian dogma is "God is love." When we think of the infinite scale of the universe, and of the dark mystery of sin and suffering in this little world, it takes a great deal of vision and courage to acknowledge that the Sovereign Potentate of all has a warm heart of love. The perhaps difficult conception of the Holy Trinity is a conception of the Godhead which makes the proposition that "God is love" at least possible to thought. There is little merit in the notion of the love of a "god" who is not the Sovereign Potentate. Some have imagined a "god" who created the universe because it brought him satisfaction and self-fulfillment to do so. He created mankind as the objects of his love because he needed them as objects of his love, that he himself might be fully blessed. This "god" is not the God of the Bible, nor of Christian theology. He is an inferior being, who because he can be improved in his mode of existence is not unchangeable in perfection. His existence inevitably presupposes the existence of a higher Supreme Being, who is the ultimate ground of existence. The wonder of the love of God is that it is the love of a mighty and self-sufficient God, who does not require the existence of anything outside Himself in order that He may be fully blessed. This is the only perfectly unselfish love which we can imagine.

The classic human example of the love which seeks only to give and to sacrifice is the tender passion of mother love. Yet even the mother loves in part because she needs to love. She cherishes her infant in part because she knows that she will be filled with grief if he sickens or dies. We cannot imagine human love which is *perfectly* unselfish. The only perfectly unselfish love of which the heart of man can conceive is the love of the self-sufficient God of sovereign majesty. It is the love of the God who when He was alone existed from eternity in unchangeable bliss. He created the universe, and man in it, as the objects of His pure beneficence, even though this love could add nothing to Himself. He set His love upon man, and in perfect foreknowledge gave to man the power to grieve His love, even though there was no necessity laid upon Him to love. This possibility is enshrined in the holy mystery of the Blessed Trinity. That happiness and self-fulfillment which man can find only in common with others God could perfectly enjoy from within the resources of His own being, when from eternity He was the solitary existence. There was love between the three perfectly inclusive self-consciousnesses, who together are one God.

This picture of God, furthermore, is the doctrine which renders conceivable the infinite condescension of the Incarnation, which act is the supreme mark of that divine love. The doctrine of the Incarnation presupposes that God the Son could in some mysterious way suspend the exercise of His bright glories, and yet continue fully to be God. This in turn presupposes a certain view of the nature of the Deity. If the Sovereign Potentate is defined only in terms of infinite and unchangeable glory, wisdom, and power, then He is the utterly remote and essentially unknowable God. He cannot, without ceasing to be what He is, give up those bright glories upon which man cannot look. The Incarnation is thus inconceivable. The conception that in the person of His Son the Highest God united Himself with His defiled handiwork, and suffered with men and for men, requires that the Sovereign Potentate be defined also in terms of perfect, eternal, unchangeable, and self-giving love. When for a season He darkened the glory the love fully shone forth, and the humiliated Son incarnate was vindicated as fully divine. To the Christian theologian the doctrine of the Blessed Trinity is the guarantee and exposition of this view of God.

Readings

Barclay, W., *The Promise of the Spirit*. London: Epworth Press, 1960.

Hodgson, L., *The Doctrine of the Trinity*. New York: Charles Scribner's Sons, 1944.

Van Dusen, H. P., *Spirit, Son, and Father*. New York: Charles Scribner's Sons, 1958.

Chapter Six

The People of God

I believe in the Holy Catholic Church

I. The Church : A Divine Plan

A. Interdependence and Community

The principle of variety is written into the very order of creation. The universe conceivably might have been created with all the stars of the same kind and size, moving upon equivalent and simple courses. Instead, there is incalculable variety and complexity. So it is in the world of organic life. There are indeed cases where the life cycle is carried on according to a very simple pattern, as when the giant panda, which eats only bamboo shoots, lives in a jungle consisting only of bamboos. Conceivably, every environment could have been peopled in this manner, but in fact such a case is remarkable on account of its singularity. The normal pattern of life is that every habitat appears to have as large as possible a variety of plants and animals packed into it, which are dependent upon one another for the means of life through a remarkably subtle and complicated system of interlocking life cycles.

The same principle holds in human affairs. Some theorists have clung to the unrealistic notion that all men are "equal." In fact, the only equality they have is one of grace, in that God chooses to love them all and value them all. They are very much the reverse of equal by natural endowments, and in the place allotted to them by divine providence in the complicated pattern of human affairs. We can see a spiritual reason behind this plan.

Were all men substantially alike in natural characteristics and abilities their "equality" would allow them to live in substantial independence one of another. They might then naturally enough be inflated with that sense of self-sufficiency which is the fundamental sin of pride. The circumstance that the human race is composed of men and women, of young and old, of natural leaders and the naturally led, of the practical and the visionary, and so forth, and that in all these partnerships the one needs the other if the business of life is to be carried on, provides the providential principle by which self-sufficiency is destroyed and mankind educated in humility. By interdependence society is cemented together as a moral discipline.

To the Christian the chief of all human affairs is man's salvation in Christ. This is the activity which illuminates the meaning of all other activities, and in which the underlying principle of all rightly-ordered human affairs is most explicitly demonstrated. Man's salvation in Christ provides the great example of that interdependence which is the cement of community. It is an important principle of theology that the Christian community, the Church, reflects a principle written into the very character of God's government of the world, and draws its existence from the eternal will of God (Ephesians 3:1–12). The Church does not take its rise from the will or convenience of man, as an expression of the principle "birds of a feather flock together." Believers do not first become Christians, and then choose to join the Church. To be incorporated into the Church is an essential part of being a Christian, and the Christian community is theologically necessary to the Christian Faith. The law of the Christian life is love, or charity. Love opens men's eyes to the fact that there are others who have rightful claims upon them, and that they themselves need others. This humbles man's natural desire for self-sufficiency, and by knitting him into the Christian community brings home to his heart and mind the spiritual principle which unites him to God.

B. Personal and Communal Religion

To speak of personal and of churchly religion as though they were in some way opposites is to obscure the character of the Christian life. On the one hand, there is a sense in which all religion is personal religion. There is no such thing as a tradition of truth or a supply of grace existing "impersonally" in the Church as such. There is only the personal action of God upon His individual children. God's method of revealing His truth to the Church is that He quickens and inspires the natural faculties of individual men to discern this truth, through their response to the experience of life and the processes of thought and imagination. New and creative apprehensions of divine truth, and new waves of spiritual endeavor in the Church, have therefore normally been associated with the lives and activities of men and women of outstanding spiritual genius, whom we may call "the prophets" and "the saints." Their influence has been mediated to the wider circles of the Church by movements of disciples who have looked to them as heroes of The Faith.

However, it does not follow from this that Christianity is essentially individualistic. The overruling principle of interdependence, which is the discipline of humility and the bond of charity, is also to be seen at work. No one man, however talented, or however completely inspired by God, can grasp all God's truth by himself. The variety of human circumstance and experience is almost infinite, and every human condition has its own lesson. Some things of the Spirit are best appreciated by the intellectualist, some by the imaginative and aesthetic temperament, and others, no less important, by the capable and common-sense man of affairs. Some lessons come in joy or success, some in adversity, sadness, or calamity. Some parts of the Christian truth are particularly the heritage of the ancient Hebrews or of the Greeks, others of the martyr Church of the early centuries, others of the ruling Church of the Middle Ages, and yet others of the age of modernity and science. Part of the discipline has been wrought out in the cloister, part in the home, and part in the workshop and the market-place. And not one of these apprehensions of Christian truth—doctrinal, devotional, or moral—is sufficient unto itself. Every man, in every condition, is in need of the discipline and fellowship of the whole body. Therefore the healthy spiritual life is communal, and the knowledge of how to think rightly about God, how best to worship Him, and how effectually to obey Him is the slowly accumulating possession of the Church. God is observed to speak to mankind most plainly, not through isolated individuals, however great, but to great individuals incorporated into the Christian community.

C. Prophetic and Institutional Religion

An important example of this principle is the relation of the "prophet" and the "saint" to the general body of the Church. If it is true that the body of ordinary believers, with their limited talents, cannot do without the vitally important leadership of the few and outstanding, it is equally true that the outstanding will commonly go astray if they are not subject to the discipline of the general body of the Church. The need of the leaders and of the led is mutual. Thus new theological truth is commonly grasped by the man of adventurous intellect, and he is often an intellectual extremist, too much in love with some brilliant theory which expresses one part only of the "manifold wisdom of God" (Ephesians 3:10). If he heedlessly goes his own way, he may easily lapse into error. If he would know the truth the Christian thinker therefore must treat the established Creed of the Church with reverence as an authoritative guide to himself. And the Church must listen to him in turn.

Much the same holds in the spheres of Christian devotion and moral obedience. The rare and splendid individual to whom the sense of the presence of God is a constant and pressing reality, who apparently finds prayer an easy joy, and who is full of spontaneous zeal for his practical duties as a Christian is himself not the self-sufficient Christian. He needs to learn many things concerning God's dealings with the human race from the experience of the multitudes of more ordinary people who often find faith and prayer hard, to whom daily affairs are a constant pressure, and who need to fall back upon the props and crutches of discipline if they are to do their duty. The spiritually able are to humble themselves gladly to bear with the less able, and to make allowances for them, for this is the very spirit of Christ's humility.

Nothing is more common in the history of the Church than the collision between prophetic and institutional religion. The established religion of the community is normally cautious and conservative, concerned with prudential rules for the discipline of frail mortals, and all too often interested in the preservation of its status and property. The awakened zealot can therefore easily write it off as hopelessly compromised, and start his own little community of like-minded zealots. This counsel of separation to form "a pure Church" is superficially attractive to many minds, but history witnesses to its eventually delusive character. With the passage of time the tempo of the new community inevitably slackens, until it also becomes an institutional religion, though an institution with less resources than the old, and of a more constricted tradition. The tension between individualist prophetic religion and institutional religion is doubtless inevitable, and to a degree even salutary. Nevertheless, the welfare of the Church is to a large degree dependent upon the avoidance of an open breach at this point, so that the new life may flow through and revivify the body of the old institution. The separation of a new denomination normally impoverishes both the old institution which is left and the new which is gradually formed. As our Lord Himself taught, there are times when a new movement of the Spirit requires new Church forms to express it (Matthew 9:17). Yet rightly understood this is not a charter for the division of the Church. It is a reminder to the institutional Church that it has a duty to be understanding with the ardent prophet, even as he has a duty to be patient with the Church.

D. Grace and the Means of Grace

The relation of personal to communal religion, and the issue between prophetic and institutional religion, is illustrated by the use of the means of grace. The means of grace are those acts of worship, and that discipline of devotion and morality, which a man is to use if he would be visited by God with His saving grace (see p. 156). It will, we judge, be agreed that man is saved by the grace of God, and that his own diligence in the means of grace does not earn salvation apart from divine grace. At the same time, if he wishes to receive God's grace he must wait upon God for it in the way which God has prescribed, that is, by expectantly using the means of grace and by trusting God's promise to honor them. Clearly, there is a balance between the due place of divine grace and of the means, and it is not always easy for the Christian to determine what this is. Some of the means of grace, such as private prayer and Bible reading, are largely individual and personal, but by and large the means of grace are communal, and correspond to the institutional side of the Christian life. Such are public worship and meetings for fellowship, the exposition of the Bible and the preaching of the Gospel, and the sacraments ordained by our Lord. These all presuppose the disciplined and ordered life of the Church. Considered in isolation, the religion of grace is inward and personal, "the walk of the soul with God." To this extent it is individual. Yet the religion of grace cannot be considered in isolation, for there are the appointed means of grace, and these are in the Church.

The doctrine which has been outlined in the preceding chapters of this book is doctrine in which the different responsible denominations of Christendom are substantially agreed. The official formularies of the great branches of the Church are recognizably at one in the doctrines of the Trinity, the creation, the Incarnation, the person of Christ, the atonement and resurrection, and the Holy Spirit. This impressive area of agreement comprises by far the larger part of essential Christian doctrine. In this sense there is truly "one body, and one Spirit. . .one Lord, one faith" (Ephesians 4:4, 5). Insofar as the denominations of the Church are divided by recognizable spiritual and theological interests, and not merely by social and political tradition and by aesthetic considerations, the divergence appears chiefly to occur in this matter of the due place of the means of grace. The collision between institutional and prophetic religion is closely associated with a difference in judgment regarding the doctrine of grace. Christians are substantially at one in what God has done for man in order to accomplish his salvation. They are not always at one in judgment as to the way in which the effect of this divine action is mediated to men and women in present experience.

The reason for this is, we think, not far to seek. Human temperament and human experience is inherently various, whereas God is always the same. It is fact of human experience that some souls are captivated in mind and imagination by worship which is highly institutional, traditional, and ceremonial, and largely for the reason that it is venerable, colorful, mysterious, and romantic. Others have been brought up in this atmosphere and found their hearts unmoved by any sense of God, or even repelled by the feeling that all this is empty formalism. God has met them in reaction to this, in an experience which appeared to be purely inward and individual. Some have felt their love and loyalty go out to the ancient institutional Churches because they are venerable, stable, and authoritative. Others have felt constrained in spirit by this institutional dignity, and have found liberty in a little informal group of familiar friends. Divergences of this kind clearly underlie different views which are held regarding the Church and sacraments, and different emphases in the doctrines of justification by faith, salvation by grace alone, election, and predestination. These are the issues which constitute a large part of the division between Roman Catholic and Protestant, and the division of one Protestant denomination from another.

It would seem from this that the Church has been divided by an insistence from one side or the other that a discipline of the means of grace which has proved profitable for some community ought to prove profitable for all. This method of devotion has then been claimed as of universal legitimacy and obligation. However, this discipline of devotion has not answered to the experience of some other group, which has rejected it. We therefore judge that the Church can only vindicate her unity by seeking unanimity in those doctrines which concern the nature of God and His saving action in Christ, and by allowing variety of approach and emphasis in those doctrines which concern the mediation of this saving action to man. The unity of the Church is not solely a matter of doctrinal confession, but insofar as agreement in doctrinal confession is required it is to be in those matters which are covered by the great creeds of the ancient and undivided Church. These are the Trinity, the Incarnation, the atonement, and the resurrection. On the other hand, reasonable liberty of interpretation is to be allowed in speculation as to the exact way in which the sacraments bring grace to man, or in questions of "conversion," "grace alone," election, and predestination. Attempts to secure uniformity of definition in things which are subject to the infinite variety of human apprehension will always divide the Church.

E. The Church Visible and Invisible

By the Church Visible is meant the whole number of those marked out as part of the organized body of the Church, by profession of Christian discipleship, and by Holy Baptism. By the Church Invisible is meant the whole company of those, known only to God, who are united to Christ by faith, and are heirs of Christian salvation. Ideally the two should be one, for all faithful disciples ought to be in the visible Church, and all those in the visible Church ought to be faithful disciples. This is indeed the unspoken assumption of the New Testament, where it is taken for granted that the turning of man from evil to God is necessarily both inward and outward. The inward change, that is, the gift of faith and of the Holy Spirit, and the outward change, that is, baptism in water and joining the Church are the two parts of the union of man with Christ. Thus, if one who is seeking to call upon God is baptized, he will receive the gift of the Holy Spirit (Acts 2:38, 22:16), and conversely, he who believes and has received the Holy Spirit, ought most certainly to be baptized (Acts 8:36–37, 10:47). The possibility of there being Christian believers outside the disciplined body of the Church is not considered in the New Testament, while un-

worthy and disorderly members of the Church are not considered as heathen
outsiders, but as under the more severe judgment resting upon apostate
Christians (Hebrews 6:4–6, 10:29). They are still part of the Church,
though only to their own condemnation.

However, later thought and experience compelled the modification of
this simple position. In the first place, St. Augustine's doctrine of election
(see p. 211) required a distinction to be drawn between the whole company
of the Elect, who are called to final salvation, and the Church as a society
in this world, united by baptism. There is the possibility that some who
have been baptized, and who are apparently members of the Church, are
not in fact of the Elect, and will not persevere to salvation. There is the
corresponding possibility that some of the Elect are not in fact at the moment
members of the Church, though to preserve the traditional doctrine that
union with the Church is requisite to salvation it is taught that before their
death these elect souls will come to Christian faith and be baptized. Thus
there is the company of the Elect, known only to God, which is as it were
"the soul of the Church," and there is the company of the baptized, known
before the world, which is only "the body of the Church." This doctrine of
the invisible Church has been perforce adopted wherever the Augustinian
notion of election has been taught, and it was re-emphasized in the
Augustinian theology of the Reformation. It has, however, been greatly
broadened in scope in the modern period by prevalent confusion as to what
constitutes the Church, and as to whether or not it is necessary for a
disciple of Christ to be a member of an organized Christian body. Questions
are thus raised which are not answered in the New Testament.

Protestantism has witnessed a proliferation of denominations with very
widely varying standards of Church membership, and the current of popular
feeling in a liberal and tolerant society has frowned upon the claim of any
one particular form of churchmanship to represent "the one true Church."
Added to this has been the spirit of criticism of any form of "organized
Christianity." Thus we have grown accustomed to the spectacle of many
persons who display in their lives and characters much of the spirit of
Christ, who yet are not active members of any disciplined Christian denomination. In addition, there are many organizations of Christians which
certainly seem to be blessed by the activity of the Holy Spirit, yet which
are difficult to bring within any intelligible and scriptural definition of the
Church. For example, some Christian societies do not observe the sacraments
ordained by our Lord. As so often, there is a mixture of good and evil in
this familiar situation. It is good that Christians should have learned to be
more tolerant and charitable toward one another than they have often
been in the past, and that they should have been reminded by modern
experience of the ancient position that the grace of God is not limited to
those means of grace which He has ordained as the regular and promised
channels of His salvation. However, it is regrettable that the majestic unity
and authority of the Church should so largely be concealed by the appear-

ance of irresponsible and even uncharitable competition, so that the thinking even of many genuinely Christlike people should be vague as to the nature of the Church and the necessity of belonging to it.

F. The Communion of Saints

In the widest sense this is the doctrine that all those who by faith are united to Christ are united to one another in a universal fellowship of mutual prayer and charity. The divisions of race, country, language, culture, and social status which separate man from man in the world are to be of no account in the Church, which is essentially one in Christ (Acts 10:34–35; Galatians 3:27–29; Colossians 3:10–11). However, the more particular theological use of this phrase, as it occurs in the Apostles' Creed, for example, is to affirm that the one Church is not divided even by death. Those in Christ who have died are not in any kind of suspended animation, nor are they excluded from fellowship with the Church on earth. The whole body of Christians as it exists in this world, living by faith and hope, compassed with infirmity, battling with evil, and growing up into Christ, is described as "the Church Militant." The whole body of Christians in heaven, living in the fuller vision of God, serving Him victoriously with ampler powers, and still growing up into Christ, is named "the Church Triumphant." The two together make up the Church, and they are in close communion with one another. Thus the Church of this world can truly feel that those who have gone before join with her in her worship and service, an invisible company having a continuing and helpful interest in the affairs of men.

It is impossible to view from a correct perspective the spiritual dignity of the Christian Church unless this doctrine of the communion of saints is fully realized. The whole world-wide company of Christians alive at the present time, with all its multiplicity of divine service, is in reality only a very small part of the Church. Most of the believers, and most of the illustrious heroes of the Faith, are in heaven. It is that wider and nobler Christian fellowship which gives meaning to ours, not vice versa. The Christian who looks only at the company on earth will be cast down by the candid reflection that the Church is an insignificant and ineffectual body, compared to those agencies which control secular society. He who has faith to look to the whole fellowship will realize that it is the existence of the Church which alone gives meaning to the entire process of world history.

Summary of Divergence: The Invocation of Saints; Prayers for the Dead

These are two devotional practices, deeply entrenched in Catholic tradition but strongly rejected by the Protestant Reformers, which express the conception of the communion of saints.

a. The Invocation of Saints

i. CATHOLIC POSITION. It is the privilege of the Church on earth to address the departed saints, who are before the presence of God in heaven, to invite them to make intercession with God on behalf of man. Of particular efficacy is the heavenly intercession of the angels, the great and illustrious saints, and above all, of the Blessed Virgin Mary, on account of the merit of their great holiness and their spiritual nearness to the throne of mercy.

ii PROTESTANT REJOINDER. It is to be agreed that it is right and helpful for the Christian to invite his fellow believers to join in prayer for him. As the Church Militant here on earth enjoys spiritual fellowship with the Church Triumphant in heaven, there is perhaps nothing inherently wrong in principle that the Church should ask departed Christians for the benefit of their prayers. However, the convinced Protestant feels that traditional Catholic devotions expressing this idea are excessive and are dangerously easy to be misunderstood by simple believers. To address the departed saints in highly reverential language is likely to be misunderstood by the simple as *worship,* such as is rightly offered only to God (Colossians 2:18). To do this before their images may admit idolatry into the Church (Exodus 20:4, 5). And even if this error is avoided, such customs may suggest that the highest God is remote and not altogether available to the unaided prayers of His humbler children. This is clearly an error, for in Christ the Mediator God has made Himself fully accessible to the believer (1 Timothy 2:5). The prayers of other Christian may be helpful, but they are not *necessary* or meritorious in purchasing divine grace. Therefore, although it is good that the fellowship of the Church Militant with the Church Triumphant should be fully and expressively symbolized in Christian worship, these traditional Catholic devotions are to be excluded from the private and public prayers of the Church, or at least allowed only with great reserve and in studied moderation.

b. Prayers for the Dead

i. CATHOLIC POSITION. Departed Christians who are in a state of grace, yet who have not performed sufficient penance to account for all their venial sins, are undergoing the balance of their discipline in the remedial punishment of purgatory (see pp. 260–61). As the Church of the unseen world is one communion and fellowship with the Church on earth, the prayers of the Church Militant can effectually assist Christian souls through purgatory, until they are accounted worthy of admission to heaven. Therefore it is the charitable duty, and the privilege, of the Church to pray for the Christian dead, and in particular to offer on their behalf the effectual and meritorious prayer of the Mass (2 Maccabees 12:41–45) (see p. 260).

ii. PROTESTANT REJOINDER. Clearly, there is no place at all for prayers for the dead in the thinking of those who accept the traditional

Protestant position that all souls go to bliss or to damnation immediately at death (Luke 16:22-26). However, some others who allow the possibility of spiritual discipline and growth in the unseen world (see p. 262) may also in principle allow the rightness of prayer for departed Christians. If intercessory prayer can help fellow believers in this life, it can also in the life beyond, because all the Church is one communion and fellowship. However, the decided Protestant will object that much traditional Catholic devotion can easily be misunderstood by simple people, and can run to excess to become the occasion of superstition. Thus, the idea that departed Christians are in a state of virtual torment in purgatory, and *require* the prayers of the Church to help them through into bliss, is felt to be an unworthy and unhealthy notion (see p. 263). The Christian need not feel that his departed loved ones and Christian friends are in some way shut out from his customary prayers simply because they are passed from sight. At the same time, they certainly need not be prayed for with anxious fear, for they are in the hands of God (Wisdom 3:1-5).

II. The Church of the Old Covenant

The conviction of the first Christians, witnessed to by the New Testament and in the writings of the early Christian centuries, was strongly to affirm the continuity of the Christian Church with Israel, the ancient chosen people of the Hebrew faith. In token of this the Jewish holy books were read in Christian worship and quoted as authoritative for Christian doctrine, as the Old Testament Scripture of the Christian Church. The spiritual heroes of old Israel were looked to with reverence as the ancestors of the Church (Hebrews 11:32-12:1). The Greek word *ecclesia* ("an assembly summoned together"), which is used of the Church in the New Testament, is the same word as used in the Septuagint, the traditional Greek translation of the Old Testament, of "the congregation of Israel," assembled in the wilderness under Moses (Acts 7:37-38). Thus in a true sense the Christian Church begins not at Pentecost, but with the patriarchs, and in particular with Abraham, the "Father of the Faithful," and founder of the Hebrew nation (Hebrews 11:1-10).

Thus it is Christian teaching that from the beginning God has declared Himself through a distinct organized community. As always, God mediated the spiritual through the natural. The natural and original bond of human community was the tribal one of physical descent. Thus we find that one tribe was selected to be the chosen people, the descendants of Abraham (Genesis 12:1-3). This Hebrew tribe started its course as one Semitic tribe among many, being essentially similar to its neighbors of the Middle East in race, speech, religion, social institutions, and so forth. Subsequent history proved it to be an altogether different nation, and particularly in the matter of religion. To this tribe was given something which distinguished it from other Semitic tribes, namely, a long series of religiously gifted and sensitive leaders, the prophets, who were able to point out to the Hebrew people the lessons which God was seeking to teach through the formative experiences of their often troubled and tragic history. The mass of the people did not learn these lessons easily or quickly, but they did nevertheless learn. Thus among all the peoples of antiquity, with the various heritages they have passed down to later civilization, the Hebrew nation was the possessor of a national religion unique for its moral and spiritual dignity and insight. The Old Testament Scripture is the story of the hammering out of this spiritual treasure upon the anvil of history, in the experience of a special tribal community enriched by the presence of the prophets.

The critic may object that every nation has to some extent felt itself to be a "chosen" people, under the immediate protection of its national gods. However, the claim of the Hebrews to have been the chosen people does not rest upon what they felt about themselves but upon the objective facts of the case. They certainly did not all show themselves always to be virtuous, but they did progressively display this unique talent for religion. Almost everything of first-rate religious value which has come down to the Christian from the ancient world has come from the Jews, and it is for this reason that their ancient books, and no others, are read today in the Christian Church. The Greeks indeed possessed a unique talent for rational argument and philosophical speculation, and provided much of the intellectual apparatus by which the Church set forth her essential faith in clearly formulated doctrine. Yet the faith which was set forth by means of this apparatus was essentially Hebrew and biblical, not Greek. Modern literary and theological criticism has abundantly vindicated the traditional proposition that the indispensable prerequisite for understanding the rise of the Christian Church and her faith is this root in Hebrew religion, enshrined alike in the books of the Old and New Testament Scriptures (John 4:22).

This proposition may be illustrated in a variety of ways. Considered in His human office as a teacher, our Lord is the climax of the prophets. He is a Jew speaking to Jews. Though our Lord's teaching shows unique comprehensiveness, balance, clarity, and beauty, the material from which it is derived is the higher and more spiritual side of traditional Jewish religion. Sometimes this derivation is expressly affirmed by Christ Himself (Mark 10:17–19); but if not, it is still there, and this long-familiar truth of traditional Christian exposition has been enforced anew by material more recently discovered, such as the Dead Sea Scrolls. In the exposition of the New Testament, it frequently happens that the correct sense is given only if the Greek words are allowed the sense they bear in the Greek Old Testament, rather than that in the pagan Greek classics. Again, the primitive Church was not uninfluenced by the pagan social environment in which it formed its institutions, yet it would appear to be an error to suppose, as some have done, that the institutions of the Church were chiefly or largely formed from pagan borrowings. The chief and formative source is to be sought in the institutions of Judaism.

The doctrine of a "chosen people" by no means presupposes the idea of divine favoritism. It is the Christian faith that God loves all men without distinction, and that of His grace He places the same value upon all human personalities. Nevertheless, it is a fact of experience that God does call some men, some communities, and some nations to distinctive tasks not open to all, and does endow them with equipment of mind and spirit suited to the task. On the one hand, these are not predetermined to be faithful and obedient. They can fall from their special calling and abuse their special gifts. On the other hand, only those with the special calling can fulfill the special task. Thus history knows of more than one nation apparently "chosen" at one time or another for a special role. So the Greeks were "chosen" to be the schoolmasters of the ancient world in philosophic argument and in art. The Romans were "chosen" to pioneer for mankind the principles of law and the administration of justice. That the Hebrews were "chosen" by God to declare the true principles of religion is the leading example of a general principle. Membership in a religiously "chosen people" was not a status of divine favor, in the sense that to be Hebrew-born made one more pleasing to God, and more certain of eternal salvation, than to be born a Gentile. The Hebrew possessed a clearer light than did the Gentile, and therefore God rightly required more of him and judged him by a more severe standard. This most uncomfortable doctrine was indeed one of the leading points of the teaching of Amos, the first great writing prophet of the Old Testament (Amos 3:1-2). To be called and equipped by God for a special and honorable spiritual office does not convey upon a man a favored position in the attainment of salvation.

III. The Church of the New Israel

A. The New Israel

The most comprehensive and fundamental definition of the Christian Church in the New Testament is that it is "the new Israel" (Galatians 3:7-9, 29; 6:16; Philippians 3:3; James 1:1; 1 Peter 2:9). The Church is the company of those who at the coming of Christ were found true and faithful "Israelites indeed" (John 1:47), and who, because they were awake to the promises of God, fulfilled the divine destiny of ancient Israel. To this nucleus was added by God the far wider fellowship of those Gentiles of many races and countries who shared the faith of the true Israelite, and confessed Jesus as Christ and Lord (Ephesians 2:11-22). Thus the Church, the community of the New Covenant, is organically continuous with ancient Israel, the community of Old Covenant. Yet she is the ancient community made new, and reconstituted upon a more completely spiritual basis.

There is a sense in which the Old Covenant was given to Abraham and to his descendants upon the basis of faith in God (Genesis 15:1–6). This higher and more spiritual side was always present in Hebrew religion, being witnessed to by many exalted passages in the prophets and psalms. However, the principle that man walks with God by faith was inevitably to some extent overlaid and compromised by the circumstance that the Covenant was given to a certain people by physical descent (though the way was open for Gentiles to become proselytes), and that the promise of God's favor was dependent upon obedience to the ceremonial and moral commandments of the Law of Moses, which was given to the people as a necessary discipline (Galatians 3:17–19). When the promised Christ came, and brought the power of the kingdom, this principle of faith, which to some extent lay concealed in the old religion, stood forth clearly. Every foretaste of spiritual good in the religion of the Old Covenant was filled to its fullness in the New, and so it could be unambiguously declared that the basis of membership in the reconstituted chosen people was faith in God through Christ. Thus membership of a particular group, and that following of communal ceremonial which was appropriate to a purely national religion, were no longer essential for membership of the people of God (Romans 3:29–31).

There is, indeed, an obligation still resting upon the Christian to observe certain outward marks of faith in Christ and of Church membership, and to follow the moral discipline of the Christian life, resting upon the ethical tradition of Judaism. Yet these outward marks and this moral discipline are such as correspond to the higher, more spiritual, and universal order of the New Covenant. Thus in the Church, with her atoning sacrifice of Christ and her spiritual ordinances of worship and morality, there was fulfilled the divine promise given through Jeremiah, that when God visited His people there would be a New Covenant of inward spiritual religion, which would bring to man a victorious power to obey the law of God spontaneously from the heart (Jeremiah 31:31–34; Hebrews 10:1–25). The Church, though soon of predominantly Gentile descent, cherished a strong sense that she was a community organically continuous with old Israel, and the legitimate heir of all divine promises made to Israel. She rejoiced in institutions corresponding to those of old Israel, but at a higher spiritual level. This is the Scriptural theology of the Church as "the New Israel."

B. The Rise of the Church

This theology of the Church corresponds to the way in which the first Church did actually take shape. St. John the Baptist, who occupies the curious but significant dual position of a Jewish prophet and a Christian saint, is the connecting link between Judaism proper and the distinctive Christian Church. The Gospels agree in regarding his preaching ministry as the mark of the beginning of the Christian movement (Mark 1:1–8). After a period of centuries during which it was apparent that prophecy had ceased in Israel, John stirred the nation with preaching which instinctively reminded all hearers of the old prophets (Mark 6:14–16). The main characteristic of his teaching was a stirring re-emphasis of the old prophetic message that mere nominal membership of the chosen people and formal participation in the religion of Israel would not suffice to put man right with God in the coming day of the Lord. It was necessary for each man born an Israelite personally to start again, and by his action in repentance and consecration to make his own the highest standards of the devotion and morality of his people (Luke 3:3–14).

This appears to be the meaning of John's baptism by water. A washing with water is a very natural rite to adopt as a sacramental "acted prayer" to symbolize turning away from the defilement of evil to good. As such it was a part of the due ceremony of making a proselyte, and the discovery of the Dead Sea Scrolls has further illustrated what importance could be attached in some Jewish circles to ceremonial religious ablutions. The significance of John's baptism apparently was that he treated as proselytes those who were Hebrews born, in accord with the principle implied by Luke 3:8. There was now within the larger community of nominal Israel, constituted by birth and formal circumcision, a smaller, awakened, and disciplined company of "Israelites indeed."

It was largely from the ranks of the disciples of John the Baptist that the nucleus of the Church was drawn. This is symbolized in John 1:35–42, where the Baptist in effect hands over some of his disciples to become our Lord's apostles. We need not suppose that when Christ called His disciples at the lake He was summoning unprepared men (Mark 1:16–20). Some or all of them had doubtless met Jesus when all went down to the Jordan together to hear the preaching of John. Jesus had made His impression upon them, and when they parted to go home He was to them their prophet and their hero. In keeping with this is the significant circumstance that the rite used by John to incorporate the unawakened Jews into the company of his disciples was continued as the initiation rite into the Christian Church. Critical scholars have much debated the question of the precise origin of the sacrament of Holy Baptism, but it remains difficult to improve upon the clear conviction of the first Christians that "the outward and visible sign" of the Church's sacrament of Holy Baptism was a washing with water which went back to the ministry of the Baptist (Luke 3:16; compare Acts 19:1–6). Thus institutionally as well as theologically the Church grew out of the awakened nucleus of the people of Israel, and was in fact the ancient people renovated.

C. Our Lord's Foundation of the Church

In the modern period some critics have claimed that our Lord did not intend to found the Church. A common argument is that as He expected to

come at an early date for the consummation of the age (Matthew 10:23),
He cannot have had an interest in the foundation of a disciplined community, because the formation of an organization implies the expectation of
a long-continued period of Christian history. Thus the eschatological view
of Christ's teaching (see pp. 45–46) seems to many to preclude an organized
Church. It is not clear that this consequence is a necessary one. However
brief the time of waiting, God's renewed chosen people were to wait in
solemn expectancy as a fully prepared people (Mark 13:32–37). That is,
there was a place for a disciplined Church. It is not claimed that in founding
the Church our Lord organized the later administrative machine.

Another form of argument, less reliable, betrays the scarcely-concealed
anti-ecclesiastical bias of many critics. It is assumed that "the spiritual" and
"the unorganized" are virtually one, so that an interest in establishing a
distinct and disciplined religious community is to be accounted largely inconsistent with the notion of our Lord as one whose care was for inward and
spiritual religion. Thus if He were a true and free prophet He "ought" to
have founded at most an informal fellowship, but not a Church with religious
rites and authoritative officers. This is decidedly to read the New Testament
through the spectacles of modern Christianity of the more "liberal" kind, and
will assuredly entrap the student into a misleading anachronism.

The traditional Christian doctrine is that our Lord founded the Church,
or perhaps better, that He refounded it, for the Church of New Testament
days was deeply aware of being old as well as new. The chief argument for
this position is the confident and unargued assumption of the first Christians
that this was so. In general, the New Testament Scriptures were composed
to meet the needs of their own time, not to answer beforehand the controversial issues of later days. Some questions regarding the Church are
extensively argued in the New Testament, particularly whether it was necessary that Gentile Christians be circumcised and adopt the national religious
customs of the Jews. This is because Christians were not all agreed. By
contrast, it is not argued whether it was the Lord's will to found the Church
and whether it was the duty of Christians to belong to it. There were no
Christians who had any other opinion, and so the matter is passed over in
silence.

The actions and words of our Lord certainly bear out the idea that He
Himself thought of the company of His disciples as "the new Israel," and as
such, a distinctive and disciplined community, even as old Israel was a community. Thus there were twelve apostles, corresponding, it would seem, with
the traditional twelve tribes of Israel (Mark 3:14). Christ described as "the
twelve tribes of Israel" those of whom the Twelve were to be the spiritual
leaders and judges (Matthew 19:28; Luke 22:30). The disciples of Christ
were "the flock of God" (Luke 12:32), which phrase is a standard Old
Testament metaphor for the people of Israel (Isaiah 40:11; Jeremiah
13:17; Ezekiel 34:3ff.; Micah 7:14). Our Lord's solemn blessing to St. Peter

as he emerges the first to make the distinctive Christian confession of faith is "upon this rock I will build my Church" (Matthew 16:18). There is both a parallel and a contrast here between the Church and the old "congregation of Israel" (Exodus 12:3), the word "congregation" in the Greek Old Testament being rendered "church" in the New Testament (compare Acts 7:38). The company founded with St. Peter as the first Christian believer, and by him led at the first public preaching of the gospel (Acts 1:15, 2:14, 3:6), is hailed by Christ as *His* congregation, His new Israel, even as old Israel was the old congregation. Finally, the distinctive Christian rite of worship which Christ ordained was a communal meal in spiritual continuation of the Jewish Passover (Luke 22:14–20), which itself was the memorial of the foundation of the chosen people as a nation, and a mark of belonging to that people.

D. New Testament Metaphors of the Church

1. THE BRIDE OF CHRIST. A frequent Old Testament figure to express the relationship of God to His chosen people was that the Lord is as a husband to His people, and Israel is the wife of Jehovah (Isaiah 62:4–5). A common variant upon this theme is that idolatry, which is the breach of the Covenant, is spoken of by the prophets as adultery (Jeremiah 3:6–10; Ezekiel 23:36–49; Hosea 2:1–5). This metaphor is naturally carried over into the New Testament, and applied to the new Israel. Thus the Church is the Bride of Christ, and the intimate union in spirit which exists between the Lord and His Church is likened to marriage (Ephesians 5:23–32; Revelation 21:2–3, 9).

2. THE BODY OF CHRIST. This doctrine is chiefly associated with the writings of St. Paul. The first stage of his argument is practical. In the passage 1 Corinthians 12:4–31, he is appealing for charity and unity in the congregation at Corinth. He points out that the Christians have a variety of spiritual gifts, some more prominent than others. However, all are necessary for the fulfilling of God's plan through the Church. The different members are like the various limbs and organs of the human body, of very different function, and some apparently more important or more dignified in use than others, yet every one necessary to the health of the body. Therefore the Christians with prominent gifts must be humble-minded, and those with only modest gifts must guard against both envy and discouragement. All must cooperate as do the organs of the body, so that the entire Church may be the healthy body of Christ.

This practical and moral line of thought is developed into a general theology of the Church in Ephesians 1:22–23, 3:6; Colossians 1:19. Here "the head," (that is, the mind) is the unifying principle of control and action for the whole human body. This holds good also of the cooperative fellowship of believers. They are united together because each one is united to Christ and directed by Him. He is therefore the head in the assembly of limbs and organs which make up the body. The final theological development displays the Church as embodying the same principle as the Incarnation. In the days of His flesh, the mind and spirit that was in Christ had a human body through which to express itself. The work of Christ is now carried on through the agency of an invisible Spirit, and it is left to the Church to make witness to the world. The Church's form and doctrine, her preaching and sacraments, her practical moral activity, and the example of fellowship which exists between her members, all visibly embody the life of the Spirit of Christ. The Church is to be Christ's lips to speak, His hands to serve. The Church's martyrs are to suffer like Christ with men and for men (Colossians 1:24). Thus the Church is the body of Christ (Ephesians 4:1–16), and is in a sense "the extension of the Incarnation."

E. The Marks of the Church: One, Holy, Catholic, Apostolic

1. ONE. Because there is but one God, who has performed the one sufficient saving act in Christ, the effect of which is mediated to mankind by the one Spirit, there can by the nature of things be only one Church. The outward disunity of the many competing denominations may disguise this essential theological unity from the superficial view, yet the unity exists in the mind of God and is the subject of the prayer and hope of faithful Christians. In token of this, believers are not baptized into the separated denomination to which they belong, but into *the Church* (Ephesians 4:4–6). Unless this principle is kept in mind it is impossible to appreciate aright either the true incentive or the aim of the ecumenical movement. Those who are discussing Church unity are not seeking to *create* the unity of the Church, as though it had to be brought into being by the amalgamation of a number of independent and self-sufficient Churches. Their task is to secure an order and practical organization of the visible Church which will express adequately the essential unity which now exists, though to do this does not require complete uniformity of worship or administration. The Church is to be made more fully the incarnation of the Spirit. And the ultimate purpose of this is not to economize human resources, nor any supposition that a large organization is more efficient or more influential than a small one. This is not necessarily so. Ecclesiastical reunion is necessary because the convincing vindication of the unity of the Church is essential if men are ever really to understand what it means to be a Christian. A divided Church is a contradiction of its own message. A divided Church, therefore, however great its zeal and devotion, cannot with full persuasiveness portray the Gospel (John 17:21).

2. HOLY. This biblical term means "separated to God, for His own use." To say that the Church is holy does not imply the claim that all its members lead very pure and upright lives, or that they are necessarily more moral than those who are not Church members. The claim of the Church is both more modest and more profound than this. It is that the Church is different from every other community because it is a society founded by God and not by

man. Its purpose is not to accomplish the will of the men who are members of it, but to fulfill the plan of God for the redemption of the race (Ephesians 3:3–6, 9–11; 1 Peter 2:9).

3. CATHOLIC. This word means *universal*. In the first place the notion of catholicity involves the doctrine that the Church as she exists in every land and place is one fellowship. Pressing closely behind this is the doctrine that the mission and fellowship of the one Church cannot be sectional. It is for "all sorts and conditions of men." He who tacitly says: "The scope of my loving sympathy, my prayers, and my evangelistic ambition, is limited to my neighborhood, or my nation, or to a particular race, or to people of culture, or to 'the workers,' or to democratic countries, and so forth," has not grasped what it means to be a Christian. He is the essential *uncatholic*.

An important secondary meaning of the word "catholic" arises from the circumstance that the guarantee of sound, balanced, and authoritative doctrine is the widest possible Spirit-guided fellowship of Christian devotion and scriptural scholarship (see pp. 3–4). The Christian message as it is apprehended only by a particular kind of temperament or human need, or by a particular nation or century with its own distinctive cultural background, is under suspicion of being possibly only a partial presentation of the gospel. The message which stands the searching test of experience from century to century, and in all manner of human circumstance, is the gospel which can be trusted as authentic, whole, and balanced. A sectional opinion within the Church may sometimes be correct, or it may be incorrect, but it is not more than a matter of opinion. The Faith of the whole, or Catholic, Church is the Catholic Faith, and the Church affirms the Catholic Faith to be the reliable doctrine, the authoritative doctrine, and the orthodox doctrine.

4. APOSTOLIC. The use of this word indicates the claim that the Church now existing is the same Church as that apostolic Church originally founded by Christ. She has maintained continuity of life and doctrine from that day to this. She rejoices in the inheritance of an enduring tradition, and repudiates the notion that one can have a "new" Church, founded by some historic Christian leader.

IV. The Doctrine of the Ministry

Many issues connected with the institutional life of the Church come to a focus in relation to the doctrine of the Christian ministry.

A. The Priesthood of All Believers

It is often assumed that this doctrine affirms either that "every man is his own priest," or alternatively, that there is in effect no such thing as priesthood in the Christian Church. Both these positions, we believe, reflect unfortunate confusion. A priest is the representative of the people. He leads their joint worship, and enables them to approach God. Having had fellowship with God he can then declare God's will to the people. Therefore the priest is also the representative of God to the people. It is Christian doctrine that the whole body of the Church collectively exercises this essentially priestly function of mediation between God and the whole of mankind.

Only some within old Israel were priests, but the whole of the "new Israel" is a "kingdom of priests" (1 Peter 2·9). Hence there is no individual in the Church, no matter how exalted his ecclesiastical office, who is a Christian priest by right of some influence inhering in his person and making him, in effect, a different sort of Christian. The priest is the organ of the whole body of the Church. Properly speaking, Christ is the Minister of the sacraments. His Holy Spirit uses the Church as the instrument of His sacramental action. He uses the local congregation, however small, as the representative in that place of the whole Church, and operates through its action that which in principle He operates through the whole. Yet in the local representative congregation not every member of the body has the same office. In the Eucharist one person must in fact say the Lord's words, and break the bread, and bless the cup, standing in the place of Christ. As he acts for all, all act in him.

The good order and the dignity of the sacrament require that this representative member be set apart for his office in such a way as will most fully bring out the meaning of what the Lord is doing in this ministerial action. In particular, it should be made plain that the representative priest is the representative and organ, not of the local congregation alone, but of the whole body of the universal Church. Only in this way can it be brought home to the local congregation that the sacramental action which they are together performing in the person of their representative, they are performing as the instruments of the one Lord as He acts through His one Church. Hence, a fully significant celebration of the sacrament requires that the minister of the sacrament should be in due ecclesiastical *order,* and that this order be recognized by the wider circles of the Church as expressive of the unity and authority of the Church. Therefore care for the ministerial order of the minister of the word and sacraments[1] is in no way inconsistent with the basic principle of the priesthood of the whole Church.

Thus one does not say that the conductor of an orchestra personally produces the music. The music is produced by a common effort, in which for a perfect rendering the part of the every player is necessary in due proportion. The conductor is a special member of the orchestra, necessary for the sake of *order.* So it is with ministerial order. This care for due ministerial order does not mean that the individual believer cannot approach God on his own. Experience proves that even the humblest believer can in his private prayer enjoy access to God, that he can have God directly speak to his soul through the reading of the Bible, and that he can on occasion speak with evangelical authority to his family, friends, and neighbors

---

[1] That is, the manner in which the minister is set apart and dedicated for his office.

concerning the things of God. Yet the apparently "private" layman or laywoman is not in fact an isolated Christian individual. He does what he does as a representative organ of the whole body, representative as is the ordained minister, though he is a different organ. The mother who teaches her child to pray, and the plain man who speaks to his fellow about Christ, are not at all in the relation of "amateurs" to the official minister as a "professional." They also are the instruments of the one Lord who operates through the whole Church. If their private and "unofficial" word is with power, it is the Lord who has spoken through His Church with the highest divine authority.

B. Ministerial Order

The manner in which the representative priesthood within the Church shall be appointed is a matter of importance. Controversy over this question of ministerial order has been, and still is, one of the chief occasions of division in the Church. In the first place, any theology of order is defective and misleading which looks upon the Christian ministry as a succession of men existing apart from the body of the Church, and handing down one to another a sort of spiritual "influence" which does not flow in the Church at large. Always, the ministry is a priesthood because it is a special limb of the priestly body. At the same time, the minister should not be thought of as the mere delegate of the Church. Christ is the Minister of the gospel and the sacraments, and uses the Church as His instrument. Therefore only Christ can make a minister, and when he acts faithfully according to his calling the minister acts with the authority, not of the congregation, but of Christ. The view held by some that the congregation for its convenience deputes the minister to exercise its own powers in its own name is to be regarded as an inadequate doctrine.

Clearly, no man is proficient enough in spiritual things to acquire a personal right to instruct others and to give them good advice. Certainly no man is holy enough to be a worthy minister of the sacraments. The minister is a sinful man speaking to sinful men, and is himself fully in need of what he offers to others. His only ground for daring to go about his ministration is that Christ has of His infinite grace called him, unworthy though he be, and sent him to the work, and that he would be unfaithful to His Lord were he to shirk this duty. Therefore the first and essential stage for the appointment of a Christian minister in due order is the divine call of the Holy Spirit (Acts 13:2). There then rests upon the authorities of the Church the responsible duty of seeking to determine whether those who profess this call are sincere, of examining their natural gifts of personality and intellect, of training them, and of appointing them in due order to whatever work seems most suitable. Yet in this essential disciplinary process the Church is seeking to discover and acknowledge the call of God, and is not herself calling the minister.

Thus the Christian ministry is the Lord's "spiritual gift" to the Church (Ephesians 4:7–8, 11–12). It is a special organ in the body, created by the Lord for a special function, by which the whole body of the Church acts. By way of illustration, the tongue is not the "delegate" of the body, as though the other limbs had shared their powers with it. The tongue has a unique function bestowed upon it by Him who created the whole body, and only it can speak. Yet it is sustained by the whole body, and when it speaks it voices the thought of the mind which dwells in the whole man. Thus the tongue is a special *representative* organ. This illustrates the relationship of the ministry to the Church. The ministry is the representative organ for the most dignified and authoritative corporate actions of the priestly society, and in this sense may be described as a priesthood.

Summary of Divergence: Views Regarding Ministerial Order

We have up to this point traced the Christian doctrine of the Church and ministry in those matters which are very widely held in common by the various recognizable parts of the Church, though perhaps with minor variations of emphasis. However, the circumstance has to be faced that there are serious divergences among Christians in judgment as to what form of ministerial order does in fact most fully and fittingly express the nature of the Church. There are also differences of judgment as to how important it is that a particular form of order be kept with strict regularity. These matters are perhaps the leading occasion and mark of the division of the Church into separated denominations.

a. Catholic View

The ancient traditional Churches feel that it is a matter of the highest theological importance that the organic continuity and the authority of the Church be fully symbolized in their ministerial order of priesthood. They account it a matter of principle that their ancient continuous ministerial and sacramental order be maintained. Thus they cannot allow that any minister of the Eucharist is in due order unless he has been ordained by a bishop who is in unbroken succession of consecration, back to the first bishops of the Church. Roman Catholics would in addition claim that for this ministerial succession to be in undoubted and fully authoritative ecclesiastical order it must own obedience to the Pope, as well as be in succession to the Church of the first days. From the Catholic view, a breach of the continuous and authoritative ministerial order occasions an actual breaking off of the divinely ordained organic continuity of the life of the Church. Baptized believers who do not possess in their congregations this organically continuous sacramental priesthood, episcopally ordained, are in some sense Christians and in a reduced sense a part of the Church. However, their denominations are not more than unordered assemblies of Christ-loving people.[2] They lack one of the essential symbolic marks of organic continuity and authority. God may indeed spiritually bless them, and use their ministrations to do His work. However, the Catholic would say that these denominations are not part of the *duly ordered* and disciplined Church.

b. Evangelical View

The evangelical denominations have had their thought and feeling largely molded by a very different set of experiences. Commonly, enthusiasts for the spiritual life found themselves in unhappy collision with the accepted ecclesiastical authorities of the day. Some then felt that a break with the older organizations of the Church was necessary in order to secure a purer witness to the gospel and a freer course for the work of evangelism. The effect of this has been to work a change of emphasis as to what constitutes the due mark of the unity, continuity, and authority of the Church. Continuity of sound scriptural doctrine, and of purity of spiritual life, has been affirmed as the true succession, in preference for the ideal of "visible" continuity of ministerial and sacramental life. Furthermore, denominations possessing a ministry not in continuous succession of episcopal ordination have found themselves to be blessed by God in the ministry of word and sacraments. This experience has led them to challenge the traditional Catholic claim that the ancient continuous ministry is essential to the due order of the Church. In some cases this effect has been further reinforced by the experience of spontaneous and relatively unordered "revivals," in which men who have had no regular ecclesiastical commission of any sort have preached with spiritual power. Thus there has arisen a variety of views regarding ministerial order. Some evangelical denominations have come to regard their accustomed ministry as not more than a matter of passing organizational convenience. Others have viewed their own accepted order as a valuable spiritual discipline. Yet even so, the due and regular maintenance of it, though perhaps important, is not to them a matter of the highest theological principle. Unlike the Catholic, the Evangelical can envisage the possibility of his order being changed in changing circumstances.

c. An Interpretative Statement

There are some genuine differences of conviction regarding the Church, between Catholics and Evangelicals, and these cannot simply be smoothed over by ecclesiastical diplomacy. Nevertheless, these differences should not be viewed out of proportion. To a large extent they are differences in judgment as to what form of order most fittingly symbolizes and safeguards a right view of the Church, and these divergences in order often disguise a good deal of latent agreement about the ideal of the Church itself. It may not be easy for a staunch denominationalist to believe that spiritual values which he prizes may at times be expressed in Church forms unfamiliar and unwelcome to

---

2 "Separated brethren."

himself. Yet such is often the case, and the attempt should be made to recognize this.

Thus the instructed Congregationalist or Baptist, who has inherited the so-called Independent form of Church polity, may sincerely profess that he does indeed regard the Church as one, and his local minister as the authoritative minister of Christ, and the minister of the whole body of the Church. He can claim that his Independent institutions do symbolize these "Catholic" qualities to him, even though the Catholic may have criticized them as inadequate in this respect. So likewise Presbyterian-type Church courts may often effectually exercise those functions of authoritative government and leadership which the Catholic associates with episcopacy. Conversely, the firm exponent of Catholic institutions may not be nearly so in love with external forms as the Evangelical fears. His real interest is in the preservation by these forms of spiritual values which are widely shared. It is important for various parts of the Church not to sit in judgment upon one another defensively or self-righteously, but to look beneath the variety of forms to what is intended by them.

The upholders of Catholic institutions have often described as "invalid" sacraments administered in churches which do not have an episcopally ordained priesthood. This is increasingly recognized to be a regrettable term, because it almost suggests to the plain man that these nonepiscopal sacraments are being dismissed as "phoney" and as unblessed by God to spiritual effect. This would be a judgment alike unrealistic and uncharitable. Actually what is being asserted is that they have not been celebrated according to those rules of order which Catholic churchmen feel are necessary to symbolize the unity of the Church, though it may still be allowed that they are means of Christian grace to those who receive them. This question-begging word, "valid," should therefore be avoided in constructive Christian discussion, as being a term which invites misunderstanding. By parity of reason, the Evangelical Christian should beware of accusing the Catholic churchman that his insistence upon the continuity of the ancient episcopal order is a mark of a legalist, unspiritual, or even "magical" view of the Christian life and discipline. The traditional order is insisted on because it is felt to symbolize a spiritual quality, that is, the organic continuity and unity of the Church.

C. Historical Development of the Ministry

The history of the Christian ministry is a subject in which history and belief run together, because what different denominations think about the ministry is chiefly determined by their historical experience. Though this is not a book of Church history, and there is no room fully to go into the details of matters which have been the subject of the strongest controversy, it is necessary to say a little upon the history of the Christian ministry, in order to complete the theological argument.

It is not surprising that difficulties about Church unity arise chiefly around the ministry, and in particular around the sacramental ministry of the Church, more even than in connection with Christian belief. On the positive side this is because there is a very wide area of substantial agreement in matters of fundamental belief between the leading denominations. On the negative side this is because the ministry is more "visible," and more intimately connected with organizational discipline in the Church, than are articles of formal belief. Questions of ministerial order carry with them issues as how the Church ought to be organized, who is to be regarded as rightly in office, who is to be deferred to in honor, and who is to be obeyed if there is a dispute regarding discipline. Disputes of this kind have all too often come down to the present day associated in the popular mind with economic, social, racial, and national rivalries. All these "outward" issues present themselves vividly to the comprehension of all the members of the Church, whereas theological questions generally appeal to the few. Thus in general Christians are more likely to be in dispute with one another about the organization of the Church, the office and dignity of its ministers, and the forms of its ceremonial, than about belief. Nevertheless, though the discussion of Church unity so largely resolves in practice into the discussion of ministerial order, it must never be forgotten that the Church's ministry cannot be considered in isolation from the Church's theology and her devotion.

The original leadership and government of the Church was clearly that of the apostles, appointed and authorized by Christ Himself. The divine commission and equipment with the gift of the Holy Spirit is indeed spoken of as in a general sense given to the whole company of disciples, corresponding to the priesthood of the whole Church (John 20:19–23). Nevertheless, from the beginning the commission to bear public witness to the gospel and to lead the Church was exercised more particularly, though not exclusively, by the Twelve (Acts 1:2–8, 12–15, 21–26). They are to be regarded as the first ministry of the Church. The first extension of this ministry was the appointment of deacons, who are spoken of as administrative officials for finance and almsgiving (Acts 6:1–6), though in fact they chiefly come to view as preachers (Acts 6:8–10; 8:5–8, 26–40). However, when the office of deacon reappears in early Christian writing after the New Testament period it is as an administrative assistant for finance and almsgiving, and to assist at the Eucharist. The work characteristic of an apostle was that of traveling preacher and founder of new local churches, in view of his qualification as a witness to the resurrection. Some not of the Twelve who to a notable degree took up this work are hence also classed as "apostles" (Acts 14:14; Romans 11:13, 16:7). However, the office of personal witness to the resurrection was essentially a temporary one. The apostleship proper belonged only to the first generation of the Church.

As their representatives for the more continuous government of local congregations the apostles appointed elders, or presbyters (the two words being alternative translations of the Greek) (Acts 14:23). The ceremony for appointment and commissioning both of deacons and elders was the laying on of hands. It would appear, in the judgment of many reliable expositors, that an alternative name for these elders was bishops, or "overseers" (the two words being alternative translations). The clearest New Testament evidence for this is a comparison of Acts 20:17 with 20:28, where the same body of men are apparently referred to by both titles.[3] Further evidence, however, is derived from Christian writings of the period immediately succeeding the New Testament. It is impossible within the scope of this work to survey the complicated detailed evidence from the apostolic fathers, which has been the subject of hotly contested controversy. In general, the following points would be agreed upon by many reliable historians of various schools of thought, though it is to be admitted that those on the Catholic side would chiefly stress the element of continuity and authority within this scheme, whereas Evangelical historians would emphasize the fluid development and variety during the first period.

1. In the Church of the period immediately following the first apostles, the government of each local congregation was in the hands of a body of officials who combined in their office the functions later separated as that of the presbyter (elder) and the bishop. These primitive officials are known to Church history as "presbyter-bishops."

2. These presbyter-bishops were appointed by continuous succession of laying on of hands from the original presbyter-bishops ordained by the apostles.

3. The presbyter-bishops were assisted by deacons.

4. From the early days of the second century onwards, first of all in the more developed and numerous congregations of Asia Minor, but rapidly in other places also, one of the presbyter-bishops became by invariable usage elevated to be president of the others. There is then a single ruling bishop in each city church, supported and advised by a body of presbyters, who now hold a lower office, distinct from that of bishop. There is also the assistant body of deacons. The succession of ruling bishops in each church, and the agreement and ecclesiastical communion of these bishops together, is accepted as the operative symbol of the authority and unity of the Church. Here is the emergence of the traditional threefold order of the apostolic ministry—bishops, priests (presbyters), and deacons. The bishop is in the first place the authoritative teacher of the Church, the father-in-God who interprets Scripture aright to the faithful. He also presides

---

[3] Compare also Philippians 1:1; 1 Timothy 3:1, 8.

at the Eucharist and other rites of the Church, assisted by the presbyters and deacons.

5. As Christianity spread, and the original city congregation formed associated Christian congregations in outlying communities, these were presided over by presbyters, who were then regarded as the personal representatives of the bishop.

It is almost impossible to answer intelligibly the frequent question as to whether this ancient polity was a "democracy." Representative government with popular elections was not the method of those days. The leadership and discipline of the Church was by the personal authority of a "father-in-God." However, the government of the Church was not on that account authoritarian, in the sense that the personal will of the bishop settled all disputes. He was to rule with the consent and cooperation of the presbyters, deacons, and whole company of the faithful. However, they made their counsel known not so much by voting for a proposed policy or office-holder, in the modern manner, but by continuing together in prayer until the whole body of the Church felt assured that it was being divinely guided by the Holy Spirit. There was more of the atmosphere of the traditional Quaker "taking the sense of the meeting" than of the typical modern "free vote" or "election."

D. Apostolical Succession

The traditional doctrine of ministerial order, derived from this position in the ancient Church, is commonly called "apostolical succession." This affirms that the organic continuity of the Church in every century and place is to be symbolized and safeguarded by a ministry in continuous succession of appointment, while the disciplinary and doctrinal authority of the Church is to be exercised through the allied principle that those admitted to the ministry are to be approved and commissioned by those who are already ministers. The ministerial succession is affirmed to go back without a break to the first ministry of the apostles, who were appointed by Christ. The effect of this is to deny the possibility of starting a "new" Church, or any claim of a body of believers to call into being anew their own ministry. The traditional procedure established from ancient times answering to this doctrine is that a bishop is to be consecrated by laying on of hands by three other bishops in the succession, and that ordination of a presbyter is to include the laying on of hands of a bishop in succession.

Some further definition is necessary, for the term "apostolical succession" is often used loosely, and in more than one sense. In the first place, there is the stricter doctrine, held generally by the Church from the third century onwards, and to the present day by the Roman Catholic and Orthodox (Eastern) Churches, and by some Anglo-Catholics. This affirms that the traditional threefold ministry of ruling bishops, priests, and deacons goes back in unbroken succession to the apostles themselves. This ministry is of divine ordinance and is essential to the due order of the Church.[4] There is also the more general and empirical doctrine which affirms that the historic ministry of the Church goes back in unbroken succession to the first ministry of the apostolic Church, but that within this succession of "presbyter-bishops" the distinction between ruling bishop and presbyter appeared by a process of *development*, in response to the experience of the Church and the guidance of the Spirit. This places the traditional threefold ministry upon the foundation of a kind of contingent divine ordinance, declared through the voice of Christian antiquity, rather than upon an express and invariable divine ordinance.

Those who adopt this latter view would generally allow that it is precarious to affirm as a matter of Christian faith any precise view as to how the Christian ministry developed in the first century. A positive doctrine on this point would require secure historical evidence for the complete succession of officers at a substantial number of representative churches. Actually the historical evidence is extremely fragmentary for the formative period. It suffices to make a continuous ministry going back to the apostles a very reasonable probability, but not more than this. In ecumenical discussion it is necessary, when the claims of "apostolical succession" are discussed, to have it clearly in mind in which of these two senses the term is being used, the stricter and dogmatic or the wider and empirical.

E. The Inward Intention and Outward Form of the Ministry

Confusion between the inward intention which is expressed by certain ecclesiastical forms, and the outward forms which have in point of fact been used by the historic Church to express this intention, has often made it difficult for churchmen of later periods to understand New Testament thought about the Church. The main stream of Christianity has firmly held what may be called the "Catholic" ideal of churchmanship, namely, that it is an essential part of Christian faith that the Church is one, visibly organized, disciplined, authoritative, and organically continuous in every age and place. Even at the best this ideal of continuity, unity, and authority has never been perfectly realized in practice, but this fact in no way denies that responsible Christian teaching has aspired after this as the ideal.

This Catholic ideal of churchmanship has been embodied through the centuries in the continuous episcopally ordained threefold ministry of the Church, together with the sacraments, the canon of Scripture, and the great

---

[4] However, the Roman Catholic Church appears to possess no authoritative definition as to whether the bishop is a minister of an order entirely different from that of the priest, or a special member of the one priestly order who is possessed of certain distinctive ruling and ordaining powers.

creeds. It has therefore become hard for traditionally minded Christians to see that much of the inward intention and spirit of Catholic church-manship can on occasion be expressed by other forms of ministry. It is not always sufficiently realized that the qualities of disciplined unity, authority, and continuity can be embodied and safeguarded by a governing conference of presbyters, and that a denomination may possess much of the essential function of episcopacy in the absence of the traditional office of bishop. It is thus dangerous for the exponent of one system of Church polity to sit in judgment upon another, unless he makes a careful attempt to look past the outward organizational form to the life which it expresses.

This is why some find it hard to grasp the New Testament doctrine of the Church. There is in the New Testament a relative degree of absence of those outward organizational and ministerial forms which historically have been associated with the continuity and authority of the Church. There is no clearly defined ruling bishop in each church, and no hierarchy to express the unity of the bishops. This has made it too easy for some to jump to the conclusion that the first Christians were not interested in disciplined church-manship and Church unity. Actually this is a somewhat superficial reading of the New Testament. The first Christians had a living sense of the majestic unity and authority of the whole Church. In spirit they were Catholic, though this catholicity was not yet fully expressed in what have come to be called "Catholic institutions." From the beginning there was an essential spiritual quality which made inevitable, necessary, and right the development of institutions to express it.

A suggested judgment from history, bearing on current ecumenical discussions, is as follows:

1. Original and authentic New Testament Christianity is Catholic, in that it holds to the organic and visible unity, continuity, and authority of the Church and her ministry.

2. The outward operative symbol by which this quality of catholicity is ministerially expressed has from very ancient days been the continuous and authoritative episcopal ministry and sacramental system.

3. The fitting basis for the future visible unity of the Church is the preservation of this continuous and authoritative episcopal ministry, suitably reformed for modern conditions. Clearly, the only possible symbol of continuity with the historic past is the institution which existed in the historic past, and which has come down from the past to the present.

However, these propositions are to be balanced and complemented by the following:

1. It is not possible to find the institution of the single ruling bishop in the New Testament Church and in the short period immediately succeeding the New Testament. Therefore the Church can in principle exist without this institution.

2. The quality of "Catholic-type" churchmanship can be found expressed and safeguarded by authoritative forms of ministry other than the historic office of bishop. These Church polities should be treated with respect.

3. The churchman's first love must be for the inward and spiritual intention of ecclesiastical institutions, not simply for his own familiar organizational setup. In discussions of Church unity this should encourage the flexible, reasonable, and adventurous approach, rather than the doctrinaire and defensive attitude.

Readings

Flew, R. N., *Jesus and His Church*. London: The Epworth Press, 1938.

Manson, T. W., *The Church's Ministry*. Philadelphia: The Westminster Press, 1948. (Protestant view.)

Miller, D. G., *The Nature and Mission of the Church*. Richmond: John Knox Press, 1957.

Moberly, R. C., *Ministerial Priesthood*. London: John Murray, 1899. (Catholic view; Anglican.)

Newbigen, L., *The Household of God*. New York: Friendship Press, 1954.

Chapter Seven

The Means of Grace

An outward and visible sign of an inward and spiritual grace

I. Grace and the Means of Grace

A. God's Action through the Church

The theology of the Church and her ministry comes to a climax in discussion of the means of grace, because these are the means by which the general saving action of God is mediated to particular congregations and to individual believers. We move from the general theology of the Church to the actual human situation. Salvation is by divine grace (see pp. 206–7). The grace of God is, in the first place, His unmerited favor toward man. The term answers to the principle that human salvation is by divine initiative. God sets His love upon those who do not deserve to be loved, and forgives those who do not and cannot merit this forgiveness. In the second place, grace is the enabling power of God which, working in man, performs this divine good will. However, experience shows, and the Christian Faith declares, that there are certain stated, regular, and divinely promised channels through which God ordinarily bestows His grace. These are the means of grace.

Man takes his share of God's gracious saving act by faith in Christ (see pp. 221–23). Just as the life of man is both inward, of thought and will and affection, and also outward, in bodily and practical action, so also is the act of faith both inward and outward. It is both the cleaving of the heart of man to Christ in loving trust, and it is the taking of the name and sign of an open Christian disciple before the eyes of the world by loyal membership in the Church. This taking of the open signs, if done sincerely, constitutes the means of grace to the believer.

B. The Use of the Means of Grace

The Church in general holds that sinful man is helpless to save himself. His sole hope is in the grace of God, and therefore he must always await the divine initiative. His action is freely and responsibly to cooperate[1] with the divine grace. Nevertheless, there is something which man can do if he sincerely wishes God to exert His initiative and visit him with His grace. He can trustfully and obediently wait upon God at the place and in the way which God has ordained. He can do this expectantly, confident that God will fulfill His promise and make Himself known. The means of grace provide this place and method of waiting. The proper use of the means of grace is that the seeker for God is perseveringly and expectantly to use them, but he is not to trust that his diligence in the use of the means of grace will *earn* or merit his salvation. His trust is to be in the grace of God alone, not in the means. Yet he is not to think lightly of his obligation to use the means of grace, or shirk the accompanying discipline or regular and loyal church-manship and the life of private devotion, for these are the divinely appointed places of waiting.

C. Grace Not Limited to the Means

It is fundamental that God is the sovereign Lord, and is not accountable to man for His actions (Exodus 33:19; Isaiah 43:13). Therefore God's grace is not limited to the appointed means of grace. God has promised to visit with His grace, and bring to salvation, those who obediently and faithfully use the means of grace; but He can nevertheless, if He sees it to be right, save those who have not used the means. It is very precarious for overzealous upholders of the ordinances and discipline of the Church to affirm that certain classes of people who are outside the means of grace cannot be saved. This is to presume upon the prerogative of God, who alone knows who are, and are not, in a state of salvation. It is the office of the Christian witness plainly to declare God's terms of salvation to all whom he can reach, and leave all matters of judgment to God. One may ask, then, what is the advantage of the means of grace in the Church, and what the nature of the obligation to use them? The answer to this is that the means of grace carry with them a certain assurance of standing before God,

---

[1] This is the usual position. The strictest Augustinians, however, wishing to affirm in the strongest terms the bondage of man's will, and salvation "by grace alone," would deny that man cooperates with the grace of God. Man is to be accounted passive in the hand of God. This is, however, an extreme position (see p. 211).

resting not upon man's merit in using the means, but upon God's faithfulness in giving His blessing in the way He has promised.[2]

By way of comparison, we do not argue that the spiritual value of home life is rigidly limited to the marriage bond. There are couples who by inadvertance have failed to comply with all the provisions of the marriage law, and some indeed who have taken to living together without any form of marriage whatever. It can happen that some of these are faithful and loving, and have rightly brought up their children. However, what is lacking is *assured status*. The union has not been bindingly pledged, in due legal form. It would appear that those who profess to love Christ and who show something of His Spirit in their lives, yet who do not use the due means of grace and who are not united with the Church, are in a condition analogous to this.

It is no business of the Christian theologian to deny that these people are sincerely good or that God's grace extends toward them or that they may finally come to eternal salvation. They may have some, or much, of Christian grace. What they lack is the *assured status* before God. They have partially or wholly neglected to take the pledges which God has ordained for those who would be marked as belonging to His people. They have not waited in the place and way which God has appointed to those who would receive His grace. This is an act of disobedience, a failure in duty toward God. Therefore, although the merciful God may in fact judge them to be in a state of salvation, they have no right whatever to count upon it. They may escape damnation, but they are not spiritually "safe," as are those who have fully united themselves to God in Christ. This is the true meaning of the traditional proposition that "there is no salvation outside the Church." This does not imply that all those who are outside the Church and her sacraments are heading for damnation, but that they have not been fully and duly admitted to the status of those who securely belong to God.

D. Grace Not Unaccountable

The divine ordinance of the means of grace shows that the action of grace is not entirely unaccountable. Grace is indeed the free action of the sovereign God, but of His own sovereign freedom God has faithfully bound Himself to visit with His grace those who wait upon Him in certain recognized ways. Therefore the searcher for God can know where he is with God. The principle of the means of grace corresponds to the reasonableness of religion. Man cannot save himself, but he never need say, "I am in the dark about God, and there seems nothing I can do about it." If he is in earnest he can

---

[2] Some would say that the sacramental means of grace carry with them this assurance in a particular way, and indeed, that this is the characteristic of a sacrament (see pp. 164–65).

reasonably obey God, unite with the Church, and expectantly use the means
of grace. Furthermore, the divine pledge of the means of grace answers to
the general doctrine that the invitation of God's grace extends to all men[3]
(John 3:16; 1 Timothy 2:4; 2 Peter 3:9) because God loves all men. All
who will may use the means of grace.

II. Worship

A. The Rationale of Worship

Worship is the action of believers as they join together to express the
faith and love which God has given to the Church, to the end that God may
be given the praise and reverence which is His due, and the Church built
up in love and faith. The principal elements of worship are therefore adoration and praise, confession of sin, profession of faith, and intercession. The
media used include visual symbolism and sacred actions, as well as the word
spoken and sung, so that man may use all his faculties in lifting up his soul
to God. Worship is the more general term which in a sense includes all the
particular means of grace, because the preaching of the word, and the
sacraments, are special and decisive actions in which the principle of worship
comes to its clearest expression. Worship is also in a sense the initial means
of grace, because the normal way in which the growing Christian child or
the convert from another religion first comes to the Christian experience of
the presence and goodness of God is by joining in Christian worship in the
home and in the congregation.

Worship is both individual and corporate. Many of its actions, in prayer,
in meditation, and in the reading of the Bible, can be informal and domestic,
and carried on without any official representative of the Church. They may
even be private (Matthew 6:6). Nevertheless, the higher forms of Christian
worship are corporate, being the acts of the whole Church. Yet it is a mistake
to suppose that individual and corporate worship are in some way opposed
one to another. Individual Christians indeed enjoy the privilege of immediate access to God, but they are not isolated individuals. When private
believers and Christian families meet for worship they still do so as part of
the Church, and their worship only comes to its fullest when they are aware
of this, and when their prayers are offered for all men, just as when the
Church meets in the public congregation.

The experience of worship is an example of the principle that God works
through the natural and the human, and uses it in order to accomplish the
spiritual. The underlying psychological rationale of worship is that "expression confirms impression." It is a general law of human behavior that to
express the inward thought in uttered word, in meaningful sign, and in
practical action, confirms and deepens the hold of the thought upon the
heart. Thus to express the sense of God deepens the sense of God. If God

---

[3] Though the strictest Augustinians would virtually deny this (see p. 212).

has first given the gift of faith "as a grain of mustard seed," then to use that rudimentary faith to take part in the act of worship provides the occasion whereby faith may grow to a more adult faith. Thus worship is a means of grace.

Worship is not on this account merely the religious aspect of "auto-suggestion," or "mass suggestion." Still less is it an example of "mass hysteria." It is a fact that individual personalities powerfully affect one another, so that for men and women to feel the same feelings in company, to think the same thoughts, and to say the same words, does imprint these things upon their minds. In mysterious ways this can often happen when the people in question are not all gathered together in the same place, if they are in spiritual rapport with one another. Yet to admit all this does not explain away worship as merely a natural psychological phenomenon, though it does illuminate the natural means which God uses to accomplish spiritual effects. It is the faith of the Church that when the Church prays the Holy Spirit is there, bestowing the sense of Christ in the midst (Matthew 18:20), so that God is the dominating personality there. Worship therefore does not consist in human beings assembling to influence one another, but in the assembly of believers in the presence of the Lord. The Holy Spirit uses and works through the natural psychological process whereby expression confirms impression, so as to bring to man a power which is not his own. The weakness, in the Christian view, of some popular psychological approaches to religion, where the emphasis is made that mental adjustment can produce "peace of mind," and in some cases, physical healing, is here. The claim may be true, so far as it goes. But to go this far is not Christian worship. The objective element of God's work through the Spirit is in danger of being forgotten.

B. The Preaching of the Word

Preaching is usually the means of grace employed by the Holy Spirit to crystallize the definite conviction of personal faith. The general Christian impulse of those who have been nurtured within the Christian community, and the goodwill of dimly awakened searchers for Christ, may be brought thereby to personal experience and personal commitment. Clearly, the Church's worship is only a means of grace if the worshipping community has some degree of knowledge of who Christ is and what His discipleship means. The outward word and ceremonial is an empty form unless there is something inward to express.[4] Preaching informs and educates the worshipping Church. Some members of the worshipping community may as yet have only a very unformed degree of Christian faith. This is the case with young children, casual adherents, or confused seekers. Preaching, with its explanation of Christian life and belief and its appeal for a thoughtful

---

[4] Though simple, young, or unsophisticated believers may have religious beliefs which mean very much to them, even though they have no power to express them in the form of reasoned propositions.

response to the appeal of Christ, enables worship to result in the growth of faith.

By "preaching" we do not mean the sermon alone. The reverent reading of the Bible can itself be a "preaching of the word." The sacraments are, among other things, a most effectual "preaching of the word." Theologically adequate hymns can preach the word, and the recital of the Creed is a particularly solemn act of "preaching." The whole business of "the preaching of the word" is essentially the painting of a vivid portrait of the living Lord of Christian devotion, so that He may make His own personal and pointed challenge to men, calling them to penitent faith in Himself, to devotion and to trustful obedience.

The Word of God is Christ (John 1:1-5, 9-14), the facts of whose life are witnessed to in Holy Scripture (see pp. 195-97). Therefore the preaching of the word is based upon the Bible. Nevertheless, that preaching which is a means of grace is not the bare exposition of Scripture. Nor is it the detailing of the facts about Christ, as in an informative lecture. It is the employment of the testimony of the Church's faith, and the preacher's own testimony, to present Christ to the people. This necessarily includes some degree of instruction in the most important facts about Christ, but it goes on from this to the appeal for faith in Christ as the crucified and risen Lord, and for a life of personal devotion to Him. In true Christian preaching the preacher is careful to give central attention to Christ, rather than to his own opinions and feelings. The Holy Spirit can use this presentation of Christ the Word so that the listener hears not the voice of a man preaching, but the voice of Christ speaking through him.

It is this element of Christ-centered preaching, based upon the scriptural record of the facts, and reflecting the Church's confession of faith, which prevents Christian worship from being a mere exercise of autosuggestion or mass suggestion. Ritual which is only an emotionally impressive ceremony, and an oration which is no more than the appeal of personal magnetism to human feeling is in just this peril. It can lead men astray into uninstructed and subjective mass hysteria. It is for this reason that the liturgy must be scriptural, and not merely aesthetic. The sermon is to be out of the Bible, and not from the daily newspaper. It is worthy of note that the four Gospels are themselves examples of "the preaching of the word," preserved in writing from the ancient Church for our instruction. They represent to us the way in which the apostolic Church presented the leading facts about Christ, not merely in the spirit of informative biography, but to interested hearers for the purpose of winning them to full Christian faith (John 20:31).

C. Intercessory Prayer

This aspect of Christian worship merits attention, on account of the difficulty which many minds have found in it. It is assumed by some that it is "unscientific" to ask for God's blessing and assistance in any affairs which concern the world of nature, for example, that He will bless the handiwork of the farmer in the gift of harvest. The objector may perhaps allow that it is reasonable to ask for spiritual blessings, but his argument really amounts to the tacit assumption that this "spiritual" intercession is in fact human autosuggestion. Thus in both these cases the objector betrays the common assumption that the world in which men live is a naturalistic system of fixed laws, and that there is no God of such a character that He can "make a difference" to events either in the realm of nature, or of human personality.

This issue has already been treated of in principle in the discussion of natural law and divine providence (see p. 28). Our judgment is that the Christian theologian will affirm that while God certainly does not "break" those fixed and reliable laws of nature which are themselves an expression of His being, His intelligent mind is in control of the universe, and He can "work through" the laws of nature to accomplish His sovereign will. If it once be allowed that the Living God exists and rules the world by His providence, then it is surely reasonable to ask for His blessing in all manner of affairs, both "natural" and "spiritual," believing that He is well able to answer those prayers if to do so is in accord with His good will. And if He indeed be a God of love who is near to man in tender sympathy and compassion, it is the natural and proper impulse of His children to make all their requests known to Him (Matthew 7:7–11). A denial of the rationality and efficacy of intercessory prayer is in fact a veiled denial of the God of sovereign power and loving providence.

However, the purpose of intercessory prayer is not to remind God of human needs, as though He were in some way forgetful or unaware (Matthew 6:7–8). Nor is it necessary to stimulate His desire to do good (Luke 18:7–8). Nor do we pray in hope of bending His will, to cause Him to alter His plan for the government of the universe. It is the Christian faith that God already knows all things, past, present, and future, and that His government is already fully and entirely good for every one of His creatures. The natural and sufficient ground of Christian prayer is that this is the expression of confidence in His goodness and wisdom. We may even venture the judgment that in some things God may choose to delay the execution of His will until such time as man recollects the duty of making intercession, because it is good for man that in this discipline he should learn both dependence upon God and confidence in asking.

The ultimate purpose of prayer is that the praying Church may become the fully sensitive, obedient, and useful instrument of God for the accomplishment of His own purpose. The Christian does not presume fully to know what is God's good plan either for the nations or for the Church, or for his loved ones or for himself. He does not, therefore, in his confident intercession try to demand or to dictate. The very spirit of Christian prayer is, "If it be Thy will." This is not an "escape clause," to the effect that if the prayer is not apparently answered the intercessor may comfort himself with the pious reflection, "Well, I did not actually ask for it." Such an attitude displays complete lack of faith. The prayer "If it be Thy will" is the prayer of the believing man, whose supreme desire it is fully to be used by God according to God's will, with God's power, and to God's glory. It is prayer after the pattern of Christ Himself (Luke 22:42). If this be so, the highest act of the Church's prayer is not for health and good success, for healing from disease, or even for the peace of the world, though all these things are rightly to be prayed for. The chief prayer of faith is for increase of faith and love, for the divine equipment of the Church, and for the conversion of the world (Matthew 6:9–10).

The critic may inquire: "If man requires faith in order to pray effectually, how can sinful man, whose awareness is of his rebellion against faith, ever bring himself to pray for the gift of faith? How can he ever start? Is there not here a 'vicious circle'?" This common dilemma illustrates that the method of the divine grace is by human cooperation. Left to himself man is indeed helpless in this vicious circle of unbelief. Yet man is not left to himself, for God's grace is still calling even the man who denies the existence of God. Man can do nothing apart from the divine initiative, but that initiative is already always there. Therefore, it is a fact of human life that even careless men, and even apparently hardened men, experience under the stress of life fleeting moments of rude awakening which cause them to have dim spiritual stirrings. This is the work of prevenient grace (see pp. 214–15). In that moment it is possible for the unbelieving man, if he will, to cry out in his agony, "Lord, I believe; help Thou mine unbelief" (Mark 9:24). And this most faltering prayer is a prayer which God can bless by the gift of a greater faith. So the opening is made for the growth in grace. Yet to the end of his life the mature Christian is still praying the same prayer, and waiting to cooperate with the divine initiative of grace.

D. Religion and Magic

It is not possible here to examine the broad question of the contrast between true religion and magical superstition, either in its primitive forms or in its modern revivals. We must confine ourselves to the understanding of Christian sacramental worship. One is aware that it is possible for even the most sacred rites to deteriorate among uninstructed and superficial worshippers into magic, and even into degrading superstition. This has in fact on occasion happened in the Church. Furthermore, it is all too easy for natural strong revulsion against one error to drive some believers, and some denominations, into error of the opposite direction. Thus there are many sincere Christian believers who fail to find in the sacraments the spiritual profit and meaning which has been the traditional heritage of the Church, because they are unduly afraid of "superstition."

The betraying symptom of magic is that it is man-centered. Its basis is the notion that it is possible, by the aid of the appropriate ceremonies and incantations, to constrain the power of the gods or spirits to the will of the worshipper. It is the attempt to harness the divine power to the protection of oneself, or one's family or one's property, or to bring "good luck" to one's enterprise. If the devotee of magic does not succeed he redoubles his request, and the spirit of his prayer is to insist that he be heard on account of the persistence and correct form of his intercessions. The Christian sacraments are exactly the opposite in spirit. They are God-centered. The sole and sufficient ground for the worshipper's confident hope of divine blessing is that the sovereign God has ordained this dependable way in which to give His blessing. The blessing is an act of *grace,* bestowed as and when God will upon those who can do nothing to establish a claim upon Him. The rite, therefore, is a means of *grace,* and its efficacy depends upon the divine promise on the one hand, and the penitent and obedient receptivity of the worshippers on the other. The prayer of the sacraments is always, "Not my will, but Thine, be done."

III. The Sacramental Principle

All worship involves the use of symbolism. However severe, and even bare, the form the worshipper may choose, the words of Scripture, of the sermon, or of a hymn, are all symbols. They are the agreed outward expressions of ideas. However, the time-honored definition of a sacrament as "an outward and visible sign of an inward and spiritual grace given unto us, ordained by Christ Himself, as a means whereby we receive the same" indicates that a sacrament is a symbol which is seen and done, as well as said. It involves a proper substance and action, as well as words to be said. That the Lord should have ordained symbolic actions and visible symbols for the central acts of Christian worship is a salient example of the principle that God can work the spiritual through the material. Sacred words may on occasion be very expressive, but in general a symbol which is seen and done has more power to move the imagination of man than has the spoken word alone.

Thus there is a place for reasoned instruction in the idea of "country," "patriotism," and "public spirit." Yet if for the sake of his country a man has to take his life in his hands upon the field of battle, the season has passed for a lecture upon the principles of the Constitution! He requires a flag—a vivid visual symbol which can in a moment focus to his imagination all that he has been taught about the idea of "country." The spoken word is essential in its place, for if the flag is not understood it can make no appeal. Yet if it is understood, the symbol can have an imaginative power which goes far beyond the unaided word. Thus in a wide variety of life's experiences men resort naturally to acted and visual symbolism at moments of climax. This is eminently true of religion, and so our Lord has taken this principle into the

Christian religion. Hence the supreme symbols have "an outward and visible sign."

The use of symbolism is not a mark of lack of spirituality. Christian theology regards it as a cardinal error to suppose that the "invisible," that is, the purely mental or the spoken, is in some way more "spiritual" than is the visible and the acted. The association of material objects with the most sacred actions of Christian worship is an expression in present Christian experience of the very principle of the Incarnation itself. Christian teaching is that God created the material universe, that He filled it with spiritual meaning, that He can have contact with it, and that He can use it and work through it to accomplish spiritual purposes (see pp. 23, 34–35). The same principle which made possible the Incarnation makes possible the sacraments. Thus the sacraments bring to the worshipper the reality of the Incarnation.

Christian theology has affirmed the spiritual dignity and efficacy of the sacraments by describing them as "operative symbols." An operative symbol both signifies a truth and is a symbol through which God will perform an action of grace corresponding to that truth. By way of illustration from human affairs, a marriage is a rite which embodies something of the "operative symbol." The plighting of troth, the giving and receiving of a ring, the signature upon a legal paper, and the consummation of the marriage are actions which outwardly symbolize the intention of the parties to be married. However, the symbols are much more than vivid and expressive ways by which the parties declare their true love to one another, though they are this. They actually marry the couple. They perform an action, and convey a status, which corresponds to the love which is symbolized. Thus they are more than symbols. They are *operative* symbols. The supreme example of this principle is found in the Christian sacraments. The Holy Communion is much more than a solemn dramatization of the truths seen in the Cross, as a visual alternative to a spoken sermon on the same subject, though among other things it is this. To celebrate the sacrament is the way by which the Church makes herself one with the Lord as He offers His atoning sacrifice, and by which she receives her share of what Christ accomplished in His death and resurrection. Thus the Holy Communion is not only a visual and acted symbol of Christ's sacrifice of obedience. It is an *operative* symbol of His sacrifice. God has pledged Himself to use it to bring to the Church, and to reverent and believing communicants, a due share of the merits of Christ's death and resurrection. Thus:

> The sign transmits the signified,
> The grace is by the means applied.

The sacraments are therefore to a unique degree *means* of grace. When believingly used they convey to man a secure spiritual status and assured standing before God, because the Lord has ordained that this shall be so. The secure and pledged effect of the sacraments does not depend upon the exact mechanical performance of certain stated acts, or the exact enunciation of certain words, so much as upon a sincere and thoughtful intention of carrying out what our Lord ordained should be done. Well-intentioned zealots for precise ecclesiastical traditions do well to remember that in carrying out His saving work in the heart God has more regard for what is within the heart of man than for the punctiliously observed outward sign. Nevertheless, if a Christian congregation is found careless in saying the sacred words required by Scripture, in performing the due action, and in using the due substances, then it is clearly deficient in intention of observing the Lord's ordinance. This deficient rite is then doubtfully a Christian sacrament, and the security of the divine pledge is lost. The rite, though not in proper ecclesiastical order for a sacrament, may, however, continue to be a helpful service of Christian worship to those who take part in it, particularly if they err because of simplicity and ignorance.

IV. Holy Baptism

A. The Sacrament of Initiation

Holy Baptism is primarily the sacrament of incorporation into the Church (Acts 2:37–41; 9:18; 10:47–48; 16:14–15, 33). By consequence it is the sacrament of initiation into the Christian life, though when the person baptized is a child the initiation requires to be completed and ratified in later years by some suitable rite involving a responsible pledge of allegiance to Christ and His Church.

B. Baptism in the New Testament and the Ancient Church

Brief note has been made of the question of the origins of Christian Baptism (see p. 139). It would seem that Holy Baptism is a combination of John the Baptist's washing with water, in token of the penitent preparation of God's people for the coming of the Messiah, and of the outpouring of the Holy Spirit which came upon the disciples of Christ to prepare and equip them for their mission. At all events, from the time of the New Testament it was the firm faith of the Church that Holy Baptism is the sacrament expressly ordained by the Lord as the symbol of self-identification with Christ, incorporation into the Church, and of the gift of the Holy Spirit (John 3:5).

The New Testament discusses this matter in terms of the baptism of an adult convert to the faith, involving confession of faith in Christ as Lord and Savior (Acts 8:36–38, 16:31–33, 22:16).[5] It is possible that at first the

---

[5] We are left to surmise the nature of the mysterious "baptism for the dead" mentioned in 1 Corinthians 15:29. Presumably it was an attempt to incorporate into the Church the righteous departed, so that they might share in the coming resurrection. This presupposes a strong sense of corporate solidarity in the Church, whereby some members might stand proxy for others. This obscurity is a standing warning against undue dogmatism regarding New Testament baptismal customs.

divine name which was invoked over the baptized person was the name of Jesus Christ alone. Many scholars think that this is presupposed by the authentic text of Acts 10:48 (R.V.). From a very early period, however, the universal formula became baptism "in the name of the Father, and of the Son, and of the Holy Ghost" (Matthew 28:19). "The name" is a very common Old Testament phrase for that which represents the person, character, and authority of anyone. Therefore to invoke upon a person or place the sacred name of God involved that God had claimed it for His own, placed it under His authority, and extended His protection over it (Deuteronomy 12:5, 28:58; 2 Chronicles 7:14; Psalm 20:5; Jeremiah 7:10). Hence baptism in the triune name signifies that the baptized person yields himself up to the possession and authority of the God who has made Himself known as Father, Son, and Holy Spirit. By invariable tradition throughout the Church, therefore, the essentials to Holy Baptism are the use of water and of the triune name of God.

The leading theological passage in the New Testament regarding Holy Baptism appears to imply that the washing is to be by immersion, for the imagery of Romans 6:4 seems to require that the baptized person be "buried" in the water. However, at an early date it was accounted sufficient if the candidate went into the water and had water poured over him. Indeed, it would appear that the leading interest of some circles of the primitive Church was that baptism should be in the running water of the river, presumably because the first baptisms in the Jordan were of this kind. In the early days of the Church it became the rule that the washing, by immersion or pouring, should be threefold, to correspond to the threefold name of God. The baptismal creed, in three clauses, recording the divine work of the Father, the Son, and the Holy Spirit, was learned by the catechumen, so that he might make a threefold confession of faith to correspond to the threefold washing. Later still, baptism by sprinkling was allowed, nominally as a concession in the case of a sickly infant, often, however, as the usual custom.

C. Baptism as Union with Christ

Union to Christ by faith and incorporation into the Church implies the taking up a stand as a Christian in face of a probably hostile world, and a life of service which must often entail self-discipline and self-sacrifice. In fact, the action of a Christian convert in submitting to Holy Baptism means that he "takes up the Cross" in order to be a disciple (Mark 8:34-35). Baptism involves adopting that attitude to life which Christ adopted, and which took Him finally to His death. Those who make themselves one with Christ, inwardly in the heart and outwardly in deed and fact by membership in the Church, will receive strength from their victorious living Head do this. Having by His grace persevered in the life of "Cross-bearing" they will share His gift of life triumphant over sin in this world, and over death in the next.

Such is the New Testament doctrine of what it means to be a Christian.

St. Paul saw this great principle depicted symbolically in the rite of Holy Baptism. To go down into the water of baptism, which act is the operative symbol incorporating the believer into Christ and His Church, was, as it were, to go down into the grave with Christ. That is to say, it involved the adoption of Christ's way of suffering love. To come up out of the water, now a confessing and pledged Christian, was like rising from the dead in company with the victorious Christ. To submit to baptism was the door into a new life of moral triumph (Romans 6:3–6).

Thus the sacrament of Holy Baptism is a symbolic preaching of the death and resurrection of Christ. It is a divinely appointed means by which the faithful, identifying themselves with their Lord, may receive their promised share in the fruits of the atonement. This, the original and most authentic New Testament theology of baptism, shows that the two Gospel sacraments embody a parallel principle. They are both symbols of self-identification with the crucified and risen Christ. Baptism is the first and decisive identification; Holy Communion is the continuing and ever-renewed identification following from this.

D. Baptismal Regeneration

This traditional theological term has been the occasion of controversy, in part due to genuine differences of emphasis, but also through the reading of different senses into the same word. The New Testament position is that Holy Baptism, by water and the Spirit, is the operative symbol of conversion to God. The turning "from the power of Satan unto God" is considered as both inward and outward. Repentance, the act of faith, spiritual union with Christ, the gift of the Holy Spirit, baptism, and union with the Church are regarded as inseparable. They are so many aspects of the same thing. The questions which have caused dispute among later Christians as to which is more important, the inward secret union of the heart with Christ or outward membership of the Church, and whether certain ordinances are essential to Church membership, had not then arisen, and are therefore not explicitly answered in the New Testament. If the New Testament position is adopted, Holy Baptism is the mark of the beginning of the Christian life. It is the sacrament of the new birth, or of regeneration (John 3:5). This has been the traditional doctrine of the Church.

However, the life and discipline of no modern denomination exactly corresponds to the New Testament position. Therefore some measure of interpretation is necessary when New Testament doctrine is applied to the Church of today. This is particularly the case with infant baptism. A believer's baptism (see p. 165) is admittedly much nearer in principle to New Testament discussions of the sacrament. Possibly the most adequate way of viewing this matter is that the change of spiritual status which God works in the infant in baptism is a real and significant change, yet it is a change in promise and potentiality, rather than of immediate actuality.

Only in this way can infant baptism be vindicated as a real means of grace which accomplishes a divine work for the child, and also be guarded against the supposition that Holy Baptism, as it were, mechanically plants some sort of divine merit in the child, which is there irrespective of the later life, morals, and churchmanship of the baptized person.

By way of parallel, a child inherits, and has, as it were, implanted in him, the legal status of the nationality of his parents. This is a real status, yet one in promise. It by no means involves that he will, automatically and for the rest of his life, be a true citizen of his country. For the potentialities of citizenship to be realized requires nurture in the community and traditions of his nation, and it likewise requires a sincere response to this environment. Nevertheless, the status is real, and if the child later proves to be a rascal and a traitor he is still a citizen of his country. The only effect of this nominal citizenship is, however, that it is the law of his own nation, rather than of another, which inflicts punishment upon him. The unrealized potentiality is there, but it brings disability and blame, rather than advantage. Something similar is true of the baptism of the infant. He is permanently marked as a member of Christ and of His Church, and a real spiritual status is conferred. Nevertheless, it is a status in promise. To bring actual Christian benefit to the child the potentiality must be realized by the response of faith, consecration, and real churchmanship in the growing child.

However, the Christian child has been placed in the environment where worship is offered, Christian nurture given, and where the Holy Spirit more expressly operates. This environment effectually, though not irresistibly, helps the growing child to respond and to realize the potentiality of the status bestowed upon him. When he becomes, of his own conviction and choice, a real Christian, he has acted in accord with his baptism. And if he neglects the opportunity given to him, and fails to respond to the drawing of the Holy Spirit and the effect of the prayers of the Church offered for him, the evil-living baptized person does not become an unbaptized person. He is an apostate Christian, having a real Christian status which works judgment upon him, rather than blessing.

The baptism of a helpless infant presents the principle that salvation is by the initiative of divine grace. Before the child can do anything, good or bad, God is already there, receiving the child as His own, blessing him, and surrounding him with the influence of the Holy Spirit. The Church is likewise already there, praying for the child, and not doubting that the prayer is with power. This conception of a real, significant, and valuable spiritual status permanently imparted by God in the sacrament, yet imparted in promise, is perhaps the fitting sense in which baptismal regeneration may be attributed to the baptism of an infant.

A venerable but less satisfactory form of theology which has been widespread in some Christian traditions is that the chief function of Holy Baptism is to wash away the guilt of original sin. The power of original sin to lead men into actual sin is a fact of experience, and so is the guilt of actual sin, in which all men are found. Nevertheless, we feel that the notion of the *guilt* of original sin is a difficult and ethically dubious one. It is hard to see how the perfectly just Judge can hold men personally responsible and guilty for an inborn weakness of nature for which they are not in fact responsible. Surely He accounts personal guilt only to those evil thoughts and deeds which men have knowingly and willingly committed. The traditional doctrine of the baptismal cleansing from the guilt of original sin appears largely to be a piece of rationalization. First the rite of infant baptism appeared, upon the sufficient ground of Christian solidarity, and was accepted as a godly ordinance. Later, when the Augustinian theology introduced into the Church the notion of the guilt of original sin, the idea of the baptismal washing away of this guilt presented itself as a natural and convenient support in theological principle for the accepted practice. This has been accompanied by the transfer to infant Baptism of the doctrine of the New Testament regarding the remission of sin in a believer's baptism. It is, we feel, preferable to avoid this somewhat uncertain ground, hallowed though it is in Christian tradition, and to discuss the theology of infant baptism in terms of its original principle of incorporation into the Church, rather than of any supposed "cleansing."

Summary of Divergence: Believer's and Infant Baptism

At the time of the Reformation some of the more radical groups of Protestants emphasized, against the Catholic tradition that infant baptism is the normal usage of a Christian community, that the scriptural and only legitimate discipline of baptism is that of a believer's baptism. That is, baptism should be administered to one who is sufficiently developed in mental powers, and in particular, in spiritual experience, to be able to testify that he has already come to a personal saving faith in Christ, in token of which he desires duly to be incorporated into the Church. This emphasis has usually been associated with the claim that the only legitimate mode of baptism is by immersion, and that pouring or sprinkling of the water is an unscriptural, and therefore defective, rite. There is, however, no necessary connection between believer's baptism and total immersion. The ancient Church often practiced the immersion of infants, and the Orthodox, or Eastern, Church still does, while believer's baptism by sprinkling or pouring is also used.

The emphasis upon believer's baptism in general answers to the principle of Christian individualism. The Church is thought of, not as the Christian side of the general community life, but as a society in some sense standing apart from, and in antithesis to, the community. Church membership is to be composed entirely of personally committed Christian believers. Thus it is assumed that one becomes a member of the Church and a Christian (in the full and proper sense of the word) by an individual, personal, and conscious conversion or act of commitment to Christ, and not merely by incorporation into the Christian community. On the other hand, infant baptism answers to the principle of Christian collectivity (see pp. 217–18). It reflects the traditional confidence of the Church that nurture from early days within the Christian community, including the Christian home and school, as well as public worship, is the regular, normal, and salutary (though not invariable) way by which individual men and women become Christian believers. Clearly, these two ideals are in some sense complementary, for there is some truth on both sides. The two may be set out as follows.

a. The Case for Believer's Baptism

The Church is for all time to be disciplined so far as possible after the manner of the New Testament Church. The Church of those days was not a generalized Christian community, but a closely knit fellowship composed of those only who acknowledged a deep personal committal to Christ. Entrance to it was by a distinct and personal experience of conversion, in token of which the believer was united to the Church by baptism (for example Acts 9:1–18). Thus a person was not baptized in order to make him a Christian, or even to help him to be a Christian, but because he could profess that he was already a Christian. One has, first, Christian individuals and then the Church, not vice versa. Baptism by total immersion is affirmed to be the New Testament custom, and is further to be defended in present practice because it constitutes entrance into the Church as a challenging rite, which is only likely to be accepted by one who is of a serious Christian purpose. It is good for the Church and her members that there should be this clear demarcation between the Church and those who are not in the Church. On the other hand, infant baptism takes away from the full meaning of the sacrament. It can too easily be taken as a customary communal ceremony by parents and friends who may be lacking in deep Christian conviction. The child thus baptized is deprived of the later salutary experience of challenge and committal. At its worst, infant baptism can open the door to superstition.

b. The Case for Infant Baptism

It is to be agreed that the baptisms actually mentioned in the New Testament in general appear to be those of adult believers. However, this is the natural outcome of the missionary situation of the early Church. Furthermore, some of the most notable passages referring to Baptism contain language which answers very naturally to baptism by immersion (see p. 166). However, the New Testament does not give a sufficiently clear witness on these points to be determinative for the Church of later times. Therefore we are rightly guided by the judgment of the ancient Church, as it understood the nature of the Christian life, rather than by the inconclusive letter of Scripture.

The custom of infant baptism began to develop from an early date in the Church, possibly even in the first Christian century. It steadily spread in the early centuries, and became the general custom as and when the Church emerged from a missionary situation into the position of the communal religion of Christian nations. In antiquity, religion was always communal and of the family. The modern notion that it is possible for a husband to be of one faith, his wife of another, and their children of yet other persuasions was an idea quite alien to the thought of the ancient world, as it is in simple tribal societies today. The early Christians did indeed discover that the new faith sometimes sadly divided the home, but this to them appeared a monstrous and unnatural thing, and one of the most painful aspects of the necessity to suffer with Christ (Matthew 10:21, 34–38).

To the mind of the times the natural event was that when the head of the household became Christian, so did the whole family, including even resident domestic slaves (Acts 11:14, 16:31–32). With this background it is plain that Christian parents would wish their children to be admitted into the new faith by baptism. This was the historical origin of infant baptism, and it is significant that the objection voiced against the custom by some in the ancient Church was not the modern one that the baptism of an infant does not mean anything, because "the baby does not know what is happening." This is the mentality of modern individualism. The objection rather was that infant baptism meant too much! It was felt to be unfair to place upon the infant the heavy Christian responsibility of living from the days of early youth a life substantially free from serious moral fault.

In a settled Christian community the normal manner in which persons become Christians is by being born into Christian homes, living in a community of at least nominal Christian standards of behavior, receiving the spiritual nurture of joining in Christian worship, and of being educated in Christian schools (1 Corinthians 7:14). The majority of believers of all denominations would place the beginning of their Christian discipleship before they can remember, in days of infancy, even though they may also be aware of moments of personal decision and consecration in later life. If effective Christian discipleship starts with infancy it is logical that the infants of the Christian community should be formally incorporated into the Church. Traditional Christianity has done this by the rite of infant baptism. The doctrine that infant baptism is an effective means of grace is in fact a token of the Church's confidence in the beneficial effect of Christian nurture.

The Christian Church is the place in which worship is offered and Christian teaching given, and where the Holy Spirit more especially carries on His work. Therefore to be incorporated into the Church is the normal first step toward becoming a Christian. This underlying philosophy of Christian solidarity has been traditionally expressed by the custom that sponsors or godparents should confess the Christian Faith, and make a promise of Christian obedience, on behalf of the child at baptism. They stand for the general body of the Church, and profess the Faith of the Church, which Faith is for the benefit of all within the solidarity of the faithful, and the infant now to be baptized in particular. Other denominations require the profession of faith and promise of Christian nurture to be made by the parents, and the congregation present, because they feel that this is a more realistic form of promise. However, the principle of this is much the same as with the traditional sponsors. It is an expression of the solidarity in Christ of the home and congregation.

V. The Holy Communion or Eucharist

A. The Name

The central act of Christian worship, in which the whole principle of the means of grace is most clearly exemplified, is the sacrament of the gospel ordained by our Lord at His Last Supper. The technical theological term which conveniently comprises this rite under all the names by which it is variously known, such as "the Lord's Supper," "the Holy Communion," "the Mass," and so forth, is "the Eucharist." This word simply means "thanksgiving," and is derived from the Greek verb *eucharistein*, "to be thankful," used in 1 Corinthians 11:24. Its use should not be understood as implying any particular theology of the sacrament.

B. The Lord's Ordinance: The New Testament Doctrine

It is not clear from the Gospels whether our Lord's Last Supper was the actual Passover meal (Matthew 26:17–19; Mark 14:12–17; Luke 22:11–16) or one of the ceremonial meals preparatory to the Passover (John 13:1). This difficult question is of historical interest rather than of importance for the understanding of the theology of the Eucharist. In either case our Lord's betrayal and death, and institution of the Eucharist, is clearly associated in the mind of the New Testament Church with the Passover. Thus if the date from the Fourth Gospel is adopted, the crucifixion took place at the time when the Passover lambs were being killed, which is doubtless what the Evangelist intends to symbolize.

At His Last Supper our Lord performed a solemn sevenfold symbolic action. He took bread, gave thanks and blessing, broke the bread, and distributed to the disciples; He took a cup of wine, gave thanks and blessing, and distributed to His disciples (Matthew 26:26–28; Mark 14:22–24; Luke 22:19–20; 1 Corinthians 11:23–26). It is clear from the narrative in 1 Corinthians 11:23–26 that St. Paul is basing himself upon a traditional formula which was always said in much the same accustomed way. He can describe it as that which was "handed on" in the Church as a recognized and authoritative tradition (v. 23). The formula he uses is apparently an attempt to weave into one all the different words and actions which the Church remembered as associated with our Lord's institution, and which are recorded in the Gospels.[6] It will be remembered, however, that the apostle does not derive his account from our written Gospels, for 1 Corinthians was written first, and is the oldest as well as the fullest written witness.

A question which has engaged the mind of some critics is whether our Lord did indeed intend at His Last Supper to found a permanent sacramental rite. It is difficult to prove unambiguously from any recorded word of Scripture that this was in His mind, though the Church has traditionally found this sanction in the phrase "this do ye, as oft as ye shall drink it" of 1 Corinthians 11:25. However, the New Testament was not written to answer modern historical or controversial questions, but to instruct the faith of believers. It is not concerned to argue the case that our Lord intended to institute the Eucharist at His Last Supper, and that this Eucharist is the permanent and distinctive Christian act of worship. This much is the working assumption of the New Testament writers, and the circumstance that the case is never argued is the clearest evidence that all the Christians were agreed on this. If acceptance of the Eucharist had been a belief which was first developed in one part of the Church, and then gradually spread to the whole, there would naturally have been in the New Testament marks of controversy over this issue. As there are none we may be assured that the Eucharist was an original part of the Christian message and institution, going back to the first apostles.

The general background of Christ's teaching on the Eucharist is that the sacrament is the new Passover appropriate to the New Israel (see p. 141). Of old times the tribes of Israel had been delivered from bondage in Egypt by the hand of the Lord at the Red Sea, and this deliverance had constituted them into a disciplined and incorporate nation. And of the Passover it was written, "And this day shall be unto you for a memorial; and ye shall keep it a feast to the Lord throughout your generations" (Exodus 12:14). It is a fundamental misunderstanding and impoverishment of Hebrew thought to suppose that a "memorial" is merely a historic *memento*, which by the aid of imaginative symbolism takes the worshipper back to the past in pious sentiment, and thus, as it were, "helps him to feel he was there." Rather is it that which takes the historic deliverance out of the past and brings it down with present effect to God's people of every succeeding generation. The faithful Israelite who joins in the "memorial" Passover can find that the effect of the Red Sea deliverance has come to him. Thus to partake of the feast is a mark of membership in the redeemed people.

The Eucharist, instituted by our Lord against a background of Passover thought, is the Christian parallel to this. The Messiah has come, bringing the promised kingdom. By His death and resurrection He is to deliver the

---

6 There is some trace remaining of a strain of tradition which apparently placed the blessing of the cup first (Luke 22:17).

people of God from the power of sin, a more signal deliverance than that from the tyranny of Pharaoh (1 Corinthians 5:7–8). The faithful among Israel, who accept Jesus as the suffering Messiah and who share in this deliverance, are to be reconstituted thereby into the new and true people of God, the New Israel of the Church. It is fitting, therefore, that the ancient Passover should be reconstituted as a new and perpetual "memorial" of this Christian deliverance. This thought is expressed in the words recorded by St. Paul: "This do in remembrance of Me" (1 Corinthians 11:24, 25).

The familiar words "in remembrance" often convey to the modern worshipper the notion that the Christian sacrament is simply a means to make the fact of Calvary dreadfully real to the imagination by the appeal of vivid symbolism. As one man may preach the Cross by word of mouth, and another in religious art, so the Eucharist is preaching in solemn drama. All this is plainly a part of the truth about the Church's sacramental worship, and it is an important truth. Nevertheless, this whole circle of thought does not at all do justice to what the New Testament intends by the word "remembrance," and would, indeed, hardly be recognized by the Christian writers of the early centuries as sacramental thought at all. The New Testament Eucharist is more than a symbolic appeal to the imagination. It is a sacramental *operative* symbol, which accomplishes an effect appropriate to the truth symbolized. The "remembrance" exists to take the historic delivering act of Christ crucified and risen, and also the personal presence of the Christ who performs the act, and bring them out of the past, so that they may be real in the experience of the Church in every place, and to the end of time. Those who faithfully celebrate the Eucharist are declaring and making themselves one with Christ as He performs His act, so that they may share the effect of dying with Him, in order to live with Him. The new Passover is the supreme mark of belonging to the New Israel.

It will be asked what is the meaning of Christ's solemn and mysterious words of institution, "This is My body," and "This is My blood," the due recital of which, together with the breaking of the bread and the sharing of the cup, constitutes the essential ritual of the Eucharist. It is very necessary that we come to this subject in a spirit of reverent reserve. If we cannot be sure of understanding fully the genius of a Shakespeare we must not too lightly assume that we can see into the mind of our Lord, particularly at this awesome moment. The exact meaning of Christ's words of institution has all too often been the subject of overconfident dogmatism, and at times of most unseemly controversy around the Table of the Lord. In general no sacramental doctrine which has endeared itself to the devotion of any responsible Christian denomination is to be dismissed as merely false, though some views may contain only partial truth. All schools of Christian thought are on the whole nearer to the truth in what they have positively affirmed of their own experience than in what they have denied in the doctrine of others. Christian doctrine is comprehensive and many-sided.

We therefore pass by controversial discussion as to which modern denominational viewpoint most nearly answers to our Lord's words of institution. The everyday language used by Jesus was Aramaic, and scholars of this ancient language have sought to reconstruct what phrases in it would most likely be translated into the Greek as it occurs in our New Testament. The result of this highly technical study would appear to indicate on the one hand that our Lord's sense was not "This stands for My body," and "This stands for My blood," in the sense of an imaginative reminder. Nor was it "This *is* My body," in the sense that some unseen and intangible entity which theologically may be described as Christ's body is now associated with the consecrated bread. Indeed, the original phrase on our Lord's lips probably did not contain any word representing "is." Rather, what Christ said was: "Behold, the body!" and "Behold, the blood!" The meaning of this is that in the whole eucharistic action, that is, in the recital of the Gospel word in obedience to Christ's command, in the breaking of the bread and the blessing of the cup, and in the partaking of the same, the effect of Christ's saving action by His victorious death is manifested to the Church. In particular, the personal presence of the dying Lord, now risen, is made known to the Church. We submit that among the various denominations, most thoughtful and sensitive believers would profess that something of this sort is what they are *trying* to say about the Eucharist as they use the various traditional doctrinal forms.

The Eucharist is an operative symbol, not so much of the Crucifixion, as of our Lord's sacrifice of victorious sinless obedience which lay behind the Cross. It is significant that what impressed the mind of the New Testament Church was that the Eucharist brought the "remembrance," not so much of Calvary, as of "the night in which He was betrayed" (1 Corinthians 11:23). Christian sentiment has often sought to make of the Eucharist a sacramental enactment of the destruction of Christ's body upon the Cross. The breaking of bread has been spoken of as a symbol of the tearing of His flesh, the pouring of the wine a figure of the shedding of His blood. In the last resort this comparison is not altogether appropriate and convincing. When St. Paul speaks of the sacramental bread he does not refer to it as that which is torn apart, but as that which is the union of many separate grains of wheat, a symbol of the unity of the Church in Christ (1 Corinthians 10:17). Had our Lord wished to ordain a sacramental re-enactment of the destruction of His body he could doubtless have adapted the symbolism of the slaughter of the Passover lamb. Actually what He left was a sacramental re-enactment of the Supper of the dark betrayal night in which He resolved to go to His death, and in which supremely He prayed the prayer of obedient submission to the Heavenly Father (Luke 22:39–42). Thus, if we may venture to read our Lord's mind, the Eucharist is the sacrament of His victorious sacrifice of sinless obedience. The Church cannot make herself one with the Lord as He dies, in a literal sense. The death of the incarnate Son was a mysterious and unique event. What the Church can and must do in her sacramental worship is to make herself one with her Lord as He *obeys*. In the Eucharist He comes to us, that we may go with Him as He offers His sacrifice of sinless obedience, and so have access to God.

Finally, the Bible makes it plain that both the Passover and the Eucharist look forward to God's deliverance, as well as backward. It is the paradoxical tragedy of the world that, though God has performed His historic saving act and redeemed His people, yet they are still oppressed by the power of evil. The Passover looked back to a great deliverance at the Red Sea, and proclaimed Israel to be a nation. Yet not all the people were righteous, and the nation was conquered first by one, then by another, pagan tyrant. Therefore the Hebrew people, as they observed the memorial of the Passover, were still looking for the fulfillment of the divine promise implicit in the first deliverance. They were awaiting the Messiah who would set up God's kingdom in open glory, in deed and in fact. The same is true of the Eucharist. It proclaims that the promised Messiah has come in the person of the Lord Jesus, and has brought the kingdom. Nevertheless, the kingdom, though authentically present to those who have the eye of faith to see it, is as yet only as "a grain of mustard seed" (Mark 4:30–32), containing the promise of a fuller divine deliverance. Therefore the Eucharist looks forward to the day when the kingdom shall be fully come, and the power of sin and evil entirely destroyed in the world. The Messiah will rule not as now, in the mystery of humiliated and suffering love, but in open glory as the acknowledged master of all human affairs (1 Corinthians 11:26). The persecuted "little flock" (Luke 12:32) which unites in the act of Christian worship, and as it meets finds itself "not many wise men after the flesh, not many mighty" (1 Corinthians 1:26), possesses in its Eucharist a pledge of the coming Day of God, when the Church shall embrace all the nations of the world. Indeed, that future perfected community is now possessed in reality, though in miniature, in the fellowship of the Church. Thus the Eucharist unites the end of time with the beginning, and gives a full view of what is meant by "remembrance."

C. Theological Terms Used of the Eucharist

Some of the chief words which have been used in connection with the Eucharist in Christian theology may now be defined.

1. SACRAMENT OF THE LORD'S SUPPER. This term emphasizes the unity in thought, intention, and spiritual experience which exists between the rite ordained by our Lord and the Church's present act of worship. The name reminds us that we are doing now what He then did, and what was done in the New Testament Church. This term therefore sums up the whole body of original New Testament sacramental doctrine.

2. HOLY COMMUNION. This word emphasizes the present experience of

the Church as she meets for eucharistic worship. It bears both a general and a particular sense. In all acts of Christian worship the faithful find the promised presence of their Lord, and in Him have fellowship one with another. The faith and experience of the Church is that this, the distinctive act of Christian worship, can be used by the Holy Spirit to grant this experience of communion with Christ in the most prevailing and precious of all ways. However, and in particular, to receive in faith the consecrated bread and wine is the due climax of the sacramental action. Thus actually to eat of that bread and to drink of that cup, that is, to *communicate,* is for each believer the operative symbol whereby he receives his share of that which Christ accomplished for the Church by His atoning death (1 Corinthians 10:16). In this special manner, therefore, the Eucharist is a sharing of Christ. It is the Holy Communion.

3. THE SACRAMENT OF UNITY. The Eucharist is the Church's act whereby she makes herself one with her dying and risen Lord. As there is but one Lord, all who identify themselves with Him are united in one spiritual body (Romans 12:5; 1 Corinthians 12:12; Galatians 3:27–28; Ephesians 4:4–5). Thus the Eucharist is not only the supreme means of communion between the faithful and their Lord; it is also the supreme means of the communion of all the faithful, one with another. To join together in the sacrament is the eminent mark of the unity of the Church (1 Corinthians 10:17). The unity expressed is not only the unity of the members of the local worshipping congregation, though this is important. The congregation which celebrates the Eucharist does so by virtue of its membership in the universal Church, and as representing locally the universal Church. By doing so it recollects and rejoices in its membership in the whole Church, on earth and in heaven, and proclaims itself to be a part of the universal Church. Thus the Eucharist is the sacrament of unity.

From this principle follow a number of important consequences. To join in the Eucharist is a pledge of unreserved allegiance, not only to Christ, but to His Church. Thus to be a communicant is the proper token of pledged membership in the Church, of full status. Similarly for Christian congregations or organizations of congregations to welcome each other's members to their Eucharists is the token that they unreservedly regard one another as portions of the one Church. Denominations which are thus "in communion" with one another profess that any divergences between them of teaching, discipline, order, and organization are in nonessentials only. Similarly, for denominations not to be "in full communion" with one another is the express and painful token that they feel some serious degree of reserve about one another's Christian standing.

Thus the true aim of the ecumenical movement is not so much organizational as spiritual and sacramental. The purpose is not to achieve a "merger," on the dubious theory that a large organization is more efficient in the service of God than a small one. The aim is to spread among the denominations such understanding of essential doctrine, such acceptance of essential order and discipline, and such growth of Christian charity that they may have the confidence to establish unreserved ecclesiastical communion with one another. However, this sacramental recognition is plainly not to be confined to an occasional and more or less formal ecclesiastical contact between religious organizations which in their normal and routine activity exist in a state of rivalry, or even of discord. This would be to make a mockery of the sacrament of unity! It is all too easy for diverse religious organizations which nominally are part of the same Christian communion practically to be separated by the spirit of rivalry and competition, and this is almost as great a scandal as the open and avowed ecclesiastical breach. To join in communion together must be the effective token of real goodwill in Christ, of genuine preparedness to learn from one another, and of regular, practical, brotherly cooperation in the work of the Church. This presupposes some effective degree of "organic union," visible and convincing to the world, though this is not the same as uniformity of worship or centralization of organization.

4. THE REAL PRESENCE. The traditional doctrine of the Real Presence is a strong affirmation of the experience of the Church that the universal presence of Christ is apprehended with unique power and certainty in the Eucharist. It certainly does not involve the naïve notion that Christ can be confined to a place. Our Lord in His risen and glorified humanity does not exist in space, and is always and equally "present" to every soul that calls upon Him. By the "presence" of Christ in worship is meant that at a certain time and place our Lord makes His universal presence effectually known to certain persons. It is the faith of the Church that Christ manifests His universal presence to the Church in a special manner in the Eucharist, which is thus seen to be the climax of all the means of grace.

We judge, however, that it is an error to suppose that in the Eucharist our Lord saves men in a different and superior manner than when He comes to man in the nonsacramental means of grace. The grace of God is the undeserved favor of God and the saving power of God, and whenever God loves and acts it is fully the work of grace. Grace is not a "thing," which can exist in different qualities. The special character of sacramental grace is not that it is "more saving" in effect, but that it is specially and securely pledged to man. Christ makes the very same saving presence known to the Church in praise and in prayer and in preaching, as in the Eucharist. Yet it is the profound religious conviction of traditional Christianity that in the sacrament He rises above the limitations and variability of human infirmity, and conveys His grace irrespective of the subjective conditions of religious emotion. Because the Eucharist is the special pledge of union with Him, He has pledged Himself with a unique guarantee to be there, which guarantee frail man can implicitly trust. Those who sincerely and expectantly take the sacramental pledge may on occasion not be able to "feel" anything.

Rather are they moved by conviction, by duty, and by discipline, and they may sometimes be painfully aware that at the moment they are unable to make any special response. Yet when from the viewpoint of later experience they look upon the long-continued practice of the Church's sacramental life, they find themselves unshakably aware that Christ *was* with His people, and *did* fulfill His promise. Thus it is not a special *kind* of grace, but a specially secure and *objective promise* of grace which is the virtue of the sacrament. The expression of this truth is the doctrine of the sacramental Real Presence of Christ.

5. TRANSUBSTANTIATION. This is the traditional Roman Catholic doctrine used to expound the character of the Real Presence of Christ in the Eucharist, or Mass. It is an attempt to express in the categories of the medieval Scholastic philosophy the secure and objective character of the sacramental manifestation of the presence of Christ. The medieval School-men drew a distinction between the outward "accidents" of any object (which correspond roughly to what in modern scientific terminology would be described as the chemical and physical properties of the object) and its "substance." The latter was conceived of as a subtle and invisible under-lying principle of existence which made the object what it was. The doctrine of the Roman Catholic Church is that at the consecration of the elements the invisible "substance" of the bread and wine is changed by divine power into the "substance" of the body and blood of the Lord, although the outward "accidents" remain the same. This change of substance is described as transubstantiation.

It is an error to charge Roman Catholic doctrine with teaching that there is a *material* change of bread and wine into flesh and blood, in the accepted modern sense of the word "material." The "accidents" remain the same, and the Scholastic notion of "accidents" most nearly corresponds to the idea of the material. The change is regarded as of an invisible and intangible underlying essence, which can only be described as non-material. Nor is it correct to charge this doctrine, when rightly understood at least, with teaching that the Lord is in a "place." The Roman Catholic Church shares the generally accepted Christian doctrine that the risen and ascended Christ is universally present. However, it is taught that the sacramental means by which the universal presence is most particularly and surely made known to the Church are the consecrated bread and wine as such, and these "means" *are* in a place. Therefore, while the consecrated elements remain in the church, the Lord is "present." This is a distinction from the more general doctrine of the sacramental Real Presence outlined in section (4) above, where the means of the manifestation of the presence of Christ is regarded as the sacramental action taken as a whole, but not the consecrated elements apart from the action of the worshipping con-gregation.

This doctrine has been the subject of violent controversy, which unhappily has done much to make the sacrament of unity into a leading occasion of Christian disunity. So charged is the issue with inherited group emotion that it is sometimes hard for the parties to bring themselves to look at the matter dispassionately. This is the more reason why the effort should be made. The devout Roman Catholic, who has experienced a deep and Christian sense of the divine presence in the Mass, and who has been taught to associate this awesome experience with the doctrine of transubstantiation, finds it hard to understand that a devout Protestant can also have the sense of the divine presence, and yet deny this doctrine. He instinctively feels that the Protestant must be seriously deficient in his understanding of Christian worship, and that in his blindness he is rejecting or even assailing that which is very sacred. Equally instinctively the Protestant, who may have been taught to reject the doctrine of transubstantiation as a dangerous and materialist superstition, feels that the Roman Catholic Church has contaminated the worship of the Church with magic.

We are not arguing here that there is no effective difference between the two sides. There is a real difference of emphasis between Roman Catholic and Protestant, but it becomes a cause of ill will and spiritual reserve chiefly when each party does not understand what the other is trying to say. It is unfitting to talk lightly of "material superstition." In passing it should be noticed that the actual Canon of the Roman Mass does not itself require a belief in this doctrine, though this belief is a definite part of the doctrine of the Roman Catholic Church. Indeed, the Canon, which contents itself with reciting our Lord's words of institution, is older than the formulated doctrine of transubstantiation.

Protestant objections to the doctrine of transubstantiation are as follows: The Scholastic distinction between "substance" and "accidents" was not known in New Testament times, and therefore it can easily prove misleading to interpret the New Testament narrative in these categories. It is safer theologically, and devotionally more reverent, to be content with the New Testament doctrine as it stands, and not to seek to expound the exact manner of Christ's sacramental presence. Furthermore, in the period prior to the Protestant Reformation the idea was commonly held that, as the consecrated elements were truly the body and blood of the Lord, the sacrifice of the Mass was in some sense a repetition of Calvary, and thus added to the effect of Christ's saving work. This in turn gave rise to the doctrine that the Church could earn merit by the due saying of Masses. The Protestant Reformers strongly condemned this latter doctrine as inconsistent with the doctrine of salvation by grace, and therefore reacted also against the associated sacramental doctrine.

Other objections spring not so much from the actual doctrine itself, but from the way in which it can be, and has been, misunderstood by simple believers not competent in theology. Although the term "substance" may have meant one thing in the technical language of learned medieval theologians, it can come to mean something quite different in the common parlance of simple people. The word "substance" ordinarily conveys the notion of "the actual solid thing itself." Many Protestants therefore feel that the term "transubstantiation" invites the uninstructed to misunderstand the Roman Catholic doctrine as teaching a gross and material change in the elements. This in turn conveys the notion that the mere presence of the consecrated elements in the Church in some way brings a divine blessing to the congregation, perhaps without too much regard for their faith and morals. Therefore, the antique term "transubstantiation" should be avoided.

The informed Roman Catholic theologian will be quick to reply that these are misunderstandings of his doctrine, and that a doctrinal statement is not necessarily to be avoided because it is susceptible of misunderstanding, for this is possible with every system. It is indeed possible for a Roman Catholic to argue as follows, by way of a mediating statement. The decree of the Lateran Council of 1215, declaring the doctrine of transubstantiation to be a part of the faith of the Roman Catholic Church, is to be upheld. The Scholastic categories of "substance" and "accidents" were used at that time as the accepted means of expression, and in terms of those categories to have denied transubstantiation would have been false to the Catholic understanding of the sacramental Real Presence. Thus the Council was not in error in affirming this doctrine at that time. However, these categories of "substance" and "accidents" are not necessarily the only ones which can be used to express the essential faith of the Church. Today other and better terms might possibly be found to express to the modern mind the same fundamental devotional intention.

6. THE COMMEMORATIVE SACRIFICE. The incarnate Son as man offered up the sacrifice of sinless obedience to the Father, which enables all those who make themselves one with their great High Priest to have access to God (see pp. 80–81). The Eucharist, furthermore, is the act by which the Church makes herself one with Christ as He does this. There is, therefore, both a difference between Calvary and the Eucharist, and also a most significant parallel.

The sacrifice of the incarnate Son was a unique divine act which has transformed the situation of the whole race. There can never be anything else like it, and it is sufficient for the needs of all men. Nevertheless, both the Cross and the Eucharist express the fundamental sacrificial principle of "a God-appointed means by which man may offer himself to God in consecration and have spiritual access to God." The former is the sacrificial principle expressed once for all in the divine saving act. The latter is the sacrificial principle expressed and ever renewed in the experience of the Church, on account of that unique divine saving act. Thus the Eucharist, though not a *repetition* of Christ's atoning sacrifice, is the Church's "commemorative sacrifice." This term may perhaps be illustrated by comparison with a great piece of music. The first composition is a unique work of creative art, never to be repeated. Nevertheless, the composer has left the score behind, and to play this through again is likewise a work of creative art, though derived from the first. It is the means by which the effect of the first unique work is mediated again and yet again to later times. These succeeding renderings are "commemorations." So the commemorative sacrifice of the Eucharist is, as it were, "playing through the score again" of Christ's unique and sufficient sacrifice of the Cross. It is the means appointed by God for the realization in the Church's present experience of the effect of Christ's sacrifice.

Readings

Baillie, D. M., *The Theology of the Sacraments*. New York: Charles Scribner's Sons, 1957.

Buttrick, G., *Prayer*. New York: Abingdon Press, 1942.

Cullmann, O., and F. J. Leenhardt, *Essays on the Lord's Supper,* trans. J. G. Davies. Richmond, Va.: John Knox Press, 1958.

Dix, G., *The Shape of the Liturgy*. Westminster: Dacre Press, 1949. (Historical Study.)

Lampe, G. W. H., *The Seal of the Spirit*. London: Longmans, Green & Company, Ltd., 1951. (Baptism and Confirmation.)

Quick, O. C., *The Christian Sacraments*. New York and London: Harper & Row, Publishers, 1927.

Chapter Eight

The Written Word

The Holy Ghost—who spake by the prophets

I. The Witness to the Christ-Centered Faith

Christian worship and preaching are delivered from subjectivity and lifted above the level of mere autosuggestion and mass suggestion by the circumstance that the center of all is Christ. When Christians assemble they are not seeking to stir up their own natural powers of mind and spirit by contact with one another, but expecting that Christ will use these natural powers as the means by which He makes Himself known. Furthermore, Christ is both the Christ of history, who was born, lived, spoke, died, and rose again, and also the living Christ of continuing Christian experience. These two are one. It cannot be too strongly emphasized that the Christ of Christian faith is not a "Christ-idea," which has been framed by the mind of the Church to symbolize certain spiritual truths. He is the Christ who at a certain place and time performed a saving act, which act has brought into the world a divine power not to be explained in terms of human personality.

Acceptance of the historical facts about Christ is not of itself saving Christian faith, though it is the foundation of faith. Thus, some even who looked into the empty tomb did not believe. Those who are confronted by the living Christ in the experience of the Church and in personal experience, are they to whom are granted saving faith. In this sense, the Christ known to the Church is "the Christ of faith," and not simply "the Christ of history." Nevertheless, personal faith in "the Christ of faith" can hardly endure without acceptance of the foundation of this experience in "the Christ of history" (see pp. 38–39).

These two kindred principles, that the Christian religion is an historical religion, and that it is a Christ-centered religion, require us to consider a further special aspect of the means of grace. This is the Christian doctrine of the record which preserves for the Church both her knowledge of the facts about Christ and the portrait of the personality of Christ. This record is the Holy Scripture. Thus it is a guiding principle of all true Christian worship and preaching that it is scriptural worship and scriptural preaching.

II. The Inspiration of the Bible

It is important to understand the nature and origin of a book which occupies this central place in the life of the Church. This is the more so because the divine inspiration and the authority of the Bible have become at times the subject of misunderstanding and of controversy. Ill-advised claims on behalf of the inspiration of Scripture have sometimes produced their unfortunate reaction in a virtual denial of this truth, and in the dismissal of the conception of the authority of the Bible. Among scholars and experts the Scripture has sometimes been treated as no more than an important "source document" in the study of Christian origins. This is a radical departure from the acknowledged Christian position. The general body of believers has often been disturbed by the erroneous impression that modern science and biblical scholarship have in some way dethroned the Bible as the book of God.

We have already defined the meaning of the term "inspiration" (see pp. 24–25). It is the quickening and stimulation of man's natural powers of mind and spirit by the indwelling Holy Spirit, to enable him more fully and clearly to understand, and to declare, the revelation which God is making known. Divine inspiration does not suspend the operation of the natural human faculties, but lifts them above that spiritual infirmity which is natural to sinful man so that they may more fully act as God originally intended. The inspired man, therefore, is not a man "lifted out of himself," but the fully *human* man, the man who is fully rational, morally responsible, and intelligent in spiritual things. All great art and creative writing is to some extent the work of divine inspiration, but it is the faith of the Church that the inspiration of Holy Scripture is the supreme example of this process. Certainly many of the writers both of the Old and of the New Testament were profoundly aware that they were writing because God had in this way laid His hand upon them and given them something from Himself to declare (Isaiah 6:7–8; Jeremiah 1:4–10; Ezekiel 2:1–3, 3:4–11; Amos 7:14–15; 1 Corinthians 2:9–13; Galatians 1:11–12; Ephesians 3:1–4; Revelation 1:10–11, 19).

The authority of the Bible consists essentially in its contents, rather than in the manner of its writing. The manner in which the book was composed under the guidance of the Spirit is of interest to the Church, but it is the actual message from God which is of importance. The special place of the Bible in the Church lies in the fact that it gives the essential, the sole, and the sufficient witness to the facts about Christ. In the Old Testament there is the story of the historical preparation of the people to whom Christ came, and the account therefore of the religious and moral thought forms of the people among whom He moved.

The New Testament is still more directly a witness to Christ, for it is the sole and sufficient account of the essential facts about Christ—His birth, His personality and character, His acts, His teaching, His death, resurrection, and ascension. In this sense Christ, who is the Word of God and the central subject of Christian preaching, is "contained in the Scripture of the Old and New Testaments." The New Testament also gives the record of the creative witness to the meaning of these facts for Christian faith. This is a witness of faith which, because it is the first in time and made by those who, historically speaking, knew Christ in a way no others ever can, is determinative for the witness of faith in all succeeding Christian generations. It is this unique content of witness to Christ which to the Church makes the Bible entirely different from all other works of Christian devotion or theology, no matter how true and divinely inspired they may be.

Summary of Divergence: Doctrines of Scriptural Inspiration

a. Allegorical

This is the view characteristic of the ancient Church, though to some extent it still lives on in traditional Christian circles alongside later views. It is assumed that the inspired writers were guided by the Holy Spirit as to the very form, wording, and literary character of their composition, so that it is possible to argue theological truth from these forms. Furthermore, the writers were so lifted above normal human faculty that they were able to utter oracles containing forecasts, often mysterious and veiled, of events in the life of Christ, though this was far in the future. However, the emphasis in ancient exegesis was not upon the significance of historical detail in the narrative, though this was not denied. The Scripture was read, by the method of allegory, as a series of symbolically appropriate pictures of Christian truth. A particular example of this approach was the finding of "types of Christ" in the Old Testament. Thus it is affirmed that the inward and "spiritual" meaning of Scripture is of a higher order than the merely literal and factual.

This method comes to its fullest development in the traditional doctrine that corresponding to the threefold nature of man—body, mind, and spirit—there is an ascending threefold sense of Scripture. The lowest, and, as it were, "bodily" sense of Scripture is the literal and historical. So we may read Genesis 22:1–14 as a narrative, that Abraham was prepared to offer Isaac in sacrifice. Next there is the moral sense, corresponding to the mind in man. Thus this passage displays an example of obedience to God which ought to be followed. Yet the really Christian and most precious sense, which alone lights up the meaning of the Scripture, is the "spiritual." This story is "a type of Christ." On this mount of sacrifice the Temple later stood, the place of the Old Testament sacrifices. It was the place also of the Lord's death, when the full meaning is seen of Abraham's prophetic oracle: "My son, God will provide Himself a lamb." This example is typical of ancient exegesis, which was fertile in reading the Scripture as a source of Christian doctrine and edification, but at the price of the danger of fanciful subjectivity.

b. Literal

This school of thought, though not unknown in antiquity, has chiefly been characteristic of orthodox and conservative Protestantism. The motive has been to emphasize as strongly as possible the clear, self-sufficient, and objective authority of Scripture against any school of thought which would give undue weight to the authority of ecclesiastical interpretation in the approach to Scripture. The tendency has been to emphasize the spiritual value of the literal and factual accuracy of the text of Scripture. This principle can be applied in various degrees. Some of this school can allow considerable room in the composition of Scripture for the play of human personality and the mental background of the times, so long as its self-sufficient objective authority is affirmed. The strictest doctrine is that of complete verbal inspiration, by which it is affirmed that the Holy Spirit so completely guided every word of the Biblical writers that the Scripture is virtually the absolute dictation of God.

c. Historico-Critical

This view is concerned to determine so far as possible the sense which was in the mind of the biblical writers as they wrote. This alone is considered the legitimate meaning of Scripture. Applied Christian allegorical interpretations are rejected as unscientific. The widest play is allowed for the free human personality and idiosyncrasy of the writers, and that they must all be understood to speak in terms of the thought forms of their own day and culture. Some critics go so far as to treat the text of Scripture simply as one source document among many others, so that the traditional sense of the authority of canonical Scripture is virtually lost. To the devout scholar of this method, however, it is evident that many of the biblical writers possessed faculties of creative genius of the highest order. Nevertheless, these vary in kind and in degree from chapter to chapter. Nor are these creative faculties different in kind from those which have gone to the composition of other great but nonbiblical literary works. Furthermore, some biblical writers are more spiritually sensitive and mature, more obediently led by the influence of the Holy Spirit, than others. This spiritual leading, furthermore, is not different in kind from that which has gone to the composition of nonbiblical Christian works.

Thus, when the manner of composition is considered, the Bible is one venerable book among others, to the Christian supreme in its class, no doubt, but not different in kind. In this sense of the word its "inspiration" may be compared to that of other books of wisdom or devotion. It is different only in degree and manner. The difference in the Bible, whereby Scripture stands apart from other books, is in its contents. For the Scripture to be fully authoritative in its content, as a witness to Christ the Word of God, does not require that its writers be lifted to a superhuman standard in their composition. It only requires that their human faculties were sufficiently guided by the Holy Spirit that they were substantially reliable witnesses.

Thus, by way of comparison, the radio transmission of an SOS message upon which the lives of men depend may be marred to some extent by interference or static. Yet provided the medium of transmission is clear enough to convey the message, the message comes with full urgency, which is not increased even if the transmission happens to be technically perfect. A reliable medium is required, but the authority is in the content of the message, not the medium. So it is with the Bible. The true task of Christian scholarship in relation to the religious authority of the Bible is not the fruitless effort to prove that it was written in a "different" and superhuman way. It is to vindicate its *content*.

III. The Canon of Scripture

The Greek word "canon" means a rule, or measuring rod. The canon of Scripture is the list of books recognized by the Church as authoritative Scripture, and as such set apart from all other books. The mark of canonical Scripture is that it may be read in Church as a regular part of Christian worship and quoted in proof of doctrine. Clearly, any doctrine of the authority of Scripture must include an exposition of the authority of the canon, for a decision must be made and justified as to which books are authoritative. This is best illustrated by the historical process by which certain writings have become regarded as canonical Scripture in Judaism and in the Church.

In general, the doctrine of an authoritative canon is a salient example of the belief that the Holy Spirit effectually guides the Church. Those who composed the biblical narratives (very often originally in the form of oral tradition, before it was recorded in writing) were aware that the Holy Spirit was moving them to set down what they felt was of high religious importance. Yet as they wrote they would hardly have looked upon it as different from other and "human" religious composition. Nevertheless, the passage of centuries showed that these writings could meet the searching test of long-continued experience. Many books of religious worth made a partial appeal to the community. They were valued perhaps by a section, and for a time. Nevertheless, they never rose beyond the status of religious literature. Other books made a more significant appeal. They increased in repute until they were accepted by the whole, or virtually the whole, of the community, as of the highest degree of religious value.

The long passage of time saw this estimate endure, and be confirmed by the experience of succeeding generations, until respect deepened into a characteristic traditional veneration. By the force of traditional judgment certain books were thus set apart from others, until the appeal could be made that a certain text is authoritative because it occurs in the sacred collection. The original sanction of the repute of the writer, or of the immediate appeal which the book made, is now superseded by this traditional sanction. The final stage is when the verdict of the whole community is officially ratified by ecclesiastical authority. In Judaism a group of rabbis, in the ancient Christian Church a council of bishops, pronounced that certain books were by long, universal, and established consent regarded as canonical Scripture.

This final stage is not to be regarded as an external and artificial process of "censorship," whereby ecclesiastical authority suppresses some books and adds its authority to others. The history of the canon shows a much more profound and spiritual process. The books were set apart by the place which they established for themselves, and authority then ratified the verdict. As we, from the vantage-point of time, look back and compare the books which were accepted as canonical with those which were set aside, we may have confidence that the early Church was guided by the Holy Spirit in the choice which was actually made. Again we see that God granted the spiritual through the natural. The process took place through a human medium, and was not inerrant. There were some "borderline cases" of choice. Some books were accepted as canonical more readily than others, and in the case of some of the minor books both of the Old and New Testaments it is possible for the critic to dispute whether there are not some other noncanonical books of equal intrinsic merit. Nevertheless, the general and substantial judgment of the Church is to be upheld as an authoritative act of guidance by the Holy Spirit.

A glance at the actual historical process illustrates the general principle that the venerable is the canonical. The classification of Luke 24:44 sets forth the threefold division of the Jewish Scriptures, as reckoned by the rabbis. The five books of the Law (Genesis–Deuteronomy) were, and still are, regarded by Judaism as canonical Scripture to the most eminent degree. They were accepted as a body of canonical Scripture by about 400 B.C. The secondary division called "the prophets," which in Judaism includes

Joshua, 1 and 2 Samuel, and 1 and 2 Kings (as Christians count them), as well as the greater and the minor prophets (apart from Daniel), was canonized later, about 200 B.C. The "sacred writings," comprising the remaining books of the Old Testament proper, became regarded in the succeeding period as in some sense Scripture, largely because of the use made of them in the Jewish worship and festivals. However, in the period when the Jews of the Dispersion increasingly came to speak and write in Greek, the accumulation of religious books still continued. Consequently the Septuagint, or ancient Greek translation of the Old Testament, contains more books than does the Hebrew canon. The traditionally minded rabbis maintained a certain reserve about these more recent books. This is the part of the Bible commonly known to us as the Apocrypha. It is noteworthy that among the Dead Sea Scrolls Hebrew originals have been found to some of these books of the Apocrypha, which traditionally have only circulated in the Church in Greek or Latin translation.

The Church of the early centuries commonly used the Septuagint, and is found to quote the Apocrypha as "Scripture," in the same way as the books of the Hebrew Old Testament. However, some of the more learned Christian fathers, and in particular St. Jerome (A.D. 347–419), the translator of the Hebrew Old Testament and Greek New Testament into the Latin Vulgate, were aware of this distinction of canonicity between the ancient Hebrew Bible and the newer Greek Apocrypha. Nevertheless, the Latin Vulgate, containing as it does the Apocrypha, was used as authoritative Scripture by the Western Church down to the Reformation, as it still is by the Roman Catholic Church. The Protestants were in general glad to revive the ancient distinction between the older and fully authoritative Hebrew Old Testament and the later Greek Apocrypha, largely because the leading traditional "proof texts" for prayers for the dead, and so forth, occurred in this latter part. The Church of England, however, as in some other things, established a compromise. Passages from the Apocrypha were continued in the lectionary to be read in public worship, but the books of the Apocrypha are not to be used for the establishment of doctrine.

The same process by which the venerable graduates upwards into the canonical may be seen to take place in relation to the New Testament writings. Where in the New Testament itself "the Scriptures" are referred to, the Jewish Scriptures are intended. In the first Christian writings after the New Testament this usage is continued, and the Old Testament is alone quoted expressly as "Scripture." However, the words of our Lord are also cited as a ruling authority, and the writings of the apostles likewise as an authority. Nevertheless, this apostolic authority is not yet that of a traditional canonical book, but a personal authority. The New Testament writings are of authority in this early period because they are the substitute for the personal presence of an apostle, who is the primary witness to the gospel. Hence is derived the traditional Christian doctrine that the New Testament canon is constituted out of "apostolic writings," that is, the writings of apostles, or of the immediate disciples of apostles, who are to be regarded as virtually their amanuenses. The leading books of the New Testament rapidly gained place during the second century as a distinct body of authoritative writings, which might be read in Christian worship alongside the ancient Scripture. By the fourth century our present New Testament canon was virtually fixed and accepted, and in the Council of A.D. 692 was expressly ratified.

IV. The Old Testament Scripture

A. Historical and Linguistic Value

The unique value of the Old Testament as Christian Scripture is that it is the story of the historical preparation of the ancient people of God for the coming of Christ. Here is the principle that Christianity is a religion embedded in history. The Christian Faith carries with it a system of thought and of ethics, but essentially it is a religion of redemption, founded upon the saving acts which God has performed in history. These acts form a long historical series, leading one from another up to the climax in the Incarnation, death, and resurrection of Christ, and proceeding down from that climax, since that time, in the acts of the Holy Spirit in the Church. It is impossible fully to understand the Christian climax without a view of the whole process. Therefore to the Church the Old Testament is Scripture speaking of Christ. The essential element in the Old Testament is that it is the story of God's choice of the chosen people at the beginning; of their deliverance from bondage, which constituted them into a nation; of the formation of their national and religious institutions; and of the subsequent long and often painful process of their education, through historical experience, in understanding of the nature and ways of God.

In this account we again see that God gives the spiritual through the natural. Most impartial scholars would allow that the history, considered as history, is not inerrant as to fact. It is history composed according to the mentality and methods of antiquity, and not according to modern critical and scientific methods. Scholars of the Old Testament have to make allowance for this. Nevertheless, the historical narrative is such that it bears effective witness to the divine process in history. Thus the deliverance at the Red Sea is certainly not described as it would be by a modern secular historian, but an authentic witness is preserved that a deliverance did take place, and in particular, an interpretation is given of the religious meaning of this event. Furthermore, it is easy to regard too lightly the value of the Old Testament narrative as a historical source in the modern sense of the word. Many critics have made haste to dismiss this or that narrative as "unreliable," or "legendary," only to discover that later historical and archaeological research has wholly or partially vindicated the biblical record.

An important aspect of this value of the Old Testament is the linguistic. Our Lord spoke to the people of the Old Testament, using their thought forms. The first apostles, who interpreted the meaning of Christ, employed the same Old Testament thought forms. Therefore the meaning of phrases and words in the New Testament cannot be fully and accurately grasped without an understanding of what these words mean in the Jewish background of Christianity. There are some elements in the New Testament which are perhaps to be interpreted, at least in part, by reference to the Gentile background of the ancient Church. By and large, however, the New Testament is to be understood in light of the Old. Thus many leading words in the Greek New Testament, such as "the righteousness of God," "the wrath of God," "propitiation," and so forth, will be misunderstood if they are given the meaning they would normally carry in pagan Greek literature. The Greek Old Testament gives the correct sense.

B. Progressive Revelation

If the Old Testament is the record of a process of historical education and discipline, some lessons will be found more advanced than others. The point of departure for the process of education was the religious outlook natural to antiquity. The Hebrew people started their history as one Semitic tribe among many in the Middle East, having a tribal religion similar to that of other kindred peoples (Joshua 24:2). By the end of the process they revealed themselves to be the people of the prophets, a nation with a unique genius for religion. However, there are many passages in the Old Testament which represent the partial process of growth and education, where the primitive background and the new lesson are mingled. Thus in some Old Testament narratives there are displayed conceptions of God and of His will which are not to be defended as fully Christian.

On the other hand, it is not to be assumed that narratives later in time are necessarily more advanced in spiritual understanding. Spiritual religion does not simply "develop" in an evolutionary manner. The disciples of great prophetic leaders can painfully lag behind, so that religious movements may deteriorate and fall into corruption, as well as advance, with the passage of time. Therefore, the Old Testament as a whole is to be interpreted both in the light of the finest things in it, and in light of the New Testament, with its clearer standards declared by Christ. The Bible, in fact, is not a collection of "proof texts" to be quoted in isolation from one another. It is to be read as a religious whole, as an historical "progressive revelation" in many stages, though all coming from one and the same God.

C. Devotional Value

Pressing close behind the essential historical revelation in value is the devotional treasure of the Old Testament. When it is stated that the ancient Hebrews possessed a unique genius for religion it is not intended that they were all virtuous. The Old Testament itself is full of rebukes for the sins of the people. What they had was a very vivid sense that God is real and important, so that religion is a matter of immense concern. God is sovereign, majestic, active, near. Even if a Hebrew disobeyed God he had a great sense that he was sinning, not merely against tribal taboo or conventional morality, but against a mighty God. This "sense of God" is a leading characteristic of the Biblical narrative, and is the surest mark of its divine inspiration.

For example, compare the Genesis stories symbolizing the creation of the world and the origin of the human race with the parallel stories in pagan mythology. Certain general similarities are to be observed, and one highly significant difference. This is the portrait of God which appears in the biblical narrative. Greek mythology may tellingly symbolize certain truths, and do so with great artistry. Yet the Greek gods, with their infirmities, their faults, and their quarrels, are not such as to command the reverence of the thoughtful and intelligent man. In the biblical narratives there may be found a prescientific and a nonphilosophical view of God, but there is a spiritually adult view of God. He is a great God, of right and truth, who commands the reverence of men. So it is when we come to the story of a military hero like Gideon. This is not told, as are the hero-stories of the Gentiles, to display from what great men the nation is descended, but "to justify the ways of God to men." The Lord is the most important character in the story, and it is told to His glory. This "sense of God" runs through the whole of the Old Testament, and comes to its climax in the splendid devotional poetry of the Psalms and prophets.

An artist looks at an apparently commonplace face or landscape and beholds in it a beauty which less sensitive eyes cannot see. As he paints he enables us to see something of what he can see, so that we come to look upon the object itself to some extent with an artist's eye. In the same way, the Bible looks on every part of life from the point of view of a man to whom God is the most pressing reality of existence. As we follow his meditations, and read his narrative, we begin in his company to look at life from that point of view. We see life no longer from the commonplace point of view, but as it exists under the eye of God. This is the first and indispensable lesson of religion. There are many humane and educated men today who have a much more developed view of the nature of God than did most of the ancient Hebrews. However, He is to them a part of the academic theory of life. They can argue about God to a nicety, but have little comprehension of what it means when one reads: "And the Lord spake unto Moses face to face, as a man speaketh unto his friend" (Exodus 33:11). This is where the Church of all ages, and of today, can learn from the Old Testament. Even narratives which express a less than perfectly Christian view of God are full of the sense of God, and so can teach the sense of God. Thus it is not necessary to vindicate at every point the morality of the stories of the patriarchs, the judges, or even of the prophets. They still make a contribution to Christian devotions.

A leading example of this principle is the use of Scripture in Church service. When the Bible is read in public worship it is read not so much informatively as *liturgically*. Rendered into magnificent, dignified, and poetic English the elevated chapters of the Scripture are read and preached from, and hymns and prayers framed in the thought forms and language of the Bible are used, in order to help the worshipping congregation to *feel* in a certain way. Having caught the sense of solemn awe men begin to exclaim, "Surely the Lord is in this place," and "How dreadful is this place!" (Genesis 28:16, 17). They have then learned the first essential lesson of religion, and can go on to instruction in Christian faith and morals. Herein is the devotional value of the Bible, and not least, of the Old Testament.

D. Prophecy of Christ

The Christian position is that the Scriptures of the Old and New Testaments together form one series, so that each part is to be understood in the light of the other. This doctrine has in Christian tradition been expressed in a particular way, which requires some measure of judicious restatement and modification if it is to be usefully preserved in the modern Church. One of the first great issues which faced the growing Gentile Church of the early centuries was whether it should preserve its living link with its Judaic past. The symbol of this dispute was naturally the position of the venerable Hebrew Scriptures in the Church as Christian Scripture. One of the chief spiritual considerations which guided the Church to keep the Old Testament was the desire to preserve the "argument from prophecy."

From the beginning it was realized that large numbers of passages in the Old Testament, hundreds of years old, could with a little ingenuity and selection be read as forecasts of all sorts of details of the life of Christ, and sometimes most unexpected and mysterious details. This gift of apparently divine prescience was treated as a sure token of the divine inspiration of the Bible, and so of its authority. By way of salient example, the accepted Septuagint text of Isaiah 7:14 read like a forecast of the Virgin Birth of Christ, an event so remarkable that no human mind could have foreseen it. To the ancient Church this demonstrated the divine origin of the prophecy, and the prophecy, thus vindicated as of divine authority, could in turn be used in proof of the Christian doctrine.

Although on the one hand many conservatively minded Christians still feel much of the force of this venerable mode of argument, and it is expressed freely in the liturgy of the Church, it must be admitted that this method of presenting the spiritual continuity of the Old and New Testaments, though immensely convincing to Christian antiquity, is much less so today. The great growth of historical and linguistic knowledge, and of the principles of scientific criticism of ancient narratives, has brought to the Church a much clearer knowledge than she has ever had of the original and historical meaning of all manner of biblical texts, which were previously often most mysterious. This process has in general demonstrated that these traditional Christian "prophetic" meanings are often not what was in the mind of the biblical writers when they composed their narratives. They are secondary meanings which have been read into the text by later Christian faith. To the scientific scholar the Old Testament is no longer a book packed with mysterious forecasts of Christian doctrine, and of details of the life of Christ. It looks as though the validity of the venerable "argument from prophecy" is overthrown.

However, reconsideration indicates that the vital Christian doctrinal interest is to vindicate the spiritual continuity of the historical process by which the religion of the Old Covenant prepared the way for Christ. Christian faith wishes to see the foreseeing wisdom of God at work in history, revealing Himself. The traditional method of stating this interest can be modified or even abandoned, if the interest itself may be preserved.

In the first place, prophecy does speak of the expectation of the Messiah, in general terms, and our Lord did claim to fulfill that expectation. The basis of the Christian faith is that this claim is true. In the second place, our Lord molded much of His teaching and activity in terms of Old Testament messianic prophecy, even to the point on occasion of literally enacting events spoken of in prophetic oracles. Thus in the most notable instance, Zechariah 9:9 had symbolized the nonmilitary character of the expected Messiah by writing of Him as "lowly, and riding upon an ass." As a sign to the people of what manner of Messiah He was, Christ literally rode into Jerusalem upon this unwarlike animal. Thus the idea of the fulfillment of detailed events is not wholly to be excluded. In the third place, however, there is another way in which our Lord "fulfilled" Old Testament prophecy, which to many thoughtful believers may well appear more spiritually satisfying. In the great passages of the Old Testament there are authentic though partial glimpses of great spiritual principles which are perfectly set forth in the person, teaching, and saving work of our Lord. Our Lord fulfilled the Old Testament prophecy in the sense that He filled it to the full. He realized the potentiality of what had been dreamed of by visionaries.

The great example of this, which serves to illuminate others, is our Lord's treatment of the great passage Isaiah 52:13–53:12. From the first days of the Church (Acts 8:30–35) the "Song of the Suffering Servant" has been the key example of "Old Testament prophecy fulfilled." We remember that our Lord Himself gave precedent for the traditional exposition whereby today we cannot read this chapter without thinking of Christ and His atonement.[1] There is thus the highest sanction for the proposition that it may be

---

[1] The Jewish exegetes did not read this passage as referring to a *suffering* Messiah.

devotionally fitting to read a secondary and Christian application into an Old Testament Scripture.

There has been much dispute as to what the original writer meant by "the Servant of the Lord." The usual construction is that he is a personification of Israel, or of the righteous nucleus of Israel, or perhaps of the ideal Israel. In drawing the figure, some actual martyred individual may also be in mind. In this passage the judgment of conventional piety is dismissed, that the overwhelming and repulsive sufferings of God's people are simply the punishment for sin. Rather are God's relatively righteous people suffering to work the blessing of the unrighteous pagans, who behold in amazement this mysterious divine plan. Here in this piece of prophetic insight is a passing glimpse of the principle which the sacrificial sufferings of Christ perfectly exemplified. As He read this passage He saw in it a picture of what He knew His own destiny to be, and so on at least one most significant occasion He expressly applied it to Himself, and to His mission of suffering (Isaiah 53:12 in Luke 22:37).[2] It is doubtless also the chief among the passages referred to in Luke 24:25–27. Thus there is a continuity of spiritual type from Isaiah 53 to our Lord's own view of His messianic death. The same God can be seen at work in both, in the first preparing the way by a partial vision, in the second "fulfilling." This remains the case even if the supposition of detailed forecasts of events in the life of Christ is abandoned.

V. The New Testament Scripture

A. The Apostolic Witness

The supreme treasure in Scripture, which gives the Bible its special place in Christian doctrine and devotion, is that it gives the historic witness to Christ. It is the indispensable, the sole, and the sufficient witness. The essential office of an apostle was to be a witness to the facts about Christ— His life, His teaching, His deeds, His death, and supremely, the fact of His resurrection (Acts 1:21–22). This was the testimony to the saving act of God in Christ, upon which Christian faith rests. As the apostles were taken from the Church by death their unique office as immediate personal witnesses came to an end. As a substitute for, and as a sufficient continuation of, their witness the Church treasured the apostolic writings. This historic witness is the heart of the New Testament.

The interest of the Evangelists in composing the Gospels is not biographical, in the accepted modern sense of the word. They are not recording

---

[2] It is only fair to note that those radical critics who do not accept the general historical character of the Gospel narratives would treat this as an example of an incident constructed by the Church to symbolize its devotion. It would be claimed that the words have been placed on the lips of Jesus so as to create a "prophecy fulfilled." This would apply also to Zechariah 9:9 (p. 194).

data for the purpose of providing raw materials for the authorship of "Lives of Jesus." A modern-style biography of our Lord would give a dispassionate treatment of every part equally of Christ's life and activity, and a clear outline of the order of events, and of the places where things happened. It is well known that the Gospels do not give this. For example, our Lord's early life in Nazareth is passed over in almost complete silence A third of St. Mark's Gospel is devoted to recording the circumstances of Christ's death, which is a curious proportion for a biography. A comparison of the Gospels will show that His teaching is recorded in a variable order, which is plainly due to the Evangelists more than to the course of events. The purpose of the Gospel writers is evangelical rather than biographical. They are recounting such of the facts about Christ as were remembered in the Church because they were important for Christian faith and discipleship, and recounting them in such a way as to bring the reader to Christian faith (John 20:30–31).

It must be clearly kept in mind, however, that this does not of itself serve to hold in question the authenticity and value, as biographical evidence, of the facts recorded. It only means that there is no secure evidence for a *complete* and orderly biography. The Evangelists were well aware that theirs was an historical faith, the advancement and preservation of which depended on the recording of facts (Luke 1:1–4). Unless some other evidence is brought forward to impugn their accuracy, the mere fact that their interest is evangelical rather than biographical does not of itself assail the historicity of the Gospels.

Another important circumstance which is at times rather overlooked in current discussion of the New Testament is that the ethical teaching of our Lord is an integral part of the Gospel message. It is the case that the essential and uniquely Christian element of the Gospel is the message about the saving act of God in Christ, in His Incarnation, death, resurrection, and ascension.[3] However, our Lord is also the master of disciples who follow Him. His teaching is their authoritative rule for ethical conduct in the new life in Christ and for the government of the Church (Acts 20:35; Romans 12:20; 1 Corinthians 7:10, cf. v. 25; 1 Corinthians 9:14, 11:23; Ephesians 5:31; James 2:8, 5:12; 1 Peter 2:21–23). The ethical teaching of our Lord is not absolutely different in kind from that of other prophetic teachers. Indeed a great part of it is reproduced from the Old Testament, being selected from the loftiest and most spiritual strain of prophetic Judaism. So also there are many parallels to be found between the teaching of Jesus and current rabbinical maxims. Furthermore, many noble principles enunciated in the teachings of non-Christian religious leaders, moralists, and philosophers show parallels in the words of Christ. However, it has never been part of the essential Christian position to affirm that our Lord's

---

[3] This essential message of the saving act of God in Christ is the so-called primitive Christian *kerygma*, "thing preached" (1 Corinthians 1:21).

unique position depends upon the character of His moral teaching. It rests upon His divine saving work.

Nevertheless, the Christian will claim that our Lord's teaching is the focus of all that is good, and that He excels all other masters in grace and balance, and in freedom from the partiality and prejudice of a particular time or race or circumstance of life. And the proclamation of this teaching as the rule of life to be obeyed by the Church has been from the beginning a part of the essential Christian message. Indeed, a leading reason why particular sayings and parables were remembered by the Church in the period of oral tradition, and so found their way into the written Gospels, was that they were of interest to the Church to provide "a word from the Lord" in guidance upon some point of Christian conduct or ecclesiastical discipline.

B. The Authenticity of the Witness

This is almost certainly the most important present-day issue of New Testament scholarship. We have seen on the one hand the manner in which Christian faith, as an historical religion of God's gracious saving act in Jesus Christ, depends upon the facts concerning Christ. On the other hand, the substantially historical character of the Gospel record has in the modern period been assailed as never before by many radical critics possessed of great academic learning. This matter has already been referred to in what has been written above on the theme of Christian faith and the historical Jesus (see pp. 35–38). A discussion of the authenticity of the Gospel portrait of Jesus must now be taken further. Those who are convinced that loyalty to traditional Christian faith compels them to adopt the literal view of Biblical inspiration will naturally reject this whole discussion as erroneous, or even impious. On the other hand, those who acknowledge that the methods of critical analysis and historical investigation developed by modern New Testament scholarship are to be accepted as technically sound within their own field are faced with a far-reaching issue of judgment.

This issue is: How far are the methods of this admitted technique to be pressed? Is it the case that the portrait of Christ, His life, character, and teaching, recorded in the Gospels is substantially reliable history, though with a few minor interpretative touches added as the narrative was transmitted through the believing consciousness of the Church? Or is the interpretative element considerable? Or has most of the Gospel portrait of Christ actually been constructed out of the believing mind of the Church, as the Christians sought imaginatively to symbolize their faith—with the consequence that we know little for certain about historic Christ? This issue, we affirm, is one of interpretative attitude brought to the New Testament, rather than of secure objective evidence contained in the New Testament narrative itself. We have stated that a mediating judgment is to be preferred, which does not seek to deny the techniques of modern New Testament scholarship, but which insists that the scholar can speak honestly and meaningfully of an authentic historic Christ (see pp. 38–41). It is now necessary to consider some reasons in support of this judgment.

The canons of interpretation to be suggested are three: (1) the consistency of the Gospel portrait of Christ, (2) the spiritual majesty of the Gospel portrait of Christ, (3) the continuity of type in Christian thought.

1. THE CONSISTENCY OF THE GOSPELS. One of the most significant facts about the four Gospels is that although they belong to different traditions there is an underlying unity of treatment. There are differences of attitude toward the Christian life between the Jewish-Christian First Gospel and the Pauline Third Gospel, and this affects to some extent the representation of Christ Himself. Yet the Christ portrayed by the two is recognizably the same figure. There is a greater divergence between the Synoptic Gospels and the Fourth Gospel, for there is a more developed element of doctrinal interpretation in the latter, and along a very definite line. Nevertheless, there would appear to be an underlying unity of doctrine between the Synoptics and St. John. A very large part of the striking superficial difference of treatment is that doctrinal implications in the earlier Gospels have been made explicit in the later. Thus in St. John the "divine claims" of our Lord are made in distinctly formulated statements from His lips, but they do not in fact claim more in substance than the *implications* of what Christ says about Himself in the synoptic narrative.

So also, when we turn to doctrinal interpretations of Christ, there are various lines of development represented in the literature of the New Testament, such as the Pauline, the Johannine, the Epistle to the Hebrews, and the Revelation of St. John. There are striking differences of treatment, yet these are not contrary one to another. Thus in the Fourth Gospel the original eschatology is greatly modified, while in the Revelation it is displayed in vivid Jewish clothing. Yet in St. John the eschatology is *modified* and restated, not merely eliminated, whereas the eschatology of the Revelation is *Christian* eschatology, not merely Jewish eschatology in disguise. Even across the widest of New Testament divergences there is a similarity of type. There are two contrasting aspects of the same Christian faith, not two faiths. In general the distinctive elements of the various schools of New Testament thought are interpretations of the same object of faith, and are complementary to one another in a full understanding of our Lord.

If it were indeed the case that the greater part of the New Testament representation of the person and teaching of Jesus Christ was the imaginative construction of the Church, it is almost inconceivable that the New Testament could present this unity. The ecclesiastical and dogmatic interests of the different groups of Christians would have had nothing to check them in their free development. There would have been no original central tradition within which local variations could arise. The "variations" would have constituted virtually the whole of Christianity. The New Testament, if by chance it had ever come together into one canon, would have contained a number of entirely divergent portraits of Christ, and a number of doctrinal interpretations having no real contact with one another beyond the bare name of Christ.

This is plainly not the case. The various interpretations must have taken their origin from an historical figure sufficient to account for the many and leading elements found in common in all the various traditions. This involves that the general picture of our Lord painted in the Gospels may be accepted as substantially trustworthy as a record of fact, and that the interpretative element due to the dogmatic interests of the Church is not more than a minor factor. It may be well argued that the minor variations in tradition confirm rather than impugn the value of the historical evidence. If there were almost complete literal and dogmatic consistency in the New Testament one would suspect that later ecclesiastical authority had been at work, carefully and artificially reducing all to order. As there is so much of freedom and variety in the New Testament writings, the independence of the various witnesses is vouched for, and the substantial underlying unity made all the more impressive.

2. THE MAJESTY OF THE GOSPELS. The portrait presented by the Gospels of Jesus of Nazareth, His person, His character, His deeds, and His words, is one of the imperishable spiritual and imaginative figures of humanity. It has won the admiration and reverence even of those who refuse to believe in Him with Christian faith. It is not to be supposed that the group mind of the primitive Church possessed the sheer genius necessary for the construction of this spiritual miracle. The Evangelists strike us as faithful but rather ordinary men, who excelled themselves in what they wrote simply because they were not constructing out of their own talent, but copying what had been remembered from the life.

We have various pointers as to the level of creative genius and spiritual insight of the primitive Church, and they all point the same way. There are the so-called Apocryphal Gospels. These are ancient works purporting to be lives of Christ, and so forth, which were not accepted as reliable or authentic by the Church. They are valuable evidence as to the sort of work which was in fact produced by the group mind when it allowed itself freedom to construct imaginative stories about Christ. These constructions betray themselves as spurious by the altogether lower level of good sense and spiritual understanding displayed, when comparison is made with the canonical Gospels. If the New Testament itself had been constructed out of the same resources it would be of the same inferior character. This effect is borne out by the character of the most ancient Christian writings following the New Testament, and which were accepted by the Church as reliable and orthodox Christian work. These are the works of the so-called apostolic fathers. They are in the main at a much higher level of good sense than the Apocryphal Gospels, but they do not compare in creative spiritual genius with the books of the New Testament. The apostolic fathers are to be venerated as outstanding figures of the heroic age of the martyr Church. They served Christ faithfully in building up the discipline of the infant Church. Yet they certainly had not the genius and insight to *create* the figure of the Christ of the Gospels.

Without disrespect it may be said that the same is true even of the New Testament writers themselves. Possibly the greatest and most formative spiritual leader of the Church in the first generation was the apostle Paul. We have examples of his work. They contain passages which display the highest degree of spiritual genius. His writings are reverenced by the Church as canonical Scripture, and are some of the most creative and influential books of religion the world has ever seen. It is harder to give higher praise than this. Nevertheless, as we read even St. Paul we find passages where we candidly say: "This is not altogether the great apostle of the Gentiles, the first great doctor of the Church! In this text we have some echo of Saul of Tarsus, the intelligent and educated first-century Jew, speaking to his day from the standpoint and conventions of his day" (for example, 1 Corinthians 11:1–15; Galatians 4:21–31). The genius even of Paul, though magnificent, is variable and beset by human limitation. He does not rise uniformly to the level of His master. Paul is not above criticism, but when men criticize Jesus it is only because He is too sublime for us!

Paul, then, did not have it in him to create the portrait of Christ, as a novelist of genius might create a character of prophetic genius. Nor could St. John. And it is impossible to believe that within the circle of those early disciples there were other men of profounder spiritual genius than these, now entirely lost to historical memory, who so fertilized the group mind that the first generation created the Gospels. This is to suppose that the effect can rise above the cause. As faithful Mark depicts the stark scene of Calvary we do not have the impression that he was a man of admirable talents. He was a good but commonplace man, and we suspect that he himself did not always have the most perfect insight into what he was writing about. How then did he come to write in this commanding way? It was simply that Peter had seen and heard, and could not forget, and that Mark had so often heard St. Peter that he could not forget either. The only reasonable explanation of the majesty of the Gospel portrait is that it was copied from the life.

3. THE CONTINUITY OF CHRISTIAN THOUGHT. It is impossible for the Christian scholar to come to the reading of the New Testament without mental prepossessions of some sort. The question is therefore raised as to what are in fact the most rational principles to bring to the study. We would affirm that experience plainly teaches the value of the principle of continuity. The Church has seen a good deal of the rise and fall of schools of theological thought, by the following process. Some stimulating writer advances a new

theological understanding. He gains repute as an intellectual leader in the world of Christian scholarship, and founds a "school of thought." He may seem for a time to dominate the theological horizon, and many hail him as the authority for Christian understanding. However, hardly have his influential books had time to accumulate a little dust than a new lead is given, in quite a different direction. A new authoritative school of thought arises, with "assured results" contradicting the old. After many years it is realized that each school of thought owed its strength to the circumstance that it was emphasizing, or rediscovering, some segment of Christian truth. The weakness of each lay in the fact that it was unbalanced in its overconfident and extreme emphasis upon this one element, and in its lack of appreciation for the many other segments of truth. The rise and passing of the new movement is found, however, to have added some small offering to the great and permanent store of Christian understanding.

Through all these disputes and discoveries there has been in the Church a principle of cautious stability in face of "new theologies," and of reverence for the heritage of the past in face of brilliant individualist innovation. The prudent Christian scholar will always be the honest reader of new researches, but he will never feel constrained radically to reconstruct the whole of the Christian religion on account of some much-discussed "new theology." This is the guiding principle of the continuity of type in Christian thought.

A valuable canon of interpretation to be used in deciding how far one may reasonably go in following the new critical techniques for the reading of the Bible is that they may be accepted insofar as they yield a greater understanding of the historic Christian Faith. Yet the historic Faith itself is not open for radical change, as though the Church did not already know the truth. Scholarly theories, no matter how brilliant, are not to be followed to the point of revolutionizing Christianity. This will be done if it is once allowed that the New Testament witnesses only to a subjective "Christ of faith," and virtually not at all to a real historical Christ.

The principle of the continuity of type makes it reasonable to suppose that the cohesion of Christian thought, which has held firm through all the long centuries covered by theological history, holds also during that all-important, formative, yet unrecorded gap which exists between our Lord Himself and the formation of our written Gospel tradition. The wise theologian will make the interpretative assumption that the New Testament Christians substantially understood their Lord, or at least, that they understood Him better than we are likely to do at this distance of time if we seek to judge apart from their witness. The skeptical assumption that they radically misunderstood their Lord, and do not reliably witness to what He really and historically said and did, is therefore to be rejected. A thoughtful reverence for the continuous historic tradition of Christianity is the rational canon of interpretation to bring to the New Testament. It is a more realistic and reliable canon than the critical assumption that the Gospel must be approximated to the prepossessions of the latest passing phase of secular thought.

C. The Apostolic Faith

The unique and indispensable treasure in the New Testament is the witness to the facts about Christ. A further element of great value is that the New Testament is the witness to the first formative ventures in theological interpretation of these facts. It is the faith of the Church that all through her history the Holy Spirit has been guiding the consensus of devout Christian scholars to a fuller understanding of the meaning of Christ and His teaching, and teaching them how to apply the fixed principles of Christian faith to the ever-changing circumstances of successive centuries (John 16:13–14). Thus the life of the Church has been marked by a series of doctrinal decisions, which, when they are found indeed to be decisions of the whole of the Church, are fully authoritative decisions for the whole Church.

In consequence, any new doctrinal decision must be built upon the foundation of the past, and must be taken within the limits of that which has been already authoritatively decided. It is not allowable to abolish the fully authoritative decisions of the past, but they can be clarified in light of new doctrinal issues arising out of new circumstances. What is acceptable to the Church is a fuller understanding of, and a clearer formulation of, the original faith (Jude 3). Superficially, so far as the wording of doctrinal formularies is concerned, the progress of Christian doctrine may look like an evolutionary process, moving further and further away from the beginning. In spiritual and intellectual substance, however, it is a conservative process, for the reformation of doctrine always consists in a recapture of its original principles.

Clearly, the criterion of this whole process is the place of the New Testament itself. If each authoritative doctrinal decision of the Church is determinative of the bounds within which later decisions may be made, the earlier the decisions the more determinative they are for the Church. The very first decisions laid down the basic structure of all later teaching. "As the sapling is bent, so is the great tree." The New Testament contains the witness to these most momentous of all doctrinal decisions. The process of doctrinal discussion, interpretation, and decision as it is seen in the New Testament must not be separated from the same process as it is observed in the Church of later times. In principle it is the same. Nevertheless, the initial stage of the process had results more significant than those of any later time. The New Testament contains the witness to these first basic decisions of the Church, which make natural and necessary the later formulations of the doctrine of the Trinity, the Incarnation, the Atonement, and so forth.

Readings

Dodd, C. H., *The Bible Today*. London: Cambridge University Press; New York: The Macmillan Company, 1947.

Kelly, B. H., ed., *Layman's Bible Commentary:* Vol. I: *Introduction to the Bible*. Richmond, Va.: John Knox Press, 1959.

Peake, A. S., *The Bible: Its Origin, Its Significance, and Its Abiding Worth*. New York: Doran, 1913.

Bultmann, R., et al., *Kerygma and Myth,* ed. H. W. Bartsch, trans. R. H. Fuller. London: S.P.C.K., 1953. (Discussion of the "demythologizing" exegesis, with a rejoinder.)

Chapter Nine

The Double Cure

I believe in the forgiveness of sins

I. Personal Religion

It has been emphasized that Christianity is the religion of an objective divine saving act performed in history. With this is connected the other fundamental, that Christianity is the religion of divine grace. The Christian Faith is the message of that which God did in His incarnate Son, and which He now does through the operation of the Holy Spirit. Therefore the Christian religion is a *gospel*. It is not the call to man that he accept a revelation, a doctrine, or an ethic, and attempt to summon up all his powers to live in accord with it. It is a gracious summons that he put his sole hope for life in what God has done for him, and will do in him.

However, answering to this historic and objective side of Christian faith there is a personal and subjective aspect. What God has done can only make an actual difference to real human beings if it makes an appeal to their minds and wills and affections, and if it produces a response from the human personality. Here is an important example of the principle that a right understanding of Christian faith is largely a matter of preserving a due balance between apparently opposite propositions, which are in fact truths complementary one to another. If one comes down too heavily upon the historical and objective side, the Faith becomes antiquarian and academic. It is then seen as a call to men to accept a set of doctrines. Such religion seems to have little contact with the practical life of ordinary men. On the other hand, if the presentation of Christianity discounts the historical and objective and becomes too purely subjective and personal, one is left with a religion of sentiments and emotions. At the best this will offend the thoughtful man, because it seems to be basing its claim for acceptance as true upon the circumstance that its devotees "feel" it to be true. At the worst it can degenerate into uncontrolled emotionalism. The due balance between historic Christianity and personal religion is a matter of no small importance.

Another aspect of this balance is that God carries on His present work of the Holy Spirit chiefly, though not exclusively, through the means of grace in the Church. However, the classic plan of personal religion, and of "the Christian experience," has been hammered out chiefly from the actual personal experience of certain outstanding Christian individuals. It also naturally turns our thoughts to the way in which the Holy Spirit works in the heart of the individual believer. Inevitably, therefore, the theology of personal religion tends to be individualist theology. Here again is a due balance to be kept between apparent opposites which are in fact complementary.

A presentation of Christian faith which is too exclusively thought out in terms of the Church may become simply communal, formal, and external, and lapse into a sterile ecclesiasticism. An understanding of faith which is too purely individual may become individualistic, introverted, undisciplined, subjective, and even eccentric. It will lack the sustaining discipline and the broad views which come of a great and ruling sense of the Church. In turning, therefore, to the theology of "the Christian experience," it is necessary to keep clearly in mind that the individual believer we are here discussing is not an isolated individual. Normally and ideally he is an integral part of the closely knit fellowship of the Church.

Although God is always the same, human nature is inherently various. Consequently the ways of divine grace in dealing with sinful men are various. It is hardly surprising to find, therefore, that the Church is not as united in the doctrines which reflect the personal religious experience as she is in the doctrines which expound the nature of God and His saving act in Christ. Indeed, there are some issues which are so much a matter of human temperament that it would appear spiritually improper for the Church to attempt to make universal doctrinal decisions upon them. They are matters of religious opinion, where the wise rule is toleration. Various denominations in the Church have on occasion made separate dogmatic decisions on some of these points, and in doing so have regrettably divided the Church. The Church can rightly insist that there is one true doctrine of God and of His divine act in Christ. Here the faithful ought to be united. Yet the ways in which souls are led to God on account of that saving act are various, and it is wrong for a section to seek to insist that the way it finds most helpful is the only correct way. It is necessary, not only to define the words which different Christian denominations use, but also to understand the spiritual intention they seek to convey by them. The divisions of the Church with regard to salvation by grace are in part due to genuine differences of spiritual apprehension. Yet divergences are also largely due to the use of words in different senses. By tradition one denomination has become accustomed to use a term in one sense, and perhaps a bad sense. Another has used the same word in another and a good sense. They may therefore be much nearer in real intention than their doctrinal formularies superficially indicate. To understand these issues is a service to the peace and unity of the Church, and through this, to its fuller understanding of the gospel.

To this study of personal religion there are two parts. In the first place, there is the doctrine of grace. This is the attempt to give a clear exposition of the way in which God exerts His initiative in the salvation of man. Then there is the doctrine of the life of Christian grace. This is the systematic account of how the heart of man may respond to this divine initiative.

II. The Doctrine of Grace

A. Grace

Two ideas are commonly united in the term *grace*. The root idea is that grace is the undeserved favor of God. The word indicates that God has set His favor upon His people not at all because they merit it, but simply because according to the mysterious counsel of His love He wills so to do (Deuteronomy 7:7–8). He forgives man, not because man can do anything to deserve forgiveness, but because He is a God of love (Exodus 33:19; Psalm 51:1; Romans 9:15–16). God does not regard man according to what he has done, but according to His own universal goodness (Matthew 20:1–16). A second idea, derived from the first, is that grace is the action which God takes to effect His gracious will. Grace is the saving and enabling power of God, indwelling man, which comes to the assistance of man's infirmity, to do for him what he cannot do for himself (Acts 4:33, 18:27; Romans 12:3, 6; 2 Corinthians 12:9; Philippians 1:7; Hebrews 13:9). Thus the believing man is in "a state of grace" (Galatians 5:4).

B. Salvation by Grace

The Christian religion is a *gospel* ("good news") of grace. That is to say, it is not God's call to man that he obey God's law by his own strength, and thus fit himself to receive God's favor. Sinful man is not able to do this (see p. 72). The gospel is God's offer to man, in his desperate infirmity, that He will give to him a strength not his own which alone will enable man to obey the law of God and so please his Maker (Ephesians 2:8). Man can turn to God only when God exerts His initiative and calls him (Isaiah 55:6–7). Man can give himself to God's service only as God summons him and equips him (John 15:16; Romans 10:14–15). Man can give to God only that which God first gave to him (1 Corinthians 4:7). In all things even the holiest and wisest of men remains completely dependent upon God, his Creator and Master.

Summary of Divergence: Catholic and Reformation Doctrines of Salvation by Grace

a. Catholic Doctrine

Catholic teaching does not exclude the conception, which has been so formative in Reformation doctrine, that God's initiative of grace in man's salvation is a personal confrontation in power and love, which moves man consciously to repentance and faith, occasioning the experience of "conversion." However, in practice this conversion experience has been thought of as characteristic of the lives of certain outstanding saints and devotees. Formative in Catholic doctrine has been the supposition that the normal Christian grows up, and is nurtured as such, in the Christian Church and community. Thus God's initial gift of grace has been thought of sacramentally and ecclesiastically. By the regeneration of Holy Baptism (see pp. 167–69), the person baptized, normally the child of Christian parents, is placed in "a state of grace." Those who in this state faithfully use the means of grace will grow in grace, and come to Christian virtues and character. To these Christian "good works" God is of His grace pleased to attribute merit. Thus man "works out his own salvation" (Philippians 2:12, 13) by cooperation with the divine grace which works in him, and having attained a Christian character and good deeds, comes to his eternal reward (Revelation 14:13). Final salvation, therefore, is by "divine grace, and the merit of good works" (Matthew 7:21–23, 25:31–46; James 1:25; 1 John 2:17; Revelation 20:13). It is by grace, for at every stage God must exert His initiative first, or man is helpless. Yet at every stage man must freely cooperate with the initiative of grace, within the discipline of the Church.

b. Reformation Doctrine

Reformation doctrine has characteristically shown a distinctly different proportion of emphasis, often associated with the Reformation formula "salvation by grace alone." The traditional Catholic idea of the initial spiritual blessing bestowed through baptismal incorporation into the Church has not necessarily been denied, and has indeed sometimes been cherished in Protestant circles. Nevertheless, the leading influence has been the theology of the personal, conscious, and individual "conversion experience." There is clearly a significant difference of Christian apprehension here. However, it should be remembered that it is a difference of proportion and emphasis, rather than of inherent principle. Pre-Reformation Catholicism did indeed assent to the principle of salvation by divine grace, but it would be widely admitted on both sides that in much popular Catholic devotion this principle had been practically overlaid by "the merit of good works," and in particular such "works" as attendance upon ceremonial Masses, ascetic practices, reverence for relics, pilgrimages to shrines, indulgences, and so forth. The Reformers characteristically were moved by a strong revulsion against all this, for they felt that the foundation principle of grace was almost completely obscured by the doctrine that man can and must *earn* his own salvation by his diligent churchmanship. Thus the Reformers wished carefully to exclude the conception of "the merit of good works." Characteristically they embraced the Augustinian theology of grace (see pp. 209–12), and in particular emphasized the formulae "justification by faith alone" and "salvation by grace alone."

This may be illustrated by the formative experience and example of Martin Luther (1483–1546).

In his young days as an exceptionally conscientious monk, Luther strove with all his powers in the customary devotional discipline to attain to the experience which he knew he ought to have, of being so filled with the love of God that he would be able to obey God spontaneously from the heart, and not merely as a stern duty. He found instead a deep frustration of spirit, until God brought him to a profound evangelical experience, in which he clearly realized that the principle of Christian salvation is loving and obedient trust in the saving love and power of God declared in Christ. In strong reaction against his background of "merit earning" he, and those who followed him, emphasized the doctrine of salvation "by grace alone." The purpose of this is clearly to safeguard the position that sinful man can of himself do nothing to accomplish his own salvation, and cannot hope to establish his own status before God. The whole saving action is of God's grace, and all the glory belongs to God.

c. An Interpretative Statement

Some would argue that the classic Protestant formula "salvation by grace alone" is acceptable as a maxim of Christian devotion, but is not by itself a sufficient principle of systematic theological thought. It belongs properly to the realm of Christian experience. The man who, having wandered far and struggled hard, suddenly comes to a profound experience of God's saving power and love in Jesus Christ finds that the instinctive cry of his heart is: "God did it all! I was not faithfully listening for Him, but He called me. I was not obeying Him. Though I did not realize it, I was wandering further and further from Him, until He chose me, visited me, overcame me by His power, and set up His throne in my heart. And as for the service I have since rendered Him—it is not at all to my credit. It is the result of His power working through me. *God did it all*, and all the glory is His!"

This experience is one of the fundamental facts of the Christian life, and no sound theology of salvation can be constructed without taking the most serious account of it (pp. 71, 220–21). We observe this form of experience is by no means limited to the Protestant or evangelical tradition. Believers of every age and place have shared something of this apprehension of the grace of God, though they have not always expressed themselves in the manner natural to a disciple of Luther. Out of the heart's cry "God did it all" is fashioned the theological maxim, "salvation by grace alone." Nevertheless, the critic would urge that if the believer wishes to advance from devotional experience to the construction of a systematic theology expounding the relation of God to all human souls, it is precarious to make the basic assumption that "salvation by grace alone" is virtually a sufficient foundation for all.[1] There are a number of other principles equally to be taken into serious consideration, such as, the love of God to all men, His reasonable dealings with mankind, human moral responsibility, and the duty of devotional discipline in the means of grace. There is a case that the Catholic position more fully answers to these considerations, in its greater degree of emphasis upon free and responsible cooperation with grace.

C. Augustinian Theology

The theology of "sovereign grace" has come to its most developed exposition in relation to the thought of St. Augustine of Hippo. The theological thought of this, possibly the most influential teacher of the Church since New Testament times, is proverbially difficult to expound on account of its diversity. When he discusses the doctrines of the Church, ministry, and sacraments, Augustine clearly displays himself as belonging to the Catholic tradition. His theology was, indeed, one of the formative influences of medieval Christianity. When, however, he turns to the theology of divine grace, the conversion of souls, the experience of personal religion, and the hope of salvation, he is the originator of that system of Christian thought commonly known as Augustinianism. It is not easy completely to reconcile the two sides of the great master's doctrine.

Significantly, St. Augustine's theology of grace was molded chiefly by his own early personal experience of conversion. His moral and spiritual bondage was much more sore than that of Luther, the upright but frustrated monk, for Augustine had tasted years of humiliation during which he unavailingly struggled with lust and unbelief. Furthermore, when he came to the gift of faith, and to an experience of spiritual release and moral purification, he continued to be a man of boldly aspiring speculative interests, who significantly did attempt to construct an intellectual system out of the theology of grace. This Augustinian doctrine places the whole responsibility for man's final salvation with the initiative of God's grace, and makes man virtually the instrument of God's action. From the time of

---

[1] As some would put it, "grace alone" is true existentially, but not wholly true as a matter of systematic doctrine.

Augustine on there was within the pre-Reformation Western Church a continuing minority tradition of Augustinian theology, or of theology verging upon Augustinianism, though it has never captured the general judgment of the whole Church.

The most influential movement of Augustinianism, however, was seen in the classic Reformation theology, which for reasons natural to evangelical Christians wished to give the strongest emphasis to the doctrine of grace. Protestant Augustinianism was most clearly and systematically formulated in the thought of John Calvin (1509–1564), with the result that fully developed Augustinian thought is now often described as "Calvinism." However, there are those who have adopted the Augustinian standpoint who are not Calvinists. "Barthianism" is a leading modern school of Augustinian thought.

The Augustinian would naturally affirm that he has adopted this doctrine essentially because he believes it to be required by Scripture, and would quote the texts which speak of man's entire depravity, divine election, and so forth. However, this leaves outstanding the question why others interpret the Scripture differently. The determinative influence appears to be the manner of religious experience by which different classes of believers have come to spiritual liberty and moral power in believing. Those whose experience has prompted the heart to cry "God did it all" have been inclined to give a leading emphasis to some texts, and to interpret others in light of them, and to find thereby the support for Augustinian doctrine. Others, with a different form of devotional discipline or religious experience behind them, have read the Scriptures in a different way.

One side of Augustinian theology has already been outlined. Its doctrine of man and of sin naturally lays a strong and distinctive emphasis upon entire depravity, the bondage of the will, and the guilt of original sin, whereby the whole human race justly merits eternal damnation because of the Fall (see pp. 70, 75). We may turn, then, to the other side, and consider Augustinian positions with regard to saving grace.

1. ELECTION. In addition to the characteristic Augustinian position there is a general doctrine of election, or of divine choice, in the Bible. The interest of this is to affirm that God is the foreseeing master of the human situation. His saving action is no mere expedient forced upon Him by man's perversity. It is the outcome of an eternal and wise plan, which will in the end fully vindicate His goodness and glory, even through the sorry processes of human disobedience (Romans 11:25–36). In this connection it is to be remembered that the Hebrew writers do not express themselves in terms of "indirect causation" (see pp. 29–30), with the result that an evil which has been *permitted* in God's world, and which has taken place under the divine order, is spoken of almost as though God had positively willed it. Thus in the passage referred to above, the proper sense of verse 32 is that the unbelieving Jews "*became* shut up in unbelief."

A second interest of the general doctrine of election is to show that according to His mysterious but all-wise counsel God chooses some persons, and some nations, to play a particular role in history. That this must be so is the conviction of one who believes that the world is overruled by the providence of God, for it is a plain fact of experience that some persons and some nations are more endowed with natural gifts than others, and are endowed in various ways, and that nations and persons are placed in historical circumstances which give differing degrees of opportunity for the exercise of their gifts. Thus the Hebrews, and no other nation, were "elected" as the chosen people. So in the passage introducing the one already referred to (Romans 9:1-13), Jacob and Esau, the traditional founders of the tribes of Israel and of Edom respectively, figure in St. Paul's theology as the "representative heads" of the two nations. The divine election, which "loved" the one and "hated" the other, was the choice which made the Israelites, and not the closely kindred nation of the Edomites, into the chosen people. However, it by no means follows from this that all Israelites, merely by the circumstance of birth into that nation, were thereby faithful to their destiny, or more righteous and more sure of eternal salvation than other men (see p. 137).

The Augustinian system, however, proceeds from this to a *particular* election. It teaches that God has chosen certain individual souls out of the mass of those destined for perdition, and appointed them to be the heirs of salvation. These are the Elect. This demonstrates God's unaccountable mercy, whereas His leaving the rest to go to the perdition which all alike deserve vindicates His justice, and hatred of sin. The leading Scripture passage cited in support of this doctrine is Romans 9, interpreted on the basis that the figures of "Jacob" and "Esau" are individual, personal patriarchs. The chapter is then viewed as a discussion of the divine destiny of individual souls, to heaven or to hell. It is clear that the doctrine of particular election is the logical outcome of the proposition "God did it all." If this is the whole of the matter, it then follows that some souls are converted simply because God has chosen that they shall be converted, and others fail to receive the gift of faith, and to be converted, simply because God's grace has chosen to pass them over.

2. PREDESTINATION. It is fundamental to the doctrine of God that His will is always the same, and that He foreknows the future. Therefore the Elect are chosen not at the time of conversion, or at birth, but from the beginning of God's dealings with the human race. Thus the Elect are called according to an eternal decree of election. This is the doctrine of predestination (Romans 8:29-30).[2]

3. IRRESISTIBLE GRACE. If those souls who are of the Elect are predestined to receive the gift of faith, and to be converted, it follows that God's grace

---

[2] A nonpredestinarian exegesis of this and similar texts would be given on the lines of the opening of the section above on election (p. 210).

is "sovereign" toward them in the sense that it is a matter of necessity that it must have its way with them. Thus it is a part of the Augustinian system that converting grace is irresistible. This does not mean that the unbelieving sinner is purely passive before it, and cannot resist. St. Augustine's own experience was that of a long and stubborn fight against grace. The doctrine of irresistible grace affirms that although a man may resist, God's purpose is bound to have its way with him. Even the most obstinate sinner, if he be of the company of the Elect, will of necessity capitulate to grace in the end, and then the grace of God carries all before it in his heart, turning his will from evil to good (Romans 9:19).

4. FINAL PERSEVERANCE. The Augustinian position is that those who are of the Elect, who receive the gift of faith, and who are in consequence in a state of grace, must necessarily continue in this state so as to arrive at a believing death, and so be confirmed to eternal glory (John 10:28, 29). Though those who have been truly converted may *seem* at times to fall into sin they will surely repent and return to faith in the end, under the influence of irresistible grace (Proverbs 24:16). And those who may seem at one time to have been in a state of grace, yet who die in a state of apostasy, have never been truly the subjects of God's saving grace, even though they may for a time have sincerely believed themselves to have been converted. The measure of divine grace granted to them may have sufficed to keep them from some degree of wickedness, but it was not *effectual, saving* grace.

5. REPROBATION. This is the culmination in logic of the whole system. The most strict Augustinians have held that God did not merely leave the non-Elect to go in their own way to the damnation which all alike deserve. He positively sentenced them to this punishment. This is the decree of reprobation.

6. EVALUATION. The Augustinian system of scriptural interpretation clearly enshrines important spiritual values, otherwise it would not have made its appeal to some of the greatest figures in the history of Christian thought. Nevertheless, its austere principles have never appealed in an unmodified form to more than a minority tradition. This would appear to indicate that taken in isolation it is not a complete apprehension of the Christian truth. The more general mind of the historic Church is that of a mediating position, namely, that the positive spiritual values of Augustinianism are to be accepted, but that the system requires judiciously to be modified by taking into account other spiritual considerations. It is good for man thus to be solemnly reminded that the Christian God of love is not a benign heavenly "buddy," upon whose goodwill man can safely presume. He is the glorious sovereign Potentate of the universe, who from eternity rules all worlds with a wisdom man cannot presume to scan. Indeed, that His love toward sinful man is the love of so great and holy a God is the very

thing which makes the love of God the unspeakable wonder that it is. The doctrine which at first sight appears so forbidding, that the aim of the work of salvation is the full vindication of the sole glory of God, as holy, just, and good, stands as a most necessary rebuke to the constant easy-going human tendency to look upon communal religion as the oil for the wheels of society, the purpose of which is to make this world a respectable, prosperous, and comfortable place in which to live.

Furthermore, the doctrine of particular election does seek to take account of the great mystery that some people appear to be born with so much more spiritual talent than others, or in circumstances of so much greater spiritual privilege, and that some respond to their spiritual opportunities and are converted, whereas others, with apparently equal opportunities, so unaccountably turn away from Christ. We cannot understand this, but have to trust that a good God overrules all for the best, in this world and the next. Finally, this forbidding Augustinian portrait of God preserves to the religion of grace the element of stern duty, and if rightly apprehended can nurture Christians who are men of iron.

However, we believe that the doctrine of "grace alone" is more safely understood as a truth of the devotional life, and as a maxim of spiritual experience, than as a speculative principle. Aspiring speculation can all too easily turn into arid speculation, which represents the God and Father of our Lord Jesus Christ as an utterly remote monarch of arbitrary might.

This limitation of predestinarian speculation is surely in accord with the spirit and intention of the Scripture. The texts traditionally quoted by Augustinians are the heart's cry of men upon their knees before the God of glory, not the musings of academics in their proverbial "ivory towers," and they must be treated as such. A judicious attempt at theological interpretation is provided, albeit in somewhat quaint and antique language, by the celebrated Anglican Article XVII, *Of Predestination and Election.* This is the work of cautious and astute men, whose care is to preserve an even balance between extremes, and to safeguard the peace and unity of a Church torn by theological factions. The opening paragraph of the Article is a statement of the positive side of the Augustinian position, and affirms that according to an eternal and mysterious purpose God has decreed the salvation by grace of those who are saved. Most significantly, however, it does not introduce the phrase "grace *alone,*" nor say that divine grace is irresistible. In particular, it is silent regarding the negative side, the doctrine of reprobation.

The second paragraph turns to the devotional experience, and away from predestinarian speculation. The practical value of the Augustinian position is observed to be in the humble assurance and confidence which it brings to those whose sole hope in life is that they are the objects of God's sufficient grace. Thus the doctrine "is full of sweet, pleasant, and unspeakable comfort to godly persons, and such as feel in themselves the working of the Spirit of Christ." This is the profound truth of the lines:

> Let me no more my comfort draw
> From my frail grasp of Thee:
> In this alone rejoice with awe;
> Thy mighty grasp of me.

However, "for curious [that is, *speculative*] and carnal persons, lacking the Spirit of Christ, to have continually before their eyes the sentence of God's Predestination, is a most dangerous downfall." Thus John Milton, the Calvinist poet of Puritanism, can write of the devils in hell:

> Others apart sat on a hill retired,
> In thoughts more elevate, and reasoned high
> Of providence, foreknowledge, will, and fate,
> Fixed fate, free will, foreknowledge absolute,
> And found no end, in wandering mazes lost.[3]

Finally, "we must receive God's promises in such wise, as they be generally set forth to us in Holy Scripture." This is a reminder that the doctrine of the Bible is many-sided. As well as passages which speak of election, and of God's sovereign power, there are also gracious promises of God's love to the whole world (John 3:16), and of His will that all men should be saved (1 Timothy 2:4; 2 Peter 3:9). Thus these high matters are not to be settled by the facile quotation of a few isolated "proof texts" in controversy. They require a unified, ordered, learned, and reverent exposition of the whole of Scripture.

D. Prevenient Grace

Prevenient grace is literally the grace which "comes before." That is, it is the action of divine grace which precedes any conscious personal experience of the life of grace. Some degree of moral and spiritual good is almost universally diffused among mankind, quite apart from whether men are definite Christian believers. The doctrine of prevenient grace safeguards the position that this good is not man's natural possession, but is a gift of divine grace (see p. 71). Associated with this is a second aspect. The notion of salvation by grace answers to the idea of the divine initiative in salvation. At every stage of the Christian experience man can only answer the call of God because God has already called him. This process of divine initiative has started long before the awakened soul is found seriously reflecting about sin, repentance, and conversion.

Psychological investigation has found itself in agreement with the traditional Christian position that the human personality can be powerfully influenced for good in the early days and years of life. Certainly the growing child in the Christian community, who is not yet old enough to have any

---

[3] *Paradise Lost*, Book II, ll. 557–61.

reflections upon sin or salvation, can have a sincere love of Jesus, and a sense of the presence of God in worship. The activity of prevenient grace is to be seen here. The proverbial careless person who, thinking nothing of religion, goes to church to accompany a friend or to get out of the cold, and is there surprisingly convicted by the truth, is likewise the object of God's prevenient grace. The spiritual choice before him when he went was a very dim and unformed one. Yet he might well have chosen differently, and that he acted as he did was a response to a preliminary leading of the Spirit of grace.

Furthermore, there are sincere seekers after truth who, on account of some unfortunate disability due to the deeply entrenched prejudice of upbringing, or to some past regrettable experience, cannot bring themselves to see the truth of the Christian position. However, if they are indeed sincere seekers it is not to be doubted that these are the objects of the leading of God's prevenient grace, even though some of them may profess to be atheists and the enemies of religion. In fact, the life of grace is not to be limited to the little company of those who seem to be very religious. The Spirit of Christ is already striving in the hearts of all men everywhere to lead them to that which is good, and ultimately to Christian faith (John 1:9). It is not for man lightly to draw any limit to the preliminary and unconscious operation of Christian grace, and to write off any abandoned creature as virtually lost to its influence.

E. Universal Grace

The majority tradition of the Church has affirmed that the grace of God is in principle universal. The chief reason for maintaining this position is that it appears to be the consequence of the fundamental doctrine that God is love (1 John 4:8). It would seem that if God loves all men He must will the salvation of all (Psalm 145:8, 9; Isaiah 49:6; Jonah 4:9–11; Matthew 5:43–48; Luke 13:29; John 3:16; 1 Timothy 2:4; 2 Peter 3:9).

A contributory reason for upholding the doctrine of universal grace is the Church's regard for God's promise of grace in the means of grace. It is true that a man cannot by his much desiring make himself believe in God or love God. To do this is the gift of grace. Nevertheless he can, if he will, use the means of grace. He can listen with a teachable mind to the reading of the Scripture and the preaching of the Gospel, and if he expectantly persists in this long enough God will honor the means of grace, and give to the seeker the gift of faith and love. The penitent and awakened seeker, who is painfully aware of the poverty of his spiritual experience, cannot make himself grow in grace. Nevertheless, he can, if he will, devoutly receive the sacraments, and God will faithfully fulfill His promise in them. Therefore honor for the means of grace appears to involve an offer of effectual grace to all sincere comers.

A number of important consequences follow from the doctrine of universal grace. In the first place, it involves the idea that the sovereignty of God's grace is a self-limited sovereignty. God allows men, if they will, to defy Him. If grace is both irresistible and universal, all men would be bound to be saved (see p. 268). In the second place, the doctrine involves that the ultimate responsibility for whether a man is saved rests finally upon man, not upon God. This is an important limitation of the notion of the bondage of the will. Left to himself, sinful man's will is indeed in bondage, and apart from the grace of God he cannot turn to God. Yet when his will is assisted by grace he is then truly free either to make or to mar himself forever.

It will be appreciated that the doctrine of universal grace holds genuine difficulties, even as does the opposed notion of particular election. The only way to Christian salvation is through faith in Christ (Acts 4:12). Yet it is not clear precisely in what way all men receive the opportunity to come to faith in Christ. In this life some, and perhaps the vast majority of the human race, never hear of Him at all. Many others, even in nominally Christian communities, never fully and intelligently hear the Christian message, so as genuinely to be confronted with the decision of Christian discipleship. There are also some who are apparently armored against the Christian appeal by a psychological "blind spot" implanted by past unhappy experience (the so-called "invincible ignorance"). Thus it is hard to defend the proposition that saving grace in Christ extends to all men without logically being led to extend the operation of grace beyond the life of man in this world (see pp. 262–63). This again may ensnare the theologian in precarious speculations and attempts to know that which man cannot know, or perhaps to affirm doctrine beyond the warrant of Scripture.

Thus, whether saving grace is affirmed to be particular or universal, God's good and wise dealings with all His creatures remain shrouded in an air of mystery, and we cannot afford to be too dogmatic. All that can be presumed is that all those who in this world have lived according to the limited light which was granted to them will find, when they awake in the life to come, that they belong to Christ, even though in this life they were not apparently Christians. This is an illustration of the general principle that it is the business of the Christian witness to declare God's terms of salvation, namely, faith in Christ, but to leave to God all judgment as to who are, and who are not, in a state of salvation.

F. Arminianism

This term is the name which has often been given to the continuance within Protestantism of the prevailing Catholic doctrine of universal grace, in opposition to particular election and reprobation. It indicates a central or mediating position.

This school of thought takes its name from the Dutch theologian Jacobus Arminius (1560–1609). He was a teacher of humanist and liberal views who, although accepting the Reformed theology prevalent in Holland, repudiated the Calvinist doctrine of reprobation. Thus in course of time the word "Arminian" came to be used in England as a term of reproach, applied by their Calvinist opponents to the non-Calvinist "Laudian" High Church divines, to indicate that these were not wholehearted Protestants, and were unsound on the doctrine of grace. The term was later adopted for himself as a title of honor by John Wesley (1703–1791) to designate his "central" or synthesizing school of non-Calvinist evangelicalism, which on the one hand strongly emphasized salvation by grace and justification by faith, but on the other hand firmly repudiated particular election, predestination, and reprobation. This judicious and moderating "Arminian Evangelicalism," which is now so largely characteristic of Anglo-Saxon Protestantism, is perhaps the most enduring and important contribution of the Methodist movement to theological understanding in the Church.

III. The Life of Grace

A. Nurture and Conversion

We now systematically consider the response of the human soul to the initiative of divine grace, and follow through the classic outline of "the personal religious experience." It is to be remembered that this outline is a *classic* outline. It is based upon the unusually distinct and formative religious experience of certain outstanding leaders of Christian devotion, and in particular, upon the teaching of the so-called "evangelical succession" of St. Paul, St. Augustine of Hippo, Martin Luther, and John Wesley. It does not follow, however, that the religious experience of more ordinary believers corresponds at every point. In the classic outline the facts of religious experience are brought out in black and white, in more order and clarity, than they often are in the more pedestrian devotional discipline of the Church.

This issue is presented in the contrast between Christian nurture within the Church and "conversion" as paths to Christian saving faith. Most Christians are such chiefly because they were born into the Christian community of the home and the Church, and were educated in Christian worship, morals, and belief. The prevailing attitude of the great institutional branches of the Church naturally corresponds to this. They lay great store by infant baptism, family prayers, Christian education in day-school and in Church school, regular habits of worship, reverence for the liturgy and the Church calendar, the status of communicant, and so forth. This devotional discipline, it is believed, will if used with sincerity and regularity bring men and women to a living faith in Christ. The great majority of believers through the centuries have lived their Christian lives substantially after this method. In this sense, the way of communal Christian nurture in the Church is the "normal" way to faith. Theologians who speak from this background instinctively lay more emphasis upon the value of man's free and responsible response to grace in works of devotional discipline and charity, and in consequence less proportional emphasis upon the mysterious action of divine grace. They speak of divine grace, but not perhaps, of "grace alone." They are not happy with the notion that those who are brought up as Christians need to be "converted," for to them "conversion" is a change from another religion, or from open unbelief, to Christianity.

It is necessary, however, also to do justice to the theology which reflects the religious experience of those outstanding individuals who have come to the apprehension of grace in an eminent degree. The importance of their witness is not to be measured by their relative paucity in number. They are men who have been led by experience to a deep conviction that God calls His children to something much more profound than a busy preoccupation with churchgoing and conventional morality, and indeed, that this preoccupation, however well intentioned, may easily become the delusive substitute for real religion. Normally such men have come to a deep frustration of spirit in the religion of ecclesiastical discipline, and then, despairing of all else, have been granted a great sense of spiritual and moral release through trust in the saving act of God in Christ. Experience has made them into "theologians of grace." Very often this experience of release has been described as a "conversion," though some would question whether this designation is entirely appropriate in the case of those who for years have been sincere churchmen. Perhaps "evangelical experience" is a better phrase to use.

In times when vital spiritual religion is reviving anew, perhaps from a background of formal churchmanship, these outstanding leaders often are joined by numbers of followers, who also share the distinctive evangelical experience. Thus a new denomination .may be formed, which naturally comes to regard a "personal decision" as the normal and expected way into Christian faith, and which may even seek to repudiate the Christianity of incorporation into and education within the Church. However, as these new groups establish themselves into the settled ways of Christian communities they normally begin to discover the necessity for the traditional discipline also. It is a great pity that the inevitable tension between the Christianity of incorporation and education and the Christianity of conversion has so often generated mutual distrust for the spiritual bona-fides of the other party, and division in the Church.

Clearly, the two approaches are not opposites, but complements one to the other. The normal path into a great releasing experience of divine grace is through Christian nurture and discipline. By parity of reason, the pastors of settled and disciplined Christian communities should certainly teach their people that mature believers ought to expect to rise above formal churchmanship to a deep personal experience of God. In many ways the two forms of Christian devotion belong to one another as partners, and can enrich one another. There is certainly a great need for the exponents of both sides to see that this is so, and to understand one another. We are now to consider the classic outline of the Christian "personal experience," as it has been traced by its outstanding and formative leaders.

B. "Preaching the Law"

By *legal* religion, or the religion of law, is meant that religion which is based on the recognition of man's absolute duty to obey the declared will of God, and thus to please God (Romans 10:5). The gospel of free forgiveness and saving grace cannot profitably be declared to men unless they first appreciate the strict ethical character of God, the gravity and guilt of sin in His sight, and the unsparing necessity of obedience to Him. Otherwise they will presume upon His mercy, and the gospel of grace will lead to moral laxity (Romans 3:5-8). Therefore the preaching of the religion of law is the due preliminary to the preaching of the religion of grace. This was true historically. The idea of God's free forgiving grace was certainly not unknown in the Old Testament (Psalm 103:8-14; Hosea 11:7-9). However, in effect it is the minor theme. For the more part, the religion of the Old Testament is the religion of law. Moral and ceremonial commandments are given, under fear of punishment for disobedience, and with hope of blessing and reward for obedience. This was the necessary preliminary discipline, until the Jewish people were thoroughly established in the religion of ethical monotheism. Then, and only then, could they appreciate the gospel of Christ (Galatians 3:23-24).

The first Christian preachers in the Gentile world well understood this principle. In Acts, when an apostle addresses Jews or proselytes, who accepted the Mosaic Law, he speaks of Jesus as the crucified and risen Messiah (Acts 2:22-36, 13:14-41). However, when we find St. Paul addressing pagans, whether they are naïve rural idolaters or more sophisticated unbelievers, he speaks chiefly as a Jew might to Gentiles, out of the Law. The distinctive Christian element is kept largely in reserve (Acts 14:12-18, 17:16-31, 24:24-25). This was typical of the evangelistic method of the ancient Church. So it is today. The necessary background to the preaching of the gospel of grace is the declaration of the sanctity of the moral law of God, and the absolute duty of man to obey it.

There is also a sense in which the common Christianity of the Church is partly *legal* still. In ideal and principle the Christian believer has advanced beyond the level of the religion of law, and no longer needs the discipline of commandments, rewards, and punishments (Romans 10:4; Galatians 3:2, 3, 25). His sufficient rule of life is guidance into all manner of loving conduct by the indwelling Spirit of Christ, and this is the Christian's "law of liberty" (Romans 13:8-10; 1 Corinthians 8:1-13; 2 Corinthians 3:17; Galatians 5:16; James 1:25, 2:12). Nevertheless, most Christian disciples are not adult enough in faith to rise wholly to this level. They find it still

spiritually profitable, even with their Christian liberty, to have some fixed
guiding rules, moral and spiritual, ready to hand, and a measure of firm
ecclesiastical discipline to remind them to keep those rules (Acts 15:22–29;
Romans 13:1–5; 1 Corinthians 5:1–13; 2 Thessalonians 3:10).

C. *Conviction of Sin*

As our Lord Himself said, "They that are whole have no need of a
physician, but they that are sick" (Mark 2:17). Men will not seek the
gift of grace unless they first come to see their unspeakable need of it. To
the Christian, therefore, the door into faith, and into all the virtues of love,
is humility (Philippians 2:3–8; 1 Peter 5:5–6). That salutary and realistic
judgment of himself as he stands before God, which makes a man at last
prepared to accept from God that which he can never hope to repay, and
which will leave him forever at the disposal of God, is worked in the heart
chiefly by the realization that he has sinned, and sinned deeply and in-
excusably, so that he can never deserve forgiveness (Luke 15:18–19, 18:13).
The purpose of "the preaching of the law" is therefore to bring to man
this conviction of sin (Romans 3:19–20, 7:9–13; 2 Corinthians 7:10).
Here is the first stage of the Christian experience, and it is worthy of note
that the deeply troubled and humiliated conscience is a work of divine
grace (Hebrews 4:12).

"The preaching of the law" does not consist in the denunciation of the
gross sins of the people who are not in Church, congenial task though this
may be to the preacher and his hearers. Men and women are not brought
to humble penitence before God by deploring the wrongs of the times,
denouncing the wickedness of communism, warning of the peril of the
hydrogen bomb, lamenting the tragedy of the divorce rate, and scarifying
the puerilities of popular television! All these considerations, though true
enough in their way, too easily encourage the hearers to say to themselves,
"God, I thank thee, that I am not as other men are" (Luke 18:11). This
confirms well-intentioned and morally decent men in that self-regarding
self-righteousness which is the condition natural to man. It separates them
still further from God. The effectual "preaching of the law" is the enforcement to the sincere and moral man of the spotless purity and inflexible
justice of the God of holy love, the absolute requirement of obedience
from the heart to Him in all things, the grievousness of slighting His offered
love, and the lamentable spiritual consequences, here and hereafter, of
alienation from God by pride, selfishness, and moral compromise.

D. *Repentance*

When the serious-minded man is confronted with the majesty of the
moral and spiritual law of God, with the dreadful consequences of disobedience, and with the blessedness promised to those who obey God, the
Spirit of grace can then work in him the response of penitence. Humble
penitence is the indispensable condition for the forgiveness of sins (Luke

7:44–48, 15:7, 18–24, 18:13–14; Acts 8:22, 11:18). Christian repentance is not merely remorse for sin, for the apostate Judas felt remorse, though he did not, like penitent Peter, return in humility to Christ to seek forgiveness. Certainly repentance is not merely regret that one is not a better and purer man, for any candid mind can feel this sentiment, even as it cherishes its self-righteousness in comparing itself with others who have done worse. Repentance involves a completely sincere purpose to turn away from evil to good, and from self-pleasing to God (Isaiah 1:16–20; Luke 19:8–9). However, the tragedy of human nature is that even the man who sincerely repents discovers that he cannot turn away from evil to good, for his moral will is in bondage. Secretly in the heart, and to some extent even openly, he continues to commit the sins which he now loathes. Thus human repentance is not fully effectual to work an actual change of life. Its chief fruit is a deepened sense of conviction of sin (Romans 7:14–24). The paradox is that the thoroughly awakened soul, which has come nearest to sincere penitence, and which is now striving with all its might to obey and please God, is the one which has the clearest realization that apart from the grace of God man cannot even truly repent. Repentance is the gift of God (Acts 5:31, 11:18; 2 Timothy 2:25).

E. Faith

The initiative of divine grace toward the sincerely penitent sinner is the offer of the gift of saving faith. It is important to appreciate what is meant by Christian saving faith, for the word "faith" is often used in reduced and variable senses, and there is much confusion. There is a distinction between "The Faith," that is, the body of reliable doctrine preserved in the Church, and "faith," which is union with God in Christ, in loving personal trust (see pp. 1–2). From the point of view of systematic theological thought "The Faith" is the foundation of "faith," though from the point of view of the actual devotional experience it is often and largely the other way about. A man first embarks upon God in personal trust and faith, and then goes on to think out the implications of this in the acceptance of a body of belief. However, in principle a man must have some reasonable ground for supposing that there is a God, and a God who has in Christ performed the saving act of power and love, before he can give himself to that God in worship, trust, and obedience (Hebrews 11:6).

This is an important point of devotional discipline, as well as of theology. Faith is not merely subjective. It is not a state of human feelings, which is "true for me because I feel it to be true." Christian saving faith is a response to the objective facts, and to the reasoned truth (Romans 10:17). However, it is equally important that Christian saving faith is not merely orthodoxy, or the candid acceptance of correct doctrinal views. It is a personal response to a personal God, who comes to meet man in Jesus Christ. If there is no personal response of loving trust and obedience toward the God who is admitted to exist, there is no saving faith (James 2:19).

If the foundation of faith is acceptance of revealed Christian truth a second element in faith is what may be called *fidelity*. This is the proverbial "betting one's bottom dollar on God," and in response to what one believes about His power and goodness, committing one's whole way of life to Him in trust and obedience. This may be described as "the faith of Abraham" (Genesis 15:6), who in obedience to the call of God "went out, not knowing whither he went" (Hebrews 11:8). This faith, or steadfast fidelity, is the faith which is chiefly spoken of in the Old Testament (Hebrews 11:1–39). This is the authentic spiritual precursor of the fuller Christian faith of the New Testament (Romans 4:1–25).

However, fidelity does not comprise everything which the Christian means by full, saving, Christian faith (Hebrews 11:40). The essentially *Christian* element in saving faith is trust in the love and power of God as it is fully declared to man in the atoning death and glorious resurrection of His incarnate Son. And the climax of this is a personal faith in a personal Savior. Saving faith takes up into fellowship with Christ the whole personality of man, the affections of his heart as well as the convictions of his mind and the resolve of his moral will (Romans 10:9, 10). It is "faith which worketh by love" (Galatians 5:6). Therefore the essence of faith is a personal "faith-union" with Christ (Galatians 2:20). The most comprehensive New Testament term to express this idea is that the believer is "in Christ." The personal presence of Christ in the Spirit is the dominating and uniting principle, and the very "atmosphere" of the whole Church, of which the believer is a living member (Romans 16:7; 2 Corinthians 1:21, 5:17; Galatians 1:22; Colossians 1:2).

Saving Christian faith is the gift of God. A sincere inquirer may to some extent seek to convince himself of Christian truth, and seek to obey God on account of what he accepts. However, this alone will not take him very far upon the path to God. He cannot by desiring and striving constrain his heart to be filled with loving obedient personal trust in his Savior. Attainment of this "personal experience" is the work of the Holy Spirit (1 Corinthians 12:3). The Augustinian position in relation to this is that at the appointed time God implants the work of saving faith in His Elect, and so converts them. The more general theological position is that there is human cooperation at this point. Indeed, this is the crucial point of all human cooperation with God, for in the moment of decision man is free to choose whether or not he will open his heart to that offered gift which alone makes possible further divine-obedience.

It is precarious overconfidently to dogmatize about this mystery of the human heart. Clearly, man has to wait upon the initiative of grace. He may heartily *wish* that he were converted, and may sincerely pray for the experience, but he cannot say to himself, "Go to now, I *will* be converted!"

Before he can say "Yes" to God he must await the time when God shall choose to call. Yet it is the general confidence of the Church that those who do sincerely and expectantly wait upon God in the means of grace will in due season, sooner or later, certainly be called, and brought to the place of decision where they may receive the gift of faith. For a man of troubled spirit, under conviction of sin, to be found thus clinging to God in the use of the means of grace is on the one hand evidence that he has not yet been granted the gift of full, saving, Christian faith. Nevertheless, it is also a mark that he has faith of a sort, a dim and unformed faith, a faith informed by hope or by duty or by fear, rather than by love. If man will not use this "faith as a grain of mustard seed" for what it is worth, and watch for God in prayer, God will not lift him any further. Yet if he uses his will to make a faithful choice, God can answer the seeker's prayer of "Lord, I believe; help Thou mine unbelief" (Mark 9:24), and bring him to the point when he can, if he will, receive the gift of full Christian faith.

F. Justification

The action which God in grace takes toward those who by loving, trustful, obedient, and penitent faith unite themselves to Christ is described by evangelical theology as *justification*.

1. DEFINITION. The Biblical word "to justify" means "to bring in a verdict of 'not guilty' "—"*to acquit.*" Our Lord taught that the loving Father freely forgives the truly penitent sinner. This fundamental doctrine of grace is in the writings of St. Paul rendered into the language of the law court. The only way in which free forgiveness of the penitent sinner can be so rendered into legal phraseology is by the use of the rather startling paradox that God "acquits the guilty," or to use the more conventional translation, that He "justifies the ungodly" (Romans 4:5). Thus "justification" is forgiveness, and acceptance with God.

2. NEW TESTAMENT DISCUSSION. The reason for this important change in phraseology is seen in the circumstances of controversy within the early Church. Rabbinical Judaism, which was the background of so much of Christianity, was largely a religion of law. Its working assumption was that due obedience to all the commandments of the Mosaic Law is the ground of man's acceptance, as he appears before the tribunal of God the Judge. Man's great question as he appears before God is always: "What is the verdict?" His hope of acquittal, or "justification," is in the works of the Law. The first major decision which faced the infant Church was whether it was necessary for Gentile believers to become Jewish proselytes, and to be circumcised and observe the whole Law of Moses. The unity of the Church was maintained by a measure of judicious compromise, and by a decision that Gentile Christians need not keep the whole Law (Acts 15:1-29). St. Paul has his place as the chief protagonist of the "freedom

party," who was against the enforcement of circumcision, and he expressed his view in the formula "justification by faith, and not by the works of the Law" (Galatians 2:16). By this he meant that Christianity was not a revived and purified form of rabbinical Judaism, but a religion of salvation by grace. Man could not hope to earn a status of acceptance before God the Judge by his merit in fulfilling the Commandments. He had by penitent faith to accept free forgiveness in Christ. Thus the notion of "free forgiveness" came to be rendered into legal phraseology.

Summary of Divergence: Roman Catholic and Protestant Doctrines of Justification

a. Reformation Doctrine

Martin Luther and those who followed him felt that popular Roman Catholic devotional practice, and also much of the medieval Scholastic theology, overlaid the fundamental gospel of salvation by divine grace with the doctrine of "the merit of good works" (see p. 207). This issue presented itself to Luther in the following way. He felt that the Christianity of "merit earning" embodied the same principle as rabbinical and pharisaic Judaism. It was the religion of law creeping in to obscure and contaminate the gospel of grace. In opposition to this he took up St. Paul's formula, "justification by faith, and not by the works of the Law" (Galatians 2:16), and extended it into a general theological principle, applying it thereby to the controversial issues of his own time. Thus the practical and specific Pauline maxim "justification by faith" (Romans 1:17, 5:1; Galatians 3:24, and so forth) is expounded as the general doctrine of "justification by faith *alone*." To the evangelical theologian, following Luther, "justification by faith alone" is a strong and necessary affirmation of the proposition that sinful man's acceptance with God cannot be earned or merited by any human performance, no matter how virtuous. Man must humbly recognize that if he is ever to be forgiven it must be a *free* forgiveness, offered by God solely for the sake of His unmerited favor to those who accept the atoning work of Christ.

b. Roman Catholic Doctrine

The Roman Catholic Church has continued to speak of the merit of good works as contributing to justification. The Roman response to the challenge of Luther's doctrine is crystallized in the authoritative canons of the Council of Trent (1547). The following propositions are there condemned as in error: "That the impious is justified by faith alone—if this means that nothing else is required by way of cooperation in the acquisition of the grace of justification, and that it is in no way necessary for a man to be prepared and disposed by the motion of his own will"; and "That justification once received is not preserved and even increased in the sight of God through good works, but that these same works are only fruits and signs of justification, not causes of its increase." It will be seen that the purpose of these condemnations is to reaffirm the traditional Catholic position that man must freely cooperate with divine grace if he is to be finally saved. The canon is directed primarily against what Roman Catholic theologians felt would be the misunderstanding into which the people would be led by the formula "justification by faith alone"—namely, the notion that it is not essential for the saved to show a changed character and conduct, and that in salvation God does not take account of a virtuous character and conduct.

c. An Interpretative Statement

There is apparently a great gulf fixed between the rival formulae "justification by faith alone" and "justification by faith and the merit of good works." Both sides have often felt that the other is guilty of a radical corruption of Christian faith. In arguing that this divergence is not so great as it looks it is well not to overstate the case. Between the two sides there is some degree of genuine difference of apprehension of the Christian religion. As we have seen (pp. 217–18), Catholic tradition has been chiefly molded by the Christianity of nurture within the Church, and of discipline within the means of grace, whereas Evangelical tradition has been more influenced by the Christianity of the personal "conversion experience." Nevertheless, the divergence is not so great as appears. A difference of emphasis or proportion has been elevated into an apparent difference of essential principle by confusion of terms and mutual misunderstanding.

It will be seen that the authoritative condemnations framed for the Roman Catholic Church at Trent are directed against what were felt to be the dangerous implication of Protestant doctrine, particularly when misunderstood by simple people, rather than against the Lutheran formula itself. Catholics have been afraid of "antinomianism" (this word means "against the [moral] law"), that is, any understanding of "salvation by faith" which would impair the link between faith and strict morality, including fidelity to the Church and her institutions. And "justification by faith *alone*" has seemed to many to involve just this. The purpose behind the affirmation of "the merit of good works" has been to safeguard the claims of morality and devotional discipline within the Church, and to enforce that God both strictly requires these things of man, and graciously approves of them in him. Yet Evangelicals would be just as firm in maintaining that their doctrine is not "antinomian." Only when man is changed by the converting grace of God into the good tree can he even begin to bring forth the good fruit of a righteous life, and when he is so changed he will inevitably do so.

The difference of terminology centers around what is meant by the word "justification." Roman Catholic doctrine has defined justification to be not alone God's initial verdict of acquittal pronounced upon the penitent sinner, but as including also His final verdict upon the believer, at the Last Judgment (Matthew 12:36–37). Clearly, if this is justification, then the maxim "justification by faith alone" does appear to imply that man is to be admitted to heaven on account of his "spiritual experience," rather than on account of his actual character of righteousness and love. Such a notion allows Christian faith to sit lightly upon Christian morals, and is contrary to our Lord's own teaching (Matthew 25:31–46; Luke 6:46). Thus Roman Catholic theology has preferred to say that man is justified by faith and the merit of good works.

However, if justification is man's *initial* acceptance with God, the Protestant position is to be upheld, because sinful man, apart from the grace of God, certainly cannot earn his forgiveness.[4] Every good thing which he possesses is already the gift of God, and any service which he can hope to render in the future is only that which it is his duty to do to the Giver of all (Luke 17:10). Thus he can never make amends for the past, and so be "justified by works." The Protestant would affirm that "justification" is St. Paul's characteristic word, and that therefore it is only rightly used in his sense, which corresponds to the Protestant exegesis of the New Testament. It would appear that the apostle's general usage is that justification is forgiveness, or man's initial acceptance by God. However, the usage is apparently not absolutely invariable (1 Corinthians 6:11).

In stating the evangelical doctrine it is necessary to avoid the suggestion that justification is only a matter of form, a bare change of legal status before God. Still less does it imply that by a legal fiction God treats the sinner as other than he really is. The God who freely forgives the sinner who does not deserve to be forgiven indeed treats him as other than he is, but this is no legal fiction. In relation to the doctrine of the atonement we have seen that man requires "a double cure" (see pp. 83–84). He needs an assurance that the saving power of God can make a real difference to sinful man in his condition of bondage, and he needs also an assurance that the saving mercy of God will actually receive him, despite the guilty past, if he goes to God to claim this saving power. These two parts of "the double cure" are connected. The load of a guilty conscience, and of the tragic frustration of self-despisings in the presence of God, is the chief factor which prevents the prodigal from rising to go to his Father, to find what He will do for him. If this be so, then release from the burden of a guilty conscience, and the assurance that the God of love has accepted him as a reconciled child, is the chief factor which releases in the heart of man a new constructive wave of moral power. To be justified, therefore, is the first and all-important stage in a renewed manner of life, actually changed for the better in mind and heart, in will and action. Justification, that is, assurance of acceptance before God, is indeed only the *initial* stage

---

4 And a Roman Catholic theologian would agree with this, for the "good works" to which God attributes "merit" are those done in "a state of Christian grace." However, this initial divine grace is interpreted normally as baptismal regeneration.

of the changed life. It is the change worked in promise, and in this sense is a change chiefly of status. Yet it is a real promise, and a real beginning.

G. Regeneration

This is an alternative word for the initial step in the life of saving faith in Christ. The legal term "justification" has in mind this step chiefly from the aspect of man's standing before God, and of acceptance with Him. The broader and more "organic" term "regeneration," or "the new birth," has the same initial step in mind, but considered chiefly as the beginning of a new course of morally changed life. Those who in Christ are accepted by God as His reconciled children are indwelt by the personal presence of the Spirit of Christ, and enabled by His power, so that they are changed in heart and mind and will and action, and enjoy a power not their own which enables them to live a life well-pleasing to God. Thus they are regenerate, or born again by the Spirit (John 3:5, 7; 1 Peter 1:23).

So it has been said that justification is that which God does *for* us, regeneration that which God does *in* us.

H. Adoption

This Pauline word is yet another metaphor used to describe the new life of those who are united to Christ in faith. They are, as it were, taken into the spiritual family of God, so as in some sense to share Christ's filial privilege of confident access to the Father. Thus the word chiefly has reference to the believer's sense, in Christ, of a confident standing before God (Romans 8:15; Galatians 4:5, 6).

I. Assurance

The use of this word raises the issue of whether, and in what way, the believer may be "sure" of his salvation. Several different answers have been given in the Church.

Summary of Divergence: the Assurance of Salvation

a. Catholic Doctrine

The position traditional to Catholic doctrine has been, and is, that while the faithful Christian need not live in a state of anxious apprehension as to his state of salvation, he cannot be "sure" of it until he arrives at a godly and believing death. He should not doubt either the goodness of God or the security of His promises to bestow grace in the means of grace. However, no man can presume beforehand that he will not fall from the discipline of the Christian life, and from the way of salvation, until death takes him beyond the power of temptation. Thus "there are no saved Christians but dead Christians." This is a common-sense though somewhat prudential view of the matter.

b. Calvinist Doctrine

The Calvinist doctrine of assurance has been based chiefly upon the doctrine of the final perseverence of the saints (see p. 212). The decree of election is fixed, and therefore if a man once knows himself to be the object of God's irresistible grace he is assured that he will persevere through life to a state of salvation. Though he stumble into temptation at times, he cannot finally fall from grace.

c. Wesleyan Doctrine

The preaching of John Wesley (1703–1791) gave much prominence to the doctrine that it is possible for the believer to enjoy the spiritual privilege of a full assurance of salvation. As in some other matters, Wesley's teaching was a mediating synthesis, and a doctrine of practical piety rather than of speculative theology. The leading text, Romans 8:16, "The Spirit Himself beareth witness with our spirit, that we are the children of God," had already been used by the Calvinist divines to establish the idea of an inward witness of the Holy Spirit, but Wesley made a fuller exegesis to substantiate his distinctive doctrine of assurance. He observed that St. Paul speaks of two "witnesses." There is first "the witness of one's own spirit." According to Wesley this is the believer's common-sense argument that since his conversion he has experienced such a distinct change of inward moral will, and of outward practical discipline, that it is impossible for him to doubt that he is the object of God's saving grace (compare 1 John 2:3, 5, 29; 3:14, 24; 4:13). This was the essential foundation of assurance, to be looked for in all who claimed the privilege.

The full and sincere believer, however, might expect that God would add to this the additional privilege of "the witness of the Spirit of God." This Wesley describes as "an inward impression on the soul, whereby the Spirit of God directly witnesses to my spirit, that I am a child of God." From what he writes one may judge that as the former "witness" is the activity of the Holy Spirit in the moral life of the believer, so this "witness" is the imprint of the Spirit upon the emotional life, though it is certainly not necessarily a matter of exuberant or ecstatic emotion. It is, in fact, the abiding mark left by the experience of "the heart strangely warmed." When the two "witnesses" are conjoined in the Christian experience, then the believer rejoices in a full assurance that he is in a present state of salvation. However, Wesley teaches that this assurance is the *privilege* of the believer. It is to be prayed for and expected, but the circumstance that one does not possess it does not indicate that one is not in a state of salvation. Furthermore, he strongly affirms that it is the moral witness which is the essential element. To claim assurance on account of a state of emotion, but in absence of the profound moral change, is rebuked as a sure symptom of most dangerous fanaticism. Furthermore, Wesley teaches that this full assurance does not entitle the believer to presume that he is bound finally to be saved. If he does not carefully watch himself in the moral and devotional discipline of the Christian life the believer may fall from grace, and lose both his assurance and his salvation.

J. Sanctification

This is the name given to the growth in Christian grace which starts with regeneration, and which is to continue progressively all the days of the believer's life (Romans 5:3–5, 6:13–14; 1 Corinthians 6:9–20, 9:24–27; Ephesians 4:20–32; Colossians 3:1–17; 1 Thessalonians 4:3). A fundamental point is that this continuing spiritual and moral improvement of inward character and outward conduct is not a self-improvement imposed by discipline. It is the fruit of the effectual operation of the indwelling Spirit of grace (Romans 8:1–13; Galatians 5:22–26). Thus all his days the Christian continues to be dependent upon God's saving grace, no matter how confirmed in good habits he may become. However, the process of morally responsible cooperation with grace continues also (Philippians 2:12–13). It is at this point that Christian theology opens out into the whole field of Christian morality, the guiding rule of which is the "law of liberty" under the guidance of the Holy Spirit (1 Corinthians 8:1–9; James 1:25), as applied to ever-changing practical circumstances of life by the authoritative pastoral guidance of the Church (John 20:23).

K. Holiness

All who seek to follow a high ideal are bound to live in a certain state of tension between that ideal and what is practicable in real life, in view of the limitations and frailty of human nature, and the fallen state of the world. The Christian has espoused the noblest ideal of all, and therefore he is more than others aware of this tension. It is not surprising, therefore, that there should be in the Church many and sharply contrasting views as to what is the realistic ideal of Christian living in this world.

Summary of Divergence: Doctrines of Holiness

a. Catholic Doctrine

The traditional Catholic doctrine of the saintly life has been, and is, that of a double Christian calling. As this has been expressed in Roman Catholic teaching, all the faithful are called by God to follow the "evangelical precepts," while the few are called to the higher standard of the "counsels of perfection." The chief scriptural warrant for this doctrine has been found in the word of our Lord to the rich young ruler, that if he would be "perfect" he should forsake all his property, and take up the austere life of a wandering disciple (Matthew 19:21).

The background of this doctrine of a double standard is the assumption that the whole of the baptized community of the "Christian" city or nation is in some sense called to Christian discipleship, even though the majority are frail and compromised human beings who can only follow the Lord from afar off. However, there are within the community a number of self-denying and devoted souls, who are called by God to a life entirely given to the service of Christ, and who are equipped with the special grace necessary to follow this calling.

Thus in the matter of property: ever since the Fall contaminated this world, the lower spiritual order of private property, with the social divisions which follow from it, has been necessary as a matter of discipline. The evangelical precept binding on all in relation to this private property is to be law-abiding, just, honest, diligent, and charitable to the poor. The corresponding counsel of perfection is that those who are called to a life of entire Christian devotion should seek the higher spiritual condition of religious poverty, in the brotherly life of communal property. In the matter of the relation of the sexes, likewise, the standard suitable to most Christian men and women is that marriage and the procreation of children is ordained by God, in order that the race be continued and vice restrained (Genesis 1:27–28, 3:16; 1 Corinthians 7:1, 2, 8, 9, 27, 28). The evangelical precept is that each man should live honorably with his wife in the sanctity of the marriage bond, and bring up Christian children (Matthew 19:1–9). However, those who are called to the higher devotion of the counsels of perfection are to remain celibate in the service of Christ (Matthew 19:10–12; 1 Corinthians 7:29–35).

This may be described as a "realistic" doctrine. It takes serious account of the admitted circumstance that it is impossible to discipline the entire nominal Christian community to live *en masse* according to the highest Christian ideals. Any attempt to constrain men to live beyond the grace granted to them will defeat its own end. It is to the spiritual advantage of most ordinary men that they discipline themselves according to a more moderate and prudential standard. However, there are a few to whom is granted an outstanding zeal for religion, and they have a calling from God to render outstanding service. For these it is good to attempt a stricter discipline. And each branch of Christian discipline has its own due place in God's plan.

The effect of this doctrine is to make Christian "perfection" virtually synonymous with the conventual life of a religious Order, under the canonical vows of poverty, chastity, and obedience. A danger in the system is that it may suggest to the general Christian community that the most which can be expected of them is a second-rate standard of discipleship, and that serious religion is the business of the separated clergy and the monastic Orders.

b. Reformation Doctrine

The Protestant Reformers strongly reacted against the medieval doctrine of the counsels of perfection, because to them it seemed to answer to the notion of "the merit of good works," and to be inconsistent with the doctrine of salvation by grace. Thus classic Reformation doctrine frowned upon the mention of "perfection" as inconsistent with an adequate view of human depravity, and of mankind as absolutely dependent upon grace. The emphasis here is that even the converted man is bound to continue all his life as a helpless sinner, though "a sinner saved by grace." Thus until he arrives in heaven the Christian is "both justified, and a sinner."

This latter maxim of Reformation theology is not intended to permit moral laxity or antinomianism, for the man who is in a state of grace ought to be living the life of the Spirit, and growing up to a thorough spiritual and moral change. However, this doctrine can display a weakness, for it may suggest the "world-despairing" attitude which regards the manifest moral ills of ordinary human society as in principle beyond repair. The conclusion is then close to hand that the most which the Christian man can do is to live the life of grace within the sphere of Church worship and private devotion and allow the social, economic, and political conventions of the community to be regulated by social, economic, and political influences. Thus the division which in the Catholic system appeared between the "secular life" and the "religious life" here reappears between the devotional life and the civic life.

c. Wesleyan Doctrine

The doctrine of holiness is another matter in which the preaching of John Wesley significantly attempted a mediating synthesis in the form of a strong evangelical doctrine of grace, which yet called the earnest believer to the hope of perfection. This system of thought, often modified in various ways, and sometimes deteriorated, has since Wesley's time been influential among Methodists, and also with other groups of Evangelicals whose tradition goes back to the revival of the eighteenth century, rather than to classic Protestantism.

The background of Wesley's teaching is not that of an evangelical Church which ministers to a whole community, but that of a closely knit society of religious devotees within the Church, banded together by unsparing discipline for the purpose of reviving the general body of the Church. Thus the appeal is avowedly made, as in the Catholic system, to the minority who are called by God to a life of outstanding devotion and service. Wesley indeed held out the ideal of holiness to all men, but his guiding interest is not prudentially to legislate for what is practicable in the general body of the "Christian" community. He is holding up an ideal to ardent devotees. However, this disciplined group is not, as in general Catholic practice, to pursue a course of monastic life more or less separate from the secular community. The expectancy of the highest standard of Christian discipleship is confidently to be held out to ordinary men and women who are surrounded by the cares of home and family, and who have a living to earn in the world.

The group seeking holiness is to be marked off from the rest of the world by its strict devotional discipline, by its austere life of diligence, frugality, and charity, and by its plain-spoken zeal in reminding men of the claims of real religion and in rebuking the sins, follies, vanities, and compromises of conventional society. Thus it is to possess something of the office and spirit of monasticism, but it is a "monasticism" to be lived out in the home, the market, and the workshop. Wesley assures ordinary men and women that if they have genuine and wholehearted faith no limit is to be set to the power of Christ completely to transform the human personality. No known and willing compromise is to be accepted as inevitable. Nevertheless, the tension between the ideal and the generally practicable inevitably reappears, though in another form. There is tension between the group seeking holiness, who are to be accounted "Christians" in the full sense of the word, and the rest of the community, who are but nominal Christians. The spiritual danger here is manifestly that the society of the zealous may slip into self-righteousness, and into alienation from the main body of the Church.

Wesley's doctrine is that Christian perfection, or holiness,[5] is to be defined as the divine gift of "perfect love." This is not "sinless perfection." The believer cannot expect to be lifted in this life beyond all human limitations. He who has the gift of holiness will still be tempted, and may sincerely misjudge other people, inadvertently doing them wrong. He may be entrapped into a fault through ignorance or inexperience, or by being taken by surprise in unforeseen circumstances. He will still be beset by his natural human limitations of temperament and mental equipment, so that he may not be able to render God all the service which man ideally ought. However, when he recognizes temptation he will turn from it with a ready instinct of loathing. When he finds himself in a fault he will not dally with sin and defile himself, but will straightway repent, and will beware of that fault again. In fact, holiness in the gift of a heart which entirely goes out in love toward God. Man cannot arrive in this life at sinless perfection, but perfect love can grant entire victory over all known and willful sin.

This condition, according to Wesley, is Christian perfection, and is the fulfillment of our Lord's promise and command, "Be ye therefore perfect, even as your Father which is in heaven is perfect" (Matthew 5:48). Those who uphold this as the due ideal of the Christian life affirm that to deny this standard is to allow that willful compromise with known sin is inevitable in the Christian life, no matter how sincere be the faith of the disciple. This is to deny the power of Christ to save to the uttermost, and in practice cuts the nerve of Christian endeavor.

Those who believe that God has in fact granted them the gift of holiness or perfect love, and who feel that in giving their Christian testimony they must witness to this, rather than deny the gift of God, do well to remember that modesty about one's spiritual attainments is one of the marks of the truly good man or woman. Such modesty adds to the spiritual effectiveness of Christian testimony. Therefore the believer will take care to speak with

---

5 Also called "entire sanctification."

discretion, remembering that the experience is a gift of divine grace, and not an 'attainment.'

It was Wesley's belief that the divine gift of perfect love was given in a moment of time. This idea is an inherently reasonable one. Profound psychological experiences of all sorts commonly work up to a sudden climax, and so it is natural to expect that if some believer were to come to an unusually enhanced spiritual illumination the experience would be granted in a flash of insight. Thus some have thought of "entire sanctification" as an instantaneous experience, parallel to "conversion," and this has given rise to the name for it of "the second blessing."

L. Mysticism

The discussion of the work of grace in the heart may be brought to a close by a brief evaluation of the mystical experience. In the wider sense a mystic is one who comes to an experience of immediate union with, or communion with, God. Thus everyone who has any experience of religion which is inward and spiritual must have at least a little of the mystic about him. If mystical communion is totally lacking, the worshipper can get no further than a conventional attendance at church service, and the bare pursuit of moral duty. However, there are some few souls possessed of exceptionally active and sensitive spiritual faculties, who are able to follow the experiences of inward and spiritual religion to an enhanced degree. These are called, in the proper sense of the word, the *mystics*.

The normal mark of a mystic is first, that the sense of spiritual unworthiness before the holy God, which in the normal believer is to be described in terms of "conviction of sin," is to the mystic deepened into a profound and agonizing sense of utter separation from God. This has been written of in the meditations of the mystics in such terms as "the dark night of the soul," during which man has to walk by "naked faith," that is to say, by faith in God utterly unsupported by any sense of joy or peace. This descent to the depths will then be followed by the other normal mark of the mystic, namely, a height of spiritual rapture which is beyond words to express. That which in the normal believer is described as joy and peace in God, and perhaps as the full assurance of salvation, is by the mystic spoken of in such terms as "the marriage of the soul with God." The witness of the mystic is that he has been granted a precious experience of complete union with the divine, such as he cannot utter (2 Corinthians 12:2-4).

First it may be said that the psychological mechanism of the mystical experience is natural, though unusual. Thus there have been true mystics in religions other than the Christian. The factor of importance, therefore, to the faith of the Church is not whether a certain man or woman has a genuine mystical experience, but whether or not he is a true *Christian* mystic. The mark of distinctively Christian mysticism is its secure attachment to the historic Christian faith, and to the historic Christian Church. The Christian Faith and Church may be likened to the filament in an electric lamp, and the intense spiritual experience of the mystic to the powerful electric current which makes the filament glow. The true calling of the mystic is to infuse a strong sense of the inward and spiritual into the familiar apparatus of worship and doctrine. Thus, when the mystic remains in the Faith, and in the Church, he can shed a clear and guiding light. However, if he yields to the temptation to isolate himself from the historic Faith and Church, as from religion at an inferior and "unspiritual" level, he may be found in serious error. The mark of delusion in the mystic is to seek to enjoy the heavenly light apart from the objective and common-sense "filament."

One or two symptoms of this error may be noted. In the first place, it has been defined above that a mystic comes to an experience of immediate union with, or communion with, God. There is an important distinction between "union" and "communion." Some mystics have spoken of "union" with the divine as though in the moment of spiritual rapture the personal distinction between God and the human soul were erased. This reflects the pantheistic doctrine that the soul of man is a "drop of divinity," that God is "the ocean of divinity," and that the destiny of man is for the drop to be lost again in the ocean. This is a notion inconsistent with the fundamental Christian doctrine of a sovereign personal God. True Christian mysticism speaks rather of the closest intimacy of personal *communion* with God, the personal distinction between God and man being carefully preserved.

Furthermore, some mystics have looked to the immediate inward and individual communion of the soul with God as an authority for new revelations of doctrine. This is a lapse into subjectivism. The true and Christian purpose of the mystical "inner light" is not to transcend historic doctrine, or to supersede reason, but to illuminate the rational and historic faith with passionate personal devotion. Clearly, also, the mystic is characteristically somewhat of a religious individualist. The most spiritually profitable Christian mystics have lived their lives of devotion within the regular institutions of the Church, even though in a sense they have sometimes been "in the Church, but not altogether of it."[6] Thus their activity has kept alive within the institutional Church the sense of inward and spiritual

---

[6] Many Roman Catholic mystics have been of this type.

religion. Other mystics have yielded to the natural temptation to write off the established ecclesiastical machine as hopelessly formal, external, and "unspiritual," and have formed private circles of their own disciples.[7] These have then gradually institutionalized themselves into new denominations, usually of a highly individualistic character, and sometimes also of an unorthodox and deviationist doctrine.[8] This is, we feel, a loss to the cause of Christian faith.

Readings

Barclay, W., *Turning to God*. Philadelphia: Westminster Press, 1964.

Hodgson, L., *The Grace of God in Faith and Philosophy*. London: Longmans, Green & Company, Ltd., 1936.

Flew, R. N., *The Idea of Perfection in Christian Theology*. London: Oxford University Press, 1934.

Watson, P. S., *Let God be God!* London: The Epworth Press, 1954. (Historical study of Luther's doctrine of grace.)

Yates, A. S., *The Doctrine of Assurance*. London: The Epworth Press, 1952.

---

[7] For example, George Fox.
[8] For example, Jacob Böhme.

Chapter Ten

The Hope of Glory

He shall come to judge the quick and the dead.
—The Resurrection of the body,
And the life everlasting

I. The Christian Hope

One of the clearest marks of authentic Christianity is that it is the religion of a reasoned and a triumphant hope—a hope for the future life of the individual, and a hope for the future of the world. This note rings out clear and plain throughout the New Testament (Romans 5:4, 5; 1 Corinthians 13:13; Ephesians 4:4; Colossians 1:27; Hebrews 6:19; 1 Peter 1:3, 3:15). This was one of the chief factors which gave early Christianity its "cutting edge" in the pagan world which was its mission field. The mythological religions of antiquity had been discredited, and the people were left with no secure religious view of life on which to lay hold. The few and educated tried to comfort themselves as best they could with the somewhat rarified consolations of philosophy, and the ignorant walked in dread of magic. There was a hope of immortality among the Gentiles, but it was the wistful hope that a reduced echo of man's present personal existence might continue for a while in the unseen world. As for the world order, the golden age was thought of in terms of the remote past, and if there was hope for a better day in the future it was conceived of in the frustrating doctrine that history is a cyclical process. Throughout all time the wheel of good and bad fortune went round and round.

What deeply impressed the pagan world about the Christians was the spectacle of men with hope. There was a hope for the world. Human history, under the hand of a mighty God, was actually going somewhere worthwhile. Therefore life was not "a tale told by an idiot, full of sound and fury, signifying nothing." And the Christians were so sure of a personal and blessed life with God, as a part of this world-hope, that they were not afraid to die, and to die the dreadful death of the arena. That proud Regulus, fortified by considerations of birth and public honor, should summon up his courage to face a patriot's death by torment was known among the Romans, and held in high regard. A doctrine which could put this heroic spirit into the lower classes, into weak women, and even into cringing slaves, was new and strange, and strangely impressive!

What was true in the ancient world is eminently true also in the modern. One of the leading symptoms of a denatured popular Christianity is a pulpit which is vague and sentimental about heaven. It is sentimental, in its implied suggestion that all tolerably decent people will surely go to heaven, and quite apart from living faith in Christ and moral obedience to Him. It is vague, in that it leaves the impression that this sentiment is no more than a sentiment, for which the Christian preacher has no more substantial support than that he wishes to say something comforting and kindly to the mourners at a funeral. He does not speak as though the Christian hope were a matter of secure knowledge.

Clearly, also, for the same reason, comfortable people surrounded by a score of pleasant luxuries in their homes are in a state of morbid excitement about the world situation. Though they profess, sincerely enough, to believe in God, they cannot bring themselves to believe in a God who is actually in control of the world. The assumption natural to "the modern man" is that human affairs are a current of events driven along by the desire to earn a living, and to win an improved standard of living. This is a view which interprets life as a process without any deep and satisfying meaning. All too often it passes unnoticed that the factor which sometimes gives a tiny Communist minority its fatal secret of iron morale in time of crisis, and which lends to it the power to browbeat the helpless driven herd of "economic men," is the very characteristic which belongs to the authentic Christian! Communists have persuaded themselves that there is a ruling process in world history, and that in their restless political activity they are the instruments of an irresistible force. This is a factor of which conventional statesmen can take no adequate measure, for it is outside their accustomed categories of practicability and sectional interest. Here is the element of hope, stolen from the Christian system! Therefore in many ways the Christian doctrine of the Christian hope, personal and historical, is the very climax of the whole conception of the life of Christian grace.

There was a spring of hope in the ancient world, and significantly it rose from among the Jews, a nation which had greatly suffered. The faith of the Jews was fixed upon one personal and sovereign God, who rules the world in justice. The history of the world, therefore, is no mere cyclical process, but a train of events flowing from the hand of a mighty God. It has a meaning, and will end in a manner worthy of God. The power of evil indeed appears to rule in this world, but in His chosen time God will show Himself to be king by visiting the world with His power. He will overthrow the might of evil, and advance His chosen righteous ones to power and glory, and this sovereignty He will exert in the person of His Messiah.

However, the mainspring of this hope was not the natural desire of the people to be free of the pagan yoke. It was a craving to see God's ways justified to men. This deeper spring of hope it was which gave to the suffering Jewish people their obstinacy of expectation. In a sad and difficult world those who are hoping for some good thing for themselves will in the end lose hope. Those whose eyes are fixed upon the sole glory of God Almighty will count it worthwhile, if necessary, to be martyrs, for they have an assurance that though they perish their sufferings are not in vain. And this preparedness to be a martyr is the sure secret of that heightened morale which can sustain the distressed cause of right in the day of adversity, and rise to opportunity in the day of opportunity. Therefore it is no accident that the theology of the Christian hope is the most Jewish-Christian part of the Faith. This Hebraic character is both the source of its strength, and the reason why it is so hard for the average modern mind to appreciate it aright.

The inquiring mind will next ask how it is possible to have a theology of hope, for hope concerns the future, and the future is unknown. It is for this reason that it is so widely assumed that when the Christian speaks of the hope of heaven he is doing no more than voicing his own private speculations, which have no more authority than his own limited wisdom. The suspicion is then close to hand that the power of wishful thinking is at work. The skeptic advances his theory that it is comforting for man to believe that he will see his loved ones again, and in a happier place, and that therefore the subconscious mind suggests the natural and sincere delusion that there is such a better life. So it is also with the Christian hope for the world order. When this is treated by the serious theologian it is often sadly the case that no part of Christian doctrine is more securely wrapped in incomprehensible jargon! And if it be treated plainly, for the plain man, it is all too often made the peculiar preserve of "Adventist cranks," who revenge themselves upon a Church which has often failed to speak plainly of the Christian hope by preaching a variant of Christianity which consists of virtually nothing but this doctrine.

In all these ways the impression has been spread abroad that the doctrine of the Christian hope is not a matter of reliable knowledge. This has gone far to subdue the spiritual expectation and relax the moral tension of our accustomed Christianity, and so to cut the nerve of heroism and confident hope. If the answer is made that the ground of Christian knowledge of the future hope is simply and sufficiently the doctrine of the Bible, the issue is still not settled. When it was commonly assumed that God inspired the Scripture by implanting mysterious knowledge on the passive minds of the writers, it could be supposed that these writers could foresee the future. However, if it is accepted that God revealed His truth through the working of the human minds of the biblical writers, then it still remains to be asked how they could be inspired to speak of the future.

As science depends so largely in her methods upon an act of faith in the *continuity of nature,* so does the Christian doctrine of the future destiny of the soul, and of the world order, depend in the last resort upon an act of faith in *the continuity of the spiritual order*. The scientist who pronounces that the sun is at a distance of 93 million miles, and is of such and such a mass and temperature, has not "been up to see." He has perfected the laws of measurement in this world of immediate experience, where his theories can be verified by practical experiment. He then makes the assumption, which the findings of science indicate to be a reasonable assumption, that these laws apply also to spheres of existence of which he can have no immediate experience. Therefore, having made his observations of the effects of the sun in this world of immediate experience, he climbs the ladder of mathematical calculation to knowledge of the distant substance of the sun.

So also, the biblical writers, and the theologians who reason from the Bible, have not "been up to visit heaven." They have, however, made the basic assumption that life is a spiritual and moral order. It proceeds under constant laws which are the expression of the will of a God who is always the same, and who can be depended upon to deal with His children in a reliable manner. If spiritual laws are to be observed in this life, it may be assumed that God's government of men will proceed according to analogous laws in the life to come. If the present spiritual and moral process, which is inevitably broken off by the dark mystery of death, appears to be leading toward some goal, then it is a rational act of faith that that goal will be reached, and that destiny fulfilled in the future. A good God, who is reasonable in his dealings with His children, will not raise hopes only to disappoint them—universally, inevitably, and completely![1]

A leading example of this process may be seen from the manner in which this hope originally arose among the Jews. The earlier Hebrew conception of the destiny of the departed was similar to that of many primitive peoples, and was of the kind which is naturally evoked by mysterious and uncanny psychical experiences such as "familiar spirits" and "haunting," and also by dreams about persons who have died. It was supposed that the spirits of the dead survived in a dim underground world called Sheol (Job 11:8), a word which is customarily though not very happily translated as "hell"

---

[1] Thus the Christian belief in immortality has traditionally been accounted a part of natural religion (see p. 24).

(Psalm 16:10).[2] Their existence there was but a reduced and disjointed continuation of the life of this world, a kind of dying echo (Isaiah 14:9–17), because "the spirit of life" had been taken from them (Job 34:14–15). In particular, the dead in Sheol had no effective communion with God, who was the God only of the living (Psalm 6:5, 115:17; Isaiah 38:18). However, God's sovereignty extended there (Job 26:6; Psalm 139:8; Amos 9:2).

Among the more spiritually sensitive Hebrews the impact of religious persecution upon this ancient system of belief was very profound. Faith suggested that in His Day God would destroy the power of evil in the world, and set up His kingdom. However, it would seem that the departed righteous would be excluded in Sheol from this promised day of divine vindication. The problem to faith was particularly acute in the case of the martyrs, who would apparently be shut out from the satisfaction of that day by the very death which was the crown of their religious merit. From this background was developed the doctrine that the righteous would rise from Sheol at the Day of the Lord. Their bodies would be reunited with "the spirit of life," so that they might live to take part in God's triumph, (Isaiah 26:19; Daniel 12:2). This doctrine of resurrection was naturally complemented by the conception of the resurrection of the wicked to judgment. It will be seen that the basis of the doctrine of resurrection was *an act of faith in the justice of God.*

As we consider the Christian hope, and the doctrine of the Last Things,[3] we face a number of propositions which *"must"* be true if God is fully sovereign, just, good, and reasonable in His dealings with men and women. As with the Jews in their hope, the ultimate ground of these beliefs is an

---

[2] Gehenna, the place of punishment of the finally impenitent (Mark 9:47), is also translated as "hell." However, the two terms are quite different.

[3] *Eschatology, apocalyptic.* We may here explain these two technical terms, for they are common in theological writing. *Eschatology* (from the Greek *eschatos,* "the extreme, the last") is the doctrine of the final destiny of the human soul, and of the world order. In the general sense it can include the conception of a far-off destiny, but it generally carries the connotation, particularly in much modern theological writing, that God's final act of history is at the present time or in the immediate future. Thus the eschatological expectation brings the sense that man is living at the crisis of the ages.

Apocalyptic (Greek "unveiling") is a distinctive form of biblical eschatological writing, in which the rise of the power of evil in the world order, and its final overthrow at the Day of the Lord, are traced out in a kind of drama of superhuman personifications and symbolical events. The vivid, and commonly even bizarre, coloring of the imagery answers to the heightened psychological tension of men who are fighting to retain their faith and hope in the most desperate of situations. Those who are summoning up their courage to die the death of martyrs cannot be content with a placid or level-headed presentation of faith. The apocalyptic writings speak out of the situation of persecution, and therefore appeal to the Church primarily in times of persecution and insecurity. The most developed example of this type of writing in the Bible is the Revelation, or Apocalypse, of St. John. Daniel 7–12 and Zechariah are also of this character, and there are many noncanonical apocalyptic books, Jewish and Christian.

act of faith in the spiritual constancy of God. Even within the confines of a life hemmed in by inevitable frustrations and limitations man has been confronted by God in Christ, and granted the gift of life in fellowship with God. Faith teaches that what God has once initiated He will bring to due fulfillment, for He is an unchanging God whose purpose none can ultimately resist. Therefore the present saving act in Christ carries implicit within it the promise of an unlimited and unfrustrated confrontation by Christ, in a world not darkened by sin.

The skeptic's charge is that this hope is a subjective delusion conjured up by wishful thinking from the subconscious. This common charge can indeed come home with devastating force to the widespread, easy-going, and sentimental delusion that in the unseen world everything will be automatically serene and happy for all tolerably decent folk, because the God with whom we have to do is an indulgent God who is bound easily and lightly to forgive. And it is well that this false hope should be deflated, even though the loss may bring pain to some. The God whom all men have to confront is a God of holy love, and the just judge of all the earth, whose love requires holy love in return. An eternal destiny of life with Him is certainly not the hope which wishful thinking will suggest as attractive to the mind of the natural man (Hebrews 10:31). The true Christian hope is an austere hope, which only those can dare to contemplate whose trust reposes in the saving work of Christ. The Christian hope, therefore, is not the illusory man-centered hope of those who are seeking comfort for themselves, but the secure and God-centered hope of those whose concern it is to see the holy love of God fully vindicated (Matthew 5:6).

The Christian doctrine of the Last Things is set forth in the Bible in imagery and symbolism. This is a necessity of thought and expression, for these doctrines concern matters which are not part of immediate human experience in this world. Therefore they cannot be described in matter-of-fact language drawn from human experience, and which can be taken literally. However, it by no means follows that this part of Christian doctrine is vague, unsubstantial, fanciful, unimportant, and not to be taken seriously as a branch of spiritual knowledge (see pp. 12–13). Provided the symbolism is properly understood, the eschatological and apocalyptic parts of the Bible contain truths of spiritual value. However, these truths do not consist so much of factual information about future events, as a sense of heightened yet solemn expectancy which is to pervade the whole of the Christian system of life and thought. This part of the Christian creed is a battle cry to be shouted, and an ode of victory to be sung, rather than a set of propositions to be reflected upon!

We do not say that our Lord's second advent, the general resurrection, and the last judgment are not events, though they are not in the ordinary sense of the word *historical* events, for they will take place when God has brought to an end the present course of history. However, the spiritual and theological importance of these events does not consist in what we factually know about them, so much as in what we *feel* about them. A vivid expectation of our Lord's victorious second advent, and a strong sense that the judgment is even now upon us, is one of the leading elements which lifts Christianity above the level of a placid and good-natured system of reasonable doctrine, customary worship, and admonitory ethics, and makes of it a fighting creed which can move men to stern endeavor, and for which they are even prepared to die. This element of Christian hope fills the New Testament, and the stories of the martyrs. It is an integral part of balanced and healthy Christianity. If this nervous tension is relaxed, one of the principle sinews of faith is severed. Nevertheless, it is also a fact that overcurious and overinsistent pressing of such questions as, "When will it happen?" "Will it happen visibly and suddenly?" "How far are we to take the Biblical symbolism *literally* and *pictorially?*" is contrary to the intention and genius of the Bible itself. It is an asking of the wrong questions, which can all too easily take the mind away from the important biblical answers. To wish for *matter-of-fact* knowledge of these future events is to desire to know the unknowable, and to find in the Bible that which is not there.

Some writers have assumed that an urgent advent hope and a care for ecclesiastical and moral discipline are interests in some way contrary one to another, because those who are daily awaiting the end of the Age will not be interested in the organization of the Church or the right ordering of human society. It is asserted that this was the case with the first Church. This surely is a mistake. A belief that the time remaining before the end is short will affect the Christian judgment as to what is appropriate moral conduct. Thus St. Paul's teaching to the Corinthians regarding marriage and slavery clearly reflects this influence (1 Corinthians 7:18–35). However, a vivid sense that the Church is living at the crisis of the ages, when every action counts because divine judgment is at the door, is generally found to be one of the most powerful of all influences to nerve the Christian community to strenuous moral endeavor and strict discipline. Those who are waiting are to be on the alert (Mark 13:34–37).

II. Hebrew and Greek Symbolism

The background of our Lord's teaching and ministry was the Jewish messianic hope (see pp. 45–46). He apparently announced that the expected kingdom had come, and spoke of Himself, at least guardedly, as the Messiah of divine promise. This message was thus framed in the thought forms of the Hebrew prophets, and to some extent, at least, in the imagery of apocalyptic. It is fundamental to an understanding of our Lord's teaching to realize that it was eschatological, though we believe that it is an error to assume, as some critics do, that it was naïvely or crudely eschatological, or that Jesus was virtually a deluded messianic dreamer (see pp. 245-46). Nevertheless, the fact remains that the symbolism which is largely used in the New Testament to express the Christian hope and the doctrine of the Last Things is radically Hebraic.

This Hebraic symbolism views the history of this world as a succession of divine acts performed under the sovereign hand of God. During the present evil Age Satan and his forces are permitted by God to exercise a certain amount of sway over the sinful human race. At the end of the Age will come God's last and most significant act. He will invade the world with the power of His sovereign kingdom, destroy the power of evil, judge all men, redeem His people, and thus, in bringing to an end the present history of the world, will show Himself to be God indeed. The dividing line between this evil world and the supremacy of the things of God is, as it were, a vertical wall, a demarcation in the future. One order will suddenly pass away, and another take its place. In terms of this scheme God's gift to man of triumph over death is the resurrection of the dead, and divine judgment is the future last judgment.

However, this is not the only system of symbolism which is used to express these truths. Thought forms which go back in the main ultimately to the more philosophical and scientific mentality of the Greeks provided the chief intellectual apparatus of the ancient Church, once it had grown away from its Jewish-Christian origins. These Greek thought forms are a main constituent of secular thought in the Western world of today. Here is another and contrasting form of symbolism for expressing the relationship between this world, and the supremacy of the things of God. A lower and material sphere of being, of less intellectual and spiritual worth now exists, and also the higher and essentially nonmaterial sphere of reason and of spiritual values. There is, as it were, a presently existent horizontal wall between them. The course of events in this lower world is regarded as a self-acting process under natural law, presided over by superior reason. When religious faith wishes to affirm the supremacy of the things of God in terms of this system of thought one arrives at the familiar proposition that human personality and eternal spiritual values are more important than "the material." God's gift to man of triumph over death is the promise that the invisible soul, which is "the real man," survives the death of the body, and lives in communion with God in a blessed immortality. Divine judgment is God's present attitude to the thoughts, feelings, and acts of man, and is a continuous process.

These two systems of symbolism for the Christian hope, the Hebraic, or biblical, and the Greek, are not mutually exclusive. Though superficially very different they are in fact complementary, for each has its own theological value. One cannot say that one or the other is "right" or "wrong." If a surveyor and an artist were both sent to visit a beautiful city, and to bring back a true representation, their work would be very different in superficial appearance. This would be due to the difference in medium of expression. Nevertheless, both the town plan and the landscape would be valid in its own medium, and useful for its own proper purpose. So it is with the Greek and Hebraic types of symbolism. Superficially they are very different, and some have pronounced them to be inconsistent. Some have affirmed that the original Jewish-Christian eschatological presentation of the Christian hope is naïve and crude, and that it was right and good that it should have been displaced in the Church by later and more philosophical conceptions. Others have seen the same change as the Hellenizing corruption of early and authentic Christianity. A more considered judgment is that both these views are partial and erroneous.

The underlying spiritual intention of both the Hebraic and the Greek forms of doctrine is to express the triumph of the things of God, and to assure the believer of the fulfillment of his life with God. The concrete and nonspeculative Hebrew system is primarily of devotional value. It serves to preserve in the Church that heightened expectancy of hope which nerves the believer to seriousness and courage. The more philosophical and scientific Greek scheme is of value in systematic theology. It fits in the Christian hope with the rest of the system of Christian doctrine. For example, the believer's triumph over death when considered in terms of the divine gift to the soul of immortality harmonizes with the doctrine of the communion of saints (see pp. 133–35). The Greek system of symbolism also harmonizes with systems of Christian philosophy. In the doctrine of the Christian hope there is therefore within the Church a twofold tradition. To keep the two sides together, and to keep them in balance, is not always easy, but the Church affirms that both are necessary to the sound body of doctrine.

It is no accident that the doctrines of the second advent, the resurrection of the body, the millennial kingdom, and the Last Judgment, which are perhaps the most distinctively Hebraic parts of the whole Christian system, have often proved some of the hardest to understand. This is on account of the immense contrast between this mode of thought and that which is customarily employed in ordinary modern secular thought. Yet the Church should not neglect to understand these doctrines, for there are important spiritual values to be preserved. The gradual reinterpretation of the Christian hope into the more philosophic terms of Greek thought was made necessary as the Church rapidly became a predominantly Gentile body, and had to make herself understood in the Gentile world which had not been nurtured upon the Old Testament.

The incipient change of emphasis is seen within the New Testament itself. Thus the twofold doctrine can be regarded as scriptural. St. Paul's original vivid Jewish eschatology was apparently misunderstood at Gentile Thessalonica, and he had to write to tell his converts that they must not live in daily and agitated expectation of the second advent, so as to give up earning a living (2 Thessalonians 2:1–8, 3:6–10). Later on he had personally to face the possibility that he might die before the coming of Christ (2 Timothy 4: 6–8). Later still, some in the Church were perplexed at the prolonged delay, and had to revise their Scripture exegesis and calculations (2 Peter 3:3–9).

In particular, we are faced with the problem of the virtual evaporation in the Fourth Gospel of the original urgent Jewish eschatology. To some expositors John 20:17 appears to imply that Christ's ascension to glory took place immediately after His resurrection, while John 14:15–18 almost seems to indicate that the promise of Christ's return after His ascension was fulfilled in the gift of the Holy Spirit. A glorious presence of Christ with His Church in current experience has virtually taken the place of the anticipated future advent in glory. In line with this, God's judgment upon man through Christ is a present and continuing process (John 3:17–18). However, although the general resurrection is immediately present in Christ (John 11:25), our Lord is still also the Son of Man (the Messiah), who is to come bringing a future resurrection and judgment (John 5:25–29). Not everything is plain in this profound and various book, but the Church is clearly feeling her way toward the later double tradition. In the Fourth Gospel there is the Greek as well as something of the Hebraic Christian hope.

The Gentile Church of later tradition did not always find it easy to keep a just balance between its original Hebraic and biblical Christian hope, and the Greek thought forms which it had to employ in order to interpret Christian faith to the Gentile world. The Greek mentality was rarely altogether at ease with the vivid and concrete imagery of the Jewish and Jewish-Christian apocalyptic literature, which is so largely associated with the doctrine of the Christian hope. This was because, unlike the Hebraic mind, it was systematic and pictorial. It would hardly have occurred to the Jewish apocalyptists to try to draw pictures of the heavenly or infernal visitants of which they wrote. Indeed, their religion forbade them to portray the human form, as in the picture of an angel. Thus when an apocalyptist speaks of an "angel" he does not think of a figure with white robes and wings, after the manner of later Christian art. He is symbolizing a concrete and embodied message.

Nor was it their interest to arrange the apocalyptic visions successively into a chronology, as though history were a process. The "half-hour" or "thousand years" of the Revelation of St. John are not measured on a clock. They are symbols of spiritual quantities. When the Greek-minded reader came to such books, if he wished to take them quite seriously he instinctively understood them in a much more pictorial and chronological manner than was justified by the original intention of the writer. The result of this was the naïve and at times crudely material millenarianism of some of the Church fathers. In the same tradition are the stirring but fantastic pictures of the last judgment found in medieval Churches, and the endless series of attempts to calculate the date of the supposed "end of the world."

And if the more philosophic and sophisticated Greek-minded Christian turned away from this, as some eventually did, he just as naturally took Jewish apocalyptic much less seriously than its due. This part of the Scripture was spiritualized away into obscure parables of speculative theology. Thus one arrived at a Christianity which was academic, philosophical, and almost entirely noneschatological. Here was a serious loss of Christian spiritual values, in the relaxation of the Christian hope. Time then took its vengeance on the Church in the rise of an opposing and equally unbalanced emphasis upon the coming of the millennial kingdom.

As we approach the details of the doctrine of the Christian hope we may therefore expect to find a comprehensive double tradition, with a strongly Hebraic eschatology subtly balanced against a more philosophic system. The main lines of the compromise which has generally commended itself to the Church are prefigured in the doctrine of St. Augustine of Hippo (354–430), who taught that the world order of his time, that is, the partnership of the Christian Roman Empire and the Christian Church, was itself the thousand-year rule of the saints (Revelation 20:4). The effect of this was to affirm that there would indeed be a momentous second advent of Christ in glory, but to place this event in the uncertain future, and quite possibly in the very distant future. Thus the Christian eschatology is preserved, but its primitive day-to-day immediacy of expectation is in the light of the long experience of the Church resolved into a less intense expectation, solemn indeed, but generalized.

This is clearly a far-reaching modification of the original Jewish-Christian hope, and yet it can be vindicated as a legitimate interpretation of the spirit and general intention of our Lord's own teaching. On the one hand, Christ did frame His message within the thought forms of eschatology, and the apocalyptist's typical urgency breathes through His teaching. Yet on the other hand, He solemnly warned His disciples against fruitless and delusive speculation as to the date of the end (Mark 13:1–7, 32–33; Acts 1:6, 7). Those parables of the kingdom which call Christ's disciples to watch in ready expectancy, also plainly carry the implication that the time of waiting may well be so long that some will be tempted to lose the sense of expectancy and settle down to spiritual slumber (Matthew 24:48–50, 25:5, 6, 19, 37–39; Mark 13:34–37). Christ's own modified advent expectation indicates for us the wise attitude to take toward the Christian hope. We are neither virtually to dismiss these high matters from serious practical consideration, nor to plunge into the less balanced type of "adventism." The judicious Christian will prudently legislate for the century-long discipline of the Church and the community, yet day by day he will remind himself that all these affairs take place under the hand of a sovereign God who disposes, however wisely man may propose. We cannot foresee the future, or know how long a time we have.

III. The Second Advent

A. The Parousia

This word (*parousia*) in the Greek New Testament is usually translated "coming," or "advent" (Matthew 24:3, 27; 1 Corinthians 15:23; 1 Thessalonians 2:19, 4:15; James 5:7; 2 Peter 3:4). The one objection to the familiar word "coming" is that it suggests the idea of movement from one place to another. Clearly, a spiritual being like the divine Son does not exist in a place, nor does the Son incarnate, in His risen, ascended, and glorified humanity (see p. 99). The idea which is symbolized in the familiar phrase that Christ "comes" is that He who at all times and in all places is immediately present, at a certain time and place makes that universal presence known to His people. It is well expressed in the lines:

> Present we know Thou art.
> But O Thyself reveal!

The New Testament word *parousia* conveys something of this conception, for by derivation it means "a being present." Among other usages, it can most significantly mean "the royal Presence" (as in the phrase "the Presence Chamber" of a royal palace). The sovereignty of a monarch extends at all times throughout his dominions, but on occasion he will visit his subjects, and grant to them, in his royal progress, the presence of his sovereignty in a personal way. They are then admitted to "the royal Presence." This is a picture of what we mean by our Lord's advent, or coming. He is truly present with all men at all times, even when they are not aware of Him. He can, however, personally manifest His presence, so as to make the fact of His sovereignty impressively real.

B. The Advent in Glory

When the divine Son united Himself with our humanity, and was born as the Babe of Bethlehem, the universal divine presence was made known to man in a special way. This was the first *parousia*, the first advent, and it was a coming in great humility (2 Corinthians 8:9; Philippians 2:8). In order to effect His presence, our Lord suffered labor, misunderstanding, rejection, contempt, torment, and death. His presence brought the kingdom of God and accomplished the saving act of divine sovereignty (see pp. 44–45). Nevertheless, the ruling power of the kingdom was then only manifested "as a grain of mustard seed" (Mark 4:30–32). The number who had faith to see the suffering Messiah for what He was, and to accept the offered hidden treasure of the kingdom, were but few (Matthew 7:14). Therefore the Church, the community of the kingdom, found herself to be a contemptible minority in the world (1 Corinthians 1:26–28),

> ...humble and unknown,
> Loved and prized by God alone.

The great ones of this world, though in point of fact they exercise their power under the providence of God (John 19:11; Romans 13:1), commonly did not recognize this fact. Therefore they snapped their fingers at Christ, His law, and His Church, and so the natural and expected calling of the people of God in this world is labor, hardship, contumely, and martyrdom (Mark 8:34; Luke 6:22–23; Acts 5:41; 1 Corinthians 4:9–13; 1 Peter 2:20–21, 3:14–17). By and large, this has been the condition of human society ever since, though the apparent outward prosperity of the Church has at times concealed this from the superficial view. It is indeed true that the power of Satan is destroyed (Luke 10:18), but this does not appear to be so (Luke 4:5–6). Christ's presence is with His world, but in great humility.

However, the Christian act of faith in the goodness, power, and constancy of God is that *"history will end in a manner worthy of God."* This is the very essence of the advent hope. It is something which "must" be if God fulfills the promise implicit in what He has already done, and can be trusted not to disappoint the hopes which He has Himself raised. The mark of this end of history will be a manifestation of the presence of Christ no longer in humility, but in glory. This is the promised Second Advent. He who is now with us will then manifest His presence in a way which will transcend in glory even the gracious and awesome presence which was seen in the Man of Galilee and the risen Christ. He will then be revealed as the rightful and undisputed Master of the whole human situation, and of all the affairs of the world (Matthew 25:31–32; Mark 8:38; Luke 17:24, 22:29; 1 Corinthians 15:24–25; Philippians 2:9–11; Revelation 5:1–7, 19:11–16). Those who in the days of His humility have loved Christ, witnessed to Him, and hoped in His despised cause, will then see the joy and desire of their hearts realized, and be filled with unspeakable bliss (Matthew 25:21; Romans 8:17–18; 2 Corinthians 4:8–18). Supremely, this is the promised reward of the persecuted, and the martyrs (Luke 6:21–23; 1 Peter 4:12–14; Revelation 6:9–11, 7:9–17). The servants of Christ will in that day be clothed with authority over men, such as answers to their divine calling (Matthew 19:27–30). Those who have neglected or refused to open their eyes to the presence of Christ will then be compelled to do so, however reluctantly, and those who have rejected Him and done Him despite will be confounded at last (Matthew 25:44–45, Mark 8:38;

Revelation 1:7). All this is comprised in the Second Advent of Christ, in glory.

C. The Visible Return of Christ

The certainty of the triumphant manifestation in this world of the royal presence of Christ is a cardinal element of Christian faith. The precise manner of it raises a number of perplexing issues. The traditional doctrine of the Church has been that at the Second Advent Christ will visibly return to the earth in glory (Revelation 1:7). However, this expectation has been widely questioned in the modern period. It is not altogether explicit what is the motive of the critics, but in general it would seem to arise chiefly from the desire to approximate Christian doctrine to the presuppositions of current secular thought, and to present Christianity as a nonmiraculous and smoothly evolutionary system. The typical secular thinker does not find it easy to accept the notion that there might in the future be a sudden and revolutionary change in world conditions, such as is presupposed by the traditional doctrine. Clearly, to the Christian this does not entirely dispose of the matter. The discussion is of events which are not part of the course of history, and which are outside the ambit of ordinary human experience. The presuppositions of current secular thought do not necessarily apply to such conditions.

A more substantial rejoinder to the traditional doctrine of a visible Second Advent is the argument that possibly this is not in keeping with the real intention of the Bible itself. A common inclination of the Greek mind in the Church was to take the imagery of Jewish apocalyptic more pictorially and chronologically than the intention of the original writers justifies (see p. 245). Without a doubt the feeling has been widespread in the Church that if the passages which speak of our Lord's Second Advent are to be taken seriously they ought to be taken literally, as of a visible descent from the heavens. Thus it is argued that the phrase, He "shall so come in like manner" of Acts 1:11 must be understood as teaching that the process by which the glorious presence of Christ will be revealed is to be thought of in terms of the ascension in reverse. It does not follow, however, that this is St. Luke's real intention. It can be maintained that a sense of the presence of Christ with His Church, discerned by the eye of interior faith as we "see" Him now, but of immeasurably greater majesty and clarity, is quite in accord with the real mind of Scripture.

Nevertheless, there is on the other side the powerful consideration that the God-given mark of Christ's risen presence, victorious over sin and death, was a *visible* presence, and in a real sense, a bodily presence, though of a glorious body. There is weight in the plea that if this experience, which was the climax of our Lord's advent in *humility,* was as impressively objective as this, Christ's Second Advent in *glory* can hardly be less than "visible." Clearly, for Christ's glorified humanity to appear in a visible and bodily form does not require that this body be a material one, in the ordinary sense of the word. This is indeed a mysterious subject, and we are warned against trying to take symbolical doctrine in a matter-of-fact sense. A certain degree of reverent reserve is fitting when we discuss whether the Scripture requires us to expect Christ's Second Advent as a visible return to earth. It is incautious either to affirm or to deny this dogmatically.

IV. The Millennial Kingdom

Lo! He comes with clouds descending,
Once for favoured sinners slain;
Thousand thousand saints attending,
Swell the triumph of His train:
Hallelujah!
God appears on earth to reign.

The Jewish expectation was that when the advent of the Messiah brought the inflowing of God's kingdom to this world the power of evil in the world order would be finally destroyed. God's chosen people, restored to righteousness of life and national integrity, would then live in holiness and happiness upon earth, to the glory of God (Daniel 7:9–18, 27–28). This hope was taken over and adapted into Jewish-Christian apocalyptic, with the Church, the new Israel, in the position of the restored and glorious people of the messianic kingdom. Our Lord Himself used the prophetic imagery of the messianic banquet (Luke 22:16; Compare Isaiah 25:6–8; Luke 14:15). He spoke of His apostles as reigning in glory in that day (Matthew 19:28), and St. Paul echoes the same idea (1 Corinthians 6:3).

However, the passage which has been by far the most influential in Christian thought on this subject is Revelation 20:1–6, which describes how Satan will first be chained, then the martyrs will rise from the dead in "the first resurrection," and reign with Christ upon the earth for "a thousand years." After this Satan will be released for his last effort in wickedness, and final overthrow, which will be followed by the general resurrection, and the last judgment of all men (vv. 7–13). It is this passage which is chiefly responsible for the doctrine, which is found in many of the ancient fathers of the Church, and which has continued to some extent in the Church ever since, that at the end of the Age, but before the final bliss of heaven, there will be the thousand-year "rule of the saints" upon earth, or millennial kingdom ("millennium," a period of a thousand years).[4]

---

[4] It will be appreciated that in detail this is a most complicated issue. There were in circulation in the early Christian centuries many noncanonical Jewish and Jewish-Christian Apocalypses, containing all manner of variants of the apocalyptic scheme. These books continued to be read and revered, particularly in the less philosophical sections of the Church, and are responsible for some of the details of the doctrine of the Christian hope found in various ancient writers.

There is here raised a perplexed theological issue which has often been the subject of unreasoning controversy. A judgment between the conflicting spiritual interests is both necessary, and not easy to come by. Here the divergence of spirituality between the Hebraic and Greek elements in the twofold tradition of the Christian hope most clearly comes to view. The insistence of some that Revelation 20, and allied Scriptures interpreted from it, must be taken literally, provides the point at which the Jewish-Christian and apocalyptic variant of the Christian hope comes to its most vivid expression. It also provides the point at which this form of the Christian hope presents the maximum of offense to the more sophisticated and philosophical mind. The position as it has stood in the history of the Church is that philosophical, cultural, and ecclesiastical schools of Christianity have generally turned away from the doctrine of the millennial kingdom. It has either been treated as an unimportant matter of vague speculation, or repudiated as naïve, crude, fanatical, and repulsive. The Scripture passages in question have been treated as of minor importance, and it has been affirmed that they must be interpreted in a symbolic sense only.

There is justice in the latter part of this plea. It has been a general tendency of the non-Jewish mind in the Church, when moved by a desire to take apocalyptic *seriously*, to interpret this Hebraic writing more chronologically and pictorially, and in this sense, more "literally," than is justified by the original intention (see p. 245). This is the leading case in point. The greatest degree of reverence for the authority of Scripture does not expressly require "the thousand years" to be taken as referring to a period of historical time as we know it. Nor is it either necessary or possible to fit all the details of all the relevant Scripture passages into one consistent chronology, as the course of biblical controversy abundantly indicates. At the same time, it is necessary to do justice to the long tradition of "adventism" in the Church, which is the testimony of history to an essential element in Christian faith.

The school of thought which has insisted upon the literal interpretation of these passages, and in consequence upon the doctrine of the *earthly* millennial kingdom, has characteristically lived in the hope that these tremendous and mysterious events would happen in the near future. This in general has not been more than an unpopular minority view within the Church. The official exponents of Christianity have normally looked upon its claims with disfavor, and at times this form of the advent hope has been treated virtually as a heresy. Nevertheless, it has shown the power of vitality and persistence. Again and again these views have appeared in the Church, despite all forms of official discouragement, and those who have adopted them have often found in their distinctive theology the secret of the strongest Christian hope and resolution. This historical phenomenon is not merely an accident to be explained away in terms of the gullibility of the ignorant.

By and large the Christian circles which have entertained the millennial advent hope have either been the socially unprivileged or culturally deprived, or else rebels, social, cultural, or political, who were standing against "the powers that be" in church or state. Times which have witnessed the shaking of established institutions and securities, of warfare, invasion, and political insecurity, or of revolutionary social changes, have also commonly seen the increased appeal of "adventism." In fact, those who find life grim, cruel, or dangerous experience the need of a heightened nervous tension such as will enable them to renew their hope when prospects are black and human hopes dead. These are they who turn with ready instinct to the Hebraic scheme of the Christian hope. The confident assurance that the Almighty is even now breaking into history to rescue the distressed cause of the right, symbolized by the vivid apocalyptic imagery—this it is which lifts up the hearts of God's people, and which strengthens their arms for the conflict. The books which came out of persecution speak in every age to the persecuted, and to those who are in a spiritual condition analogous to persecution.

There is enough of embattled wrong, of tragedy, and of uncertainty in life to make this an important part of the Christian gospel. Nevertheless, uncertainty, tragedy, and embattled wrong are not the whole of human life. Not all Christians are all the time so engaged to face the persecutor or oppressor that they have no leisure to consider wider human affairs. Indeed, there comes a day when there exists a university of "Christian" learning, a communal or national "Christian" religion, and even a "Christian" civil government. There is therefore a legitimate place for that more reflective Christianity which seeks to present Christian truth as an integral part of the whole intellectual and cultural activity of men. There is the place likewise for the churchmanship of prudential pastoral discipline, even though this is but a crutch to assist unheroic Christians in the performance of routine spiritual duties. And there is a place for the religion which seeks to be preservative of law and order in the community at large, the cement of the conventional morality of decent society.

This communal, prudential, reflective Christianity is not the faith of men who are contemplating the end of the Age. It is the religion of those who are legislating for the welfare of their grandchildren. It is "low tension" Christianity. Yet it answers to a part of life. The Christianity of the relaxed eschatological tension instinctively moves into the Greek scheme of presentation for the Christian hope as being more humane, reflective, and philosophical. The apocalyptic chapters of the Bible are then interpreted in a symbolic, and not a literal sense. Our Lord's Second Advent is affirmed indeed in principle, but contemplated as though it were likely to take place only in the remote future.

We may ask, "What is the just balance between these two legitimate Christian interests? What is the ground of common understanding which will suffice to hold together these two traditions, the majority and ecclesiastical, and the minority and "adventist," both of which have in their own way vindicated themselves upon the stage of history?" Surely true Christianity is the religion of divine intervention, but not of an utterly unaccountable divine intervention. It is also an evolutionary religion, but certainly not a merely evolutionary religion. It is faith in a process of reasonable and providential development, set within the background of divine intervention.

The expectation of the millennial kingdom vividly symbolizes the cardinal truth that Christianity is not a world-despairing religion. It is a world-subduing faith. This answers to the principle displayed in the incarnation and the sacraments, that the material creation is the handiwork of God, created in order to signify a spiritual purpose, and visited and used by God for the accomplishment of spiritual ends. The fitting climax of this principle is the doctrine that the ultimate destiny of this material world is not to be "cast as rubbish to the void." The whole world order is to be radically redeemed (Romans 8:19–22). The ideal of the Christian is not, therefore, to flee as a hermit to the wilderness, or to wait for a reward in a heavenly sphere, while the nations of the world go to the devil in their own way. Christ's final and complete triumph is to be vindicated in this very world which rejected Him and put Him to an open shame (Philippians 2:10–11). The whole life of nations is to be radiantly transformed under the mastership of Christ so that the glory of God may be fully revealed therein (Revelation 11:15).

It follows that there is implicit within Christianity a world-affirming and active spirit, and even, in its due place, a socially idealistic, reforming, and "progressive" spirit. The New Testament teaches that the civil government, though not "Christian" in the fullest sense of the word, yet exists under the providence of God, and by its legal rewards and punishments can do something to uphold human morality and minister to the will of God (Romans 13:1–5). It is therefore very much the business of the Christian to practice civic virtue in every way open to him (Mark 12:17; Acts 25:10–12; Romans 12:9–21, 13:6–10; 1 Peter 2:11–22). Furthermore, experience shows that wise and humane political constitutions and social conventions, improved educational and cultural standards, and better conditions of housing and hygiene, will often help ordinary men and women to live a decent and dignified life. These good things do not indeed bring Christian salvation, but they may avoid human degradation, and this is no light matter. Thus Christian history indicates that the civic virtues of Christian men and women have often, as a kind of by-product to their service of God, decisively helped in the upbuilding of helpful cultural, educational, social, and political institutions. Christianity therefore by no means despairs of the social, economic, and political order, but cherishes the ambition to conquer it all for Christ. The "rule of the saints" is the promise of God.

Nevertheless, the attitude of the Christian to "the kingdoms of this world" is not one of evolutionary utopianism. The Christian citizen wishes to help his fellow citizens to better citizenship, and accounts this an important part of the service of God. Yet he does not rest his hope for the reconstruction of the world order upon anything so insecure as this. Associated with the Christian doctrine of the Second Advent in glory and the millennial kingdom there is the conception that as history proceeds to its close there will be a greater and greater overflowing of human wickedness, bringing world strife and unparalleled persecution of God's people (Mark 13:3–13; Revelation 6:1–17, 8:6–9:21). Indeed, this consummation of wickedness is in apocalyptic passages personified as *Antichrist,* who will appear at the head of the forces of evil, only to be overthrown and judged to make room for the final triumph of right (2 Thessalonians 2:1–10; 1 John 2:18; Revelation 9:11, 20:7–10). There can hardly be any doctrine more repugnant than this to the presuppositions of ordinary secular thought on social subjects. It is the tacit working assumption of well-intentioned humanist thinkers that as history proceeds and human society develops, human righteousness ought generally to advance, and culture and happiness to increase. If the course of sad events disappoints this hope, we see evidenced the spread of disillusionment and bitterness, and the rise of "angry young men" who spend their days and talents in cynical criticism because the human race has so signally failed to take their good advice!

Christian doctrine takes a more realistic and more balanced view. The intention of the Bible in speaking of Antichrist is not so much to declare that the world is actually and positively becoming more wicked as time goes on, but to teach that both good and evil are showing themselves ever more plainly to be what they are. Human affairs are a mixture of right and wrong, and as human institutions develop both the right and the wrong develop together (Matthew 13:24–30). That right and wrong reach their climax together is symbolized in the conception of the appearance of Antichrist, and of the Messiah. We have already indicated that active Christian service in the world can prevail to some extent. Nevertheless, the somber fact of human life remains that human nature is infirm and human institutions even at best are painfully mixed in character. Therefore spiritual, moral, cultural, and social advance is limited and variable, and its triumphs inherently insecure.

Thus the ancient Hebrews excelled at religion, but not at art; the Greeks at art, but certainly not at religion. The social structure of the Middle Ages gave man a secure place in society at the expense of freedom, the society of today freedom at the expense of contentment and security. The Renaissance produced magnificent works of art, literature, and architecture from a society stained with cruelty and corruption. The modern Western world is much more humane and kindly, and this has contributed greatly to the sum of human happiness, yet one's heart sinks as the tawdriness and vulgarity apparently inseparable from the machine age goes all around the world. And so examples might be multiplied, in personal life as well as in communal. It is not that human striving achieves nothing, for the spirit of man has accomplished wonderful things. Yet as he moves forward in one activity he slips back in another. There is a principle of limitation and frustration woven into the very fabric of human affairs.

Nor are the feats of man secure. Long centuries can build up great civilizations, but civilizations can also decline through loss of political nerve, through social corruption, through invasion, or merely from the effect of soil erosion. As the Christian looks upon this world process his heart does not fail. The moral of all is not that God repudiates social endeavor, or that social endeavor is not worthwhile. It is simply that man is not to put his trust for the final and secure salvation of the world order in human endeavor toward educational, cultural, social, and political advancement. The ideal society is to be set up by the power of God.

It is fruitless to argue whether the dropping of the atom bomb was a greater or a lesser crime than the sack of Magdeburg. There is no way of comparing either the human suffering or the human guilt. It is simply that the age of science and mechanical production can work both human welfare and human destruction on an unparalleled scale. We are assured by some men of science that it is now technically possible to extinguish the human race. The Christian does not pretend to more wisdom in these matters than other men, and it is difficult to know the truth. We suspect that when publicists declare "war would be the end of civilization" they really mean "war would be the end of comfortable urban civilization, replete with automobiles, washing-machines, and television." The Christian is not so easily shaken in his faith. On the one hand, he does not argue, "This is too horrible to think of. It cannot happen here!" In a world which crucified the Lord of glory crimes sufficient to consume civilizations both can happen, and have happened. Historical experience shows that God does not suddenly step in to prevent man reaping the recompense of human pride and folly. The real but horrible possibility that the climax of man's knowledge and power should indeed be used to accomplish the most universal of all crimes is exactly what the Bible symbolizes when it speaks of the revealing of Antichrist.

Yet the Christian, who takes this most severe and realistic view as to the possibility of all manner of evil in a sinful world, also has a spring of hope not known to other men. The natural process of human affairs is that one sin makes another easier, one wrong provides the incentive for another. If this were all, final ruin would be inevitable. However, if this were all, final ruin would have taken place long ago! The Christian holds that if human affairs had been left to the natural process of development, sin would have in past centuries produced sin to such effect that the world today would be nothing but a squalid and brutal shambles. That this is not so indicates that there is "a power not ourselves that makes for righteousness."

God providentially overrules the sins, crimes, and follies of humanity so as either to rescue man from the utmost consequences of his own actions, or else to work his moral discipline through those worst consequences. Therefore by divine intervention the world order holds together. This is why the Christian, alone of all realistic thinkers, can look upon the future even in this perilous day with a sober measure of hope. Discreet statesmanship, moved by fear of awful consequences, may skirt around one international confrontation, and another, and another. Yet some fool is bound to press the button in the end! This is the most that the worldly-wise can rationally hope for—because he forgets the sovereignty of God.

The processes of human development take place within the overriding context of divine intervention. As man matures in power his wickedness flowers, but the purposes of God bear fruit as well. The ideal society is therefore not to be built by the power of man alone. It is the work of the majestic power of God. This is what is symbolized in the doctrine of the millennial kingdom. The biblical doctrine is to be taken seriously as reputable theology. It describes a real divine act. Nevertheless, it must not be forgotten that the biblical doctrine is a symbolic one, and as such is to be understood.

V.   Human Destiny

A. Eternal Life

> Thy love I soon expect to find,
> In all its depth and height;
> To comprehend the Eternal Mind,
> And grasp the Infinite.

As we turn from the Christian hope for the world order to the Christian hope for the child of God we take up again the theology of the life of grace, and continue it through the gates of death. The broadest term for the gift of God to man is eternal life (John 10:28, 17:2; Romans 6:23; 1 John 5:11). It is unfortunate that this phrase is so often misunderstood. Eternal life is not simply the survival of death, to an existence of endless duration. This would be a very mixed blessing, even though the human mind shrinks naturally from the thought of passing out of existence. Eternal life is the life of the heavenly sphere, or to put the matter in a more distinctively Christian and personal manner, it is life in fellowship with God (John 17:3; 1 John 1:2).

Eternal life is a present possession. It is something which man now has, if by faith in Christ he is joined to God, not something which he hopes to possess only after death (John 3:16, 18, 6:54, 10:28; 1 John 1:2, 5:11,

13). Thus in a true sense the Christian believer is already in possession of heaven and the gifts of the age to come (Luke 10:20; Philippians 4:20; Hebrews 6:5). The central point of Christ's original gospel of the kingdom was that the blessing which had been so long expected was in Him now granted (see pp. 44-46). Yet paradoxically, what He has already granted is but the first installment, and token of good faith, of the fullness of God's gift in the day of the Lord (Romans 8:23-25; 2 Corinthians 1:22, 5:5; Ephesians 1:13, 14).

Here again is an example of the master principle of the continuity of the spiritual order. The ultimate ground for the biblical and Christian hope of a personal life of blessedness with God beyond the grave is the same as that which prompted the faith of the Hebrews to evoke the hope of resurrection. It is an act of faith in the goodness of God. By way of comparison, let it be imagined that an artist is at work. He lavishes all his genius upon a piece of great creative art, and then, before the paint is dry, he thrusts it into the fire and starts to paint again. Every picture is thus destroyed; not the rough sketch only, not the imperfect attempt, but the perfect work— and for thousands and thousands of times. One would say, "This artist is no true artist. He has a divided personality, for he destroys that which it is his very nature to create. He is a maniac!" If what the Christian believes about God be true, it is impossible to imagine that He can be like that. It would be a denial of His own rational constancy for God to call into being His sublimest work, and then, before the work was finished, to annihilate it.

Yet man is not God's creative art. He is God's created child. Suppose a couple were to say to one another, "It is a nuisance to have this child about the house. Had we not desired; he need never have been born. Therefore he is at our disposal, to do with what we will. We will put him in an orphanage, so we can enjoy our liberty." Such would be a profoundly immoral act, because freely to procreate a living personality which can be loved, and which requires love for his happiness and welfare, brings upon the parents a binding moral obligation to bestow that love.

So God need not have made us, and we are at His absolute disposal. Nevertheless He has made us, and made us capable of knowing and loving Him, and made us so that we have no true blessedness apart from fellowship with Him. Therefore, it would seem that the sovereign God, who has created us men and redeemed us in Christ, has freely taken upon Himself a binding moral obligation, if He indeed be good, to give that blessedness of which His children are capable. To raise the hope of fellowship with Himself by the Christian experience of this life, and then inevitably, uni- versally, and utterly to disappoint this hope by annihilating man at death would be inconsistent with what God has shown Himself to be in Christ. The affirmation of Christian faith is that the constancy of the spiritual order requires that the gift of life with God in this world shall continue to its proper and rational fulfillment. Eternal life, therefore, is life of such a quality now that it will continue beyond the grave. As the poet puts it:

Thou wilt not leave us in the dust:
Thou madest man, he knows not why;
He thinks he was not made to die;
And Thou hast made him: Thou art just!

It will be noticed that the conception of eternal life largely answers to the Greek presentation of the Christian hope. It reflects the idea that the higher side of the life of man, in which his faculties of mind and spirit are taken up in fellowship with God, is a present possession of an imperishable character. Therefore it is not surprising that this doctrine is particularly prominent in the Johannine literature. However, the doctrine of eternal life is not inconsistent with the Hebraic conception of resurrection. That future act of God can be regarded as the fulfillment of the present possession (John 6:54).

B. Immortality and Resurrection

The personal Christian hope as presented in Greek terms is also well expressed by the use of the word "immortality." This speaks of the imperishable character of the spiritual personality of man, which continues its sentient and moral life after the death and decay of the material body. This doctrine has been accounted a legitimate part of Christian theology, even though it is not altogether the biblical way of expression. It has several advantages. It accords with the conviction, which to most thoughtful people appears a reasonable one, that the mental and spiritual aspects of man's life are of a nobler order, and more significant for the evaluation of his personality, than are the bodily and material. Furthermore, it harmonizes with the doctrine of the communion of saints. The faith that departed Christians are at this moment alive to nobler powers, and in a blessed existence of communion with God, excludes the erroneous notion that they are in a state of suspended animation, awaiting the resurrection, as well as the inadequate idea that they are in a frustrated and limited Sheol-like existence (Luke 23:43; Philippians 1:23; Revelation 7:13-17). The doctrine of immortality makes it possible to affirm in an unqualified manner that the departed saints are in spiritual fellowship with the Church Militant (see p. 133).

However, justice must also be done to the other side of the Christian tradition, and to the spiritual values preserved in the biblical doctrine of the resurrection of the body and the general resurrection, even though it requires a certain degree of mental effort if the modern man is to carry himself back into the categories of thought employed. The guiding principle is that the ancient Hebrews did not look upon man as twofold, composed of a nonmaterial "soul" or "spirit" dwelling in a material body. Still less would they have found it natural to say that the nonmaterial "soul" was "the real man." To the Hebrew, man was a unitary organism. That which we so naturally separate in thought as "body" and "soul" was not separated. Just as the body of a man without "the breath of life" was not a man, but a corpse, so by parity of reason, a disembodied spirit was not "the real man," but the shadow of a man, a mere ghost.

Once this background of ancient thought is granted, it is natural for the triumph of man over death to be spoken of as "resurrection." Thus the Jewish hope was that at the Day of the Lord the spirits of the departed would be released from their dim existence in Sheol and reunited with their risen bodies. They would again be fully and entirely alive. In the time of our Lord the more conservative Sadducee priests rejected this relatively late development of doctrine, but otherwise it was generally accepted among the Jews (Mark 12:18–23; John 11:24; Acts 23:6–9). Thus the intention of the biblical doctrine of resurrection is strongly to affirm that the man who will be alive at the day of God's triumph is not to be thought of as a pale ghostly copy of the man who lives now. Christian doctrine knows nothing of the "spiritualist" expectation of mere "survival," and the survival of a somewhat disordered or reduced echo of the personality. "The resurrection of the body" symbolizes the conception of "the whole man alive again," complete in every vital faculty. The implication is that the Christian believer need not fear that the life of heaven will be a somewhat rarified and chilly existence, "all passion spent." We will be more fully alive then than now.

However, in order to symbolize this truth it is not necessary to insist that the resurrection of the body must be interpreted as the mysterious reconstitution of the actual material and physical frame in which man has lived. In his great chapter St. Paul wrestles with this very point, and apparently seeks to restate the traditional Jewish doctrine of resurrection in light of the one resurrection which had actually taken place. In raising Christ from the dead God had set His seal upon the general idea of resurrection as triumph over death, and also had modified and spiritualized the expectation (see pp. 98–99). Christ's resurrection body was a "glorified" body which truly corresponded to the purely physical body which had died, and which yet transcended it. St. Paul affirms that this will be the case also with the human body at the general resurrection, though to express himself he has to employ the somewhat paradoxical phrase "a spiritual body" (1 Corinthians 15:35–54).

The two sides of this Christian tradition, the belief in immortality and in resurrection, are to be reconciled by the doctrine of a future life which is not purely static. It is the Christian faith that the departed are fully alive, and that the dead in Christ even now rejoice before Him, and serve Him with nobler powers. However, it can hardly be the case that at the moment of death the development of the soul is suddenly arrested. We may believe that there is still room for man, in ever fuller response to the

grace of God, to be changed "from glory to glory" (2 Corinthians 3:18).
We must be cautious in speculation, and not seek to know the unknowable.
We cannot affirm positive doctrine beyond Scripture, and it is to be remembered always that the scriptural teaching is symbolic. However, general
Christian tradition does allow the position that the life beyond the grave
is not static. The dead in Christ are already in a state of spiritual well-being,
and useful in God's service, and yet there is the mysterious prospect of
bliss still greater, and service more noble, when God brings to its final
culmination His good purpose for the whole creation. This idea is symbolized
in Christian theology by the doctrine of a present paradise, and also of the
general resurrection at the last day. Thus the symbols of present immortality
and future resurrection are complementary one to another.

Summary of Divergence: Doctrines of Human Destiny

a. Ancient and Eastern

In the Jewish background of the Church the idea was known that
the departed might have to undergo discipline on account of past sins,
and that the prayers of the faithful might help them in this (2 Maccabees 12:42–45). It is not surprising, therefore, that this same idea is
voiced by some of the ancient fathers of the Church. The Eastern, or
Orthodox, Church has continued conservatively, remaining more or less
on this ground. It teaches that the souls of the faithful departed, who
may not have had occasion fully to bring forth the fruits of repentance
in this life, will continue in discipline and spiritual growth in the
unseen world. The prayers of the Church, particularly at the Eucharist,
can assist them in this. Philosophically minded Orthodox theologians
have guarded against the notion that this purgatory is in a "place,"
or that the purging "fire" is a physical flame.

b. Roman Catholic

The Roman Catholic Church has developed from the above simple
teaching to a much more elaborated doctrine of purgatory. The basic
principle is that those who are in a state of Christian grace must demonstrate penitence for their sins by the due performance of penance, or
disciplinary punishment. This leads to divine forgiveness. Those who
are not able in this life to perform sufficient penance to secure the discharge of all their sins must make up the balance by undergoing the
remedial punishment of purgatory before they are admitted finally to
heaven. In this discipline they can be assisted by the prayers of the
Church, particularly at the Mass. It is to be noted that this is not a
doctrine of a "second chance" for those who have died in wickedness or
unbelief. Those who die in the *mortal* sins which separate the soul from
God, such as pride and unbelief, are irrevocably lost. It is only those
departed in a state of grace, and who are on the sure road to final

salvation, who are admitted to purgatory to make amends for their lesser, or *venial,* sins.

This doctrine clearly provides a wide scope for spiritual discipline and development in the unseen world (Matthew 12:32; 1 Peter 4:6). The general assumption of Roman Catholic teaching is that some period in purgatory is the destiny of the general body of believers. The great and illustrious saints, however, who have died full of the good works produced by grace, may go straight to heaven. Infants dying unbaptized cannot be admitted to heaven in the fullest sense, but exist in a state of relative happiness. Traditional Roman Catholic teaching has often spoken of purgatory as though it were a "place" of purging "fire," and its remedial discipline as occupying a period of "time." This language of popular piety is, however, more authoritatively and reliably regarded as symbolic.

c. *Protestant*

Classic Protestantism reacted strongly against the Roman Catholic doctrine of purgatory, and has in general affirmed that at death all souls go immediately either to heaven or to hell (Luke 16:26; Hebrews 9:27). The basic theological reason for this is that the Roman Catholic doctrine of purgatory answers naturally to the conception of "salvation by grace and the merit of good works." The opposed Protestant principles of "salvation by grace alone," and "justification by faith alone" would appear to exclude the principle of meritorious remedial suffering, and therefore the notion of purgatory. Some would maintain, however, that what is excluded by these Protestant principles is not so much the idea as such of remedial discipline and spiritual growth in the life beyond, as the notion that the merit of remedial discipline can atone for the unresolved guilt of venial sins. The latter idea is clearly denied by Protestant principles.

However, it can hardly be doubted that the wider popular Protestant abhorrence of the very idea of purgatory was due to its association with Masses for the dead, and indulgences for the benefit of souls in purgatory. These practices undoubtedly became the occasion of widespread abuse, both devotional and financial, in the period leading up to the Reformation. Protestant feeling reacted very strongly against these abuses and tended to shun everything apparently associated with them, even indirectly. It is not surprising, therefore, that Protestantism abandoned the traditional belief in purgatory.

d. *A Constructive Statement*

It is necessary to approach the doctrine of human destiny in the unseen world with a measure of reverent reserve. Our knowledge is derived in part from general spiritual probabilities, which are not more than probabilities, but still more from Scripture. Yet is it not always clear how far the Scripture in question is to be interpreted literally, and how far symbolically, as a parable of truth.

Those who do not accept the doctrine of purgatory, either in its simple form, or in its developed and Roman Catholic form, still have to admit that there may be some difficulties attendant upon the total abolition of the conception of remedial discipline and growth in the unseen world. The abandonment of the doctrine of purgatory appears to consign to eternal damnation all those who are not saintly enough to go immediately with rejoicing into the presence of God. A thorough-going Augustinian is indeed prepared to accept this stern result. Just as popular Roman Catholicism has worked upon the general presumption that the destiny of most ordinary people in the nominally Christian community is the pains of purgatory, and afterward Heaven, so the assumption of some schools of evangelical teaching has been that all those who are not "soundly converted" are lost. This implies the damnation of the great majority of the human race (Matthew 7:13–14). This in turn is a conclusion so fearsome that the mind of the average humane person refuses to take it altogether seriously. The reaction has been the spread of that prevalent, sentimental, and delusively comforting notion that all tolerably decent folk go straight to heaven, and quite apart from any genuinely devout Christian discipleship. This is to short-circuit the whole Christian faith, and to produce that "modern man who is not worrying about his sins."

It is not easy to strike a judicious balance in this matter. There is little explicit direction from Scripture, which perhaps indicates that this is a matter of speculation in which it ill becomes the Christian teacher to be too exclusively dogmatic. The parable of Dives and Lazarus (Luke 16:19–31) perhaps gives us a glimpse into the mind of our Lord. Christ both speaks most seriously of "a great gulf fixed" between the morally careless and the hope of salvation, and also significantly places the torment of Dives in Hades, the abode of the departed awaiting the resurrection, and not in Gehenna, the place of the finally lost (v. 23). Already there seems to be some stirring of compunction in his formerly hardened heart, and some thought for the welfare of others (v. 28). All this, moreover, is the imagery of a parable. It is not systematic theology, nor even the raw materials for systematic theology, but a guide to practical devotion. We suggest that the Christian teacher who follows the doctrine and spirit of Christ will warn men that there is a most dreadful judgment awaiting the morally and spiritually careless, but he will also allow himself to hope that the very rude awakening of the unseen world may quite possibly be the occasion of an awakening of many to penitence, faith, and righteousness. This is not the doctrine of "a second chance." There appears to be no basis for this hope either in Scripture or in logic. There is no ground for supposing that those who have deliberately turned away from Christ in this life will be able to turn to Him in the next (see p. 264). Yet this is not really the problem.

The number of those is small who, like Judas, have clearly faced Christ, and then unaccountably turned from Him in deliberate apostasy. The burden upon Christian thought is the vast company of those who have apparently passed through life without ever making a clear decision, for Christ or against. Many of these are perhaps Church members and Church attenders of a sort, through social habit or a vague instinct that this is "right." They are the multitudes of kindly, decent folk, who have sincerely intended to stand for the right, yet who by preoccupation, confusion, or apathy have failed effectually so to do. Here is the real moral and spiritual problem of the world, for most of the human race is in this condition.

When these souls pass into the clearer vision of the life beyond, there will be stripped from them all those preoccupations which have enabled them so easily to shuffle through their days on earth without ever making a decision. Then there will surely be a rude awakening indeed, and pangs of remorse! And it is by no means inconceivable that many of these will then discover, in that remorse, that passing gleams of Christian truth which they had before accepted, and faint kindlings of Christian resolve which they had entertained, will have some degree of hold upon them. This may very well be the beginning of spiritual discipline and of spiritual development. It would seem that this may be a reasonable view of the destiny of most ordinary folk after death. Perhaps their immediate lot is neither that highest bliss which will be the reward of those who on earth have made it their joy to love and serve Christ, nor the pains of everlasting damnation, but a state of growth. Yet this does not necessarily involve the Roman Catholic doctrine of purgatorial suffering as penance.

One proviso is, however, to be made in this doctrine. It should not be presented as though one would terrify men and women into good ways. Here was in fact the abuse which destroyed the spiritual repute of the common medieval doctrine of purgatory. In the end men came to feel that their ignorant fears had been unfairly exploited, and they rebelled. One of the mysteries of Christian experience is that in Christ the goodness and the severity of God are eternally conjoined (Romans 11:22). As the serious-minded Christian turns his mind to the God of holy love who has come to him in Christ, he is bound to feel that his moments of religious realization bring to him life's most searching pain. He can probably assure himself that he has played his part not too discreditably as a citizen, a businessman, a Churchmember, as a husband and father, considering always the limitations of human nature. But what of his standing as a child of God? What man dare seriously consider the wealth of the offered love of God, and the utter poverty of his own response? This is a thought to chill the spine with apprehension! Yet by a strange alchemy, that moment of serious contemplation also brings into the believer's life the joy which in all human joys is the very spirit of joy: "That unsparing Judge loves *me*, and in Christ suffered for me, and has freely forgiven me! Therefore I must fear—and yet I need not fear." If this be so now, it will surely be more so in the life beyond. Men must be seriously warned that the pain of realization will be greater. Yet they may be comforted that to those who have sought to love Christ, the conjoined bliss will be the greater too. Therefore discipline and growth beyond the grave are to be taken seriously, but not dreaded, for man's hope of standing boldly in the presence of God rests ultimately in divine grace, and not in human performance.

C. Judgment

The Bible teaches that judgment is both present (John 3:18–21, 12:31), and future (Matthew 12:41; Romans 14:10; Hebrews 9:27, 10:27). There is no true inconsistency between the two sides of the Christian tradition, for here is another example of the principle of the continuity of the spiritual order. It is a dreadful fact of experience that to see the good and deliberately to turn from it makes it for the future harder to see what is good, and to do it when it is seen (1 Timothy 4:2). On the other hand, to respond to grace and to go through the open door into the good, opens the door into a higher good choice and makes it easier to go. In the present spiritual order both good and bad choices tend to confirm themselves. The conclusion of this is plain. If this process of choice continues in a consistent and rational manner there is inherent the dreadful possibility that those who continue long enough to resist the drawing of grace will finally confirm themselves in evil. They will then no longer be able to see the good as good when it is presented to them, but will account it to be evil (Mark 3:28–30). And even if they could see the good, they would no longer have any desire to turn to it. By parity of reason there is inherent in the process the possibility also that those who continue fully to open their hearts to grace will arrive at a condition when they will be able fully to see the good, and fully to love it when they see it, and to do the good with a will no longer in the slightest divided. They will then be confirmed in good. God will have given them the power to live sinlessly. Thus the process of present choice leads to a climax in a final and all-decisive choice. Present judgment leads to the last judgment.

Divine judgment is not an act of arbitrary power. The sovereign Lord certainly has the right to punish breaches of His holy law (Romans 3:5, 6). However, it must be understood that the God of universal love punishes for man's own ultimate good, and not just to vindicate the divine dignity or to compel man to acknowledge the divine sovereignty (Hebrews 12:5–10). Therefore God's judgment upon sinners is not an external penalty of suffering which God of His sovereign will attaches to man, but which, if He willed, He could quite rightly forego. The punishment for sin is something which man's free choice of evil makes inevitable, because the world is God's moral order. The final judgment upon the impenitent sinner is not, then, a last act of divine vengeance, but a culmination of the principle of the continuity of the moral order.

This is seen in the New Testament usage of the phrase "the wrath of God." "The wrath" is thought of as a spiritual entity existing in the world, as it has been created by the holy God. It represents the principle that out of self-centered and rebellious pride, which is idolatry, and its fruits in sinful action, come the inevitable effects of moral degradation and final utter ruin (Romans 1:18-32). Thus it is "the wrath of God," for it exists in God's world, and He is responsible for it (Ephesians 5:6). Nevertheless, the New Testament avoids making the verb active, and saying "God is angry," because in the last resort "the wrath" is not something which God *does*. It is something which *happens*, and God's positive action in the matter is to rescue from it those who will be rescued. It is not the case that after a certain limit of forbearance God will not accept repentance. When man has finally hardened himself he cannot repent, even though God call him with all His grace.

The climax of the Last Judgment differs from the present process of judgment in two important ways. In the first place, the present judgment is a secret judgment, known with certainty only to God. The men of this world judge right and wrong largely by the standards of outward conventional morality, and by canons derived in the main from prudential considerations of the preservation of human society. This is a dim and shifting standard. Therefore the world goes on its way substantially ignoring the judgment of Christ upon its affairs, and putting Him to an open shame. Also, the Christian understands that he has no right to judge his neighbor, for he cannot know how clear light his neighbor has, and what is the strength of his temptations. Only God, who can see into the heart, can decide who is the righteous and the unrighteous man, and who is in a state of salvation (Matthew 7:1; Romans 14:13; 1 Corinthians 4:5). The Last Judgment, however, will be an open judgment, of which all men, however unwillingly, will be compelled fully to take account (Matthew 25:31-32; Romans 2:5-10, 14:10; 1 Corinthians 3:13; Revelation 20:11-13). In the second place, the present judgment is a provisional judgment. Even the obstinate sinner, if he repent, can yet find mercy (Ezekiel 33:10-11; 1 Timothy 1:12-15). And it is possible for believers to fall away if they do not keep themselves in the means and discipline of grace (1 Corinthians 9:27, 10:12). The judgment of the last day, however, is a final judgment, and seals man's fate forever (Matthew 25:46; Revelation 22:11).

God's action of judgment is taken according to man's attitude to Christ. Thus Christ is the mediator of judgment (John 5:22; Romans 14:10; Revelation 22:12). This is true of the present judgment. Men are now being judged according as they accept or reject Christ (John 3:17-21). This process will come to its due climax of open and final judgment when Christ appears in glory (Matthew 25:34-36, 42-43; Mark 8:38; Revelation 14:14-16, 20:4).

The question has been discussed whether man's final acceptance with God at the Last Judgment depends on faith in Christ or on "good works." This chiefly depends on what is meant by these terms. Clearly, the moral character and Christian service even of the holiest of men cannot of themselves win acceptance with the holy God, for the utmost man can do is

only that which is his duty, and none has done this (Luke 17:10). In
this sense, man's sole hope for an unashamed appearance before God at
the judgment is divine grace, made known to those who are in Christ
(Romans 8:1). Nevertheless, men are judged at the end not according
to the profession of faith they have made (Matthew 7:21-23), or even
by the "experience" they have enjoyed, but according to the constructive
response they have made to the offer of grace. God judges men as they
really are in character, and life, and deeds (Matthew 25:31-46; Revelation
14:13, 20:13). In this sense, although man's initial acceptance with God,
or justification, is by faith alone (see pp. 225-26), his final acceptance is by
the works of love which faith brings forth (1 John 4:17-19). The two
errors to be avoided are that man can and must earn his final salvation by
his own merits, apart from grace, and that he can be vindicated at the
Last Judgment apart from a thoroughly changed life and character.

1. HELL.

> Every eye shall now behold Him
> Robed in dreadful majesty;
> Those who set at nought and sold Him,
> Pierced and nailed him to the tree,
> Deeply wailing,
> Shall the true Messiah see.

In Jewish eschatology Gehenna was the name given to the place of punishment of the finally lost.[5] This vivid and somber symbol was, like so much
of current imagery, adopted by our Lord (Matthew 5:29; Mark 9:43-48).
Traditional Christian theology has therefore drawn the tragic logical consequence from the fact of a final and irrevocable divine judgment. This
consequence is the doctrine of hell, the everlasting perdition of the finally
impenitent.

Clearly, this is a doctrine of almost inconceivable dreadfulness, which
is almost impossible for the thoughtful mind to accept, were it not that the
difficulties implicit in rejecting it are so great. Christianity can be made
to appear repulsive, and even ludicrous, to sensitive minds through an incautious zeal in stating the doctrine of hell. It should therefore never be
spoken of "unadvisedly, lightly, or wantonly," but with every care taken
to avoid misunderstanding. In the first place, like all doctrines of the unseen
world, this teaching is framed in symbolic language which, though it expresses an important fact, is not to be taken materially. Nor is it needful
to suppose that our Lord, in using on occasion the vivid symbolism of Jewish

---

[5] The name "Gehenna" comes from the Vale of Hinnom, outside Jerusalem, where
in times of idolatrous backsliding obscene and barbarous human sacrifice had been
offered. Ever afterwards it was regarded as a place of ill omen, and the name was
adopted in Jewish apocryphal literature for the place of punishment of the wicked. It
is not the same as Sheol, Hades, the abode of the departed who await judgment.

eschatology, took it in a crude and material sense. Thus hell is not a "place," nor a place of "fire."

Second, we should follow our Lord in stating the doctrine with great reserve. Christ spoke as one who believed in the dreadful possibility of the endless loss of the finally impenitent, but He was decidedly not a "hell-fire preacher." In the background of our Lord's mind there plainly lurked a grim and shuddering foreboding of an inconceivable fate awaiting those who finally rejected Him (Luke 17:1-2). Yet it was not His central point of appeal. The chief appeal which Christ made in summoning men to repent and turn to the good was always the goodness of God, and the blessedness of responding to this goodness (Matthew 5:43-48). This is the rightful proportion for Christian teaching and preaching. It is most significant that although the general framework of our Lord's gospel of the kingdom was eschatological, He avoided that note of strong denunciation of God's fiery judgment against sinners, which was so usual and natural an element in the apocalyptic scheme. In nothing does He more clearly rise above the limitation of the thought forms of His background.

Three leading difficulties arise in connection with the doctrine of everlasting damnation. First it is asked how heaven can be a condition of bliss if the righteous know that some of their loved ones, or indeed, any sentient creatures, are suffering eternal loss. The traditional answer to this difficulty is that the final judgment, and the sentence of damnation, includes the loosing of the ties of nature, so that the former loved ones are no longer loved. The righteous are loosed from the duty of feeling pity for them, and think of them no more. This grim doctrine at least brings home to the mind the horror of sin.

Next it has been objected that the notion of final loss is inconsistent with God's sovereignty. If some souls eternally resist His saving purpose, His plan for the universe remains forever partially marred, and this would be inconsistent with the perfection of His glory. In answer it may be said that this objection depends upon an assumption regarding the divine perfection and sovereign glory, which is not necessarily a valid one. It is assumed that for God to be fully God every creature must submit to His will. The Christian conception is that God's highest glory consists in the loving and willing obedience of all His creatures, and not merely in their obedience. It would not contribute to His glory to compel the finally impenitent to submit, and it is not inconsistent with His sovereignty to permit them forever to continue in the way they have chosen.

The fundamental difficulty is that everlasting punishment would appear to be purposeless because, if there is no hope of it ending, there is no hope for it to prove remedial. It is felt that only remedial punishment is consistent with the conception of the love of God, everlasting punishment being purposeless torture. Here is one of the last dark mysteries of human thought, and no entirely satisfactory answer is possible. One solution which has been suggested is that God will ultimately annihilate the finally impenitent, so as to bring their useless sufferings to an end. Surely this is a matter of speculation, and it is precarious either to assert definitely that this will be so, or that it is absolutely impossible.

There is a certain speculative difficulty to the doctrine of annihilation. The only ground upon which it appears possible to reconcile the goodness of God with the continued existence of man after his fall, in view of the untold wrong, degradation, misery, and cruelty which have flowed from sin, is that the continuance of sin is a tragic necessity if God is to respect and preserve the moral freedom which He has Himself given to man. And this freedom is in turn a necessity if man is to obey God freely and lovingly, as a child and not as a slave. Therefore God's universal love and perfect goodness is more fully vindicated in the creation of the higher order of moral freedom, even at the price of the possibility of moral tragedy, than it would have been in the creation of a lower order of mechanical obedience to His laws, though orderly and painless. If God has once decreed this order as the highest and best, it is so to eternity, and He will not alter it because some have proved impenitent. Or to put the matter the other way around, if it is required by God's perfect goodness and universal love that ultimately He annihilate obstinate sinners, we may with all reverence say He ought to have done it long ago!

In so uncertain a realm of speculation it would appear to be safer to abide by the simple word of Scripture, which knows nothing of the ultimate annihilation of the wicked. Nevertheless, we are reminded that the passages which speak so plainly of the endless punishment of the wicked (for example, Matthew 25:46) are symbolic, and we may have some reserve in insisting that these *must* be interpreted literally. The guiding principle is that in the last resort the Scripture is not a book of cosmological speculation, written to answer abstract questions about ultimate human destiny. It is rather a practical book of guidance, spiritual, devotional, and ethical, addressed to man's actual situation. In this situation a doctrine of the unlimited tragic consequence of unrepented sin is more salutary for the soul of man than are more easy-going doctrines, even though the traditional doctrine of hell is accompanied by some speculative difficulties. In the last resort Christian doctrine is not molded by speculative interests, but by care for the devotional and moral life of man. Man does not know all. Life is mysterious. A doctrine is not false because it leaves the mind of man with unfathomable difficulties. Yet this austere scriptural doctrine of the possibility of eternal damnation for the finally impenitent is for man's practical good. And the Christian believes that in the end all God's purposes will be vindicated as good.

2. HEAVEN.

> The dear tokens of His passion
> Still His dazzling body bears;
> Cause of endless exultation
> To His ransomed worshippers;
> With what rapture
> Gaze we on those glorious scars!

The process whereby the free response to grace brings a more effectual drawing of grace, and the choice of good confirms man in the power to choose good, logically culminates in a final and decisive choice for good, which yields up the soul wholly to the sovereignty of grace. This is Heaven, for the final great reward of good is good. In classic phrase St. Augustine struggles for words to express this conception of the final confirmation of the saints in the love of good and of God. "It does not follow that they will not have free choice because sins will have no power to attract them. Nay rather, it will be more truly free, when set free from the delight of sinning to enjoy the steadfast delight of not sinning. For the first freedom of choice, which was given to man when he was created upright, gave the ability not to sin, but also the ability to sin. This new freedom will be the more powerful just because it will not have power to sin; and this, not by its unaided ability, but by the gift of God."[6]

This is the counterpart to the inability of the finally hardened to see the good and to repent. The Last Judgment upon the righteous is freely to be lifted by grace forever above the battle with sin. This is no mere reward of pleasure, however "spiritual," arbitrarily bestowed on the righteous by God. It is the fitting, natural, and inevitable reward for good, in a world which is a continuous and rational moral order. The reward of good is to be made into the man who can fully delight in good, which is to delight in God.

The Christian doctrine is that this created universe is not eternal in existence. The eternity of creation would appear to make the creation necessary in some way to the fullness of the Deity, which would be to infringe upon the absolute sovereignty of God (see p. 25). Therefore it is taught that when the material creation has fully served its purpose as the expression of the goodness and wisdom of God, and when it has been completely restored in the millennial kingdom, it will then pass away. The notion of an end to the present material creation is expressed in typical apocalyptic imagery by the doctrine of the "conflagration" of 2 Peter 3:9–13. However, in this passage this is expected apparently at the Second Advent, and therefore presumably before the millennial kingdom. The obscurity reminds us of the error of seeking to take apocalyptic imagery chronologically.

---

6 *De civitate Dei*, XXII. 30.

More notably, the Revelation of St. John expresses the idea by saying that after the millennial kingdom there is to be "a new heaven and a new earth: for the first heaven and the first earth were passed away" (Revelation 21:1). There is then a description of a permanent and more glorious, and apparently nonmaterial order. However, the essential of the Christian hope is clear. The final blessedness of the perfected is to see God face to face, and forever to join in His worship (Revelation 22:3, 4). Thus the Summum Bonum is the Vision of God. When Christian theology, which is the greatest and most august system of thought which has ever entered into the heart of man to conceive, comes to the limit of its aspiration, and all things go out in mystery, the whole purpose of creation is fulfilled in the gracious promise of our Lord: "Blessed are the pure in heart: for they shall see God."

Readings

Baillie, J., *And the Life Everlasting*. London: Oxford University Press, 1934.
Cullmann, O., *Immortality of the Soul or Resurrection of the Dead?* London: The Epworth Press, 1958.

Indices

Index of Names and Subjects

Index of Scripture References[1]

---

[1] Numbers referring to Bible chapters and verses are printed in roman type; page numbers
are in italic type.

285

Printed in the United States
2936

THE ART *of* DESIRE

THE ART *of* DESIRE

CHERIE FEATHER

HEAT

New York

THE BERKLEY PUBLISHING GROUP
Published by the Penguin Group
Penguin Group (USA) Inc.
375 Hudson Street, New York, New York 10014, USA
Penguin Group (Canada), 90 Eglinton Avenue East, Suite 700, Toronto, Ontario M4P 2Y3, Canada
(a division of Pearson Penguin Canada Inc.)
Penguin Books Ltd., 80 Strand, London WC2R 0RL, England
Penguin Group Ireland, 25 St. Stephen's Green, Dublin 2, Ireland (a division of Penguin Books Ltd.)
Penguin Group (Australia), 250 Camberwell Road, Camberwell, Victoria 3124, Australia
(a division of Pearson Australia Group Pty. Ltd.)
Penguin Books India Pvt. Ltd., 11 Community Centre, Panchsheel Park, New Delhi—110 017, India
Penguin Group (NZ), 67 Apollo Drive, Rosedale, North Shore 0632, New Zealand
(a division of Pearson New Zealand Ltd.)
Penguin Books (South Africa) (Pty.) Ltd., 24 Sturdee Avenue, Rosebank, Johannesburg 2196,
South Africa

Penguin Books Ltd., Registered Offices: 80 Strand, London WC2R 0RL, England

This is an original publication of The Berkley Publishing Group.

This is a work of fiction. Names, characters, places, and incidents either are the product of the author's imagination or are used fictitiously, and any resemblance to actual persons, living or dead, business establishments, events, or locales is entirely coincidental. The publisher does not have any control over and does not assume any responsibility for author or third-party websites or their content.

First edition: June 2008

Library of Congress Cataloging-in-Publication Data

Feather, Cherie.
    The art of desire / Cherie Feather.—1st ed.
        p.   cm.
    ISBN 978-0-425-22160-0
    1. Women museum directors—Fiction.   2. Women artists—Fiction.   3. Indians of North America—
Fiction.   4. Man-woman relationships—Fiction.   5. Diaries—Fiction.   I. Title.
    PS3623.H5798A78   2008
    813'.6—dc22

                                                                                        2008008109

PRINTED IN THE UNITED STATES OF AMERICA

10   9   8   7   6   5   4   3   2   1

To Karen Solem and Cindy Hwang,
for believing in this book. To my family,
for their love and open-minded support.
To Chris Marie Green and Judy Duarte,
for being there every day.

PROLOGUE

TEXAS
1895

The first time I saw him he was naked, morning-dappled water lapping at his skin, swirling around tendon-tight calves. His rifle, a gun he'd probably stolen from a rancher, was at the edge of the stream, well within his reach.

A hawk soared above his head, screeching like a red-tailed devil, creating a strangely spiritual arc. Mesmerized, the Indian followed its every move.

I knew he was unaware of me. Although I was no more than twenty to thirty steps away, I was crouched amongst a copse of cottonwoods. Earlier I'd been napping there, and upon awakening, I'd lifted my head and spotted him through a branch-scattered gap in the foliage, a stunned gasp locked in my throat.

Was this my punishment for dozing in the sun? Or my reward? I'd gone to that location to work, to sketch the scenery.

I longed to draw him instead. But I couldn't find the will to move, to do more than stare. Curiously handsome, his bluish black, cheekbone-length hair framed the hollowed angles and mysterious shadows that sculpted his face. Muscled ridges and flat planes defined his body, with wide shoulders and a powerful chest. His thighs, I decided, had been built for straddling the horse that grazed nearby. A stolen mount, no doubt. A prize that went with his rifle.

Taking a swift breath, I centered my gaze, filling my vision with his penis. I measured the length and fullness, but I imagined how it would look fully erect, with his testes drawn tight, his foreskin pushed back, and the sensitive head exposed.

Queen Victoria shame me.

In my own country, I was a rumored bohemian, London-born, Paris-schooled, an artist seceding from conventionality, an upper-class girl who'd cast her morals to the wind, who'd stroked many a cock with her hands, even with her ruby red mouth.

But the gossip wasn't true. Not completely. I fantasized about those carnal acts, but the only cocks I dared stroke were with a collection of Asiatic marten brushes.

The hawk flew away, abandoning its circling post. The Indian snapped out of his trance and continued his bath. My heart pounded like the drums of his people. I knew who he was. He was an Apache prisoner of war who'd escaped from a military fort in Oklahoma Territory. Last week U.S. Army soldiers had scoured this area in search of him. They'd ridden into town with a photograph, asking if anyone had seen him. They'd gone to ranches and farms, too. When they'd come to my house, I'd gazed curiously at his picture.

2

And now here he was.

I should have remained motionless until he went away. But somewhere in the peril of my soul, I found the strength to sit upright, to lift a piece of charcoal from my ready-made paint box. The paper clamped to my stretching board was cold-pressed, better suited for rough effects than a detailed portrait of a bared man. But I was willing to compromise. Desire burned like a hot-wick candle beneath the folds of my skirt.

I had moved to America to study its ethnic, geographic, and religious diversity, to paint its fading frontier. So why not study him? Make him my secret project?

"Atacar." I whispered his name. It was of Spanish origin, and in English it meant "to attack."

Suddenly he went still, his dark gaze shooting through the trees like an obsidian-tipped arrow. He couldn't have heard his barely audible name on my lips, yet he'd found me out.

The charcoal slipped from my fingers; my paper remained blank.

Our eyes met, and he reacted like a hound on the heels of a fox. Before I could blink, he grabbed the rifle, jammed it against his water-damp shoulder, and aimed it at me.

I did the unthinkable. I looked at his penis again, challenging the air between us. His face remained an indiscernible mask, devoid of emotion, of any kind of lust. But in his fire-ready stance, his stomach muscles jumped, giving him away, making his cock stir.

From there, neither of us moved.

Finally he motioned with his chin, ordering me out into the open. I didn't hesitate. I lifted my arms in surrender and walked toward him.

Praying he would take me.

3

CHAPTER ONE

Dirty sex with a dirty boy.

That was all Mandy Cooper, the proper, professional, highly organized director of the Santa Fe Women's Art Museum, could think about.

She was addicted to Jared Cabrillo, Atacar's great-great-nephew, a man who sizzled in the art scene, who was notorious for having public liaisons, who wielded his celebrity like the party-on-the-edge charmer he was.

Mandy could feel him watching her from across the museum. She and her staff were hosting a summer reception, and he'd crashed the event.

She tried to avoid him, but she couldn't. His gaze was too strong, too persistent. She gave up the fight and looked at him, too.

Their eyes met, and he lifted his wine and toasted her before he put the glass to his lips and drank the bloodred liquid.

She gripped the silver chain on her evening bag, locking it

around her wrist like a handcuff. He was drop-dead, imprison-a-woman gorgeous. There was no other way to describe him. He walked toward her, and her panties stuck to her skin, making her want to rub her thighs together.

"Nice party," he said, as they came face-to-face.

"It's going well." She'd been sleeping with him for almost a month, yet she couldn't stop herself from staring.

He sported a retro-style, black Western shirt, decorated with white piping and tucked into crisp jeans. His face, diamond-blade dazzling and stone-quarry tough, mirrored his heritage. Both ears showcased tiny silver hoops. He had an intimate body piercing and tribal tattoos, too.

He was everything she shouldn't want. At thirty-eight, she was supposed to know better. He was ten years younger than she was, but he wasn't her boy toy. He controlled their affair, enticing her into carnal situations.

He set his empty glass on a nearby table. "You look beautiful, Mandy."

"Thank you." Her black dress scooped modestly in front, and the delicate silver and turquoise cross around her neck offered a hint of adornment.

Aside from their naked urges, they didn't know each other very well. They didn't have meaningful conversations. But at least she knew he wasn't seeing anyone else. He didn't cheat on his lovers. Of course that didn't change who and what he was. He treated monogamy like a courtesy, not a commitment.

Needing a diversion, Mandy turned toward the famous portrait of Jared's ancestor. They were standing in front of Atacar's exhibit.

He was the museum's most prized possession, a Catherine Burke treasure, a portrait remarkable for its depth and passion, for its stunning realism. But Atacar was more than Catherine's greatest work. So much more. The nineteenth-century artist was rumored to have loved him, just as he was rumored to have loved her.

But no one knew for sure.

Catherine had abandoned her Texas home, never to be heard from again, and soon after she'd disappeared, Atacar had been shot and killed by a trio of soldiers.

As Mandy looked into his eyes, an air-conditioned chill blasted from the ceiling, sending goose bumps along her arms.

He was an imposing figure, his head cocked just so, his expression dark and serious. Positioned in a straight-back chair, he gripped the barrel of a Winchester rifle. She tried to imagine him sitting for Catherine while the daring girl painted his image. His clothes consisted of Anglo gear, reminiscent of ranchers and farmers, but he was Chiricahua Apache, an enlisted army scout who'd become a prisoner of war.

Mandy blinked, but Atacar's gaze remained constant. The museum had acquired his portrait nearly forty years earlier. Prior to that, it had been hidden inside the walls of the farmhouse where Catherine had lived.

Upon its discovery, their romantic legacy had begun. Rumors spawned that they'd been lovers. That she'd disappeared because of him. That their desperate hearts would remain forever entwined.

But once again, no one knew for sure.

The only ray of hope was that Catherine had kept a secret journal, writings that had never been found.

By now, most of the art world thought the journal was a

myth. But Mandy chose to believe otherwise. She had the museum historian searching for it.

Suddenly Jared moved closer, close enough to invade Mandy's space, to attack her senses. She could smell the spicy notes of his cologne. She turned to face him, his ancestor fading into the background.

"Why did you come here tonight?" she asked.

He smoothed the front of his hair. He wore it plaited into a single braid, leaving the hardened angles of his face unframed. "To fuck you."

Her addiction jabbed her hard and quick, like a needle to a starving vein. "I'm working, Jared."

"That's what makes it so fun." Fun or not, he didn't smile. He just looked at her with the same driven expression as when he'd toasted her with his merlot or cabernet or whatever he'd been drinking. "Like when we do it at my work."

She didn't respond. He was a highly successful breeder, trainer, and showman who managed his own horse farm. Banging each other's brains out in his barn wasn't the same as getting naked at the museum.

His gaze turned darker, more intense. "You could take me to your office. You could make me do things to you."

Hedonic chills vibrated her spine. By now, they were just inches apart. He kept moving closer, drawing her in to his seductive sphere, doing what he always did.

"What things?" she asked.

"You could take off your panties, order me to my knees, and lift your dress in front of my face. You could make me taste how sweet you are."

The room started to spin. She wanted his mouth between her legs. But envisioning herself standing in front of him, *making* him do it was almost more than she could bear.

"Does that excite you?" he asked.

"Yes."

"What else turns you on? What other games do you want to play?"

"I don't know." Her voice shook. "I honestly don't know." At the moment she just wanted to crawl all over him, to fall like a sugared gumdrop at his feet.

"I'll bet she did it," Jared said.

"What? Who?"

"Catherine." Jared moistened his lips. "I'll bet she lifted her skirts in front of Atacar's face. I'll bet she came all over him." His voice was soft and low, dangerously demanding. "Do it, Mandy. Be bad for me."

Heat flooded her lungs. If her guests weren't milling around, eating canapés and socializing, she would've removed her panties right then and there.

"Meet me at my office," she said. "But give me a head start. I need to unlock the door."

His demeanor didn't falter. "Hurry up."

"I will." She did her damnedest to regain her composure, to not give away what she was about to do.

She walked toward the stairs, moving quickly so no one stopped her, so she didn't get trapped into small talk. Finally she ascended to the second floor, her low-heeled pumps assaulting terrazzo-topped concrete, ringing like bullets in her ears.

Her office door came into view, and she fumbled with her

purse. What if she got caught? Her affair with Jared wasn't a secret, but doing it at work . . .

She removed her keys, and footsteps sounded. She nearly jumped out of her skin.

"Easy, baby, it's me."

Jared. He'd barely given her a head start. Mandy glanced his way, her heart thudding between her thighs.

He came up behind her, bumping his fly against her rear. "You're so conventional. So ladylike. But here you are, wanting this as badly as I do."

He had no idea. She crammed the key into the lock and pushed open the door. Her drug of choice was crashing in on her, rushing perilously through her veins.

They crossed the threshold and locked themselves inside. Her office housed an executive desk, a sofa, and matching side chairs. But she didn't move in that direction. She paused just beyond the entryway, beside a floor-to-ceiling bookcase, with a security light burning low.

Caught in a sexual whirlwind, she reached under her dress and removed her panties. She wasn't wearing hose. Her legs were bare.

"Get on your knees," she told him.

He dropped down with a grateful thud. Gorgeous Jared with his head tipped back, his jaw jutting forward. While he waited, a thick, naughty beat of silence swallowed the air.

One. Two. Three. Let him see.

She hiked up her dress, bunched the fabric around her hips, and exposed herself.

"Damn." His voice pulsed, the tendons in his throat strained.

He was staring at her. Ravenously. Mandy gripped her hem a little tighter. She knew he liked her Brazilian. He thought the process that left a small strip of pubic hair above a woman's vulva was hot and sexy. He'd talked her into getting waxed, convincing her that it would make her feel prettier, even when she was alone. He'd told her to touch herself and think about him when he wasn't around, to make it her guilty pleasure. She couldn't begin to count how many times she'd followed his advice, imagining that he was watching her.

She moved closer, teasing Jared with her guilty pleasure, widening her stance to give him a better look, to show him the cleft of her labia. But that wasn't enough. Anxious, she took her dress completely off, dragging it over her head. Her basic underwire bra came next. She wanted to be naked, all the way bare, except for her conservative black pumps.

He swallowed, eager to taste her. He looked half-starved.

"Do it," she commanded, spreading herself for him. "Do it."

He didn't waste a second, not one delicious moment. He went right for her clit, sucking hard and fast, then slowing to deliberate strokes. He knew how much pressure to apply, how much saliva to spread. Excitement gathered low in her belly.

She watched him lavishing every taut, tingling taste. The sight was roughly, fiercely erotic. His hungry mouth. Her damp, swollen sex. She pitched forward, and he made a primal sound. Mandy got even more aroused.

"Are you hard?" she asked, trailing her hands through his hair and snagging his thick, silky braid.

He paused to answer her question, moisture glistening on his lips. "I'm so turned on, I could come in my pants."

Her knees nearly buckled. "I'm going to do this to you. When you're done with me."

"What if I don't want to stop? What if I want to keep going?" He snaked his tongue so she could see him make contact with her clit. He banged her with his fingers, too.

All the way in. All the way out. He even rubbed his sticky digits down the front of his shirt and along his bulging fly, smearing himself with her juices.

Dizzy, she rotated her hips. Sooner or later he would have to stop; if he didn't, she would explode into a pool of pollinated liquid.

Reaching out, she grappled for something to brace the blinding pleasure and fisted the edge of a shelf. A moment later, she caught the binding of a hardback book and clutched it between her white-knuckled fingers.

He made a sudden move, cupping her rear and pulling her toward him. They both went crashing until she landed on top of him, sprawled across his handsome face.

This was even wilder, she thought. Sexier. She rode his mouth, her body flexed, her back bowed in a fluid arc. She'd never felt more graceful, more ladylike. The irony should have made her laugh. Instead, she came in convulsing waves.

All over her dirty boy.

Jared and Mandy sat on the floor and gazed at each other. He wiped his mouth with the back of his hand. He'd just devoured her orchid-soft, pussy-sweet flavor, enjoying every warm, wet, orgasmic taste.

"That was the hottest thing ever," he said, before she got shy and glanced away. "So don't even think about blushing."

She lifted her chin. "I'm not."

Sometimes she did. Regardless of how nasty they got, she still had an innocent quality. Her mink-colored hair skimmed her shoulders, and her eyes were framed with sweeping lashes.

She was the first proper girl he'd fucked, and he was hooked. He didn't know for how long, and he didn't want to know. For him, it was easier living from day to day, walking the sexual tightrope that drove him.

"Now it's your turn," she said. "Take off your clothes."

"Are you still going to blow me?" he asked, upping the ante on the offer she'd made. "Are you going to suck me as deep as you can? Deeper than you ever have?"

"Yes." She released a shuddering breath. There was a damp spot on the carpet beneath her, where some of her wetness had leaked onto the floor. "I am."

His nerve endings went electric. He got to his feet and offered her a hand. She stood up, and he grabbed her and swung her into his arms.

"What are you doing?"

"Carrying you to bed."

She looped her arms around his neck and kicked off her shoes. "It's a sofa. Not a bed."

"Close enough." He tossed her onto the sofa in question, planted his knees on either side of her face, and shoved down his boxers and jeans in one fell swoop.

His penis sprang free, and he felt good enough to grin. The head of his cock was pierced, and he knew it fascinated her.

"Up close and personal," she said.

"Just for you." He imagined her tongue sliding over the curved barbell. He got harder just thinking about it. Not that he wasn't already rock solid, not that he hadn't meant what he'd said about creaming his jeans earlier.

"I like touching it," she told him.

"Then what are you waiting for?" He wanted her to get aggressive.

But she didn't. She traced the barbell with the tip of her finger. Softly. Tentatively. He thought he might die.

"You never told me what it's called."

"It's a PA." His own breathing engulfed him. "A Prince Albert. They pierce it from the outside of the frenulum and into the urethra."

"Is this the frenulum?" She gestured to the band of tissue under the head of his cock, where a portion of the barbell was.

He nodded. "It's a common piercing for a guy."

"Not in my world." She touched him again. No, not him. The jewelry. "Every time I see it, I keep thinking that it hurt."

"When I first had it done? It didn't. No more than getting your ears pierced." His stomach muscles jumped. He wanted her to lean forward, to give him a silky blow job. Her gentleness was exciting him. "It takes about the same amount of time to heal, too. But I've had it forever." Since he was a rebellious teenager, seeking a rite of passage, a way to define who he was.

"If feels amazing when we have sex," she said. "I didn't expect it to. But it does."

"It's supposed to give both partners more pleasure. Not painful pleasure. Tingling sensations. It increases the sensitivity."

Mandy looked up at him, and their eyes met, making him more aware of his erection popping in her face, of the promise she'd made.

They moved toward each other at the same time, at the same exhilarating instant, and she parted her lips, taking the tip of his cock inside.

She toyed with the barbell, creating a rippling sensation, then pulling back to lick him, to run her tongue along the underside of his shaft and over the top, until she nursed the head again.

He fought the urge to relinquish control. But he didn't. He held on, letting Mandy play, letting her decide when she would take him deeper. While she experimented, he watched her, heightening the game.

It got better from there.

She shoved his jeans farther down his hips. "Lie on your back," she said. "I want to crawl between your legs."

Who was he to argue?

He did what she told him to do, even though they had to fight the sofa to make it happen. Once he was in position, she opened the snaps on his shirt and exposed his chest and stomach.

She took her time, kissing his abs, leaving wet marks on his skin. By now he wanted to push her down and make her suck him all the way to the back of her throat.

He didn't wait for long. He tried, but he couldn't. She put her mouth on him again, and he lost the battle. He did what he was craving to do. He pushed her down.

She made a girl-hungry sound. She liked his roughness, he thought. Jared spread his legs and lifted his hips, grinding one booted heel into the cushion and planting his other foot on the floor, supporting his weight. He set the rhythm, and she took over, sucking greedily.

She was sowing her blow-job oats, reaping him for all he was worth, the way he'd wanted her to. But even so, he didn't spill into her mouth. Not because he was being polite. He loved watching her swallow. But tonight he wanted to come inside her. So he lifted her up and told her to stop, whispering gruffly in her ear, telling her it was time to fuck.

Mandy watched him undress. Her eyes were bright, and her hair was tumbled. She was still feeling her oats.

Anxious, he ditched his boots and went to work on his jeans, then his pricey Western shirt, tugging the sleeves to get himself out of it. He hadn't brought protection. He and Mandy were clean and safe. They'd talked about it on the night they'd first gotten together.

"I love your tattoos." She pawed his triceps, where he had matching armbands. "Do you have any idea how exotic you are?"

"Do you have an idea how hard I'm going to give this to you?" He nudged her with his steel-tipped sword.

"I'm ready."

"You better be." He told her to straddle his lap in a reverse cowgirl position, so he could see her ass, so he could reach around and cup her tits, so he could pinch her nipples.

His lover accommodated him. She turned around and spread her thighs nice and wide, creating the slick leverage she needed.

He gripped her waist, and she went rodeo, giving him a thrill. Not only could he admire the curve of her ass, he got an erotic view of her sliding up and down, milking his cock.

She gulped her next breath. "It feels so good."

He knew she meant the barbell. The sensation rocked him, too. Her pussy caressed him, and he nearly growled, his heart machine-gunning his chest.

"Touch yourself." He struggled to steady his voice. She kept riding him, only now she was going slowly, forcing him to feel every luxurious glide. "Do it the way you do it when you're alone."

She moved her hand, and he could tell that she was rubbing her clit. He couldn't wait to bring her deeper into his realm, to seduce her even more.

"Turn around," he said. "I want to see."

They made the switch, with her sitting forward on his lap, stroking her sex.

He watched her come, thinking how incredible she was. She smiled when she was done. Her lashes fluttered, too. How pretty could she be? Warm and soft in the barely-there light.

"Is that what you wanted to see?" she asked.

He wasn't about to respond, not now, not in the wake of wanting her so badly. Desperate for more, he pushed her down and opened her legs until they were almost straight in the air. She gasped, and he thrust full hilt, pumping hard and fast.

She had another orgasm, poised like an acrobat. Her stomach quivered, and she reached out and clawed the back of the sofa.

When she wrapped her legs around him, the familiarity of being this close to her shattered his mind. Jared tunneled his hands in her hair, heat surging through his blood and burning his loins. He went off like a geyser, coming deep inside her.

In the minutes that followed, she clung to him, breathing

softly against his neck. He wanted to be gentle for her, to hold her close, but he didn't know how to pull it off, not without getting out of his comfort zone. So he settled on a quick kiss, got dressed, and went downstairs ahead of her.

Once he hit the party, he didn't have another drink or wait for Mandy to reappear. He left the museum, and on his way out, he frowned at Atacar, knowing the other man would've stayed.

CHAPTER TWO

"Turkey with avocado and coleslaw on the side. Pink lemonade, lots of ice."

Kiki Dion, the museum's colorful historian, placed Mandy's lunch on her desk. The other woman's wavy red hair peeked out from beneath a geometric-printed bandanna-style scarf, and freckles dusted her nose.

"Thanks. It's been one of those days."

"For me, too. We deserve a moment to rest our bones." The redhead sat across from her. She'd also gotten a sandwich, cramming in a quick lunch together.

"How's the research going?" Mandy asked.

"I don't have anything new to report, but not from the lack of trying. I'll keep working on it."

"I know you will." The journal quest was still in its early stages. Mandy had worked at the museum for a little over a year, and Kiki had only been there for eight months, so it had taken some time for them to settle into their jobs before they'd made the journal a priority. But now that they had, they weren't letting go.

The historian unwrapped her food. "So what's up with you? Any more hot romps with Jared?"

"Not since the party." Mandy wasn't surprised by Kiki's blatant question. She'd been confiding in the other woman about her affair.

They seemed like unlikely friends, but they weren't. Although Kiki was closer to Jared's age than to Mandy's, they'd both survived mundane marriages, with ex-husbands who'd left them wanting more, not just sexually but emotionally. Not that Jared came anywhere near to fitting the emotional bill for Mandy. But she kept telling herself that wicked sex wasn't supposed to be steeped in life-altering conversations and hand-holding walks.

Kiki glanced at the sofa and shot her a teasing grin. "I hope you had that cleaned."

She smiled, too. "I did. Right away." But the memory of him remained. She'd been focused on Jared all week, anxious for him to call, to tempt her into another be-bad-for-him encounter. "I spilled coffee on it the next day to cover my tracks."

"Good thinking." Kiki dived into a grilled roast beef and swiss, eating heartily, crumbs falling onto her napkin-draped lap. "Why don't you ever call him?"

"I don't know. Maybe I like waiting for him to get in touch with me." Mandy removed a pepperoncini from her sandwich and bit into it. The juice squirted into her mouth, the spicy hotness reminding her of her lover. "Maybe it's part of my addiction. Part of the thrill."

"He is exciting. Remember the first night you slept with him?"

"How could I ever forget?" Mandy had always been keenly

aware of Jared's reputation, but she rarely saw the art-celebrity bad boy out on the town. They didn't run in the same circles. Then last month, she'd been seated next to him at a hotel ballroom charity dinner, and sexual sparks flew. "I told him that I was half in love with Catherine and Atacar."

"And he used that to seduce you."

"Yes, he did. By the end of the night, he'd convinced me to check into a room with him."

"You were the talk of the town. Atacar's great-great-nephew and the Women's Museum director. People are still gossiping, wondering how a nice girl like you fell for a guy like him." Kiki flashed another playful grin. "But I know the real scoop."

"That he turned me into a Jared junkie?"

"Exactly." Kiki paused. "Does he know you're trying to find the journal? That you're hoping to acquire it for the museum?"

Mandy nodded. "Yes, but he doesn't think it exists."

"He's a nonbeliever?" Kiki sounded surprised.

"He tried to find it, too. A long time ago. But he never did, so he thinks it's a lost cause."

"Then I'll do my darnedest to prove him wrong."

The phone rang, and they quit talking as Mandy took the call. A few seconds later, she exhaled a quick breath and hung up.

"That was Gloria," she said, referring to the curatorial division secretary. "She wanted to know if she should accept my flowers or have the delivery boy bring them directly to me."

"Your flowers?"

Mandy struggled to keep her cool, to not make a fuss, even if her heart was heading toward a girlish patter. "Apparently someone sent me a bouquet."

Kiki reacted openly, her voice boosting a notch. "Do you think it was Jared?"

"I doubt it. It doesn't seem like something he would do. It's probably work related." Mandy reached into her bottom drawer for her purse, removing her wallet for some bills, preparing for the tip. "But I told Gloria that I'd take them. Just in case."

They waited, Kiki perched on the edge of her chair, and Mandy standing near the door, lying to herself, insisting it didn't matter who the flowers were from.

When the bouquet arrived, the women gazed at each other. A stunning spray of long-stemmed, deep red roses in a sleek crimson vase. Maybe it *was* something Jared would do.

Mandy asked the delivery boy if he knew what kind of roses they were since they were so dark, and he said they were a hybrid tea called Black Magic.

After he left, she snagged the miniature envelope that accompanied the bouquet. But there wasn't a traditional gift card inside. Instead, she discovered a business card of an adult store in Albuquerque. It was called Black Magic, too. She turned the card over. Jared had written a note for her to meet him there tomorrow at three o'clock.

"So?" Kiki asked. "Are they from him?"

"Yes." She couldn't think of anything to say except that one little word.

"Can I see?"

Mandy extended the Saturday-afternoon invitation, and the other woman studied both sides, her eyes going wide.

"He's full of surprises, isn't he?"

"Always." Mandy wet her lips and tasted the lingering pepper juice. "I wonder what he'll talk me into buying."

"Something that will make you want him even more?" Kiki asked without expecting an answer. "Black Magic is right. That man is casting a spell on you."

"I know." Heaven, how she knew. Without thinking, she leaned in to inhale the roses' sweet, light fragrance, to touch their bewitching petals.

Jared waited in the parking lot, leaning against his truck, a customized fifty-seven Chevy big block, Prussian blue with polished centerline wheels. It wasn't his ranch vehicle. He drove it for fun.

Life was supposed to be fun, wasn't it? Especially with Mandy. So here he was, keeping things light, telling himself not to feel guilty. He'd lied to Mandy from the start. He knew Catherine's journal existed because he had it. He'd searched for years and then had uncovered the book unexpectedly. But that wasn't something he could reveal. The journal was a secret he'd promised to keep.

He glanced up and saw that Mandy had arrived. She parked next to him and got out of her midsize sedan. He didn't start a conversation. He let her do the talking. She was fifteen minutes late.

"I didn't know what to wear to a place like this," she said. "I changed three times."

Was she kidding? He broke into a smile. "What you have on is fine." Slim-fitting jeans, a blouse that shimmered in the sun, jeweled sandals. She'd painted her fingernails red for the occasion. Her toenails, too. Normally she wore pink polish.

"I hope I don't see someone I know."

He tapped her chin. Her face was shaped like a heart, with a cute little point at the end. "If you see someone you know, you'll both pretend it never happened. You won't discuss it at the next stuffy fund-raiser."

"The last one wasn't stuffy. You were there."

He knew she was referring to the night their affair had begun. The charity dinner had been for a Native American cause, so Jared had bought a ticket and paid an astronomical price for his meal, hoping to do his part. He hadn't intended to get side-tracked by the museum director whose job included keeping his ancestor's portrait in her care. Her interest in Catherine and Atacar should have kept him away. But it had intrigued him instead.

He reached for her hand and led her toward the sex shop. She stalled for a moment, studying the shaded windows and shiny black door. He urged her forward. Black Magic wasn't a dungeon, even if it seemed dark and cavernous from the outside.

He escorted her into the building, and she made a pleasant sound.

"It smells good in here," she said. "Like cinnamon."

He didn't comment, but he'd heard that cinnamon produced heat within the body, increasing physical and sexual appetites.

The store was big and well-lit with an array of toys, BDSM gear, fetish clothes, lubes, lotions, books, and DVDs.

Sensual accoutrements, he thought. For all types. A group of young women who appeared to be planning a bachelorette party were waving rainbow dongs at each other and giggling about wedding colors.

Mandy glanced at Jared, and they both laughed. "Are you still nervous about seeing someone you know?" he asked.

"Not anymore." She walked over to a female-friendly display, a glass table showcasing massage oils and bath products.

"Try this." He reached for a tester on another display and pumped clear liquid onto her hands.

She rubbed her palms together, as if she were analyzing a department-store moisturizer. "That's nice. Silky." She spread the lingering wetness over the backs of her hands. "It's not drying very well, though."

He bent forward to whisper in her ear. "It's a silicone lube. For the toy I'm going to buy for you. To make it nice and slick."

She caught her blunder and grabbed ahold of his shirt, a basic white tee, keeping her body close to his. Their pelvises would've bumped if they'd been the same height, but he was taller.

"Are you getting a toy, too?" she asked.

"No." They separated, and he led her to the dildo section. The giggling girls were gone. He gestured to a wall of rubber phalluses. "Check them out. Touch them."

She blinked at him. "Is one of these going to be my toy?"

"No. But I want you to touch them anyway."

She stepped forward and examined the samples, weighing them in her hands, running her fingers along their sculpted shapes.

Jared stood back and watched. He'd created this game for her, and he thrived on every inch of it. "Do you like the realistic ones?"

"Yes. Like this." She fondled a model equipped with a thickly veined shaft, hefty balls, and a bulging head.

"Good. Because you're going to make one of me. When I'm big and hard."

She looked up. By now her cheeks were flushed, giving her a warm glow. "Make one?"

He led her to another shelf, where he showed her a dildo-making kit. Her cheeks turned pinker.

"It'll include anatomical details," he said, enjoying her reaction, the shyness that made seducing her exciting. "Veins, ridges, balls. Just like the one you said you liked."

"Only it'll be an exact replica of you." She picked up the kit. The box depicted a picture of an erect penis. "I can use it when I'm alone."

"Not the first time. You're going to use it when you're with me. I want to watch you slide it between your legs. In your bedroom, with the lights turned low and candles burning."

She clutched the box, pressing the cardboard against her chest. The good girl. The want-to-be-bad girl. "That sounds romantic. Sort of," she added softly.

Jared didn't respond. Sort of romantic was the best he could do. In the silence, they gazed at each other. Was she imagining him in her bedroom, instructing her how wide to spread her thighs, how deeply to insert her homemade toy? A copy of his cock. He knew it made him seem arrogant, but he didn't want her to use a device that was fashioned after another man. He wanted to be her lover in every way.

"Will you do this for me?" he asked. "Will you use it and let me watch?"

"Yes." The word came out in a sensual rush. "But we have to pierce it. It won't feel like you if it doesn't have your PA."

Damn, she was sweet. Multiorgasmic Mandy. "We can use one

of my barbells." He would be sure to go home and get one before they went to her place to make the mold.

"What about the candles?" She glanced around. "Can we get them here?"

"Sure. But the only kind they sell are shaped like body parts. Or full nudes. Like statues of people."

"I think I'd like to get some of those."

"Okay." He knew what area of the store they were in, so he pointed the way.

She chose two white candles, one shaped like a man, the other molded as a woman. She went for a red candle, too, where a couple was together in a Kama Sutra position called Flower in Bloom.

"This is beautiful," she said.

It was, he thought, wondering how it would look with a flame burning at the tip, making the lovers melt into each other.

She glided the wax creation under his nose. "It's scented."

He caught a fragile whiff of roses, like the bouquet he'd sent. Suddenly he worried about losing her, about their affair ending before he was ready to let her go.

"Don't ever say no to me," he said. "Don't ever not be there when I need you."

"I won't," she responded. "I swear I won't."

～

A naked man in her bathroom, Mandy thought. Tall and dark and waiting for her to make him hard.

She'd already read the directions on the kit and mixed the

molding powder with water. The specially designed container was ready. But Jared wasn't. He'd asked her to do the honors.

He sat on the closed lid of the commode and opened his thighs. He was so unabashed, so comfortable with his nudity. And why not? Between his gym routine and endless hours on horseback, he had the body of a modern-day god.

Mandy knelt on the contour rug at his feet. Her bathroom was decorated in dusty blue and sea-foam green, with a clear white shower curtain. She lived in a one-bedroom condo in a fast-growing urban area.

Jared skimmed her hair away from her face, and she darted out her tongue. He'd removed his piercing, so the cast would be smooth.

"That's my girl," he said.

She smiled against his growing erection. One lick, and he was half-hard. He leaned back against the commode and widened his legs.

She gripped the base of his shaft and lowered her mouth, stroking and sucking at the same time. He smoothed her hair again, keeping it from falling forward, from obstructing his view.

His testes were drawn tight. She cupped the tender sacs, and he pushed deeper into her mouth. He was cheating, she thought. By now he was hard enough for the negative mold. He just wanted to get sucked some more.

Mandy gave him what he wanted until he groaned and told her to stop.

Before he inserted his cock and balls into the container, she dabbed a little petroleum jelly onto his pubic hair to be sure the molding material didn't grab any of it.

Sixty seconds later, the negative casting portion was done. The next step was pouring the liquid rubber into the container.

"It'll take hours to set," she said. "It won't be done until later tonight."

"Then we'll hang out together and wait." He reached for a washcloth and dampened it with soap and warm water, cleaning himself, getting rid of the jelly. He slid his piercing back in, too.

They both stood beside the sink, their reflections in the vanity mirror. She wanted to spend the evening with him, to have dinner, to sit on the patio and watch the sun go down. But she wasn't fooling herself into believing that they were headed toward an emotionally committed relationship. Earlier when he asked her to never say no to him, to be there when he needed her, she was well aware that he meant sexually.

He tossed the washcloth into the hamper, and she glanced at his cock. He was still half-hard, hungry for more attention. Apparently she'd left a lasting impression.

"Do you want me to finish what I started?" she asked.

Jared looked down, then back up at her. "Is that a rhetorical question?"

Mandy smiled. "I think maybe it was."

She guided him back to the commode. The moment she knelt at his feet, he sat down and assumed the fellatio position, spreading his thighs the way he'd done before.

She stroked and sucked, and he went back to playing with her hair, running his fingers through it, keeping it away from her face so he could watch.

"You're getting good at this," he said.

Enjoying his praise, she relaxed her throat and took him as deeply as she could, the way he'd made her do at the museum.

Although he tasted clean and sexy, he tasted salty, too. Semen was already beading at the tip.

He scooted to the edge of the commode lid, getting as close to her as possible. His breathing hitched; his legs went taut. His stomach tightened, too.

He thrust forward, fucking her mouth. She couldn't think of another way to say it, not with the way he was moving in and out.

When he bucked his hips, she felt the pressure of his oncoming orgasm. He spilled into her, and she swallowed every drop.

Afterward, she returned to the sink to sip some water, and he came up behind her. Once again, they were standing in front of the mirror. He didn't say anything. Instead, he put his arms around her, then unzipped her jeans and wedged his hand between the denim and her skin.

Instantly aroused, she exhaled a quick breath, and he worked his way into her panties.

"Do you know what I was fantasizing about when you were sucking me?" he asked.

She pressed against his fingers. By now, he'd found her clit.

"What you're going to do to yourself later," he said, answering his own question. "I can't wait for the damn thing to set so I can watch you use it."

She shivered against his touch. She was getting slick and wet. "You were watching me go down on you, too."

"Can you blame me?" He grazed the side of her neck with his teeth. "You're my bad girl."

She had an insane urge to ask him to give her a hickey, to

brand her in a visible way. But she wasn't a smitten teenager letting her high school boyfriend get to second base. He'd already been to third and back. He'd scored at least a dozen home runs.

He trapped her gaze in the mirror. "I want a key to your condo. Will you give me one?"

"Yes." The tension between her thighs got thicker. He thrust two fingers inside of her, banging her in that dirty-boy way of his.

"Do you know why I want it?"

"To come over in the middle of the night when I'm asleep. To kiss me. To climb on top of me." But not to cuddle, she thought. He never did that.

"That's right. Spontaneous sex. I can't get enough of it with you."

"Me, neither. With you." She angled her hips to give him better access, to show him how wet she was. She was more than willing to let him steal into her bedroom at whatever ungodly hour he chose, to give her a fix, to feed her addiction.

Losing control, she climaxed, staring at her haunted image in the glass. All she wanted was Jared. Just him. Her lover. All the time.

The way Catherine had probably wanted Atacar.

Mandy pitched forward against the sink and closed her eyes. She didn't want to think about Jared's great-great-uncle or the woman who was rumored to love him.

Not now. Not while Jared was standing behind her, with his hand still wedged in her pants, working her into another frenzy.

And making her come again.

CHAPTER THREE

Atacar didn't take me. He didn't sweep me into frenzied passion. For what seemed like the longest minutes of my life, he continued to hold me at gunpoint.

Should I tell him my name? That I am Catherine Burke, a twenty-two-year-old virgin artist with a wanton reputation? That I want him to kiss me? That I long to feel his nakedness against mine?

What if he didn't speak English? Then what? My words would be lost on him. But my actions wouldn't. I repeated what I'd done earlier and looked at his cock. I could see his genitals in much greater detail now that I was standing only a gun barrel away from him. He grew bigger, aroused by my visual attention, and I got bolder.

I brought my gaze to his face and stared him down, biting my bottom lip, sucking it lustfully between my teeth. His granite-cut features didn't soften. They were as hard as his penis. I felt triumphant. His eyes burned for more. My boldness made them darker, pitched like a midnight fire.

At that point, I expected him to lower the rifle, to sweep me into the passion I craved. But he didn't. He appeared to be waiting for me, to see what I would do next. Nervous energy skittered through my blood.

What would I do next? I'd never seduced a man before. I couldn't just stand there like an inexperienced ninny and stare him into ejaculation.

So I did what I assumed a seductress would do. I curtailed my fear and removed my clothing. I got as far as my dress, petticoat, and corset cover and stopped, letting him look at me in my ribbon-trimmed corset, lace-hemmed drawers, and high-top boots. To heighten the image, I loosed my daytime coiffure, which was already messy from my nap, allowing my wheat-colored hair to fall in long, unbound waves.

Atacar finally lowered his gun, resting the butt of the weapon on the ground. He looked at me as if I were a divine delicacy, the best sweetmeat he would ever taste. My breasts tingled. The juncture between my thighs went moist.

He jutted his chin, telling me, without words, to complete my state of undress. I prepared to unfasten my corset, and a sudden noise caught both of our attentions.

The rustle of foliage, of riders approaching.

Atacar moved at a spinning pace, and so did I. We gathered our clothes and dashed for the cottonwoods. He latched on to my arm to speed me up, and I felt as if I were being dragged. He was much taller than I was, making quicker strides. His horse spooked and ran, too. The animal disappeared out of sight. The riders were still coming from the opposite direction.

Once we were hidden in the trees, Atacar pushed me down and thrust his water-damp body on top of mine. He was heavy, big and muscular, and the air whooshed out of me.

He lifted his head and arched his torso to see who would appear. All I could see was his naked chest, which bore varying scars. War wounds, I presumed. I knew he was clutching his rifle. If the riders threatened us, he would attack, living up to his name.

The strangers arrived. I heard them dismount. I heard them talking, too. They were cowboys, filling their canteens at the stream, discussing the stray cattle for which they were searching.

Atacar's posture relaxed a bit, and I realized that he understood what they were saying. I could have spoken to him after all. Either way, I suspected that he was relieved that the other men weren't associated with the army. Luckily, they didn't linger. They were gone soon enough.

Leaving Atacar and me alone once again.

This time I waited to see what he would do. Would he lift his body from mine and don his clothes so he could track his missing horse? Or would he stay where he was, pressed intimately against me?

He stayed.

Our gazes locked. My heart rapped in raw excitement. His hips bumped mine, creating friction. His arousal returned, stone-hard and insistent.

"I'm aware of who you are," I said.

"And I'm aware that you're bewitching me," he responded in

a strong, choppy accent I'd never heard before. But that was prob-
ably how Indians sounded when they spoke English.

Dangerous. Exotic.

"Soldiers came through this area last week," I told him. "I saw
your picture."

"And now you want to lie with me?"

I nodded, feeling my pulse rise. "Yes."

After that, we quit talking. Our words no longer mattered. I
battled my corset, and he tugged at my drawers. I didn't show him
that the crotch seam was open. I let him pull them down instead.

I knew that women could have orgasms, and I was anxious to
experience what my bohemian friends in Paris whispered so deli-
ciously about. They'd told me that I could make it happen myself,
but I'd wanted to wait for my first lover.

And here he was.

Atacar kissed me, his tongue fornicating with mine. He tasted
wild and forbidden, and I hungered for more. Liquid heat, as
powerful as the sun itself, rained down on us.

Experimenting, I rubbed his cock, circling the head. It was
silkier than I'd imagined. I felt as wonderfully wanton as my rep-
utation, sliding my hand up and down, enjoying the gliding sensa-
tion. He groaned and kissed me harder. Our teeth clashed, and I
bit his lip. He pinned me down and told me do it again, and I
made a drop of his blood spill into my mouth.

We rolled over in the dirt, the grass-patched, leaf-laden ground
abrading the exposed portions of my skin. My corset, which laced
in back and contained a front opening, was partially undone, and
my drawers were halfway down my legs. A twig scratched my
bare bottom.

Atacar used his fingers, parting the curls that covered my mound, and I spread my thighs for him. He looked down, aroused by how willing I was to expose myself, to let him see. I looked down at him, too. His cock was even more engorged. I imagined him spending his seed all over me.

He played with the secret folds of my flesh, making me sinfully wet, making me squirm. I didn't need to wonder if the nub he tended was my clitoris. I knew it was. My bohemian friends whispered deliciously about that, too. I finally understood why.

The world burst at my core. I shuddered and shook, lifting my hips in jerking motions. He dipped two fingers inside, spreading even more wetness, more of what I needed. I panted until there was barely breath left in my lungs.

Then I heard a familiar voice call my name. "Catherine!"

Atacar rolled away and grabbed his rifle.

"No!" I told him, scrambling to right my undergarments, pulling up my drawers and fastening my corset. "That's my nanny. I'm from England, and she came to America with me." I managed to put my petticoat in place, but I couldn't find my corset cover, so I climbed into my dress the way I was, nearly tripping over the fabric. Nanny kept calling out to me, expressing her concern. I'd been gone a long time.

Atacar shoved on his clothes, too. But he couldn't get his cock to behave. In spite of our predicament, he remained half-hard, the buttons on his pants straining. He still desired me.

For all the good it did. By now, he looked as if he wanted to rip my hair from my pretty little head, to make me suffer for his unresolved erection. I hoped that scalping one's enemies wasn't a practice in his tribe.

Nanny called my name again.

"Hurry," he snapped. "Go to her. Before she finds you here with me."

"I'm trying." I had leaves in my unscalped hair, and my hastily fastened corset was threatening to come undone. I was an abomination.

It was to no avail. Nanny discovered us. She came puffing through an opening in the trees, stopped in her tracks, her gaze darting from me to him, then back to me. Although my appearance was ravished, she didn't accuse Atacar of hurting me. She must have recognized a seductress when she saw one.

"Goodness, child." She shook her head, her double chin quivering. "What have you done?"

~

It was done.

Jared leaned against the sink while Mandy popped the dildo out of the cast. She traced the naughty phallus, and his cock went hard.

"It's you." Her fingers caressed the rubber form, moving from the head to the shaft to the testes. "Every sexy detail."

"You're making me excited." He leaned over to kiss her, the toy pressed against her blouse.

"Pierce it," she said.

He used a needle. Mandy seemed intrigued, studying the procedure. He put a circular barbell in the same location as his piercing to give her the familiarity she craved. He washed the dildo with an antibacterial solution, cleaning it for her.

Once it was dry, Mandy licked the newly decorated head. He

thought about the blow job she'd given him earlier and got even more excited. He wanted her to suck the dildo, too.

"Let's go." He took her hand, and they went into her bedroom.

Jared removed the quilt and top sheet from her bed, leaving the bottom sheet and two pillows. Her room was soft and feminine with whitewashed furniture, pastel prints, and hints of lace. It was perfect for tonight, ideal for a man's voyeuristic obsession. He angled a chair, positioning it at the footboard, where he intended to watch the show. He put the dildo in the center of the bed, along with the lubricant they'd brought.

She dimmed the lights and lit the candles, placing them on the dresser beside several ornate bottles of perfume. The stage was set, he thought.

Jared took his seat, and Mandy turned toward him. The Kama Sutra candle began scenting the air, the light rose fragrance enhancing the ambience.

"Take off your clothes," he said.

She stripped, removing her sandals first, then her blouse and jeans. Her flesh-colored bra and panties came next. She had small breasts with full, pink nipples. Her stomach was flat, and her hips flared. As always, her pussy was delicately waxed. She was so beautiful, she looked like a centerfold come to life.

"Give me your panties," he said.

She walked forward and handed him her daintily laced underwear. He tucked them in to the front right pocket of his jeans, taking them as a trophy, wanting to keep something that belonged to her close to him.

All pink and pretty, she blinked, seeming unsure of what to do next.

He motioned with his chin. "Get on the bed."

She did as he instructed, kneeling on the sheet, waiting to fulfill the rest of his needs.

He gave her another aroused order. "Lick the dildo. All of it. Every inch. And imagine it's me."

"It is you." She darted her tongue over the head and played lavishly with the piercing.

By the time she worked her way down, he scooted to the edge of his seat. She held the phallus high enough for him to see her scoop one of the balls into her mouth.

Damn, he thought. Hot fucking damn. "Do that to the other one. Then give it a really nasty blow job. Hot and dirty, the way I like it."

She didn't disappoint. Clutching the base, she wrapped her lips around the dildo and sucked, pumping the device as if it really were his dick. She tipped back her head, exposing the ladylike column of her neck.

Somehow, someway, Jared was going to get through this without jerking off. Looking but not touching her or himself was part of the fantasy.

Mandy made the dildo come. Or that was how it seemed in his mind. He imagined white-hot liquid spurting into her mouth. She even made a swallowing sound. When she released the dildo, she licked her lips.

This was the best fantasy he'd ever had, and it was just getting started. "Put the lube on it now. Make it as slick as you can."

She used a generous amount, gliding the silicone solution over the rubber form. He could almost feel her sleek, smooth strokes. She took her time, favoring her new toy.

"Lie back and spread your legs," he told her.

Mandy propped both pillows against the headboard and opened her thighs. But it wasn't enough.

"Wider," he said. "All the way."

She inched them open a bit more.

He didn't back down. It was part of the game, and they both knew it. "More. Show me how pretty you are. Show me what I want to see."

She did it. She went as wide as she could, exposing her inner folds. He didn't ask her to do anything else. He just sat there, staring at her cunt.

Mandy flexed her hips, offering him an even prettier view of her labia and the hood of her clit. She glistened in her own juices. He could only imagine how much wetter she was going to get.

He lifted his gaze to her face, and she gave him her best naughty-girl smile. He'd never met anyone like her. Good. Bad. Shy. Wild. He wanted to grab her panties out of his pocket and press them against his fly.

"Tell me to put it in," she said.

"Not yet." He needed a minute.

She clutched the dildo. "When?"

He took a steadying breath. "Now. But don't insert it very deep. Go slow so I can see it happen."

Mandy followed his direction, soft and easy, and he watched the pierced head disappear.

"A little more."

She gave the dildo another tender push, and he marveled at how sweet and sexy she was. She was looking down at herself, watching, too.

When she glanced up, they stared at each other. He unzipped his jeans to ease the pressure, to make his hard-on more bearable. His boxers tented through the opening.

"Go deeper," he said. "But not all the way. Just enough to hit your G-spot."

She made a curious expression, biting the inside of her cheek, looking girlish and womanly at the same time. "I don't know how far that is. I've never tried to find—"

"Try it halfway. At an angle." He knew it was difficult to reach during regular sex, but devices like dildos and vibrators were easier to maneuver. Some vibrators were made especially for that spot.

"Like this?" She repositioned the dildo, angling it with each stroke.

"Yeah. Like that." Jared spread his thighs. He wanted to give up the fight. He wanted to jerk off, as hard and fast as he could, but he gripped the underside of his chair instead.

Mandy stimulated her G-spot, using both hands to hold the tool, going at a watch-me pace that drove him half-mad. Her rhythm was steady: shallow, then hard, then shallow again.

She went faster, and her firm little tits bounced with each pumping stroke. Her nipples were as hard as rock candy. He wanted to dissolve them on his tongue.

"I like doing this for you." She arched her back against the pillows and thrust her hips. "Just for you." She thrust again, showing him how good it was.

He tightened the hold on his chair.

"Jared." She panted his name, making sure his gaze was locked on the point of impact.

He dragged a gust of rose-scented air into his lungs. He felt as if he were going to explode. He knew she was going to come.

Her orgasm ignited the bed, shooting imaginary sparks straight at him. He could have sworn that she'd made the flames on the candles dance. The Kama Sutra couple melted all over each other.

When it was over, Jared gave Mandy and himself time to recuperate.

Before he told her to do it again.

~

Atacar scowled at me. He'd planned to cross the hills and ride into Mexico, where he could escape the law. But he didn't recover his horse.

He blamed me for his dilemma, claiming his desire for me had affected his judgment. He should have tracked his horse before it had gotten so far away from him.

"I bewitched you," I bragged, making his scowl deepen. He wasn't amused, and neither was Nanny.

He formulated a new plan, pulling her and me into it. He assumed that we lived within walking distance of the stream, or else we wouldn't have traveled on foot. He questioned me, making sure we resided alone, just the two of us. We did. At a farmhouse I'd purchased from the bank. Up until last week, we had a farmhand, but he'd left our employment to marry the widow he'd been courting. Nanny and I had yet to replace him.

Rifle in hand, Atacar nudged us forward, insisting that we offer him food and lodging until he raided a neighboring ranch for another horse to steal.

I carried my stretching board and paint box, and Nanny
trudged beside me, complaining that Atacar was forcing us to the
farm so he could steal our horse. We only had one, and we needed
it to pull our buggy when we went into town for supplies.

"That red Indian will leave us on the plains to starve," she
said, even though I caught her darting wistful glances at him.

Nanny was rather plump, with graying brown hair and sag-
ging bosoms. I'd heard that she was quite voluptuous in her
youth. Long before she'd become my nursemaid, she'd been a
fetching farm girl. She'd also been accused of having a forbidden
tryst with a notorious London thief. She'd denied the allegation,
but I always wondered if the story were true. Now, seeing the way
she looked at Atacar, I suspected it was. My old nanny missed her
thief.

Hours later, Nanny served supper. The three of us sat at a simple wooden table and ate in silence. Compared to the genteel
dwelling in which I'd been raised, the farmhouse was primitive.
But in this area, it was considered quite nice. Nanny and I each
had our own bedroom, and I used the third for my studio.

I watched Atacar beneath my lashes, trying to get his attention. I caught Nanny's instead. She scolded me, squinting her eyes
and pursing her lips. It wasn't unlike me to misbehave during
a meal. I'd done so at society events, poking fun at my already
soiled reputation. My parents were greatly relieved when I'd
expressed an interest in moving to America. Father bestowed a
portion of my own dowry upon me, providing means for my survival. He was certain I would never snare a respectable husband
anyway.

Nanny pursed her sour-plum lips again. I ignored her and

resumed flirting with Atacar. He finally turned his frustrated gaze upon me.

"How long are you going to be uncivil?" I asked.

"When you stop bewitching me."

"I won't stop," I countered.

"Then I'll be civil," he said, leaning toward me and speaking directly in my ear, keeping his words from Nanny, "after I fuck you."

His harshness aroused me. But it frightened me, too. Had I taken my seductress game too far? Would he thrust hard and fast upon entering me? Would losing my maidenhead be more painful than it should be?

"You'll be the first," I whispered back, too stubborn to let my fear show.

His expression changed. He seemed confused. How could such a brazen girl be a virgin?

"I've been waiting for a man who makes me feel the way you do," I admitted.

Atacar didn't dispute my claim. He didn't say anything. He just looked at me as if I'd bewitched him even more. I relaxed, sensing that he would be gentle my first time.

The farmhouse had a sleeping loft in the barn. At bedtime, Atacar told me to meet him there. I knew it was because he wanted to lie with me where Nanny couldn't hear us. She knew it, too. She'd figured out that she'd interrupted us in the cottonwoods before he could deflower me.

I changed into my finest undergarments, a red corset and matching drawers that were fashionably called lingerie. I brushed my hair until it shined, pinning a portion of it up and allowing the remainder to fall freely. I removed a buttercup from the glass jar beside my bed and worked it into my coiffure.

Before I left for the barn, Nanny draped me in a blanket. She insisted that I drink a special blend of tea, too. She told me that it would help me relax. So I took a few sips of the brew she offered.

"While you were getting ready, I asked Atacar why he speaks English so well," she said. "And do you know what his response was?"

I shook my head. The blanket was soft and fluffy, providing the comfort she wanted me to have. The tea helped, as well.

"He scouted for the army," Nanny told me. "He translated for them, too."

"If he served the army, then why is he a prisoner of war?"

"After the Chiricahua hostiles surrendered, the entire tribe, including the scouts, were exiled to military installations. First to Florida, then to Alabama, and now Oklahoma Territory. It didn't matter that Atacar served the army; the government treated him and the other scouts as if they were hostiles, too."

"He's lived a complex life," I said.

"Yes, he has." She tucked the blanket tighter around my shoulders. "And if he doesn't steal our horse, he'll probably steal your heart."

"The way the London thief did to you?"

She didn't answer. She took my empty teacup and handed me a kerosene lamp. I turned away, slipping off for my rendezvous, the moon a silver crescent in the sky.

I entered the barn and climbed to the loft. Atacar waited for me. He was stripped to the waist. I held up the light to admire him and to let him appreciate me.

Neither of us spoke. I stepped forward and placed the brass lamp on a hook on the wall, then spread the blanket on a bed of straw.

We came together and kissed, standing on the fluffy floor covering. I showed him that my fancy silk drawers were slit between my legs, and he smiled. It was the first time I'd seen his lips curve. He looked wickedly handsome.

He knelt down and licked me there, right through the opening. I gasped and widened my stance. I knew this was called cunnilingus, and it elicited the warmest, wettest, most naughty sensation. I could scarcely wait to orgasm, to shake and shudder against his tongue.

Atacar gazed up at me, making sure I was watching. I was. Totally. Completely. How could I not? I felt like a wild-hearted bride on her secret wedding night.

He stopped pleasuring me, but only long enough to order me to lie down and remove my drawers. I did his bidding, and he knelt between my thighs and lifted my legs onto his shoulders, licking me some more.

He told me how womanly sweet I tasted, calling my private place my cunt. My bohemian friends had familiarized me with that word, and like all of the other definitions they'd taught me, they'd whispered it scandalously. From Atacar, it sounded rough and dangerously romantic.

I removed my corset so my breasts would spring free. He laved my clitoris and reached up to stimulate one of my nipples, to roll it between his thumb and forefinger.

I scooted even closer to his mouth. I was drenched with his saliva and my own honey-slick moisture. He stilled his tongue, and I rubbed against his face, teasing him the way he teased me.

Finally he resumed his skillful ministration, and I put I my fingers down there, encouraging him to lick them. He turned my boldness into a game and told me to do it, too. So I did. I tasted my own fingers after they'd been inside me.

Heat danced between us. I couldn't take my eyes off of him, and he couldn't stop looking at me. I'd aroused him, and myself, beyond reason.

I climaxed, even more powerfully than before, streams of fire bursting through my quaking body.

After it was over, Atacar wiped the wetness from his face and rose up to hold me. I clung to his neck, and he said something in Apache. I had no idea what it was, but I could tell it was an endearment. He removed his pants and slid between my legs, his rock-hard penis poised at my soft, slick entrance. My heartbeat quickened, and I exhaled a virginal breath.

Desperate for him to take me.

CHAPTER FOUR

Jared paid an unexpected visit to Mandy. He arrived at her office, dressed in his work clothes: a practical denim shirt, jeans, and durable boots. His hair, as always, was combed away from his face and plaited into a thick, shiny braid. A canvas satchel was slung over his shoulder.

A cowboy, she thought, with a bag of tricks. She didn't ask him what was inside of it. Silent, she waited for him to open the flap and release the zipper, to see what sort of magic he would produce.

They both stood with the barrier of her desk between them. From the moment he'd entered the room, they'd barely spoken, barely done anything but exchanged magnetic eye contact. Mandy and Jared hadn't seen each other in a week, since he'd sat at the foot of her bed and watched her play with the toy they'd made. She wanted to tell him that she'd been using it every night since, all alone, reliving the fantasy, but she kept quiet instead, focused on the satchel he'd yet to open.

Finally he got into the bag and removed swatches of silk, velvet, and lace, fanning them across her desk in a composition of color.

"Jared?" she queried, looking at the little squares of material, then back up at him.

"I'm having a Victorian gown made for you. For a costume ball. You'll be wearing a decorative mask, too. Jewels, feathers, that sort of thing."

Her heart skipped a thrilled beat. The sun shone through the window, making the swatches shimmer. She'd never been to a masque, at least not where she'd participated. She'd attended street fairs and carnivals, but not in costume. As a child she'd gone door to door on Halloween, but that didn't count, certainly not in a glamorous way.

"When and where is the party?" she asked. "Who's hosting it? Are—"

He held up his hand, halting her questions. "We'll discuss the details after you choose the fabrics for your gown."

Mandy's mind whirred. She wanted answers, but she wanted to browse the materials, too. The feminine finery intrigued her. She stepped around from the other side of her desk and stood beside Jared.

"Pick one of each," he told her. "Silk for the main part of the gown, velvet and lace for the trim."

She took her time, laboring over the luxury. She examined the silks first, zeroing in on different shades of pink. It was her favorite color.

Jared remained patient throughout the process. Finally she handed him a swatch that was labeled Cherry Blossom. "This one."

He studied it for a moment.

"Is something wrong?" she asked.

"No, it's a good choice. I like this, especially for you. In China, cherry blossom is the symbol of female dominance, beauty, and sexuality."

"It is?"

He nodded. "That's what I've heard." He smiled a little. "But I'm not an authority on female dominance."

No, but he was pretty damn good at male dominance, at controlling their affair. He was the aggressor, and she couldn't stop herself from craving him. He gripped the pink silk lightly between his fingers. The same fingers that stimulated her. Mandy shivered. She wanted him to touch her right now, to put his hands all over her.

"Keep going," he said.

She struggled to stay focused, but she could barely breathe. Sex had never mattered before she'd met Jared, not like this, not to the point of consuming the air that chopped in and out of her lungs.

"The swatches. Pick out the other two."

His voice cut into her thoughts, stealing more oxygen, making her more light-headed. Being addicted to him was a bitch. But it felt incredible, too.

"*Mandy.*"

"Oh, yes, of course." She returned to the fabrics on her desk.

For the velvet, a rich emerald caught her eye. As for the lace, all of it was white. Virginal, she thought. The needlepoint style she chose had an intricate floral pattern and finely scalloped edges.

Jared placed her selections on the corner of the desk. Then he reached into the satchel and removed a clear plastic container filled with decorative trim and faux jewels.

"Should I pick through those, too?" she asked.

He nodded. "As many as you want."

Mandy went for satin ribbon and an array of sparkling ornaments, assuming that some of these items were for her mask.

She glanced up, anxious to know more. "Will you give me the details now?"

He shook his head. "Not until I take your measurements."

She dropped the jewels into their container, and they scattered like stones in a fishbowl. "*You're* going to measure me?"

He made a macho expression, squinting his eyes and tightening his jaw. Tiny lines bracketed his mouth. "I can handle it. The seamstress showed me what to do."

"I'm sure you can. I just didn't expect . . ."

"What?" he pressed.

She searched for an explanation that would make sense to a man she'd masturbated for. It was odd, she knew. She'd fucked herself with a dildo for him, but this was different. This was like telling him how much she weighed. "My measurements won't be impressive. They—"

"Don't get shy. Not about this." He moved closer, and before she could collect her senses, he took her in his arms.

Transfixed, she breathed in his scent. He wasn't wearing cologne. He smelled faintly of the earth, of the ranch where he lived.

He kissed her, tugging her bottom lip, using his teeth in a soft, sexy fashion. She sighed into his mouth. Her skin turned explicitly warm; her nipples went hard.

When he released her, she blinked at him. She wanted to keep holding on, to rub against him, to get down and dirty.

"Are you going to be a good girl and let me pull out my tape measure?" he asked.

She couldn't stop the smile that ghosted around her lips. Her self-consciousness was gone. "Is it big?"

"Are you kidding? It's"—he stepped back and whipped out the article in question—"a hundred and twenty inches."

Playing along, she feigned a shocked expression. "I hope it doesn't hurt."

"It will if you don't hold still." He positioned her, making sure both of her feet were planted firmly on the floor. He told her not to inflate her lungs, expand her chest, or stretch her height.

Mandy obeyed his commands. She'd never had a dress made, but she recalled the day the wedding gown she'd chosen had been fitted.

Of course, this wasn't the same. She wasn't headed for an altar-bound mistake with her mother and sisters gathered in the bridal shop, exchanging fussy opinions. On this sunny afternoon, she was being measured for a glittering costume with her lover at the helm. This was far more compelling.

Jared went around her bust, shoulders, chest, back, waist. He took lengthwise measurements, too, pinning the tape measure when it was necessary, following the lines of her body, recording every inch. Instinctively she swayed toward him.

"You need to stand straight."

"Sorry." She corrected her posture.

By now he was doing a center-front measurement from her waist to the floor. The last time he was on his knees in her office, she'd removed her panties, lifted her dress, and straddled his gorgeous face.

She looked down at him, but he didn't offer to repeat the performance. He was too busy writing numbers on a sheet of paper in a spiral notebook.

"You're teasing me," she said.

"Am I?"

"You know you are."

He stood up. "I've got something planned."

Desire zinged through her blood and zapped into her pores. Was he going to flip up her skirt and bend her over the desk?

"For the night of the party," he added.

He took a side-front measurement, going down on his knees again. Then he got to his feet once more. Finally he finished, rolling up his big, bad tape measure and putting it away. It might as well have been his cock. He wasn't going to make her come. Not today.

"What size shoes do you wear?" he asked, keeping his notebook handy.

She scowled at him. Sexual frustration battered her like a rutting ram, defying her femininity, the silk, the velvet, the lace—the masque she'd been so eager to attend. "This party better be worth it."

"Don't worry, baby. It will be."

"Fine." She huffed out her shoe size, giving him several brands for reference. He jotted down the information.

Her phone rang, and he indicated that she was free to answer it. Mandy wasn't about to.

"You owe me details, Jared."

This time he didn't protest. He responded casually. "Pia Pontiero is hosting the ball."

The fashion designer? Mandy had heard that the aging blonde diva owned a mansion in Santa Fe, along with a villa in Rome, a town house in London, and beachfront property in Malibu. "You're friends with her?"

"I know her fairly well."

Of course he did, she thought. Or else Pia wouldn't have put him on the guest list. This was his social circle, his glamorous peers. Mandy wondered how many of his former girlfriends would be there. Not that she was about to ask. They didn't talk about old lovers. He'd never even questioned her about her ex-husband. Sometimes she wished that he would, and sometimes she was glad he hadn't brought it up.

Mandy crossed her arms, then uncrossed them, battling her body language. Was she afraid of sharing her emotions with Jared, of creating more than a sexual bond with him?

"It's a history-of-fashion theme," he said, watching her the way a hawk watched a field mouse. "Guests can wear a costume from any time period."

Another crossing. Another uncrossing. More vulnerable body language. Why couldn't she just stand still? "When is it?"

"A week from Saturday."

"Oh, my goodness." She couldn't help it; she gave him a startled look. He never failed to make her head spin. "You're having a dress made for me that soon?"

"Yes." Cool and calm, he cleared the swatches and jewels from her desk and put them away. "The gown and everything that goes with it will arrive on the day of the party. And at seven 'o clock that night, a limousine will pick you up."

"We're taking a limo?"

"Yes, but we're not riding together. I'm going earlier." His smile was slow, sinful, as smooth as a brandy-and-cigar salute. "By the time you get there, I'll already be at the mansion, and you'll have to figure out who I am."

Images of searching for him among the other guests twirled in her mind. She pictured a Spanish Colonial Revival mansion with wrought-iron window grilles, hundreds of colorful tiles, and a courtyard leading to a sprawling Southwestern garden. A house designed for gallant men and finely clothed women.

"Do you think you'll be able to recognize me?" he asked.

She refused to think otherwise. Surely she would know her own lover, even if he were cloaked and masked. His height, she thought. The width of his shoulders. The confident way in which way he carried himself.

"Yes," she told him. "I'll recognize you."

"You better. Because you're going to proposition me at the party." He latched on to her wrists and brought her, full-force, next to him. "You're going to get this close to me, then you're going to whisper in my ear."

Already her pulse was fluttering at her neck, eager for what came next, to participate in the carnality he'd created. "What am I going to say?"

"That you want me to fuck you. There. At the mansion. But if you don't choose the right man, if it isn't me, you'll be making a sexual advance to a stranger." He smoothed her hair away from her cheek, grazing her skin. "And he just might take you up on your offer."

She reacted to his touch, needing him, wanting him. "That won't happen."

"What won't? You choosing the wrong guy? Or him banging you breathless while both of you have your masks on?"

"It's going to be you, Jared. You're the only man who's going to do that to me."

He stepped back, but his gaze remained fixed on hers. Strong. Hard. Possessive. "Did you ever make me a key to your condo?"

She nodded. "It's in my purse. I'll get it for you."

"I don't want it now. Slip it into my pocket when we're at the party. When I'm making you come." He reached for the satchel and looped it over his shoulder, pausing at the door. "I'll see you at the masquerade."

"You, too." Caught up in his game, she watched him leave, her heart beating in her chest just as deeply as it pounded between her legs.

~

On the night of the masque, Mandy stood in front of the closet-door mirrors in her room, wearing her underwear. But it wasn't a bra and panties. She'd donned the undergarments that had arrived with her dress. So there she was in a lace-and-ribbon-trimmed corset, a decorative corset cover, embroidered stockings, and a pair of wide-legged drawers, also trimmed in ribbon and lace, with the crotch seam open.

She felt positively decadent.

She had expected a gown and mask, but she hadn't considered time-period undergarments, too. She hadn't realized that Jared would go this far.

"Look at you," Kiki said from behind her. The historian had come over to help her get ready.

Mandy reached for her petticoat and put it on. The stiff garment flounced and frilled at the bottom. "I'm being transformed."

"Yes, you are. The lady of the Victorian manor." The other woman pointed to a makeshift vanity table they'd set up. "Now let me do your hair."

Mandy took a seat, allowing herself to be pampered. Kiki dived right in, enjoying her self-appointed role in all of this. She'd researched hairdos that had been featured in *Harper's Bazaar* in the mid-1890s and wanted to try her hand at a fancy evening coiffure.

First she curled Mandy's hair, forming a profusion of ringlets in front and dividing the rest into three sections, where she created a soft, intricate bun. For the finishing touch, she used jeweled combs Jared had provided, working them into the design.

"Women were so elegant then," she said, seemingly pleased with her work.

Mandy was pleased, too. She gazed at her own reflection. She was becoming more and more Victorian. "You did an amazing job."

"So did Jared." Kiki walked over to where Mandy's dress was hanging. "This is an exquisite replica. It's sewn exactly the way it would have been in that era."

"Jared is a stickler for detail." Mandy thought about the dildo they'd made and got warm in the vicinity of her open-crotch drawers. "He likes things to seem real."

"He must really be into you." Kiki took a lingering look at the gown. "This must have cost him a fortune."

"He's a successful horseman. Rich clients and all that." Her heart went a little haywire, but she reined it back. "He's made a name for himself in this town."

"He's making one for you, too. Of course, tonight no one will know who you are."

Mandy nodded and glanced at the bed, where she'd placed the mask that accompanied her costume. She knew the history behind masked balls: to disguise oneself to create confusion or anonymity, to have bouts of harmless fun. But what Jared had in mind wasn't harmless. It was dangerously erotic.

Like him.

"I better finish getting ready," she said, butterflies winging their way to her stomach.

Kiki reached for the gown, offering to fasten the back closures.

The cherry blossom dress fit Mandy beautifully, with sleeves that puffed at her shoulders and a skirt that flowed into a bell, balancing her figure and creating a striking silhouette. The neckline was trimmed in velvet with a row of iridescent beads, as was the hem, which erupted into embroidered lace. A matching wrap, a capelet, went with it.

Kiki smoothed the back of the gown. "You look gorgeous. He's going to die when he sees you."

"Thank you." The butterflies went crazy. "I chose the colors."

Mandy stepped into her shoes, evening slippers that complemented her dress. The winged eye mask came next, adorning her face with glass jewels and ostrich feathers.

By the time Kiki left and the limousine arrived, Mandy had blotted and refreshed her lipstick three times. She kept imagining how Jared was going to taste. All she wanted to do was kiss him.

She rode in the back of the long, black car, fingering the drawstring on her small, beaded purse. It, too, had been fashioned after the Victorian era.

Although she considered pouring herself a drink, she refrained. She was already drunk on Jared. She kept thinking about his disguise, anxious to discover what type of costume he'd chosen.

Surely he would be in Victorian garb, as well.

As the vehicle traveled farther into the mountains, she gazed out the window, watching the nighttime landscape go by.

She refused to believe that she would falter at the party. She would recognize her lover, no matter what his masquerade.

Wouldn't she?

Now that the time grew near, her confidence wavered. What if he'd disguised himself beyond recognition? Mandy wet her mouth, tasting her pretty pink lipstick. What would happen if she propositioned the wrong man?

Nothing. Because Jared wouldn't let someone else touch her, not while they were involved, not while she belonged to him. He was possessive that way.

Wasn't he?

She shifted in her seat. If she weren't in jeopardy of wrinkling her dress, she would've bunched her skirts and touched herself through her slit drawers.

For Jared. For the excitement he'd created.

She actually wanted to come in the car, to close her eyes and imagine that Jared's cock was buried deep inside her.

Damn. She squeezed her thighs together.

Earlier, she'd closed the glass partition that separated her from the chauffeur. Now all she had to do was lower the electronically operated blind. Then she would have even more privacy.

Her clit throbbed, desperate for attention.

Should she do it?

No, she thought. She wasn't about to arrive at the party a rumpled mess, with her fingers creamy from her own come. Instead she would sit here like a good girl, squirming in her glittering gown, coiffed like the proper lady she was supposed to be.

The limo wound its way along a private road, finally taking her to a sprawling estate hidden in the hills.

The chauffeur opened her door, and she climbed out of the car, holding up the hem of her lavish dress, feeling like Cinderella exiting her coach.

She thanked the driver and presented her invitation to a tuxedoed man at an iron gate. He allowed her access, and she walked along a brightly lit path toward the front door, passing a tiered fountain and a spray of indigenous foliage.

The house was what she'd imagined: an enormous two-story Spanish Colonial Revival mansion with a clay roof, stuccoed archways, and prominent pillars.

Music spilled into the air. Voices echoed festively into the night. The moon was decidedly half-full, adding a bewitching ambience.

Another tuxedoed man was stationed at the door. He directed her to the coat check, where she left her wrap. From there, she was guided to a ballroom with stained-glass windows, malachite floors, and carved wood accents. It was breathtaking.

And so were the other guests.

Costumes varied. She noticed Renaissance, Regency, Romantic, Victorian, Edwardian, flapper, as well as trends from the 1940s to the 1990s. Power-dressing and haute couture were represented, too.

No fashion stone was left unturned, particularly with the women: flounced ruffles, ladylike fans, feather boas, vinyl, leather, pearls, diamonds, hats, bonnets, long, flowing scarves. It was endless.

Masks ranged from simple to extravagant, from swan shapes to butterflies to shiny stars and eclipsed moons. One curvy redhead could have been a panther on the prowl, with an exotic mask and a jet-black gown plunging to her navel.

The men were equally dashing. She scanned the crowd for Jared, but there were hundreds of guests in attendance, spilling into the buffet room and onto the dance floor. The patio was occupied, too.

Mandy didn't know where to begin.

She decided that she needed the drink she'd neglected to pour in the limo, so she twined her way through the fashion extravaganza and beelined to the nearest bar. She went for a Between the Sheets, a cocktail consisting of rum, cognac, passion fruit mixer, and lime juice. Jared had introduced her to Between the Sheets, in more ways than one.

Now she wished she would have strummed her clit in the car. The bartender handed her a rocks glass. He'd given her an extra cherry.

In case she lost one? She sipped the drink. It was too late for that. A woman couldn't get her cherry back. And this woman didn't want to. She just wanted to find Jared, to hold him close, to whisper naughty words in his ear. Her dirty-boy lover.

Where the hell was he?

Mandy took a deep breath and started her search, looking at every masked man she passed. Some of them looked back. But none of them had Jared's granite-cut jaw, six-foot-one frame, or cocky swagger.

No, that wasn't true. There were plenty of tall, square-jawed men with fuck-me attitudes, but she could tell that they weren't him.

Because they didn't make her hot or hungry or desperate to get laid. The eye contact she'd made with them didn't arouse her; it didn't ignite the fire in her veins.

She sipped more of her Between the Sheets, letting the liquid slide down her throat. Trying to conjure Jared, she imagined that she was tasting his come. That he was kneeling over her, spilling into her mouth.

"That's my favorite drink, too," a female voice said from behind her.

Mandy spun around.

An incredibly leggy blonde in a micro-miniskirt and plastic, peek-a-boo top clanked her glass against Mandy's. She was one of the most dazzling creatures at the party. Her hair, which could have easily been a wig, was long and thick and flatiron straight. But even if her hair was fake, the rest of her was real. Model-thin with perky breasts quite visible through her geometric-printed top, she embodied a 1960s mod girl. Her mask made her eyes look big and wide. It even had overly exaggerated, spiky eye-lashes attached. The effect was stunning.

"Here's to Between the Sheets," she said.

"And to men who make women weep," Mandy added, know-ing instinctively that the glossy girl with the fishnet stockings, flashy go-go boots, and killer legs was one of Jared's former lovers.

CHAPTER FIVE

"By the way," the mod girl said, her voice lilted with a unique accent. A bit British. A bit Italian. A bit American. A lot sexy. "We made your dress."

Mandy blinked beneath her mask. "We?"

"Our company. Pia Pontiero, Inc."

"You work for Pia?" Was she a showroom model? An assistant designer? An illustrator? Surely she wasn't the seamstress Jared had mentioned.

"I'm Amber. Pia's daughter."

Damn. It wasn't the designer who'd put Jared on the guest list. It was her young, gorgeous daughter.

"When I was little, Mama used to buy me things to make me behave," Amber said. "She still does." The announcement came on the heels of a pretty, if not self-indulgent, smile. "I'm what they call a spoiled heiress. I also fucked the twirling daylights out of Jared."

Mandy wasn't used to these kinds of situations. These kinds

of women. But she was in Jared's world now. Who fucked who was par for the course. The *inter*course, she thought, determined to keep her sense of humor. "I already figured out that you and Jared used to be lovers."

Amber brought her glass to her lips, leaving pearly pink marks on the rim. "We met at the club scene in London, then reconnected here when Mama bought this house."

Jared had been to England? He'd partied on another continent? Mandy frowned. There was so much she didn't know about him. So much he hadn't revealed.

Amber continued. "On our first Santa Fe date, we went to a local bar and discussed the appeal of erotic-named drinks."

"Like Between the Sheets?"

"And others. He enjoys watching women having Sex on the Beach, a Kiss in the Dark, or a Screaming Orgasm. Hand Jobs make him crazy, too. But Blow-Job Shooters are his favorite. Has he gotten you into those yet?"

Mandy tried to keep her voice neutral, to not sound as clipped as she felt. "No. Not yet."

"They're delightful. Bailey's Irish cream, Amaretto, and whipped cream. The correct way to shoot a Blow Job is to place your hands behind your back, pick up the glass with your mouth, tilt your head back, and drink."

Screw not sounding clipped. Mandy had just earned the right to act catty. "What about a Hand Job mixed with a Blow Job? Or haven't you ever tried that?"

"Mixing cocktails isn't a good idea. Or did you mean the real thing? I'm quite proficient at that."

"So am I." She didn't used to be, but she was now.

A beat of silence passed before Amber asked, "Did you know that I'm part of the game? Of what Jared arranged for you tonight?"

Damn him all to hell. Him and his go-go girl. "He told you to approach me?"

"No. I wanted to meet you on my own. To tell you who made your dress." Amber's accent softened. "Do you like it?"

"Yes." Mandy relaxed a little, glancing down at the front of the skirt. It was a gown Catherine could have worn. "I love it."

"Jared has been planning this for a while, but he didn't want to tell you until the time got closer. That's why we had to put a rush on your costume."

"My friend said it probably cost him a fortune."

"It did." The other woman angled her head, making her hair—or her wig—sweep her cheek and fall to one side. "But men should pay for sex. Girls like us shouldn't give it away."

Was Amber putting Mandy in the same sexy league as herself?

The designer's daughter smiled, and so did Mandy. Suddenly knowing that they'd fucked the same man seemed hot. Gloriously naughty. A secret between strangers.

They smiled at each other again, as "Masquerade," a song from *Phantom of the Opera*, vibrated from the DJ's sound system, receiving an instant response from the crowd.

"Paper faces on parade," Amber said, reciting a portion of the chorus.

"Hide your face," Mandy added, "so the world will never find you." She paused, thinking about her lover's disguise. "So exactly how are you part of Jared's game? Of what he arranged for me tonight?"

"Besides my involvement with your costume? I know what he's wearing, too. How he intends to trick you."

Intrigued, Mandy moved closer, catching a hint of Amber's perfume. She smelled as fresh as a new rain. "You could tell me."

"And spoil the fun? Not a chance." Amber finished her drink and placed it on the tray of a passing waiter. The bartender had given her two cherries, too. But she'd left both of them in the bottom of her glass.

"Not even a hint?" Mandy asked. She'd eaten her cherries. She'd sucked them right down to the stems.

"Sorry, no. But maybe you and I get can together sometime. We can do some Blow Jobs. The cocktail kind," the heiress clarified.

"That sounds good."

"To me, too." One last smile, and Amber was off, gliding through her mother's multimillion-dollar mansion.

As Mandy watched her go, she realized how unusual their encounter had been: polite, then bitchy, then strangely, sexually empowering.

Jared's former bedmate was gone, and Mandy's body tingled beneath yards of silk, velvet, ribbon, and lace.

She craved her dirty boy even more.

So she set out to find him. She wandered through the party, examining the men, but more carefully this time. She checked them out in every way. She even glanced down at their flies. It was crazy to think that she would recognize Jared's cock beneath a pair of pants, but it gave her wicked pleasure to try.

Then it happened. Mandy caught sight of a tall, broad-shouldered, slim-hipped man headed for the buffet who could be

Jared. His long, dark hair was banded into a ponytail, and he was dressed in Victorian formalwear: a Tombstone shirt, an elegant silk puff tie, a classic gray vest, black Highland pants, and a matching frock coat. On his lapel, he wore a pink rose.

The same shade as her dress.

Her heart went volcanic, nearly erupting on the spot. She dashed across the room to follow him, to get a closer look at his masked face.

She lucked out, managing to get directly behind him in the buffet line. He reached for a plate, and she noticed his hands were gloved. He glanced her way and gave her a gentlemanly nod. But that was it. He wasn't behaving as if he knew her. His attention returned to the food that awaited him.

Mandy picked up a plate and silverware, too. But her mind wasn't on their upcoming meal. She studied his profile. His black satin mask altered the contours of his face. It completely covered his forehead, reshaped his eyes, and molded around his cheeks and down his nose, leaving only his nostrils visible. His mouth was exposed, too. But she didn't know if he was Jared, not for certain.

Were those the lips she'd been kissing? Was he her lover? The man who'd been making her come?

He filled his plate, selecting various meat dishes, along with chipotle-spiced potatoes and herb-braised vegetables. For dessert he chose rice pudding. He'd skipped the salads altogether.

She'd seen Jared eat salads, hadn't she? He wasn't opposed to leafy greens. Or was he? Mandy furrowed her brow. She should know Jared better than she did.

Since his mannerisms gave nothing away, she focused on his

hair. It was the right color, the perfect length, the correct thickness. It was Jared's hair. Wasn't it?

Before he carried his meal to one of the many linen-draped tables in the dining room, she asked if she could join him.

"Yes, ma'am," he responded, his deep, rich timbre tinged with a slight Southern drawl. "You're more than welcome to dine with me."

For a moment, Mandy went still. She didn't move. She barely breathed. His slow, sensual drawl slid straight to her drawers, making her sweet and creamy. Could another man besides Jared do that to her?

"Where did you learn to talk like that?" she asked.

He guided her to a window-seat table. "I was raised in Oklahoma."

Was that a clue? Was that where Jared was originally from? As far she knew, most of the Chiricahua Apache hailed from a reservation in New Mexico, where their ancestors had gone after their incarceration at Fort Sill had ended. Of course, there was a small group who'd stayed behind and had become the Fort Sill Apache of Oklahoma.

She sat across from him. He didn't remove his gloves to eat. A waiter came by to take their drink orders. She decided to have another Between the Sheets. He asked for a Coca-Cola, using the formal name for Coke.

"It was invented in 1885," he said, after the waiter departed.

She spread her napkin on her lap, preparing to taste her meal, sparse as it was. She'd barely put any food on her plate. "What was?"

"Coca-Cola. It's Victorian, too."

"Like us?" She gazed into his eyes, but they didn't give him away. She wondered what he would do if she came over to his side of the table and put her hand on his thigh, if she rubbed his cock through his pants, if she made it swell.

He would love it if he were Jared, she thought. He would encourage her to play, to go through with their plan, to proposition him.

And if he was a stranger?

"Is something wrong?" he asked.

"No." Nothing but the hot and cold chill snaking her spine. When the waiter brought their drinks, she took a desperate swig.

Her Victorian-garbed partner smiled, and she went sweet and creamy again. She imagined him thrusting inside her. If he wasn't Jared, then she was in trouble. His masquerade, his similarity to Jared, aroused her.

"Who are you?" she finally asked.

"A guest at the party," he told her, keeping his identity to himself. "Who are you?"

She almost said her name, but she caught herself before it slipped out. What good would introducing herself do?

He turned away from her, noticed someone he knew, and motioned to whoever his acquaintance was. Mandy shifted in her chair, hoping to see Amber with a couple of Blow-Job Shooters. At least that would prove that her dinner companion was Jared.

But it wasn't Amber he'd solicited. He'd just invited two men to their table, and both of them looked *exactly* like him: the same mask, height, body type, hair, clothes. The only difference was the color of the roses on their lapels; one was red, and the other was blue. Both carried dinner plates brimming with Southwestern delicacies.

The red-rose man sat beside her, and the blue sat on the other side of the table next her original companion, the Coca-Cola drinker sporting the pink boutonniere.

So this was the game Amber had helped create. She'd found two men, probably models or actors, who resembled Jared enough to pull off this deception, especially with masks covering most of their faces. For all Mandy knew, a touch of Hollywood makeup had been added. Hair extensions. Whatever it took to clone them.

No one spoke. The waiter reappeared for more drink orders, did a triple take, and raised his eyebrows at Mandy, almost as if she were headed for an orgy. What the hell, she thought, as she shrugged back at him. At the moment, it seemed like a pretty good plan. She didn't have a clue who was who.

As the waiter darted off, she divided her gaze between the sexy trio. "I think I want all of you."

Pink Boutonniere smiled, Red speared a roasted pepper on his plate, and Blue sat back in his chair.

"You can't have all of us," Blue said, his voice slow and sinfully Southern, too. "You'll need to choose one."

"You?" she asked.

He didn't respond, and suddenly his hard-edged silence made him seem like the real Jared.

But that didn't mean he was. He could be as phony as the dyed flower on his lapel. Blue roses didn't exist.

She turned toward Red. He'd yet to speak. But at least his

rose embodied the Black Magic bouquet Jared had sent to her office, at least that was genuine.

"What do you think?" she asked him.

"I think you should dance with me," he responded. "After we finish our meal."

Another Southern boy. His voice mirrored the other candidates. She got goose bumps. "Are you from Oklahoma, too?"

"We all are. We're all Jared," he added, reminding her that she was caught in a carnal charade.

The waiter returned with Red and Blue's drinks, but this time he didn't raise his eyebrows at Mandy. He left her to her orgy.

Red leaned closer to her, close enough to cast a Black Magic spell. Mandy was tempted to kiss him, to taste the roasted peppers on his lips. He seemed to have Jared's mouth. But all of the men's mouths were shaped the same. Damn. Now Red was arousing her, the way Pink had done earlier.

She looked at Pink, getting his reaction. He liked watching her and Red. He seemed turned on by seeing her flirt with someone else. He dipped into his dessert and swallowed the frothy pudding on his spoon.

"Bad girl," he said.

"I'm always bad for Jared," she told him, casting a glance at Blue.

Blue returned her eye contact, but only for a stolen moment, an instant in time. Compared to the other men, Blue hadn't done anything to entice her. But his aloofness compelled her more than Pink's playfulness, more than Red's charisma.

Was he Jared?

Blue ignited her entire body, from the top of her intricately coiffed hair, to the hood of her swollen clit, to the tips of her satin-covered toes. She wanted to fuck every hard-edged inch of him. She even drew her thighs apart to ease the pressure.

"Dance with me," Red said, catching her attention. By now, they'd finished their meals.

"Yes, of course." She hesitated before she stood up, curious to see what Blue would do. But he didn't do anything except flag down the waiter for another beer.

"Be good," Pink told her. "Until we get our turns."

"You mean be *bad*," she corrected him, anxious for Blue's turn. But she had a feeling he was going to make her wait. He didn't seem to be in a hurry to dance with her, and that made her want him even more.

Stupid girl, she thought. She should have the sense to ignore him. But as she walked away with Red, she looked over her shoulder at Blue. He didn't return her interested glance. He'd made eye contact with another Victorian woman in the room. Mandy wanted to kill him.

She hoped he wasn't Jared.

"Screw Blue," she said out loud.

Red chuckled beneath his breath and swept her onto the dance floor. The song was soft and elegant, so she swayed in Red's arms. Throughout the night, the music had been changing, going from fast to slow to somewhere in between, accommodating all of the guests, all of the eras from which they were attired.

"This is an amazing party," she said.

"It is," he agreed. "Especially this part. We've never danced together before."

That was true, whether he was Jared or an imposter. Either

way, Red was an impeccable dancer. He was light on his feet, the way a society-schooled Victorian man should be. Mandy had learned to waltz for her wedding, but that was a lifetime ago. But at least she knew the basics.

"You're good," she said.

"I try." He embellished his next move and made her laugh. She wondered if he was as creative in bed.

"You're not Jared," she said suddenly.

He quit smiling. "Now why would you say that?"

Because if he were Jared, she wouldn't be wondering if he were a creative lover. She would already know. She would feel it. As well as she and Red moved together, their sexual rhythm was off.

"I've never danced with you before," she told him. "But I've never slept with you before, either."

"Dear lady." He kept the Southern drawl. He stayed in character. Or maybe it was his real voice. "We could remedy that. You could pick me anyway."

Her face went hot. Was she blushing? Were her cheeks turning rosy? Was she behaving like a Victorian miss with her skirts all aflutter? "You'd sleep with a girl you don't even know?"

His smile returned. "I'm trying to get to know you. I'm giving it my best shot."

Yes, she thought. He'd admitted that he wasn't Jared, but he wasn't succumbing to defeat. "What about the other man? Would he pursue me, too?"

"I don't know."

"Do you know who he is? What color of flower he's wearing?"

"No." Red glanced in the direction of the dining room. "We've had quite a few dress rehearsals that included the three of us, but we got ready separately this evening. We didn't see each other until our roses were in place."

"So you don't know who Jared is, either?"

"Not this evening, no." The song ended, and Red took her hand. "Shall I escort you back to the table?" He paused. "Unless you'd prefer to slip away for a tryst with me?"

Mandy smiled in spite of herself. He was quite the charmer. "It's tempting, but I came here to rendezvous with my lover."

"He's a lucky man."

"He better think so."

Red looped his arm through hers, and they walked side by side, probably looking as if they belonged together, as if they were a tight-knit couple.

As they passed beneath a hand-painted archway, Mandy glanced up at the Mayan symbols above her head. The mansion was adorned with ancient-style artwork.

Red stopped walking. "Which one do you think he is?"

"Pink or Blue? I honestly don't know. Pink isn't possessive enough, and Blue isn't attentive enough. They both confuse me."

"That's too bad." Red made a last-ditch effort to woo her. "Maybe you should just go for me."

"Maybe I should." She bumped his shoulder, and he laughed. He knew she didn't mean it.

He removed the rose from his lapel and handed it to her. "You might as well take this. Maybe keep it as a memento or something."

Mandy pinned his boutonniere to her purse. She thought him offering it to her was a nice gesture.

They returned to the table and found Pink sitting by himself. Blue was gone.

Mandy's heartbeat quickened. Her pulse went deliriously mad. The game kept twisting and turning, coiling her emotions with it. Deep down, she wanted a chance with Blue. She wanted to win his affection.

"Where's Blue?" she asked Pink.

"Who's Blue?" he responded.

"Your partner in crime."

He shook his head. "Good God, woman, if he's Blue, have you been calling me Pink?"

Behind her, Red burst into a chuckle, amused by Pink's reaction to his own nickname. She almost nudged Red to shut him up. Her sense of humor was wearing thin. The least Blue could have done was stay at the damned table.

"So where is he?" she asked Pink again.

"Hell if I know." Pink shrugged as if his partner in crime didn't matter. "He got up and walked away. I didn't see which direction he went."

Mandy snared his gaze. It seemed darker than before, less flirtatious, less playful than Pink's. Everything about him seemed different. Harder. Edgier. Sexier.

Something wasn't right.

"Did you switch flowers?" she asked, her nerves skittering to a halt. "Did you used to be Blue?"

"Who? Me? The Coca-Cola man? No, I've always been Pink." His lips twisted into a grimace. Red chuckled once more, but he quieted down when Pink told him to piss off.

"You're Blue," Mandy said. "You're him."

"Then prove it," he told her.

She accepted his challenge. "I will. But first you have to dance with me."

"If that's what you want." He stood up and moved toward her, pausing as if he were going to lean in to kiss her. But he didn't. He removed the pink rose and pinned it next to the red one on her purse.

"Now I'm Jared," he said.

"You're still Blue, and you're going to be Blue until *I* decide that you're Jared."

"She's a hellcat," Red interjected.

"I hope so." Blue was smiling now. The first time he'd smiled all night.

He offered her his arm, and they entered the dance floor. He was a better dancer than Red, and Mandy hadn't thought that was possible. But Blue moved with such masculine grace that even her heart followed his lead.

Her heart?

No, she thought. No. That wasn't part of the plan. She almost pulled away, lifted her skirts and dashed into the night, leaving him in her panicked wake.

But she stayed where she was, stumbling on her next step, inwardly cursing her discomposure.

"What's the matter?" He held her close. "Haven't you ever seduced a stranger?"

Mandy's breath rushed out. She went hot beneath her corset, her petticoat, her modesty-free drawers. "Are you a stranger?"

"I might be."

She looked into his eyes, searching for the man she knew. She wanted to prove that he was Blue and that Blue was Jared. But what if he wasn't? What if he was Pink playing a trick on her?

"You're not sure who I am," he said.

Once again, Mandy had trouble concentrating on the waltz. Other couples twirled around them, jeweled masks catching the light. The floor was filled with Renaissance, Regency, Romantic, Victorian, and Edwardian dancers.

Finally she snapped out of her shell. She refused to stumble again, to be as stiff as her petticoat. The music was sweet and melodic, wonderfully fluid. She wanted to be part of it.

"Kiss me," she told her partner.

"Not now. Not yet."

Damn. Whoever he was, he was following the rules of the game. Her hunger went unfed. He wasn't going to give himself away with a kiss, not unless she propositioned him for more.

"Maybe it would be better if you were Pink," she said.

His voice went a little more Southern. "And why is that?"

She wondered if Oklahoma had truly been his home, if he'd grown up there as a child. "Because there's no such thing as a blue rose."

"Isn't there?" Without missing a beat, he removed a blue boutonniere from inside his frock coat and gave it to her. The flower was identical to the one she'd seen him—or was it the other man?—wearing earlier.

"It's fake," she chided, trying not to be awed by him.

"That one is. But I heard that scientists have been working on making them real, and that someday they'll be available."

Without thinking, she pinned the boutonniere to his lapel,

moving to the music while she did it. "They'll never be this bright. This vivid."

"That's what scientists are working on. Getting the color just right." He rejoined their hands. "Did you know that in the Victorian era, they used flowers to communicate? Lovers weren't allowed to express their feelings for each other in public, so they sent coded messages through flowers." He paused, his mouth set in a serious line. "There were even dictionaries on the subject."

It was impossible not to be awed by him. "How do you know all of that?"

"I read about it."

The song ended, and she stepped back and gazed at the rose, studying its cobalt petals. It fit him beautifully. He'd been Blue all along.

But was he Jared?

"I saw you looking at another Victorian woman," she said, reminding him that he'd offended her earlier.

"Maybe I was envious of you and those other men."

"Then you shouldn't have created this charade. You shouldn't have put Red and Pink in my path."

"Maybe I did it to test you."

"To see if I would recognize my own lover?"

The music started again. Another classic song. Another gliding melody. Without the slightest hesitation, he reached for her. They were quarreling, but Blue still took what he wanted.

Silence tick-tocked between them. Sway, turn, promenade, chassé. She followed his every lead. She didn't stumble; she didn't falter. On the outside she was floating across the floor. But inside she felt as if she were being branded.

"I didn't look at her the way I'm looking at you," he said.

He was right. She couldn't deny his claim. Even with all of the people, with all of the festivities surrounding them, he was riveted to her, as she was to him.

Mandy couldn't stop herself if she tried. She wanted him inside her. Deep and wet. Hard and powerful. Her addiction was crying for relief. She needed a fix; she needed the man in her arms.

She moved closer, pressing her mouth to his ear. "Fuck me," she whispered. "Here. Tonight. At the mansion."

He nuzzled her delicately coiffed hair, and she envisioned him ravishing it, tugging at the pins, one by one.

"Are you sure?" he asked. "Are you sure I'm him?"

"Who else could you be?" She held him with all of her might. No one made her feel the way he did.

Good, bad, naughty, nice.

"I could still be a stranger," he told her.

She held him tighter. He was Jared. He was her lover. But she liked that he was offering to be a stranger. "Then fuck me," she said, heat spiraling through her core. "As if you've never fucked me before."

CHAPTER SIX

My heart wouldn't quit pounding. Atacar's body was so close to mine, I could smell the hunger on his skin. A male scent. Hard. Primitive. Animalistic.

"Are you ready?" he asked.

I nodded and looked up at him. He was on top of me, supporting his weight with his arms. I marveled at his face, just inches from mine. I still wanted to paint him, to immortalize him in a way only an artist could. I knew he would be my greatest work, my deepest challenge. He was dangerously handsome, as wild as the land that had borne and bred him.

The lantern flickered, and I caught my breath. Shadows danced like demons inside the barn, shifting across our bodies.

"Say it." His gaze pierced mine. "Tell me you're ready."

"I am," I insisted. To prove my point, I spread my legs wider. Tingling with anticipation, I glistened in my own juices. I was a

virgin, hungry to be had. But that wasn't enough for him. He wanted more from me.

He cuffed my wrists with his hands, holding me down, using the masculine power that compelled him. "Are you sure?"

Heat coiled in my belly. A girlish sheen of sweat broke out across my forehead. My nipples peaked like mountaintops.

"Yes," I whispered, my voice barely audible, barely recognizable. I couldn't imagine being more ready, more eager to lose my maidenhead.

He gentled his hold on me, lowering his mouth to mine, kissing me softly, making me sigh. I put my arms around him and prayed that he would stop teasing me. I needed him. I needed his hardened length thrusting inside me.

Concern edged his voice. "It's going to hurt."

I wet my lips, tasting the aftermath of his kiss. "I know."

He reached down, and I scooted closer. When he pushed the tip of his cock inside, I tensed. I didn't mean to, but suddenly he seemed too big for my tight passageway. He didn't stop. He kept pushing, going deeper, filling me, packing my body with his.

I curled my toes. It didn't hurt. Not yet. But I was bracing myself for the pain.

Boom. He thrust all the way, nearly shattering me in two. I gasped from the invasion, digging my fingernails into his back. Every time he moved, I clawed him. He told me to relax, but I didn't know if I could. We were immersed in shadows, fire demons licking our skin.

"Watch it go in and out," he said.

Needing a diversion, I glanced down at our joined genitals.

His penis was thick and heavily veined, and my vagina was soft and pink, the delicate folds stretching for him. His pubic hair bumped mine. He was as dark as I was blonde.

"We're beautiful," I said.

Atacar laughed, the sound rich and husky. Apparently beautiful wasn't the word he would have used. But I couldn't think of a more fitting description. He was all man, and I was all woman. What could be more beautiful than that?

I lifted my bottom in the air, experimenting with the position I was in. His penetration didn't hurt quite as badly. It still stung, but I decided that I liked it. Having him inside me, making me ache, gave me a vivid sense of being alive.

I was like a wolf, breathing in my mate. His scent, the male arousal I smelled earlier, got stronger, assailing my nostrils.

His stomach muscles rippled with every stroke. Deep. Shallow. He went forward, he withdrew, heightening the pleasure, intensifying the ache.

I hoped that Nanny was wrong. That he wouldn't steal my heart. Or worse . . . that he wouldn't break it. He was watching me now, analyzing the expression on my face. I tried to level my emotions. But it didn't work.

He touched my cheek with such tenderness he almost made me cry. I wasn't a girl prone to tears, but this was a monumental moment in my life. I turned my head and kissed his fingers.

"I had a wife," he said suddenly. "I was married."

His confession nearly knocked the wind out of me. I clutched his shoulders to sustain the blow and gouged his flesh so sharply I drew blood. He was still inside of me, still stretching my inner folds.

"*Did she die?*" *I asked.*

"*No. I threw her away.*"

I assumed that was the Apache way of saying he'd divorced her. I didn't have the courage to ask him why he'd left his wife. Not now. Not while our slick, naked bodies were entwined.

We both went silent. The only sound was the meeting of our flesh, the hot, desperate sin between us.

He covered my mouth in a searing, scorching, soul-burning kiss, plundering me with his tongue, bewitching me as deeply as I'd bewitched him.

Unable to control my passion, I rasped a dirty word in his ear, encouraging him to pound me into the blanket. My body was like a wooden bow, arched and ready to snap. His cock was so hard and his balls so tight I feared he might explode.

His driving rhythm torched my womb, but I didn't care. I didn't want him to be gentle. I didn't want him to touch me in a way that might trigger tears. I was already getting too attached.

"*Don't stop,*" *I said.*

"*I won't.*" *He kissed me again, wedging his fingers between us, strumming my clitoris.*

He played me like the piano in my mother's gilded parlor. A thundering concerto filled my head, and I reached beyond the blanket and grasped handfuls of straw. By now, I'd locked my legs around his waist. He rocked my body, bouncing my breasts. His powerful chest heaved.

The music got louder, more demanding. I slammed my hips against his, meeting his generous strokes. My cunt was wet and sore; my clitoris was on fire. His callused fingers kept playing me.

He looked down, and so did I. Together we watched ourselves make forbidden love. Being with him was more scandalous than anything I could've imagined.

"You're beautiful," he said.

"We're beautiful," I countered.

He didn't expel a husky laugh, not this time. He accepted my opinion. He allowed me to speak my feminine mind. I wanted to tell my Paris friends about him, but how could I? The best I could do was document our affair within the pages of my leather-bound journal.

I dropped the straw in my hands, scattering prickly stalks. Desire flooded my core, bubbling beneath the surface of my mound. Atacar used his fingers like Merlin's magic, his cock like King Arthur's sword. We were both sticky with my juices.

An orgasm lashed my body, whipping me into a fevered cry. He followed with a raw growl, thrusting, pounding, until he soaked me with his seed.

Our breathing slowed to a hush. Sweat evaporated from our skin. He sat up and produced a canteen of water Nanny had given him. He offered me a drink, and I took it readily. He swigged after I did, putting his lips where mine had been. I was still feeling sexual. But I felt vulnerable, too. I hadn't forgotten about his wife. That there was a woman he'd thrown away.

Without speaking, he reached for his shirt and dampened the edges, cleaning the redness from my thighs and around the opening of my vagina. Some of the stickiness had been blood. How foolish of me to forget what losing my maidenhead meant.

Discomfort overcame me. I tried to close my legs, but he insisted on bathing me. I furrowed my brows. He was soiling his only shirt.

After he was done he cast the garment aside. Then he noticed *that the buttercup I'd pinned into my hair had fallen onto the blanket sometime during our copulation. He retrieved it, tucking it back into my tousled coiffure.*

I wondered if he knew about the language of flowers. If not, would I have time to teach him? Or was I dreaming of things that would never be? I wasn't sure how soon he intended to steal a horse and leave.

He took me in his arms, and I put my head on his chest and listened to the masculine patter of his heart.

For tonight, he was mine.

~

Mandy waited for Jared to lead her to one of the mansion's guest rooms, to make love with her in a richly draped bed. But he didn't.

"Let's go for a walk in the garden," he said.

"The . . . garden?" she parroted, unable to stall the confusion in her voice.

He lifted her chin, angling her face so her eyes met his. "Did you think I was going to take you upstairs? I can't do that. I don't have access to any of the rooms."

"I just assumed . . ." She stalled again. "Are you sure we can . . . in the garden . . . I mean . . . how can we . . . ?"

"Don't worry about it. We'll figure out a way."

She tried to quit fretting. But as they exited the ballroom and entered the flagstone patio leading to the garden, she took inventory of the guests enjoying the outdoors. They were everywhere, seated at wrought-iron tables, nestled on rustic benches in torch-lit corners, standing out in the open with cigarettes and/or cocktails in their hands.

"I told you not to worry about it," he said.

"I'm not," she lied.

"Yes, you are. I can feel your apprehension."

But he couldn't see it. Her expression was hidden behind her mask. Which was the beauty of a masquerade, she thought, of having your features concealed. No one but Jared knew how she was feeling, no one but the man who was going to fuck her senseless.

She looked around again. At a populated party.

As Mandy moved forward, she snagged a chip in the stone walkway, latching on to his arm to brace her unladylike stumble.

"Relax." He stopped to give her a chaste kiss, feathering his lips across hers. "I promise, it'll be fine."

Her heart tagged torridly after his, the way it had when she'd faltered on the dance floor. But she made an excuse. "My skirts are too long."

"You're nervous. You're afraid someone might come by and see us. And they might." They stood at the edge of the patio. "But trying not to get caught is part of the thrill."

She looked toward the garden. What properly reared woman wouldn't be nervous? "I've never done anything like this before."

"I have. I'm good at it."

She studied him. Moonlight cloaked his clothes and highlighted the inky darkness of his hair. "Now why doesn't that surprise me?"

"It's not supposed to." He took her right hand into his left hand and drew her closer. From there he cupped her shoulder blade with his other hand, placing his fingertips against her spine. "Dance with me again."

"Here? Now?"

"I can still hear the music. Can't you?"

"Yes." A Nat King Cole song drifted through the air. "Unforgettable."

He smiled, his lips curving softly, sensuously, devilishly. "You are, you know."

Mandy went breathless. The Jared she knew wouldn't have teased her with a love song. But he wasn't behaving like himself tonight. He was still talking like Blue, still using the Oklahoma accent. It was part of the game, the stranger fantasy. He swept her into an elegant waltz, and she swayed in his arms.

"The garden is terraced on three acres," he said. "With lots of paths, lots of trees, lots of areas to stop, to appreciate the elements."

"And each other?"

"Definitely each other," he whispered against her cheek, creating a relentless surge of warmth. "I can't wait to fuck you."

A deliberately romantic dance. Rough, carnal words. Mandy couldn't begin to describe the conflicting sensations.

After the song ended, they kissed, mouths questing, tongues tangling. The ostrich plumes on her disguise fluttered, but his mask didn't move. It remained securely molded to his face.

He released her, and they explored the garden, where scores of plants and flowers bloomed. Some areas were well lit, and others contained a sprinkle of light. A few tall, leafy corners were completely dark.

While on a brightly lit path, they approached a bentwood arbor and passed another costumed couple, decked out in 1940s fashions. The man's hat dipped in front, and the woman's gown presented an austere image.

Mandy's nerves kicked up again. How many guests were

strolling the grounds? How many people were shadowed in the shrubs? Quite a few, she suspected. But she doubted that any of them were looking for a place to have sex.

A sense of propriety told her what they were about to do was wrong. But a deeper sense of naughtiness made it seem right.

They kept walking, and she thought about the language of flowers he'd mentioned earlier. She noticed poppies, daisies, cosmos, marigolds, and petunias.

"Do you know what any of these mean?" she asked.

He pointed to the cosmos. "Those represent modesty. The pure love of a virgin. And those"—he indicated the daisies— "embody innocence."

"Really? Oh, my goodness. I don't we think we should mess around in this area."

He laughed and pulled her into a kiss. "Maybe we should find some snapdragons. They mean dazzling but dangerous."

"I'm impressed that you know all of this."

He shrugged. "I only know some of it. There are hundreds of flowers. Hundreds of meanings."

While on the snapdragon hunt, Mandy and Jared came upon a gazebo. It wasn't a private spot. A trio of Elizabethan ladies graced the hedge-flanked structure.

As they passed berries and currants, Jared said something about this being like an English garden. Mandy thought about him partying in London, but she didn't question him about it. For now, she wanted to retain the fantasy that she and Jared were strangers. That they didn't know anything about each other. She liked the romantic in Blue. Jared's alter ego fascinated her.

"There," he said. "Snapdragons."

She looked across a sloping field and saw their bounty. The ruffled, tubular flowers ignited in a range of colors: white, pink, red, purple, orange, and yellow.

He took her hand, and they crossed the field. A breeze caressed the air, stirring the snapdragon scent.

"They're beautiful," she said. "Dazzling but dangerous," she added, repeating what he'd told her.

He agreed, and when they got close enough to touch the magical flowers, he picked one, squeezing the top and bottom of the bloom to make the dragon roar. Mandy laughed, and he smiled, enchanting her even more.

"There are thirty to forty different species of snapdragons," he said. "Some of the hybrids are bicolored. Like those." He indicated a pastel mix. "They're called Peaches and Cream."

"Your knowledge of flowers really is impressive."

"Maybe I learned it for tonight. For you."

"Maybe you did." She looped her arms around his neck. "Some men will do whatever they can to get laid."

"Damn straight." He scooped her up and carried her through the snapdragons, taking dirt pathways that divided rows and rows of rainbow blooms. He didn't stop until he came to a weather-beaten chair, positioned next to a rustic little table.

She gazed at the cozy niche. "You knew this was here." And he'd known the exact location of the snapdragons, too.

He set her on her feet. "Does it matter if I did?" He unscrewed the bulbs in the nearby floodlights, making the area dark. Mandy's breath lodged in her throat. This was where they were going to make love, where he was going to fuck her.

He didn't remove one stitch of clothing. He didn't even loosen his tie. Mandy didn't adjust her costume, either. She remained the way she was, wearing an old-fashioned gown and clutching a delicately beaded purse, waiting for him to make the first move.

"Rub against me," he said.

She moved forward, pressing her pelvis against his. Although her heavily tiered dress hindered the intimate contact, he made an appreciative sound. She suspected that his cock had gone hard. That being surrounded by silk and lace was arousing him.

Their mouths came together, and he sucked on her tongue as if he were half-starved, as if she had the capacity to feed him. She kissed him back with the same hungry fervor, the same passionate need.

Finally he removed an article of clothing. His gloves came off. He bunched up her skirts and invaded her open-crotch drawers, teasing her with bared fingers. When he found her clit, she squirmed with honey-sweet pleasure.

"I was going to do this to myself in the limo," she said.

"Really?" His Southern accent went rough. "Why didn't you?"

"I didn't want to mess up my dress, to get wrinkled. To make my fingers sticky."

"Mine are getting that way. I'm going to have to lick them clean. Or maybe I'll make you do it."

"We can share them, can't we?" She impaled herself on his sticky digits, creaming them even more. She couldn't help her reaction to him. He made her nasty. He made her desperate to do dirty things.

"You first." He freed his fingers and offered them to her.

She took a ladylike lick, tasting the musky flavor of her own juices. She could barely see him in the dark, but she could tell that he was watching, gazing at her through slivers of moonlight.

"Your turn," she told him.

He didn't hesitate. He laved the sexual treat, roughly, diligently, like a mountain lion cleaning his paws. Mandy got wet again.

"Touch me some more," she said.

He gave her what she wanted, and she gripped the hem of her dress, holding the petticoat with it, allowing him better access.

"Do you like messing around with a stranger?" he asked, heightening the game.

She pitched forward a little. "Yes."

"Then stay there, and I'll put my mouth on you. I'll eat you until you come."

She wasn't about to refuse. She wanted him to taste her, to push his tongue through the slit in her drawers.

He knelt on the grass and put his face under her skirt. She lowered the hem of her dress and petticoat, letting the materials curtain him.

He ate her deep and slow. She sank onto the wetness, rocking back and forth. Her sex swelled, craving more and more.

Being completely clothed while a masked man lapped deliciously between her legs was almost more than she could bear. She told him to lick her clit, too.

He did, feverish, sucking the sensitive nub. Her dirty boy was doing his job, making her crazy for him.

Mandy widened her stance. The fabric around the opening of her Victorian drawers was soaked.

In the distance, she heard voices, other guests strolling the lush garden, talking in party-chipper tones. But she didn't care. Nothing mattered but her impending orgasm.

Finally she convulsed, jerking her hips, bucking forward, coating her lover with her juices. In her mind's eye, the moon burst in the sky, raining over the snapdragons, making their colors explode.

Voices sounded again, but she barely heard them. She was too dizzy from climaxing so hard. Jared climbed out from under her dress. Then he shifted his gaze and grabbed her, pulling her deeper into the darkness.

Suddenly she realized how close those voices were. Two sets of couples encroached the snapdragons. She could see the foursome clearly. The path they strode was generously lit.

"Shit," Jared said. He spoke barely above a whisper.

"I thought trying not to get caught was part of the thrill," she chided, keeping her tone as quiet as his.

"It is. But I'm hard as a goddamn rock, and I want to fuck."

"We're going to have to wait it out."

"Easy for you to say; you already came."

"I'm ready to come again." She watched the couples stop to chat. "I'm still wet."

"Yeah? Well, you have no idea how wet you're gonna be by the time I'm done with you." He put his arms around her, holding the back of her body tightly against the front of his.

She leaned back, enjoying his possessive touch. He hissed out a breath, giving her chills. The other people hadn't budged.

"What the hell are they doing?" Jared complained. His hold was getting tighter, more aggressive.

"I think they're tipsy." Mandy focused on their overly jovial voices. "They probably drank too much moonshine." The four-some was dressed from the speakeasy era, the women wearing flapper fringe and long pearls.

"I don't care if they've been chugging turpentine. They need to get their asses moving."

She turned in his arms, smiled, teased him. "You're impatient."

"I'm tired of waiting."

But wait they did, standing together, pressed against some scratchy shrubbery. One of the speakeasy men cracked what appeared to be a silly joke, and his companions chortled.

"Screw this," Jared said.

Mandy nibbled the inside of her lip to keep from giggling, until her lover shocked her into silence. Within the span of a heartbeat, he lunged for the chair, sat down, and plunked her on top of him, so she was straddling his lap, hip to hip, face-to-face.

She held her breath, waiting for the other couples to notice them, to hear the rustle they'd created. But nothing happened. She and Jared remained in the dark, and the partiers kept talking and laughing.

Jared reached down and undid his pants. Mandy did her damnedest not to gasp. He freed his cock, spread her skirts to cover them, and pulled her onto his erection, determined to have his wicked way with her.

No matter who was around.

CHAPTER SEVEN

Jared pushed deeper, and Mandy reveled in the familiarity of his touch. His passion. His piercing. Sometimes he wore only slightly curved barbells, and sometimes he wore circular jewelry. Tonight he was in a circular mood. And so was she. For her, the circular barbells created stronger sensations.

He kissed her, possessing her mouth and making the moment even more intense. His rhythm was smooth and sexy, hot and hard. Her purse fell from her lap and dropped onto the ground.

"I like this position," he whispered. "I like how your skirts drape over me."

"Me, too." The entire scenario felt like a color-hazed dream: their timeless costumes, the mansion in the clouds, the half-moon, the aroma of plants and flowers, the other people's voices buzzing like bees.

"This isn't going to be enough for me," he told her. "After I come, I'm going to want to come again. And again. I don't think I'll ever get enough of you."

She looked into the darkness of his mask. He seemed like a shadow, a flesh-and-blood mist. But he was real. She shaped her hands over the breadth of his shoulders and onto his lapels. On his left side, she encountered his boutonniere.

"What do blue roses mean?" she asked.

"Mystery."

She touched the petals. Now she understood why he'd chosen it. Blue, the man he'd personified this evening, created a mysterious effect. He nuzzled her neck, gently, roughly, kissing and nipping.

She sank onto his lap and made her skirts rustle. "Are you going to come home with me later? Are you going to spend the night?"

"Yes." He'd stopped using the Oklahoma accent. He was no longer talking like a stranger. He was completely himself. Or was he? He'd never been this romantic.

"Will you hold me when we're in bed?"

"Yes," he said again.

Her skin tingled. Her heart sparkled. While he was still inside of her, she reached for her fallen purse.

He circled her waist, keeping her balanced, keeping his sweeping rhythm. "What are you doing, baby?"

Her desire spiraled higher. She loved it when he called her baby, when he used endearments during sex. "Getting the extra key to my condo. The one I had made for you." She pressed her lips to his satin-covered cheek and rasped his name, sending chills up and down her own spine.

Suddenly he stopped moving. She almost complained. She almost told him to keep going, to quit teasing her, until she realized why he'd gone motionless.

The other people's jovial voices grew louder.

Mandy held her breath. She didn't know exactly how close the intruders were. Her back was to them. So she waited, knowing Jared was watching the foursome, tracking their garden-strolling path. She tried to gauge his reaction, but between his mask and the lack of the light, she could barely see him.

A second later, his face seemed to disappear completely. She glanced up at the sky. The moon was the culprit, peeking in and out of trees, sending nighttime shadows across Jared's face.

She waited, and so did he. Finally, the other voices faded, along with shuffling sounds that she assumed were retreating footsteps.

"They're gone," he said, affirming her assumption.

Mandy's breathing returned to normal. She opened her purse and dug around for the key. *There.* She ran her fingers along the metal teeth. Leaning forward, she kissed Jared, dropping the key into his coat pocket.

He resumed their activity, thrusting his cock again, filling her with rapture. The chair beneath them creaked, rebelling from his aggressive motion, from their combined weight. Beneath her lace-trimmed corset and the equally decorative corset cover, her nipples went sweetly, sensitively hard.

"I'm going to go down on you in the limo," she said.

He thrust harder. "So I can fantasize that I'm a lord and you're a naughty Victorian lady?"

"Yes." His imagination stirred hers. "The limo can be our

carriage." She wanted to give him a blow job while he destroyed her properly coiffed hair. She wanted to suck every engorged inch of him.

In the distance, birds sang a nighttime song, and suddenly this place seemed like the Garden of Eden. Breathtaking. Beautiful. Dangerous.

"Do the Apache believe in Heaven and Hell?" she asked.

"Why? Am I tempting you into Hell?"

"I think maybe you are. But it's like Heaven, too." She was wet and creamy, and it was all for him. He was an angel. He was a demon. He was everything good, everything bad.

She climaxed with her breath panting and her pulse skittering. He came at the same time, shooting his essence into the very core of who she was, of who she'd become.

She put her head on his shoulder. The birds were still singing. Crickets chirped, too. She didn't want to let go, but she knew they couldn't stay there forever. He lifted her up, setting her on her feet, and his semen trickled between her legs. She clenched her inner muscles, trying to keep the sticky warmth inside.

He stood up and adjusted his pants and buttoned his coat. From there, he screwed the floodlight bulbs back into their sockets. Within seconds, the area was illuminated again.

Mandy smoothed her skirts. Some of his come was still leaking out of her, but between her lacy drawers, silk hose, and stiff petticoat, there was plenty of fabric to absorb the moisture.

"You don't need those anymore," he said.

She blinked. "What?"

"The other flowers."

He pointed to the roses pinned to her purse. Some of the

petals were missing, and the leaves were slightly bent, but the boutonnieres remained attached to her bag.

"Who were Pink and Red?" she asked, curious about the men who'd participated in the charade. "What are their real names?"

"It isn't important." He snagged the other roses and flung them, destroying the symbolism. "I'm the only guy who matters. I'm the one you're going to be waking up with tomorrow. Me, and me alone."

~

I awakened alone in the barn. Dawn had barely broken. Only a sliver of light streamed through the breezeway.

Had Atacar left me after our night of lovemaking? Was he gone for good? Or had he stayed and breakfasted with Nanny? I imagined her preparing a hearty-size platter for him. Nanny was an accomplished cook, and she believed that the first meal of the day was the most beneficial.

I searched for my undergarments and put them on. I suspected that I looked quite wanton in rumpled red silk with my hair mussed and my lips swollen from a man's lustful kisses. Needing to feel closer to my lover, I picked up the blanket we'd slept on and draped it over my shoulders. It smelled of moonlit sex and summer straw.

The lone horse on the other side of the barn whinnied, capturing my attention. I descended the loft ladder to visit with her.

She was a sturdy mare with varied colors, a breed that had gained popularity in Buffalo Bill's Wild West. I'd seen the smashingly successful show when it had toured Europe. I'd been young at the time, but still mature enough to appreciate the striking beauty of the painted horses they'd used.

And to be fascinated by the Indians.

They'd looked so grand in their feathers and breechcloths while they'd re-created historical battles for the crowd.

Was it any wonder I'd been instantly attracted to Atacar? I touched a finger to my lips. How I longed to kiss him again, to press my body against his.

I wanted to know more about him, to learn of his youth, his battles, his escape from the fort. There was the matter of his wife, too. That weighed heavily on my mind.

I headed into the daylight. My feet were bare, but I often went barefoot. Nanny said it was the bohemian in me.

I walked toward the house, a frame structure with a porch across the front. The kitchen served as a place to cook, but it was our conservatory, as well, with a hothouse arrangement so vegetables grew year-round. We had an outdoor garden, too.

At one time, there had been a sod house on this property, but that was before the railroad had arrived in this area, bringing lumber, brick, and other materials.

I entered the house, hoping to find Atacar, but he wasn't there. I approached Nanny. She was scrubbing the kitchen. She looked up and saw me.

"You slept late," she said. "You neglected your chores."

I defended my position. "It's barely dawn."

"Farm life starts early," she countered.

Nanny had been reared on a farm, and she had the annoying habit of touting her authority. Of course, our Texas settlement wasn't a crop-producing farm. Everything we did was for our own consumption, but there was still a lot of work, especially since our farmhand had quit.

Yesterday I'd neglected my chores, too. I'd gone off to paint and had met Atacar. And now I wondered where he was, but I was too fearful to ask. I didn't want to hear that he was gone.

"I'll tend to my chores," I said.

"Atacar already milked the cow, fed the chickens, and gathered the eggs. He's familiar with farming. When he was in Alabama, he and some of the other men in his tribe labored at farms near the military post."

My pulse spiked. I'd barely heard what she'd said about his work experience. I was too excited to think beyond his presence at my farm. "He's still here? Where is he now?"

"Making repairs to the wagon shed."

I turned on my heel to leave, to dash off, to be with my lover, and Nanny grabbed my arm. I tried to pull away from her, but she held tight.

"You shouldn't flitter about like that. You should wash the sex from your skin and don some modest clothes." She removed the blanket from around my shoulders and placed it on top of her laundry pile. "I'll heat the water for your bath."

"Did Atacar bathe?" I asked, wondering if he'd washed the sex from his skin.

"As soon as he arose this morning, he went down to the stream."

"Mmm." I made an appreciative sound. "He was bathing in the stream when I first met him."

Nanny shot me an exasperated glare, warning me not to discuss his nakedness any further. I focused on my nakedness instead.

She helped me haul the tub into my room, and I soaked in the water she'd heated. I was impatient to see Atacar, but Nanny had been right. Not only did I need to bathe, I needed to soothe the lingering soreness that came with losing my maidenhead.

After I dried off, I pinned my hair neatly to my head and put on a practical daytime dress fashioned from pastel-printed cotton and decorated with a row of simple buttons.

I returned to the kitchen, and Nanny fixed me a cup of tea, the same special blend from last night. I wasn't hungry, but she insisted that I eat some bread and jam. As I'd suspected, she'd fed Atacar a big, scrumptious meal, and according to her, he'd devoured every bite. She seemed to like that he had a strong appetite. So did I, but I was thinking of his appetite for me.

I couldn't sit at the table any longer. I left my bread half-eaten and my tea half-sipped. Eager to greet Atacar, I walked briskly to the wagon shed. The property was littered with out-buildings. The family who'd built the farm had returned to the East, allowing me the opportunity to finance a ready-made home and make payments to the bank.

I entered the shed and found Atacar engaged in the repairs Nanny had mentioned. He heard me approach and turned to face me. Our gazes met and held, but no words were spoken.

We didn't exchange a proprietary "Hello." We didn't say, "Good morning." We did nothing except look at each other.

Finally I broke the silence, stunning him, and myself, with an emotional question. "Why did you throw away your wife?"

He tensed. He frowned. But he responded just the same. "She had sex with another man."

I gaped at him, then closed my mouth before I swallowed a flying insect. "Why did she do that?"

"Because I didn't love her."

I doubted that many men loved their wives the way they should. Papa barely tolerated Mama. But Atacar seemed plagued by his distant feelings toward his wife. So I asked, "Why did you marry her?"

"It was arranged by our families."

"Is that common in your culture?"

"It can be. Some of the old people think it's foolish to marry for love. Our families were close, so her parents perceived me as a good match for her."

"But you weren't?"

"No. She was congenial. She tried to be a good wife, but I felt nothing when I was near her." He made an empty gesture. "I should have refused the match."

"How long ago was this?" I needed to see the time line in my head, to picture him as he was then. He looked to be in his mid-thirties now.

"Twelve years have passed." He paused, as if he were gathering his thoughts. "I touched her at night, but my passion for her was forced." He repeated the empty gesture. "She didn't please me, in or out of bed. I kept hoping that she would, but she never did."

Another question. More curiosity. Atacar was a mystery that had just begun to unfold. "Did the other man love her?"

He nodded. "I threw her away so she could be with him. They're still together. But what I did was considered unmanly." He frowned again, tiny lines creasing his eyes. "I didn't punish my wife for being unfaithful. I didn't beat her or cut her nose to make her look ugly. I didn't go after her lover, either. I would've had the right to kill him."

I frowned, too. How could anyone consider Atacar unmanly? He was strong and fierce. He emitted power. "Why didn't you do those things?"

"It didn't seem right to destroy her. Or the man who cared for her."

I was impressed by the mercy he'd bestowed upon his wife and her lover. "I think what you did was noble. Compassionate."

He disagreed. "I should have tried harder to love her, to make her feel special. But mostly I ignored her. I made the marriage bad."

"Sometimes a person can't help who they love." I stepped closer to him. His gaze was nailed to mine. "But if you'd been my husband, I wouldn't have gone to another man. I would've waited for you to favor me, no matter how long it took."

He responded in kind. "If you'd been my wife, you wouldn't have needed to wait. I would have favored you from the start."

Silence engulfed us once more. We weren't saying that we loved each other. How could we? We were scarcely acquainted. But our physical attraction seemed strong enough to sustain us.

"Will you stay?" I asked.

"For how long?" he wanted to know.

I wanted to say "Forever," but instead I said, "Until I can find a permanent farmhand. Maybe a month or so? I can give you room and board and a modest wage."

He accepted my offer, deciding that having currency to take to Mexico would enhance his trip. "But if someone discovers that I'm here and who I am, you and Nanny must say that I forced you into giving me a job and hiding me from the authorities."

I was touched that he was trying to protect us, but I knew he was right. Aiding a prisoner of war was dangerous business. I accepted his terms.

He leaned in to kiss me, lightly, briefly, and I sighed and put my arms around his neck.

I'd found a way to keep him. If only for a while.

～

At nightfall while Nanny slept in her room, I led Atacar to mine, and he glanced around. Most of the furnishings were basic, items I'd purchased locally. My journal sat on a simply constructed desk, the pages burning with my writings. As for my bed, it was far more luxurious than it should have been. I'd ordered it from a catalog and had it shipped to Texas. It didn't fit the farmhouse, but I didn't care. The wooden frame was ornately carved with fabric draped over the top and front of it. The mattress was a soft, feather-stuffed luxury to which I'd become accustomed.

"My family has these kinds of beds at home," I told Atacar. "They're called testers. This one has been reduced in size. It's not as big as they normally are."

"It's still big," he commented.

"I suppose it is, considering the size of the room. It takes up a lot of space."

He gazed at the bed once more, then asked me to remove my clothing and lie upon it, with my legs spread for him. His request was bold and erotic, and I tingled, eager to do his bidding.

I took my time, lingering for his benefit. He watched me with keen interest. I suspected that he'd gotten used to my fancy undergarments since he'd seen me in them several times by now, but I could tell that he enjoyed how I looked in my corset and drawers.

When I was bare, I climbed on the mattress. He stared at my pink-crested breasts, my quivering stomach, the exposed juncture between my thighs. He studied my face too, watching my expression.

Did he know how excited I was? How nervous?

"Turn over," he said. "On all fours."

I stalled. That wasn't what I had expected to hear. He gestured for me to follow his command, and I nibbled my bottom lip, tugging it between my teeth. But I didn't refuse him. I rolled over and got into position. I realized that he was going to mate me this way. It made me feel like a mare that was about to be mounted by the biggest, roughest stallion in the herd.

I heard Atacar getting undressed. He would need some new clothes, especially since he'd stained his shirt with my maiden's blood. But that was last night. Tonight I was no longer a virgin.

I wondered if he would lick me, the way a stallion tasted a mare's vulva before they copulated. I hoped he would. I wanted his tongue inside me.

He got onto the mattress. I could feel his weight shifting the soft feather stuffing. I didn't twist my body or try to look at him. I faced forward and let him crawl up behind me.

He placed his hands on either side of my hips, smoothing them across my bottom, tracing the rounded shape. After he admired my derriere, he moved on to my vagina, using his fingers, spreading me like the folds of a flower. He spoke in Apache, and I went desperately wet. I had no idea what he was saying, but the guttural sound of his language, coupled with his touch, aroused me. I could tell he was preparing to taste me. By now, he was lowering his head, putting his mouth in place.

I gazed at the burgundy and gold fabric on the front of the bed, the colors swirling before my eyes. He darted his tongue, tasting my juices. But he couldn't get enough of me that way, so he positioned himself below me and pulled me down. I gulped the air in my lungs. He'd seated me right on his face.

He licked; he kissed; he rubbed saliva all over me. He inhaled my scent, too, savoring it. I couldn't see what he was doing, but I felt every primitive sensation.

I climaxed in undulating waves, rocking back and forth. I undid the pins in my hair and let the loose waves fall over my shoulders and down my back. I wanted to look like a palomino for him, to allow my blonde mane to entice him.

When my orgasm ended, I raised my hips so I was on all fours again. He crawled out from beneath my legs and got behind me, fitting his cock against my cunt.

He entered me so hard, I gasped. But I loved it, too. He buried his face in my hair. He seemed pleased that I'd freed it from its ladylike confinement.

His heavy testes slapped against me as we fucked. Or made love. Or copulated. I wasn't quite sure what word to use to describe our second encounter.

He plowed through the silkiness of my hair so he could nibble, quite roughly, on the back of my neck. This kind of mating seemed to come naturally to him. He penetrated me with powerful thrusts.

In my mind's eye, I imagined how we looked, kneeling on a tester bed, naked as the days we were born, his big, dark hands wrapped about my small, fair waist, his penis sliding in and out of me. I wanted to paint us, to relive this moment forever. But I knew I couldn't. A painting of that nature would be far too scandalous, so

I decided that I would do a small sketch in my journal. I might even draw a heart around it. I realized how girlish of me that would be, but I couldn't seem to control my strangely romantic thoughts.

Atacar plunged even harder, taking what he wanted, what we both seemed to need. He impaled me, he stretched me, his body claiming mine. My breasts bounced with each rough movement. He reached around to cup them, to make me whimper. Fire spread from my nipples to my clitoris, then burned deep and low in my belly.

I was going to climax again.

My lover was going to orgasm, too. I heard the rumbling in his breathing and felt the thick, driving pressure in his loins. He growled in my ear, and I turned, trying to kiss him, but I couldn't reach his mouth.

Spasms shook my core. I grabbed a pillow and clutched its downy softness, digging my fingers into it. Atacar shot his seed, filling me with white-hot fluid.

He collapsed on top of me, and I hit the mattress with a thud, the pillow wedged beneath me.

He said something, but I didn't comprehend him. He was speaking Apache again. A second later, he caught his mistake and switched languages.

"Am I too heavy for you?" he asked.

"No." He was, but I didn't want him to move. He was still hard, and he was still inside of me.

"I think I am. This can't be comfortable for you."

He withdrew, leaving me naked and exposed. I rolled over to look at him. He touched my cheek, and I concluded that drawing an image of us with a heart looped around it made perfect sense.

"I'm glad I'm you're first," he said. "That you're exploring sex with me."

"So am I." I wondered how many positions he would encourage me to try, how many different ways he would shape and bend my body.

He lay down next to me, and we faced each other. I loved how he looked in the kerosene-lit glow. The light illuminated his deeply hollowed features.

"I want to paint a portrait of you," I said. "Will you sit for me?"
He shook his head.

"I don't mean right now. In the daytime. When you're fully clothed. You can pose with your rifle," I added, hoping that would tempt him.

"I won't let you seize my soul."

Was that some sort of Apache superstition? Or was he speaking metaphorically? "My painting wouldn't do that to you."

"Yes, it would. You would capture me for all time. Even after I was gone, I would belong to you."

I looked into his eyes. He wasn't being superstitious. He was worried about falling in love with me. I went fluttery inside. I was happy it had crossed his mind.

"That could happen even if I don't paint you," I said.

"It would be worse if I allowed you to create a portrait of me. It would be like leaving a part of myself behind. I can't do that. I won't."

Mortally wounded, I frowned at him. "You might have already left a part of yourself behind. You filled me with your seed. Last night and tonight." I glanced down at my stomach. "You could have made me pregnant already."

111

"I told Nanny about a tea you should use. I've heard medicine men speak of it."

My frown turned to surprise. The tea Nanny had been brewing for me was a preventative? I wondered how effective it was. Nonetheless, I was grateful that he'd considered me in that regard. In Europe, sometimes men used penile sheaths as implements of protection, but widespread use of them was rare.

"So, are you going to sit for me?" I asked, pressing him about the portrait.

"No." He remained firm in his conviction. "We shouldn't get too close." But even as he said it, he gathered me in his arms, holding me close.

So very, very close.

CHAPTER EIGHT

After the party ended, the limo picked Mandy and Jared up at the mansion's front gate, and the driver got out and opened the door. Jared helped Mandy inside and told the chauffeur to take them farther into the hills, to keep driving and not disturb them. They weren't ready to go to Mandy's house yet.

As the car pulled away, Jared closed the glass panel and lowered the privacy blinds. He removed his mask, and so did Mandy. They gazed at each other, and the moment turned hot and emotional.

She'd offered to give him oral pleasure, and he couldn't wait for her to nurse his cock. Earlier, she'd refreshed her lipstick, and he noticed that the glossy cosmetic complemented the cherry blossom color of her gown. Female dominance, beauty, and sexuality, he thought.

"I want to see you in your underwear," he said.

"Right now?"

He nodded. "Yes, right now. I want to push the envelope with the fantasy you inspired. The lord, the lady, the Victorian carriage."

She agreed, but he knew that she wouldn't deny his request. Whatever he craved, she gave to him. He couldn't ask for a more thrilling lover. She was dominant in a submissive way, the perfect partner for his lustful games.

"Turn around, and I'll help you remove your dress," he said.

She obliged, presenting him with her back. He went after the hooks and stripped her to her corset and drawers, tossing the rest of her garments aside. The petticoat had a life of its own, sitting stiffly by itself. The gown took a lot of room, too. But being surrounded by her feminine finery made him more aroused.

"My Mandy," he said, as she faced him once again. The tops of her breasts spilled out from her corset, but he'd had it designed that way. "My *multiorgasmic* Mandy."

Her voice went soft, sexy. "Is that what you've been calling me?"

"It's what you are." She was also a woman who'd asked him to hold her later. A woman who needed sex, but who needed affection, too. But he didn't want to think too deeply about that. Not now. Not while she was going to get him off.

"Have I told you how beautiful you look tonight?" he asked.

"No. But thank you."

She leaned forward to kiss him, and he plundered her mouth, practically swallowing her tongue and bruising her lips. Nothing had ever felt so right. When they separated, he could barely breathe. She amazed him, the way she sat on the seat with her thighs pressed demurely together and her breasts partially bared.

The good-bad girl.

Anxious for more, he removed his tie, unbuttoned his shirt, and opened his pants. Making his intentions known, he pushed his pants down his hips, exposing his cock and balls. He wanted her to lick and suck his testes, too. He wanted the package deal.

Mandy got onto the limo floor and knelt in front of him. He glanced down at her. He'd meant what he'd said about how beautiful she was.

She reached out and circled the head of his cock, running the tips of her fingers over his piercing. He went shivery. She was teasing him, making him wait for her mouth.

"Why is this called a Prince Albert?" she asked.

"No one knows the true origin, but it's alleged that Queen Victoria's consort, Prince Albert, wore a ring attached to his penis, which was then strapped to his thigh."

She played with the barbell. "Why would he do that?"

Damn. Jared went shivery again. "To maintain the smooth line of the tight trousers that were fashionable at the time. In the nineteenth century, this kind of piercing was referred to as a dressing ring. Or that's one of the theories. As I said, no one knows for sure."

"You dress on the left. That's the side you keep your cock on."

He skimmed her cheek. "I'm glad you noticed."

"I notice everything about you." She paused and licked the skin around his jewelry. "And I like that your piercing has Victorian roots. That makes it even sexier, even if it's a myth."

He delved into her hair, dislodging the decorative combs and unearthing pins. If she didn't hurry up and suck him, he was going to fucking die.

She finally lowered her head all the way and took him in her mouth. He lifted his ass off the seat and pushed deeper. She cupped his balls, gently abrading the sacs.

He continued to ravage her hair. Curls tumbled and fell, draping her heart-shaped face. She sucked him harder, bobbing her head.

She did everything he wanted her to do. She alternated his balls, licking and sucking each one, until she returned to his cock, taking his granite length all the way to the back of her throat. He groaned, deep and rich and guttural. Her eyes drifted closed; her cheeks went hollow.

The limo slid along a mountain road, and he watched Mandy make love to him. She paid special attention to the circular barbell, flicking her tongue along its horseshoe shape. He'd worn it especially for her. He knew it was her favorite.

"I'm so into you," he said.

She stopped to nuzzle his thigh, to think about what he'd said, to look up at him with depth in her pretty blue eyes. "I've been calling my attraction to you an addiction."

"Really?"

She kept nuzzling his thigh, tickling the tiny hairs on his legs. "I'm going to need a twelve-step program to get you out of my system. You and all of the things you tempt me into doing. You're corrupting me, Jared."

"I know, baby. But I can't help it. You tempt me, too." He liked sweeping Mandy into his world. He liked having control of their affair. But even more than that, he liked how she responded to him, how much she enjoyed being corrupted.

Beyond aroused, he pushed her down, making her suck him

again. Thinking about the sexual side of their relationship made him hot as hell. All he wanted to do was come.

She gave him the blow job of his life. His modern Victorian lady. His lover. The woman driving him to agonizing distraction.

He tugged at her gorgeous hair, rocking back and forth, fucking her cherry blossom mouth. When it happened, when he ejaculated, she tipped her head back so he could watch. She swallowed every milky drop, then licked him clean. She even mewled like a cat, a feral little kitten, mink-soft and dirty-sweet.

Adrenaline shot through Jared's veins. His heart beat rapidly in his chest. Every nerve ending in his body burst into flames. He waited for the feeling to end, but it didn't go away. Not until she sat back on her haunches, not until she quit touching him.

As air chopped through his lungs, he yanked up his pants and adjusted the rest of his clothes. She blotted her mouth with a delicate handkerchief from her purse. Always the lady, he thought. She put on her corset cover and petticoat. Jared helped her with her gown, fastening the hooks in back.

She turned around to face him once more. "I used to hate the taste of come."

He lifted his eyebrows. "But you like it now?"

"I like knowing it's yours. That it's part of you. I even fantasized about it earlier, when I was drinking a Between the Sheets." She angled her chin. "That's when I got acquainted with Amber."

He started. "She approached you? She told you who she was?"

Mandy nodded. "We agreed to get together, do some Blow-Job Shooters sometime."

That was just what he needed, his current lover partying with his ex, or whatever the hell Amber was to him. "Sometimes she's a bitch. And sometimes she can be a good friend."

"That's the impression I got of her. She said that you met in London."

He didn't want to talk about England, but if he avoided it, Mandy would wonder why he was being evasive. "It was just a couple of trips I took."

"A couple? You've been there more than once?"

"The first time, it seemed like an interesting place to see, to do the tourist thing. The second time, I enjoyed it enough to go back." A lie, if he'd ever told one. The weeks he'd spent in England were more than a vacation, more than a holiday dalliance.

"I'd love to go there someday."

"I'm sure you'd like it." On his second trip, he'd met Amber, but he hadn't been honest with her, either. She didn't know real reason he'd ventured onto British soil. He'd told her the same bullshit story he'd just told Mandy. Jared switched subjects. "Are you ready to head home? Should I tell the driver to take us to your condo?"

"Okay." Mandy removed the stray pins that remained in her hair and shook the rest of her curls free. "He's going to know we messed around."

"I imagine he's to used it. People mess around in limos all the time."

"This has been the most erotic night of my life," she said. "The party, the charade, the garden, and now what I just did to you."

"For me, too." He kissed her softly, preparing himself for the promise he'd made: to hold her while they were in bed.

He just hoped that he didn't disappoint her. Jared did erotic well. But being warm and romantic made him uncomfortable. Suddenly he wanted to put his mask back on, to hide behind the man she called Blue.

~

The sky was a brilliant shade of blue. I stood on the porch, gazing at the horizon and waiting for Atacar. But he was still completing his chores. As our new farmhand, he'd taken on most of the outdoor work, leaving Nanny more time for domestic duties and me for my art. Of course, my art was done for the afternoon. Mostly because I'd worked on secret sketches in my journal. For the past two days, since Atacar had agreed to stay, I'd been drawing us in various states of arousal. And, yes, I included those girlish hearts, too.

"Catherine!" Nanny called from the kitchen. "Come inside and fetch the food."

I turned and entered the house. As soon as Atacar finished his work, he and I were going on a late-day picnic. Nanny had prepared roast chicken. She'd even baked a gingerbread cake.

She handed me a carefully packed basket with a blanket folded on top, and I thanked her. It hadn't taken Nanny long to grow extremely fond of Atacar. She fussed over him like a cackling hen, making sure that he was well fed and well cared for. Tomorrow, she and I were going into town to purchase fabrics for his new clothes.

"It'll be a shame to lose that man," she said. "He's a good worker."

I nodded, a lump forming in my throat. I didn't want to think about Atacar leaving in a month. "I could implore him to stay a bit longer. But I don't think he will."

"Maybe he'll change his mind later." She heaved a laden breath. "Or maybe it's best if he moves on before you two get too close. Before what you feel for each other gets too deep."

"I'm trying not to fall in love with him."

"I know, child. He's trying not to fall in love with you, too."

I put down the basket and reached for my old nanny, hugging her, needing her comfort. She wrapped me in her ample arms. Finally, I stepped back and rubbed my eyes. They'd begun to water, and I didn't want Atacar to see me this way.

Nanny righted her appearance, as well. She smoothed the wisps of hair escaping her gray-streaked bun and flattened her apron. Then she shooed me back onto the porch, picnic supplies in tow.

My lover arrived with his hands and face freshly washed. I could tell that he'd cleaned up at the pump. He smiled at me, and I warned my heart to be still. He was wearing a Western hat Nanny had given him. When I first bought the farm, she'd found a few cowboy items the previous tenants had left behind in the barn: a torn neckerchief, holey gloves, a battered hat marked by John. B Stetson Co. She'd kept everything, fascinated by their rugged appeal. And now she'd put those articles to good use. Not only had she given Atacar the hat, she'd repaired the gloves and neckerchief for him.

I stepped forward. I was ready for our picnic. I'd already decided that we would eat at the cottonwoods near the stream. As always, Atacar had his rifle with him. He was never far from his gun.

As we headed to our destination, I fantasized that he was courting me. That he'd come calling, and I'd invited him on an outing. Of course, if I were living with my parents, Mama would've insisted on a chaperone. She never would've allowed me to be alone with him. I smiled to myself. I was grateful to be living with Nanny. She'd permitted me to have sex with him.

"If someone crosses our path, we should try to hide," he said, interrupting my thoughts. "But if we can't and they recognize me, I'll have to raise my rifle, and you'll have to tell them what we agreed upon."

"That you're forcing your company on me." I wondered how that would fare in a picnic setting. I paused to look more closely at him. "With the hat, you could pass for Mexican. Especially if you keep your head down and shield most of your features." I created a story. "If we are seen, I could say that your name is Juan, and you're my new farmhand." At least the farmhand part was true, I thought. "I could tell them that you showed up at my door, looking for work. You speak Spanish, don't you?"

"As well as I speak English." He considered my plan, then sent me a cheeky grin. "You could say that you brought Juan along on your picnic to keep you safe from renegade Indians."

I scolded him. "That's not funny."

"Yes, it is." His grin broadened, and we both laughed.

Silence befell us for a moment after that. Everything we did was a risk. In the quiet, I studied him. His skin was dark, but sometimes he behaved the way a white man would. Atacar knew Anglo customs well. I imagined he knew how to behave in a Mexican manner, too. At one time, the Apache had warred with the Mexicans, just as they'd warred with the whites. But those battles were over now.

"*My plan has merit,*" *I said.*

"*It does,*" *he agreed.* "*But we still need to be cautious.*"

We arrived at the cottonwoods and spread the blanket in the copse where we'd first touched and kissed. I set up the picnic, and we settled in to eat.

"*Why did you enlist as a scout?*" *I asked, handing him some chicken.*

"*In the beginning, we helped the army fight our enemies. It elevated my status as a warrior.*" *He bit into the meat, chewed, and swallowed.* "*It allowed me to have a horse and a gun. We didn't have those things anymore.*"

"*Because you were confined on a reservation?*"

"*Yes. Later, when the army started using us to track our own people, we were sometimes called traitors.*"

By his own people, I knew he meant the Chiricahua Apache who'd been considered hostiles.

He continued. "*I was loyal to the army. But in the end, it was futile. They held all of us accountable for Goyathlay and his followers. Geronimo,*" *he clarified when I gave him a blank stare.*

Ah, I thought. The infamous Geronimo. I noticed that Atacar spoke his name with respect. Maybe it was because Geronimo had eluded capture for so long. Or maybe because he'd fought so hard for what he believed in.

"*We've been prisoners of war for nine years,*" *Atacar said.* "*The government continues to make promises they don't keep.*"

"*Nine years?*" *I shook my head, understanding why he'd chosen to escape and wondering how much longer his tribe would remain in military custody.*

He changed the subject, clearly uncomfortable with his memories, with the choices he'd made. "Tell me about your life. Before you came to America."

"It was difficult," I admitted. "I'm from an upper-class family, and they put a lot of restrictions on me."

"You misbehaved?"

"Every chance I got." I nibbled playfully on my chicken, lightening his mood and making him smile. He knew how easily I misbehaved. "I convinced my parents to send me to Paris to study art, and then I took up with a bohemian crowd. That mortified them."

"What is bohemian?" he asked.

"Impoverished and marginalized artists who live nontraditional lifestyles."

"They are improper?"

"Yes. Quite so. I learned about sex from my bohemian friends."

Like the man he was, Atacar disputed my claim. He wanted responsibility for my lustful ways. "You learned about sex from me."

"True. But I already knew what was what." I gestured to my skirt. "When you lick me down there, it's called cunnilingus." I paused, making sure he was watching every move I made. "And if I were to suck you . . ." I let my words drift, right along with my gaze. By now, I was looking at the front of his pants. "It would be called fellatio."

He stopped eating. I'd actually shocked him. As bold as I was, he hadn't expected me to talk about sucking cock, at least not at a picnic.

I continued. "I've heard the taste of man's seed is salty." I steadied my gaze. "I like salty flavors."

123

"Don't tempt me," he said. "Not here."

"Why not here? We're surrounded by trees." I popped some cake into my mouth. "I want to learn how to do it."

Atacar made a strangled sound. "Not here," he reiterated.

"You put your fingers inside me here. We rolled around in the leaves." I pointed. "Right over there."

He cursed in English. He didn't repeat the vulgarity in the other languages he spoke, but he didn't need to. His arousal was evident.

"You're wicked," he said.

"I'm trying to be." I was teasing him, playing a game. He was right about not having oral copulation at this location. We needed to stay on guard, to be aware of our surroundings. But it was fun to fantasize.

He caught on to my game. He bit back a smile and handed me more cake. I refused to eat it. I drank some water instead, pretending to cleanse my palate, to prepare for the taste of his cock. "I want something salty."

He rifled through the basket, searching for the right food to satisfy me. He found pretzels Nanny had baked and salted, using a recipe she'd acquired from an neighbor. She enjoyed knotting the dough, and they kept well as a snack or meal accompaniment. But nonetheless, I shook my head no.

He continued looking and came up with a pair of pickles. He analyzed them.

"Those aren't salty," I said.

"No, but you can suck on them." He extended the largest of the two. Its length and girth was impressive—for a pickle. "Try this one."

I burst out laughing. He had a diabolical sense of humor. He laughed with me for the second time that day. I would miss him terribly when he was gone.

I stopped laughing. I missed him already.

"What's wrong?" he asked.

"Nothing," I lied.

"We can be together later," he told me.

"You'll teach me to perform fellatio tonight?" I asked, focusing on sex, even though we both knew there was more between us than carnal urges. "When we're in bed?"

He drew a rough breath. "Yes."

"Will you hold me afterward?"

"Always," he responded. "For as long as I can."

CHAPTER NINE

At our sleeping hour, I donned a white nightgown with an eyelet collar and ruffled hem, and Atacar stripped down to his skin. I longed for the sensation of being clothed while he was naked, and he didn't deny my request.

My heart thudded wildly. His penis was already hard, and I hadn't even touched him. We smiled at each other, and he moved forward to kiss me, to put his lips softly against mine.

Anxious to begin my fellatio lesson, I ended our kiss and got to my knees. I was close enough to inhale his musky scent, so I breathed him in. He didn't indicate that I should suck him right away. Instead, he allowed me a visual exploration, where I studied the bulbous head, the slit at the tip, and the heavily veined shaft that comprised his cock. I gazed at his testicles, as well. To me, they were a powerful testimony to his manhood, the place where his seed was stored.

Curious, I darted my tongue and tasted each sac. Growing

bolder, I got far enough below him to lick the seam of skin between his genitals and his buttocks. He shivered when I did that, and I knew I'd struck a highly sensitive spot. Finally, I lapped at his cock, swirling my tongue over the head.

He put his hands in my unbound hair, twining the long strands between his fingers. Then he ordered me onto the bed so he could kneel over my face. I followed his lead, aroused by his aggressiveness, by his desire to control me.

Once we were in bed, I did what I always did when we were together. I imagined how we looked, me in my flowing nightgown and him completely naked, wielding his erection over me.

I opened my mouth and took him inch by inch. I was careful not to graze him with my teeth. He watched me with divine interest and told me to take more. I gripped the base to give myself better leverage and took as much as I could.

But it wasn't enough for him. He pushed deeper. I actually felt him jabbing the back of my throat.

For an instant, I was stunned. I hadn't expected to fit all of him into my mouth, but he'd just proved that it was possible. His lesson was rough and sensual, and it aroused me.

I sucked him in earnest, sliding my lips up and down. I worked hard, bobbing my head with each motion.

After I gave myself a moment's rest, Atacar rolled over onto his back and opened his legs, encouraging me to pleasure him in that position, too.

Flushed with excitement, I crawled between his thighs and resumed his oral stimulation. He moved with me, pumping his hips in a steady rhythm.

He leaned forward and caressed my face. His touch was warm

and tender, but it was carnal, too. He withdrew so I could lick his testicles and the sensitive seam I'd tasted earlier. He admitted that I was the first woman who'd dared put her mouth there.

Feeling deliciously decadent, I returned my attention to his cock. I used my hands, stroking while I sucked. He groaned his hunger, and I triumphed even more. I wanted to bring him to completion. Already I could taste a few beads of ejaculate seeping from the tip. It was as salty as I'd imagined. I had no idea how much would spill out when he climaxed, but I was prepared to take what he gave me.

Reveling in my own wickedness, I squirmed naughtily against the bed. If a pillow had been handy, I would've tucked it beneath my legs and pressed down on it. I was bare beneath my nightgown.

Atacar groaned again, deeper this time. His entire chest rumbled, making me keenly aware of his pending orgasm. As his body continued to tighten, as his stomach muscles clenched, I did my best to keep my jaw and throat relaxed. His hands were in my hair again, tunneling hard and fast.

His groan turned to a growl. He lifted his buttocks and fisted my scalp. Within seconds, his seed shot out like lava issuing from a volcano.

Atacar watched me, his gaze fixed on my semen-filled mouth. I swallowed as quickly as I could. I didn't want to miss a drop. I was thrilled that he couldn't seem to take his eyes off me.

I waited, giving him time to breathe. Then I sat up and smiled. He smiled, too.

"You're a fast learner," he said.

I ran my tongue across my lips. I could still taste him. "I've always been a good student."

He pulled me down on top of him, and we rolled over the bed. He tickled me, and I laughed.

"The man who marries you will be lucky," he said.

We were still playing, still wrestling like children. "Because I enjoy sex?"

"And because you're smart and witty and beautiful."

His words made me dreamy, but I didn't want to give myself away. "I'm a deplorable cook. And I can barely sew a straight stitch."

He winged his eyebrows. "Then why did you offer to make me new clothes?"

"Nanny is going to help me. Without her, I couldn't have made the offer."

"A man will still be lucky to have you." He tickled me again. "As long as Nanny is part of the bargain."

I pinched him, and he grinned. He had the most dashing smile. It made the expression in his eyes dance.

The lamp flickered, shadowing the room in a ghostly fashion, and we stopped teasing each other. Our emotions turned serious.

He looped his arms around my waist, bringing me close to his chest, where his heart pattered next to mine.

A few raven black strands of his hair fell across his forehead. His hair wasn't long, but it wasn't short, either. He wore it chopped to a medium length. I reached up to run my hands through it.

"Tell me about the status of your family," I said, wondering if he'd left anyone behind at Fort Sill. "Are your parents still living?"

"No. But I have a sister. She is married with a baby daughter. I love my niece dearly. My sister and brother-in-law, too. But I couldn't stay at the fort."

Because he needed to be free, I thought. "What's it like?"

"It's far better than what we endured in Florida. Many became ill and died there. My parents were among them." He paused a moment before he continued. "It's better than the post in Alabama, too. At Fort Sill, there are mountains, not as big as our homeland, but the soil is good. The first winter was harsh, but sod has been broken for planting now, and a cattle herd is under way."

"To help your people become self-sufficient?"

"Yes. But we're still at the mercy of the War Department." Atacar kept his arms around me. "I tried to escape once before."

My pulse jumped. "When?"

"Toward the end of our stay in Alabama, when I labored at a farm outside the post. But I was captured and brought back."

I inhaled a sharp breath. Had he been punished for running away? If so, it hadn't deterred him from making another attempt.

"My sister begged me not to escape again," he said. "She wanted me to remain in Oklahoma Territory. To comply with our new life there."

But he didn't, and now he was here with me. "I have a brother." I pictured my tall, trim, fair-haired sibling, impeccably groomed and gallantly spoken. "He begged me to comply, too. With the rules of society."

"But you turned bohemian instead."

"Yes." Seductress that I was, I rubbed against my lover. "I most certainly did."

"Maybe I am bohemian, too." His voice went rough. "From your bewitching."

"Maybe you are."

"And maybe you are in need of your turn."

131

I shuddered. I understood what he meant. I'd sucked him, and now he was going to lick me.

He raised my nightgown and bunched the fabric around my waist. I watched him lower his head, captivated by his exploration. I parted my thighs, letting him play sweet havoc with my clitoris. He kissed me down there, circling the bud of my womanhood with his tongue.

I asked him if he liked my cunt, if he thought it was pretty. I knew that he did, but I wanted to say something provocative.

He responded in an erotic whisper, the words warm against my skin. Yes, yes, he liked it. He liked my yellow curls, my delicate pink folds, my creamy moisture.

He behaved as if I were his favorite dessert, devouring me with his entire mouth. He laved my juices, and I nearly flew off the bed. He knew how much I loved cunnilingus. He knew it drove me mad.

I couldn't hold still. I rocked back and forth, clenching my bottom and thrusting my hips toward him. He continued to ravish me, making my slit wetter than it already was.

With my hair strewn across a pillow and my nightgown twisting beneath me, I climaxed.

In the moments that followed, he gave me one last, lingering lick, then righted my ruffled hem, smoothing it over my legs and down my ankles. I sighed my sheer and utter contentment.

"Next time we'll do it at the same time," he said.

I knew he was talking about mutual oral copulation, where the pleasure was simultaneous. I'd heard of it, of course. Intrigued, I envisioned us in that highly naughty position, certain I would like it. "I'm eager to do everything with you."

"Me, too. With you. But for now, we should sleep."

I agreed. I was sated, and so was he.

He extinguished the lamp, and we snuggled, the front of his body pressed against the back of mine. I closed my eyes, and he slipped his arms around my waist, holding me for the rest of the night.

~

Jared didn't know how long he was supposed to hold Mandy. Were they supposed to sleep in each other's arms? That wasn't his style. When he spent the night with a woman, he banged her brains out, then rolled over onto his side of the bed. Of course, he and Mandy had already had sex tonight. They'd gotten hot and heavy in the garden, and she'd given him head in the limo. This wasn't a booty call. Yet here they were at her front door.

After they entered the condo, he analyzed himself. What the hell was wrong with him that he couldn't hold a woman without panicking? That he didn't know how to give or receive affection? That he was so damned detached?

What indeed? How about an abusive father? And a mother he barely remembered? That was classic Freud, right? Psych 101 all the way.

"Do you want a nightcap?" Mandy asked, as they stood awkwardly in her living room.

"Okay." He figured a drink might help. Maybe she figured that, too. "What do you have?"

"How about some brandy?"

"That sounds good."

She went into the kitchen and opened a cabinet, where she

kept her liquor. He could see her from his vantage point. Her condo had an open floor plan.

She returned with two snifters of brandy. He thanked her and took a sip. She lifted her glass to her lips, too. Neither of them could think of anything to say, but at least the brandy hit the spot.

She finally spoke. "Are you tired?"

"Are you?" he responded.

She nodded. "Yes, but I probably won't fall asleep right away."

Which meant what? That they were going to lie in bed, cozy as you please, stumbling through a conversation? Freud be damned. He wished he'd never agreed to do this.

They finished their brandy, and she put their glasses in the sink.

"I'm going to take a bath," she said.

He noticed that she didn't invite him to join her, but it was just as well. He assumed that she wanted to do the girly thing and use the scented products she kept on the side of her tub.

"Will you undo me?" she asked.

"No problem."

He helped with the hooks on her dress, and she left him in the living room. Uncertain of what else to do, he sat on the sofa, turned on the TV, and flipped the remote control. If he thought he could bail out on his promise without hurting Mandy's feelings, he would head straight out the door. But he couldn't, so he watched a late-night talk show and waited for her.

Twenty minutes later, she reappeared, looking soft and clean and fresh. Her face was scrubbed free of cosmetics, and she wore a lace-trimmed nightshirt in an angelic shade of blue.

"The bathroom is free if you need it," she said.

"Thanks." Jared turned off the TV. He kept extra toiletries at her house. He had a few extra clothes hanging in her closet, too. He'd stayed over plenty of times. But tonight was different, and they both knew it.

He washed his face and brushed his teeth. When he entered Mandy's bedroom, he stripped down to his boxers. She was already in bed and had left a night-light burning.

He got under the covers. She moved closer, and they faced each other, but he didn't reach for her. It was too soon to cuddle. He needed time to ease into it.

He complimented her instead. "You smell good."

"It's a Hawaiian orchid body wash. I used the same lotion, too." She angled her head, making her pretty brown hair sweep the side of her face. "Do you know what orchids mean?"

"In Hawaiian? I have no idea."

"I meant in the Victorian language of flowers."

"Oh, that." He wondered if he should admit that he knew the answer, that he'd studied the language of flowers far more than he'd let on.

She waited for his response, gazing directly at him, and he realized that he couldn't avoid her question.

"There are different meanings," he said.

"Like what?"

"Luxury. Beauty. Lust." He gave a pause. "Love." He hesitated again. "It depends on what source you use."

Her gaze remained riveted to his. "I'm going to have to learn that language. It's fascinating."

"It is." He hedged, thinking about Catherine and Atacar, about the couple who'd lived and loved and lost. "Not that I'm an expert."

"You seem pretty good at it to me." She waited a beat, as if she were gathering her thoughts, her emotions. "You really are a blue rose, Jared. Full of mystery." She studied him with affection, with tenderness, with awe. "So, are you from Oklahoma?"

"Yes." Her attention made him uncomfortable. He wasn't used to this kind of intimacy. The Freud factor, he thought. In the past he'd avoided women like her, women who cared, who made men weak, who stripped them of their machismo.

"What about the accent?" she asked, questioning him further.

"I used to talk like that." But over the years he'd purposely rid his voice of the Southern inflection, determined to become someone new. He'd only incorporated it into the party charade to fool Mandy. "I moved here when I was eighteen."

"With your family or by yourself?"

"By myself." He gave her a condensed version. It was the best he could do. "My parents were divorced when I was a baby, but my mom died when I was seven, so I don't remember her very well. After that, I went to live with my dad."

She seemed to sense what was coming. "Did he treat you badly?"

"He used to push me around and tell me how worthless I was. But he quit doing that when I got big enough to fight back." Jared glanced at his hands. How many times during his teenage years had he balled them into knuckle-scraping fists, had he stood toe-to-toe with his dad?

Mandy looked as if she was going to wrap her arms around him, but he tensed his shoulders, letting her know that he didn't want that kind of solace. When they cuddled, it would be for her, not for him.

She didn't do it, so he relaxed a little and continued. "Dad resented having to raise a kid by himself. It didn't matter that I was *his* kid. That I looked like him. That I fell into his footsteps and started working with horses. That I was really good at it."

"Does your mom have any family left?" she asked. "Is there anyone from her side that you're close to?"

"No. She was an only child, and her parents were already gone before I was born."

"Was Atacar her ancestor? Are you related to him through her?"

"Yes." Jared blew out the breath he'd been holding. "And that was always a point of contention with my old man. A jealousy thing, I guess. He said Atacar's portrait didn't mean anything. That it wasn't important. But it was to me."

"So you moved here when you were eighteen, got embraced by the art world, and found success in the horse industry."

"All of that didn't happen overnight, but yes, that about sums it up."

She leaned on her side, watching him in that tender way of hers. Apparently she wasn't ready for their conversation to end. "How did your mother die?"

"It was a car accident." Most of his memories were vague, but he recalled that day vividly, as if it were a video that looped in his mind. "She was supposed to pick me up from school, but she never made it. I waited in the principal's office. They gave me crayons or a puzzle or something to play with, but it didn't help. I was scared, and I wanted my mommy. She'd never been late before. The administration didn't know what was going on, either. Not until the hospital called."

Mandy didn't keep her gentle hands to herself. She tried to console him, skimming her fingers along his cheek, his jaw, the tendons in his neck. "Do you have anything of your mother's? Any kind of keepsake?"

His throat went tight, and he pulled back, making her drop her hand.

Finally he responded, "I used to have this trinket-type box that belonged to her, but I broke it about six months ago."

"Was it made of glass?"

"No. It was made of wood, but it was really old. It had been in her family for generations. After she died, Dad gave it to me." Another vivid memory, Jared thought. Funny how the painful ones were the most clear. "He was packing up Mom's stuff for the Goodwill, and I was crying. He turned around and thrust the box at me. Then he explained that it was special to her, and she probably would've wanted me to have it. After that, he told me to shut up, to never cry again. I stopped bawling and clutched the box like my life depended on it."

Mandy made a troubled face, as if she wanted to console him again.

He kept talking. "When I was little, I kept my favorite Hot Wheels in it. When I got older, I used it as a men's valet, for my wallet, keys, extra coin."

"How did you break it?"

"I was reaching for something on my nightstand and knocked it over. The box hit the floor, and the bottom of it splintered and cracked."

"Did you try to repair it?"

"No."

"Why not?"

"I just didn't."

"Maybe it was subconscious. Your way of telling yourself that you couldn't bring your mother back."

The tightness in his throat returned. It was more than that. Breaking the box had changed his life, but he couldn't reveal that part of the story. Because that was how he'd found Catherine's journal.

By chance. By accident.

Or had it been fate? The journal had been sealed into a secret compartment, and there was no way to open that portion, short of breaking it.

Apparently his mom hadn't known of its existence, either. Once he'd read the journal, he'd discovered that the book had been there since the nineteenth century, since friends of Catherine's had put it there.

"I wish for your sake that your mother hadn't passed away," Mandy said. "That things would have turned out differently for you."

He didn't respond, and she added, "I understand why you moved to Santa Fe. Why you needed to be near Atacar."

Jared frowned. "You make him sound as if he's still alive."

"Sometimes when I look into his eyes, it seems as if he's looking back at me, as if he's inside Catherine's painting. Sometimes he gives me chills."

Jared was getting chilled right now. Atacar had been worried about Catherine capturing his soul.

"I hope I can find her journal," Mandy said. "That it's out there somewhere."

He protected his lie, repeating what he'd been telling her all along. "I don't think it exists."

She disagreed. "Look how the painting was found. Hidden inside the walls of the farmhouse where Catherine lived."

"That doesn't mean the journal was hidden, too." Jared had read it hundreds of times since he'd found it. He knew almost every word by heart. But he wasn't keeping it a secret for himself. Someone in England had asked him not to make Catherine's writings public.

"I'd rather cling to the hope that it was hidden. That it's in a spot no one has discovered yet."

Too late, he thought. "You should stop looking."

"I'm not giving up until I know for sure. Until Kiki exhausts her research. I've got her working on it. You know how important Catherine and Atacar are to me, to the museum."

They were important to him, too. More than he could possibly say. He changed the subject. "It's getting late. We should get some sleep."

Before she could protest, he turned out the light, and as darkness pitched the room, he realized that he still hadn't snuggled with her. That he hadn't kept his promise.

Shit.

His anxiety kicked up again. He could tell that Mandy was waiting, hoping he would come through.

So he sucked in a shallow breath and did it. He pressed the front of his body to the back of hers and put his arms around her waist.

An instant smile sounded in her voice. She even sighed. "This is nice."

He nuzzled her hair. It smelled as good as the rest of her. But that didn't calm his nerves. "I'm glad you think so, but don't get used to it. I'm not doing this every time I spend the night with you."

She got sweetly bossy. "Yes, you are."

"Listen to you. The dominant woman."

She laughed and nudged him in the ribs. He laughed, too. At the absurdity of his situation. Of being afraid of a little affection.

He breathed her in again, all warm and scented, all floral and soft. "It's not that bad," he heard himself say. "But it'd be better if I was inside you. Cuddle fucking. That sounds good, doesn't it?"

Another nudge. Another laugh. "Not on your life, buster. You're not using sex to get out of this."

"Buster?" He pinned her arms, teasing her right back. Sex was what he knew, what he did.

She wiggled. She squirmed. She played his silly game. But within minutes, they quit goofing around. So he did the best he could, mimicking what he'd read in Catherine's journal. He closed his eyes and held Mandy as close as he possibly could.

The way Atacar used to hold Catherine.

CHAPTER TEN

Mandy awakened to the aroma of fried food, then sat up and hugged her knees to her chest. She needed to give herself a moment to get her bearings. Jared was cooking for her? On a Sunday morning after they'd cuddled all night?

Before she got too giddy, she went into the bathroom and freshened up. Still in her nightshirt, she padded to the kitchen and stood in the entryway.

Yep. There he was, looking like a hunk-of-burning-Elvis-song love. Chest bare, jeans slung low on his hips, and hair in a ponytail, he manned a pan at the stove.

He noticed her right off. He turned and smiled. She told her runaway heart to behave. So he'd held her tenderly in the dark. So he was fixing her something to eat in the light. That didn't mean she should fall at his feet.

"What are you making?" she asked.

"Fry bread. I figured the smell would wake you."

"It did." She came forward. She was familiar with fry bread. She'd eaten it on a couple of occasions and had loved it. You couldn't live in the Southwest and not know that it was an American Indian staple served at powwows and selective restaurants. "I had the ingredients?"

He turned the disk-shaped dough, frying the other side to a golden brown. "It's a simple recipe. Flour, baking powder, salt, water, oil." He teased her with a playful wink. "Lots of calories. From me to you."

"Please, fatten me all you want." Mandy gazed at the greasy treat, and he removed it from the fire and put it on a paper-towel-lined plate to absorb the oil. Traditionally fry bread was topped with honey, powdered sugar, or taco fixings.

"I'll get the honey." She rummaged through the cabinet. "I might even have a box of powdered sugar that's been gathering dust."

She found both items, and he finished frying the rest of the dough. By the time he was done, he'd made enough to feed a tribe.

Unable to help herself, she grabbed him and kissed him. But not lightly. She planted a hard, head-spinning lip-lock right on him.

"Damn." He caught his breath. "What was that for?"

"The food." The kiss was for holding her last night, too. But she wasn't about to admit it. Her heart was misbehaving again.

She stepped back and noticed that he'd made a pot of coffee. She could've kissed him for that, as well. She poured a cup and doctored it with her favorite creamer.

"Ready?" he asked.

"Absolutely." For her this was like eating donuts in the morning, something she rarely did.

Jared set the glass-topped table, and they sat down to scarf. He sprinkled powdered sugar on his fry bread, then drizzled honey over it.

She watched him. "You're using both toppings?"

"Damn straight. The sweeter, the messier, the gooier, the better."

What the heck. Mandy tried it that way too, moaning when she took her first bite. The flavor melted in her mouth. "Can you cook anything else?"

"I grill a mean steak."

"We'll have to barbecue sometime."

He lifted his eyebrows. "Like a real couple?"

"Why not?" She let herself dream. "We could do it tonight. On my patio with citronella candles and a bottle of sparkling wine."

"I think maybe we should concentrate on one meal at a time, especially since I'm going to jump your bones after we're done with breakfast."

She met his calculating gaze. He wasn't kidding. He had a hungry look in his eyes that had nothing to do with food.

"To make up for not getting cuddle fucked last night?" she asked.

"Yep. Sweet, sticky, oral sex." He let her know exactly what he had in mind. "Right here in your kitchen."

The promise of decadent pleasure blasted through her body. This time she wasn't about to deny him. Or herself. She shifted in her chair, her pulse beating between her legs. "Can I pour honey down the front of your pants?"

He sent her a lethal smile. "As long as I can do it to you. Inside your pretty little panties," he added, reminding her that she was sitting there in a lace-trimmed nightshirt and matching underwear.

Eager, Mandy reached for another piece of fry bread and drenched it with the substance in question. "Do real couples have sex as much as we do?"

"How would I know? I've never been in a real relationship." He went for seconds, too. "You're the one who was married."

Mandy stopped eating. He was looking at her as if he expected her to discuss her marriage and divorce, to give him the lousy details before he dragged her onto the floor and oral sexed her to death.

"Fair is fair," he said.

She fought to stay focused. "What?"

"I sold my soul to you last night. It's only right that you sell yours to me today. Do you know how difficult it was for me to tell you that crap about myself?"

She nodded. The pain was still there, deep and dark within his psyche. She couldn't imagine losing your mother at such a young age, only to have your bastard of a father resent you for it.

"So?" he said, pressing her to open up to him.

She did, knowing that she had little choice. "My husband should have been my best friend, but he wasn't. We were married for fifteen years and got nothing out of it. Meals in front of the TV, average sex, work-related conversations." She fussed with her coffee, clanking the cup against the table. "We took vacations when we could arrange our schedules accordingly, but even that was dull. Empty," she clarified, using a more fitting description.

Jared squinted at her. "Was it more exciting when you were dating?"

"Not really."

"Then why did you marry him?"

"Because that's what good girls from Iowa do. They marry their college sweethearts and tell themselves that a diamond ring and a big church wedding will make a difference."

He ignored the ring and vow. "You're from Iowa?" The lethal smile returned, brimming with mischief. "I'm banging a farm girl?"

"I wasn't raised on a farm." She balled up a paper napkin and tossed it at him, hitting him square in the chest and making his grin widen.

"Damn. Spoil my fantasy, why don't you? I was picturing you as a milkmaid. All cute and corn-fed, with your boobs spilling out of a gingham dress and your hair in pigtails."

She sent another balled-up napkin flying. He laughed, and she broke down and laughed, too.

"I used to shop at the Piggly Wiggly," she said. "Does that count?"

"Sure. Why not?" He sat back in his chair, serious again. "What's your ex-husband's name?"

"Ken. Kenny, when we first got together."

"What does he do?"

"He's an audit manager. He has a degree in finance. And his career always came first. Every time we relocated, it was for him. Not that I couldn't find curator positions in the cities he chose, but do you know how many years I wanted to move to Santa Fe? This is my dream town, where I wanted to be."

"Did you come here after you got divorced?"

"Yes. Ken is still in Seattle. That's the last place we lived." Mandy looked across the table at her lover. The sun shone through the window, highlighting the bluish black streaks in his hair. "I'm not saying that I was a perfect wife. When a relationship fails, it's rarely one-sided."

"Did either of you cheat?"

"No. But I don't know why we hung on to our marriage for so long. Maybe it was the nonquitters in us. Or maybe we just got used to the rut we were in."

"Did you ever want to pour something sweet and sticky down the front of his pants? Did you ever fantasize about anything like that?"

Her heart struck her chest. Trust Jared to throw her off-kilter, to shift gears without warning. "No."

"But you want to do it to me?"

"Yes." Just like that, she got blatantly aroused. She even spread her thighs to combat the heat.

He left his chair and stood beside hers. "Because I turned you into a bad girl?"

"Yes," she said again, as he unbuttoned his jeans.

She got up, and with a snap of his wrist, he tugged the waistband of his boxers away from his skin, giving her the opportunity to seize the honey. Like a woman possessed, she gripped the plastic bottle and squirted the syrupy liquid into the opening he'd provided. She aimed for his cock and balls, but some of it clung to his pubic hair.

Whatever the case, he seemed to thrive on the sensation, on watching her do it. He sucked in his breath, and the ripple of muscle along his abs vibrated. She decided to blast some honey there, too. And all over his chest, coating his flat brown nipples.

"Damn." He inhaled another shuddering breath. "You're a girl on a mission."

"Yes, I am." She reached for the powdered sugar box.

"Shit," he said, even though he seemed more than willing to be her dessert, as long she was going to be his. "You're next, Multiorgasmic Mandy."

"I know." She dusted his chest and stomach with sugar, and it stuck to the honey. He was still wearing his jeans and boxers. "Take those off."

He peeled them down. His pierced cock sprang free, fully aroused and scrumptiously sticky. She sprinkled a light coating of sugar on it.

She glanced up at his face, and he went full-bore, dragging her nightshirt over her head. She held her panties open for him, and he grabbed the honey. Because she was waxed and her Brazilian only left a landing strip of hair, he was able to hit his mark easily, drenching her nether lips.

"Feel good?" he asked.

She nodded, dizzy on her feet, the sticky sensation ratcheting higher. By now, he was aiming a stream of the gooey substance toward the hood of her clit. She pulled open the waistband of her panties even wider, giving him as much room as he needed.

"We're going to sixty-nine," he said. "Then we're going to fuck in the shower."

He lifted the container and shot some honey across her nipples and down her stomach. The powdered sugar came next, and she relished every tantalizing second of their insane foreplay.

He removed her panties and tugged her down. He stretched onto the cool, tiled floor, and she straddled his face and lowered her head.

Their bodies stuck together like glue. He laved the sweetness between her legs, and she sucked him. He tasted like the topping on the fry bread, only better. Her Jared. Her addiction. She couldn't take all of him from this position, but she took enough to make him moan, right against her clit.

No matter how hard they tried, they couldn't eat each other clean. A warm, slick residue remained.

Mandy rubbed against him, glorifying in the swirl of his tongue. There was hunger in his touch, but reverence, too. Jared kissed and licked her silken folds, sweeping her into a delicious frenzy.

She couldn't imagine a more erotic setting. Here they were on her kitchen floor, painted in honey and dusted in sugar. Lovers without boundaries, she thought.

Animalistic. Beautifully wild.

With her senses spinning in prismatic colors, she climaxed, rocking back and forth. In the midst of her spasms, she did her damnedest to stroke him, to bring him to fruition, but he didn't come. He pulled away before it happened, saving his release for the shower.

He scooped her up and carried her to the bathroom. Thoroughly enthralled with their affair, with the way he made everything so passionate, she clung to him.

He put her on her feet, turned the spigot, and adjusted the nozzle. They stepped into the tub, water falling like rain. He kissed her, long and slow, then stepped back, preparing to shower, to get rid of the gooiness so he could fuck her nice and clean. She noticed that his big, gorgeous cock was still hard. She handed him a bottle of body wash.

"This isn't the orchid stuff, is it?" he asked.

She smiled, shook her head. "It's ginseng."

He took a whiff, then decided it smelled okay for a guy to use. She watched him pour a dollop into his hand and lather his long, muscular body.

She washed, too. But she couldn't look away from her lover. He consumed her. "Why haven't you ever touched yourself for me?"

He rubbed liquid soap over his chest and down his stomach. "Because you've never asked me to."

"You'd do it if I asked?"

"Yes, but not right now." He scrubbed his pubic hair and moved on to his cock and balls, then took her hand and made her wash him.

She pumped his soapy penis, and they kissed again. Steam filled the tub and floated over the shower curtain. Sharing the spray of water, they rinsed their hot, naked bodies.

He spun her around and pressed her against the wall. She widened her stance, knowing he was going to enter her this way. He cupped her breasts and caressed them, tweaking her nipples and making them ache. She moaned and waited for his cock, her sex soft and slick and swollen.

He went for the kill, swooping like a predator and thrusting so hard, so deep, rough, she gasped and begged for more. She even rasped, "Please, please . . ."

"Please, please . . . what?" he echoed in her ear.

"Do it harder."

He worked her like a jackhammer, and the power-tool motion was nearly her undoing. Her hips vibrated. Her boobs bounced. Her teeth rattled. She put her hands flat against the wall to hold herself up.

"Think about something dirty," he said. "Fantasize while I'm fucking you."

"I—"

"Do it," he commanded. "Use that naughty imagination of yours."

She closed her eyes and felt a rush of excitement.

"Are you doing it?"

"Yes."

"That's my girl," he praised, feeding the fire. "Now tell me what it is."

The excitement spiraled, hurtled, broke free. "I'm asleep in bed and you come into my room. You whisper my name, and I wake up. You turn on the light. It's bright, and I squint at you, my heart pounding in my chest. You start undressing me, taking off my pajamas and my panties. You strip me bare, and I lie there, wondering what you're going to do to me."

He thrust deeper, waiting for her to continue.

"You take off your clothes, too," she said, picturing the scenario in her head. "And then you kneel over my face."

"Damn." Jared pushed her harder against the wall. "Am I going to jack off?"

"Yes, but you don't use any lubricant. Nothing except saliva. You lick the palm of your hand."

"Then what?"

"You grip your cock and stroke yourself. From shaft to tip. Up and down, strong and hard. No man has ever masturbated for me before, and watching you fascinates me. I like that you're doing it so close to my face. But it's not enough. I want more. I want to put my mouth on you while you're doing it."

His voice all but vibrated. "Do I move closer?"

"You move close enough for me to lick whatever part of you I can reach. My tongue is everywhere. All over you."

"Fuck."

He sounded so aroused, so excited by her story, he could barely breathe. But he didn't come. He slowed his thrusts, pacing himself inside her. She could feel him, making her inner walls contract.

"While I'm licking you, you keep stroking yourself, getting off on what I'm doing." She paused to absorb the details. She didn't know that this was her naughty-girl fantasy, but it was. Heaven help her, it was. "You taste so hot and sexy, I can't get enough."

"How long do you lick me?"

"Long enough to drive you crazy."

"I'm already crazy. Fucking certifiable. You've got to tell me more."

"I will. Just give me a minute." She held on to the shower wall, hands fanned, fingers spread. She was getting certifiable, too.

Impatient, he withdrew and spun her around so they were face-to-face.

Suddenly Mandy went horribly, terribly shy. She didn't want him looking at her while she spun her sexual tale, while her imagination clawed its way to her cunt.

"Tell me the rest. I want to know how it ends."

Her face flushed, but there was so much steam, so much moisture, her skin was probably pink already. "I don't know. I—"

"You know, damn it. It's your fantasy."

She tried to think, to concentrate. His gaze was locked directly on hers.

He dragged her onto the tub floor and thrust into her again. "Come on, baby, tell me what I want to hear. Tell me what happens next."

She gripped the sides of the tub. The water was still running, and her bottom was sliding against the surface as he fucked her.

"By now your cock is leaking," she said, her shyness fading, her hunger burgeoning. "With beads of pre-come. So you rub it against my mouth and let me taste it."

He rocked back and forth, sloshing the water, intensifying the sex. "Am I close to coming for real?"

"Yes, and so am I. I reach down and stroke my clit. I can't help it. I need some relief."

His breathing went labored.

Mandy wrapped her legs around him, making him plunge deeper. "We masturbate together. Then you move down and position yourself over my tits."

"So I can splash your nipples?"

"Yes. And when it happens, it feels so good, so milky and warm that I rub it all over, across my breasts, down my stomach, and deep between my thighs. I use it like lotion."

Jared gave up the fight. He grabbed a handful of her wet hair, tangled it around his fingers, and kissed her. As their tongues collided, he spilled into her. The force of his orgasm triggered hers, and she shuddered through an equally desperate climax.

Seconds ticked by. Then minutes. But neither of them moved. He was still inside her, and she was still clutched around his waist.

Finally he helped her up, and they turned off the water. He wrapped her in a towel, and she nearly stumbled in his arms, reeling from the erotic aftermath. He held her a little tighter, promising that on one of these long, hot summer nights, he would mirror her imagination.

And make her fantasy come true.

CHAPTER ELEVEN

Mandy sat at one of the brightly colored patio tables in front of the museum, where a food vendor sold snacks and sodas. She sipped an Orange Crush and waited for Kiki to join her so they could discuss Kiki's research.

Alone with her briefcase at her feet, Mandy reflected on her surroundings. The Santa Fe Women's Art Museum was located within walking distance of the Plaza, a downtown area that served tourists with hundreds of gift shops and a host of restaurants and galleries.

In spite of its commercialism, Mandy loved the Plaza. Santa Fe meant "Holy Faith" in Spanish, and for her that epitomized the depth and beauty of this city. After her divorce, she'd come here to start a new life, to find faith in herself. In that regard, she and Jared were the same. He'd come here to start over, too.

She hadn't seen him since the morning after the masquerade. But it had only been a week. Besides, he'd invited her to have dinner at his house tomorrow. He'd offered to grill one of his mean steaks for her. Nothing could have pleased her more. Not that she wasn't anxious for him to fulfill her other fantasy, but she figured he was building the sexual tension, keeping her busy until he slipped into her room one unsuspecting night and made it happen.

Mandy glanced up and saw Kiki headed toward her. The historian's wavy red hair shimmered in the sun, and her gauzy dress billowed. She was a Santa Fe transplant, too.

"Sorry I'm late." Kiki sat beside her. As always, she'd accessorized with Southwestern jewelry. Today she wore a collection of coral, turquoise, and spiny oyster. "I got caught up at a last-minute meeting."

"That's okay. I was little late myself." Their workdays rarely ended on time, but they both loved what they did. They never complained. As for Kiki's research, Mandy made a pleading face. "Please, tell me you found the journal."

Kiki laughed. "Don't we wish it could be that easy? Still, I thought you might be interested in what I compiled on Catherine's nanny. Other historians have created files on her, but I'm hoping to make mine more complete. It might help us find the journal."

Mandy sat a little more upright. It was common knowledge that Catherine's nanny had moved to America with her, and that the other woman had probably been with her when she'd hidden Atacar's portrait and abandoned the farmhouse. But whatever had become of them after that was anybody's guess.

"In England she was known as Nanny Perkins," Kiki said. "But Catherine just called her Nanny."

"What was her full name?"

"Hattie Grace Perkins. Most nannies were from the lower classes, and she was no exception. She was a country girl who'd gone to London to seek employment. Staying on the family farm wasn't an option. Her family had too many mouths to feed."

Mandy tried to picture Hattie, to imagine what she looked like, but she couldn't get past Jared's lusty fantasy of a farm girl. Somehow she doubted that Hattie wore pigtails and too-tight gingham dresses. "Was Catherine her first charge?"

"No. She worked for other families before the Burkes hired her to look after their children. She was Catherine's older brother's nanny, too. But it was Catherine who captured her heart."

Mandy smiled. All of this made Catherine seem more real, more tangible. Mandy had seen pictures of Catherine in the museum's archives, and the artist always seemed to have an undeniable gleam in her eye, much like the mischief Jared sometimes got in his eyes. Who wouldn't be drawn to that type of charm?

Kiki continued. "No one else could handle Catherine, certainly not her parents, and not the string of governesses who came and went. Nanny was it for Catherine. They shared a special bond. I think it was because Nanny understood Catherine's wild streak."

Mandy could tell there was more to the story, so she sipped her soda and waited for Kiki to tell it.

"There were rumors that when Nanny was fresh off the farm, she'd had an affair with Thomas Boydell, a notorious London thief. Not only was he a thief, he was a social activist. Thomas robbed from the rich and gave generously to the poor, determined to improve the conditions of the city, to combat the poverty and filth."

Intrigued, Mandy leaned forward. "A nineteenth-century Robin Hood. He sounds sexy."

"Supposedly he was. Tall, dark, and dashing."

"What ever became of him?"

"He was killed in a mob riot. Nanny denied the allegation that they were involved, but supposedly she was never the same after he died. Part of her spirit floated away. Right into the muddy water of the Thames," Kiki added, putting her own spin on the British tale.

"Now I feel sad for her," Mandy said.

"I know. It's like Catherine and Atacar. What ever happened to happily ever after?"

"You're asking me?" Mandy pictured the wedding dress she'd preserved, then shucked; the ring she'd removed; the vows she shouldn't have recited.

Kiki had a ready answer. "At least you're dating a gorgeous guy who takes you to sex shops and masquerade parties."

"That's not synonymous with happily ever after."

"Who says Prince Charming can't buy his ladylove a dildo-making kit, wear a black mask, and bang her in someone else's garden?"

"I shouldn't have told you that stuff. Now you're being cynical."

"No, I'm not. I think he's turning out to be just what you need. Exciting, sensual, obscurely romantic."

The mere suggestion sent Mandy's pulse reeling. "He wasn't romantic in the beginning."

"Maybe not. But apparently he's trying to tap into that part of himself. And he's doing it for you."

Yes, Mandy thought, like the upcoming dinner at his house. But nonetheless, she countered Kiki's assessment of him. If she didn't, she was afraid she'd get too attached, that she'd let herself feel too much. Wanting him to hold her every night was bad enough. "You have no idea how emotionally guarded he is."

"Sounds like a match made in dysfunctional Heaven to me. You're guarded, too."

"Not like him." She thought about what his father had done to him. The damage that had been caused. "He hasn't been loved since he was seven, since the day his mother died."

"That pretty much says it all, doesn't it? The reason he turned into a bad boy. Bad boys are always tortured. If they weren't, they'd be corporate assholes like our ex-husbands."

"Now you really are being cynical."

"Sorry." Kiki flashed her signature grin. "I couldn't resist."

Caught in a gal-pal moment, they laughed. A moment later, they went reverently quiet, the city of Holy Faith shimmering around them. Soon the sun would be setting, painting desert hues across the sky.

"I won't give up," Kiki said, revisiting their original conversation. "I'll keep researching the journal."

Grateful for her friend's determination, Mandy asked, "Are you going try to locate Nanny's ancestors?"

The redhead nodded. "I'm working on that now."

"What about Catherine's family? Are you going to contact them, too?"

"I already did. Catherine only has one significant heir, and I knew she would refuse my calls. She won't discuss Catherine with anyone."

"Who is she?"

"Catherine's grandniece, and she's a reclusive old bird. Proper, prestigious, powerfully rich."

"What's her name?"

"Minerva. She's Paul Burke's granddaughter. Paul was Catherine's brother, and he had one son, who in turn had one daughter."

"Making her the matriarch," Mandy concluded. "Of a dwindling family."

"Yep. She's in her eighties now. But you want to know the ironic part? When she was young, she favored Catherine. Long, wavy blonde hair, blue eyes, fragile complexion."

"Really?" Mandy's interest in the old bird piqued. "That must have been a curse, to look like the black sheep of the family. Not that Catherine wasn't beautiful. She was stunning. But you know what I mean."

"I surely do. Minerva's lineage to the Burke dynasty runs deep. And so does her refined breeding. She married an equally proper man, but she's widowed now, and they never had any children. She lives in a country estate, but she still owns the house where Catherine grew up, too."

Mandy tried to envision it. "I wonder if it has one of those winding stairways with austere portraits, and if there's a missing spot where Catherine's picture should be."

"I don't know." Kiki glanced up at the predusk sky, but she didn't prepare to leave. She remained seated. "But as I said, I'm not giving up on Catherine or her nanny. Not until we know what happened to them."

～

Nanny drove our buggy, and I sat next to her. We were on our way to town to get the materials for Atacar's new clothes.

The ride was bumpy, but it wasn't Nanny's fault, as she couldn't control the condition of the roads. Our carriage, known as a runabout, was built for two with room in the back for supplies, and Nanny was good with the reins. We also had an old, broken-down wagon that had been left by the previous tenants, but we had no reason to repair or use it.

I gazed out at the land, searching for prairie dogs peeking out of their holes. In spite of their names, they weren't wild dogs. They were robust rodents, grizzled and fat, and they never failed to make me smile.

I spotted a mother with her young and thought about what Atacar had said. That a man would be lucky to have me as his wife. Marriage had never appealed to me before, but I was getting swayed by it.

Unable to quell my romantic notions, I turned to Nanny and said, "Do you think I'd make a good wife?"

She kept quiet, staring straight in front of her. A moment later she gazed at me and asked, "Why? Did Atacar propose marriage?"

"No. But he thinks a man would be lucky to have me."

"He's already having you."

I made a priggish face at her, and she laughed at how silly I looked. She never told me whether she thought I would make a good wife, but she probably didn't want to encourage me. I glanced back to catch another glimpse of the prairie dog and her pups, but they were no longer visible.

A deep sense of longing overcame me. If I found a kind-hearted husband, if I bore him rosy-cheeked children, if I lived to be a hundred, I would never forget Atacar.

Nanny frowned, as if she sensed what was on my mind. Because of her thief, I surmised. I opened my mouth to ask her about him, but I clamped it shut just as swiftly. I knew how protective she was of her memories.

We hit another pocket in the road, and the runabout wobbled. After that, we rode in silence without incident.

The town we frequented was the county seat. A courthouse dominated the community, along with a bank, a livery stable, a hotel, a post office, a general store, and a few smaller enterprises. On the edge of town was a railroad depot, a Methodist church, and a newly constructed school.

Nanny secured the horse and buggy to a hitching post, and we gathered our skirts, took to the walkway, and headed for the general store. The proprietors, Mr. and Mrs. Mayes, were some of the first to settle in this area and had watched their business grow.

The Mayeses were friendly and helpful. They were especially helpful to me because I was a spendthrift. I'd purchased my bed from a catalog they'd provided, and my extravagance had both staggered and pleased them.

Mrs. Mayes rushed forward to greet us. Although she wasn't a comely woman, she carried herself as if she were.

"Miss Burke," she said. "And Miss Nanny."

We responded to her in the same gracious manner, and she asked if there was anything special we needed.

I told her that we were interested in fabrics and sewing sundries. As we made our selections, it didn't take her long to conclude that the articles of clothing we intended to make were for a man. But Nanny and I were prepared for Mrs. Mayes's assumption. We'd discussed it ahead of time and decided that we should admit that we'd replaced our old farmhand, adhering to the story that Atacar was Juan.

I said to the lady proprietor, "He only has one set of clothes, and they're threadbare and permanently soiled. I believe that a man should look presentable, no matter what the nature of his work."

Mrs. Mayes seemed to appreciate my standards, citing that cleanliness was next to godliness. Then she suggested that I browse the store clothes, garments that were ready-made. "That way, you can outfit him right quick," she said. "We're nicely stocked. We received a shipment just yesterday."

Naturally I was compelled to shop. Nanny gave me a warning glare, but I ignored her. Some of the items were practical, and others were a bit smarter, garments Mrs. Mayes called go-to-meeting clothes. I chose a sturdy work shirt and a pair of denim blue jeans for Atacar. For the sizes, I used measurements Nanny had taken of him.

Mrs. Mayes draped my selections over her arm and proceeded to show me some dresses I might fancy. A two-piece ensemble caught my eye, along with some matching ribbon for my hair.

On our way home, Nanny scolded me. "You shouldn't draw that kind of attention to yourself."

"The dress I chose was simple." Not that I have could have done otherwise. *The general store didn't stock Paris fashions.*

"You know full well I was talking about what you purchased for Atacar. Store clothes for a farmhand? It's enough that we're sewing for him."

"Mrs. Mayes didn't seem to think I did anything wrong. It was her idea."

"That woman just wants your money. There were other patrons nosing about. You need to be more cautious."

I told Nanny to quit fretting. Atacar would be gone in a month, and no one would be the wiser. But even as I said it, I felt ill inside. Not about his clothes, but about losing him.

~

Before the sun went down that day, I invited Atacar into my studio. He was wearing his new shirt and jeans, and I thought he looked crisp and handsome.

"This room has many windows," he said.

"George, our previous farmhand, installed them for me. When I paint, I need extra light."

Atacar turned away from the windows. *"Why doesn't George work for you anymore?"*

"He moved to town. He got a job at the livery stable and married the young widow he'd been courting. She has two little boys, and George seems quite fond of them. I suspect that factored into her accepting his proposal. George is a simple man, but he's kind." I waited a moment before I asked, *"Why didn't you and your wife have children?"*

"Because she didn't conceive."

166

"Was she drinking the tea Nanny has been giving me?"

"No. It just didn't happen. I think she is barren. She has no children with her new husband, either."

"Do you hope to have a family someday?" I asked, pressing him further.

A frown furrowed his brow. "Not now. Not while my life is so unsettled."

I tried to seem unaffected by his words, by his future without me. "Maybe you'll meet a woman in Mexico, a pretty senorita who will help you settle your life."

"Catherine." He whispered my name, almost as if he shouldn't have said it at all. Then he moved closer, the light surrounding him like a sun-sparked halo.

I got teary-eyed. I didn't mean to. I so hated to cry. I blinked the wateriness away. I could see him watching me, wanting to take me in his arms.

I stepped out of reach, and his breathing went rough.

He continued to speak. "I wish you could come to Mexico with me. But I could never ask that of you. As long as my people are prisoners, as long as soldiers continue to search for me, no one can help me settle my life."

Whose heart was I trying to fool? His or mine? I walked toward him like the lovesick girl I was.

He embraced me, and I nestled against his new shirt. It was rough and scratchy, and I relished the masculine texture. He caressed my back, gliding his hand along my spine, and I looked up at him. I'd only known him for a short time, but I'd already begun to memorize his features. The corded muscles in his body, too. I even knew the placement of his scars.

"I want to teach you a new language," I said.

He regarded me with a curious expression: a quirk of one eyebrow, the slightest angle of his head. "I don't speak enough languages already?"

"This one is for lovers," I told him.

He didn't hesitate. "Then I am ready to learn."

Although my heart wrenched, I began his lesson, refusing to let the tightness in my chest stop us from having this moment.

I sifted through my botanical paintings and showed them to him, explaining that each flower, herb, tree, and shrub had been assigned a meaning.

"Lovers send each other nosegays," I said. "They used to be round tussie-mussies. Mostly they're corsage bouquets now, where the flowers are bunched loosely with longer stems. But no matter what the style, lovers must know the definition of each botanical so they can decipher their messages to each other."

He listened with rapt attention, so I proceeded. "My paintings aren't a complete study. But this is." I offered Atacar my floral dictionary, a book Mama had passed on to me. She, too, had studied this language. Some of the sentiments had changed over the years, but I knew the definitions from her time, as well as what was considered current.

Mama and I despaired over each other, but we shared the love of flowers. She was proud of my botanical paintings, and I cherished her dictionary.

Atacar examined the book and returned it to me. He didn't know how to read or write English, but he seemed fascinated by the concept of florigraphy.

"To express a thought, you must present a flower upright,"

I told him. "To express the opposite of that thought, you must allow the flower to hang in a reverse position. Otherwise the sentiment won't be clear, and your lover will misinterpret your message."

"Do you have a favorite flower?" he asked.

I considered his question. "I have many."

"Then which one speaks of us? What would you send to me? Here and now. On this day."

Something came to mind. But I hesitated.

"Tell me," he said.

I took a swift breath, preparing to respond. "I would give you flowers from a spindle tree. In England, they bloom in May and June, followed by an abundance of fruit."

"What is their meaning?" He motioned to the dictionary in my hand. "What do they represent in your book?"

"Leaves, flowers, or fruit from a spindle tree would say, 'Your image is engraved on my heart.'"

Atacar's gaze locked deeply onto mine. "What would I send to you to say that I share your sentiment?"

My response nearly stuck in my throat. We were admitting that we were falling in love, even if our words were coded. "Double-flowered asters."

He glanced at my paintings. "Do you have a picture?"

"No. But they're shaped like stars, and they mean precisely what you said."

He wanted to know more. "Do they grow in Texas? Can I pick them from the plains?"

The tightness in my chest returned. "I think so, but they don't bloom until late summer or early fall, and you'll be gone by then."

"What could I pick in Mexico that would have a similar sentiment?"

"A dahlia. The type with variegating colors." I sorted through my paintings. "Like this." I tried to sound light of spirit, to let him know I appreciated his romantic gesture, but I was still heavy inside. "Dahlias are indigenous to Mexico. They grow splendidly there."

Atacar queried me further. "What is their precise meaning?"

"They say, 'I think of you constantly.'"

"Then envision me in Mexico, gathering them for you. Imagine that my arms are filled with them."

In the silence that followed, my heart—the heart in which his image was engraved—collapsed. I didn't want to envision him so far away. I didn't want to reach out and not be able to touch him.

If Atacar felt the same crushing ache, he was doing a keener job of hiding his discomfort beneath the darkness of his eyes. I probably looked as if I'd been flayed.

"Maybe you should stop teaching me this language," he said.

"No." I gathered my wits. "I want us to create conversations this way. To use the plants and flowers available to us, as well as imagining using those which are not."

"So do I." He stroked my cheek. "What were you wearing in your hair on the first night we made love?"

"A buttercup. It means 'rich of charms.'"

He smiled. "You are rich of charms. Dangerously so."

Ah, yes, my bewitchment of him. I smiled, too. "I'll wear one tonight for you. I'll wear one every night."

Until my lover was gone.

CHAPTER TWELVE

Jared waited in his front yard for Mandy to arrive. His house was an adobe structure surrounded by sagebrush, trees, and towering mesas. It was his sanctuary, a place that made him feel spiritual, as if he truly belonged to the earth.

His dogs, two active Border collies, were off somewhere, romping the grounds. Probably zigzagging through the barn, with its rows of stalls and treasured occupants. Jared's horses were his life.

Suddenly Mandy's car appeared, turning onto the private road that led to his graveled driveway. He hooked his thumbs in his pockets and wondered what compelled him to want her so badly, to keep going out of his way to seduce her.

She parked and exited her vehicle. He moved forward to greet her.

"Hey," he said, sounding like he was in middle school again.

"Hey," she echoed, sounding like a pubescent kid, too. Sometimes he forgot that she was nearly ten years older than he was, and sometimes their age difference was part of the allure. It depended on his sexual state of mind.

He gave her a French kiss to break the ice, and she got breathy and flushed. Was it any wonder he got off on seducing her? If he slipped his hand down the front of her summer skirt and into her panties, she would probably be wet.

They went inside, and she put her purse beside a battered end table. He knew Mandy liked his flea-market style, the eclectic Southwestern furnishings he'd chosen. She hadn't been to his house as often as he'd been to hers, but they'd been known to fuck up a storm in his barn. In his big wrought-iron bed, too.

"Let's get the barbecue started." He escorted her onto a patio designed for entertaining.

"Wow. Look at this."

She seemed impressed that he'd dressed the table with flowers and candles and already had a trio of salads ready. He'd tossed the mixed greens, but the pasta combo and coleslaw had come from the deli.

He offered her a drink, and she accepted a raspberry-flavored malt liquor. He went for a Corona with salt and lime.

"We're having filet mignon and vegetable kebobs." He fired up the gas grill. "Corn on the cob, too."

She smiled. "You're planning on getting laid tonight, aren't you?"

He laughed and swigged his beer. "Do I ever plan on *not* getting laid?"

"Nope. You're a hot-blooded guy."

"Who's having an affair with a hot-blooded girl." He clanked their alcohol bottles, toasting their tryst. He was still focused on fucking Mandy, only now he was learning to hold her, to give her the tenderness she craved to go with it. That seemed like a fair trade.

She sat at the table, and he went into the kitchen to get the steak and vegetables. When he returned with a platter, she peered at the raw food. He'd already marinated everything.

"How do you want your steak?" he asked.

"Medium."

"Me, too." He manned the grill, glancing up to study her. "I like your hair that way." She'd banded it into a low ponytail with loose strands falling around her face. It made her look soft and breezy.

"Thank you." She motioned to the floral arrangement on the table. "That's a gorgeous centerpiece."

"They're variegated dahlias." He couldn't help using the flowers from Catherine's journal. He wanted to make them part of his and Mandy's affair, too. Part of the tenderness, he thought. "Dahlias were first cultivated by ancient Aztecs, but there's an interesting story about how they were introduced to England in the early nineteenth century."

She scooted forward on her chair, prepared for him to enlighten her. She seemed captivated already.

"Lady Holland is responsible for sending dahlias to England," he said. "She'd seen them in Spain, where they'd originated from Mexico."

"Who's Lady Holland?"

"She was a divorcée who was unwelcome at court. She used to be married to Sir Godfrey Webster until she ran off with Lord

Holland and had a scandalous affair. Holland was younger than she was. Just by a few a years, but he was considered a young lord."

"They sound like a sexy couple."

"They were, I suppose. Oddly enough, their affair blossomed into a long and happy marriage. When they lived in Spain, she saw the dahlias and sent them home to England. Lord Holland even wrote her a dahlia poem."

Mandy glanced at the centerpiece, then back at him. "That's a beautiful story. Did you hear it when you were in England?"

"No. I picked it up on the Internet when I researched dahlias. You know, the language of flowers thing. Dahlias have a few different meanings, but the variegated variety says, 'I think of you constantly.'"

"You still need to teach me all of those meanings."

"I will." He turned the filets and rotated the vegetables. "In fact, I bought you a book about it. It's in my room. On my bed."

Her eyebrows shot up. "We're going to read in bed?"

"Yes, ma'am." He wasn't giving her the dictionary Catherine had mentioned in her journal. Catherine had never specified the title, and even if she had, those old editions were difficult to find. But there were plenty of modern books about Victorian florigraphy. "We're going to have a little flower fun."

"I'll bet." She laughed, making him laugh, too.

He hoped she liked his upcoming surprise. He'd gotten her more than a book, more than words on a page. He'd spent all day preparing for her lesson.

They lingered over dinner, enjoying the night air. She complimented him on how good the meal was, and he had to agree. The steak was thick and juicy.

For dessert they sliced into a strawberry pie that had come from a restaurant bakery. The berries were big and ripe, the glaze sweet and gooey. Like the sugar gluttons they were, they topped it with whipped cream from a can.

"In the language of flowers, strawberries mean 'You are delicious,'" he said.

"Really? Fruits have meanings, too?"

"Some do, as well as herbs. All sorts of plants."

"I'm anxious to get my book."

"Then finish your pie."

She didn't finish, not completely. She left some of the crust. But he figured that she'd had plenty to eat.

A short while later, after they'd taken a breather from stuffing themselves, she helped him clear the dishes. He kissed her when they were in the kitchen.

"You taste like strawberries," he said.

"So do you. We're both delicious."

"Yes, we are." Another kiss. Another taste. "Let's go to my room."

She agreed, and he took her hand and led her down the hall. He paused at his doorway. "Close your eyes."

"Why?"

"Just do it."

"This better be good." She got a kid-at-Christmas expression on her face and squeezed her eyes shut.

He wondered if she used to shake her packages before she tore into them. He swung open the door. "You can look now."

She gasped, and he smiled. He'd filled the room with potted plants and flowers tagged with their common and scientific names. But more important, the bed was dusted with soft, silken petals. Mostly they were rose petals, but he'd included petals from other flowers that either mattered to him and Mandy or to Catherine and Atacar. The delicately dismantled blooms looked like big, rainbow-colored confetti. The book he'd promised sat on top.

"Oh, my God. This is so beautiful, Jared. I don't know what to say."

He slipped his arms around her waist. They were still standing in the doorway. "I told you we were going to have a little flower fun."

"I know. But I didn't expect anything like this." He released her, and she walked into the room and gazed at all of the botanicals. "I'm overwhelmed."

"The potted plants are from a nursery, and the petals are from a florist. I ordered everything last week, and it was delivered today."

"I would've died if Ken had done something like this for our wedding night. Or for one of our anniversaries. Or for any occasion."

Jared shrugged off her comment. He figured it was natural for her to compare him to her ex, considering how long she'd been married.

She picked up the book, making the petals surrounding it flutter. She didn't ask him why he'd chosen to combine those particular flowers, and for that he was grateful. He'd been prepared to lie about the ones associated with Catherine and Atacar.

"Kiki said that you've been trying to be romantic for me, and she was right. You are." Mandy clutched the publication to her chest. "You totally deserve to get laid for this."

"Damn." He grinned, glanced down at his fly. "Now you're giving me a hard-on."

She came forward and kissed him, tongue to luscious tongue. "I might even give you one my famous blow jobs."

He pulled her tight against him. "They're famous?" He couldn't stop from teasing her. She had a sparkle in her eye, and he knew he'd put it there. "Should I start calling you Mandy *BJ* Cooper in front of your friends and work associates?"

She teased him right back. "Not unless you want to get smacked."

To make her point, she swatted him with the book. Then she looked through it, connecting the plants in the room to their definitions. She was taking her lesson seriously.

She laughed that there was a succulent called hen and chickens and that it meant "welcome home, husband, however drunk ye be."

Jared chuckled, too. He hadn't realized that the nursery had sent that along. That he'd included it on the list. "I guess that's the kind of husband I'd be."

"Your wife would be happy to see you even if you were wasted? Somehow I don't think it works that way."

Mandy continued to thumb through the book and scan the plants in the room. She took her time, but he didn't mind. He appreciated her attention to detail.

Finally she started plucking flowers, leaves, and stems. When she was done, she handed her compilation to Jared.

"Let's see." He worked on deciphering its messages. He knew the language well. He'd been studying it since he'd found Catherine's journal. "The daylily is 'coquettish,' the azalea is 'romance,' the African marigold means 'vulgar-minded,' and the chickweed represents a rendezvous." He put it all together. "You're flirting with me so we can have a romantic, vulgar-minded rendezvous. In other words, my sweet, noble lady, you're telling me that you're ready to fuck."

She flung her arms around his neck. "You're good at this."

He scooped her up, and they landed on the bed. As they rolled around, kissing and touching, the petals stuck to their hair and created a snowflake effect on their clothes. Jared couldn't get over how radiant Mandy looked, and she was just as fixated on him.

They took turns getting undressed and watching each other strip. She went first, unbuttoning her blouse. The eyelet fabric had embroidered holes in it, too small to see through, but pretty enough to notice. Her bra was even prettier, but she didn't unhook it. She waited for him to take off his shirt.

He dragged the casual cotton tee over his head. Just for good measure, he unbuttoned the top of his jeans, too.

She undid her bra and exposed her breasts. Jared leaned forward and tossed some petals there. He loved her small tits and big, pink nipples.

Joining in his game, she tossed some petals at him, and they landed on his bulging fly. He pinned her down and kissed her. She still tasted like strawberry pie, but he supposed he did, too.

They finished removing the rest of their clothes. Steeped in flowers, they rubbed their nakedness all over each other, and the heady aroma of botanicals mingled with the scent of human lust.

She went down on him, making good on her "famous" blow-job offer, and he thanked the day he'd met her. She fondled his balls and sucked sensuously on his cock, flicking her tongue over the piercing.

While he toyed with loose strands of her hair, he told her that he was going to eat her, too. That he was going to dive between her legs and lap her up.

He could tell that his zealous admission turned her on. She swallowed him deeper, and the sensation of getting sucked off so thoroughly blasted through his veins. But when it got too deep, too aggressive, too flat-out torturous, he stopped her.

He switched positions with Mandy, but he didn't go directly for her pussy, even if it was the flower he craved. He kissed his way down, licking her nipples and trailing a damp path to her navel. He slid lower, and she moaned and spread her thighs to accommodate him.

As he absorbed the delicate warmth of her sex, he encouraged her to fantasize, to think about the night he was going to slip into her room and come all over her.

"I have been thinking about it." She ran her hands over her breasts and down her stomach, as if it were happening right now.

"You're so beautiful. So fucking sexy." He laved her clit, and the sensitive nub tightened.

She went breathy. "We're both beautiful, Jared. When we do things to each other, we're the most beautiful people on earth."

Familiarity seized him. Catherine had said something similar to Atacar. On the night he'd taken her virginity, she'd talked about how beautiful a man and woman could be when they were together. Atacar had been inside her at the time, but the sentiment had been the same.

Jared teased Mandy's clit, over and over, desperate to make

her come. He couldn't help it. He needed to feel that beauty against his tongue, to draw it toward him and back to her.

She caressed his face, and he looked up. Their gazes met and held. The intimacy struck him straight in the chest. It grabbed hold of his dick, too. Especially when she came, when her juices flowed like nectar into his all-too-willing mouth.

He waited for her spasms to subside before he reared up to fuck, to fornicate, to copulate, to have sexual intercourse, to bang, to boff, to screw, to mate, to make love. He didn't know which words to choose. He just knew that he needed to join his body with hers.

Jared entered her hard and deep. She wrapped her legs around him, and he couldn't remember the missionary position ever feeling this good, this right.

He didn't know why their affair mattered so damn much, but now he wished it didn't. There was a part of him that wanted to walk away, to quit seducing her, to quit creating parallels between their relationship and Catherine and Atacar's. But some of it wasn't his fault. Some of the parallels seemed to be happening without his intervention.

Confused, he drove himself into her. She held him while he pounded his way to relief. He couldn't have slowed his pace if he tried. He needed to come inside her, to spill every pulsing drop.

His heart hammered. His brain fogged. His vision blurred. At that explosive moment, he wasn't even sure of his own name. All he wanted was his release.

Locked good and tight, he thrust back his head, shuddering, until there was nothing left.

Afterward, he collapsed on top of Mandy. He tried to move, but he couldn't. Finally he asked, "Am I too heavy?"

But before Mandy could respond, déjà vu blasted him like a bullet. Atacar had asked Catherine the same thing. Shit, Jared thought. Had he done that subconsciously to see what Mandy would say?

She kept her arms around him. "You're fine."

Jared recalled that Atacar had been too heavy for Catherine, even if she'd liked his bulk.

He rose on his elbows, lifting most of his weight from Mandy's body. But he didn't disengage their hips. He was still inside her. "Did you come?"

She laughed a little. "Couldn't you tell? I clawed your back. I gasped your name."

"You did?" He hadn't heard her voice; he hadn't felt the sting of her nails. He'd never blanked out like that before. He'd never had an orgasm that intense.

She tried to hug him, but he wasn't up for cuddling, not while his mind was befuddled. He withdrew and rolled away from her, scattering flower petals onto the floor.

So much for being tender.

Silence befell them until she said, "I told Kiki you were guarded."

His frustration flared. He rolled back over to look at her. "Why do women have to tell each other everything? How would you like it if I told my friends personal stuff about you? That you used to have crummy sex with your husband? Or that you—"

She cut him off. "It was *average* sex."

"Crummy. Average. It's the same damn thing." Annoyed that she'd defended her ex, he sat up and thrust his hand through his hair, tugging his braid.

She sat up, too. Just as edgy, just as snappy. "What's wrong with you? Why did you do all of this if it's pissing you off?"

"It's not the flowers." He glanced around, assessing the jungle he'd made of his room. Tomorrow he and his gardeners were hauling everything outside to be planted. "It's just me."

She didn't respond, and he cursed himself for destroying the sparkle he'd seen in her eyes earlier.

"Say something, Mandy."

She sighed. "I'm sorry for talking to Kiki about you, but she's the only friend I have who I can confide in."

"It's okay. I don't care. You can tell her whatever you want." He zeroed in on his problem, his frustration. He was guilty for keeping secrets, for using Catherine and Atacar to seduce her. "But I wish you and Kiki would give up on the journal. That you'd quit fooling yourselves into believing it's real."

"What can I say?" Her voice went soft. "We're die-hard romantics. Women who look at Atacar and see what he felt for Catherine."

Jared pushed his secret to the limit, trying to dispel the truth, even if he knew how much Atacar had loved Catherine. "What if it's bullshit? What if he didn't care about her?"

Mandy got stubborn. "He did. I can feel it. And you should, too. He's your ancestor. You should have more faith in him than that."

Jared frowned. He had plenty of faith in Atacar. It was himself that he didn't trust. His own feelings. His own emotions. "Fine. Whatever."

She swung her feet to the edge of the bed. "I should go."

"No." He grabbed her before she could leave. "No fucking way. I'm not done with you yet."

"Done with me?" She tried to jerk free of his hold. "I'm not your property."

"I didn't mean it like that." He rained gentle kisses along her shoulder, doing what he should have done after they'd fucked. Or made love. Or whatever the hell it had been. "Stay with me, baby. Let me fix this. Let me hold you."

She fought her vulnerability, her addiction to him. He could hear the struggle in her voice. "You're maddening, Jared."

"I know. I'm an ass." He tucked her against him. What else could he do? He was addicted to her, too. "A shitty boyfriend."

She turned to face him. "You're not that bad. Girls like me dream about this kind of stuff."

He knew she meant the plants and flowers. "I owe you an apology bouquet. I'll pick one tonight."

She smiled and settled into his arms. "If I had any sense, I'd find a nice white-picket-fence guy and teach him how to have sex like you."

"That can't be taught." He paused, grinned, tapped her chin. "No one has sex like I do."

She laughed and cuddled closer, and he realized they'd just weathered their first fight. He held her, making the best of what they had.

Even if it wasn't meant to last.

CHAPTER THIRTEEN

I paced my studio, the wooden floors creaking beneath my feet. Whenever I attempted to create a new art study, I thought about Atacar. I couldn't focus on anything except him. He was the ever-present subject on my mind, the portrait I longed to paint. But he still refused to sit for me.

He was outside tending to his chores, and Nanny was in the kitchen preparing dinner, which in Texas was our midday meal, served hot and hearty. A light midday meal or picnic would have been considered lunch. Supper, whether hot or cold, came later.

"Catherine!" Nanny screeched my name.

I poked my head outside the studio door and acknowledged her. She rarely disturbed me while I was painting. Not that I had been painting, but she couldn't have known otherwise.

"Hurry!" Her voice screeched again. "Someone is coming."

My heart skipped a frantic beat, and my thoughts spun back to Atacar. Was it soldiers? Were they coming for him?

I dashed into the kitchen. Nanny was at the window. I peered out, as well. A carriage approached, not uniformed riders.

"I thought—" My voice nearly broke.

"What, child?"

"It was the army."

Although Nanny patted my shoulder, quieting my fears, she looked as frazzled as I felt. Wisps of gray hair escaped her bun, and perspiration dotted her brow. But she'd been tending a hot stove. She probably would've looked that way even if company hadn't besieged us.

The carriage moved closer, and I recognized its occupants: George, our former farmhand, his wife, and her two small children. The youngest squirmed on her lap.

George had promised to bring his new family around, but I hadn't expected a visit so soon after his nuptials.

"We'll have to invite them to stay for dinner," Nanny said.

"Yes, of course." It was the proper thing to do.

Nanny and I walked onto the porch to greet our guests. By now, they'd climbed out of the carriage, and George was hitching the horse.

He gave us a crooked smile. Even at thirty, he seemed boyish: tall and gangly with feet that were forever shuffling.

His wife, attired in a simple blue dress, was petite and commonly pretty. Although I'd met her during their courtship, this visit would give us the opportunity to get further acquainted. I just wished it wasn't happening while I was hiding my Apache lover at the farm.

"Mrs. Horn," I said, greeting her formally.

She smoothed the front of her hair. The light brown strands puffed into a delicate pompadour, then narrowed into a ribbon-garnished braid in back. "Please, call me Alice."

"Then call me Catherine."

The children were Jack and Peter. They did their best to behave, as their mother corrected them often. But they were only two and fours years old.

The Horns accepted our dinner invitation, and Nanny returned to the kitchen to continue the meal preparation. I sat in the parlor with George and his family.

George was as fidgety as the boys. "Maybe I should leave you ladies alone till you call me to the table."

"Your company is perfectly acceptable," I told him, trying to ease his obvious discomfort.

"I appreciate that, ma'am, but I don't cotton much to sitting still. I'd prefer to head on down to the wagon shed. Maybe pick up a hammer and get some work done. I should have fixed those broken boards before I quit on ya."

I tried to appear poised. "The wagon shed has already been repaired. Didn't you hear that we hired a new farmhand?"

"Who was I supposed to hear it from?"

"I told Mrs. Mayes when we were in town."

"She don't discuss other people's business with me." He scooted to the edge of his chair. He'd removed his hat when he'd come inside, and his ears were sticking out the sides of his head. "I'd still prefer to leave you ladies alone. How about if I go for that stroll anyhow? Maybe seek out your new hire?"

I wanted to exclaim, "No!" but I knew better than to overreact. "That would be for naught. Juan doesn't speak English."

"Juan? He's Mexican, then?" George wasn't deterred. "I can talk Spanish. Not much, but some."

Now what was I supposed to say? I looked toward the kitchen at Nanny, but she seemed unaware of my dilemma. "How about this?" I managed. "Before you stroll the farm, I'll invite Juan to dinner. I wouldn't want him to think that he isn't welcome at our table when we have guests."

It was the best I could do, the only solution I could fathom: Dash off to warn Atacar that George wanted to meet him.

"How'd you learn Spanish good enough to converse with Juan?" George asked. "You being from England."

"My family holidayed in Spain." Although that was true, my use of the language was sorely limited. I was embellishing my skills.

George didn't query me further, so I excused myself and entered the kitchen, telling Nanny what I was about to do. She gave me an anxious look.

I searched the farm and found Atacar working in the garden. He wore his hat dipped low, and his face was smudged with dirt.

"We have visitors," I said.

"I know. I saw the carriage."

Apparently he'd sullied his face purposely, hoping to mask his features. I explained the situation, and we discussed our options. We agreed that he should refuse to dine at the table, claiming that he preferred to eat alone in the barn. But allowing George an introduction seemed unavoidable.

"I'll send him out to meet you," I said.

Atacar nodded, and I was tempted to kiss him. But I knew I

couldn't. This wasn't the time to promote our romance, to transfer the dirt from his person onto mine.

I returned to the parlor and relayed the message to George. He hopped out of his seat, eager to get his shuffling feet moving, and my nervous wait began.

I chatted with Alice and gave her children paper and pencils with which to scribble, but my pulse pounded the entire time.

George wasn't gone for long, and he reappeared seeming flustered. I hoped it was because his Spanish had given him more trouble than he'd assumed it would. That he'd fumbled between "Hola" and "Adios."

While Alice helped Nanny set the table for our meal, George motioned to get my private attention.

"Ma'am," he whispered. "I don't mean to scare you, but something don't feel right about Juan."

Heaven help me, I thought. "I don't know what you mean."

"He barely lifted his face to mine. I don't trust a man who won't look ya in the eye."

"He's reserved."

"I don't think that's it. I think he was trying to hide his appearance from me."

My knees threatened to buckle. Since when had George become so observant? "That's nonsense."

"Have you looked at him clearly?"

"Most certainly. He works for me."

"Then I want to look upon him clearly, too. Without his face being smudged up. Without him keeping his head lowered. I ain't even sure he's Mexican."

I kept my expression stern, my attitude unyielding. "Juan doesn't owe you anything, George."

"Don't he? He could be that Apache them soldiers was hunting. Don't you remember them showing us his picture?"

I folded my hands together, squeezing them tight. "Of course I remember, and Juan isn't him."

"I think he could be. But until I get a clearer look, I can't be sure."

"He isn't," I reiterated.

"No disrespect, ma'am, but—"

I interrupted. "His name is Juan, and he's from Mexico."

"You need to listen to what I'm saying—"

"No, you need to listen," I interrupted again, more adamantly this time. "If I say he's Juan, then that's who he is."

George gaped at me, the truth dawning in his eyes. By defending Juan so diligently, I'd just revealed Atacar's identity. I wanted to fall to the floor and weep my remorse, to curse the day I was born.

"Lordy," George said. "Oh, Lordy."

I resorted to begging. "He's a good man, and you have to promise to keep my secret. Please. He'll be leaving in less than a month."

George glanced at his wife. She was boosting her youngest boy onto a dining chair. "Alice says that all men have the right to be free. Her family is dead now. But they was abolitionists."

"Then Alice should understand. She might even want to help an Apache prisoner of war. The army wronged him. They wronged his people."

"Yes. But I—"

"Please," I implored once more, drawing George and his family into my plight.

A moment later, George spoke to Alice about Atacar, and she convinced her husband to take up my cause, to keep my secret. I wanted to wrap my arms around her, to thank her in a way words of gratitude never could. But I kept a proper distance.

Alice requested to meet Atacar, so I fetched him to dine with us. He washed up at the pump, gazing at me as if I'd betrayed him.

"How do you know you can trust them?" he asked.

I explained that Alice's family had helped free slaves during the American Civil War. And that she sympathized with Indians, too.

"And George?"

"I think his heart will keep him pure. That he's a man of honor."

"And if he isn't?" Atacar dried his face with a clean rag, his mouth taut, the frown lines near his eyes stark against his skin. "Promises have been broken to me before."

I didn't debate his point. How could I? What he'd said was true. I'd even told George that Atacar had been wronged. "If you're concerned about him contacting the army, then you should leave for Mexico tonight. You're welcome to my horse. You can take her on your journey."

"I won't take your horse from you." He reached out to touch my cheek. "Nor am I ready to leave. Not without spending more time in your arms."

I touched his cheek, too. I would never love anyone the way I loved him.

We went inside and gathered at the table. Everyone addressed Atacar as Juan. The children were too young to comprehend the situation, but not too young to learn Juan's name, to repeat it on other occasions.

Nanny had prepared stewed chicken with dumplings, accompanied by peas and potatoes. For dessert, we had coffee, tea, and cake.

I made fast friends with Alice, and she suggested that we continue to socialize. "George and I can stop by next week. He can play his fiddle, and the rest of us can dance." She smiled at her children. "The boys, too."

"That's a glorious idea," I responded, truly meaning it.

Nanny was pleased, as well. The men neither disagreed nor reacted favorably. But they did speak a few cordial words to each other.

It seemed like a good start.

~

As I lay in the dark with Atacar, moonlight drifted into the room, dusting the bed in silvery hues.

"Do you regret your decision?" I asked.

"To stay? To trust your friends?" He rolled sideways to face me. "No."

"Then why are you sullen?"

"Because when the time comes for me to leave, I will miss everything about you."

"Then invite me to go with you. Me and Nanny."

"I can't."

My chest turned tight, aching for more. "Can't or won't?"

"Won't," he admitted.

I considered turning away from him, but I didn't. He touched the buttercup in my hair, treating it with fragile care. The tightness in my chest deepened.

"I need to steal a horse soon," he said. "To have a mount available if I have to leave in a hurry."

"I'll purchase a horse from the man who owns the livery stable. He trades and sells. George can help me fetch a good price."

He lowered his hand. "You'll do no such thing. I've taken enough charity from you already."

I addressed the flaw in his plan. "You can't raid one of my neighbors and keep a stolen mount in my barn."

He frowned at me, his moonlit features partially shadowed. "Then you can purchase a horse and deduct the cost from my wages."

"You need that money for Mexico."

"Do not tell me how to spend my earnings."

"You're a stubborn man."

He tugged me into his arms. "And you're a stubborn woman."

I remained frustrated. "You're going to remedy our argument with a kiss?"

"No." He removed my nightgown, baring my body for his pleasure. He was already naked. "With more than that."

I cursed him for sliding his hand between my thighs. But I couldn't control my erotic reaction. I tingled from his touch.

He pressed his fingers against my clitoris. I sighed my acquiescence and opened my legs, giving him permission to make me climax. Not that it would have made a difference. He would have done it regardless.

He rubbed me until I shuddered, but that wasn't enough for him. He wanted to have mutual oral copulation, too.

Shivers slid up and down my spine. We hadn't performed that act yet. We'd spoken about it, but we hadn't brought it to fruition.

He told me to straddle his mouth, backwards, so I was facing his cock. I did his bidding, feeling quite naughty from atop his face.

From my vantage point, I admired the outline of his penis, big and hard against his stomach. The foreskin was already pushed back, exposing the bulbous tip.

He put his tongue inside me, and I lowered my head. I inhaled his musky scent, using my hands and mouth to stimulate him.

Doubled-edged hunger assailed my senses: him licking me while I sucked him. I took as much of him as I could, and he helped me set the rhythm, thrusting his hips.

But even as he moved, as he fornicated with my mouth, he didn't break his other stride. He continued to lave my vagina, to make it wet and slick.

I rocked back and forth, enjoying our wantonness. His cock was leaking ejaculate, pearly drops dissolving on my tongue.

We moaned our pleasure. The moonlight faded, and I could no longer see him. The room was pitched in inky darkness, and the sensation of being so close to him intensified. I could feel every vein, every ridge in his cock.

Nerve endings fluttered inside me, and I verged on another orgasm. My second that night. I wondered how many a woman could experience without pooling like candle wax.

Atacar laved ruthlessly, spearing my silken folds, and I relinquished the battle and climaxed, my juices warm and sticky. I pressed down on him, wanting him to savor my moisture, and he obliged, giving me the wickedness I craved.

As I shuddered and shook, he had an orgasm, too. His hot seed filled my mouth, and I swallowed, allowing the milky wetness to slide down my throat.

After it was over, we stayed like that, letting the intimacy of what we'd just done settle softly between us.

Finally we shifted, getting face-to-face so we could kiss. I tasted myself on his lips, and I suspected that he tasted himself on mine.

"This makes me want to fuck," he whispered.

"It does?"

He nodded in the dark. Or I thought he did. I couldn't be sure. "A warm fuck. Later tonight. After we rest. I don't want it to be over. I want as much of you as I can get."

I wrapped my arms around him. "Me, too. With you."

He kissed me again, and we stayed silent for a while. The moonlight reappeared, the glittering rays bathing our skin.

I thought about the dinner conversation that had transpired earlier. "Do you dance, Atacar?"

"Not white man's dances."

"You don't waltz, polka, gallop, or mazurka?"

"No."

"Then I shall have to teach you."

"The way you're teaching me to speak with flowers?"

"Yes." I wanted to share all of my favorite things with him. "When Alice and George return to socialize with us, we'll dance to his fiddle like the grand couple we are."

"How will I learn before then? Without music?"

"I can hum the songs for you. We'll practice every night beneath the stars, with crickets chirping and fireflies glowing." I smiled to myself. "Scientists say that they illuminate when they're courting."

"We're courting," he said.

"Yes, we are."

He moved closer. "We're illuminating, too. Inside."

I sighed, thinking how roughly romantic he was. His nakedness teased mine, creating sweet shivers. We kissed and rolled over the bed, locked in each other's arms.

He slid between my legs, and I felt his hardness nudging me. He was fully aroused and ready to mate. A warm fuck, I thought, enjoying the adjective he'd used. I clutched his buttocks, encouraging him to join with me.

We moved in perfect unison, our tempo slow, then dreamy, then swift. Changing positions, I landed on top, riding him the way a cowgirl would straddle a stallion. He gripped my waist and moved me up and down in a sleek and sensual manner.

I felt his cock so deeply, I wondered if he were stroking my womb. He told me how glorious I was, and I tried to imagine what he saw: a naked woman, shrouded in semidarkness, her limbs spread across his lap.

He put his hand against my mound and rubbed me while we mated. He'd been born to be my lover, to pleasure me, just as I'd been born to arouse him.

"We'll start tonight," he said.

I knew what he meant. After we climaxed, we would slip outside for his first dance lesson, to absorb everything we could from each other.

From now until the day he went away.

CHAPTER FOURTEEN

Jared was gone. He'd left town to attend a horse auction and wouldn't return until Monday. But for now it was Friday afternoon, and Mandy was at work with the phone cradled to her ear.

"Are you ready to shoot some Blow Jobs?" the female voice on the other end of the line asked.

Mandy bit back a grin, thinking how odd the invitation sounded coming from a woman. Then again, it wasn't just any woman. It was Amber Pontiero, the spoiled, sexy heiress who used to sleep with Jared.

"When?"

"Tonight. You can bring a friend, too. We can make it a ménage, metaphorically speaking."

Mandy immediately thought of Kiki. "I know just the girl."

"Perfect. Meet me at Clay's Corner at seven. It's a little place on the outskirts. Do you know it?"

"I've heard of it."

"Take a cab. Or hire a chauffeur. We're going to get obnoxiously drunk."

"That sounds good to me." Mandy needed a girl's night out, especially since Jared was gone.

"Do you want to do some Cocksucking Cowboys, too?"

Mandy blinked. "What?"

"Cocksucking Cowboys."

"Please tell me that's a drink."

Amber laughed. "It is."

"At the masquerade, you said that mixing cocktails isn't a good idea."

"It's a fine idea when you're planning to get drunk enough to dance on the tables. To flash your panties at other patrons."

Mandy crossed her legs, even though she was alone at her desk. She couldn't imagine dancing on tabletops. "I think I better wear pants."

The other woman laughed again. "Spoilsport." Her sexy accent drifted through the phone. "You're such a good girl, except for when you're with your man."

"He inspires me."

"Is that all he does to you?"

"I don't know what you mean."

"Are you falling in love with him? No offense, but you seem like the type."

Mandy's heart punched her chest, and she stalled, unable to answer the question, to consider the possibility. Instead, she fidgeted with a paperweight on her desk.

Amber went silent too, as if she were contemplating the delayed reaction. "Maybe you should fuck someone else. Maybe even have a real ménage."

Just in case she was falling in love? "That wouldn't work. Besides, I don't want anyone else."

"What about Pink and Red? I can arrange for you to be with them."

"I was only attracted to them because they looked like Jared."

"They can put their costumes back on."

"Honestly, I'm not interested."

"All right, darling. But you don't know what you're missing. I already fucked them, and they were fabulous. I'll give you the details when I see you." A smile sounded in Amber's voice. "Until tonight. Ciao."

Mandy didn't have time to say good-bye. The line went dead. She stared at the phone. A second later, she snapped out of her trance and dialed Kiki's extension, inviting her to join the drinking, tell-all sex fest.

Kiki accepted readily, and at precisely 7:00 p.m., they entered Clay's Corner, a woody establishment with a jukebox in front, a billiards table in back, and ceramic chili peppers decorating windowsills and doorways.

Mandy and Kiki snagged a booth. Clay's served appetizers, too. They ordered potato skins and chips and salsa. The food arrived before Amber did. Apparently she intended to be fashionably late.

Kiki lifted a potato skin from the platter and dunked it into the dipping sauce. "I'm anxious to meet this girl."

"I don't even know what she looks like. Not beyond her costume at the ball. Or those killer legs."

"You didn't Google her?"

"No." Mandy reached for her glass. They'd gotten ice water to drink. They didn't want to start boozing until Amber showed up.

"I did, and there are quite a few pictures of her on the Net. She's a gorgeous, short-haired brunette."

"Her hair was long and blonde at the party, but I suspected that it might be a wig."

Kiki leaned in close. "Can you believe she slept with your guys? Do you think she did it at the ball?"

"They aren't *my* guys."

"Not technically, but they *were* masquerading as Jared. Can you imagine having multiple partners? I can't."

"An orgy crossed my mind at the party. Which Jared is which? Maybe I'll take all of them. But in reality, I never would have done it. I'm too monogamous."

"So am I. But I think watching other people would be hot. Threesomes, foursomes, fivesomes." The redhead clamped a hand over her mouth, mumbling her shame. "I can't believe I just told you that." She freed her mouth. "Is fivesomes even a word?"

"I don't know. But don't worry about it. You can tell me anything. Besides, we all have fantasies."

"Lately I've had some doozies."

"Me, too." Mandy thought about the fantasy Jared had yet to fulfill. "Sometimes we even shock ourselves."

"No kidding." Kiki flashed a cockeyed grin, returning to her usual self. She glanced up. "Oh, wow. Our drinking buddy just arrived, and she's even more gorgeous than her pictures."

Mandy turned around. Sure enough, Amber Pontiero had

walked through the door, causing everyone in the bar to look her way. Sporting a white tank top, a denim skirt, and wedged sandals, she was a sight to behold. She wore her short, dark hair in an angular-cut bob, a style originated by Vidal Sassoon in the 1960s. Amber was still a mod girl, with or without the long blonde wig, fishnet stockings, and go-go boots.

As for her unmasked face, she had bluish green eyes smudged with nutmeg shadows and smoky liner, a slightly crooked nose, and a full mouth. All of it worked on her.

Amber smiled at a trio of male admirers at the bar and headed for Mandy and Kiki's table.

Mandy made the introductions, and Amber settled deeper into her seat. "Are you ladies ready to get drunk and cause a scene?"

Kiki drenched a tortilla chip with salsa. "You're already causing a scene. Just look at you."

"You, too. A genuine redhead. I know a dark and brooding artist who gets off on girls like you. Those cute little freckles across your nose would drive him mad. You wouldn't happen to be into bondage, would you?"

Kiki nearly choked on her chip. "Why? Is that his fetish of choice?"

"That's what he paints. BDSM depictions."

Mandy stifled a laugh. Kiki looked as if she'd been sucker punched. Apparently she hadn't taken her erotic fantasies quite that far. Or maybe she had, but she wasn't willing to admit it.

A round of Blow-Job Shooters was ordered, and upon their arrival, Amber instructed Mandy to go first.

"Make us proud, darling."

"I'll do my best." Mandy put her hands behind her back, leaned forward, and gripped the glass with her mouth. She struggled for balance and prayed that she didn't drop it all over herself. She could hear Kiki cheering her on.

"Come on! You can do it."

Mandy went for it. She tilted back her head and drank. By the time she was done, she had whipped cream all over her face. She wiped it off and grinned. The cocktail had tasted pretty damn good, but the process of drinking it was even better.

Kiki took her turn. She struggled and made a mess, too. But in the end she accomplished the task, receiving high fives from her companions.

Amber didn't spill a drop. She sucked and swallowed like a pro, treating her shot like the biggest, hottest, cream-filled cock she'd ever tasted.

"Good Lord." Kiki all but gaped. "If I were a guy, you would've given me a boner."

The three of them burst out laughing.

"The same drink with a cherry on top is called a Muff Diver," Amber said. "I've watched Jared down a few." She addressed Mandy. "As you recall, he got me into erotic-named drinks."

"And now I'm going to be hooked. Not to mention drunk and hungry for him. But he's out of town."

"So you can take him muff diving when he gets back." Amber flashed a knowing smile. "He's good at it."

"Really good," Mandy admitted. By now they were referring to the real deal.

Amber kept the party going. She flagged down the waitress and ordered Cocksucking Cowboys, shots made with two parts butterscotch schnapps and one part Irish cream. The Irish cream floated on top.

Amber lifted her glass in a toast. "To old friends and new acquaintances."

"Hear, hear." Kiki clanked her glass.

So did Mandy. Socializing with Jared's former lover wasn't the least bit awkward. Amber was so casual about the affair she'd had with Jared, Mandy didn't feel threatened by it.

"Tell us about Pink and Red," Mandy said.

"Oh, yes. My new playmates. They didn't have anything to do after you figured out who Jared was, so I hit on them." She winked teasingly at Kiki. "What man in his right mind would turn me down? Right, darling?"

"Right," the redhead confirmed. She seemed to be enjoying the other woman's vanity-driven charm.

Amber turned toward Mandy. "At that point, you and Jared were off somewhere."

"We were in the garden. That's where we spent the last half of the party."

"Ah. Then that explains your missing whereabouts. Well, anyway, I invited Pink and Red upstairs to my suite. It's not as if they were strangers to me. I knew their real identities. I'd helped Jared hire them."

"What do they look like when they're not in costume?" Mandy asked.

"They're both L.A. actors. Pink has light brown hair and a scrumptious tan. He surfs and snowboards and does all of those sexy California things. Red is part Native American and is originally from the South, so the accent wasn't much of a stretch for him. He also has a naturally exotic flair. Without the mask he looks more like Jared than Pink does. It took a bit more work to transform Pink."

"Your makeup people did an amazing job," Mandy said. "I was stumped when I saw all of them together."

"That was the idea. Do you want to know their names?"

Mandy nodded.

"Pink is Jay, and Red is Luke. But I did my darnedest to forget who was who. When I slept with them, I told them to keep their masks on. It seemed more fun that way. We kept the lights off, too."

"You did two masked men in the dark?" Kiki asked.

Amber nodded. "At first we just stood in the room and kissed. I was in the middle, and they were on either side of me. I kept turning to kiss one, then the other."

Kiki went after a handful of chips. Mandy followed suit, riveted by Amber's story.

"They undressed me, and one of them dropped to his knees. I can't tell you how aroused I was."

Mandy had to ask, "What did the other man do?"

"He stood behind me, kissing my neck, rubbing my nipples, playing with my belly button. There I was, getting oral sex from one lover and getting teased by the other."

Kiki asked the next question. "Did they switch places?"

"Oh, yes. They took turns, one right after the other. I gave both of them head, too. Speaking of which—" She stopped talking and ordered a third round of drinks, waited for them to arrive, and made sure that everyone did a Blow Job before she continued.

Mandy wiped the whipped cream from her chin and down the front of her blouse. Her shots were getting messier. Kiki's, too. Even Amber had to lick white froth from the corners of her lips.

"They didn't take their clothes off when I gave them head. They undid their pants and sat on the edge of my bed."

"Oh, my goodness." This from Kiki. "You went back and forth?"

"Yes, I did. Right there on my knees. I didn't do it long enough to make them come. I knew we'd be crawling all over each other later."

Mandy stuffed a potato skin into her mouth. "I'm calling Jared when I get home. I don't care if he's out of town. After all of this, I'm going to need to hear his voice."

Kiki scowled. "Who am I supposed to call? The Maytag repairman? Oh, I know—how about the Mac computer guy? He's young and hot. Of course, with my luck, the PC guy would answer instead."

Amber looked at Mandy, and they sputtered into laugher. Kiki rolled her eyes, but she laughed, too.

"There's always the artist I told you about, darling."

"Mr. BDSM?" Kiki looked downright panicked. "I think not getting laid is safer."

"He's not as dangerous as he sounds."

"Says the ménage mistress."

The storyteller laughed again. "You're so adorable. So feisty. I can just see him trying to restrain you."

"Don't even think about setting me up. That's all I need. A blind date with a guy who'll want to blindfold me."

"You think I'd set you up?" Amber batted her lashes. *"Moi?"*

"Yes, *moi*. Now finish your ménage. I want to hear the rest."

"But of course. Jay and Luke got undressed, and we climbed into bed. We started kissing again. They put their hands all over me, and I caressed them. Strong shoulders. Muscled abs. Big, silky cocks. And those masks. I think that was the sexist part of all."

"What about your mask?" Mandy asked.

"I ditched it. I'm not sure when, but by the end of the night, it was gone. The foreplay was incredible. Luke straddled my face while Jay went down on me." She made a confused expression. "Or maybe it was the other way around. All I know is that I was giving and getting at the same time."

She paused to reminisce. "I had condoms in my dresser, so I fitted both of them. They took turns, bending my body, spreading my legs, telling me how perfect I was. It was the most romantic threesome I've ever had. All that kissing, all that caressing. They even sent me flowers the next day. Pink and red roses." She tucked a strand of her choppy hair behind her ear. "Not that flowers matter that much to me. But it was sweet."

"Sometimes flowers matter," Mandy said, thinking about Jared. "Sometimes they're really important."

Amber shrugged, and Mandy considered the bouquet the other woman had received. Pink roses meant "grace and beauty" and red embodied "love and passion."

"We're all so quiet now," Kiki said.

Amber nodded, but she didn't comment. Mandy got the impression that the heiress wasn't as indifferent as she seemed, that in her own way, she'd gotten attached to Jay and Luke.

Finally Amber spoke. "Let's have one more round. I don't think we're drunk enough."

Mandy and Kiki agreed, but the tone of the evening didn't change. After they quit drinking, the tipsy trio hugged and said a girl's-night-out good-bye, then went home with an assortment of men on their minds.

～

Mandy entered her condo and peeled off her clothes. Naked, she brushed her teeth and wiped off her makeup, gazing at her hungry image.

Once she was in bed, she grabbed the phone and dialed Jared's cell.

He answered on the third ring. "Multiorgasmic Mandy," he said by way of a greeting.

She got warm inside. She even parted her thighs ever so slightly, making the sheet pool at her hips. "Is that how you have me programmed into your phone?"

"No, but I should put you in that way. How are you, baby?"

She tried to picture him in his hotel room. Was he naked, too? God, she hoped so. "Drunk and horny." Emotional, too. But she left that part off.

"Really?" He sounded amused. "How'd that happen?"

"Amber did it to me. With Blow-Job Shooters and Cock-sucking Cowboys. Kiki was there, too. Amber told us a sexy story. Do you know what she did?"

"No, baby. What did she do?"

"She had a threesome with Pink and Red. At the ball. And they sent her flowers the next day."

He didn't respond, and she wondered if the call had gotten dropped.

"Did you hear me?"

No more humor. Irritation edged his tone. "Yeah, I heard you."

Mandy frowned at the phone. He was jealous of his ex being with two men who'd been masquerading as him? "Thanks a lot, Jared."

"I'm not pissed at what she did."

"Then what are you pissed at?"

"If I know Amber, she probably suggested that you fuck them, too. She probably offered to arrange it."

Mandy snapped at him. "So what if she did? I'd never do it."

"You wouldn't?"

"No." And she wasn't about to mention why Amber suggested that she mess around with Pink and Red. She might be drunk, but not inebriated enough to admit that the other woman thought she was falling in love with Jared.

Silence hung in the air, until he said, "I've done it."

"Done what?"

"Had ménages."

"With who?"

"I'm not bi, so being with two girls works better for me, but I've shared my lovers with other men. I'd never do it with you. I'd freak out if I had to share you with another guy. Or even another girl. I couldn't handle watching you with someone else."

"I couldn't handle you with anyone, either." Just thinking about him kissing another woman made her stomach churn. But even so, she didn't want to consider why their affair had gotten so intense, so committed, so emotional. "Are you going to go back to having threesomes when we stop dating?"

"I don't know. I doubt it. It's been a while since I've done it. Mostly I was experimenting, just being wild, I guess. Are you still horny? Or did I kill it for you?"

"It's dead."

"Sorry."

"It's okay."

"Want me to get you there? To talk you back into it?"

She smiled in spite of herself. "As long as it's just the two us. No talk of other people."

"That's more than fine with me. Are you on speaker?"

"No."

"You're going to need to have your hands free."

She egged him on. "To do what?"

"To bang yourself, baby. With that big, blasting dildo you made of me. This is our phone-sex ménage. You, me, and him."

She laughed. "So much for not involving anyone else." She hit the speaker button. "I'm ready."

"Get the dildo and the lube."

She stood up and went to her dresser, retrieving the necessary items. She even stroked the rubber phallus. "He's already hard for me."

"So am I. Now lie down and open those pretty legs."

She got back in bed. "Are you going to touch yourself, too?"

"Not this time. I'm going to save it for when I come on you. You still want me to jerk off on your tits, don't you?"

"Yes." Oh, God, yes. "But first you have to do it over my face so I can watch."

"I know. I remember. I'll do it exactly the way you want it. Now grease down the dildo."

She slathered the lubricant over the copy of his cock, her pulse already pounding at her clit. "When are you going to slip into my room, Jared? When is it going to happen?"

"Soon."

She fondled the pierced head. "How soon?"

"As soon I get back in town. Is the dildo ready?"

"Yes." She slid the phallus between her thighs, and he proceeded to give her orders, to make her wet and aroused, to tell her how deep and fast to use it.

Drunk and naughty, she fucked herself while he listened to every hot, hammering breath she took. She loved what he was making her do. But she refused to believe that she loved him more than the sex, more than the addiction.

Even if she didn't want to hang up the phone when it was over, even if she couldn't bear to let him go.

CHAPTER FIFTEEN

We lit a brass lamp and got dressed. I paired my nightgown with satin slippers, and Atacar climbed into the blue jeans I'd purchased for him in town. He wore his work boots, the only shoes he owned. He didn't bother with a shirt. We glanced at each other and smiled. Our dancing attire was most unusual.

We took the lamp outdoors to illuminate our way. As we walked arm in arm scouting our farmland ballroom, a gentle breeze enhanced the summer air, making scents from the night sweep and swirl.

We chose a spot near the barn. Atacar placed the lamp on a tree stump, and I admired him. As always, he looked stunning in the kerosene light.

I moved forward, running my hands along the masculine contours of his chest, encountering his nipples and the slightly raised ridges of old scars. My fingers trailed to his stomach.

"Is this what you do to all of your dance partners?" he asked.

I knew he was teasing me. "Only those I fancy."

"I like being fancied."

I was tempted to slip my hand lower, to invade the waistband of his pants, but I stepped back to regain my composure. "We'll start with the waltz."

He nodded, eager to learn. His attention was rapt, his gaze unwavering.

First, I taught him the proper way to bow. As he stepped to the side, closed in, and made the gentlemanly motion of bending forward, I smiled. He looked far more handsome than any man with whom I'd ever danced, even with his bared chest, blue jeans, and work boots.

I recalled the Indians who'd performed with Buffalo Bill and wondered how long it had been since Atacar had worn tribal adornments.

As we proceeded, I said, "The waltz is a turning dance in three-quarter time."

He gave me a quizzical look.

"The main pulse of the music is every three beats." I demonstrated, humming a song and counting off the beats, emphasizing the pulse.

He understood instantly.

I taught him the song so he could hum it, too. He was quite musical, and our voices blended in chilling harmony. I suspected that once he mastered the steps, we would partner in dance as splendidly as we partnered in bed.

With the Texas soil beneath our feet, I encouraged him to lead me into a basic waltz. We did quite well until he moved forward when he should have moved backward, and we bumped into each other.

We laughed and resumed the lesson. He was determined not to repeat his error, but he did it again.

"I'll get it right," he said.

I marveled at his focus. We practiced for hours, but he didn't want to stop. He continued to learn from his mistakes.

I instructed him in a polka-dot waltz, teaching him how to embellish the footwork. It was one of the sweetest, shortest versions of the dance, and I thought it suited us.

Afterward, we stood beneath the sky, our bodies pressed close. He ran his hands through my unbound hair, and I slipped my arms around his waist.

We separated, and my thoughts drifted to my youth, to the balls, soirees, and dinner parties I'd attended.

"I came out when I was seventeen," I said.

"Came out?"

"Formally presented to society. With the purpose of landing a husband," I added. "But I wasn't interested in marriage. Not at the time."

He didn't comment on my "Not at the time" remark. Instead, he said, "My people have a similar practice. We have a ceremony that announces when a young girl is ready to marry. At the end of the ceremony is the lover's dance, and that's when a man can propose. If she accepts, he consults her father and bargains for her."

"Did you propose to your wife at this ceremony?"

"No. Our marriage was arranged in a less romantic fashion."

I waited, hoping he would offer to teach me the lover's dance, *but he didn't. He'd already made me ache when he'd declined to take me to Mexico, and now he'd made me hurt again. But what did I expect? For him to get an impulsive notion? To propose?*

"Are you weary?" he asked. "Do you want to end the lesson?"

"I'm fine," I lied. I hadn't meant to make him aware of my distress. "I'd like to keep dancing."

"So would I." He began humming the song I'd taught him.

I curtsied to his bow, and he led me across patches of dirt and grass. Crickets chirped from their hiding places, making music with other nocturnal creatures. I looked for courting insects, but I didn't see any.

"In England, we call them glowworms," I said, thinking out loud.

Atacar blinked at me.

"Fireflies," I explained.

He didn't respond, but he stole a kiss while we waltzed, his mouth warm against mine.

"I want you to paint me," he said suddenly.

I faltered on my next step, gripping his shoulder to keep myself steady. He had gotten an impulsive notion, not to take me to Mexico, not to marry me, but to be the subject of the portrait I'd been longing to create. Although the woman in me wanted more, the artist in me nearly wept. He'd just eased a portion of my ache.

"You'll sit for me?" I asked.

"Yes."

"What if I need more time to paint you? Will you stay longer than you originally intended?"

Our dancing ceased, but we continued to hold each other. "I'll stay until you complete it."

The breeze turned stronger, blowing my hair and making my nightgown cling to my body. "What made you change your mind?"

"When I go away, I want you to keep part of me, to have it for all time."

I couldn't seem to find my voice, to engage in a response, not with my heart clamoring to my throat.

Atacar didn't fault for me for my silence. As I nestled against him, he rocked me in his arms, even after the lamplight went out, leaving us in the dark.

❧

Groggy, Mandy awakened in the dark. She blinked at the shadows in her bedroom. Why did it seem as if she wasn't alone? As if someone was watching her?

Jared, she thought.

No, that made no sense. He was still out of town.

She squeezed her eyes shut. She was losing it, imagining Jared's presence when he wasn't even there.

"Mandy," a man whispered. Deep, low, sensual.

Oh, God. Her eyes flew open, and she shifted her gaze in the direction of his voice. He was standing in an inky black corner of her whitewashed room. He looked like a ghost, a hazy apparition. "You really are here."

"I came back early."

She inhaled a choppy breath and glanced at the digital clock on her nightstand: 2:58. "How long have you been standing there?"

"A while. I've been watching you sleep."

She followed his footsteps, trying to focus on his long, lean, shadow-shrouded body. This was her fantasy, the one she'd been waiting for. He was here to make it come true.

And now she was nervous. Anticipation curled low in her belly, and even lower, pulsing in reckless invitation. Jared had taught her to talk dirty, to think dirty, to be his bad, bad girl.

Then why did this feel so forbidden? She should be used to her nasty urges by now. But she wasn't. The conventional side of her rebelled, and she clenched her thighs. But that only managed to intensify the hunger.

Jared turned on the light, and the brightness illuminated the room in a blinding glow. She squinted, struggling to make her eyes adjust.

He walked toward the bed, stopping just short of it. Mandy sat up and leaned against the headboard, the sheet twined around her legs. She glanced at the clock again: three on the dot.

Her gaze drifted back to his, and boom! Her heart hit her chest. Beautiful Jared. His hair was combed straight back, plaited into its customary braid, exposing chiseled angles and sun-burnished skin. He sported a denim shirt and timeworn jeans. Like the cowboy he was, he'd looped a distressed leather belt with a traditional Western buckle through the frayed waistband. She zeroed in on his fly. He already had an evident bulge.

"What are you looking at?" he asked.

Desire pounded at every pulse point of her body. She didn't respond. They both knew exactly what she was looking at, what she wanted, what the naughty girl inside her craved.

He raked his lethal gaze over her, and she fidgeted with her oversize nightshirt, a faded garment with an image of Tinker Bell splashed across the front of it. Beneath it, she wore thin cotton panties.

"Interesting pajamas," he said.

Dare she admit that she had a Sleeping Beauty ensemble, too? "I wasn't expecting company. You tricked me by coming back early."

"And now I'm going to peel those sweet clothes right off you."

He climbed onto the bed, scuffing her sheets with his boots, adding another dimension to the game. The flecks of dirt aroused her. The roughness. The maleness.

"Lift your arms," he said.

She obeyed his command, and he tugged at her Tinker Bell top, lifting it over her head and messing up her already sleep-tousled hair.

He bared her breasts and stared at her nipples. He kept staring until they stood at attention.

If he touched them, she would cream the bed.

But he didn't. He merely took his visual fill, making her desperately aware of her fantasy. She could barely wait for him to take off his clothes, to kneel over her, to stroke himself.

But he wasn't ready. He was still teasing her. He hadn't even removed her panties, and according to the scenario she'd created, she was completely naked before he masturbated on her.

Damn. That sounded so dirty, so hot, so nasty.

"You're blushing, baby."

"No, I'm not."

"Yes, you are."

She quit protesting. Being at his mercy was driving her crazy. "You're making me wet."

"How wet?" When she just sat there, he tore away the sheet. "Show me."

She spread her legs, revealing the crotch seam of her underwear, letting him see what he was doing to her.

"Naughty miss. You've got a damp spot."

He latched on to her panties. Working them off, he skimmed them down her hips, her thighs, her knees, and then over her feet.

"Lie down," he told her. "And keep your legs open."

Blatantly bared, she scooted onto a pillow. She waited for him to get undressed. Instead, he slid his fully clothed body between her legs, his denim fly almost chafing her delicate skin.

Almost.

He kissed her, slanting his mouth over hers. That hadn't been part of the fantasy, but it was so warm, so tender, she nearly melted. Now she was romantically aroused, too.

"My Mandy," he whispered.

Yes, she thought. She was his. She belonged to him. He nuzzled her neck, and she could smell the woodsy scent of his cologne. She touched his cheek, skimming her fingers along his jaw.

"I've never done this before," he said.

Stunned, she met his gaze. "You've never touched yourself for any of your lovers?"

"Yes, but not like this. Not so"—he paused, his voice quiet—"intimately."

She understood what he meant. Even with all of his sexual experience, with all of his bad-boy wildness, he'd never stroked himself so close to someone's face. "Do it for me, Jared."

He kissed her again. "I will. All over you."

Mandy shivered. Already her skin felt warm and liquid soft. She could only imagine how it was going to feel after he ejaculated on her.

He sat up, and his demeanor changed. He was rough again. Hard. Demanding. The slight edge of shyness was gone. She shifted her legs a fraction, and he grabbed her ankles.

"Stay put."

She wasn't about to move. She was more than willing to lie there with her heart pounding and her fingers itching to calm her clit.

Eager for more, she watched him get undressed. He did it roughly, tugging off his boots, pulling at the snaps of his shirt, thrusting open his belt, jerking down his pants, and freeing his cock.

Mandy's breath lodged in her lungs. His big, erect cock. Barely able to contain her excitement, she waited for him to put it in her face.

"Are you ready?" he asked.

"Yes." Please, yes. Her clit throbbed like a bitch.

He crawled over her, and she fisted the sheet strewn at her side. He got into position, planting his knees.

More throbbing. More hunger.

His penis, surrounded by a dark patch of hair, jutted forward, the pierced head aimed right at her. Like a missile, she thought, primed to launch.

Not only could she see his heavily veined cock, she could see the weight of his balls. He looked so powerful, so strong and masculine she couldn't take her eyes off him.

He licked his hand and lubricated his palm, and when he gripped the thickness of his shaft, Mandy caught her breath.

This was a first for him, but it was an even bigger first for her. Aside from a few scattered X-rated movies, she'd never witnessed male masturbation, and even in the movies she'd watched, the men hadn't done it from start to finish. A few strokes were all she'd seen.

But now . . .

She loved how aggressive Jared was. He treated himself as if he were his own prey. Although he moved his hand slowly at first, he was rough.

Kneading his thumb over the head, he pressed the piercing. His crown prince, she thought. She couldn't wait until it jeweled with come.

He stroked harder and faster, and Mandy moaned her pleasure. He glanced down at her, and their gazes locked.

"You're going to lick me," he said. "I'm going to move closer, and you're going to use your tongue."

Yes, she thought. *Yes.* When she'd relayed her fantasy to him, she'd told him that she'd wanted to lick whatever parts of him were closest to her mouth.

He widened his knee stance and moved lower, positioning his balls within her reach. She separated the tender sacs and laved each one, inhaling his musky scent. It was far more primitive than his cologne, but just as appealing. She buried her face against him, and he bucked like a stallion.

"Oh, fuck, baby. That feels good."

A wicked thrill spiraled through her. He was still stroking himself, moving his hand in a rapid motion. Empowered, she ran her tongue along his perineum, the sensual seam between his genitals and his ass, and he rocked against her touch. She knew it was a highly sensitive area. Sometimes when he gave her oral sex, he licked her there. Women had perineum regions, too.

Mandy didn't stop. She put her mouth all over his hot, male flesh. While she tortured him with her tongue, he kept milking himself, fulfilling her fantasy.

On the brink of ecstasy, he pulled back to show her his cock. Pearly drops of pre-come moistened the tip and leaked onto the barbell.

He rubbed the moisture against her lips, and she tasted the salty flavor. Together, they made ragged sounds. Desperate for relief, she reached down and stroked her clit, creating feminine friction.

"Naughty girl," he said.

"Naughty boy," she parroted.

They masturbated in unison. Mandy slid her fingers from her clit to her opening, smearing her juices, and he leaked more and more come.

"I can't hold on . . . I'm going to . . ."

She braced for the ultimate orgasm, for getting splashed with his semen. He moved down and ejaculated on her breasts, soaking her with his essence.

She went mad, coming when he did. In the silky minutes that followed, she massaged his seed over her nipples, across her stomach, and between her legs. She used it like lotion, just as she'd been dying to do.

He watched her, a dirty-boy smile on his handsome face. "You're incredible, baby."

She purred her pleasure. "I'm not done yet."

"You're not?"

"No." She wanted to have another orgasm, so she rubbed the milky wetness in tiny circles around her clit, renewing her arousal.

"Lord have mercy, woman." Jared sat beside her, taking in the show.

She noticed that he was still half-hard, that his erection wouldn't go away. Focused on his cock, on the memory of his warm, wet ejaculation, she frigged her clit until she ached, until she shuddered and thrust her hips in the air.

Slowly, slowly, the peak subsided, and she smiled at her lover. "Promise we can do this again."

"I promise." He looked as if he could barely breathe. "Any-time."

Feeling playful, she grabbed him and pulled him on top of her, gumming their naked bodies together.

"Shit!" He cursed in her ear, but he laughed, too.

They rolled over the bed, bunching the sheets and knocking pillows onto the floor.

Finally he pinned her down, cuffing her wrists with his hands. "I'm going to get you for that."

She feigned a struggle. "You and whose army?"

"Okay, now you did it. Now you're going to get it even harder."

But even as he professed his machismo, he released her from his bonds and kissed her, holding her close, so close she couldn't distinguish her heartbeat from his.

In that life-harrowing moment, she feared the worst. That she was a stone's throw from falling in love with him.

CHAPTER SIXTEEN

As I prepared my studio for Atacar's first portrait sitting, my confidence wavered. I'd been desperate to paint him since I'd first laid eyes on him, but now that the time was here, my nerves threatened to shatter.

This portrait was all I would have left of my lover after he was gone, and I wanted everything to be perfect. What if I didn't do him justice? What if I couldn't capture his true spirit? What if my talent wasn't worthy of him? I'd been convinced in the past that he would be my greatest work, but what if I'd been wrong?

Frowning at a chair I'd strategically placed in front of a blank wall, I moved it ever so slightly, reangling its position.

I thought about my previous works, portraits I'd been commissioned for in Paris. Female artists weren't sought after, but I'd managed a small measure of success, even with the restrictions of my gender. Yet here I was, losing faith in my ability.

"Catherine?"

Atacar's voice sounded behind me. I turned to look at him. Up until now, he'd remained quiet, clutching his rifle, waiting for me to make my final adjustments.

"Yes?" I responded.

He leaned his gun in a corner of the room. "I can't do this."

My heart dropped to my stomach. Had he lost confidence in me, too? Or had his original concern resurfaced? Was he uncomfortable about leaving a piece of himself behind? "You won't sit for me? You won't allow me to begin your portrait? Last night you said that you would."

"I'm not going back on my word. I was talking about leaving you behind after the painting is complete."

A gust of breath left my body. I reached out to grip the edge of the easel where I'd placed the canvas for his picture. Had I heard him correctly? Was he considering an alternative?

"I kept telling myself that creating a life with you would be wrong," he said. "But leaving you behind feels wrong, too. I want us to have more than memories. More than my soul locked inside of a painting."

I whispered a prayer to the heavens. Another gust of air expelled from my lungs. "Are you asking me to go to Mexico with you?"

He nodded. "If I had columbine and pennyroyal, I would give them to you."

Tears flooded my eyes. The sentiment attached to columbine was "I cannot give thee up," and pennyroyal meant "Flee away."

"What would you give me?" he asked.

I moved closer to him. By now I was trembling, but somehow

I was floating, too. As if I were in the midst of a dream. "Dandelions."

"To say that your wish has come true?"

"Yes." I took another heart-winging step in his direction. "I would give you red chrysanthemums, too."

Atacar's boots vibrated the floor. He was moving toward me, as well. Red chrysanthemums meant "I love you."

He reached for me, and I practically fell into his arms. His chest rose and fell; his breathing quickened.

"I love you, too," he whispered against my hair.

I lifted my face to his, and we kissed, the taste of our commitment rising like a wave. My fear of losing him was over. He was mine. He belonged to me.

"Nanny will come with us," he said.

"Yes, of course. She'll be pleased to be part of our future." I clutched him as closely as I could. I inhaled his scent, too. He smelled like the elements: the wind, the earth, the fire in his blood.

He kissed me again, deeper this time. We separated, our hearts full. We agreed to begin his portrait as we'd originally intended. Only now, when the painting was complete, we would be leaving for Mexico together.

He retrieved his rifle, and I instructed him to sit forward on the chair. He followed my direction, gripping the barrel of his gun and resting the butt on the floor.

He lowered his chin and looked up at me. The effect was stunning. For a moment, I could do little more than stare.

Daylight scattered across his shoulders, and shadows hollowed his cheekbones. His gaze caught mine, his eyes dark and serious.

Faint lines bracketed his mouth, fading into the sun-cloaked texture of his skin.

I approached the canvas, the passion I felt for him bubbling inside me.

He didn't move. He didn't flinch. His expression remained constant. He was the most brilliant model who'd ever sat for me. I opened my paint box, ready to work.

To capture every detail, every nuance of the warrior I loved.

⟋

Mandy wasn't going to let it happen. She wasn't going to fall in love with Jared. Yet here she was, drenched in his semen and emotional from the tender way in which he held her. Surviving a mundane marriage had been easier.

He lifted his sticky body from hers. "We need a shower. Or a bath. Or both. Do you want to rinse off in the shower, then take a long, hot bath with me?"

"That sounds good." Too good, she thought. But refusing wasn't an option. They couldn't sleep the way they were. "We'll have to change the sheets, too."

"You think?" He shook his head, laughed a little. "I can't believe you did this to me."

It wasn't as bad as what he'd done to her. At least he wasn't worried about falling in love. She stalled and gazed into his eyes. Or was he? She didn't have a clue what went on in Jared's mind.

"Do you want to light some candles in the bathroom?" he asked. "We could use the ones from Black Magic." He turned toward her dresser, motioning to the trio of candles they'd bought at the sex shop. "We could have a drink, too. Brandy, wine, whatever you've got."

She fought a frown. "Are you trying to be romantic?"

"I guess, yeah. Is that a problem? I thought you liked it when I did nice things."

"I do." Trapped in turmoil, she put her arms around his neck. "I do."

"Then why are you so tense? What's wrong, baby?"

"Nothing. Honestly, I'm fine." To prove her point, she pressed her lips to his, warning herself to accept their affair for what it was, to quit stressing about the tightness in the vicinity of her heart.

The kiss seemed to satisfy him, to solidify her sincerity. He reached for her hand, and they entered the kitchen and uncorked a bottle of sparkling rosé. Upon gathering the wine and two glasses, they returned to her room and collected the candles.

After rinsing off in the shower, they filled the tub, poured the wine, and enhanced the air with scented wax.

Jared sat down first and bent his knees, making room for Mandy. She slid into the open space he'd provided and leaned against him, the back of her head nestled in the crook of his shoulder. Even in the tight quarters, they were comfortable. Cozy, she thought.

As she sipped her wine, she weighed the past with the present. She'd wanted these sorts of moments with Ken, but he wasn't the bath-and-candle type.

"Do you believe that people have a compatibility quotient?" she asked.

"I don't know. I suppose they do." Jared skimmed her nipples, then lowered his hand and drew imaginary rings around her navel. "We're sexually compatible."

She sighed from his touch. "Do you think we have anything else in common?"

"We love Santa Fe. Neither of us will ever leave this place. We've made it our home."

She wanted him to keep going. She wanted to hear more. Needing to concentrate, she abandoned her wine, placing the glass on the side of the tub. "Anything else?"

He circled her navel again. "We appreciate art, music, and flowers. We have a similar sense of humor, and we make pigs of ourselves when we eat dessert." He stilled his hand. "We don't like to talk about our feelings, but we end up doing it for each other anyway. But most of all, we crave excitement. If we didn't, we wouldn't be having this affair."

She sat up and turned around to look at him. "I never thought of myself as a thrill seeker." Nor had she expected him to say such poignant things.

"Are you kidding? The good-bad girl?" He smiled and flicked some water at her.

She smiled and splashed him back. He always managed to make her feel young and vibrant. "If Ken had been more like you, he would have been a heck of a lot more fun."

Jared ended the swashing game. "You do that a lot."

"What?"

"Compare me to your ex."

Damn. "I'm sorry. It's a bad habit. I'll try not to do it again."

"Its okay, I guess. I'm learning to deal with it."

"Me and my crummy marriage?"

He shrugged. But a second later, he zapped her with a personal question, an issue they'd never discussed. "Why didn't you have kids? Isn't that what most couples do? Start a family, even if their marriage sucks?"

Mandy couldn't deny his logic. There was truth in his words, in his assumption. "We decided in the beginning that we would wait until we established our careers. And then we just let it pass. We didn't talk about it anymore."

"What about now? Would you take another stab at marriage and babies if the right guy came along?"

Oh, God. She went flip. If she didn't, she feared her feelings for him would betray her. "Is there such a thing as the right guy?"

He considered the question. "Probably not. But I've heard women talk about it. Even Amber says that kind of stuff. Of course, she's probably looking for two Mr. Rights."

Mandy couldn't help but laugh. Jared laughed, too. But their mirth died as quickly as it had erupted. In the interim, she reached for her wine.

He cut into the quiet. "I almost donated my sperm."

"What?" She gaped at him. "To who?"

"A sperm bank."

She drained her glass. He was full of surprises. "When?"

"I'd just turned eighteen, and I was saving money to move here. I heard that sperm donation paid about seventy-five to a hundred dollars per specimen, and that it required weekly specimens for up to six months. When you do the math, it sounds pretty good. But it's not that simple. They reject ninety to ninety-five percent of the applicants."

"Were you rejected?"

"No. I passed all of the screenings. I was young and gene-
tically healthy. I hadn't gotten tattooed or pierced yet. Not completely. I had my ears done, but they were old. So that wasn't a
concern."

"Why? Is there a time frame involved?"

He nodded. "You can't be tattooed or pierced within a year of
the donation. I think the same rule applies to giving blood. Or it
used to. It might be less time now." He shifted his legs, bending
his knees a bit more, making Mandy aware of his height, even in
his seated position. "But passing the screenings didn't matter. I
backed out on my own. I couldn't go through with it."

She assumed he was talking on a deeper level, more than ejac-
ulating in a cup. "What made you change your mind?"

"I didn't want to procreate that way. I didn't want to look
back years later and wonder if I had a kid out there."

She battled her next question, hoping his response, regardless
of what it was, wouldn't affect her. That she wouldn't get emotional about it. "Do you think you'll ever settle down? Maybe
have a family of your own?"

"I don't know." He made a perplexed face, as if no one had
ever asked him that before. "But I'll tell you this much. I'd be the
best dad I could be. I'd never do what my old man did to me."

So much for not getting emotional. She wanted to put her
arms around him and never let go. "Of course not. You're a good
man."

"I'm not that good."

Needing a diversion, Mandy tried to focus on something else.
To her, he was starting to seem perfect. Searching for a change of
topic, she glanced at his matching armbands. She took a quick

perusal of his jeweled penis, too. She could see it below the surface of the water.

"So, when did you get your Prince Albert and your tattoos?"

He glanced down. "I got the royal treatment a few months after I decided not to donate my sperm." He looked up and met her gaze. "I was going through a rough time, trying to identify myself, to get rid of the old me, to bury the kid my dad used to kick around."

"And getting an intimate body piercing helped?"

"Yes, it did."

"What about the tattoos?"

"I got inked after I'd been in Santa Fe for a while. I couldn't afford any major artwork until then." He turned one of his arms toward her, explaining the design. "This represents White Painted Woman. She's a deity who bore a child from the rain." He indicated a symbol that represented rain. "She called him Child of the Water. My mom used to read me folklore about him. The slaying of monsters was my favorite."

"It's nice that you remember her reading to you."

"Yes, but it's scattered. Not the stories. My memories. I kept up on the folklore myself. I kept that part of my culture alive. My dad certainly wasn't going to do it." Jared lifted his wine and brought the rim of the glass to his lips. "Dad didn't follow the old ways, and neither did his family. They're not spiritual people. They're hard and violent."

And he'd disassociated himself from them a long time ago. "Your tattoos are beautiful. Thank you for telling me about them."

"You're turning out to be a pretty good friend. You know that, Mandy?"

She warned her heart to be still. "You, too."

They went silent until he asked, "Do you think the water is getting cold?"

"Maybe a little."

"Should we refresh it, or do you want to get out?"

"We can refresh it." She didn't want to break this bond with him. "If that's okay with you."

"It's fine. The bath was my idea."

She drained most of the water and added more, and he refilled their wine. Once the tub regained its warmth, she returned to her original position of leaning back against him. The candles continued to burn, making shadows dance on the shower curtain.

Jared circled her waist. "That looks ghostly."

"It does," she agreed before she closed her eyes and sank into the haunting comfort of being wrapped in his arms.

❧

I asked Atacar to bathe with me, so we hauled the tub into my room and filled it with hot water. We lit some candles, too. At one time, candles had been a primary source of household lighting. Now they seemed old-fashioned and romantic.

The tub hadn't been constructed for two people, but we made do. We leaned back and sat across from each other with our legs bent. Some families had piped-in water and built-in tubs, but not in this area. This was as close to luxury as we got.

"Are you going to sell the farm?" Atacar asked.

I shook my head. "I don't own it outright. I'm making payments to the bank. They can reclaim the property after I'm gone."

"I can repair your old wagon to take to Mexico."

Ah, yes, I thought. The broken-down vehicle the previous owners had left behind.

"I can paint it so it looks good," he said. "And I can make a top for it."

"That's a brilliant idea." I could afford to buy a covered wagon, but Nanny kept warning me that the income Papa had provided for me wouldn't last forever, and I should be more frugal. Besides, if I purchased a shiny new wagon, the townsfolk would wonder why I needed it, and Nanny and I were keeping our move a secret.

Atacar planned our trip. "I'll have to stay in the back of the wagon when we're on main roads. But we'll still need to be cautious."

"We will. We'll be careful."

"When the time comes, you should darken your hair. You'll be less noticeable in Mexico. We'll want to attract the least amount of attention possible."

I patted my blonde mane. I'd piled it on top of my head for the bath. "Do you know of a plant that will make it brown?"

He nodded and leaned forward to give me a gentle kiss, reassuring me that everything would be all right.

"Turn around," he said. "I'll wash your back."

I changed my position, and he ran the soap along my spine. He nibbled the side of my neck, too.

"Will you marry me when we're in Mexico? Will you become my wife?"

His words, his proposal, made me shiver. I latched on to his arms and wrapped them around my body.

"Yes," I said. "Oh, God, yes."

He continued to nuzzle, to nibble, to graze my damp skin. "We'll have beautiful children, Catherine. Babies for Nanny to spoil."

I tightened his hold on me; I made certain that he didn't let go. "We'll have a perfect life. We'll be together until we're old and gray."

"We can farm in Mexico. We can do what we're doing here. And we can pick variegated dahlias and put them in glass jars all over our house. To think of each other constantly."

"We can pick yellow dahlias, too." They meant "I am happy that you love me," and Atacar and I would always be happily in love.

Wouldn't we?

"Promise that the army will never find us," I said. "That they won't take you away from me."

"They won't," he whispered. "This is meant to be. We are meant to be."

As water lapped at my body, Atacar shifted me to my knees. I pitched forward and gripped the tub. I could feel his cock pressed against me. He was on his knees, too.

The arms that had been circling my waist dropped lower, a strong hand slipping between my legs. He stroked the bud of my womanhood while he entered me.

He thrust deeply, and I watched the candles burn, mesmerized by the erotic drip of wax. I arched my hips, wanting to feel more of him. He pushed all the way inside, riding me full hilt.

The candles flickered. The water sloshed. My mind spun.

"Who will marry us?" I asked.

"A mission priest," he responded.

I wasn't Catholic, and neither was he, but that was the faith in Mexico. I suspected it would become our religion, too. Our baptism. "I'll have to improve my Spanish."

"I'll give you lessons." He tugged on my hair, loosening pins, making strands fall. "Turn your head. I want to kiss you."

I angled toward him, and his mouth crushed mine. Our tongues twisted and danced, the sensation warm and wet. He pumped into me, swaying back and forth. I reached back to cup his balls.

I knew how he liked to be fondled. I knew almost everything about him, sexually and otherwise. He was more than my lover. He was my dearest friend, too. There was nothing I wouldn't do for him.

He thrust in and out until I climaxed, until flames burst in front of my eyes. But he didn't stop. He kept moving at a feverish pace, pushing toward his own release, filling me with his heat, his passion, his seed.

Afterward, we slid into the tub and steadied our breaths. I turned around to face him, and we completed our bath, drying off with the same towel and kissing each other again. From now on, we would share everything.

Our future, I thought, as I hugged him desperately close. The rest of our lives.

CHAPTER SEVENTEEN

The following week, George and his family came to visit, and we enjoyed a lighthearted afternoon. Nanny prepared a picnic-style meal, and the men moved the dining table outside. The weather was lovely, perfect for a social gathering.

We weren't far from the house, just a short distance from the porch. A butterfly winged its way past the table, and little Peter tried to catch it. He was Alice's youngest son. At two years old, he was an active child with rosy cheeks and wispy brown hair. Jack, the four-year-old, had a similar look. He was more interested in the pie Nanny had baked than helping his brother snare the butterfly. I could hardly blame him. The aroma of sugared apples wafted through the air.

Atacar glanced at me and smiled. The children were a pleasant reminder of the family we hoped to create someday.

We confided in George and Alice about our plans to move to Mexico, and they supported our decision. George promised to help us acquire extra horses. He offered to help Atacar repair the old wagon, too.

After everyone finished eating, I discussed my upcoming nuptials with Alice. As a second-time bride, she was an accomplished wedding organizer.

She accompanied me inside, and we sorted through my gowns to choose one in which I could be married. I wanted to be prepared for my special day. As soon as Atacar, Nanny, and I arrived in Mexico, we intended to arrange the ceremony. Atacar already knew the town in which we would settle.

I opened a wooden trunk that housed my best gowns, and Alice sucked in her breath.

"Oh, my," she said.

"Most of them are from Paris. Some were featured in fashion magazines."

"They're exquisite." She placed a pink dress on my bed, followed by a yellow, then an emerald green. "But you should wear white."

"Even if I'm not a virgin anymore?" I teased.

She gave me a conspiratorial smile. "Neither was I the first time I married. I was already carrying Jack in my womb. But I wasn't far enough along to show."

It felt wonderful to have a new friend, a young woman willing to share her secrets with me. "I've been drinking a preventative tea."

Alice tilted her head. "I've never tried anything like that. When Rowan, my late husband, and I were courting, we practiced coitus interruptus. Withdrawal," she clarified. "But it wasn't effective every time. That's how I conceived Jack."

I analyzed the science of intercourse. "Some of Rowan's seed must have leaked out before he withdrew."

She nodded. "There are physicians who say that coitus interruptus can be detrimental to men's health, and others who believe it isn't so. Rowan didn't behave any differently when he spilled inside of me or when he withdrew. He derived the same pleasure."

"Atacar and I want to conceive after we're married." I considered the alternative. "But it would be all right if it happened sooner. The way it did with you and Rowan."

Alice glanced at the flatness of my stomach. "You'll know if you miss your menses."

"I haven't yet."

"Then the tea must be working." She paused, smiled. "But no matter, you'll have charming children."

"You have charming children. Your sons are adorable."

"I love them dearly. I want to have another with George. Hopefully a little girl. But after that, I'd like to stop." She furrowed her brow. "Maybe I should try your tea. They don't sell preventatives in town, and it's illegal to obtain them through the mail. Such nonsense. Such prudery."

In her own quiet way, Alice was as independent as my bohemian friends. I would miss her once Atacar, Nanny, and I were gone.

"I'm glad we're getting to know each other," I said.

"Me, too."

"I'd offer to write to you, but I don't know how reliable the postal service is in Mexico. Besides, I—"

"Worry that soldiers could intercept the letters?" she provided.

I nodded. "Atacar says we'll be safe in Mexico, that the U.S.

Army has no power there. But how can we be sure?" I sighed, hating to lose touch with her and George. "Maybe you can visit us. That way we could see each other again."

She brightened. "That would be lovely. Maybe we can plan a trip for next year and bring the boys."

I shared her enthusiasm. "I'll look forward to it."

We proceeded to sort through my gowns. I had three white dresses. The design that seemed the most appropriate for a wedding had a trained underskirt and yards of lace. Alice thought it was breathtaking. It was a favorite of mine, as well. With a bouquet of flowers and a delicate veil, I would make a stunning bride.

As for Atacar's attire, I would ask Nanny to make him a white shirt and a black jacket. We could buy the materials in town and say they were for a tailored suit for me. Some modern girls were wearing mannish skirt ensembles. They even sported bow ties at the collars.

Alice helped me put away my gowns, and we sat quietly for a moment.

"How did Rowan leave you widowed?" I asked.

"He was thrown from a skittish horse and broke his neck. I miss him something fierce. But I'm grateful I have George now."

I, too, was glad that she had George. But if I ever lost Atacar, I could never replace him. I'd just as soon die.

We returned to the outdoors and found the men playing games with the children, behaving like boys themselves. As I watched Atacar with Peter, my heart went pitter-patter. The two-year-old toddled on his chubby legs, and Atacar scooped him up and made him squeal.

Nanny sat in the shade, monitoring the activity with a smile.

George turned and noticed Alice and me. He'd been spinning Jack like a windmill. "Our womenfolk are back."

Atacar turned, as well, making my heartbeat stronger. "So they are. Your wife and my betrothed."

His betrothed. I walked toward him, a lump forming in my throat, a prayer for our future.

"Play some music," Alice said to her husband, lightening my mood.

George complied, entertaining us with his fiddle. His wife danced with Jack, and Nanny gave the youngest a twirl, bouncing him in her arms.

Atacar bowed to me, and we joined in the fun, doing a whimsical polka we'd been practicing.

As the day quieted down and the children grew sleepy and napped on the grass, Atacar requested one last song.

A romantic waltz. Just for me.

~

"Are they doing a country western waltz?" Mandy asked.

Jared glanced at the dance floor. While a cover band played honky-tonk ballads, jean-clad couples moved counterclockwise in a promenade position. "Yep. That's what they're doing."

"It looks fun."

He returned his attention to Mandy. She sat across from him at a rustic little table. He'd invited her out for a night on the town, so here they were at one his favorite cowboy haunts. "I can teach you, if you want to learn. It's similar to a ballroom waltz, but it doesn't use as many diagonal patterns, and it's more relaxed."

"Sure. You can teach me. After I finish this." She lifted her Silk Stockings, an iced cocktail that paired tequila with cream and cinnamon.

Not that Jared minded watching her sip a lingerie-inspired concoction. He'd started the sexy-drinks cycle with her, just as he'd done with Amber.

"So where did you learn to ballroom waltz?" she asked.

"I took lessons."

"For the masquerade?"

He nodded. "But I've been country dancing most of my life, and as I said, it's not that different."

"Your ballroom technique was amazing. I was impressed."

"Thanks." Uncomfortable with her praise, he glanced away. Atacar had been a natural-born dancer, too. "Maybe it's in my blood."

"Did the other men take waltz lessons for the masque, too?"

The other men. She meant Pink and Red, or Jay and Luke, as they were known in the real world. "Yes, but Pink wasn't picking it up fast enough, so that's why he never got his turn to dance with you."

She laughed. "God forbid that one of your impersonators would be stepping all over my feet."

He laughed, too. Even if he felt serious inside. "That would have blown the polished Victorian image was I was trying to create."

"So what's your image tonight, Jared?"

"Nothing. I'm just being me." Before he frowned, he swigged his beer, quenching an uneasy thirst. Was there even such a thing as being himself anymore? He'd gotten so caught up in the journal, in mimicking Atacar, in comparing himself to his ancestor, he was starting to wonder who Jared Cabrillo was.

And then there was Mandy.

He studied his lover, with her mink brown hair and pretty blue eyes, wondering when he'd gotten so attached to her, when she'd started to matter so damn much, when she'd become more than just a hot lay.

She returned his intense gaze, and he kept his hands wrapped around his beer, clutching the base of the sweating bottle.

"Are you all right?" she asked.

"I'm fine."

"Are you sure?"

"I was just thinking about how powerful women are." Especially her. If she wasn't making his dick hard, she was making him emotional. "Have I ever told you about Coyote?"

"No. Is that a woman?"

"He's a trickster in my culture."

"What does he have to do with women being powerful?"

Jared tried to ignore the music. The band was playing a twangy version of "Could I Have This Dance," a song about falling in love on the dance floor. "Coyote discovered the power of a woman." He scooted his chair closer to the table, bumping the edge of it. "Of her pussy."

Mandy's glass rattled. She grabbed it and gave him a suspicious look. "Are you making this up?"

"It's folklore." But it was starting to seem frustratingly real. "Coyote found a pretty woman and wanted to have sex with her, but he got scared because he saw teeth inside of her vagina."

She raised her eyebrows, but she didn't comment.

"When the woman wasn't looking, Coyote got a long stick and a rock. Instead of inserting his penis, he put the stick inside of her." Jared paused, frowned. "Her pussy ground up the stick, so Coyote was glad he hadn't used his cock."

She winced. "I'll bet."

He made a face, too. The fall-in-love song was still being sung. "Coyote used the rock next. He used it until he knocked off all the teeth, until her vagina became what a woman's is today." Soft and warm, he thought. Alluring.

"So did Coyote ever have sex with her?"

"Yes. And do you know what she told him when he was done?"

She leaned closer. "No. What?"

"She said something like, 'Hereafter I shall be worth a lot. Many horses and many things.'"

"Smart girl." Mandy angled her head. "Is that the folklore behind Apache men offering gifts for their brides?"

Jared nodded, grateful when the romantic song ended. "But I think it's just another way of paying for pussy."

She toyed with the cherry garnish in her Silk Stockings, teasing him, going coy. "Maybe I should start making you pay. You've got lots of horses."

Was she kidding? He was already paying, sitting here with his heart twisted around his cock.

The band slid into another love song, and Mandy showed him that she'd finished her drink and was ready for her county western waltz lesson.

He stood up and offered her his hand, wishing she had teeth in her vagina. If she did, he would know better than to get bitten.

But it was too late for that. Because when he took her in his arms, all he wanted to do was keep her.

~

Hours later Jared drove Mandy to a secluded spot with a hilltop view. He parked his truck, and they gazed out the front windshield. He wasn't sure why he'd brought her here. Maybe it was to look at the stars.

"This makes me feel like a teenager," she said. "Like we're high school sweethearts."

He turned toward her, thinking how pretty she looked in the moonlight. He considered lifting the hem of her dress and sliding his hand along her thigh, the way a teenage boy would do, but he tempered the urge.

Instead he asked, "What was your favorite subject?"

"In high school?" She provided a ready answer. "I took an art appreciation class that blew me away."

"That makes sense. Considering your career path."

"What about you?"

He didn't glance back at the stars, but they were there, scattered across the night sky. "Astronomy. But I liked anatomy, too."

"Human anatomy, I'll bet." Her smile went crooked.

"Are you accusing me of stealing kisses between the lockers?" The urge to lift her dress returned, but he held off. "I partied and played around, but I managed to stay on track. I got good grades in all of my classes. I didn't mind studying. It gave me something to focus on."

Her voice went soft. "Other than your dad and the way he was mistreating you?"

Jared nodded. "No one expected a kid like me to be an honor roll student, least of all him. He wanted to see me fail. It pissed him off when I didn't."

"Nothing you did made him proud."

"No, nothing." He shifted the dialogue to her family, needing to rid his mind of his. "So, do your parents ever come to visit? Or any of your brothers or sisters?"

"Not too often. Mostly I go back to Iowa since everyone still lives there."

"I wonder what they'd think of me." He got closer to sneaking his hand up her dress. "The cowboy you're boning."

"Since you put it that way . . ."

"What?"

"Truthfully? My parents would think you're too young and too wild for me, my brothers wouldn't trust you, and my sisters would whisper to each other about how gorgeous you are. Then they'd warn me to be careful."

He tried to shrug it off. He was often judged in that manner. But deep inside where it counted, her honesty stung.

"I'm sorry," she said. "That sounded harsh. But I come from a conservative family. Their opinions are predictable."

"It's okay," he lied. "It doesn't matter."

"Yes, it does. If you ever did meet them, I'd insist that they give you a chance. That they look deeper. That they see you for the man you really are."

"I'm just a guy who's fucking you, Mandy."

She shook her head. "You're more than that. You're strong and kind and wonderfully impulsive. You're thoughtful and romantic, too. You've done things for me no man has ever done." She cleared her throat, battling a sudden hoarseness. "Amber even accused me of being in love with you."

Holy shit. He tried to breathe, but he couldn't exhale. His lungs expanded like a balloon.

"But I'm trying not to love you," she added quickly. "I'm trying not to complicate our lives that way."

"Good. Good." He released a chop of air, then another. Finally he steadied his breathing. "Sex is best. Lots of sex." But even as he said it, he knew they were spiraling toward more.

The balloon came back.

He should end it now. He should take her home and never see her again. But he was still itching to touch her, to slide his hand under her dress, to claim her under the stars.

He scooted across the bench seat of his vintage truck, moving closer. Then he did it. He hiked up her hem and exposed her panties.

She parted her legs, letting him have his way. But that was the dynamic of their relationship, the heat that drove them.

"Are your panties blue or purple?" he asked, creeping his fingers along her thigh. It was too dark to distinguish the color.

"Blue."

"You'll have to get a purple pair, too."

"Why?" She widened her thighs a little more.

"There's a drink called Purple Panties." He eased toward the waistband. "Vodka, triple sec, pineapple juice, grapefruit juice." He slid inside the fabric. "You shake the ingredients with crushed ice, then add seltzer and lime."

"That sounds refreshing." She tightened her rear, pushing her pelvis toward his hand.

He stalled, teasing her, making her wait. She was trying to get him to make contact with her clit.

He told her, "Pink Panties and Edible Panties are drinks, too."

"I wear lots of pink underwear. But I've never worn the edible kind." Another pelvic lift, another attempt to make him comply.

He didn't give in. He let her crave his touch even more. "What about Slippery Panties?"

Her head seemed to be swimming. She gave him a dizzy look. "What?"

"Slippery Panties. That's another drink."

"If you touch me, my panties will get slippery. Creamy. Wet. Please, Jared. Move your hand. Do something."

He let it happen. He stroked her, and the energy between them splintered. His cock went hard, straining against his zipper. But he wasn't looking to get himself off. It was her he wanted to please.

He dipped into Mandy's center, spreading her juices while he thumbed her ever-swelling clit.

She still had her ass flexed. Tight and sexy. He leaned in to French her, to capture her mouth. As their tongues tangled, the pressure built.

They stopping kissing, and their aroused breaths steamed up the windows. By now her thighs were wide-open. They could have been teenage sweethearts, he thought. Getting nasty on a school night.

She climaxed in a feminine flurry, biting down on her bottom lip and making girl-sweet sounds. He didn't remove his hand until the shuddering stopped and he'd absorbed every gentle quake.

In the afterglow, she leaned her head against the back of the seat and smiled at him. Miss Blue Panties. He gave her a chaste kiss and righted the hem of her dress.

"What's your full name?" he asked, realizing that he didn't know one of the most basic things about her. "Is it Amanda?"

"Yes, and my middle name is Lynn."

"Amanda Lynn Cooper." He turned the key in the ignition and set the defroster. "Is Cooper your maiden name? Or is it left over from Ken?"

"It's my maiden name. I went back to it after the divorce. What about you? What's your middle name?"

"Michael." He watched the windows clear. "Jared means either to rise or to descend, and Michael was an archangel. It's a strange combination."

"No, it's beautiful. Jared Michael. Will the angel rise or will he fall?"

He didn't comment on being called an angel. "Remember when you asked me if the Apache believe in Heaven and Hell? Christian Apache do. And those who follow the old way believe in the underworld. It's a place where spirits go, with mountains, rivers, and trees. Whatever you did on earth, you do there. If you were a warrior, then you stay a warrior. You're the same, only you're dead." He paused, fought a self-induced chill. "A ghost."

"Do you think that's where Atacar went after he died?"

"I don't know." He hadn't instigated this conversation to pull Atacar into it.

"If he did, I hope Catherine was able to meet him there."

"What makes you think she died, too?"

"She had to have died eventually. It's been over a hundred

years." Mandy sighed. "But I still wish I knew what happened to her. That her journal would surface."

Jared turned toward the stars, feeling guilty for keeping secrets, feeling sad for knowing the truth. "Like you said, eventually she died, too. Eventually it was over for both of them."

CHAPTER EIGHTEEN

I set down my brush and stepped back. The portrait was finished. I'd reached my artistic vision. Everything I'd ever learned, my entire craft, seemed centered on this moment, on this painting.

I told Atacar, and he responded, "Truly? It's done?"

I nodded and smiled.

He rose from his chair and leaned his rifle against the wall, coming around the other side to view his image. I hadn't allowed him to see it before now. I'd been keeping it covered in between sittings.

But this was the final unveiling.

He didn't speak, not at first. He gazed at the canvas for what seemed like a very long time. Suddenly I got nervous. While I waited for his reaction, my pulse bumped like a rough carriage ride.

"It's me," he said. "Only better." He turned toward me. "Because it came from you. From your heart, from your hand."

"It's the man I love."

"It's the man who loves you, too." Atacar turned back to the painting. "You captured him."

He was right. I did. I captured him in every way possible. "The seriousness in his eyes, that comes from the pain in which he has lived. But it comes from the power of who he is, too. The warrior who escaped. The Chiricahua Apache who found his freedom."

"He found more than freedom. He found a woman. The perfect woman."

"Perfect for him," I said.

"Yes, for him."

He leaned in to kiss me, and I looped my arms around his neck. His clothes smelled of the herbs he sometimes burned when he prayed.

I wondered if there was another couple in the world who loved each other as much as we did. I didn't think it was possible, but I was biased.

We separated and faced his portrait again. I could still taste him on my lips, lingering, always lingering. I got eager for nightfall, for the things he did to me in the privacy of our room.

"We should show the portrait to Nanny," he said. "She'll be impressed."

"Yes, we should." Nightfall was hours away.

We went into the parlor, where Nanny was using her sewing machine, a hand-operated model we'd purchased from a catalog. She glanced up, with spectacles clipped to the bridge of her nose. They were a common style of eyeglasses, and she wore them to read and to sew. She couldn't see well close up.

"The portrait is complete," Atacar said.

"Is it?" Nanny pushed away from her chair and got to her feet, anxious to view what I kept telling her would be my greatest work.

She removed her spectacles, which were attached to a ribbon around her neck, and abandoned her sewing.

The three of us entered my studio, and upon seeing the painting, my dear old nanny pressed a hand to her heart. She got teary-eyed, too. She'd never expressed that kind of emotion in front of me before, and certainly not over one of my paintings or sketches.

"It's grand," she said, her voice awed. "Oh, it's so grand."

I thanked her, humbled by her praise. Atacar smiled at me, and I reached for his hand.

We returned to the parlor, where Nanny resumed her sewing. I offered to prepare supper, and she and Atacar exchanged a humored glance.

I rolled my eyes. I was a pitiful cook, but I could manage cold meats and cheeses. I could slice fresh fruit and arrange it festively on a platter, too.

I donned an apron, intending to look official, as wifely as I could. Beneath the practical cover-up, my work clothes were mottled with paint. I was a silly sight.

But somehow I was enchanting, too.

I knew this because when I glanced back over my shoulder, my future husband was admiring me.

～

Later that night, Atacar guided me to the mirror on my wardrobe cabinet and stood behind me. We were fully clothed, but I could tell that he had other intentions.

I gazed at our reflections. I'd never considered making love in front of a mirror. But it was titillating, so very right for me. I liked to envision how we looked while we mated, and now I would be able to watch, to see everything.

He slipped his arms around my waist and turned his head to kiss the side of my neck, to graze me with his teeth.

In the glass, my expression went soft and womanly. He undid the tiny buttons that marched down the front of my dress. His technique was slow and painfully sexy. The more buttons he worked, the more my dress gaped, exposing my corset cover.

He paused to nibble my neck again. He was torturing me purposely, making the process last. Finally, he removed my dress, peeling it down my body and allowing it to pool at my feet. I stepped out of the circle of fabric and waited for his next move.

He pillaged my hair, one pin at a time. I was wearing a la concierge, a style in which my long hair was pulled to the top of my head and fastened into a knot.

Silky strands tumbled in disarray, making me look like a siren. I was more beautiful than I'd ever been, but my beauty was coming from him, from what he was doing to me, from the way he was making me feel.

He divested me of my corset cover and petticoat, leaving me in my ribbon-trimmed corset and lace-hemmed drawers. On the day I'd met him, this was how far I'd gotten in my state of undress before we'd been forced to hide in the trees.

I searched his gaze in the glass. My Atacar. My love. Someday I wanted to take him to Paris, to show him the city that influenced me. Eventually I wanted to take him to London, too. Home, I thought. To introduce him to Mama and Papa and my brother, Paul. I didn't know if they would accept him any better than they accepted me, but it would be nice to form a bond with my family, especially for the sake of the children I hoped to have.

Atacar removed a buttercup from his pocket and tucked it behind my ear. I'd been wearing a buttercup in my hair every night, but today I'd gotten sidetracked by our guests and had forgotten to pick one from the nearby field where they grew. My lover had remembered for me.

His seduction continued. He opened the front closures on my corset and caused my breasts to spill out. He caressed me, rubbing my nipples, then moved forward and bent his head, taking a pointed tip into his mouth.

My reflection went breathy, and I put my arms around him, holding him close. As I watched, I listened to the sounds of his suckling. He shifted from one nipple to the other, enjoying his treat.

I waited for him to move lower, to give me cunnilingus. He teased me instead, kneeling to toy with my navel, to dart his tongue in and out of the indention.

"Does this feel good?" he asked.

My voice vibrated. "Yes."

"Are you getting wet?"

"Yes."

He undid my drawers, pulling them down my hips. Once they were all the way off, he faced me forward. By now, I was completely naked, desperate for him to lick me.

But he didn't. He stood up, approached my vanity table, and retrieved my hand mirror, an ornate object with silver backing.

He returned to his knees and positioned the small mirror between my legs. I tried to remain poised, to not seem shocked. But I was. Shocked and curious.

"I want you to see what I see when I look at you there," he said.

I glanced down and saw my nether lips, surrounded by a tuft of blonde hair. I took a swift breath and looked up at my head-to-toe nakedness. Then down again at my private place. I was wickedly aroused.

Atacar kept the hand mirror in place, angling it just so. "Use your fingers. Open yourself up."

I obeyed his erotic command. I exposed my dewy folds. The flesh inside was soft and pink. I imagined Atacar's tongue delving into it.

"Keep looking," he said. "Keep touching."

I rubbed my clitoris, making it swell.

Finally, too aroused to continue, I begged him to lick me. Atacar discarded the smaller mirror and gave in to my plea, grasping my hips and pulling me toward his mouth. I shivered, wildly excited.

I watched from the bigger mirror as he made his luscious foray. I pressed closer to him, rocking in a forward motion. I sank my hands into his hair, fisting his scalp.

He painted me with saliva. He sucked and nibbled. He did everything imaginable with his hot, hungry mouth.

I climaxed like a tornado. Before I pitched over, he steadied me, sliding his hands along the sides of my body as he rose to his feet.

"We're not done yet," he said, passion alight in his eyes. "We're just getting started."

I curled up to him, purring my pleasure, a wind-ravaged kitten anxious for more. "Are we going to use the mirror again?"

He nodded, opening his shirt and pushing down his pants. "And the floor and all of the furniture in the room. I'm going to press you against the wall, too." He spun me around and made my heart hit my chest. "I'm going to take you as many ways as I can."

"Forever," I gasped.

"Yes," he responded. "Forever."

Jared closed the leather-bound book and returned it to the floor safe in his closet, spinning the combination lock until the numbers blurred before his eyes. He'd been reading Catherine's journal, as he often did when he was alone. But this time, he panicked.

Forever.

The word reverberated in his mind. He couldn't do forever. He couldn't make that kind of commitment, and if he kept mimicking Atacar, that's what would happen. He would get so far into Mandy that he wouldn't be able to live without her.

The other night beneath the stars, he'd considered ending their affair. But he hadn't done it, even after she'd admitted that she was trying to keep herself from falling in love with him.

So what the hell was he waiting for? For her to stumble and fall? To love him?

He needed to let her go, for both of their sakes. No more dancing. No more candlelit baths. No more language of flowers.

He reached for the landline phone on his nightstand, prepared to ring Mandy, to tell her that they should call it quits. But he stalled. Already his body was craving hers.

One last time.

All night, in every position imaginable, the way Atacar had taken Catherine: in front of a mirror, straddled on a chair, up against a wall, on the floor . . .

Shit.

He glanced around his room. He couldn't do it here. He needed to make a clean break, which meant her condo was off-limits, too.

A hotel, he thought.

The first time they'd fucked had been at a hotel, so why not let it be their last?

He got out the phone book and dialed the place where they'd started their affair. Focusing on the tightness beneath his zipper, he requested the same accommodations. He didn't stop to consider why he remembered their old room number, other than that his first night with her had been pretty damn memorable.

There, he thought, as he hung up, the wheels were in motion. He ignored the other tightness, the clenching near his heart, and called Mandy, catching her on her cell phone.

She answered in a customary greeting. "Hello?"

"Meet me at the Hôtel de Terrasse. The same room as before."

"Jared?"

"Who else would it be?"

"What's going on?"

"I just said what's going on. Meet met at the hotel. Room four ten."

"What for?"

"To have sex." He glanced at his watch: 2:04. Check-in was at three. "In an hour."

"You sound strange. Are you all right?"

"I just need to get laid. We're going to do it all night, over and over, as many times as we can."

"Oh, my goodness. Are you at least going to buy me dinner first?"

He could tell that she was teasing him, joking about his impatience. But she was right. He needed to slow down, to catch his breath. Besides, food was fuel, energy to keep going. He'd meant what he'd said about making it a marathon. "We can order room service."

"I was kidding, Jared."

"I know, but I think we should eat. I think dinner is a good idea."

She didn't disagree. "I need to get ready. And to pack a bag."

"So do I. I'll see you at three."

He ended the call and threw his belongings in a leather satchel. He wasn't going to tell Mandy that this was their last date, the end of their relationship. He would do that in the morning, when the sex was over, when he could think clearly.

Atacar would hate him for this, and so would Catherine. But they'd been dead and gone a long time. They weren't in any position to save him.

An hour later, Jared got to the hotel and checked in. Mandy was late, so he waited. The familiar room, with its hand-painted furniture, beamed ceiling, and kiva fireplace, did nothing to ground his emotions.

He walked onto the balcony. He could see a view of the Plaza, where historical Santa Fe sprawled out before him.

Finally Mandy arrived, and he greeted her with a powerful hug. "Thank you for doing this," he said. "For being here."

She gave him a passionate kiss. "I promised that I'd never say no to you, remember? Besides, why wouldn't I want to be here?"

"No reason." He hugged her again, holding her as if he would never let her go. But letting her go was exactly what he was doing. After tonight, he thought. After he thrust his desperate cock inside her.

He stepped back. "Let's order dinner."

They scanned the room service menu and chose the same meal: mango gazpacho and beef fajitas. For dessert, they ordered chocolate mousse.

Jared admired his companion. She looked amazing in a backless dress, a halter or whatever it was called. He'd never seen her in anything that required her to go braless.

"That's sexy," he said.

"Thank you." She turned in a pretty pirouette. "It's new. A gift to myself."

"It suits you. The good-bad girl." What the hell was he going to do without her?

Get on with his life, he told himself a second later. Become a bachelor again.

"You look sexy, too," she said. "All rough and ready."

Jared ran his hand along his jaw, where he'd neglected to shave. He would probably give her a beard-stubble burn. Everywhere, he thought, all over her naked body. But he doubted that she would complain. He suspected that she would like it.

He frowned, wondering who would share her bed after he was gone. Envisioning another man in his place packed a punch, in more ways than one. It made him want to rip the nameless, faceless guy apart.

THE ART OF DESIRE

Christ, he thought. He needed to get a grip.

A short while later, a knock sounded on the door. Jared dashed off to allow their food server into the room.

Once they were alone, Jared and Mandy settled in to eat. She spooned into her gazpacho, a cold soup designed for warm weather. He tasted his, too.

"This is good," she said.

Good?

No, he thought, his chest going tight. This was bad. The shittiest thing he'd ever done. He was going bang her in nearly every sexual position known to man, and in the morning when she was wrapped securely in a hotel-monogrammed robe, he was going to break up with her. He deserved the bastard-of-the-year award for that, and he would probably get it, too. She would probably hate him forever.

Forever.

There was that word again. The word that panicked him. The word that Catherine and Atacar had tried—and failed—to claim as their own.

They kept eating, and when they were nearly done with their meal, Mandy said, "It's been almost two months."

Jared glanced up from his dessert. "What?"

"Since we first got together." She looked toward the bed. "Since our affair started. Being in this hotel feels like an anniversary, especially in the same room. It's nice that you remembered."

He didn't want to talk nice. Because he didn't feel nice. Because he wasn't. "I just want to touch you, Mandy."

She swallowed the last spoonful of her mousse and stood up.

He pushed back his chair and tugged her onto his lap. With the flavor of chocolate on their lips, they kissed.

He skimmed a hand down her back, where the dress left her skin exposed. She straddled him, rubbing against his jeans.

"Guess what color my panties are," she said.

His thoughts drifted to the other night. "Purple."

She shook her head.

"Pink."

Another headshake.

He didn't guess again. "Why don't you show me?"

She climbed off his lap and lifted the hem of her dress, inch by inch. He waited for a color to appear. But what he saw was her Brazilian-waxed pussy, sans underwear. She'd gone commando for him. His mouth all but watered.

He shoved their dishes aside, making room for his lover. "Take off your dress and sit here."

She blinked. "On the table?"

He nodded. "With your legs open. I want to eat you."

She did it. Only she placed her dress below her, using it like a napkin between her ass and the tabletop. He smiled, thinking how mannered she was.

He sat in front of her, lowered his head, and feasted like the sexually starved man he'd become. She was better than the chocolate, better than anything he'd ever tasted. He glanced up and noticed how willing she looked, spread out like a sacrifice.

He returned his attention to the dampness between her thighs. He licked and swirled. He kissed and nibbled. He ate her as erotically as Atacar had eaten Catherine in front of the mirror.

"Have you ever looked at yourself?" he asked.

"Looked?"

"In a mirror."

She nodded, seeming shy yet seductive, Mandy at her most alluring. "Sometimes when I . . ."

"Touch yourself?"

She scooted closer to his mouth. "Yes."

Damn. He pushed his tongue all the way inside, and she thrust her hips in a bang-me motion. He made her come, but he didn't give her time to rest. Right after she shuddered and shook, he lifted her off the table started the sex marathon.

Jared peeled off his clothes, and they christened the floor, where he penetrated her, doggy style, with him kneeling behind her. He wanted to start this way because they could watch themselves in the closet-door mirror.

As he pumped into her, their gazes locked in the glass. She was on all fours with her little tits hanging down and her hands and knees ground into the carpet.

But she liked it. He could see how turned on she was. He clutched her hips and thrust harder. She moaned and lowered her head and torso, making the position even more exciting.

Hotter. Naughtier.

He didn't care if he came a hundred times tonight, if he used up every ounce of semen his body could produce. All he wanted was her—Amanda Lynn Cooper—in every dirty, sexy way he could take her.

They stood up, and he fucked her against the wall, backward, where he was behind her. But soon he spun her around so they faced each other and one of her legs was wrapped around his waist.

"You feel so good," he said. "So good."

"So do you." She kissed him, making his head spin.

They tumbled into bed and went missionary for a while, then she straddled his lap and rode him home.

He came in an explosion of lust, and she collapsed on top of him. He held her, their bodies slicked with sweat.

They stayed that way, nuzzled close, then cooled off with ice cubes, rubbing each other down, letting the frozen water melt and drip.

She leaned over to suck him, getting him ready for a second round. He stroked her hair and watched her blow him.

Within no time, they were at it again, going for an edge-of-the-bed position with a pillow propped under her hips and him standing over her. All she had to do was put her legs in the air and let him hammer away.

Which he did, as deeply as he could.

He tried not to think about anything but his primal need, his hunger. Tomorrow he would deal with the ache of letting her go, of freeing himself from emotional bonds. Tonight, all that mattered was being tangled up in her sinuous body.

She arched and flexed, and they found their way into a kneeling lotus, a soft and gentle position that made Mandy sigh. They kissed and caressed, but it was still sex, Jared told himself.

Just sex.

His partner climaxed, rocking back and forth. She moved like a mermaid, fluid and luxurious. He could feel every sway, every rhythm of her wavelike peak.

He gave her a minute to snap out of her trance, and she graced him with a smile. Before he lost what was left of his needing-to-escape heart, he pulled her back into down-and-dirty fucking.

They used every stick of furniture at their disposal. They even boffed on the balcony, where evening had crept in, shrouding their nakedness.

Hours later Jared struggled to sleep. He lay awake for most of the night. But his lover didn't. She nodded off in his arms, unaware of what morning would bring.

CHAPTER NINETEEN

Mandy awakened next to Jared, the smell of sex clinging to her body. She looked longingly at her partner in crime. He was still crashed out, his hair covering half of his face. A portion of his braid had come loose.

Although she tingled to touch him, she let him sleep. She eased away from the bed and headed for the bathroom. She took a long, hot shower and toweled off. She brushed her teeth and combed out her shampooed hair, too.

Getting cozy, she slipped on a thick, white robe provided by the hotel. Then she made a pot of coffee and poured herself a cup.

She returned to bed and sat on the edge, steam rising from her cream-doctored brew. What a night. She was sore, but it was a good kind of ache.

Jared squinted and opened his eyes. Mandy smiled, thinking how rough and rumpled he looked, a sexy male in his prime.

"Hi," she said.

"Hey," he rasped back.

As he sat up and leaned against the headboard, the sheet circled his waist. His penis was hard, tenting the fabric. But she knew it wasn't for her. Fully functioning men got erections during the dream stage of sleep, even if their dreams were nonsexual. Jared had awakened with what was commonly referred to as "morning wood."

He jabbed at the loose strands of his hair, struggling to smooth it in place. "You're wearing one of the hotel robes. Just like I figured you would be."

She angled her head. He sounded odd, dark and pensive. "Isn't that why they give them to us? To wear?"

"Yes, of course." He glanced at the clock. "I hadn't meant to sleep this long."

She checked the time, too. "It's still early. How about some breakfast? We can order in."

"I'm not hungry. But you can get something if you want."

"I made coffee." To her, he seemed like he needed a caffeine boost. "Do you want a cup?"

He shook his head. "I just need a shower."

She understood that he was groggy and tired from their marathon, but his moodiness was killing her morning-after glow.

He stood up and paused for a moment, as if he meant to touch her, to twine a finger around her damp hair, to fold down the collar of her robe, to kiss the pulse at her neck, to show her affection.

But he didn't. He grabbed his overnight bag and disappeared into the bathroom.

Okay, so fine. Maybe he would feel better after he showered. In spite of his refusal of food, Mandy ordered a continental breakfast big enough for two, in case he gained an appetite. An assortment of rolls, bagels, and pastries might do him some good. The fresh-squeezed orange juice would be an extra pick-me-up, too.

She didn't get dressed. She stayed belted in her robe, intent on remaining cozy. She'd always enjoyed the hotel experience. Refusing to sit in a dimly lit room, she opened the drapes, allowing the sun to shine through the sliding-glass balcony door.

Jared emerged from the bathroom, fully dressed with his hair rebraided and his jaw free of day-old whiskers. She caught a whiff of his cologne, a spicy, sea-breeze scent. As crisp as he looked, as fresh as he smelled, he still seemed sullen.

"What's wrong with you?" Mandy asked.

"I can't do this anymore," he responded.

"This?"

"Us." Nerve-frazzling seconds ticked by. "I think we should stop seeing each other."

She gripped the back of a dining chair. "You're ending our affair? After a night like last night? After . . ." The guilt in his eyes hit her square in the stomach. The wariness. The betrayal. She released the chair and clenched her middle. "You did this on purpose, didn't you? You planned it. That's why last night happened the way it did."

"I'm sorry. I just needed—"

"To fuck me over? Literally and figuratively?" Her breath rammed out her lungs, scratching past the lump in her throat. She shouldn't care. She'd always known an end was in sight, but not like this, never like this. "Is it because of what I said about trying not to fall in love with you? Is that why?"

He thrust his hands in his front pockets, hunching his

shoulders, going James Dean. "That's part of it. We weren't supposed to get close enough for either of us to worry about falling in love."

She fought to steel her reaction, the way she'd been fighting her feelings for him. She wasn't going to let him see her come unglued, even if she was headed toward destruction. "And the other part?"

"I feel as if I'm losing my identity. Like I don't even know who I am anymore. I need to go back to being Jared. The old me."

She studied him: deep-set eyes, slightly winged brows, hard-cut cheekbones, a sensual mouth. He looked the same, but she knew he was referring to the party boy, the man who didn't cuddle at night.

A knock rattled the door, and they both flinched. She'd forgotten about breakfast until a disembodied voice announced, "Room service," from the other side.

"I have to get that," she said.

Jared stepped back, and she answered the summons. Instead of allowing the server to come inside, Mandy took the tray and placed it on the unmade bed.

After signing the bill, which would be charged to Jared's credit card, she closed the door and left the food untouched. She wasn't the least bit hungry. Not anymore.

She gazed at her now former lover, and he frowned.

"I'm sorry," he said. "But I think it's better this way."

Better for whom? The ache between her legs throbbed, but the pain that knifed her heart was a thousand times worse.

"If it's over, it's over." She made a sweeping gesture. All she wanted was for him to go away, to vanish before she cried.

He stalled, almost as if he couldn't bear to leave on such a hard, cold note. That gave her a gleam of satisfaction. The jilted woman.

With a snap of feminine bravado, she carried her continental breakfast to the table as if she meant to eat it. When she turned her back on him, he released a jagged breath.

But he didn't apologize again. Nor did he change his mind. She heard him gather his last night's clothes, which were still strewn on the floor, and shove them into his overnight bag. She heard him place something on the nightstand, too. She suspected it was the key to her condo.

She waited, the sound of his booted footsteps moving farther away from her, and with the click of the door, he was gone.

The time had come. We were leaving for Mexico. Instead of traveling at first light, we'd chosen to depart in the afternoon, so our friends could see us off. Alice was already at the farm, and George was scheduled to arrive later, after his workday ended.

Up until today, Nanny and I had been sorting through what seemed like an endless amount of personal effects and supplies. We were leaving many things behind, but it didn't matter, as long as Atacar and I were going to be together.

"I'll miss you so much," Alice said, as she glanced around the partially barren house.

"I'll miss you, too," I responded.

"We'll visit when we can. But for now, it's going to be difficult to say good-bye."

I hugged her, and Peter toddled between us, eating a treat Nanny had given the boys. His face and hands were sticky. He grinned at us with his tiny teeth. Alice and I laughed, and she cleaned him up.

I went outside and approached Atacar, where he was fastening a wire chicken coop on the back of the wagon. We were taking our chickens, as well as our cow. Nanny intended to cook some of the chickens along the way, and the cow would provide milk on our journey and in Mexico.

Atacar smiled at me, and I returned his affection. The sun shimmered, highlighting the blue blackness in his hair. He was so handsome, so big and strong, and he was mine. All mine.

The sound of hoofbeats snared our attention. We spun around and saw George racing toward the farmhouse.

Panic rose in my bones. "Something is wrong." The other man had left work early.

We dashed toward him, and he reined his horse to a frantic stop and dismounted. Nanny and Alice appeared on the front porch. They'd heard the thunderous hoofbeats, too. The children followed, but Alice shooed them back inside, protecting them from the drama that was about to unfold.

"An Indian was spotted near the watering hole this morning," George said.

"Oh, God." I clutched Atacar's hand. He'd gone to the stream earlier to gather the spiritual herbs he used when he prayed.

"There was no one around," my lover said. "How could I have been seen?"

George explained. "A couple of boys was hiding in the trees. They'd sneaked off to chew tobacco and have a spitting contest. They didn't tell nobody at first. If they admitted that they'd seen you, then they would've had to tattle on themselves, to say they wasn't home doing their chores."

"But they did tell." This from Alice.

George nodded to his wife. "After their pappy discovered their chores wasn't done, they spilled the beans, and their pappy took them into town to talk to the marshal." He addressed Atacar once again. "The boys wasn't sure if the man they seen was you. But they was sure he was Indian. And when they described him to the marshal . . ."

I clutched Atacar's hand more tightly.

George continued. "The town is all abuzz. I came here as soon as I heard."

"Did the marshal telegraph the army?" Atacar asked.

"Yes. And now soldiers are going to be searching this area again, from here to the border."

Which meant that Atacar needed to travel alone, to mount a horse and ride as fast as he could, to take the back roads, to make headway. The wagon would be too slow, too cumbersome for him to outrun the army.

I turned to my lover. "You leave now, and Nanny and I will head out on our own. We'll meet you in Mexico."

He touched my cheek, making me ache. "Promise me you and Nanny will be safe."

"We came to America by ourselves. We won't falter on this trip." Tears flooded my eyes. "Promise me the same thing."

"I'll do whatever I can to make our destination." His hand lingered on my cheek. "For you. For us."

George helped Atacar pack his saddlebags, and Nanny provided him with dried meat and hardtack. Within minutes, he was ready for his lone journey.

He kissed me, more deeply than he'd ever kissed me before. "I love you, Catherine."

I put my arms around his neck, my voice quavering. "I love you, too."

As I watched him ride away and disappear in a cloud of dust, my knees threatened to buckle.

Silence fractured the air. Nanny put her hand on my shoulder, and Alice and her husband stood like scarecrows.

George finally spoke. "You have to unpack his portrait," he said to me. "You can't take it with you. If you encounter soldiers along the way, they might stop you and search the wagon. They might search every wagon they see."

As a precaution, I thought. To be sure no one was harboring a runaway Indian. Or that he wasn't a stowaway without the traveler's knowledge.

"I understand," I said. If the army uncovered Atacar's portrait in my possession, they would know I was willingly connected to him. "What about my journal? I keep a memorandum book. It's filled with his name, with my thoughts, my feelings."

"Is it small enough to hide on your person?" Alice asked.

I nodded, deciding that I would tuck it into the waistband of my drawers. Soldiers would never look beneath a woman's skirt, not unless they intended to rape her, and I would fight to the death if they attempted to violate me.

"What shall we do with the portrait?" Nanny asked.

"We can hide it here," George responded.

We went inside, and he removed a row of boards in the parlor wall. I placed the carefully wrapped painting inside and watched him hammer up the opening.

That was it. The final act before Nanny and I bade our friends farewell and began our journey.

Without the man I loved.

~

Mandy stood in front of Atacar's painting, gazing at his image. A wall of glass protected him from the modern world, from vandals, from thieves. But a safety shield hadn't surrounded him when he'd been alive.

She looked into his eyes and battled an ever-present ache, an emptiness that grew deeper with each day. She missed Jared. She missed him so much. Two weeks had passed since he'd ended their affair, and she couldn't stop thinking about him.

Footsteps echoed off the museum floor, and she turned to the quick-paced sound. Kiki headed toward her in a gypsy-inspired dress with her hair rioting around her face.

"I figured I'd find you here," the other woman said.

Mandy nodded. She visited Atacar for a few minutes every day. But she'd always done that.

Kiki sighed. "You look sad."

"I'm hanging in there." Mourning a man who was still alive. How lovesick was she? How lost without him? God, she hated herself for that. She glanced at the painting. Was being near Jared's ancestor making it worse? Or better? At this stage, she didn't know how to feel.

"Sometimes life sucks," Kiki said.

Mandy nodded, still gazing at the portrait, still locked within its oil-on-canvas embrace. "Do you think the old army report about Atacar is accurate?"

"That he aimed his rifle at the soldiers who attempted to apprehend him, and they returned fire in self-defense?" The historian went silent for a moment. "I don't know. But I could see him doing that. Fighting to maintain his freedom."

"So could I." According to the report, he'd taken several bullets to the chest, one of which had been fatal.

Before Mandy's mind wandered further in that direction, Kiki exhaled an audible breath and said, "I hate to do this to you right now, but we need to talk. There are some things I need to tell you."

"About what?"

"The journal. First of all, I located one of Nanny's ancestors. A cousin, a working-class Londoner. He says his family doesn't know anything about it nor do they have it in their possession. If they did, they would've sold it to the highest bidder long before now."

"Do you believe him?"

"Yes. But it doesn't matter, because I think your former lover has it."

"Jared?" His name all but bruised her lips. "Oh, my goodness. Why?"

"Because Nanny's ancestor told me that he heard a rumor that Jared stayed at Minerva Burke's estate when he was in England."

"Catherine's grandniece? The reclusive old lady who won't speak to anyone about Catherine?"

Kiki nodded. "I checked into the rumor, and it's true. From what I uncovered, Jared has been to England twice."

"Yes, he told me that."

"Did he also tell you that on his first trip, Minerva contacted a historian, and she and Jared had something authenticated?"

Mandy's pulse jiggered. "Something?"

"I wasn't able to find out what it was. But I'd bet my ass in a sling that it's the journal. What else could they possibly have in common?"

Mandy's stomach clenched. "If it is the journal, then Jared lied to me the entire time we were together."

"I hope you're going to confront him."

"Damn right I am. Oh, God. I feel so betrayed. On every level. What was he trying to prove? What kind of game was he playing?"

"I have no idea. But he sure played it well."

A tour guide entered the room, and when she led her group toward Atacar's exhibit, Mandy and Kiki moved out of the way.

"I'm so sorry," her friend said, as they stood off to the side. "I wish I'd delivered better news."

"Me, too." As strangers gathered around Atacar, Mandy noticed their heightened interest in the tour guide's commentary about the warrior's rumored romance with the artist who'd painted his portrait. "Me, too."

~

While en route to Mexico, I darkened my hair with the plant dye Atacar had suggested. I did everything I would have done if my lover had been with me. Everything except lie in his arms, except touch him, except listen to him breathing while he slept.

I missed him painfully, and I prayed for every mile of our trip that he would be there when we arrived.

No one stopped us, and no one searched our wagon. We passed other travelers, but we didn't see any soldiers. Nanny kept saying that was a good sign, but I wasn't sure.

We crossed the border on a gruelingly hot day. Amid the countryside, I saw dahlias growing wild, rich with color. I insisted that Nanny stop so I could pick some. I gathered them in my arms, as many as would fit.

"They're for Atacar," I said.

"You'll see him soon," she responded, reminding me that we were on our way to the region where he would be waiting, the town in which we'd agreed to make our home.

I clutched the flowers, holding fast to their sentiment: "I think of you constantly."

We drove to our final destination, the wagon bumping along dusty roads, where farmland and orchards shimmered in the distance.

My lover was nowhere to be seen, and within days, the dahlias wilted. I spoke to everyone in town, describing his appearance in my limited Spanish. The mission priests were especially kind. I told them of his true identity, and they offered to help me discover what had happened to him.

Nanny tried to reassure me. "If he was captured and taken to Fort Sill," she said, "he'll find a way to escape again."

But he never did. Because the priests learned that he'd been shot and killed. That he'd died right before he'd reached the border. He'd fallen from his horse and bled into the earth with his rifle by his side.

CHAPTER TWENTY

"I'm going to tell her," Jared said. He was on his cell phone, talking to Minerva Burke, doing what he'd been doing for the past two weeks: missing Mandy.

"Her?" the elderly woman asked. "The museum director?"

"Yes."

"Why?"

"Because I . . ."

"Love her?" came the inquisitive reply.

He stalked the office in his barn, where ribbons and trophies boasted his horse-industry status. He was supposed to be working, catching up on paperwork.

"I don't know," he said.

"Yes, you do. Or you wouldn't have called me. And certainly not at this hour."

He winced. He'd forgotten about the time difference between New Mexico and England. He'd probably gotten Minerva out of bed. "Sorry."

"Do you love her?" she asked again.

He wanted to curse, but what good would it do? He'd been having this conversation with himself, over and over, until his mind threatened to burst.

"Yes," he said, finally admitting it out loud.

"Does she love you, too?"

"She told me that she was fighting it."

"Then do what you have to do to make things right, even if means making Catherine's memorandum book public."

He stopped pacing. Aside from the British historian who'd authenticated the journal and whose job it was to keep quiet, Minerva and Jared were the only people who'd read the book in its entirety. "You'd be okay with that?"

Her voice didn't slip. She maintained the same polished tone. "Truthfully? I'd prefer that it remain private, but not at your expense. When I asked you to keep it a secret, I never expected it would cause you so much pain."

"It didn't. Not until I fell for Mandy."

"Yes, and now I feel responsible for your troubles. You wouldn't have lied to your young lady if it weren't for me."

He thought about his deception at the hotel. "This isn't your fault. I did things to her that have nothing to do with you." And he could only hope that Mandy would forgive him.

After work, Mandy went home to change her clothes, to freshen up, to take a deep breath before she climbed back in the car and drove to Jared's house.

She considered calling to tell him that she was coming over, but she decided the element of surprise would work in her favor. If she caught him off guard, it would be easier to catch him in his lie. Or so she hoped. He'd done a damn good job of fooling her into believing that he didn't have the journal. That he didn't even believe it existed.

He was in possession of the one thing she wanted most, not only for the museum, but for herself. He knew how much Atacar and Catherine meant to her, how deeply she'd become rooted to uncovering their past, but he'd breezed in and out of her bed without saying a word. The way he'd used her and cast her aside, especially their last night together, hurt beyond words.

Mandy opened the door to leave and—

Boom!

There he was: a tall, dark mirage standing on her stoop. Talk about getting caught off guard. Suddenly she couldn't think straight.

Silence slammed between them, and they made rocky eye contact. She forced herself to take the lead, to speak first. "I was just on my way to see you."

"Then my timing is okay?"

He sounded humble. Too humble? Was he here to embark on another game, another lie? To seduce her back into his handsome clutches? "Your timing has never been right. You always seem to get the upper hand."

"I'm so sorry I hurt you, Mandy. What I did to you—"

She cut him off, stopping him from taking advantage again. "Do you know what I found out today? What Kiki figured out?"

He made a face. "That I have the journal?"

Lucky guess, she thought, giving him a sarcastic look. "Kiki said that you and Minerva Burke had it authenticated."

"We did. But only because Minerva wanted proof that it was real. I already knew it was authentic. I'm the one who found it, who brought it to her."

"And now you're on my doorstep on the same day I discovered the truth. How convenient for you."

"Maybe it's coincidence. Or fate. I don't know. But I came here to tell you everything. The whole story."

Mandy didn't soften her expression.

"You don't believe me? Why else would I be here?" He made an open gesture. "With my heart in your hands?"

She wanted to trust him, but she was afraid of letting go. How many nights had she hugged her pillow and wished it were him, had she cried herself to sleep?

What if he hurt her again?

Once bitten, twice shy. She'd never quite gotten the impact of that idiom until now.

"Give me a chance, Mandy. Please."

Oh, God, she thought. He was making this difficult, so damn hard. She allowed him into her condo. He sat on the sofa, and she took the chair farthest from him, struggling to keep her distance.

He cleared his throat, and his Adam's apple bobbed, making him seem boyish, nervous. He blew out a rough breath. "Remember the trinket box I told you about that belonged to my mom? That I broke earlier this year?"

She nodded, and he continued. "The journal was inside of it. When I knocked the box onto the floor and the wood splintered, I discovered that there was a sealed compartment."

She scooted to the edge of her seat, envisioning what he was describing.

"I can't even begin to express how I felt. I'd been searching for Catherine's journal for most of my adult life, and there it was right under my nose. I sat down and read it, every word. I've read it hundreds of times since. It's beautiful, Mandy. Sexy, romantic, sad. Catherine and Atacar loved each other so much."

"Why didn't you trust me with the truth?"

"It wasn't a matter of trust, not in the way it seems. I'd agreed to keep the journal a secret before I met you. I promised Minerva that I wouldn't make it public. She's been avoiding rumors about Atacar and Catherine for nearly forty years, since his painting was found at the farmhouse, and she was worried the journal would stir up everything again."

"The proper, prestigious Burkes." Mandy heaved a sigh. "Even after all this time, they still want to sweep Catherine under the rug."

"That's what I thought at first, too. But once I got to know Minerva, I realized it went deeper. She resembled Catherine when she was young. In her family, that was a cross to bear."

"I know," Mandy said. Kiki had mentioned that a while back, when they'd first discussed Catherine's grandniece.

Jared explained further. "Minerva won't admit it, but somewhere deep inside, she identifies with Catherine. I think Minerva would have run free if she thought she could have gotten away with it, but she followed the rules of society instead. I think she's afraid of the journal going public because it represents everything she isn't supposed to feel. Or wasn't supposed to feel when she was young."

"Why did you show her the journal to begin with?"

"Because I discovered that I was related to Minerva, to the Burkes." He held Mandy's gaze. "Catherine is my great-great-grandmother." He paused, still making eye contact. "And Atacar is my great-great-grandfather, not my great-great-uncle."

"Oh, my goodness." Her heart bumped her chest. "They had a baby? And you're a descendant of that child?"

"Yes." Jared's breath went rough again. "But Atacar didn't know about the baby. Catherine didn't find out that she was pregnant until after he died."

~

Without Atacar, I wanted to die. Life was a seamless blur of pain. I cried endlessly for the man I loved. I mourned him every day, alone in the dark, clutching our wedding clothes against my body.

Nanny tried her best to console me, but she missed Atacar, too. She'd treasured him like a son, and now he was gone.

Instead of getting our own farm, we stayed at the mission. I donated money to the church, and Nanny cooked and cleaned for the priests. I tried to paint, to put brush to canvas, but I couldn't. I was empty inside.

Then everything changed. My menses that month never arrived. I told Nanny, and we waited for signs of life to appear in my womb. When I struggled through bouts of dizziness and nausea, we rejoiced. In my final days with Atacar, the preventative tea I'd been drinking had failed, and I've conceived his child.

I wrote to Alice. I was no longer worried about the army intercepting my correspondence. My whereabouts wouldn't interest them, not without Atacar by my side.

Three months later, I received a reply from Alice. She was thrilled about my baby. She gave me news from Texas, too.

She wrote, "George and I heard about Atacar soon after he'd been shot. The army notified the marshal that the 'Runaway Apache' was dead. George and I mourned him silently. We were heartbroken for your loss."

She added, "The bank already sold the farmhouse, and as far as we know, Atacar's portrait is still there, hidden in the walls. Now, in retrospect, it seems like a grave. But George says it's all right because Atacar had been happy at the farmhouse, so it's a good resting place for his picture."

I folded the letter and pressed it against my heart. Alice promised to visit this summer with George and the boys. She was anxious to see Nanny and me. By then, I would have the baby, and all of us could be together.

Atacar wouldn't be at our reunion, but he was never far from my thoughts. When I went to sleep each night, I rubbed my protruding tummy and whispered to the little one about its father. I had a reason to keep living, to be happy once again.

⌒

"Was she happy?" Mandy asked, after listening to Jared recount Catherine's story. He'd given her a condensed version of what had been written in the journal, retelling it in his own words.

"She was happy while she was pregnant, but she never got to raise her son. She died in childbirth."

Mandy turned emotional, deeply pained inside. Hurting for Catherine, she walked onto the patio to get some air. Jared followed her, but neither took a seat at the colorful mosaic table. They stood on a small slab of concrete, near a potted plant, and gazed at each other.

"Did Nanny stay in Mexico?" she asked.

"Yes, but soon after the baby was born, she became ill. Her life was ending, too."

"So there was that little boy with no one."

"The priests took him to an orphanage."

"What was his name?"

"Adán. It's the Spanish form of Adam."

"How you know all of this? Did Nanny document it before she died?"

"It was Alice," he said. "She wrote the last entry in the journal, summing up what happened and how she felt about it. When she and George arrived in Mexico to visit Catherine and Nanny, they were met with tragedy. Catherine was gone, Nanny was gravely ill, and the baby was at an overcrowded orphanage."

A breeze stirred the air, blowing a strand of Mandy's hair across her cheek. She tucked it behind her ears, concentrating on Jared's tale. "What did Alice and George do?"

"They stayed with Nanny until she passed. But before she died, they promised her that they would find a loving home for Adán. They wanted to keep him, but they couldn't."

"Because of his heritage?"

"How could they bring a dark-skinned baby home and raise

him? They knew that he would be scorned. That he wouldn't be accepted. So they devised a plan to take him to Fort Sill to be with Atacar's sister and her husband."

Mandy frowned. "Wouldn't that make Adán a prisoner of war?"

"Yes, and Alice struggled over that, but she decided that Adán should be with Atacar's family, even if it meant being under military custody."

Mandy pictured the fort as it had been. From what she knew, the prisoners lived in picket houses, raised cattle, and farmed. Later, after their captivity ended, they were supposed to acquire Fort Sill as their permanent home, but they never did.

"Alice and George pretended to be missionaries," Jared said. "That gave them opportunity to roam freely and sneak Adán inside. They located Atacar's sister and gave her the baby. After that, they all sat down and composed a lie, working out details of how to pass Adán off as Tiana's child."

"Tiana? That's Atacar's sister?"

Jared nodded. "This is the story they came up with: Tiana would approach the fort officials and reveal that she had a two-month-old baby, but that she'd kept her pregnancy and Adán's birth a secret because she was trying to avoid registering him. All of the prisoners were supposed to have enrollment numbers. Births and deaths were supposed to be reported."

Mandy contemplated the lie. "I can see how she fooled the fort officials, but what about the people Tiana was close to? Friends? Family? How did she fool them? Wouldn't they have known that she wasn't pregnant? Or nursing?"

"Apache women wore full skirts and long, loose blouses. Her figure wouldn't have been an issue. As for nursing, she was able to feed Adán from her breast. She had another child who was still taking milk from her. A daughter who was about fifteen months old. Women nursed their kids for a long time in those days."

"Do you think Tiana or her husband ever told Adán the truth? About who his real parents were?"

"I doubt it. The whole point was to protect him from being labeled a half-breed. In that environment, Adán would have been treated badly for his mixed genetics, not just by the military, but by other Apache."

When Jared stopped talking, another question occurred to her. The final one. The end of the saga.

"What about the journal?" she asked. "Who put it in the box? Who sealed it?"

"Alice asked George to make a box to preserve it. Then she gave the box to Atacar's sister for Adán when he grew up, to treat it as a family keepsake. That was Alice's way of honoring Catherine without anyone knowing that her journal was being passed from generation to generation."

Now that the story was over, Mandy went silent. She couldn't think of anything to say. But apparently Jared could.

"I'm sorry I lied to you," he told her. "And I'm so sorry for what I did at the hotel."

She longed to touch him, to hold him, but she didn't. She questioned him instead. "Is your heart really in my hands?"

"Yes. Totally. Completely. I love you, Mandy."

He ventured closer, and the heat, the scent, the familiarity of him made her ache. But she didn't reach for him, so he stopped moving toward her.

She needed to know more, to be sure that what he claimed

was real. "On the night you broke up with me, you said something about losing your identity. What did you mean?"

"I seduced you because your interest in Catherine and Atacar intrigued me. But later, I got confused." He squinted into the waning sun. "I started living through the journal. I created parallels, similarities between their affair and ours. I mimicked Atacar. I behaved the way he did."

"Then maybe you're still confused. Maybe you're mimicking Atacar now."

"I'm not. This is coming from me, not from the journal." He thumped against his chest, his heart. "Me," he reiterated with another light pounding. "I broke up with you out of fear. I was fighting my feelings, but you said that you were doing that, too."

Her breath hitched. "I was."

"Are you still?" He searched her gaze. "Or did I blow it? Is it too late for you to love me?"

"No, it's not too late." She couldn't stop herself from latching on and closing the gap between them. "It's not too late at all."

"Will you say it?"

She was grateful that he needed to hear the words, because she needed to say them, to let herself feel them, to stop fighting what was in her heart.

"I love you," she said. "I do."

He wrapped his arms around her. "I'm never letting you go again."

"I'm never letting you go, either." She put her head on his shoulder. "I want us to have what Catherine and Atacar lost."

"The chance to stay together? We'll have that and more." He

paused. "But we'll have to decide what to do about the journal, whether to keep it private or make it public. I spoke to Minerva earlier, and she's willing to go public, but she'd only be doing it for me."

"You care about her, don't you? That's why you kept the journal a secret for her, why you protected her feelings."

"The first time I went to England was to show her the journal and see how she would react to me. The second time, she invited me back so we could try to get to know each other a little better. So, yes, I care. She's cautious and reclusive, but she seems to care about me, too."

"Then it's your choice what to do about the journal, Jared. I won't intervene. I'll respect your wishes, no matter what they are." She reached for his hand and led him to her bedroom, hungry to have him, to make every being-in-love moment count. "All I want right now is you."

Jared was desperate for Mandy, too. To breathe her into his pores, to press his body against hers.

"I feel like a kid who's going to come too fast," he said.

She teetered toward him, reaching for the buttons on his shirt. "We don't even have our clothes off yet."

"That's what I mean." He nudged her hand down, encouraging her to cop an intimate feel. "See? Instant hard-on."

"Like that's anything new." She smiled and cupped him through his jeans. "You're the most hard-on guy I know."

"Because you're the most orgasmic girl I know. We've got this chemistry thing going." Love, he thought. How amazing was that? He stepped back, stopping her from undressing him. He wanted her naked first. "Strip for me. Let me look at you."

"Are you going to make me get in bed and spread my legs? Are you going make me touch myself?"

Damn. He more than loved this girl. She was the epitome of lust, of sin-swept temptation. There she was, his Mandy, with her eyes bright and blue and her hair caressing her shoulders.

"Yes," he said. "I'm going to make you do that."

She took her sweet time removing her blouse. He waited and watched. Her expression turned soft and sultry, like twilight, like the hour between waking and sleep.

He imagined spending the rest of his life with her. Commitment, he thought, in the midst of erotic dreams.

"This is going to work out just fine," he said.

"What is?" She dropped her blouse on the floor.

He admired her, standing before him in her bra, a modest piece of lingerie with soft cups and a bit of lace. "Us."

Ziiip. She went after the front closure of her pants, tugging the linen garment down her hips. Her panties exhibited the same innocent appeal as her bra.

His hard-on got harder.

Off came her undergarments.

She was beautiful, so damn beautiful with her small, flushed breasts, slim waist, and curvaceous hips.

"I kept my favorite toy," she said. "But I didn't use it when we were broken up. I was afraid it would make me miss you even more."

He knew she was talking about the dildo they'd made of him. "Use it now, baby. Get naughty for me. Be my bad girl."

That was all it took. She got the device, climbed in bed, and lubed it. Once it was slick and wet, she rubbed the pierced head over her nipples, down her stomach, and around her clit.

She spread wide, exposing her labia, letting him take a greedy look. She made the insertion, and desire fevered through his blood, making him hotly, romantically aroused.

She bit down on her bottom lip, and her breathing elevated to shallow pants. But before long, she was inhaling and exhaling in a deeply sensual way, in and out, like the motion of the dildo.

Jared removed his clothes and got into bed. He stretched out next to Mandy and gripped the toy, taking over for her. She moaned low and sexy, and her eyelashes fluttered. She was close to coming, but not quite there.

He ditched the rubber phallus and fitted himself between her thighs, giving her the real deal. She wrapped her legs around him, and they kissed . . .

And kissed . . .

And kissed some more.

He rocked his hips, claiming her in ways he'd never claimed her before. The carnality was the same as it had always been, but the feeling was new.

Heart sex, he thought.

She climaxed with his cock thrust full hilt, and while it was happening, they looked into each other's eyes. This was it. Love in its deepest, purest, most primal form.

Jared resisted the urge to come. He took it slow, setting a sinuous rhythm, wanting to give Mandy another orgasm before he let himself fall.

The onset of dusk seeped through the blinds, shadowing the

room. He wasn't looking for a marathon, just more of her, of what she made him feel.

She was warm and silky soft, and they moved fluidly together. He linked both of his hands with hers, holding on to a word that was no longer forbidden.

Forever, he thought, as he kissed her again.

Forever.

EPILOGUE

ONE MONTH LATER

"Are you nervous?" Kiki asked.

"A little," Mandy responded. She and Kiki were at the museum, standing in front of Atacar's portrait and waiting for Jared and Minerva. He was picking up Minerva from the airport, and this would be Mandy's first time meeting her. "I want to make a good impression."

"You will."

"I'm going to try." Jared had left the fate of the journal in Minerva's hands. And after much thought, the older woman had decided that it should be made public and that Jared should proclaim his birthright. But before Catherine's memorandum book was turned over to the museum, Minerva wanted to meet Mandy and discuss the details of how it should be exhibited. Minerva wanted to see Atacar's portrait, too.

"I appreciate you hanging out with me," Mandy said. "For helping me wait out my nerves."

"No problem. I'll just say a quick howdy-do to Minerva and scoot off afterward."

"Thanks." Mandy started another conversation, killing time. "So, what's going on with you? Anything new?"

"Except for Amber calling me all the time and bugging me to meet that guy?"

"What guy?"

"You know, Mr. BDSM. The bondage artist."

"Oh, that's right. The one who has a thing for redheads. Are you going to take a chance and meet him?"

"Are you kidding? I'm not setting myself up for something like that." Kiki lifted her wrists above her head, as if she were being restrained. "Could you see me like this? Strung up in some wacko's playroom? Begging him to do Lord only knows what to me?"

Mandy laughed. "Actually, I could."

"Oh, shut up." The historian laughed, too. Then she made a guilty face. "I checked out his art."

Aha, Mandy thought. Curiosity in bloom. "In person or online?"

"Online. I have to admit, his work is amazing. I saw his picture, too. Jet-black hair. Sizzling blue eyes. And get this— according to Amber, he's a history buff. He just bought a house that used to be a turn-of-the-century hotel. Of course, he can buy whatever he wants. He inherited billions from his family."

"Wow. He sounds like quite a catch."

"Oh, right. He's a dream, except for the whips and chains and muzzles and gags part." Kiki glanced toward the door. "Speaking of rich families . . ."

Mandy turned and saw Jared and Minerva enter the museum.

Kiki leaned over and whispered, "Look at her. It's like we're holding court for a royal."

"Shhh." Mandy nudged her friend, even if the same thought had just crossed her mind. At eighty-three, Minerva carried herself like a noblewoman. Sheathed in an elegant dress and a triple strand of pearls, she clutched Jared's arm. Her snow-white hair was classically coiffed.

Jared escorted his elderly cousin closer, and Mandy took a deep breath. After the initial introductions and small talk were exchanged, Kiki excused herself and slipped away. As for Jared, he turned quiet, letting Mandy and Minerva get acquainted.

"You're lovely," the older woman said to her.

Mandy relaxed. "Thank you. So are you." She wondered if Catherine would have aged in a similar manner if she'd gotten the chance to grow old, if her hair would have turned a brilliant tone of white, if her eyes would have faded to a paler shade.

"I packed a family photo album in my luggage," Minerva said, as if she sensed that Mandy had been comparing her to Catherine. "With pictures of my ancestors. And me when I was young."

When she'd resembled Catherine, Mandy thought. "I'd love to see the album."

"And you shall." Minerva turned toward Atacar's portrait. "Oh, my. He's stunning, isn't he?"

"He made my heart pound the first time I saw him," Mandy responded. "I can only imagine what he was like in person."

"I suspect that he was as captivating as Catherine described. Can you fathom what she felt for him? What he felt for her?" She turned back to Mandy. "Well, of course you can. Jared and you . . ."

Yes, Jared and me, she thought. He'd made her heart pound the first time she'd seen him, too. She glanced at him, and he smiled. They were living together now. She'd rented out her condo and moved in with him, becoming his partner in every way.

As Minerva studied the portrait again, Jared said, "The journal itself should be exhibited here, but I don't think we should make all of it available for the public to read. We should protect Catherine and Atacar's most intimate moments."

The Burke matriarch agreed. "All we need to do is release excerpts that will prove what they felt for each other was real."

"Very real," Mandy said, as the three of them gazed into the warrior's painted eyes.

"Do you think this will reunite them?" Jared asked.

Mandy reached for his hand. "I hope so." They were giving Atacar the journal, every word Catherine had written about their life together.

To stay beside him for all time.